PAINTING AT THE EDGE OF THE WORLD

01

DOUGLAS FOGLE, EDITOR

WALKER ART CENTER, MINNEAPOLIS

Published on the occasion of the exhibition **PAINTING AT THE EDGE OF THE WORLD**, organized by Douglas Fogle for the Walker Art Center, Minneapolis, February 10–May 6, 2001.

The exhibition catalogue for **PAINTING AT THE EDGE OF THE WORLD** is made possible by major support from the **BETLACH FAMILY FOUNDATION**. Additional support for this catalogue was provided by the **ELIZABETH FIRESTONE GRAHAM FOUNDATION** and the **ANDREW W. MELLON FOUNDATION** in support of Walker Art Center publications.

PAINTING AT THE EDGE OF THE WORLD is made possible by generous suppport from **THE BUSH FOUNDATION**, **AMERICAN EXPRESS MINNESOTA PHILANTHROPIC PROGRAM**, **ROSINA LEE YUE** and **BERT A. LIES, JR.**, and **JUMEX FOUNDATION**.

Major support for Walker Art Center programs is provided by the Minnesota State Arts Board through an appropriation by the Minnesota State Legislature, the Lila Wallace-Reader's Digest Fund, The Bush Foundation, the Doris Duke Charitable Foundation through the Doris Duke Fund for Jazz and Dance and the Doris Duke Performing Arts Endowment Fund, The Pew Charitable Trusts, the Target Foundation on behalf of Target Stores, Dayton's, and Mervyn's California, The McKnight Foundation, General Mills Foundation, Coldwell Banker Burnet, the Institute of Museum and Library Services, the National Endowment for the Arts, American Express Minnesota Philanthropic Program, Honeywell International, The Regis Foundation, The Cargill Foundation, U.S. Bank, Star Tribune, The St. Paul Companies, Inc., and the members of the Walker Art Center.

Northwest Airlines, Inc. is the official airline of the Walker Art Center.

CONTENTS
03

Painting is an ancient practice, found in caves alongside the earliest tools. Despite the longevity of the medium, we still do not fully understand the role it initially played in the lives of both the makers and those who watched light dance across the surface of these images. Perhaps these paintings, which we now regard with modernist self-consciousness, were not seen or made as fictions at the time. Despite the ravages wrought by climatic changes and the human breath of recent visitors, these renderings in pigment remain palpable, even heroic representations of the desired object, be it animal or spirit. Still, this question concerning the role played by the human invocation of patterns, gestures, and pictures in our collective life remains with us today.

Though we live in a world where the pixel has seemingly replaced the paintbrush, we continue as human beings to need to *make* sense of the things that bring us pleasure, tame our fears, taunt the unknown, or elevate the spirit. While children today are as likely to explore the intricacies of computer-imaging programs as they are the wet pigment of finger paints, the challenges posed to painting by this new technology are hardly new. The viability of painting has undergone a number of examinations precipitated by factors ranging from the onset of photomechanical reproduction to the revolutionary attempt to forge a new aesthetic erasing boundaries between art and life. Over and over again, these crises of modernism have been linked to the death of painting as a progressive form of aesthetic expression. Today, however, with the apparent resurgence of painting, it has become clear that reports of this medium's demise continue to be greatly exaggerated. The medium persists in being an inclusive one, capable of suggesting both the inner necessities of the artist and the world(s) in which the artist operates.

PAINTING AT THE EDGE OF THE WORLD brings together thirty artists from across the globe to explore the conceptual as well as technical issues imbedded in painting today. Many of these artists purposefully test the traditional definitions of the medium, while others elect to work within well-defined parameters (including those related to the position of viewer). In each case, however, these artists ask us not only to look at the possible permutations of painterly practice today, but to consider how painting itself interacts with and illuminates the world around us. As Douglas Fogle ponders in his essay, where does the edge of the canvas end and the edge of the world begin? This is the central question that frames both this exhibition and the remarkable collection of essays in this publication.

Like any project of this scope and complexity, **PAINTING AT THE EDGE OF THE WORLD** would not have been possible without the very generous contributions of those who share the Walker Art Center's commitment to new scholarship and practice in a world that is often more susceptible to the lure of the gilded frame. We are deeply grateful for the major and, happily, ongoing financial support of the Betlach Family Foundation, whose generosity made this publication possible. Additional support for this catalogue was provided by the Elizabeth Firestone Graham Foundation and the Andrew W. Mellon Foundation in support of Walker Art Center publications. The exhibition itself is made possible by major support from The Bush Foundation in support of the Walker Art Center's mission to better understand the complementary as well as competing values that are shaping an increasingly global and interdependent artistic universe. Others who shared our aspirations and were of assistance include the American Express Minnesota Philanthropic Program, Rosina Lee Yue and Bert A. Lies, Jr., and the Jumex Foundation.

I want to thank curator Douglas Fogle for digging into the history of painting in order to better understand its present; while this book contains many voices, its orchestration is due to Douglas' penetrating research and expansive vision. His curiosity, tenacity, and engagement with artists, as well as his willingness to stretch beyond conventional wisdom about the medium and its message, resulted in this provocative project. I am pleased that the exhibition makes visible work by artists that is too little known while offering others the opportunity to create new work, some of it on-site, suggesting the elasticity of this enduring medium.

KATHY HALBREICH, DIRECTOR

I would like to extend my heartfelt gratitude to everyone who has helped me in the conception and realization of this exhibition and publication.

First and foremost, I would like to thank the artists in this exhibition, all of whom have contributed to the rethinking of the medium of painting as we enter a new millennium: Franz Ackermann, Haluk Akakçe, Francis Alÿs, Kevin Appel, Marcel Broodthaers, John Currin, Marlene Dumas, Andreas Gursky, Eberhard Havekost, Arturo Herrera, Mike Kelley, Martin Kippenberger, Udomsak Krisanamis, Jim Lambie, Margherita Manzelli, Paul McCarthy, Lucy McKenzie, Julie Mehretu, Takashi Murakami, Nader, Chris Ofili, Hélio Oiticica, Laura Owens, Michael Raedecker, Thomas Scheibitz, Thomas Schütte, Rudolf Stingel, Hiroshi Sugito, Paul Thek, and Richard Wright. Their vision and innovation are the heart of this project and it has been our honor and pleasure to provide them with a modest edge of the world on which to paint.

I am also deeply grateful to the authors, whose intelligent contributions to this volume open many doors and pose many questions. Their considered words both challenge and enlighten us as they examine the expanding boundaries and ever-promising potentialities of painting today.

PAINTING AT THE EDGE OF THE WORLD would not have been possible without the generosity of the numerous lenders to this exhibition who have shared important works from their collections or the commitment of the funders who provided crucial financial support. I would particularly like to thank Charles J. Betlach II (Betlach Family Foundation), Rosina Lee Yue and Bert A. Lies, Jr., Eugenio Lopez (Jumex Foundation), and Ray A. Graham III (Elizabeth Firestone Graham Foundation) for their forward-looking commitment to emerging artists and their willingness to take a financial leap of faith with me on this project.

Among the many individuals and organizations that helped to facilitate this exhibition, special thanks go to Marcella Beccaria at Castello di Rivoli Museo d'Arte Contemporanea, Rivoli, Italy; Kirsty Bell and Gavin Brown at Gavin Brown's enterprise, New York; Tim Blum and Jeffrey Poe at Blum & Poe, Santa Monica, California; Tanya Bonakdar and Marc Jancou at Bonakdar Jancou, New York; Ted Bonin at Alexander and Bonin, New York; Jörn Bötnagel and Yvonne Quirmbach at BQ, Cologne; Will Bradley and Toby Webster at The Modern Institute, Glasgow; Gisela Capitain and Johannes Wonseifer at Galerie Gisela Capitain, Cologne; Sadie Coles at Sadie Coles HQ, London; Jeffrey Deitch at Deitch Projects, New York; Fondazione Lucio Fontana, Milan; Marc Foxx at Marc Foxx Gallery, Los Angeles; Fundació Antoni Tàpies, Barcelona; Barbara Gladstone at Barbara Gladstone Gallery, New York; Claudio Guenzani at Studio Guenzani, Milan; Steve Henry and Paula Cooper at Paula Cooper Gallery, New York; Michael Jenkins and Brent Sikkema at Brent Sikkema, New York; Chiaki Kasahara; Anton Kern at Anton Kern Gallery, New York; Samy Kinge at Galerie Samy Kinge, Paris; Martin Klosterfelde at Klosterfelde, Berlin; Frank Lehmann and Ralf Lehmann at Galerie Gebr. Lehmann, Dresden; Jenny Liu and Christian Haye at The Project, New York; Lawrence Luhring at Luhring Augustine Gallery, New York; Patricia Martin at Jumex Foundation; David McAullife at Angles Gallery, Santa Monica, California; Martin McGeown and Andrew Wheatley at Cabinet, London; Jake Miller at The approach, London; Victoria Miro and Glen Scott Wright at Victoria Miro Gallery, London; Birgit Müller at Jablonka Galerie, Cologne; Yuko Nagase and Tomio Koyama at Tomio Koyama Gallery, Tokyo; Tim Neuger and Burkhardt Riemschneider at neugerriemschneider, Berlin; César Fihlo Oiticica at Projeto Hélio Oiticica, Rio de Janeiro; Jeffrey Peabody at Matthew Marks Gallery, New York; Photofest, New York; Andrew Richards at Marian Goodman Gallery, New York; Andrea Rosen and Steven Sergiovanni at Andrea Rosen Gallery, New York; Rich Shelton, St. Paul, Minnesota; Monica Sprüth at Galerie Monica Sprüth, Cologne; the Estate of George Paul Thek, New York; Jack Tilton at Jack Tilton/Anna Kustera Gallery, New York; and Henry Urbach at Henry Urbach Architecture, New York.

I am indebted to Sandra Antelo-Suarez at *Trans* for her generous intellectual input into the conception of this publication; to Paulo Herkenhoff, Adjunct Curator at the Museum of Modern Art, New York, for his advice and encouragement; and to Francesco Bonami, Manilow Senior Curator at the Museum of Contemporary Art, Chicago, for his friendship, risotto, and acute intellectual insight. (Che fare?)

At the Walker Art Center, I would like to thank Director Kathy Halbreich for the open and productive intellectual environment she has created and encouraged in the visual arts department and the institution at large; Chief Curator Richard Flood for his curatorial vision and for allowing my Italian lessons to wait a few months; Curator Philippe Vergne for providing a valuable intellectual sounding board; and Curatorial Intern Elizabeth Thomas, for writing the articulate artist biographies and for her incredible dedication, which informs every aspect of this exhibition and publication.

In the visual arts department, I would like to acknowledge Administrative Assistants Henrietta Dwyer, who deftly handled the myriad organizational details of the exhibition, and Lynn Dierks, who pinch-hit when necessary. In the registration department, Registrar Gwen Bitz continued to amaze us as she heroically and meticulously organized the complex details of shipping and handling the artworks. For their incredible installation of the works, I am indebted to Cameron Zebrun and his entire staff in program services, especially Bob Brown and Peter Murphy, who continually outdo themselves with their innovative craftsmanship, miraculous problem solving, and minute attention to every aesthetic detail. In the development department, I would like to thank Director Christopher Stevens and his colleagues Kathryn Ross and Sarah Sargent for their unflagging efforts in making this exhibition financially solvent so that it wouldn't fall off the edge of the world. Thanks also go to the exhibition's fiscal caretakers, Administrative Director David Galligan and Finance Director Mary Polta, and to Director of Program Planning Howard Oransky for his institutional counsel. My appreciation goes to Director of Education Sarah Schultz and her talented public programs staff, including David Logan and Meredith Walters, who organized the exhibition-related educational programs.

I am extremely grateful to the staff of the Walker's design department, including Design Director Andrew Blauvelt and Senior Graphic Designer Santiago Piedrafita, who masterminded the artful and intelligent design of this publication. Editor Michelle Piranio brought clarity and subtle attention to the poetics of language, and Publications Manager Eugenia Bell deftly ensured that this book arrived in the building on time against all odds. Additional support was provided by Photographer Dan Dennehy, Walker Librarians Rosemary Furtak and Mary Ellyn Johnson, and Slide Librarian Barb Elam.

Finally, this exhibition and publication are dedicated to those who would paint the world and those who live at its edge.

DOUGLAS FOGLE

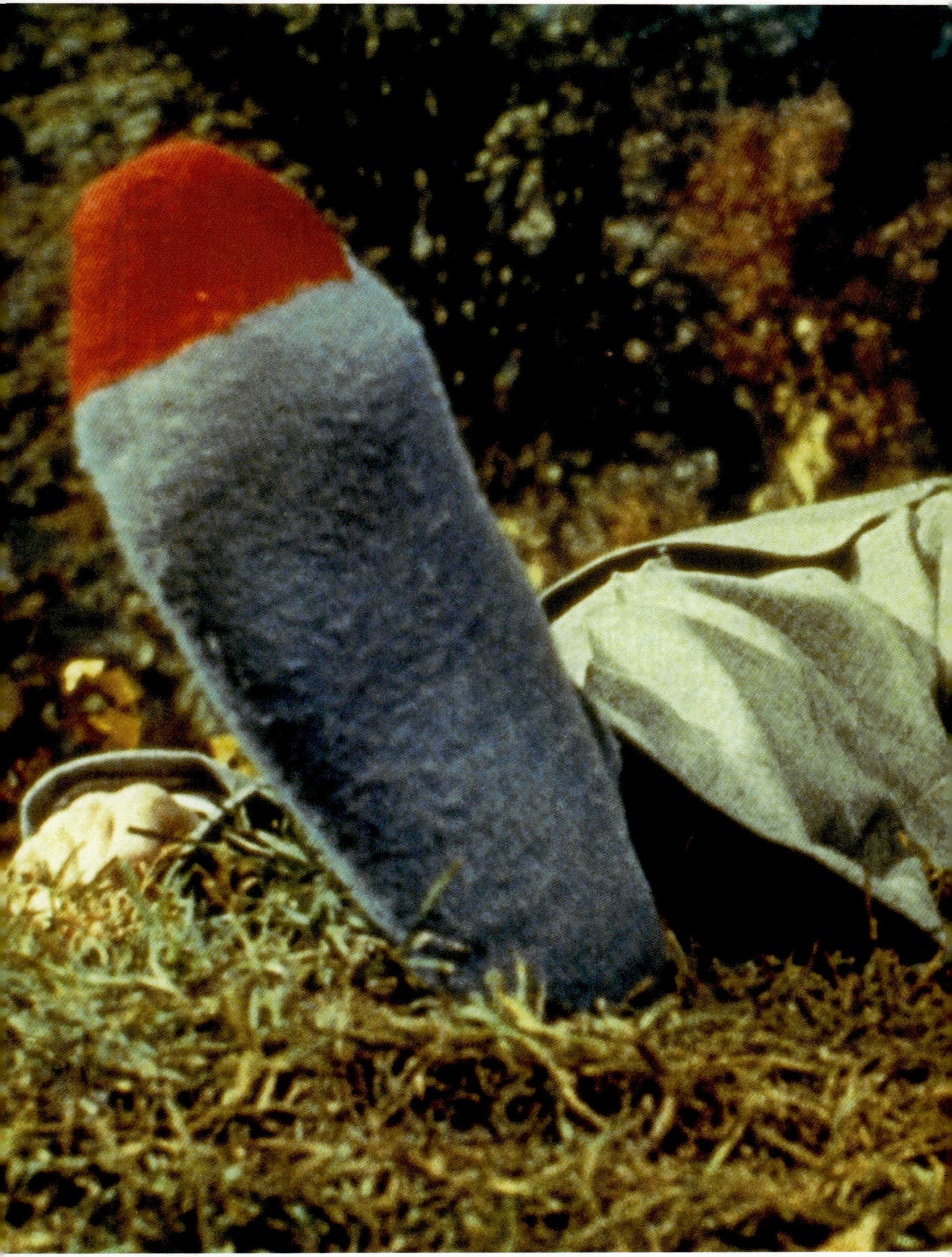

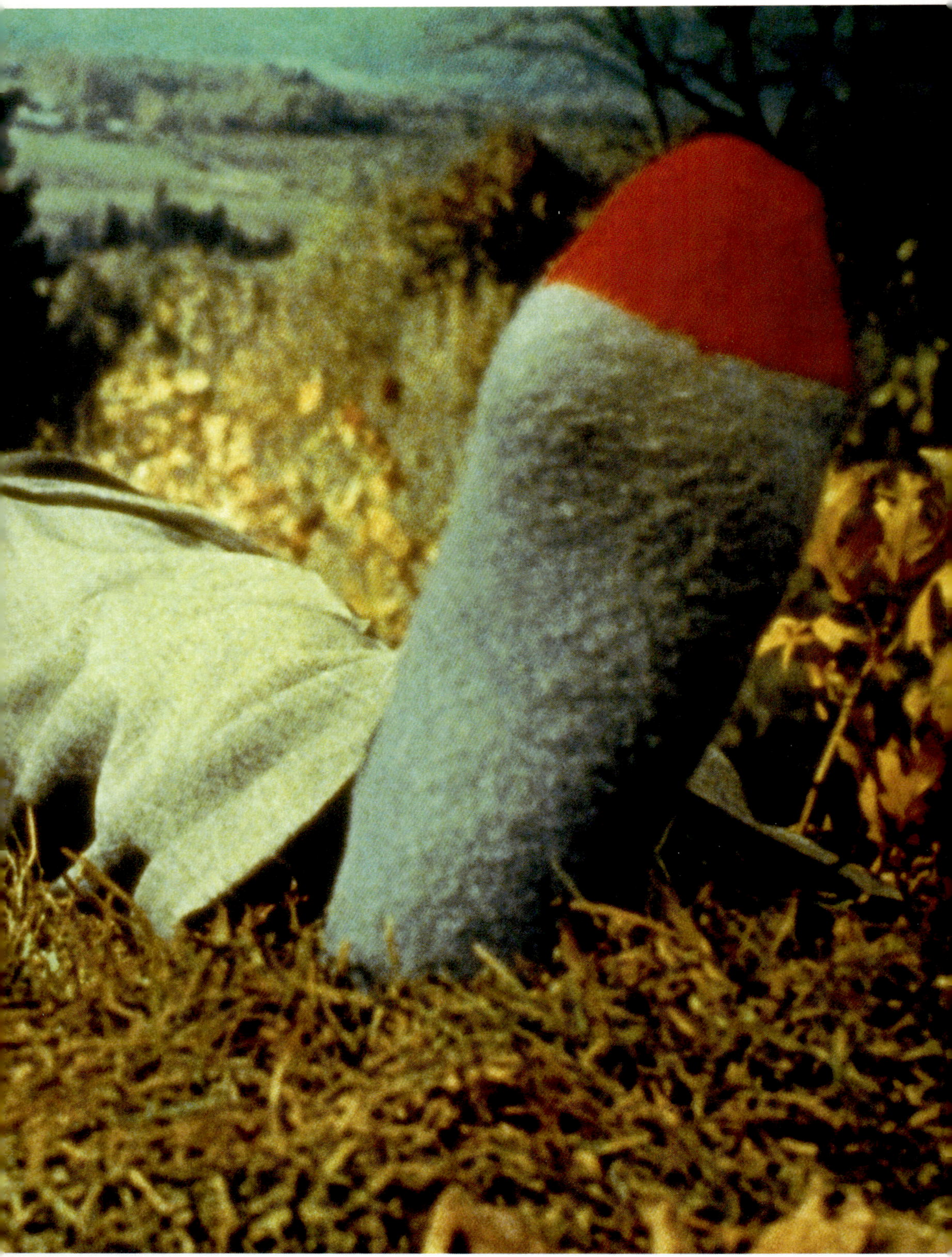

FIG. 1 Alfred Hitchcock still from the film **The Trouble with Harry** 1955 Courtesy Paramount Pictures

11

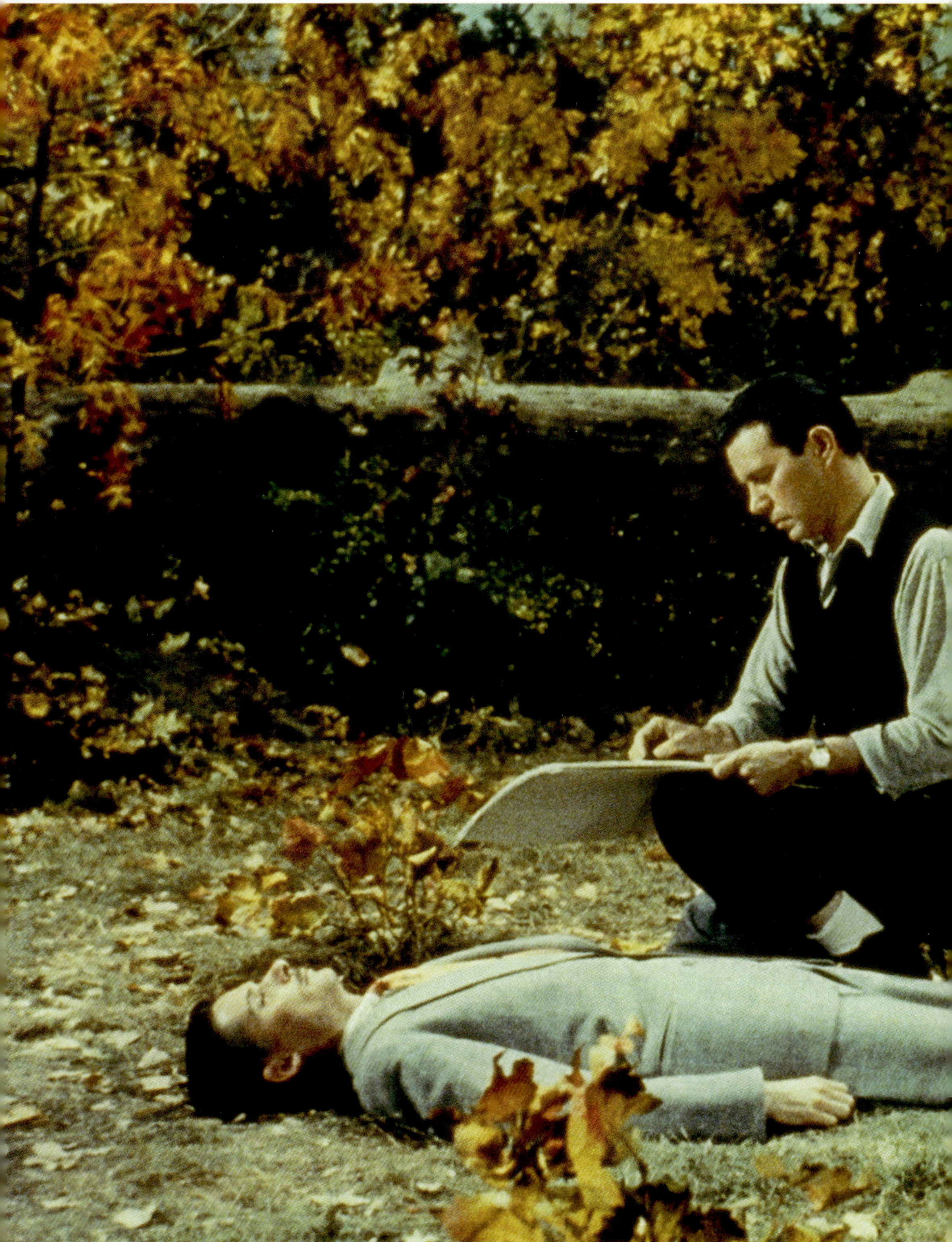

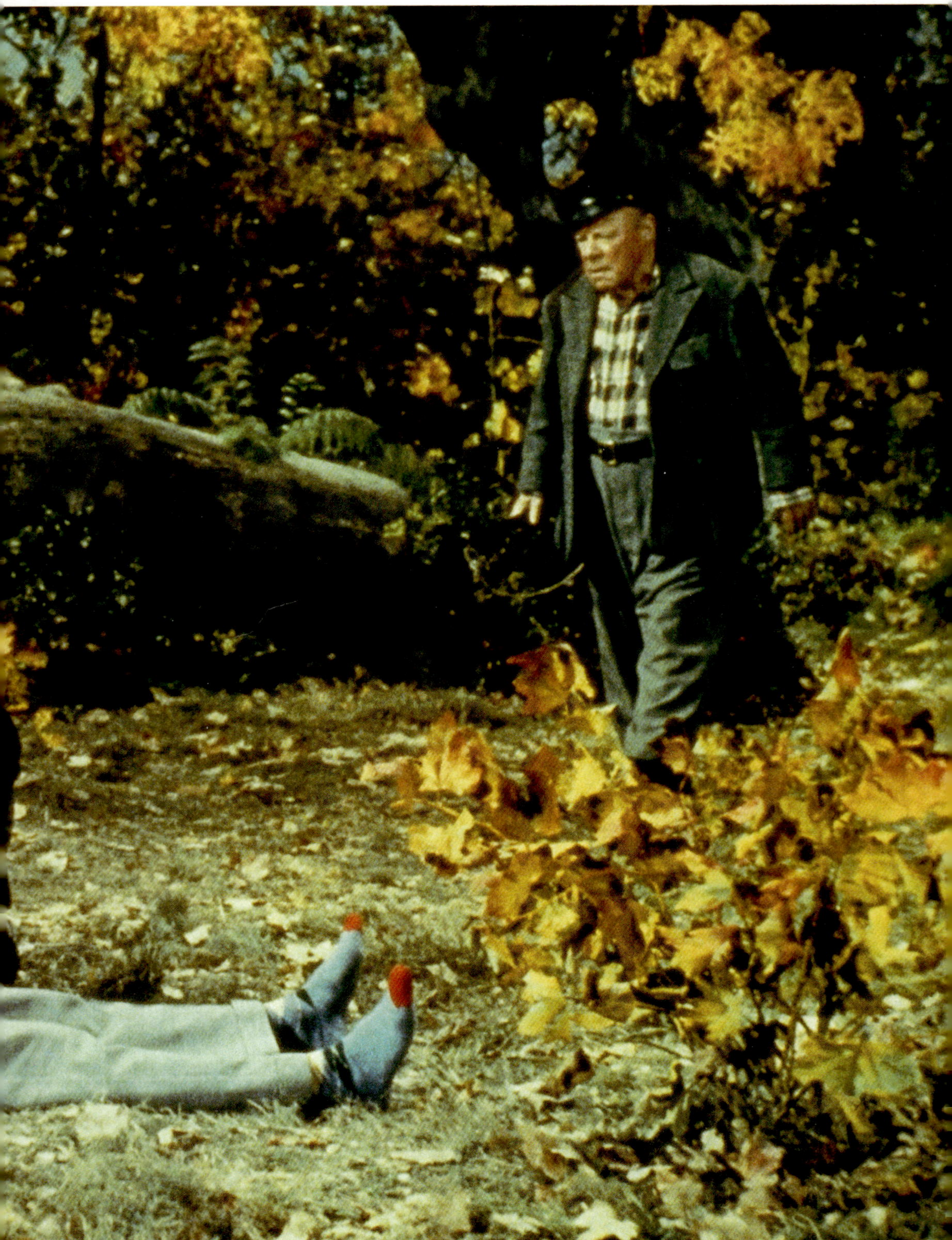

FIG. 2 Alfred Hitchcock still from the film **The Trouble with Harry** 1955 Courtesy Paramount Pictures

Douglas Fogle is Associate Curator of Visual Arts at the Walker Art Center and organizer of the exhibition *Painting at the Edge of the World*. During his tenure at the Walker he has initiated a series of exhibitions with emerging artists such as Daniel Oates, T. J. Wilcox, and Bonnie Collura, as well as a number of larger exhibitions including *Stills: Emerging Photography in the 1990s* (1997) and *Diana Thater: Orchids in the Land of Technology* (1997), and *Unfinished History* (1998) with Francesco Bonami. As a writer he has published widely in exhibition catalogues and journals such as *frieze*, *Flash Art*, and *Parkett*.

The Trouble with Painting

Douglas Fogle

"The question was: Why do painters still paint? For me the reason is clear. Because the world is flat." — Marlene Dumas[1]

The opening scenes of Alfred Hitchcock's film *The Trouble with Harry* (1955) present a montage of the beautiful autumn landscape in rural Vermont. Taking in pastoral vistas reminiscent of the Hudson River School paintings of the mid-nineteenth century, Hitchcock's camera shatters the arcadian beauty of this serene setting as it trains its unmoving focus on the dead body of Harry Worp. Shot from an extremely low angle, the forced perspective is similar to that in Mantegna's classic Renaissance painting *The Lamentation Over the Dead Christ*. As the film progresses, Harry's dead body provides the motivational force of the narrative, being buried, unearthed, and buried over and over again. After Harry's final exhumation, his body is washed, his clothes are laundered and pressed, and he is yet again put out to pasture, where he was originally found—becoming once more part of the landscape, a corpse waiting to be discovered by the authorities at a later time. The film ends with a stunning view of this New England countryside, with over-titles that read "The trouble with Harry is over." A dead body enters this hypernormal American rural community, strangely disturbing the peace, hijinks ensue, a community of conspirators is formed, and finally the dead body is disposed of unceremoniously. Up comes the Bernard Herrmann musical score and social order is seemingly restored. Or is it? In the end, is a troublesome body really so easily disposed of?

In many ways Hitchcock's black comedy is a film about painting, employing or invoking motifs and elements from this medium such as the still life, the memento mori, and the landscape. More to the point, the film's central male character, Sam Marlowe, is the filmic embodiment of a modern painter circa 1955, living in isolation in this sleepy rural community and exhibiting provocative but tasteful amounts of expressionist eccentricities as he creates his abstract paintings. One of the final moments of the film bears out Sam's recognition as a brilliant painter, when a sophisticated Manhattan millionaire—equally reminiscent of the cartoon tycoon from the board game Monopoly and of the contemporary British art collector Charles Saatchi—"discovers" the genius of these paintings and purchases the whole lot. (Enter the art market, stage left.)

But in a more metaphorical sense, *The Trouble with Harry* provides an apt backdrop for a discussion about the nature of painting today. For the trouble that Hitchcock's dead body provokes throughout this film is similar to that caused by the corpse of painting, which seems to be uncovered with great regularity every few decades or so. Throughout the last 150 years, with the precision of a finely tuned art-historical clock, painting has appeared at the hospital emergency room "dead on arrival." But, like the inert body of Harry, painting lies there in plain sight, dead yet very much present, and strangely lacking the rigor mortis that is characteristic of cadavers as we know them. Like the characters in Hitchcock's film, many of us seem troubled by the status of painting's fluctuating life signs. But what exactly is the trouble with painting? Why does it confound us so much? What is the power of this medium, which we profess to love and to hate so virulently? And more significantly, why has its status as living or dead become so important to us?

We, too, try to bury our body—the body of painting—over and over again. And while at times the heralding of these deaths seems downright apocalyptic ("Really, this is the end . . . seriously"), in the end it seems much more like a nuisance than like an aesthetic *Götterdämmerung*. Though collectively troubled by painting's status, we barely flinch when it miraculously rises from the dead again and again. This continual death and rebirth of painting, what we might call its Lazarus effect, has become a common feature of the artistic landscape over the past 200 years, ranging from Paul Delaroche's perhaps apocryphal declaration upon seeing his first Daguerreotype more than 150 years ago that "from today painting is dead" to Mondrian's Neo-Plasticism, Ad Reinhardt's "last paintings," and the constant allusions to the "death of painting" in the critical discourse of the 1980s.[2] Like Harry, however, the body of painting never seems to go away. In a manner similar to the doctor in Hitchcock's film, we continually stumble over the body of painting, get up, and keep on walking down our path. The millionaire also seems to be equally present, buying up painting without regard to how much dirt remains on its body after its exhumation.

Today, however, with another so-called resurgence of painting at the dawn of the new millennium, it has become clear once again that reports of this medium's death have been greatly exaggerated. In fact, painting has never gone away, but, like a virus exposed to an antibiotic, it has mutated, imprinting its genetic code on an entire new generation of descendants. But is the question of painting's vitality really the one that we should be asking? Perhaps it's rather a question of the ontology of painting, the very nature of its being. If we move the discussion of painting out of the realm of its death and rebirth, maybe the questions we should be asking are these: Is painting a mode of thought? Is there a philosophy of painting that extends beyond the confines of the medium? Where does the edge of the canvas end and the edge of the world begin?

The edge of the canvas and the edge of the world. These two liminal spaces have been intricately linked since the origin of the technology of the portable picture plane in the Middle Ages. Writers and theoreticians of perspective of the Italian Renaissance, such as Leon Battista Alberti, suggested that a system of painting could provide a window on the world and thereby make that world intelligible and available to the viewer. The *Weltanschauung* that these Western systems of perspective reflected was, of course, intimately tied to the spirit of exploration that would once and for all disprove the flat earth theory and clear the way for the following 500 years of creeping globalization. Strangely enough, it was the same intellectual moment that both disproved the idea of a radically defined "edge" of the world and pioneered the translation of this new global view onto the flat picture plane. One kind of flatness brazenly replaced another, while the edge of the world was displaced from a hypothetical point of geography to the edge of an easel-based canvas. It is this connection between the birth of the pictorial representation of the world and the material exploitation of that same world, pioneered by the so-called "age of discovery," that has been at the crux of a number of ideological critiques of painting, from those of critic Walter Benjamin in the 1920s and 1930s to the aesthetic interventions of artists such as Daniel Buren from the 1960s onward.

Buren first came to prominence for his attempt to reach what Roland Barthes termed a "zero degree" of painting with his installations of neutral stripes applied directly to the wall. One of Buren's earliest and most memorable "refusals" of painting was enacted with his colleagues Oliver Mosset, Michel Parmentier, and Niele Toroni under the aegis of their group participation in the 1967 Salon de Jeune Peinture held at the Musée d'art moderne in Paris. Working in the gallery space, the artists fabricated their own reductive individual motifs on a series of canvases of equal size. Buren employed his now characteristic vertical red and white stripes; Mosset painted black circles on a white ground; Parmentier painted horizontal bands of gray and white; and Toroni painted square blue marks on a white ground. At the end of the day, their work was withdrawn from the gallery except for an empty sign reading "Buren, Mosset, Parmentier, and Toroni are not exhibiting."[3] This performance as refusal was accompanied by the following text, handed out by the artists in the form of a flyer explaining why they refused to exhibit:

Because painting is a game,
Because painting is the application (consciously or otherwise) of the rules of composition,
Because painting is the freezing of movement,
Because painting is the representation (or interpretation or appropriation or disputation or presentation) of objects,
Because painting is a springboard for the imagination,
Because painting is spiritual illustration,
Because painting is justification,
Because painting serves an end,
Because to paint is to give aesthetic value to flowers, women, eroticism, the daily environment, art, dadaism, psychoanalysis, and the war in Vietnam,
We are not painters.[4]

This suspicion of painting was part and parcel of the dramatic challenges to the dominant tradition of the visual arts that was being mounted in the 1960s through conceptualist

FIG. 3 Daniel Buren Photo-souvenir: "Manifestation n°1: Buren, Mosset, Parmentier, Toroni," Salon de la Jeune Peinture, Musée d'art moderne de la Ville de Paris 1967 © D.B.

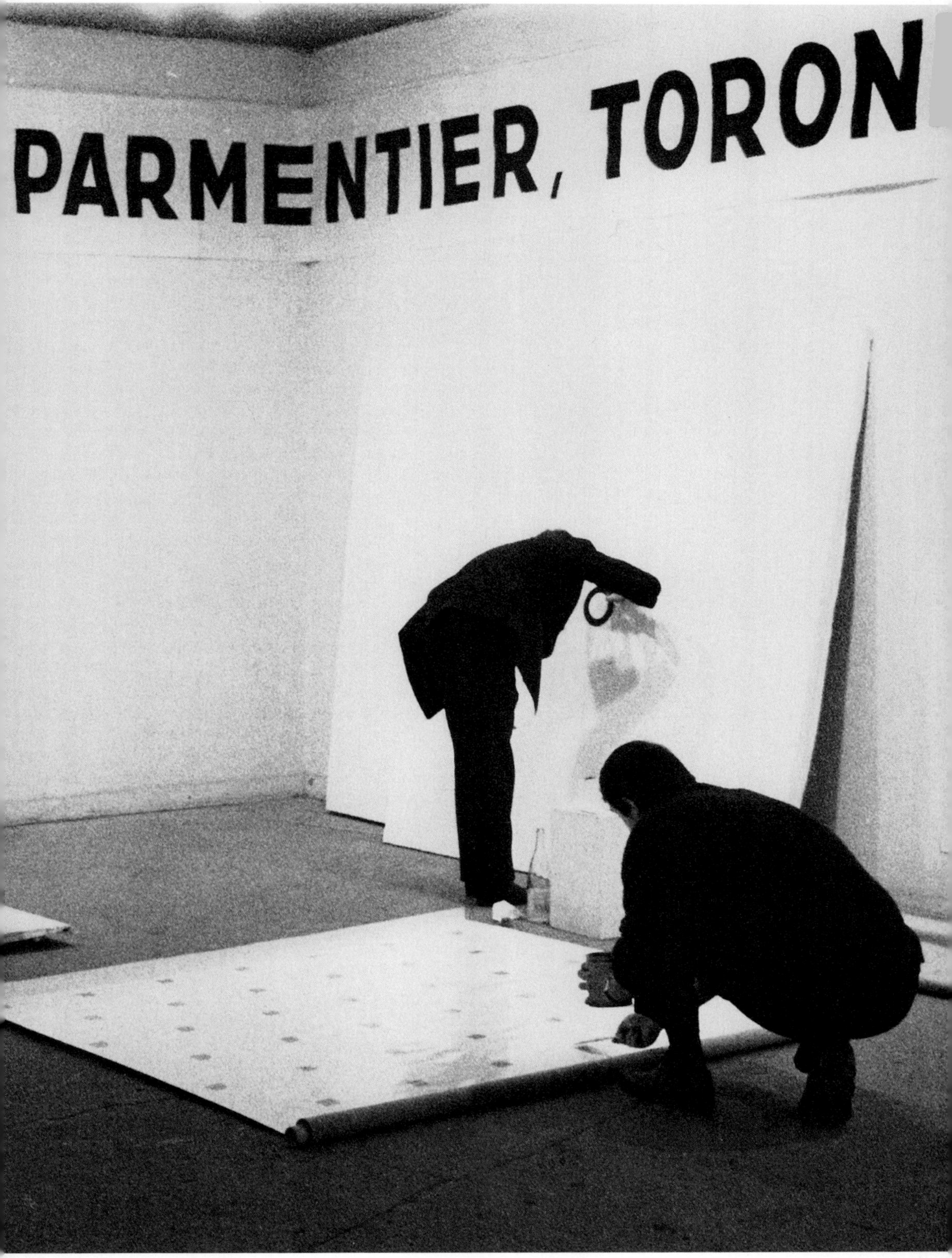
PARMENTIER, TORON

critical approaches to artistic production. One could devote an entire volume to this particular topic, tracing the multitude of different manifestations of the "refusal" of painting in an increasingly globalized artistic community. Coming of age intellectually in the 1980s, I myself am the educational product of a generation of artists and critics who developed this suspicion, which I am calling our trouble with painting. Raised on equal doses of the Picture Theory photographers (Cindy Sherman, Sherrie Levine, Barbara Kruger, Richard Prince), the psychoanalytical iconoclasm of *Screen* magazine theorists such as Laura Mulvey and Stephen Heath, and the writings of Walter Benjamin, we developed our own trouble with painting. In this intellectual climate, Clement Greenberg's apotheosis of Abstract Expressionism in the construction of his own Kantian reduction of "modernist painting" seemed equally suspect and *retardataire*. And despite the increasing ascendance of a number of major artists and painting movements—from Francesco Clemente and the transavanguardia to Anselm Kiefer and the Neo-Expressionists and on to the American contingent that included Julian Schnabel, David Salle, and Eric Fischl—Buren's refusal of painting seemed to me aptly justified.

But what if painting today is no longer what Buren and his cohorts imagined it to be? What if the refusal to paint implicit in their work—their attempt to reach a zero degree of painting—no longer holds the power it once did? What if the ground has shifted beyond the parameters in which their refusal was enacted? Ironically, these questions were first suggested to me in part while reading a review of an exhibition of Andreas Gursky's photographs by critic Howard Halle. Upon viewing this exhibition, Halle came to the conclusion that "'painting' is a philosophical enterprise that doesn't always involve paint." Referring specifically to what he saw as the painterly mode of Gursky's photographic compositions, Halle reformulated his understanding of the ontology of painting in order to suggest that it is "a way of organizing the world that represents neither truth nor fiction exclusively but rather a little of both. Whether an artist uses a brush or a camera to achieve that goal scarcely matters."[5]

It was after reading this review that I finally began to think about my own trouble with painting, the gnawing feeling that my iconoclastic philosophical indoctrination had led me to a similar critical refusal of painting (but also of the pleasure of viewing). As I began to reflect on the state of painting today—its ontology—I started thinking about a number of Buren's own contemporaries who might offer us a way out of this endgame and who perhaps cleared the ground for an entirely different range of possibilities for painting in a new generation of artists working today. The exhibition *Painting at the Edge of the World* begins with three of these historical precedents, emphasizing artists who began to question the traditional modernist definitions of painting that were popular in the 1960s.

Brazilian artist Hélio Oiticica (1937–1980) attempted both in his art and in his writings to answer the question of painting's relationship to the world, suggesting in 1961 that "never has painting so approached life, the 'feeling of life.'"[6] In his *Spatial Reliefs*, *Nuclei*, and *Penetrables*, Oiticica expanded the definition and the physical manifestation of painting by exploring the notion of painting in space and radically altering the viewer's relationship to both the object of painting and the plane of representation. In his work *Nucleus NC 1* (1960, p. 317), for example, the artist's experiments led him to an evolution of the notion of the painting's support surface by removing it from the wall, contorting it, and merging it with color in a radical hybridization of painting and sculpture that he termed a "non-object." This action was also seen by the artist to give the work a temporal dimension lacking in traditional wall-bound painting. In his *Bolides*, on the other hand, Oiticica attempted to overcome the limitations of traditional painting by "incorporating" the medium, giving color a body in a series of containers that held raw pigment. As he suggested, "The problem of painting is resolved by the destruction of the picture, or by its incorporation into space and time."[7] In his formulation, rather than refusing to paint, the artist merges color, structure, space, and the dimension of time in a radical redefinition of painting at the edge of an expanding notion of the world.

The paintings of American artist Paul Thek (1933–1988) offer another possibility for thinking about the ontology of painting. Operating against the grain of the mainstream versions of modernism in ascendance in the 1960s, Thek painted works on newsprint and canvas that eschewed the heroic mannerisms of the Abstract Expressionists in favor of a consciously "minor" position. His intimately scaled "picture light" paintings (pp. 343–345), for example, which were installed low on the wall in gilt bamboo frames and illuminated by small overhanging lamps, intensified the viewer's awareness of the act of looking at painting while additionally offering a critique of the high seriousness of both modernist painting and museological practices. Employing a consciously naive style, these paintings explored a field of sentimentality and an aesthetics of failure through the use of a vernacular, anti-heroic vocabulary. Thek's intentionally "bad" paintings are iconoclastic in their execution as well as their content, which is riddled with humorous irreverence. With subjects ranging from landscapes to religious iconography (*Pink Cross and Green Buds*, 1975–1980) to cartoon imagery (*Bambi Growing*, 1979–1980) to a continuation of Jasper Johns' number series (Thek began with number 11) to his send-ups of abstraction (*Abstract Pattern on a Cave Wall*, 1980) and of petroglyphs (*Neolithic Porno*, 1979–1980), Thek takes on the history of painting in a sincere if pointed manner, while insisting on its irrepressible necessity.

Ironically, perhaps the most radical gesture in Thek's paintings from the 1960s to the 1980s was his insistence on the possibility of visual beauty and the pleasure of looking, which was critical anathema in many artistic circles at that time. As he himself suggested, "The paintings [in his exhibition *A Lot of Little Paintings*, 1980] were about theology, psychology, philosophy, art, and, hopefully in all of them, humor. Though in some, I got caught in beauty. I thought, 'Let's just make this one be beautiful, not have anything to do with anything else!'"[8] Retroactively, one can see in Thek's work an opposition to the critical dogma of the day operative in Minimalism and Conceptual Art as he navigated a troubled path between an ecclesiastical desire for enlightenment and the banality of the modern world around him.

Belgian artist Marcel Broodthaers (1924–1976) took another approach to the question of our trouble with painting, negotiating a strangely ambiguous position between this medium and those of photography and film, as in his slide installation *Tableau-Bateau* (1973, pp. 247–249). In eighty color slides that meticulously record and dissect fragments of a small amateur painting of a fishing boat at sea, Broodthaers enacts a parody of the formalist close readings characteristic of traditional art-historical analysis. This circa 1900 anonymous seascape, having been acquired by the artist at a curio shop in Paris, would become the subject not only of this slide installation but also of three other works: two 16mm films entitled *Analyse d'une peinture* (1973) and *A Voyage on the North Sea* (1973–1974), and a companion book entitled *A Voyage on the North Sea* (1973). In each, Broodthaers enacts a conceptual deconstruction of this painting and of painting in general, but he also constructs a strangely sympathetic homage to an anonymous Sunday painter working at the turn of the century. At the same time, Broodthaers foregrounds the tension between time and movement in a world where painting is confronted by the power of photography and film.

In their own unique ways, each of these three artists opened up a field of possibilities that has enabled us to think outside of the endgame exemplified by Buren and his colleagues. One materialized the plane of the canvas into the space and time of the three-dimensional world. Another opted to remain within the confines of the picture plane and the genre of paint on canvas but adopted a style and a manner of presentation that challenged the heroic sanctity of modernist painterly practice. The third took a conceptual approach to the question of painting by photomechanically analyzing an amateur work as if it had been painted by an old master. As the example of these artists suggests, the works in *Painting at the Edge of the World* do not always conform to the traditional definition of painting on canvas or to what we might expect of paint on canvas. And while these examples offer no more than a skeletal genealogy of a contemporary ontology of painting, we can at least provisionally speculate that artists such as Oiticica, Thek, Broodthaers, and even Buren were integral in establishing the apparent freedom and heterogeneity of painting today—the multiple permutations of possible methods with which to approach it as a question.

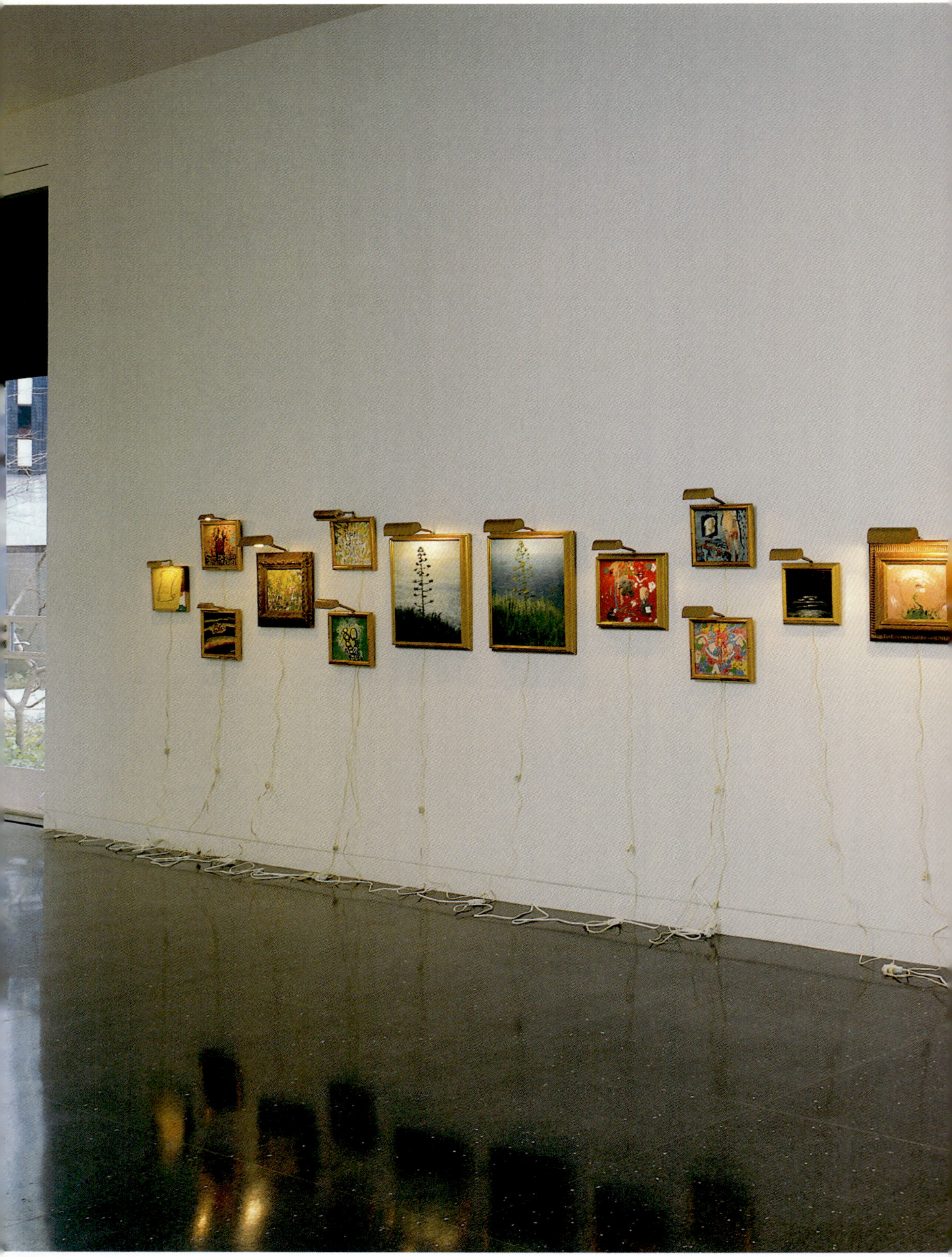

FIG. 4 installation view of Paul Thek's "picture light" paintings from the exhibition **Paul Thek: Paintings, Works on Paper, and Notebooks 1970–1988** at The Arts Club of Chicago, 1998 Courtesy The Arts Club of Chicago

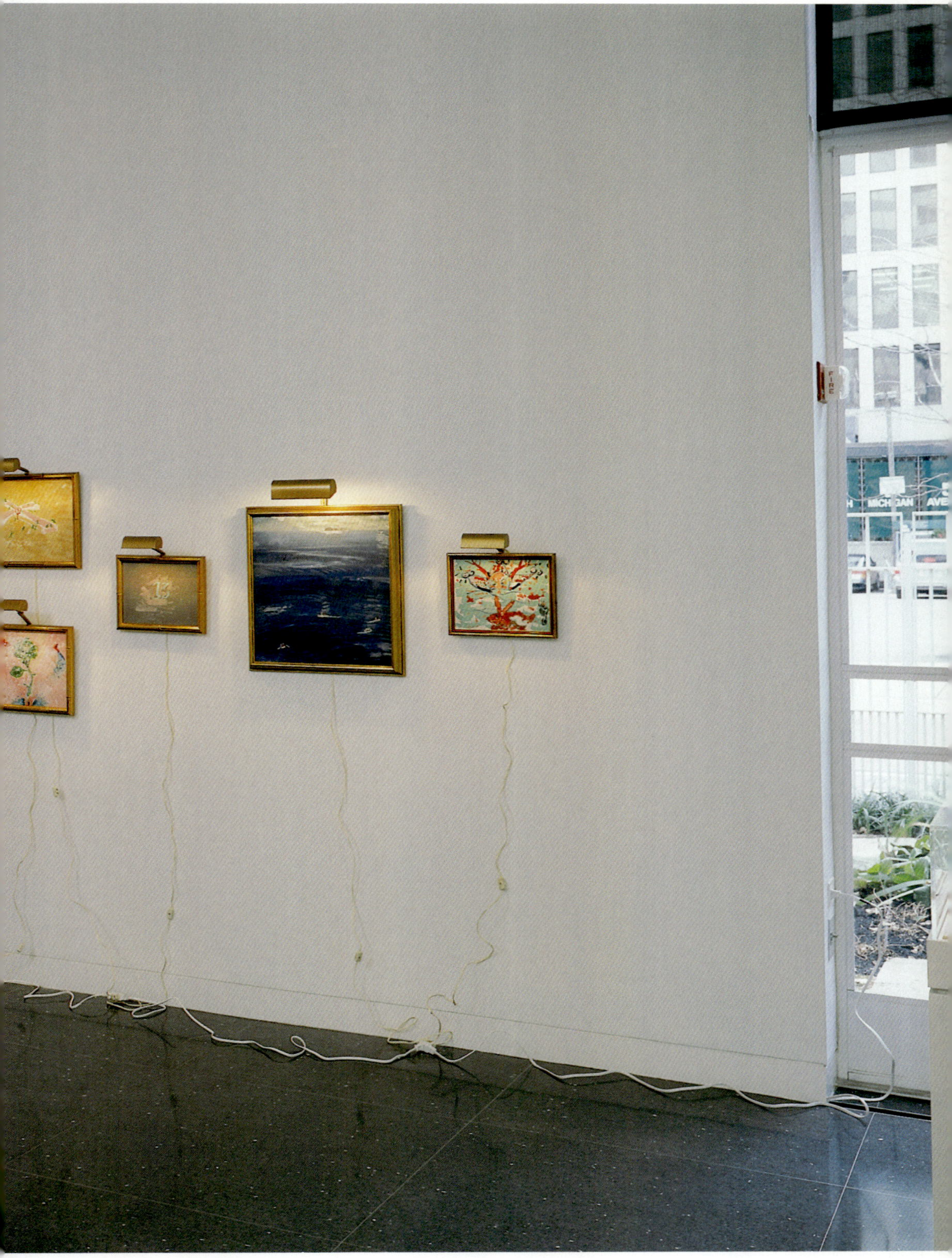

What has become clear today is that, in light of all our trouble with painting, its practice is no longer solely bound by such traditional categories as figuration, abstraction, portraiture, and landscape, or even by the conventional definition of the medium as paint on canvas. The artists in *Painting at the Edge of the World* demonstrate that a philosophy of painting is found today not only in these genres but also in a photograph (Andreas Gursky), in a walk through a city (Francis Alÿs), in a club culture–inspired application of vinyl tape on the floor (Jim Lambie), in cast rubber "paintings" (Martin Kippenberger), or in paint applied directly to a wall (Arturo Herrera, Richard Wright, Franz Ackermann, Haluk Akakçe).

Classical figuration takes many forms in this exhibition, from a variety of approaches to portraiture (John Currin, Marlene Dumas, Margherita Manzelli, Laura Owens) to the televisual (Eberhard Havekost) to the merging of decorative illustration and the cybernetic (Haluk Akakçe) or the provocative marriage of traditional Japanese Nihonga painting with the iconography and temporal dimensions of *manga* and *anime* (Takashi Murakami). Likewise, abstraction is no longer the purely reductive act popularized by modernism but now begins to look like techno-organic topography (Udomsak Krisanamis), a hybrid blurring of the decorative, the figurative, and the abstract (Chris Ofili), an explosion of cartoon iconography (Arturo Herrera), or an intersection of the volumetric geometry of architecture with the flatness of the picture plane (Kevin Appel, Julie Mehretu). The genre of landscape painting manifests a similarly heterogeneous set of approaches as well, ranging from contorted scenarios rendered with accreted amalgamations of paint and embroidery (Michael Raedecker) to the quiet and psychological flattening of pictorial space in childlike renderings of battles (Hiroshi Sugito) to the highly graphic depiction of the architectural landscape with an impure palette drained of its energy (Thomas Scheibitz).

The content of the work in this exhibition is equally wide-ranging, with, for example, one artist confronting the relationship between the philosophical mode of thinking and painting (Nader), another looking at her own fascination with the mass spectacle of sports as embodied in the Olympics (Lucy McKenzie), and another directly confronting the traumatic legacy of modernist painting and the underside of American popular culture (Mike Kelley). In the end, at least one of the artists in *Painting at the Edge of the World* cuts across all of the traditional genres and subjects of painting in an exploration of the vicissitudes of the multiplicitous vocabularies of painting (Paul Thek).

In each of these cases, painting's traditional function as a window on the world has been circumvented, or rather someone has left the window open and a number of things have crawled in. Whether working in performative (Paul McCarthy, Francis Alÿs), sculptural (Hélio Oiticica, Thomas Schütte), or conceptual veins (Marcel Broodthaers, Rudolf Stingel), or in the traditional category of paint on canvas, the artists in *Painting at the Edge of the World* redefine both the nature and the continued relevance of a philosophy of painting at a time when the space between the edge of the canvas and the edge of the world has been radically blurred.

It is important to note that *Painting at the Edge of the World* is a two-fold project, each part complementary to but independent of the other. On the one hand, it is an exhibition that includes work by thirty artists from across the globe and spanning a number of generations. On the other hand, *Painting at the Edge of the World* is a book of essays by a number of today's most provocative established and emerging voices in the field of criticism, each of whom poses a new set of questions about the particular manifestations of the discourse of painting today. Yve-Alain Bois' influential essay "Painting: The Task of Mourning," for example, is perhaps the only text on the death of painting written in the 1980s that addresses what I have referred to as painting's "Lazarus effect." Unlike many of his contemporaries, who were content to grimly herald the death of this medium, Bois set out to examine the apocalyptic tone of the discourse that infused the debates around the viability of painting from the birth of modernism to the 1980s. In examining the end of painting, Bois suggests that while "mourning has been the activity of painting throughout this century," only a nonpathological mourning holds the hope of any future possibility of painting.

The troublesome nature of the "tableau" is the topic of Hubert Damisch's 1991 essay "The Trickery of the Picture." Looking at the double entendre of the word "tableau" in French, which suggests both a picture and the support on which it is painted (table), he asks us to think about whether or not the picture is a thing of the past. Discussing its historical, chronological, dialectical, and ontological manifestations, the author suggests that the picture form continues today, in a covert way, even in the aftermath of the death of painting. Asserting its presence through a kind of "trickery," the picture form of classical painting, according to Damisch, "has not ceased to function as a model and ideal standard, even though the concept as such has been radically transformed."

Jörg Heiser's essay "The Odd Couple" approaches the question of painting's troubled history from the perspective of the "uncanny resemblance between the discourses around the contemporary status of painting and that of rock music." In diagnosing a mutually imbricated crisis of legitimation for both painting and rock music, Heiser asks us to consider the parallel responses of each to the threat to their continued relevance in an age defined by the ubiquitous presence of electronic media.

Andrew Blauvelt also challenges the sanctity of the reductivist vision of modernist painting championed by the likes of Clement Greenberg by bringing it into a proximate relation with another medium. In his essay "No Visible Means of Support," Blauvelt gives center stage to the relationship between architecture and painting in an examination that unearths their mutual dependence both historically and in a contemporary cultural context.

Daniel Birnbaum's essay "Late Arrivals" continues the focus on a notion of painting in the extended field, stressing the philosophical importance of delay and repetition as operative structures in the history of art. Looking specifically at the utopian impulses of the state-sponsored modernism of 1960s Sweden—as exemplified by Olle Bærtling's public works for the Stockholm Culture Center—and their "deferred action" today in shelter magazines such as *Wallpaper** as well as in the work of contemporary artists such as Tobias Rehberger, Birnbaum suggests that there is indeed difference in repetition.

The question of difference—cultural, political, and aesthetic—is the topic of Paulo Herkenhoff's essay "Monochromes, the Autonomy of Color, and the Centerless World." For Herkenhoff, the white monochrome can be seen as having reemerged simultaneously and independently across the globe in the 1960s and 1970s, thereby providing a provocative paradigm that stresses the assertion of cultural difference and the displacement of eurocentric models of viewing the history of art. As he suggests, "White monochromes reveal the world marked by solitary differences" and chart a course "from the notion of zero to the critical recording of history."

Midori Matsui's essay "New Openings in Japanese Painting" investigates the question of cultural difference in contemporary Japanese painting from the perspective of Gilles Deleuze and Felix Guattari's notion of "minor literature," which stresses the importance of the subversion of the dominant language from within by its nonindigenous users. Specifically addressing the work of Takashi Murakami, Tam Ochiai, Hiroshi Sugito, and Yoshitomo Nara, Matsui looks at the different ways each of these artists has forged an aesthetic identity by "deploying their cultural past as technical resources and ideological prototypes" while subverting both these traditions and the colonial legacy of Western modernism.

In his essay "Painting and Trance in Severo Sarduy's *La simulación*," Reinaldo Laddaga brings to light the little-known work of Cuban poet and critic Severo Sarduy. As Laddaga points out, Sarduy's untranslated book *La simulación* (Simulation) brings together a wide range of divergent cultural references—from the mimicry practices of an Indonesian butterfly to the "simulation drive" inherent in the act of transvestism—in order to elaborate a theory of painting that highlights its relationship to trance and the slow dispersion of death.

The relationship between speech and painting is at the heart of Frances Stark's meditation

on painting, "Scared to Death." In a peripatetic linguistic sojourn, moving with equal affinity from the work of Robert Ryman to her stint faux-painting Mel Gibson's Beverly Hills home, Stark acts out not only the dissonant gap between language and vision but also our incessant desire to attempt to speak about images, as suggested by her epigraph from Emily Dickinson indicating that "speech is a symptom of affection."

This volume also includes a number of artist's texts that each address a particular relationship to the discourse of painting. In Hélio Oiticica's 1960 essay "Colour, Time, and Structure" and Takashi Murakami's recent essay "A Theory of Super Flat Japanese Art," we see two very distinct attempts to map out a new course for painting in the global context of the 1960s and 1990s respectively. Writing in the context of the Brazilian Neo-Concrete movement, Oiticica delineates a new relationship to painting in which the artist theorizes the fusion of color, structure, space, and time, which becomes materialized in the quasi-paintings that the artist termed "non-objects." Murakami's essay, on the other hand, makes a provocative case for the emergence of a unique Japanese aesthetic sensibility, which he calls "super flat," by tracing a genetic link between the innovations of the "eccentric artists" of Japan's Edo period with the unique treatment of images and cinematic timing that emerged in Japanese *anime* of the 1970s.

Mike Kelley and Marlene Dumas describe very personal relationships to painting in their texts. Kelley's essay "Goin' Home, Goin' Home," originally published on the occasion of his 1995 painting exhibition *The Thirteen Seasons (Heavy on the Winter)*, exposes the so-called normalcy of a painting's "aura of completion" as the masking of an originary psychic trauma. Looking at his own paintings as "willful perversions" of his modernist training, Kelley ponders whether it is ever possible to transgress without reinscribing the laws of the very normalcy that one is trying to circumvent. Marlene Dumas, on the other hand, takes on the question of gender in painting in an equally personal if oblique manner in her 1993 essay "Women and Painting," arguing that "If painting is female and insanity is a female malady, then all women painters are mad and all male painters are women." Poetically mapping out the reasons why she paints, Dumas charts a territory of painting that traverses the realms of domesticity, manual labor, and femininity while staking a claim for the messiness, intimacy, and visceral materiality of the medium.

Finally, Marcel Broodthaers' 1963 poem "Questions of *Painting*" asks us to consider the aura that the institutional frameworks of the museum and of art criticism impart upon painting, a fitting query for a book and an exhibition devoted to a consideration of the contemporary status of painting and the questions it provokes.

In the end, however, what is to be done about all this trouble with painting? If we keep tripping over this dead body and it keeps getting buried and exhumed over and over again, will we ever really be done with this trouble? In Hitchcock's film, the dead man is the star and the driving force of the narrative. In fact, Harry is perhaps more fully present in death than he ever was in life. Strangely, while all the characters experience a certain level of anxiety (and in some cases, complicity and guilt) regarding the presence of a corpse in their midst, none of them actually mourn Harry's passing. In his essay in this volume, Yve-Alain Bois suggests that mourning the death of painting is the condition for the possibility of its renewal. At the conclusion of "Painting: The Task of Mourning," Bois paraphrases the Austrian writer Robert Musil, who suggested in 1936 that "if some painting is still to come, if painters are still to come, they will not come from where we expect them to." Sixty-five years later, at the beginning of a new millennium, Musil's words still ring true. No exhibition can hope to give a definitive and final answer to the question of our "trouble with painting." In the best of cases, the works and essays that comprise this project will provoke more questions than they are able to answer. But looking for these unlikely painters in unexpected places is precisely the kind of trouble we should embrace. The trouble with painting is over. Or is it?

NOTES

1 Marlene Dumas, "The World Is Flat," in Marlene Dumas, *Sweet Nothings: Notes and Texts* (Amsterdam: Marlene Dumas/Galerie Paul Andriesse, 1998), p. 54.

2 Numerous discussions of the "death of painting" have been published over the past twenty years, among which stand out Douglas Crimp's essay "The End of Painting" (1981), Thomas Lawson's "Last Exit: Painting" (1981), and Yve-Alain Bois' essay "Painting: The Task of Mourning" (1986).

3 Jeffrey Deitch, "Daniel Buren: Painting Degree Zero," *Arts Magazine* 51, no. 2 (October 1976), p. 88.

4 Daniel Buren, Oliver Mosset, Michel Parmentier, and Niele Toroni, statement issued as a flyer for the Salon de la Jeune Peinture, Musée d'art moderne de la Ville de Paris, January 3, 1967. English translation published in Michel Claura, "Paris Commentary," *Studio International* (London) 177, no. 907 (January 1969), p. 47.

5 Howard Halle, "Photo-unrealism," *Time Out New York*, December 30, 1999–January 6, 2000, pp. 55–56.

6 Hélio Oiticica, "February 16, 1961," from *Aspiro ae grande labirinto* (Rio de Janeiro: Rocco, 1986). English translation published in *Hélio Oiticica* (Rotterdam: Witte de With and Minneapolis: Walker Art Center, 1992), p. 43.

7 Ibid.

8 Paul Thek interviewed by Richard Flood, "Paul Thek: Real Misunderstanding," *Artforum* (October 1981), p. 51; reprinted in *Paul Thek: The Wonderful World that Almost Was* (Rotterdam: Witte de With, 1995), pp. 105–112.

An influential conceptual artist represented in *Painting at the Edge of the World*, Marcel Broodthaers (1924–1976) produced voluminous writings in consonance with his work in other media. Challenging the formal possibilities of language, his writings range from critical essays and exhibition reviews to prose and poetry, many of which are collected in *Broodthaers: Writing, Interviews, Photographs* (1988), edited by Benjamin H. D. Buchloh. The following poem is included in that volume and was originally published in *October*, no. 42 (© 1987 Massachusetts Institute of Technology and October Magazine, Ltd.); reprinted with the permission of MIT Press.

Marcel Broodthaers
Questions of *Painting*
1963

**Is the painting of Frans Hals
done with poisonous matter?
And the one of Goya?
Both treating the human face
in a subtle manner.
Have these paintings a perverse odor
like the monstrous praise of which
they are victims?**

**Is it to critics that one should
address these questions?
Or to the organizer of exhibitions?**

TRANSLATED BY JOHN SHEPLEY

Yve-Alain Bois is Professor of Modern Art and Chair of the History of Art and Architecture Department at Harvard University. He was a founder of the French journal *Macula* and is co-editor of *October*. A renowned philosopher of art, Bois has published numerous books, including *Painting as Model* (1990), *Formless: A User's Guide* (1997) with Rosalind Krauss, and *Matisse and Picasso* (1998). As a curator he has organized major exhibitions such as *De Stijl and French Architecture in the 1920s* (1985), *Piet Mondrian Retrospective* (1994), and *Ellsworth Kelly: Early Drawings* (1999). The following essay was originally published in the exhibition catalogue *Endgame: Reference and Simulation in Recent Painting and Sculpture* (© 1986 Massachusetts Institute of Technology and the Institute of Contemporary Art, Boston); reprinted with the permission of MIT Press.

Painting: The Task of Mourning
Yve-Alain Bois
1986

"[My paintings] are about death in a way: the uneasy death of modernism."
— Sherrie Levine

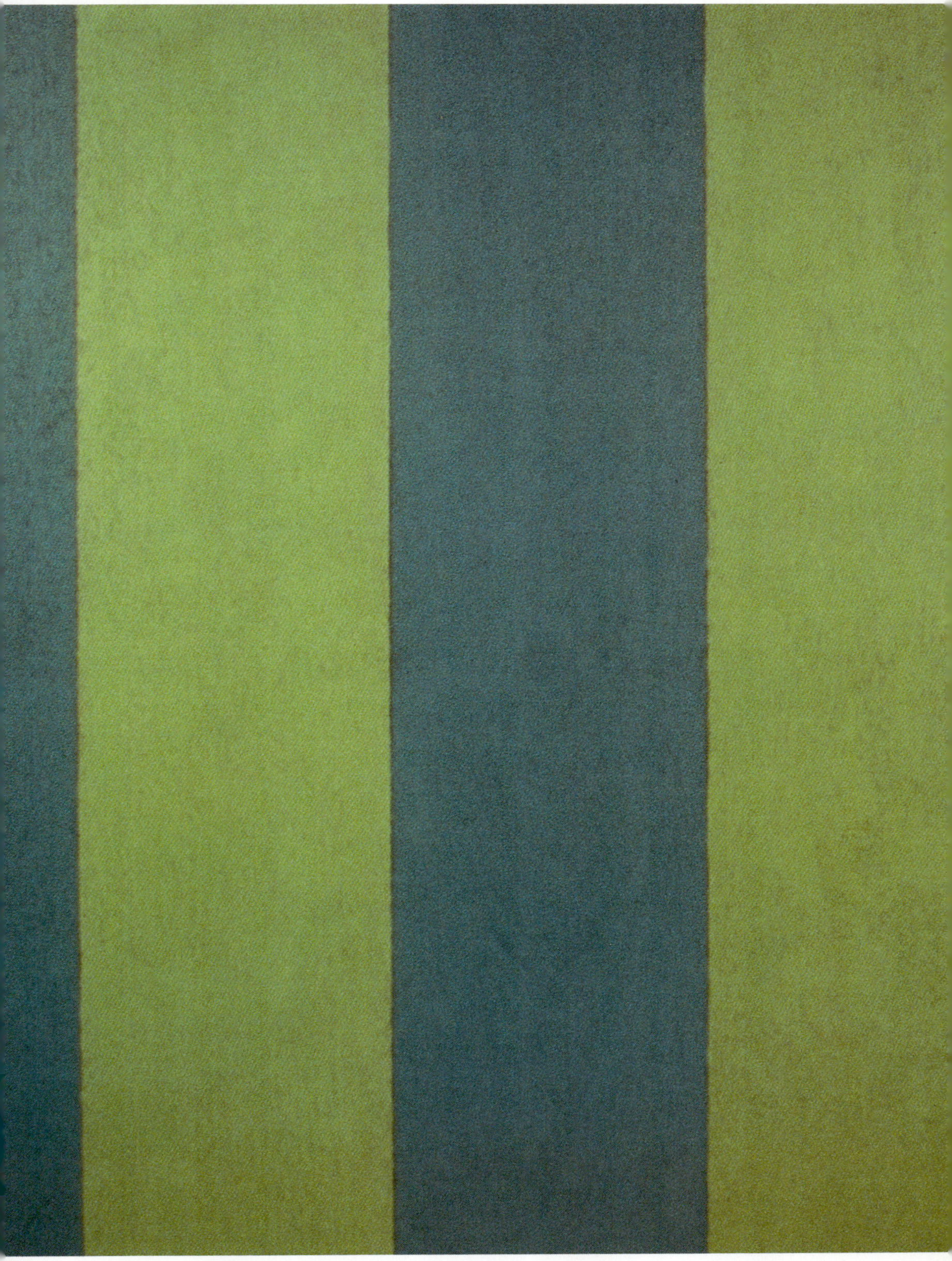

FIG. 1 Sherrie Levine **Broad Stripe #6** 1985 casein, wax on mahogany 24 x 20 in. Courtesy the artist and Margo Leavin Gallery, Los Angeles

Nothing seems to be more common in our present situation than a millenarianist feeling of closure. Whether celebratory (what I will call manic) or melancholic, one hears endless diagnoses of death: death of ideologies (Lyotard), of industrial society (Bell), of the real (Baudrillard), of authorship (Barthes), of man (Foucault), of history (Kojéve) and, of course, of modernism (all of us when we use the word postmodern). Yet what does all of this mean? From what point of view are these affirmations of death being proclaimed? Should all of these voices be characterized as the voice of mystagogy, bearing the tone that Kant stigmatized in *About a Recently Raised Pretentiously Noble Tone in Philosophy* (1796)? Derrida writes:

> **Then each time we intractably ask ourselves where they want to come to, and to what ends, those who declare the end of this or that, of man or the subject, of consciousness, of history, of the West or of literature, and according to the latest news of progress itself, the idea of which has never been in such bad health to the right and the left? What effect do these people, gentile prophets or eloquent visionaries, want to produce? In view of what immediate or adjourned benefit? What do they do, what do we do in saying this? To seduce or subjugate whom, intimidate or make come whom?[1]**

Each time, which means that there is no generic answer to this question: there is no single paradigm of the apocalyptic, and no ontological inquiry about "its" tone. Because the tone of their writings is so different, it would be particularly misguided, and perverse, to connect Barthes to Baudrillard, Foucault to Bell, Lyotard to Kojéve—but it is done in the theoretical potpourri one reads month after month in the flashy magazines of the art world. Derrida's proviso, *each time*, means that in each instance one must examine the tone of the apocalyptic discourse: its claim to be the pure revelation of truth, and the last word about the end.

I will focus here on a specific claim: that of the death of painting, and more specifically, the death of abstract painting. The meaning of this claim is bounded by two historical circumstances: the first is that the whole history of abstract painting can be read as a longing for its death; and the second is the recent emergence of a group of neoabstract painters who have been marketed as its official mourners (or should I say resurrectors? But we will see that it is the same). The first circumstance leads to the question: when did all of this start? Where can we locate the beginning of the end in modern painting—that is, the feeling of the end, the discourse about the end, and the representation of the end? The existence of a new generation of painters interested in these issues leads to the question: is abstract painting still possible? In turn, this question can be divided into at least two others: Is (abstract, but also any other kind of) *painting* still possible? And is *abstract* (painting, but also sculpture, film, modes of thought, etc.) still possible? (A third thread of the question, specifically apocalyptic, would be: is [abstract painting, but also anything, life, desire, etc.] still possible?)

The question about the beginning of the end and the question about the (still) possibility of painting are historically linked; it is the question about the (still) possibility of painting that is at the beginning of the end, and it is this beginning of the end that has been our history, namely, what we are accustomed to name *modernism*. Indeed the whole enterprise of modernism, especially of abstract painting, which can be taken as its emblem, could not have functioned without an apocalyptic myth. Freed from all extrinsic conventions, abstract painting was meant to bring forth the pure *parousia* of its own essence, to tell the final truth and thereby terminate its course. The pure beginning, the liberation from tradition, the "zero degree" that was searched for by the first generation of abstract painters could not but function as an omen of the end. One did not have to wait for the "last painting" of Ad Reinhardt to be aware that through its historicism (its linear conception of history) and through its essentialism (its idea that something like the essence of painting existed, veiled somehow, and waiting to be unmasked), the enterprise of abstract painting could not but understand its birth as calling for its end. As Malevich wrote: "There can be no question of painting in Suprematism; painting was done for long ago, and the artist himself is a prejudice of the past."[2] And Mondrian endlessly postulated that his painting was preparing for the end of painting—its dissolution in the all encompassing sphere of life-as-art or environment-as-art—which would occur once the absolute essence of painting was "determined." If one can take abstract painting as the emblem of modernism, however, one should not imagine that the feeling of the end is solely a function of its essentialism; rather it is necessary to interpret this essentialism as the effect of a larger historical crisis. This crisis is well known—it can be termed industrialization—and its impact on painting has been analyzed by the best critics, following a line of investigation begun half a century ago by Walter Benjamin.[3] This discourse centers around the appearance of photography, and of mass production, both of which were understood as causing the end of painting. Photography was perceived this way by even the least subtle practitioners. ("'*From today painting is dead*': it is now nearly a century and a half since Paul Delaroche is said to have pronounced that sentence in the face of the overwhelming evidence of Daguerre's invention."[4]) Mass production seemed to bode the end of painting through its most elaborate *mise-en-scène*, the invention of the readymade. Photography and mass production were also at the base of the essentialist urge of modernist painting. Challenged by the mechanical apparatus of photography, and by the mass-produced, painting had to redefine its status, to reclaim a specific domain (much in the way this was done during the Renaissance, when painting was posited as one of the "liberal arts" as opposed to the "mechanical arts").

The beginnings of this agonistic struggle have been well described by Meyer Schapiro: the emphasis on the touch, on texture, and on gesture in modern painting is a consequence of the division of labor inherent in industrial production. Industrial capitalism banished the hand from the process of production; the work of art alone, as craft, still implied manual handling and therefore artists were compelled, by reaction, to demonstrate the exceptional nature of their mode of production.[5] From Courbet to Pollock one witnesses a practice of one-upmanship. In many ways the various "returns to painting" we are witnessing today seem like the farcical repetition of this historical progression. There were, it is true, simple negations: for instance, van Doesburg's *Art Concret* (the dream of a geometric art that could be entirely programmed) and Moholy-Nagy's *Telephone-paintings*. But it is only with Robert Ryman that the theoretical demonstration of the historical position of painting as an exceptional realm of manual mastery has been carried to its full extent and, as it were, deconstructed (fig. 2). By his dissection of the gesture, or of the pictorial raw material, and by his (nonstylistic) analysis of the stroke, Ryman produces a kind of dissolution of the relationship between the trace and its organic referent. The body of the artist moves toward the condition of photography: the division of labor is interiorized. What is at stake for Ryman is no longer affirming the uniqueness of the pictorial mode of production vis-à-vis the general mode of production of commodities, but decomposing it mechanically. Ryman's deconstruction has nothing to do with a negation (contrary to what most of its readers think, what is called deconstruction has very little to do with negation per se. Instead, it elaborates a kind of negativity that is not trapped in the dialectical vector of affirmation, negation, and sublation). Ryman's dissolution is posited, but endlessly restrained, amorously deferred; the process (which identifies the trace with its "subjective" origin) is endlessly stretched: the thread is never cut.

If I insist on Ryman, it is because in his art the feeling of an end is worked through in the most resolved way. Although he is claimed by some as a postmodernist, I would say he is more accurately the guardian of the tomb of modernist painting, at once knowing of the end and also knowing the impossibility of arriving at it without working it through. Asymptotically, his paintings get closer and closer to the condition of the photograph or of the readymade, yet remain at the threshold of simple negation. His position is difficult to maintain, yet it is perhaps, historically, the most cogent one.[6] To understand this, we must look again at the historical development that preceded him. "If we could describe the art of this, the first half of the twentieth century, in a sentence, it would read as the search for something to paint; just as, were we to do the same for modern art as a whole, it must read as the critical preoccupation of artists with solving the *technical* problems of the painting medium. Here is the dividing line of the history of art," writes Barnett Newman, reminding us of Schapiro's insistence on the importance of touch, texture, and gesture.[7] But the para-

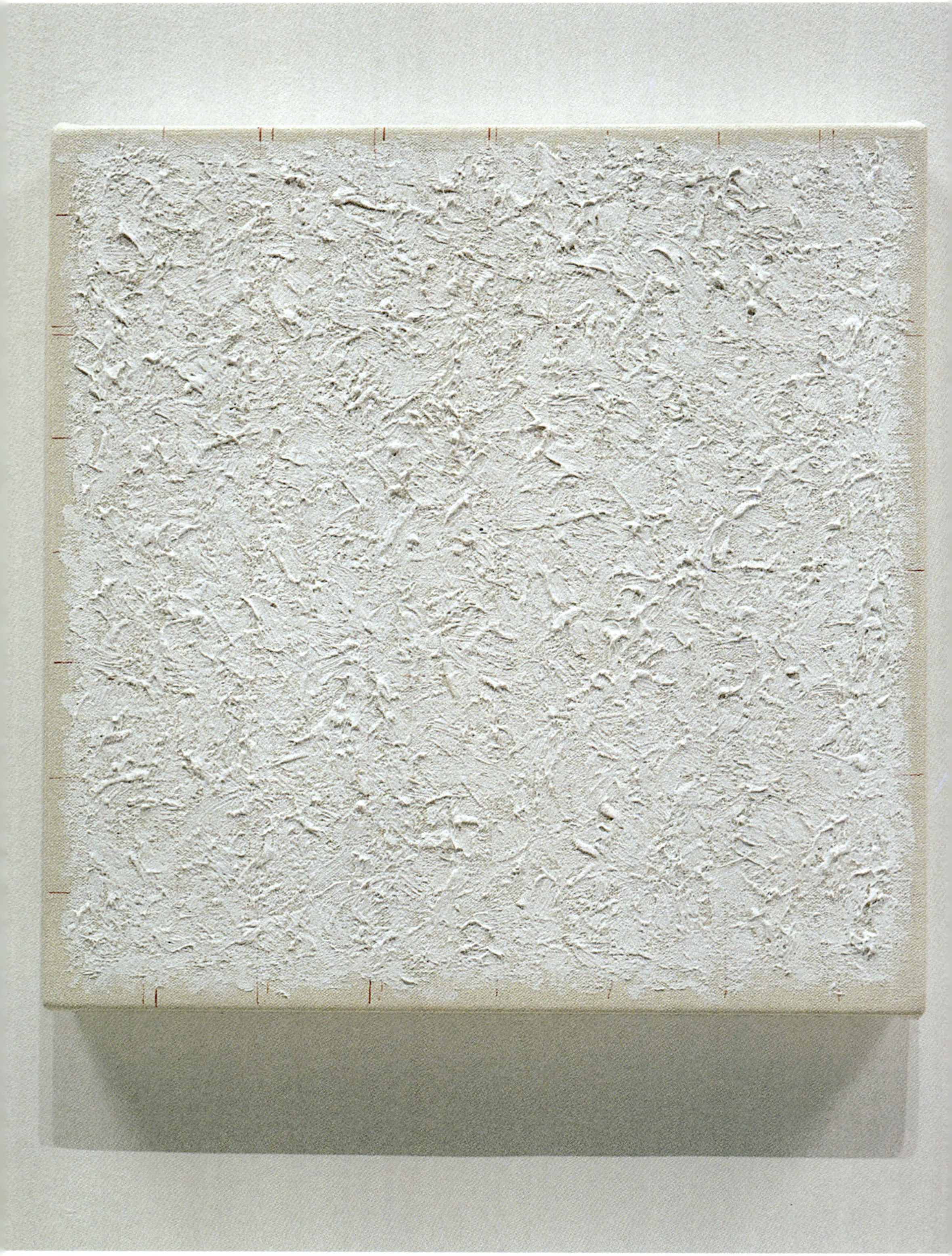

FIG. 2 Robert Ryman **Group** 1998 oil, acrylic varnish, dark ground on stretched cotton 14 x 14 in. Courtesy the artist and PaceWildenstein, New York

dox here, brilliantly enunciated by Thierry de Duve, is that the modernist opposition to both traditional painterly finish and the mechanical (which were fused by academic art of the late nineteenth century) bore within itself the stigmata of the mass-produced:

> **Although tin or copper tubes were already in use in England at the end of the eighteenth century for the preservation of watercolor, it was only around 1830–1840 that tubes of oil paints began to be available on the market. . . . For John Constable or the Barbizon painters to leave their studio and paint outside, directly from nature, the availability of tubes of paint was a prerequisite. One cannot imagine them carrying along the bulky equipment that the preparation of paint on the premises would involve. Certainly, pleinairism was one of the first episodes in the long struggle between craftsmanship and industrialization that underlies the history of "Modernist Painting." It was also one of the first instances of an avant-garde strategy, devised by artists who were aware that they could no longer compete, technically or economically, with industry; they sought to give their craft a reprieve by "internalizing" some of the features and processes of the technology threatening it, and by "mechanizing" their own body at work.[8]**

It is this internalization of the mass-produced that led to Duchamp's disgust for paintings and his invention of the readymade. ("Let's say you use a tube of paint; you didn't make it. You bought it and used it as a readymade. Even if you mix two vermillions together, it's still a mixing of two readymades. So man can never expect to start from scratch; he must start from readymade things like even his own mother and father."[9]) The historical condition of modern painting as a return of the repressed is also exposed in Seurat's art (Duchamp's favorite), and then deconstructed—not negated—in Ryman's. Industrialization first produced a reaction within modernist painting that led to the emphasis on process—but this reaction had only become possible through the incorporation of the mechanical within the realm of painting itself. Seurat's art marks the moment that this condition is recognized. After him, a long period of analytical decomposition followed—the strongest moment probably being Pollock—which culminated in a conscious incorporation of the mechanical in painting and a reversal of the original reaction to industrialization. Painting had reached the condition of photography. Ryman is the key figure in this historical development, but he has been backed up by a host of related practices in the 1970s.[10]

Even at the outset, industrialization meant much more for painting than the invention of photography and the incorporation of the mechanical into the artist's process through the readymade tube of paint. It also meant a threat of the collapse of art's special status into a fetish or a commodity. It is in reaction to this threat that the historicism and essentialism of modernism was developed. There is a tendency in America to believe that Clement Greenberg was the first advocate of the modernist teleology. On the contrary, as I have mentioned, the work of the first abstract painters was guided by the same teleology. It therefore seems more telling here, no matter how eloquent Greenberg's discourse has been, to seek the absolute beginning of such a construct: in other words the "beginning of the end." It seems that the first proponent was Baudelaire, who conceived history as a chain along which each individual art gradually approached its essence. Nobody has better perceived the function of the threat of industrialization in Baudelaire's work than Walter Benjamin. The greatness of Baudelaire, according to Benjamin, is to have recognized that the fetishistic nature of the commodity-form (analyzed by Marx at the same time) was the threat that capitalism posed to the very existence of art. "When things are freed from the bondage of being useful," as in the typically fetishistic transubstantiation accomplished by the art collector, then the distinction between art and artifact becomes extremely tenuous. This tension lies, according to Benjamin, at the core of Baudelaire's poetry.

Except for the Italian essayist Giorgio Agamben, it has been little recognized how much the famous chapter of Marx's *Capital* on the fetishistic nature of the commodity, its "mystical" or "phantasmagoric character," owes to the German philosopher's visit to the Great Exhibition in London in 1851, where industrial products were given the kind of auratic pres-

entation previously reserved for works of art:[11] "By means of this exhibition the bourgeoisie of the world is erecting in the modern Rome its Pantheon in which to exhibit with proud self-satisfaction the gods it has made to itself. . . . [It] is celebrating its greatest festival."[12] According to Marx, the fetishistic character of the commodity, what he called its "metaphysical subtlety," is grounded in the absolute repression of use value and of any reference to the process of production, or the materiality of the thing. And if Agamben is right in pointing at the connection between Marx's fundamental analysis and his visit to the London fair, then another connection brings us back to Baudelaire: Courbet's one-man show, in the bungalow he had built for this purpose next to the Beaux-Arts section of the Exposition Universelle in Paris in 1855, which contained among other works his famous *Studio* where Baudelaire is portrayed. As is well known, eleven works by Courbet had been accepted by the exhibition committee—and not minor ones—but he was dissatisfied with the way they were displayed: not exhibited together, but dispersed among an undifferentiated mass of hundreds of paintings exactly as, in the next building, machines and machine-made products were exhibited, competing for the gold medal. "I conquer freedom, I save the independence of art"[13] are the words Courbet used to explain the motivation of his parasitic show of some forty works, which he managed to install only six weeks after the inauguration of the fair and to maintain until it closed five months later. With these words, Courbet characterized what is for me the first avant-garde act, an act of defiance against the ever-growing realm of the commodity.

The universal commodification under capitalism is what, according to Benjamin, Baudelaire's genius was to perceive as the terrifying and endless return of the same. I cannot go deeply into Benjamin's extraordinarily complex analysis in this essay, but only note that beginning with Baudelaire's startling characterization of the writer as a prostitute, Benjamin sees the poet's successive identifications with the ragpicker, the flaneur, the bohemian, the dandy, or the "apache" as the adoption of heroic roles bearing the stigmata of commodification: roles that were doomed to failure and were superseded by Baudelaire's final phantasmagoria, his conception of the new. Benjamin writes, "This vilification that things suffer by their ability to be taxed as commodities is counterbalanced in Baudelaire's conception by the inestimable value of novelty. Novelty represents an absolute that can neither be interpreted [as an allegory] nor compared [as a commodity]. It becomes the ultimate entrenchment of art."[14] The shock of the new, in other words, is an expression that derives from Baudelaire's aesthetics. But there is more to it: Baudelaire sees modernity, the value of novelty, as necessarily doomed by the inevitable process by which the novel becomes antique. The quest for the absolute new in art becomes a moment that can never stop, endangered as it is by its devolution into the realm of interpretation or comparison. "But once modernism has received its due," writes Benjamin, "its time has run out. Then it will be put to the test. After its end, it will become apparent whether it will be able to become antiquity."[15] This is the banal process that was called *recuperation* in the 1960s, but has been better analyzed since then as an effect of the simulacral.

This urge toward the new, which is at the core of the historicist teleology of Baudelaire, is doubly a myth, both because of the immanent perishability of novelty, and because novelty is the very guise that the commodity adopts to fulfill its fetishistic transfiguration. Baudelaire indeed saw the connection between fashion and death, but he did not recognize that the absolute new he searched for all his life was made of the same stuff as the commodity, that it was governed by the same law as the market: the constant return of the same. Benjamin recognized this blind spot of Baudelaire's: "that the last defense of art coincided with the most advanced line of attack of the commodity, this remained hidden to Baudelaire."[16] Needless to say, it also remained unseen by the numerous avant-garde movements that followed him. We must recognize, however, that the insistence on the integrity of specific media that occurs in every art of the last quarter of the nineteenth century was a deliberate attempt to free art from its contamination by the forms of exchange produced by capitalism. Art had to be ontologically split not only from the mechanical, but also from the realm of information—it had to be distinguished from the immediate transitivity of information that amounted to a general leveling of every fact of life. Mallarmé is certainly the most articulate on this point, and his awareness formed the basis of his theory against the instrumentalization of language by the press. If he insisted on the materiality of language, if he claimed that the poet must remunerate language, if he spoke of the intransitivity of language, it was because he tried to advocate a mode of exchange that would not be abstract, nor based on a universal interchangeability through the medium of a single general equivalent, nor reified in a mystifying fetish split off from the process of its production. I would say that although few artists were as consistent as Mallarmé and Baudelaire, one can certainly read the whole history of avant-garde art up to World War I as following in their wake.

There were many reasons for a shift in the situation of the art object to occur around World War I, and I would be a fool to claim one or two events as the origin of a complex set of transformations that were sometimes abrupt, sometimes gradual. But to pursue my thread concerning the market, I would like to consider two pivotal events: the famous sale of the Peau d'Ours, which occurred on March 2, 1914, and Marcel Duchamp's invention of the readymade, already mentioned, which happened at around the same time (I take his *Porte-bouteille* of the same year as more to the point than his *Roue de bicyclette* of 1913, which still involves, although ironically, a compositional procedure). The sale of the Peau d'Ours marked the astonishing discovery that far from being laughable, the avant-garde art of the past—novelty as antiquity—was highly profitable as an investment. Not only works by Gauguin, Vuillard, or Redon were sold at very high prices, but also paintings by Matisse and Picasso. It was discovered, in short, that investment in contemporary painting was much more profitable than the typical investments of the time, including gold and real estate. Needless to say, the speculative logic that emerged from this sale (buy today the Van Goghs of tomorrow because the new will become antiquity) was to shape the entire history of the twentieth-century art market.

Now Duchamp. His readymades were not only a negation of painting and a demonstration of the always-already mechanical nature of painting. They also demonstrated that within our culture the work of art is a fetish that must abolish all pretense to use value (i.e., the readymade is an art object through its abstraction from the realm of utility). Furthermore, the readymade demonstrated that the so-called autonomy of the art object was produced by a nominalist institution (the museum or art gallery) that constantly buried what Marx called the point of view of production under the point of view of consumption (as the ethnologist Marcel Mauss noted once, "a work of art is that which is recognized as such by a group").[17] Finally, and more importantly, Duchamp's act presented the art object as a *special* kind of commodity—something that Marx had noted when he explained that "works of art properly speaking were not taken into consideration" in his account, "for they are of a special nature."[18] Having no use value, the art object does not have any exchange value per se either—the exchange value being dependent on the quantum of social work necessary for its production (Seurat demonstrated this *ad absurdum* through his desire to be paid *by the hour*). What Duchamp was keen to observe is that works of art—as much as oyster pearls or great wines (other examples given by Marx)—are not exchanged according to the common law of the market, but according to a monopoly system maintained by the entire art network, whose keystone is the artist himself. This does not mean that the exchange of works of art is beyond competition or any other manifestation of the law of the market, but that their sometimes infinite price is a function of their lack of measurable value. Value in the art world is determined by the "psychological" mechanisms that are at the core of any monopoly system: rarity, authenticity, uniqueness, and the law of supply and demand.
In other words, art objects are absolute fetishes without a use value but also without an exchange value, fulfilling absolutely the collector's fantasy of a purely symbolic or ideal value, a supplement to his soul.

Duchamp's discovery led him to a range of experiments meant to reveal the mechanisms of the art network: I only need mention his 1917 *Fountain* (fig. 3), his various appearances as a transvestite, and his *Chèque Tzank* of 1919, all of which pointed to authenticity as the central theoretical construct on which the art network is based. In Duchamp's wake, artists like Daniel Buren as well as Cindy Sherman and Sherrie Levine have analyzed the nature of authenticity. This analytical strategy has often been characterized as the "deconstructive

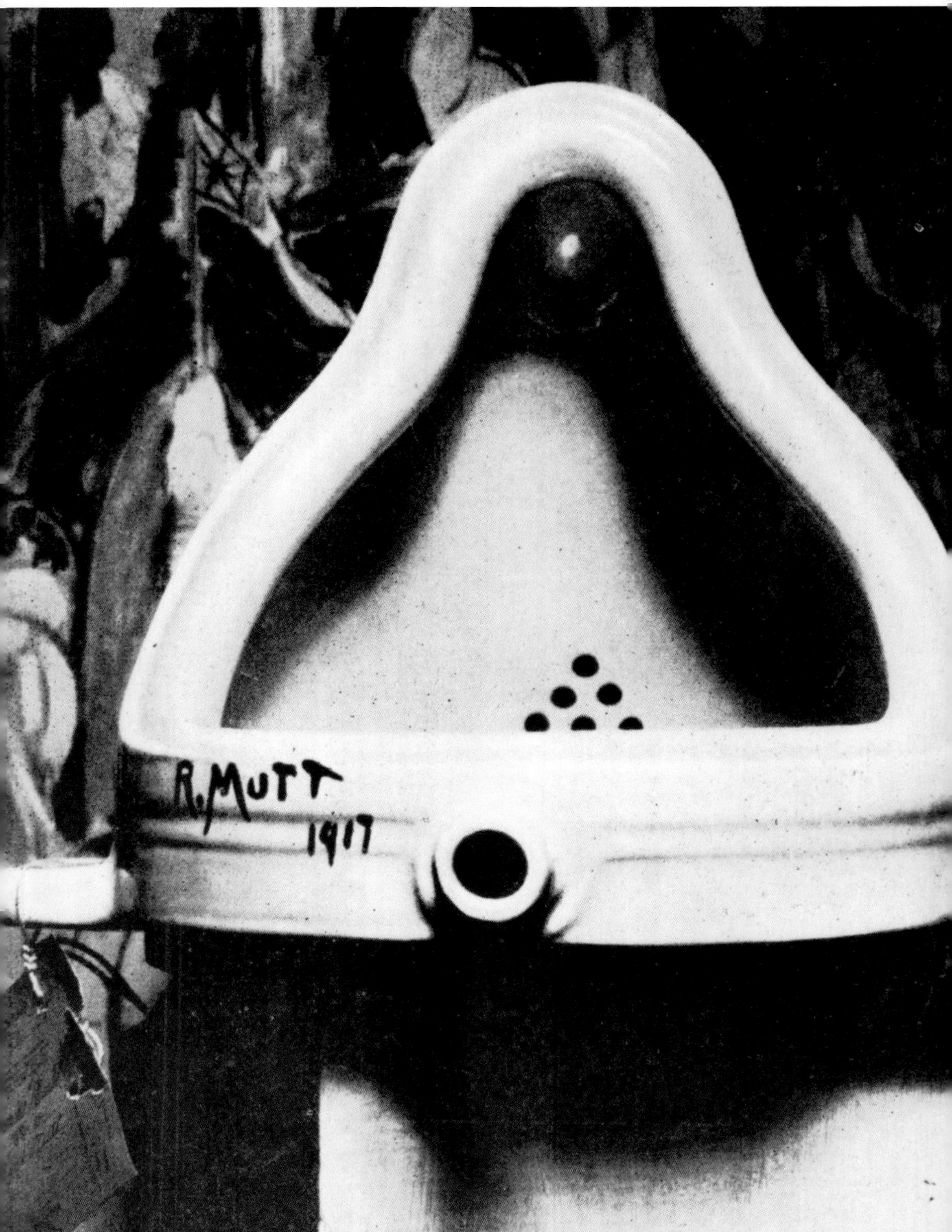

FIG 3 Photograph by Alfred Stieglitz of Marcel Duchamp's **Fountain**, 1917, as reproduced in *The Blind Man*, no. 2 (May 1917), p. 4. Collection The Philadelphia Museum of Art; The Louise and Walter Arensberg Archives © 2001 Artists Rights Society (ARS), New York/ADAGP, Paris/Estate of Marcel Duchamp

tendency" of postmodernism, yet I am not entirely confident with this labeling (which does not diminish at all the interest I have for such practices). In so far as I interpret Duchamp's art as a negation, I interpret his heirs as explicating and radicalizing his negation. Or rather, if one wants to stay with the term deconstruction, I would say that Duchamp and his heirs are deconstructing one aspect of what they negate (painting): specifically the imaginary aspect of painting, which these artists consistently associate with its fetishistic nature (deconstruction means also the sense of inescapability from closure). But there remain, if I am allowed to borrow *metaphorically* the Lacanian terminology, two other aspects of painting that must be considered: the real and the symbolic.

Both the Peau d'Ours sale and Duchamp's invention of the readymade had the potential to spawn a kind of cynical conservatism: if the new was doomed to its transformation into gold by the market, and the work of art was by its very nature an absolute fetish, then it might seem that the avant-garde's ideology of resistance was obsolete. In fact, such a cynical position was undertaken by what is called the *return to order*, which started with Picasso's *Portrait of Max Jacob* in 1915 but which became a massive phenomenon in the 1920s with Pittura Metafisica in Italy and the Neue Sachlichkeit in Germany. These movements share a lot with the neoconservative brand of postmodernism that has recently emerged (whether it's called new wild, neo-romantik, transavanguardia, or whatever), as Benjamin Buchloh has brilliantly demonstrated.[19] The market itself induces this kind of cynicism.[20] The cynical attitude, however, was not the only one available. The feeling of the end could also be reclaimed by a revolutionary aesthetics. This is what happened in Russia, where artists immediately responded to the situation created by the events of October 1917. In a revolutionary situation, art cannot but sever its ties with the market and its dependence upon the art institution: it seeks to reestablish its use value and to invent new relationships of production and consumption: it breaks with the linear, cumulative conception of history and emphasizes discontinuity. In other words, in such situations art can open up a new paradigm, something that was eloquently advocated by El Lissitzky in the brilliant lecture he delivered in Berlin, in 1922, about "The New Russian Art."[21]

Of all of these gestures of the Soviet avant-garde, one of the most significant is Rodchenko's exhibition, in 1921, of three monochrome panels, which he later described with these words: "I reduced painting to its logical conclusion and exhibited three canvases: red, blue, and yellow. I affirmed: It's all over. Basic colors. Every plane is a plane, and there is to be no more representation."[22] If Rodchenko's gesture is important, it is not because it was the "first" monochrome—it was not the "first" nor the "last"—and not because it was the first "last picture" (not only does Duchamp's readymade better deserve this title, but, as we have seen, in a way all modernist abstract paintings had to claim to be the last picture). If Rodchenko's gesture was so important, as Tarabukin saw when he analyzed it in *From the Easel to the Machine*, it was because it showed that painting could have a real existence only if it claimed its end; Rodchenko's "meaningless, dumb and blind wall . . . convinces us that painting was and remains a representational art and that it cannot escape from these limits of the representational."[23] Rodchenko's painting needed to attain the status of a real (nonimaginary) object, which meant its end as art. Again we are confronted with a negation—not a deconstruction—which accounts, according to me, for what must be called the failure of the productivist program in painting that followed Rodchenko's gesture logically (the dissolution of the artist's activity into industrial production). Or, to use again the terminology I borrowed before, Rodchenko deconstructed only one aspect of painting: its pretense to reach the realm of the real—a deconstruction that was carried out again, and further elaborated, by minimalism in the 1960s.

Rodchenko's was still not the only alternative to Duchamp's negation, nor to cynicism. In August 1924, shortly before he broke with the Dutch movement, Mondrian published his last article in the magazine *De Stijl*. Entitled "Blown with the Wind," it is a denunciation of the *return to order* that was invading the galleries and had almost led him, three years earlier, to abandon painting altogether. He writes:

> **If artists now reject the new conception, critics and dealers reject it even more**

> **strongly, for they are more directly exposed to the influence of the public. The sole value of abstract art, they openly assert, was to raise the level of naturalistic art: the new was thus a *means*, not a *goal*.** [And there I intervene to mention Picasso's remark to a baffled Kahnweiler that his neoclassical works of the *return to order* period were *better* than those of his precubist naturalistic period. Back to Mondrian's text. This is, he writes,] **an open denial of the essence of the new, which was to *displace and annihilate* the old. They too swing with the wind and follow the lead of the general public. Though quite understandable, this is temporarily disastrous for the new, for its essential nature is thus *lost from sight*.**

I give you this long quotation for its insistence on the momentary nature of the *return to order* phenomenon: the whole article is suffused with a kind of optimism that would sound utterly incomprehensible if the role of the new were not laid down at the end of the article:

> **Abstract art can evolve only by *consistent development*. In this way it can arrive at the *purely plastic*, which Neo-Plasticism has attained. Consistently carried through, this "art" expression** [the quotation marks are Mondrian's] **can lead to nothing other than its *realization in our tangible environment*. For the time will come when, because of life's changed demands, "painting" will become absorbed in life** [again, the quotation marks are Mondrian's].[24]

For anyone who is familiar with the voluminous writings of Mondrian, this sounds typical, and indeed, as I already noted, the myth of the future dissolution of art into life is one of his most frequent themes. Far from being a compulsive quest of the absolute new, structurally doomed to failure, as in Baudelaire's formal teleology, Mondrian's affirmation of the new is geared toward a definite *telos*, that of the advent of a classless society, where social relationships would be transparent and not reified, and where there would be no difference between artists and nonartists, art and life. The new art must be, within itself, the model and augury of such a liberation: this future liberation, or socialist state, is envisioned through the principle of neoplasticism, of which neoplastic art can only be a "pale reflection," albeit the most advanced possible at the time. This principle, which Mondrian also called the "general principle of plastic equivalence," is a sort of dialectic whose action is to dissolve any particularity, any center, any hierarchy. Any entity that is not split or constituted by an opposition is a mere appearance. Anything that is not determined by its contrary is vague, particular, individual, tragic: it is a cipher of authoritarianism, and it does not take part in the process of emancipation set forth by the "general principle of equivalence." Hence the complicated task that Mondrian assigns the painter is the destruction of all the elements on which the particularity of his art is based: the destruction of colored planes by lines, of lines by repetition, and of the optical illusion of depth by the sculptural weave of the painterly surface (fig. 4). Each destructive act follows the previous one and amounts to the abolition of the figure/ground opposition that is the perceptual limitation at the base of our imprisoned vision, and of the whole enterprise of painting. There is no doubt that Mondrian sets a task of the highest order for art: he prescribes a propaedeutic role. Painting was for him a theoretical model that provided concepts and invented procedures that dealt with reality: it is not merely an interpretation of the world, but the plastic manifestation of a certain logic that he found at the root of all the phenomena of life. In an article he wrote under the shock of the Nazi-Soviet mutual nonaggression pact, Mondrian says: "The function of plastic art is not descriptive. . . . It can reveal the evil of oppression and show the way to combat it. . . . It cannot reveal more than life teaches, but it can evoke in us the conviction of existent truth";[25] "the culture of plastic art shows that real freedom requires mutual equivalence."[26]

Arthur Lehning, an anarchosyndicalist leader of the 1920s, said that his friend Mondrian was a child in politics, and nothing could be more evident.[27] However, this naiveté, which appears to have been the only possible alternative to Duchamp's negation and to the cynical strategies of the *return to order* in Western Europe, should not blind us to Mondrian's remarkable position. One is struck by the fact that he never felt any compulsion toward the monochrome, which could easily have provided, so it seems, the kind of absolute flatness he was striving for. But as an iconoclast readymade, the monochrome could not have functioned for him as a tool to deconstruct painting or more specifically to deconstruct the order of the symbolic in painting (of tradition, of the law, of history). Mondrian felt that within the economic abstraction engendered by capitalism, painting could only be deconstructed abstractly, by analyzing, one after the other, one against the other, all of the elements that (historically) ground its symbolic order (form, color, figure/ground opposition, frame, etc.). This painstaking formal analysis was for him the only way painting could reach its own end. Because it was conceived of as an abstract model, painting could resist the abstract commodification that is the fate of every (art) object; it had to postpone its own dissolution into the real until the symbolic order on which it is grounded had been "neutralized." Painting was therefore engaged in the necessarily interminable task of this neutralization. It might seem strange to speak of Mondrian, whose system of thought owed so much to Hegel's dialectic, in terms of deconstruction, yet unlike any dialectician he never expected any leap, never paid any tribute to the modern ideology of the *tabula rasa*: he knew that the end of painting had to be gained by hard labor.

But is the end ever to be gained? Duchamp (the imaginary), Rodchenko (the real), and Mondrian (the symbolic), among others, all believed in the end—they all had the final truth, all spoke apocalyptically. Yet has the end come? To say no (painting is still alive, just look at the galleries) is undoubtedly an act of denial, for it has never been more evident that most paintings one sees have abandoned the task that historically belonged to modern painting (that, precisely, of working through the end of painting) and are simply artifacts created for the market and by the market (absolutely interchangeable artifacts created by interchangeable producers). To say yes, however, that the end has come, is to give in to a historicist conception of history as both linear and total (i.e., one cannot paint after Duchamp, Rodchenko, Mondrian; their work has rendered paintings unnecessary, or: one cannot paint anymore in the era of the mass media, computer games, and the simulacrum).

How are we to escape this double bind? Benjamin once noted that the easel painting was born in the Middle Ages, and that nothing guarantees that it should remain forever. But are we left with these alternatives: either a denial of the end, or an affirmation of the end of the end (it's all over, the end is over)? The theory of games, used recently by Hubert Damisch, can help us overcome this paralyzing trap. This theory of strategy dissociates the generic *game* (like chess) from the specific performance of the game (Spassky/Fisher, for example), which I will call the *match*.[28] This strategic interpretation is strictly antihistoricist: with it, the question becomes "one of the status that ought to be assigned to the *match* 'painting,' as one *sees* it being played at a given moment in particular circumstances, in its relation to the *game* of the same name."[29] Such questioning has the immediate advantage of raising doubt about certain truisms. Is the "alleged convention of depth"—rejected by the pictorial art of this century because, according to Greenberg, it is unnecessary—necessarily of the order of the *match* more than of the *game*? Or rather, should we speak of a modification of this convention within the *game*? Without thereby becoming a theoretical machine encouraging indifference, since one is obliged to take a side, this strategic approach deciphers painting as an agonistic field where nothing is ever terminated, or decided *once and for all*, and leads the analysis back to a type of historicity that it had neglected, that of long duration. In other words, it dismisses all certitudes about the absolute truth upon which the apocalyptic discourse is based. Rather, the fiction of the end of art (or of painting) is understood as a "confusion between the end of the game itself (as if a game could really have an end) and that of such and such a match (or series of matches)."[30]

One can conclude then that, if the match "modernist painting" is finished, it does not necessarily mean that the game "painting" is finished: many years to come are ahead for this art. But the situation is even more complicated: for the match "modernist painting" was the match of the end of painting; it was both a response to the feeling of the end and a working through of the end. And this match was historically determined—by the fact of industrialization (photography, the commodity, etc.). To claim that the "end of painting" is finished

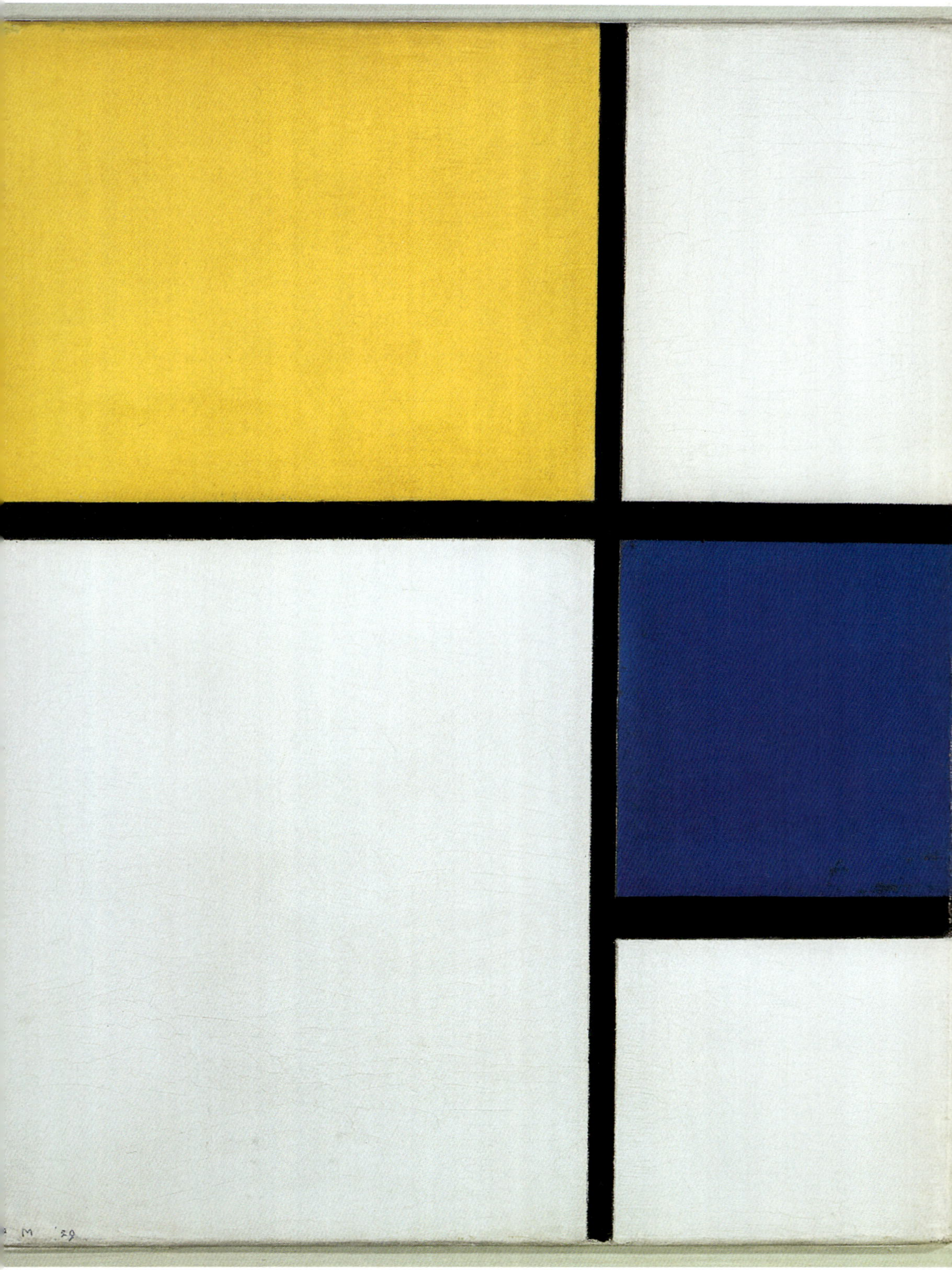

FIG. 4 Piet Mondrian **Composition** 1929 oil on canvas 16 x 12 ¾ in. Collection The National Museum of Modern Art, Kyoto

FIG. 5 Peter Halley **White Cell with Conduit** 1985 acrylic, day-glo acrylic, Roll-A-Tex on canvas 64 x 64 in. Courtesy the artist

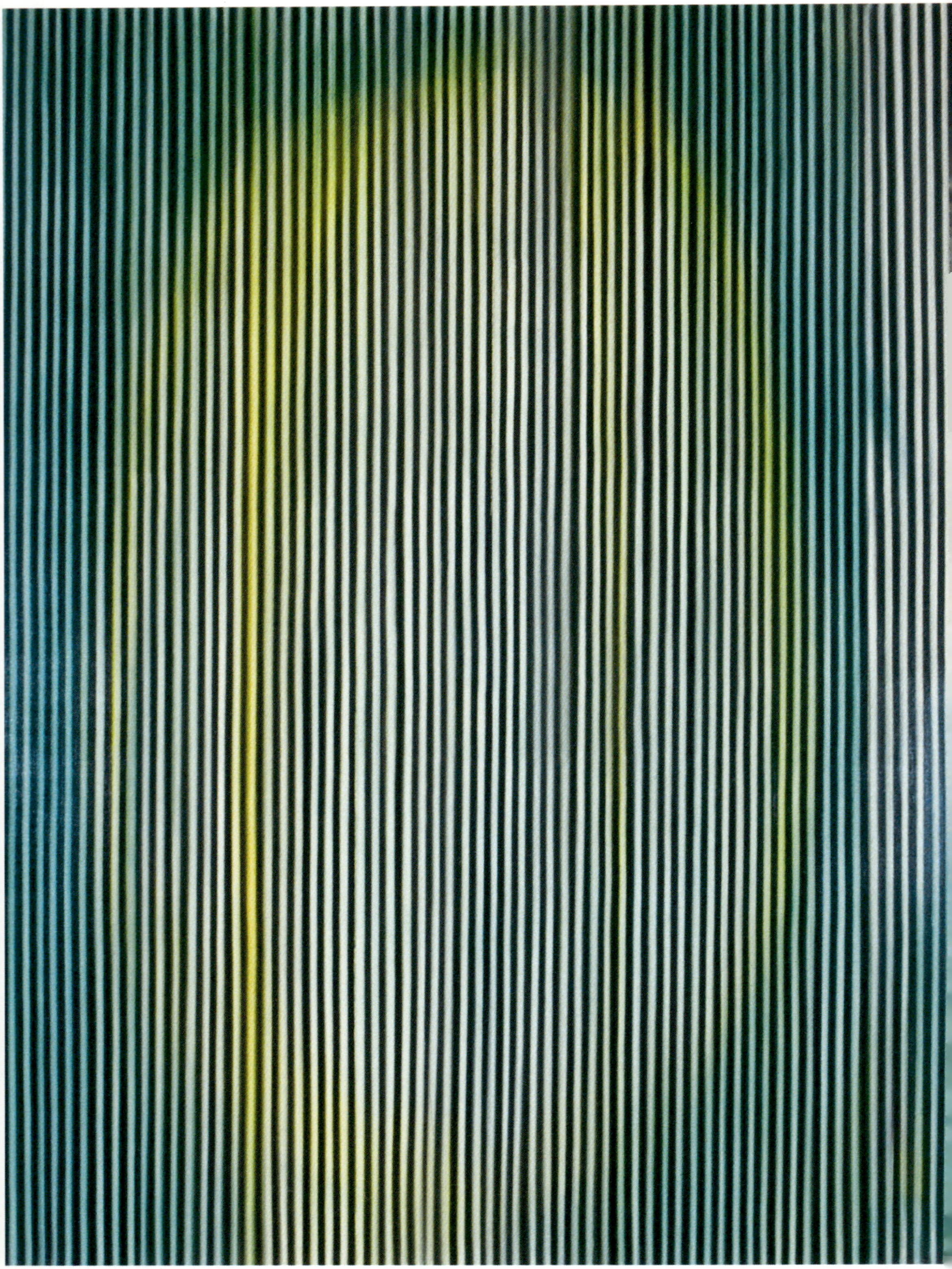

FIG. 6 Ross Bleckner **The Forest** 1981 oil, wax on canvas 120 x 96 in. Courtesy the artist and Mary Boone Gallery, New York

is to claim that this historical situation is no longer ours, and who would be naive enough to make this claim when it appears that reproducibility and fetishization have permeated all aspects of life: have become our "natural" world?

Obviously, this is not the claim of the latest group of "abstract" painters, whose work, as Hal Foster has rightly remarked, has been presented as either a development of appropriation art (which is supported by the presence of Sherrie Levine in the group) or as a swing of the pendulum (the market having tired of neoexpressionism was ripe for a neoclassical and architectonic movement: the "style" after the "shout," to make use of an old metaphor that art criticism proposed to distinguish between two tendencies within the realm of abstract art: one whose emblem was Mondrian and the other, Pollock).[31] The work of this recent group of painters wishes to respond to our simulacral era, yet paradoxically in their very reliance upon Jean Baudrillard, emphasized by Peter Halley (fig. 5), who frequently writes critically about these issues, they all admit that the end has come, that the end of the end is over (hence that we can start again on another match; that we can paint without the feeling of the end but only with its simulacrum). As Foster writes, "In this new abstract painting, simulation has penetrated the very art form that . . . resisted it most."[32] Starting with a critique of the economy of the sign in late capitalism, Baudrillard was driven, by the very nature of his millenarianist feeling, to a fascination for the age of the simulacrum, a glorification of our own impotence disguised as nihilism. It seems to me that although the young artists in question address the issue of the simulacral—of the abstract simulation produced by capital—they have similarly abandoned themselves to the seduction of what they claim to denounce: either perversely (as in the case of Philip Taaffe, who refers to Newman's sublime while he empties it of its content); or unconsciously (as in the case of Halley, who seems to believe that an iconological rendering of simulacra—through his pictorial rhetoric of "cells" and "conduits"—could function as a critique of them). Like Baudrillard, I would call them manic mourners. Their return to painting, as though it were an appropriate medium for what they want to address, as though the age of the simulacral could be represented, comes from the feeling that since the end has come, since it's all over, we can rejoice at the killing of the dead. That is, we can forget that the end has to be endlessly worked through, and start all over again. But this, of course, is not so, and it is in flagrant contradiction to the very analysis of the simulacral as the latest abstraction produced by capitalism (perhaps this illusion is rooted in the abuse of the term postindustrialism, whose inveterate inadequacy to describe the latest development of capitalism has been exposed by Fredric Jameson).[33] Appropriation art—the "orgy of cannibalism" proper to manic mourning—of which this movement is obviously a part,[34] can then be understood as a pathological mourning (it has also its melancholic side, as noted by Hal Foster about Ross Bleckner (fig. 6) and Taaffe in their fascination for the "failure" of op art).[35] Bleckner writes about Taaffe: "Dead issues are reopened by this changed subjectivity: artists become transvestites and viewers voyeurs watching history become less alien, less authoritarian."[36] I would correct the latter assertion this way: ". . . viewers watching oblivion become more alien, more enslaved." For "simulation, together with the old regime of disciplinary surveillance, constitutes a principal means of deterrence in our society (for how can one intervene politically in events when they are so often simulated or immediately replaced by pseudo-events?)."[37]

Yet mourning has been the activity of painting throughout this century. "To be modern is to know *that which is not possible any more*," Roland Barthes once wrote.[38] But the work of mourning does not necessarily become pathological: the feeling of the end, after all, did produce a cogent history of painting, modernist painting, which we have probably been too prompt to bury. Painting might not be dead. Its vitality will only be tested once we are cured of our mania and our melancholy, and we believe again in our ability to act in history: accepting our project of working through the end again, rather than evading it through increasingly elaborate mechanisms of defense (this is what mania and melancholy are about) and settling our historical task: the difficult task of mourning. It will not be easier than before, but my bet is that the potential for painting will emerge in the conjunctive deconstruction of the three instances that modernist painting has dissociated (the imaginary, the real, and the symbolic). But predictions are made to be wrong. Let us simply say

that the desire for painting remains, and that this desire is not entirely programmed or subsumed by the market: this desire is the sole factor of a future possibility of painting, that is, of a nonpathological mourning. At any rate, as observed by Robert Musil fifty years ago, if some painting is still to come, if painters are still to come, they will not come from where we expect them to.[39]

NOTES

1 Jacques Derrida, "Of an Apocalyptic Tone Recently Adopted in Philosophy" (1983), trans. John P. Leavey, Jr., *The Oxford Literary Review* 6, no. 2 (1984), pp. 22–23. This essay is a reading of Kant's pamphlet mentioned above.

2 Kasimir Malevich, *Suprematism. 34 Drawings* (Vitebsk, 1920), English trans. in Malevich, *Essays on Art*, ed. Troels Andersen, vol. 1 (New York: Wittenborn, 1971), p. 127.

3 I refer here to the critical work accomplished in the magazine *October* by Rosalind Krauss, Douglas Crimp, and Benjamin H. D. Buchloh; but also to Hal Foster's recent anthology of articles, *Recodings: Art, Spectacle, Cultural Politics* (Port Townsend, Wash.: Bay Press, 1985), and to various articles by Thierry de Duve.

4 Douglas Crimp, "The End of Painting," *October*, no. 16 (spring 1981), p. 75.

5 See Meyer Schapiro, "Recent Abstract Painting," in *Modern Art: 19th and 20th Century (Collected Papers)* (New York: Braziller, 1978), pp. 217–219. The text appeared first under the title "The Liberating Quality of Avant-Garde Art" in *Art News* during the summer of 1957.

6 I take the liberty to refer to my article "Ryman's Tact," published in *October*, no. 19 (winter 1981). See also the excellent article by Thierry de Duve, "Ryman irréproducible" (1980), reprinted in de Duve, *Ecrits Datés I 1974–1986* (Paris: La Différence, 1987), pp. 119–158, which deals explicitly with Ryman's relationship with modernism and photography.

7 Barnett Newman, "The Problem of Subject Matter," c. 1944, as quoted by Tom Hess in *Barnett Newman* (New York: Museum of Modern Art, 1971), pp. 39–40.

8 Thierry de Duve, "The Readymade and the Tube of Paint," *Artforum* (May 1986), pp. 115–116.

9 Marcel Duchamp to Katherine Kuh (1961), quoted in ibid., p. 113.

10 See Rosalind Krauss, "Notes on the Index" (1977), reprinted in *Originality of the Avant-Garde and Other Modernist Myths* (Cambridge, Mass.: MIT Press, 1984).

11 Giorgio Agamben, *Stanze* (1977), French trans. Yves Hersant (Paris: Christian Bourgois, 1980), part two ("Dans le monde d'Odradek—Oeuvre d'art et marchandise"), p. 75.

12 Karl Marx and Friedrich Engels, "Review—May to October [1850]," in Marx and Engels, *Collected Works*, vol. 10 (New York: International Publishers, 1978), p. 500. The original text was published, although not in its entirety, in the *Neue Rheinische Zeitung*, nos. 5–6, 1850. The editors of the *Collected Works* ascribe the text to Marx (see ibid., p. 695, note 348).

13 *Lettres de Gustave Courbet à Alfred Bruyas*, ed. Pierre Borel (Geneva: Editions Pierre Cailler, 1951), p. 87.

14 Walter Benjamin, "Paris, Capital of the Nineteenth Century," second version (1939), in *Das Passagenwerk, Gesammelten Schriften*, vol. 5 (Frankfurt: Suhrkamp, 1983), p. 71.

15 Walter Benjamin, "The Paris of the Second Empire in Baudelaire" (1938), English trans. in *Charles Baudelaire: A Lyric Poet in the Era of High Capitalism* (London: New Left Books, 1973), p. 81.

16 Walter Benjamin, *Das Passagenwerk*, pp. 71–72.

17 Marcel Mauss, *Manuel d'ethnographie* (1947), second ed. (Paris: Payot, 1967), p. 89.

18 Karl Marx, *Oeuvres* (Paris: Gallimard, 1968), vol. 2, p. 1871.

19 Benjamin H. D. Buchloh, "Figures of Authority, Ciphers of Regression," *October*, no. 16 (spring 1981). (I am not so sure anymore that Picasso's *Portrait of Max Jacob* should be heralded as the point of departure of the vast movement of the "return to order." In fact, Picasso's irony there implies a distance that is very much in keeping with his cubist enterprise. I hope to be pursuing this angle in further studies.)

20 See "Mythologies: Art and the Market," Jeffrey Deitch interviewed by Matthew Collings, *Artscribe International* (April–May 1986), pp. 23–26. Almost any assertion made in this interview with Deitch, a corporate art advisor, would require a commentary, starting with his denial of having a cynical position. Nevertheless, it provides valuable information on the present situation: while Marcel Duchamp could say in 1966 that "the museums are run more or less by the dealers" and that "in New York, the Museum of Modern Art is completely in the hands of the dealers" (Pierre Cabanne, *Dialogues with Marcel Duchamp*, trans. Ron Padgett [New York: The Viking Press, 1971]), we are now confronted by the omnipotence of the collector. He has made the dealer into a mere appendage of his own body: this is the situation that is well described in Deitch's interview.

21 Reprinted in Sophie Lissitzky-Kuppers, *El Lissitzky* (London and New York: Thames and Hudson, 1968), pp. 330–340.

22 Alexander Rodchenko, from the manuscript "Working with Maiakovsky" (1939), quoted in *From Painting to Design: Russian Constructivist Art of the Twenties* (Cologne: Galerie Gmurzynska, 1981), p. 191. On Rodchenko see also Benjamin H. D. Buchloh, *Niele Toroni—L'Index de la peinture* (Brussels: Editions Daled, 1985), pp. 40–42 (unpublished in English).

23 Nicolai Tarabukin, *From the Easel to the Machine* (1923), English trans. in *Modern Art and Modernism: A Critical Anthology*, eds. Francis Frascina and Charles Harrison (New York: Harper and Row, 1982), p. 139. It is worth noting that Tarabukin was totally immersed in millenarianism: his major reference is Spengler's *Decline of the West*.

24 Piet Mondrian, "De Huif naar den Wind," *De Stijl* 6, no. 6/7 (1924), p. 88; translated in *The New Art—The New Life: The Collected Writings of Piet Mondrian*, ed. and trans. Harry Holtzman and Martin S. James (Boston: G. K. Hall, 1986), p. 181. For Picasso's remark, see Daniel-Henry Kahnweiler with Francis Crémieux, *My Galleries and Painters* (1961), English trans. by Helen Weaver (New York: Viking, 1971), p. 54.

25 Piet Mondrian, "Liberation from Oppression in Art and Life" (1941), reprinted in *The New Art*, p. 323.

26 Ibid., p. 327.

27 See Yve-Alain Bois, *Arthur Lehning en Mondriaan—Hun vriendshap en correspondentie* (Amsterdam: Van Gennep, 1984), p. 39.

28 See Hubert Damisch, *Fenêtre jaune cadmium* (Paris: Seuil, 1984), p. 167.
29 Ibid., p. 170.
30 Ibid., p. 171.
31 One remembers the book by Michel Seuphor, *Le Style et le Cri* (Paris: Seuil, 1965), which helped to vulgarize such a critical distinction.
32 Hal Foster, "Signs Taken for Wonders," *Art in America* (June 1986), p. 90.
33 See Fredric Jameson, "Postmodernism, or the Cultural Logic of Late Capitalism," *New Left Review* (July–August 1984), pp. 53–92.
34 "Orgy of Cannibalism" is an expression of Karl Abraham to characterize the manic state in "Esquisse d'une histoire du développement de la libido basée sur la psychoanalyse des troubles mentaux" (1924). In this article, Abraham completes the famous but very short text by Freud on "Mourning and Melancholia." See Abraham, *Développement de la libido, Oeuvres Complètes*, vol. 2 (Paris: Payot, 1973), p. 293.
Dwelling on the early essays of Freud and Abraham, Melanie Klein shows how the feelings of triumph and omnipotence that characterize manic mourning prevent the *working through* of mourning. (See "Mourning and Its Relation to Manic-Depressive States," in *Contributions to Psychoanalysis 1921–1945* [London: Hogarth Press, 1950]. See particularly pp. 322 and 336.)
35 Foster, "Signs," p. 83.
36 Ross Bleckner, *Philip Taaffe* (New York: Pat Hearn Gallery, 1986), p. 7.
37 Hal Foster, "Signs," p. 91. Peter Halley is perfectly aware of this, as is shown by most of his texts and particularly by his brilliant article entitled "The Crisis in Geometry," *Arts* (summer 1984). But he believes that this state of affairs can be represented, and through representation, criticized. Both of these claims are dubious (and contradictory with his Baudrillardian theory).
38 Roland Barthes, "Réquichot et son corps," in *L'Obvie et l'obtus, Essais Critiques III* (Paris: Seuil, 1982), p. 211.
39 Robert Musil, "Considérations Désobligeantes," *Oeuvres préposthumes* (1936), French trans. Philippe Jaccottet (Paris: Seuil, 1965), p. 87.

Midori Matsui is Associate Professor of American Studies at Tohoku University. She has written extensively on contemporary art and culture in Japanese and English. Her publications include "Little Girls Were Little Boys: Displaced Femininity in the Representation of Homosexuality in Japanese Girls' Comics" in *Feminism and the Politics of Difference* (1993) and "Beyond Signs: Hybridity in Japanese Art" in *The Age of Anxiety* (1995).

New Openings in Japanese Painting: Three Faces of Minor-ity

Midori Matsui

Since the mid-1990s, a new figurative painting has emerged in Japan. Coinciding with the revival of figurative painting in the United States, represented by Elizabeth Peyton and John Currin, for example, the idiosyncratic creations of Japanese innovators, including Takashi Murakami, Yoshitomo Nara, Hiroshi Sugito, and Tam Ochiai, signify a break with previous tendencies in Japanese painting. Rather than conforming to institutional versions of Post-Painterly Abstraction, or following the latest fashion, they pursue the "third way," mining their cultural past for technical resources and ideological prototypes, while playing up their postmodern sensibility to the fullest advantage. Never explicitly forming a group, these artists are characterized by an increased degree of cultural hybridity: growing up in an overblown consumer society, they possess a common cultural reference with their contemporaries worldwide, while their keen awareness of the problems and challenges facing contemporary art place them in the ranks of "migrant" artists. Such independence inevitably puts them in competition with prevailing expressions of Japanese painting, which are still polarized by the dichotomy of an uncritical reception of foreign influences and a sentimental embracing of domestic traditions.

The innovations of Murakami, Nara, Sugito, and Ochiai present possibilities of resolving this dichotomy. These artists strive to gain individuality and establish a unique style of Japanese painting that runs against the grain of its incomplete modernity. Since modernization in Japan has meant Westernization, its critique and modification inevitably take on an aspect of postcolonial struggle, which provides a backdrop for each artist's individual struggle.

Prehistory

The dichotomy of Japanese painting began in the late nineteenth century at the inception of the modernizing, or Enlightening, process brought about by the Meiji Restoration. The wholesale import of Western political and cultural institutions also resulted in the creation of the category of art (*geijutsu*, or *bijutsu*) as part of the Japanese participation at the World Exposition held in Vienna in 1873.[1] Western-style painting, or Yōga, was made an official category of modern painting at Kōbu bijutsu gakkō, the official conservatory. Acknowledging the crisis of traditional Japanese painting, Ernest Fenolosa, then a guest professor, and Tenshin Okakura, an art historian and the first president of Tokyo bijutsu gakkō (Tokyo Art School), urged the unification of traditional Japanese painting into a new style called Nihonga, in opposition to both Yōga and the old-fashioned tendency to blindly preserve traditional aspects of Japanese painting.[2] They offered an alternative of innovating within the Japanese tradition, reviving lost techniques of ancient painting as well as incorporating the latest experiments of contemporary Western painting.[3] Eclecticism was an important factor in shaping this new category of national art. From the modern Western perspective that favored autonomy and originality, Fenolosa commended in his influential book *Bijutsu shinsetsu* (1882) the ability of Japanese painting to create a unique pictorial reality, while Tenshin argued that the new painting must strategically "integrate many assets of Western civilization in order to revive the Asian spirit."[4] Tenshin's private educational institution, Nihon bijutsu in, was established in 1889; Nihonga and Yōga were officially adopted as two major genres of painting at the art exhibition held by Monbusho (the Ministry of Culture and Education) in 1907.

The crisis of identity perpetuated by its colonial origin caused Japanese painting to fluctuate between looking outward and returning to the domestic. For example, Ryūsei Kishida and Tetsugoro Yorozu, innovators of Yōga in 1930s, turned to traditional Japanese styles in search of individual reality.[5] The fluctuation continued after the 1950s when *gendai bijutsu*, or contemporary art imported from France and the United States, stole the attention from Yōga and Nihonga. After the eclipse of painting in the 1960s and early 1970s by the indigenous conceptual arts of Hi Red Center, Bi-kyoto, and Mono-ha, in reaction to the appropriation of the action painting of Gutai by the imported styles of Art Informel, the late 1970s and early 1980s saw a belated attempt to claim the significance of modern formalist painting from theoretical viewpoints.[6]

Encouraged by the revisionist strain of such exhibitions as *American Painting: The*

Eighties, curated by Barbara Rose in 1977, the influential critics Teruo Fujieda and Toshiaki Minemura curated exhibitions in order to enhance their formalist-influenced theories of painting.[7] Not questioning the legitimacy of sanctioning formalist painting at that point, both critics defended their positions in the leading theoretical art magazine of the time, *Bijutsu Techo.* Whereas Fujieda endorsed the thicker texturality of the painted surface, reversing his previous sanctioning of flatness, Minemura criticized Fujieda for maintaining an admiration for the continuous pictorial plane.[8] Designating this attitude as Occidental materialism, Minemura called upon domestic artists to recover the specifically Japanese ability to create "a discontinuous pictorial plane," modeled on Bunjinga (landscapes in ink), in order to reclaim the innate experimentalism of the Japanese spatial composition appropriated by the nineteenth-century Western modernists.

Despite their hopes for authentic innovation, the painters promoted by Fujieda and Minemura merely presented domestic modifications of Post-Painterly Abstraction and the late 1970s work of Frank Stella, as well as Minimalist paintings in the manner of Robert Ryman and Agnes Martin.[9] Although theoretically opposed to each other, both Minemura and Fujieda helped to consolidate academic styles in Japanese painting.

In the 1980s Japanese critical discourse was characterized by the defense of painting from polarized perspectives: academicism versus the faux-postmodern loosening of cultural canons under the auspices of "the New Wave" or New Painting. The latter position was loudly asserted between 1983 and 1985.[10] Regarding New Painting as a "postmodern genre," critics ascribed its "return to images" to an abandonment of avant-garde experimentalism in favor of the wealth of quotidian experience or personal and mythical memory.[11] The celebration of this eclecticism was frequently accompanied by discourses indicating that the avant-garde had given way to immediate reality.[12]

Neither academicism nor populism could have influence beyond the domestic field. This polarization between official, imperfectly translated Western theories and the return to undisciplined self-expression was characteristic of modern Japanese culture as a whole. They are the two faces of colonial intellectualism discussed by philosopher Masao Maruyama in his seminal book *Nihon no shisō* (The Japanese mind).[13] Critic Noi Sawaragi also criticized the same closure in *Nihon, gendai, bijutsu* (Japan, contemporary, art); blaming the preceding generations of Japanese artists and critics for indulging in a false game of "authenticity" and "deviation" in a closed circuit, which bore no relevance to international art history, Sawaragi urged the younger generation to break open this closure by using its "weakness" as a springboard for new creation.[14]

As a critic promoting the theories of postmodern appropriation, Sawaragi helped a new generation of Japanese artists to emerge in the early 1990s, which he collectively named Neo-Pop (or New Pop).[15] A Japanese equivalent to American Simulationism, Neo-Pop included Takashi Murakami, Mariko Mori, and Kenji Yanobe. Projecting an ironic awareness of the phantasmal nature of their identity through large sculptures and installations that simulated the metallic glitter and wild fancy of Japanese *manga* and *anime* images, Neo-Pop artists pushed painting to the periphery. In contrast to the academic defense of textured abstract paintings, appropriationist paintings ironically referenced painting as an institutional representation to be attacked, or as empty images mirroring the vacuity of postmodern existence, like simulations of cartoon figures in Takashi Murakami's *Sansei no hantai nanoda.*[16]

Appropriationist irony started to wane around 1995, with the closing of Rontgen Kunst Institute, the gallery that was headquarters to the information-savvy, "bad-boy" aesthetic. To the surprise of many, Murakami was the first to detach himself from the critical irony of Neo-Pop. In 1994, at his solo exhibition at SCAI the Bathhouse, *Which is Tomorrow? —Fall in Love*, Murakami featured large hand-painted canvases depicting his original cartoonish character DOB, mixing the antimimetic, ornamental aesthetics of traditional Japanese painting and *anime.* While the cheeky grin of DOB reflects the artist's self-irony as regards the derivative nature of both *anime* and art in Japan, the decorative precision of *Zuzazazazaza* (1994) and *And then and then and then and then* (1995) indicated his turn from cynicism toward the construction of a new concept of beauty (fig. 1). As if to reflect the general public tendency after 1995 to celebrate everyday pleasure and simple feelings —itself a consequence of the prolonged recession—"beauty" and "emotion" became keywords for understanding the gradual recovery of painting as an innovative genre. Yoshitomo Nara would also play a crucial role in renewing interest in painting; in his first solo exhibition at SCAI the Bathhouse in 1995, Nara captivated the jaded art-world audience with the brilliant reminder of innocence in his emotionally gripping paintings. With solo exhibitions in Tokyo in 1996 and 1997, Hiroshi Sugito and Tam Ochiai steadily developed yet a newer aesthetic of marginality by employing figurative images as indices of painterly elements, downplaying emotion but intensifying the strangeness of perception.

Articulation and Deterritorialization—Conceptual Models for Painterly Innovations

In order to explain the ideological strategies of Murakami and the technical innovations of the other three, I apply the theoretical categories of "articulation," "adolescence," and "deterritorialization," as defined respectively by Stuart Hall, Julia Kristeva, and Gilles Deleuze and Felix Guattari. Kristeva's theory will be discussed later in connection to the rise of the painters of adolescent sensibility; the theories of articulation and deterritorialization, however, require a lengthier explanation.

Articulation is essentially a term used to explain the relationship between ideology and social forces, revealing that their connection is not necessary or absolute. First developed by Marxist sociologist Ernesto Laclau, it was modified by Hall for postcolonial application.[17] In his frequently cited interview, "On Postmodernism and Articulation," Hall defines articulation as the deployment of the dominant ideological language by the subjects of a colonized country in order to equip themselves with logic and terms of struggle. Building on the Althusserian idea of ideology as a set of socio-cultural practices and beliefs that shape class or national identity, Hall suggests how an "ideology," or the mechanism of rule, can be advantageously used by the subjected people:

> **The theory of articulation asks how an ideology discovers its subject rather than how the subject thinks the necessary and inevitable thoughts which belong to it; it enables us to think how an ideology empowers people, enabling them to begin to make some sense or intelligibility of their historical situation, without reducing those forms of intelligibility to their socio-economic or class location or social position.[18]**

The appropriation of the language of domination can have an explosive effect on the cultural practices deeply embedded in the feelings of a colonized people. Hall gives the example of the Rastafarians in Jamaica who subversively used the language of the Bible to create a new expression. This new expression or language belongs neither entirely to the indigenous development nor to the culture of the colonizers. Its formation gives its participants a new identity; if its practice involves many people from different social spheres, then it shapes a new political group. Hall calls this enunciation of a new political identity "articulation."

Deterritorialization is a way to break down legitimized areas of signification, using a word, or a pictorial element, in such a way as to direct attention from the denotative meaning of a sign to the "act," or the state of transition in which things remain perpetually unformulated. Deleuze and Guattari introduced this term in their book *Kafka: Toward a Minor Literature* (1975). "Minor literature" is defined not as the literature of a minority group, but as a radically heterogeneous expression invented by those who write (create) in a major or dominant language that is not their own, frequently subverting common usage by using words as mere sounds or gestures.[19] "Minor" here means a form of subversion, a deterritorializing ability to transform the familiar into the strange, a principle of "escape" or indeterminacy, a tendency that exists within any major (legitimate) language or means of expression to make it radical.[20]

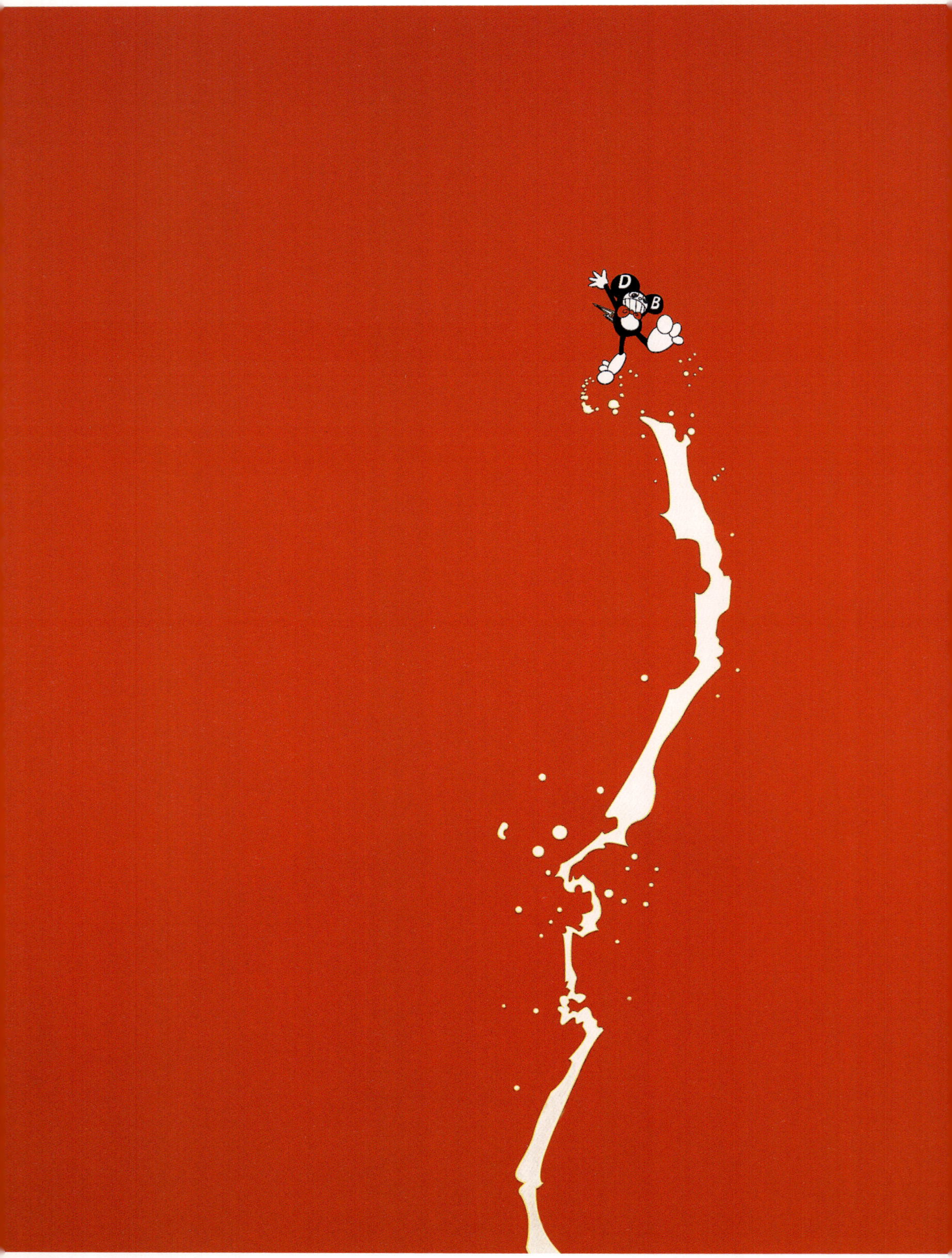

FIG. 1 Takashi Murakami **Zuzazazazaza** 1994 acrylic, silkscreen on canvas 59 x 67 in. Collection Ryutaro Takahashi; Courtesy Tomio Koyama Gallery, Tokyo photo: Norihiro Ueno

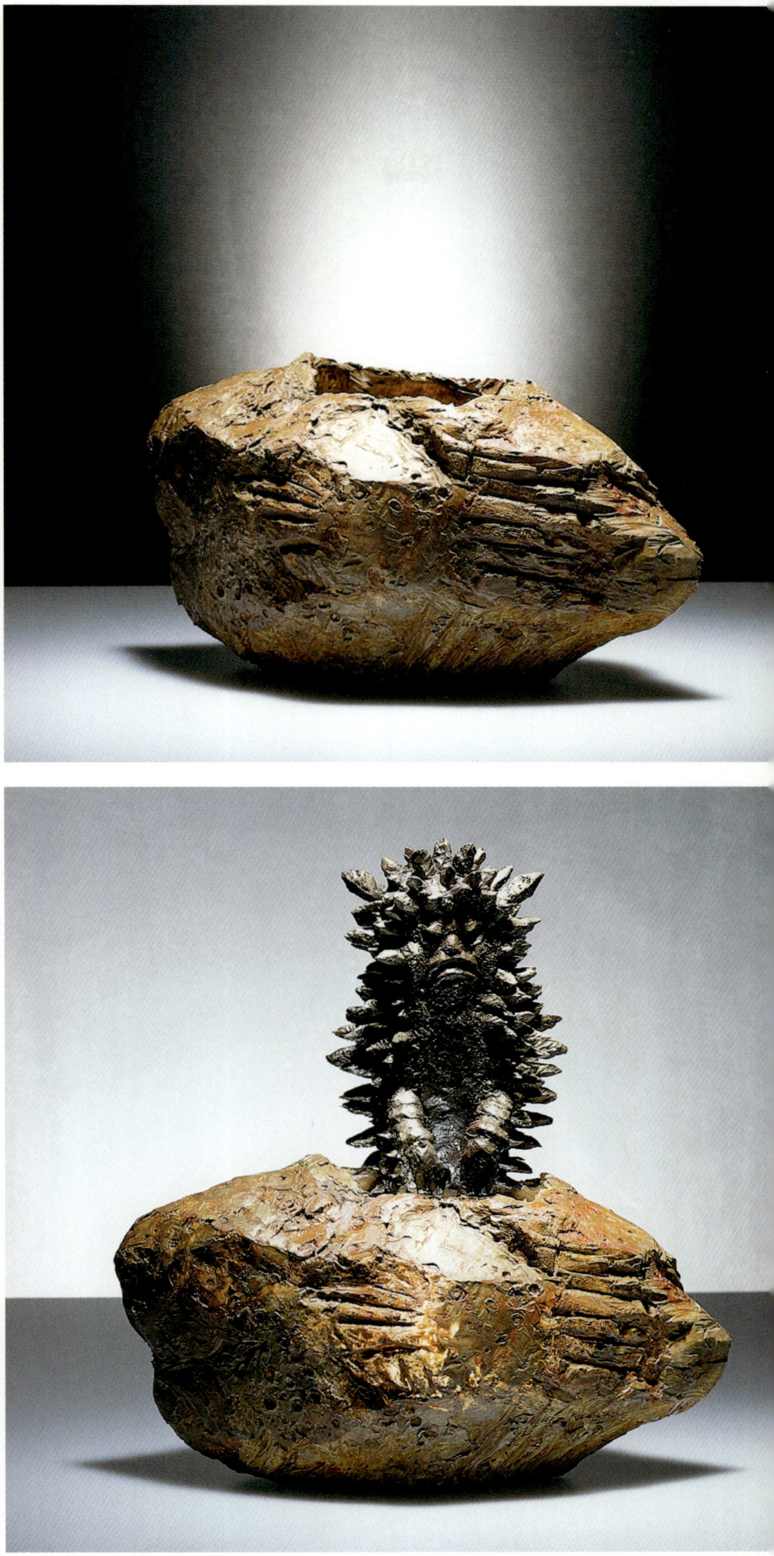

FIG. 2 Tohl Narita **Garadama** (Garamon's Egg) and **Garamon** 1999 plaster Private collection photos: Noritaka Harada

These theories provide the strategies for a marginalized subject to define a radically unique identity, existing between fixed areas of belonging such as the "global" and the "domestic." While Murakami, through his conscious reappropriation of his Nihonga heritage and re-centralization of the marginalized *anime* and premodern aesthetic, practices postcolonial articulation, Sugito and Ochiai, children of the age of global migration, idiosyncratically distance the influence of modernist painting. Nara unfolds the visual transcription of the in-between realm of childhood and adolescent fantasy, integrating "naive" and regional characteristics. What emerge through the study of their innovations are three modes of radically redefined "minority."

Redefinition of the Japanese Vernacular—Takashi Murakami

As Murakami turned steadfastly to painting, his treatment of *anime* motifs changed from appropriationist referencing to a positive aesthetic element.[21] He also transformed the cynical strategy of Neo-Pop into a unique theory of Japanese vernacular art by revealing a significant ideological and aesthetic link between traditional Japanese painting and *anime*. In his recent publication, *Super Flat* (see his essay "A Theory of Super Flat Japanese Art" on pp. 187–205), Murakami integrates his past theoretical and artistic practices into a coherent theory by forcefully manifesting stylistic affinities between the mannerism of *anime*—in which human proportions are playfully distorted, exploiting the two-dimensional composition—and *kiso*, or eccentric composition, characteristic of eighteenth-century Edo and Kyoto Mannerists.[22] His ambition was to formulate a theory of Japanese Pop by uniting marginalized premodern and postmodern vehicles of popular imagination.

The idea of Pop is crucial to Murakami, since it simultaneously embodies the shameful inauthenticity of its identity and is a paradoxical source of its own transcendence. This is partly because *anime* and *manga* constitute a common frame of reference for Murakami's generation. More significantly, *anime* presents a model of postcolonial subversion. Japanese *anime* and *manga* had an inauthentic origin, imitating Disney animations; they soon developed amazing visual features unseen anywhere outside of Japan. Unlike Japanese high culture, which fed on translations of Western philosophies and literatures, *manga* and *anime* achieved uniquely Japanese styles, capturing a large popular audience. A wild imagination was evidenced by the masterful distortions of animators such as Yoshinori Kanada, Tohl Narita, and Rhosaku Takayama, art-school graduates who went into the commercial profession of *kaijyū* design—making monster figures for science-fiction films aimed at children (fig. 2).[23] In a special issue of *Kōkoku hihyō* featuring "Tokyo Pop," Murakami explicitly states that it is the task of his generation "to create original [art] without depending on the existing intellectual system," making Japanese animation a point of reference for his own artistic practice, which needs to establish its unique positionality precisely where no proper systems of legitimation exist.[24]

Bringing together the threads of repressed Japanese popular imagination, Murakami practices cultural genealogy. Grounding his own artistic practice in this rediscovered heritage of the Japanese vernacular, he performs an act of cultural articulation. This act endows him with a postcolonial pride, which enables him to exercise his artistic agency in the international field of "contemporary art."

Murakami's ambivalent relationship to Nihonga demands further explanation. Originally trained as a Nihonga artist at Tokyo University of Music and Art, Murakami has always demanded that an artwork possess formal precision and transcendent character. A belief in art's ability to offer something that transcends mere hobby—an "absolutely amazing" experience—as well as an appreciation for the aesthetic rigorousness of *otaku* taste (connoisseurship of Japanese *anime* culture) distinguishes Murakami from his Neo-Pop peers Kenji Yanobe and Kodai Nakahara.[25] Observing the Nihonga practice decline into the inert production of investment materials, Murakami abandoned contemporary Nihonga, seeking to reconstitute his identity as a "contemporary artist."[26] In his appropriationist phase, Murakami disguised his Nihonga sensibility as a kind of *otaku* craftsmanship; *Polyrhythm* (1991), a resin panel adorned with minute plastic soldiers, undermines the preciousness of traditional craft by blending it with a despised *otaku* taste, while at the same time paying homage to both (fig. 3).

His present position, nevertheless, strongly evokes the productive eclecticism of Tenshin. As stated earlier, Tenshin's Nihonga was created in reaction to colonialism, an "apparatus invented to conduct an aesthetic struggle."[27] As Tenshin stated in his influential book, *The Ideals of the East with Special Reference to the Art of Japan* (1903):

> **When the first decade of the era was passed, . . . a band of earnest workers strove to found a third belt of art-expression, which, by a higher realization of the possibilities of ancient Japanese art, and aiming at a love and knowledge of the most sympathetic movements in Western art-creations, tried to reconstruct the national art on a new basis, whose keynote should be "Life true to Self."[28]**

The Nihonga painters who emerged from Tenshin's schooling successfully united revived techniques of traditional painting, including the Kano school's powerful lines, the Yamatoe school's exquisite coloring, Rinpa's use of ornamental patterns as structural and symbolic principles, and Post-Impressionist experiments.[29] There was a more than superficial exchange between Japanese techniques and Post-Impressionist experiments; Japanese painters saw in the flat spatial composition and structural use of ornamental color planes of Gauguin or Cézanne, for example, a theoretical deployment of their familiar aesthetic.

Art historian Noriaki Kitazawa claims that Fenolosa's and Tenshin's invention of Nihonga was an Orientalist institutionalization of modern Western aesthetic standards disguised as a domestic form.[30] It is, on the contrary, a conscious act of turning the colonial situation into an occasion to create a new political identity, which Murakami's contemporary practice updates. It is not accidental that *Bugi rinsen* ("Maiko" in a garden) (1924) by Bakusen Tsuchida (fig. 4), a follower of Tenshin's philosophy, consciously mixed the Yamatoe manipulation of coloring—painting every tiny flower pattern of the kimono with utmost elaborateness and arranging high-toned bright colors in bold contrast—with the construction of flat geometrical shapes into a cubic mass derived from Cézanne and Picasso, realizing similar effects of decentering the pictorial plane to those achieved in Murakami's *The Castle of Tin-Tin* (1998). In the latter, the flat, even application of colors to every detail undermines the thematic division between the center and the periphery, while the ornamental accentuation of brightly colored dots suggests a different principle of spatial composition than that governing mimetic representation (fig. 5).

Murakami's reinstatement of the inherent modernity of traditional Japanese painting contrasts favorably with Toshiaki Minemura's failed attempt in 1977. Minemura's urging that Japanese painters construct a "discontinuous pictorial plane" by reviving the line inherited from Bunjinga—the painting of ideal landscapes by reclusive intellectuals—misfired largely due to his incorrect historical reference to sixteenth-century wall-painting master Hasegawa Tōhaku as a model Bunjinga painter, as well as his arbitrary championing of the Mono-ha as Bunjinga's modern heir.[31] Minemura also ignored a significant characteristic of Bunjinga: the juxtaposition of writing and drawing to project a poetic vision of the world, which disrupted the autonomy of painting. It was a characteristic that made Fenolosa attack Bunjinga as a premodern category in his influential book *Bijutsu shinsetsu*, based on the belief that poetry and painting should be separated (figs. 6 and 7).[32]

Favoring elaborately finished, autonomous pictorial planes, Murakami undoubtedly "internalizes" what Minemura calls the Western materialist aesthetic. The rules of *Naikokukaiga kyoshinkai* (the National Exhibition of Painting)—the earliest government-funded exhibitions in the Meiji Period—demanded that painting be displayed as separate from ornamental upholstery, framed as an individual, autonomous piece.[33] The challenge to Murakami's "institutional" aesthetic is brought about by the narrative evocation of Yoshitomo Nara and the creation by Hiroshi Sugito and Tam Ochiai of a heterogeneous pictorial surface juxtaposing visual metonyms, opening up its associative field to many different contexts.

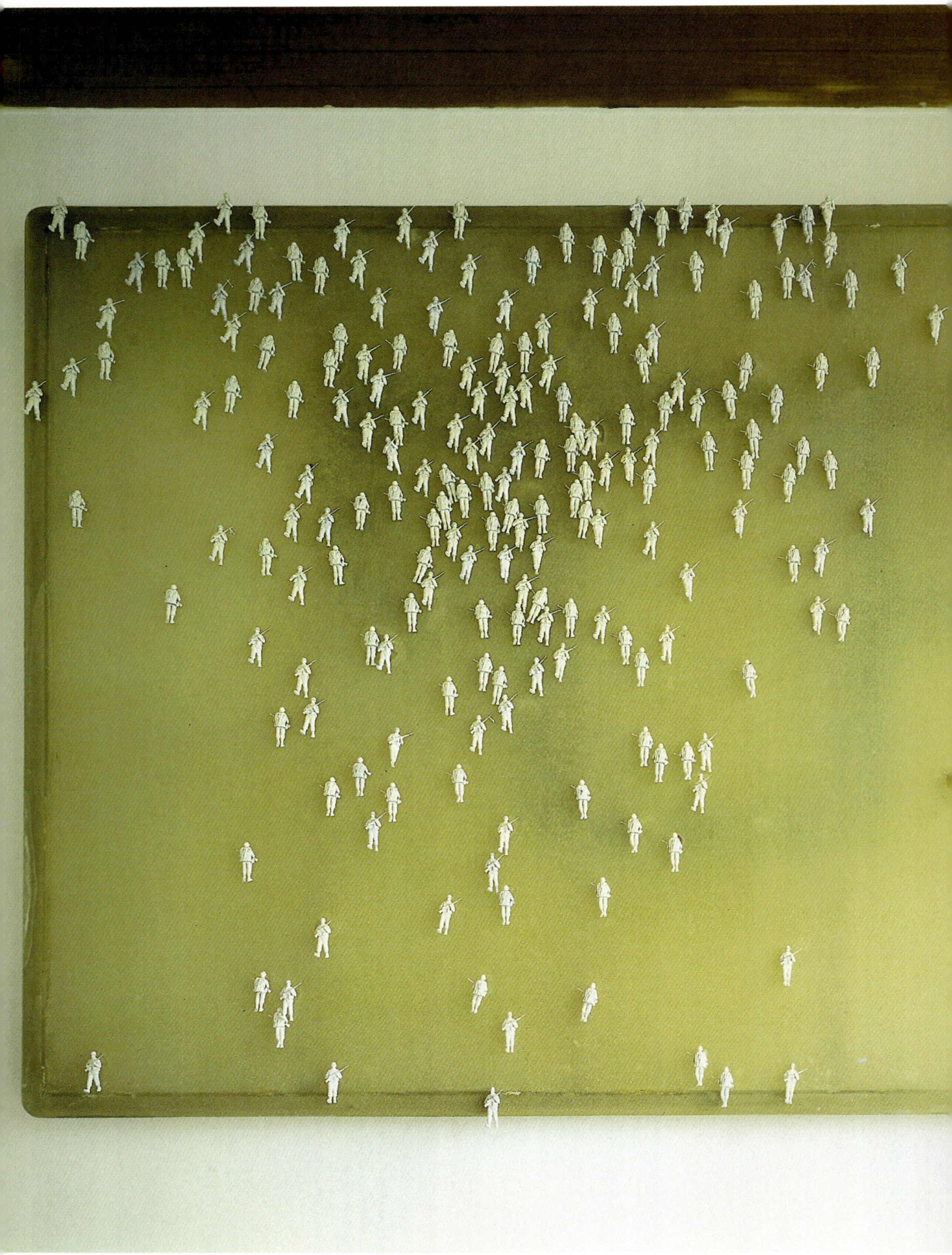

FIG. 3 Takashi Murakami **Polyrhythm** 1991 synthetic resin, stainless steel, Tamiya 1/35-scale plastic models 47 ¼ x 70 ¾ in.
Collection Tsutomu Ikeuchi; Courtesy Tomio Koyama Gallery, Tokyo

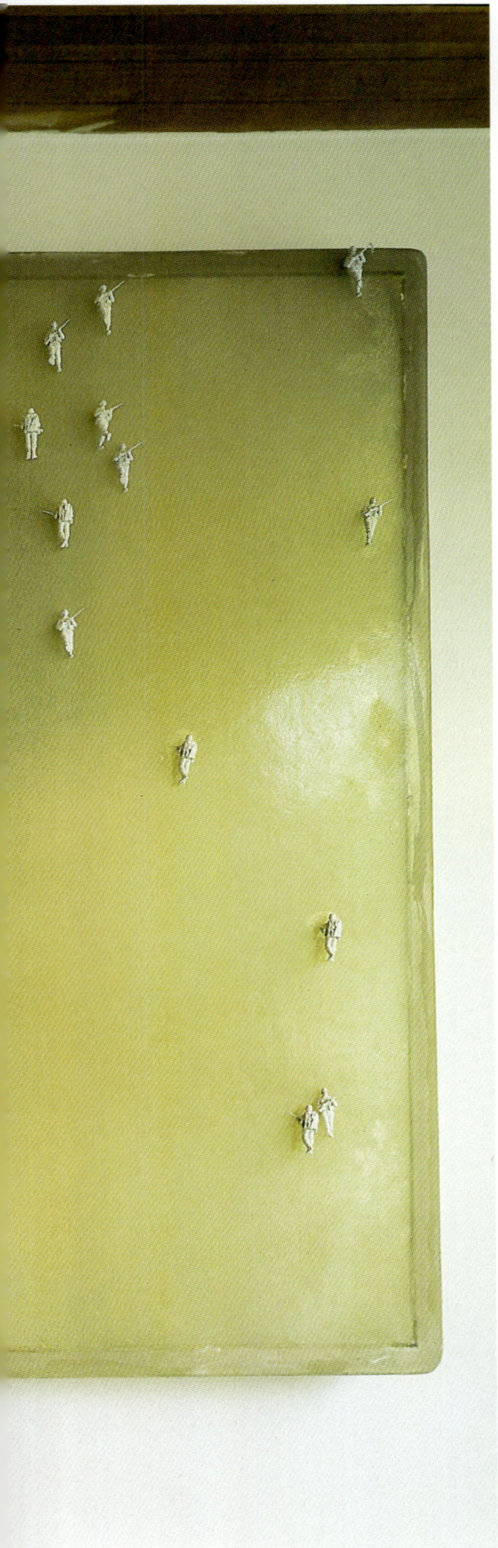

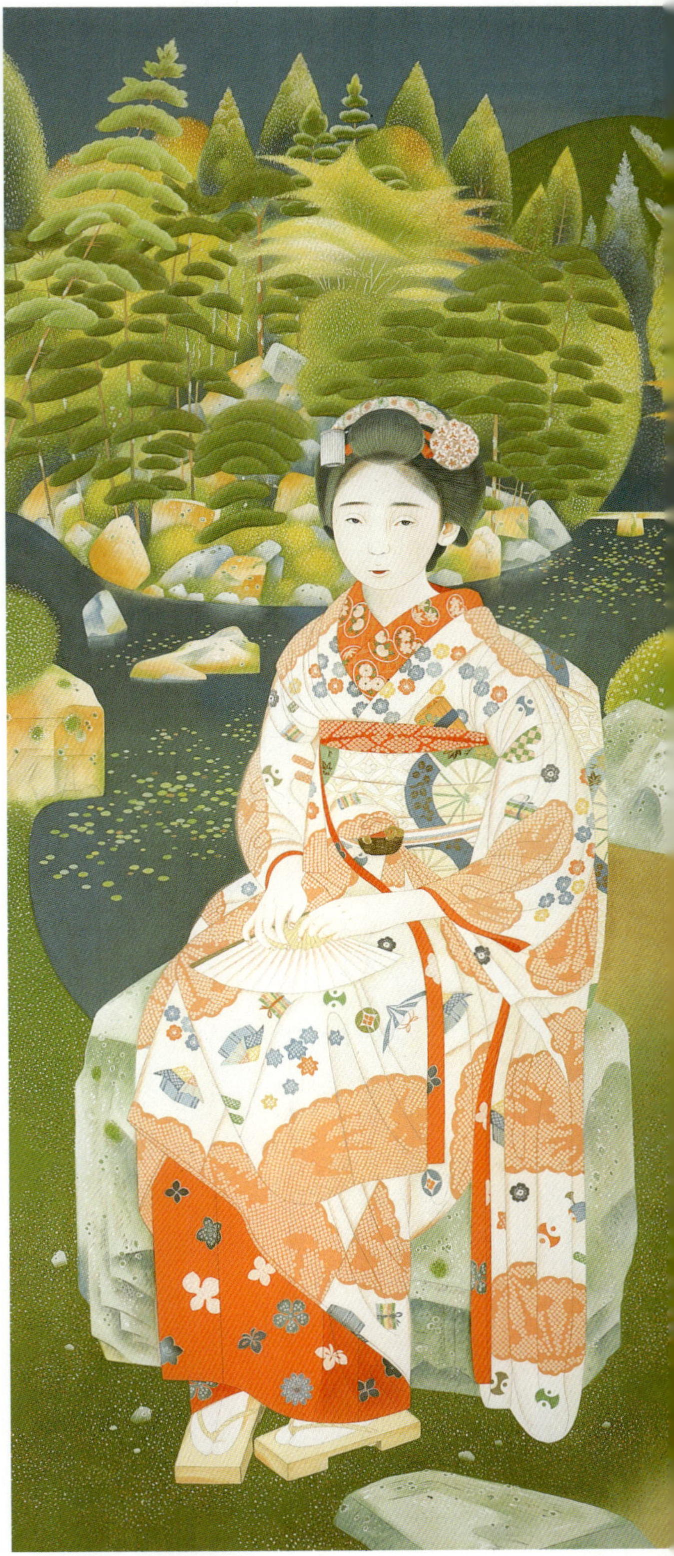

FIG. 4 Bakusen Tsuchida **Bugi rinsen** ("Maiko" in a garden) 1924 color on silk 86 ¼ x 40 ½ in. Collection National Museum of Modern Art, Tokyo (Indefinite Loan)

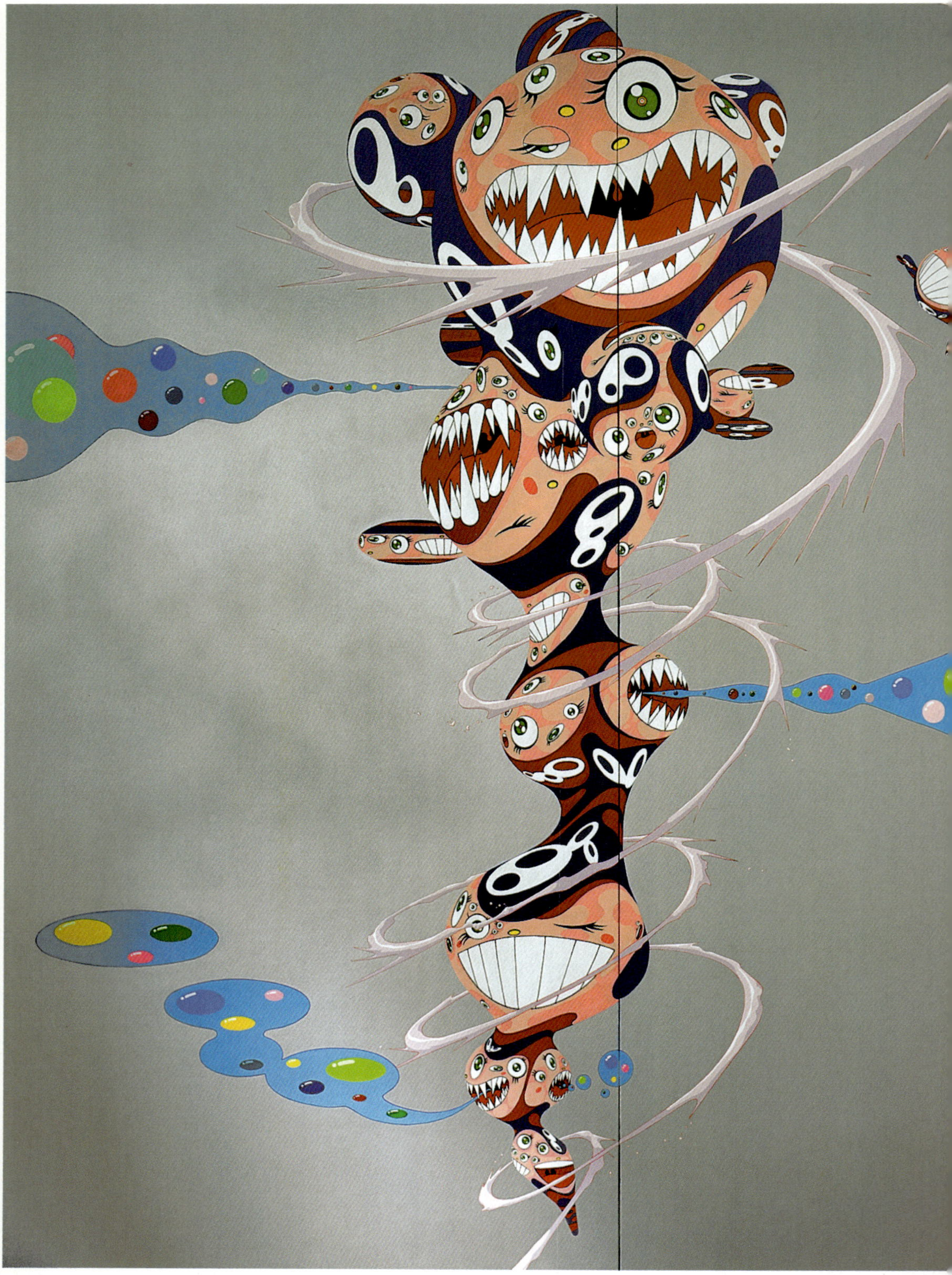

FIG. 5 Takashi Murakami **The Castle of Tin Tin** 1998 acrylic on canvas on board 120 x 120 in. Collection Ruth and Jake Bloom, Los Angeles; Courtesy Blum & Poe, Santa Monica, California

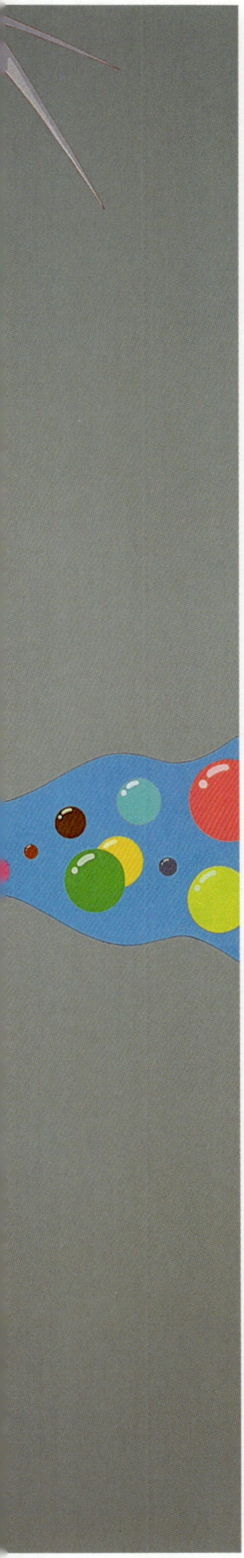

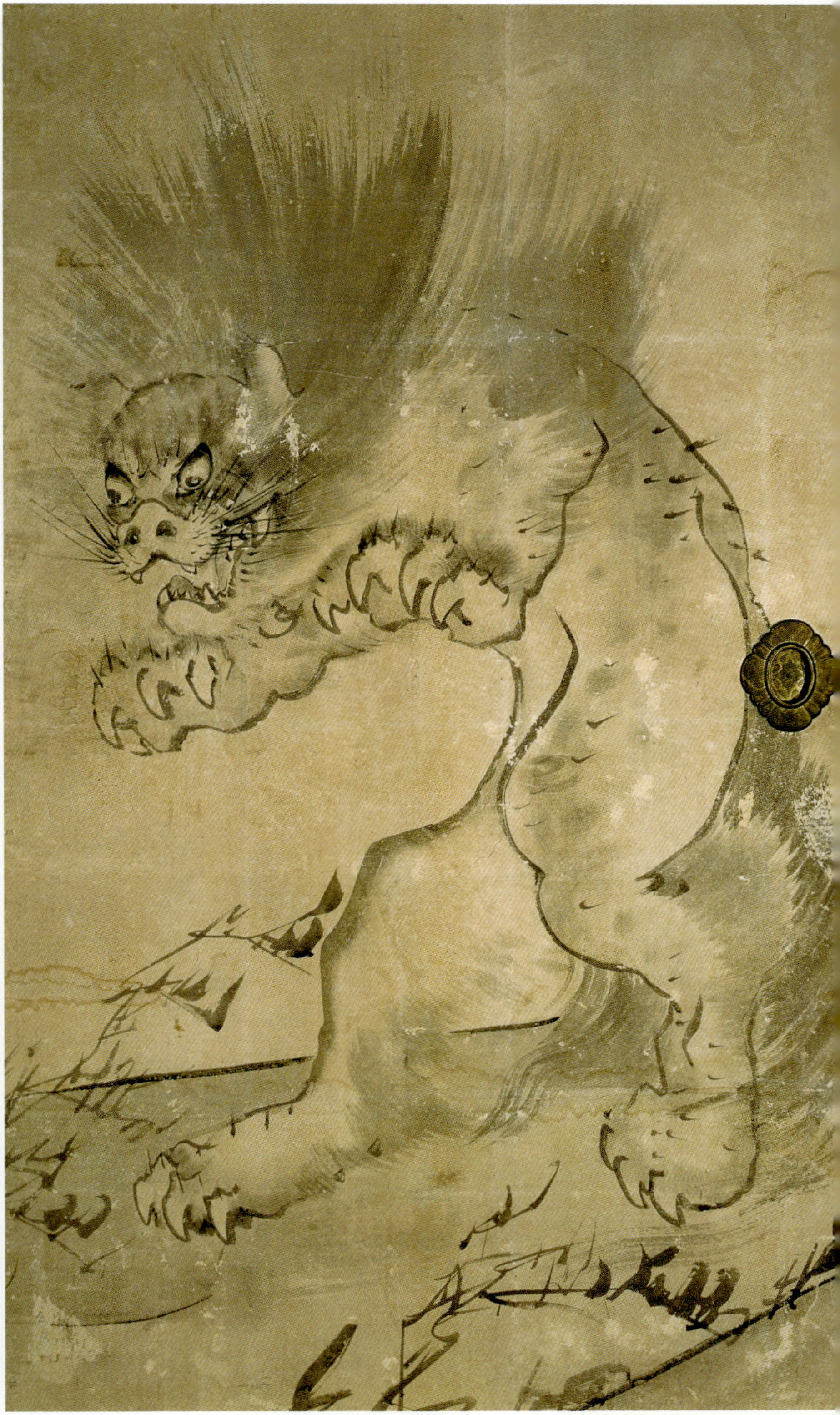

FIG. 6 Nagasawa Rosetsu detail of **Karajishizu** (Chinese lions) 1786 ink on paper twelve sliding door panels
Collection Jyojuji Temple, Kushimoto Okyo Rosetsukan Museum

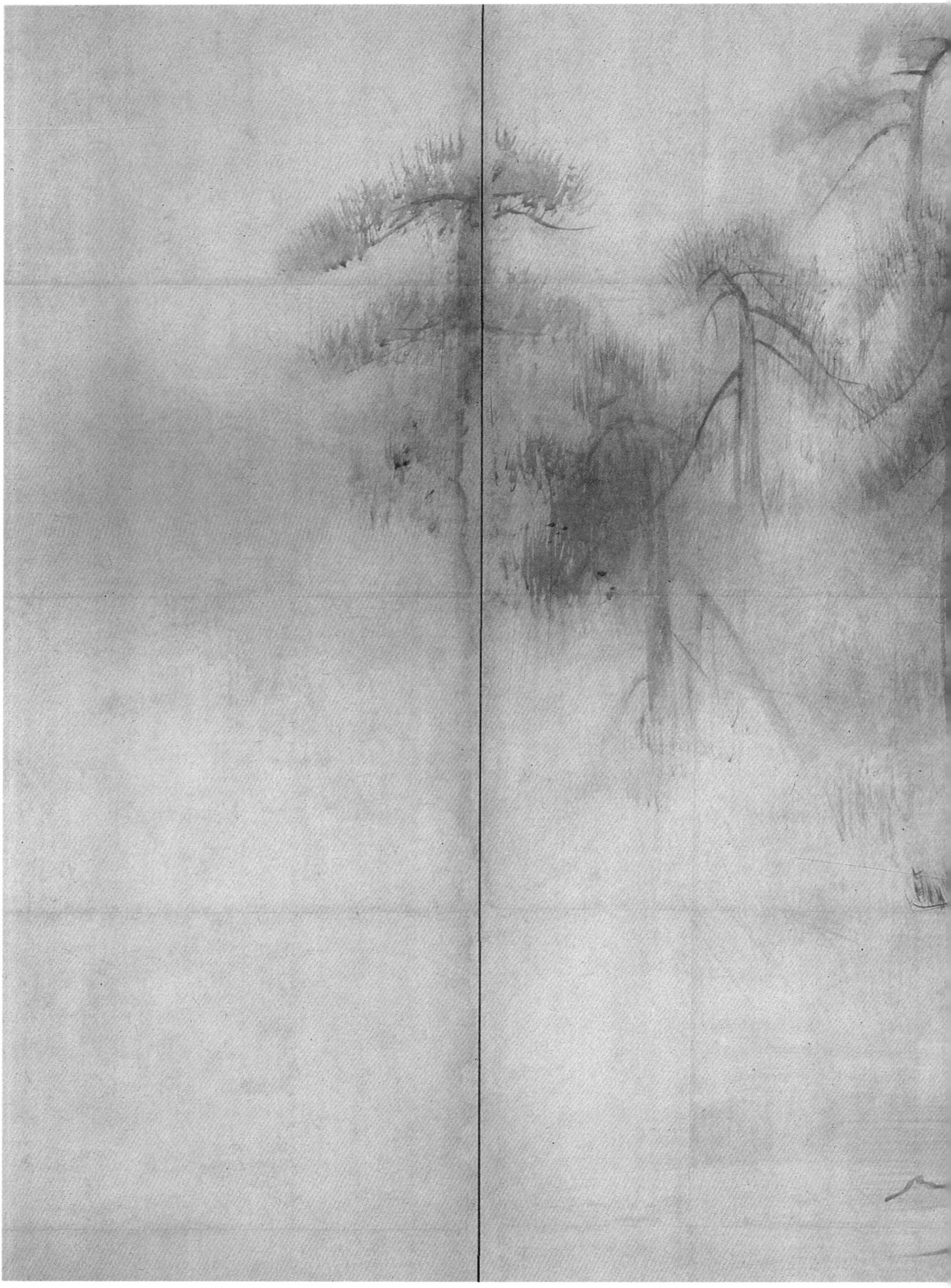

FIG. 7 Hasegawa Tōkahu detail of **Shōrinzu** (Pine trees) Momoyama period, 16th century ink on paper pair of six-fold screens 61 ½ x 136 ½ in. Collection Tokyo National Museum

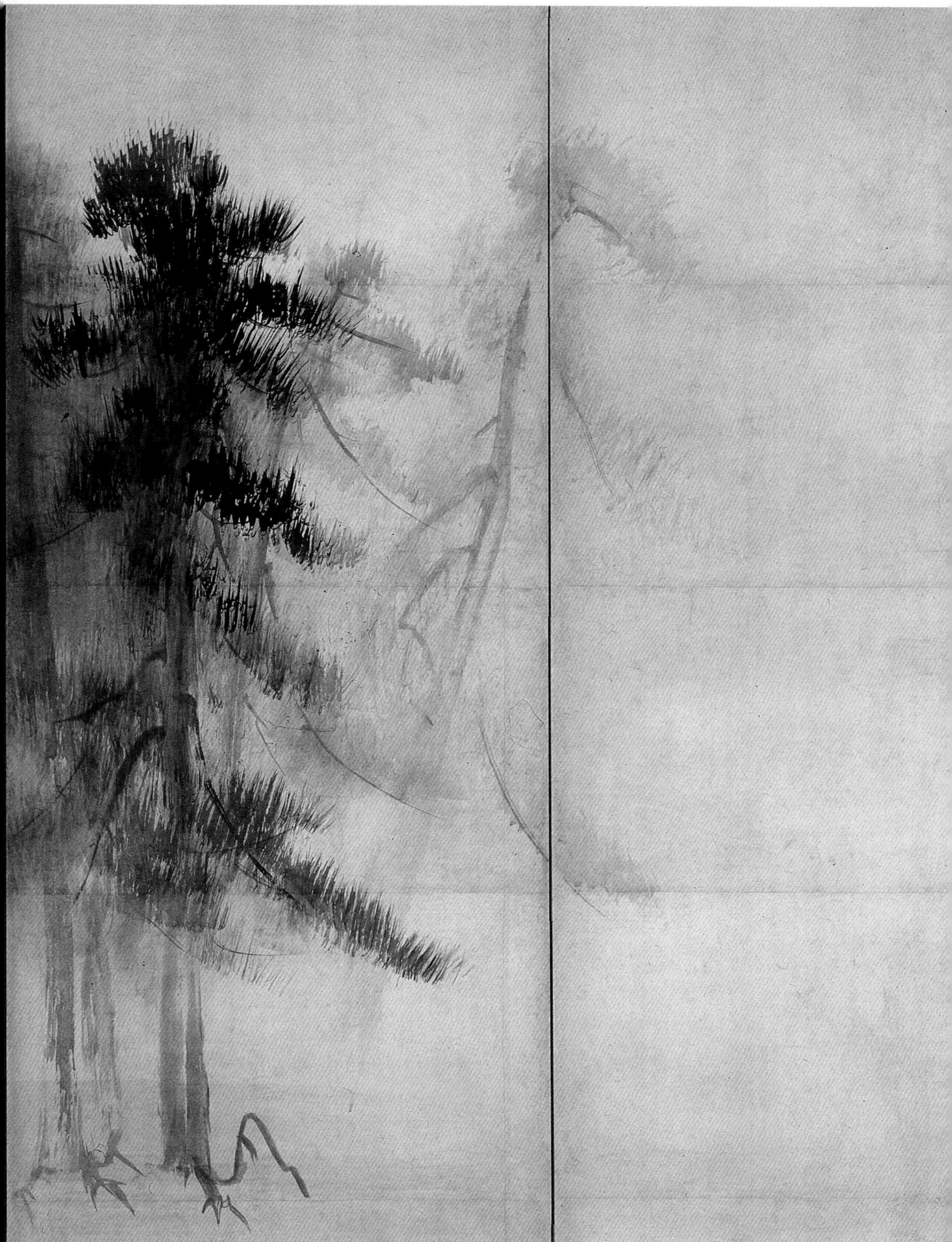

The Adolescent Recaptured—Yoshitomo Nara

Yoshitomo Nara has played a central role in reestablishing interest in figurative painting since 1995. As documented in the July 1995 and November 1998 issues of *Bijutsu Techo*, Nara and Takanobu Kobayashi, among a few others, became extremely popular within a few years as masters of *kairaku kaiga*, or the "painting of pleasure," passionately supported by an audience outside the regular art clientele. Their popularity was contemporaneous with the return of "beauty" and "emotion" as a reigning paradigm in the New York art world following the Whitney Biennial of 1995, which saw the emergence of Elizabeth Peyton, Rita Ackermann, and Karen Kilimnik as painters of disturbing adolescent portraits. These artists shared with outsider painter Henry Darger and photographers Wolfgang Tillmans and Jack Pierson the unabashed celebration of adolescent desire and androgyny, a juxtaposition of sensuous beauty and psycho-sexual violence, and a deceptively amateur outlook that suggested their fresh discovery of the quotidian and their dangerous proximity to popular kitsch.

The Japanese boom of figurative painting did not form as strong a current as its American counterpart. This was partly due to the failure of individual painters to sustain their poetic intensity, but mostly owes to the absence of a system of legitimation in the Japanese art world to incorporate even blatantly outsider elements into the art-historical discourse. While his peers gradually lost strength and appeal within five years, Nara survived because of his special ability to transcribe dream logic and to evoke a memory of the undifferentiated consciousness of infancy fluctuating between animal immediacy and human will. His paintings are inhabited by disproportionately large-headed children, contorted bodies, and extended limbs. The works embody a hybridization of the human and the animal, or the organic and the inorganic, and compose a narrative space in which people and animals communicate with one another. The sense of magic is eloquently conveyed in his earlier paintings, including *In the Deepest Puddle II* (1995), in which a girl with an enormous bandaged head looks back, chest-deep in a puddle, and *Kumo no ueno minnna* (Friends on clouds) (1989), populated by hybrid creatures, in which bold lines drawn over the richly textured meshes of color lead the viewer's thought from the material plane to its imaginary outer space (figs. 8 and 9). Mixing distortion and ellipsis, these paintings perform allegorical evocations. They strongly suggest Nara's kinship with the "magical realism" of the 1930s Neue Sachlichkeit movement in Weimar Republic Germany; one also thinks of the paintings of Balthus, very early Lucien Freud, and early Yasuo Kuniyoshi (fig. 10).[34] Nara's precursors were practitioners of figuration in doubt of its own representational illusion.

A style such as Nara's escapes the evolutionist categorizations of art history. Its radicality can best be explained in analogy with a literary category. Julia Kristeva's idea of the "adolescent novel" provides a useful conceptual model. Itself a variation of her earlier theory of a "polyphonic novel," the theory of the adolescent novel reevaluates the rich mixture of diverse narrative styles—immediate dramatic address, poetry, fairy tale—exemplified by the premodern picaresque fiction of the fifteenth century.[35] The undifferentiated narrative, which typically featured the adventures of an androgynous youth whose identity constantly shifts, embodies an "open psychic structure," provisionally called "adolescent." According to Kristeva, this "adolescent structure opens itself to the repressed," initiating "a psychic reorganization of the individual."[36] She also points out that such open structures "easily traverse the frontiers between differences of sex and identity, reality and fantasy, art and discourse," because they "immediately [echo] the fluidity, i.e., inconstancy, of a mass media society," and that "the adolescent is found to represent naturally this structure that can be called a 'crisis' structure only through the eyes of the ideal, stable law."[37]

Filled with signifiers of liminality and even incorporating writing as part of its poetic vision, Nara's pictorial world precisely transcribes the fluidity and heterogeneity of the "adolescent structure" (fig. 11). Its faux-naive style incorporates elements of kitsch, reflecting the impurity of mass cultural representation, while extending beyond commercial kitsch to tap into the primary resources of popular imagination.[38] As such, Nara's work shares the disturbing charm of paintings by Karen Kilimnik and Henry Darger, mirroring the dangerous seductions of adolescent anarchy and mass culture.

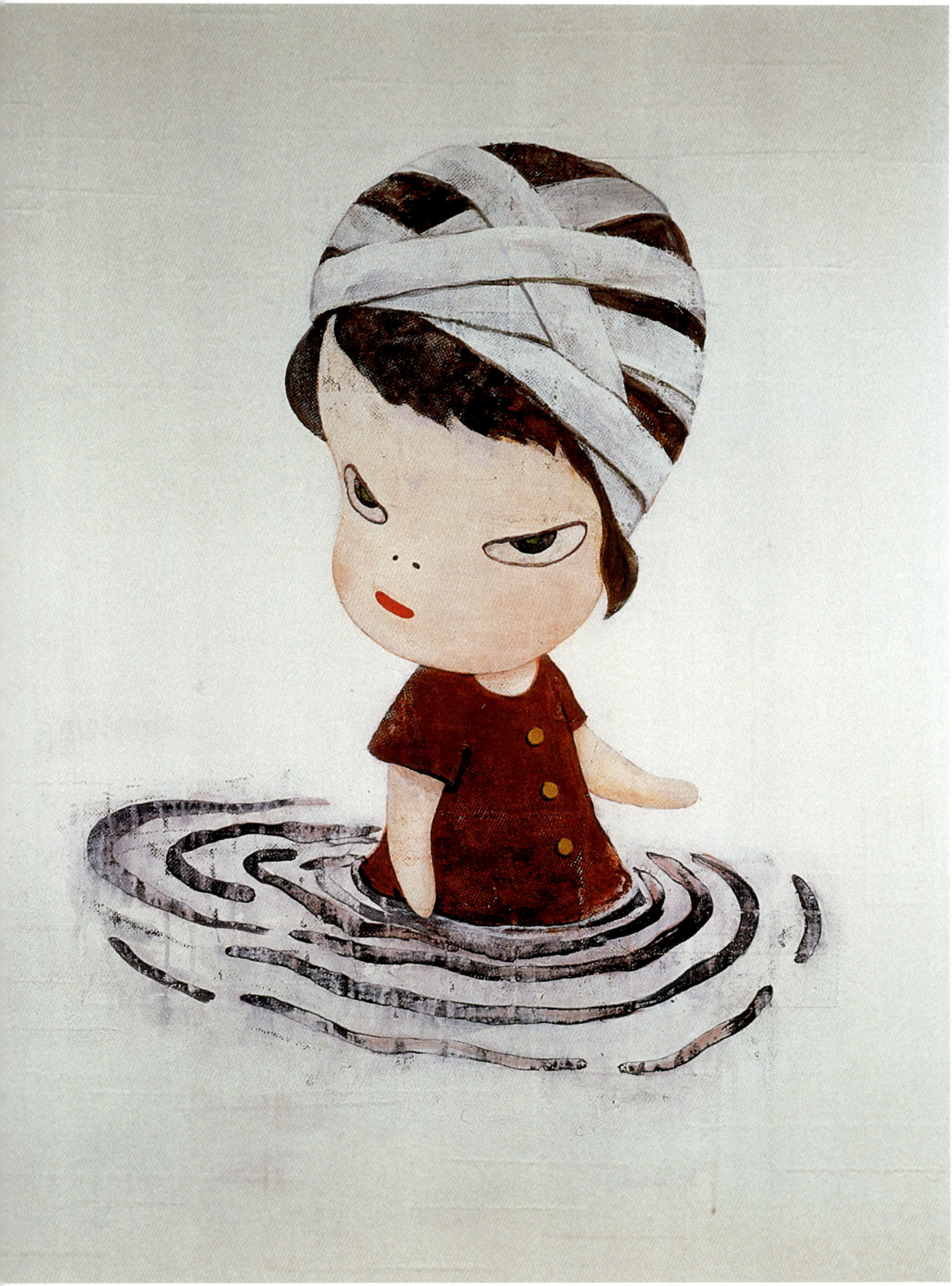

FIG. 8 Yoshitomo Nara **In the Deepest Puddle II** 1995 acrylic on canvas 47 ¼ x 43 ¼ in. Collection Masako Sanoji; Courtesy Tomio Koyama Gallery, Tokyo

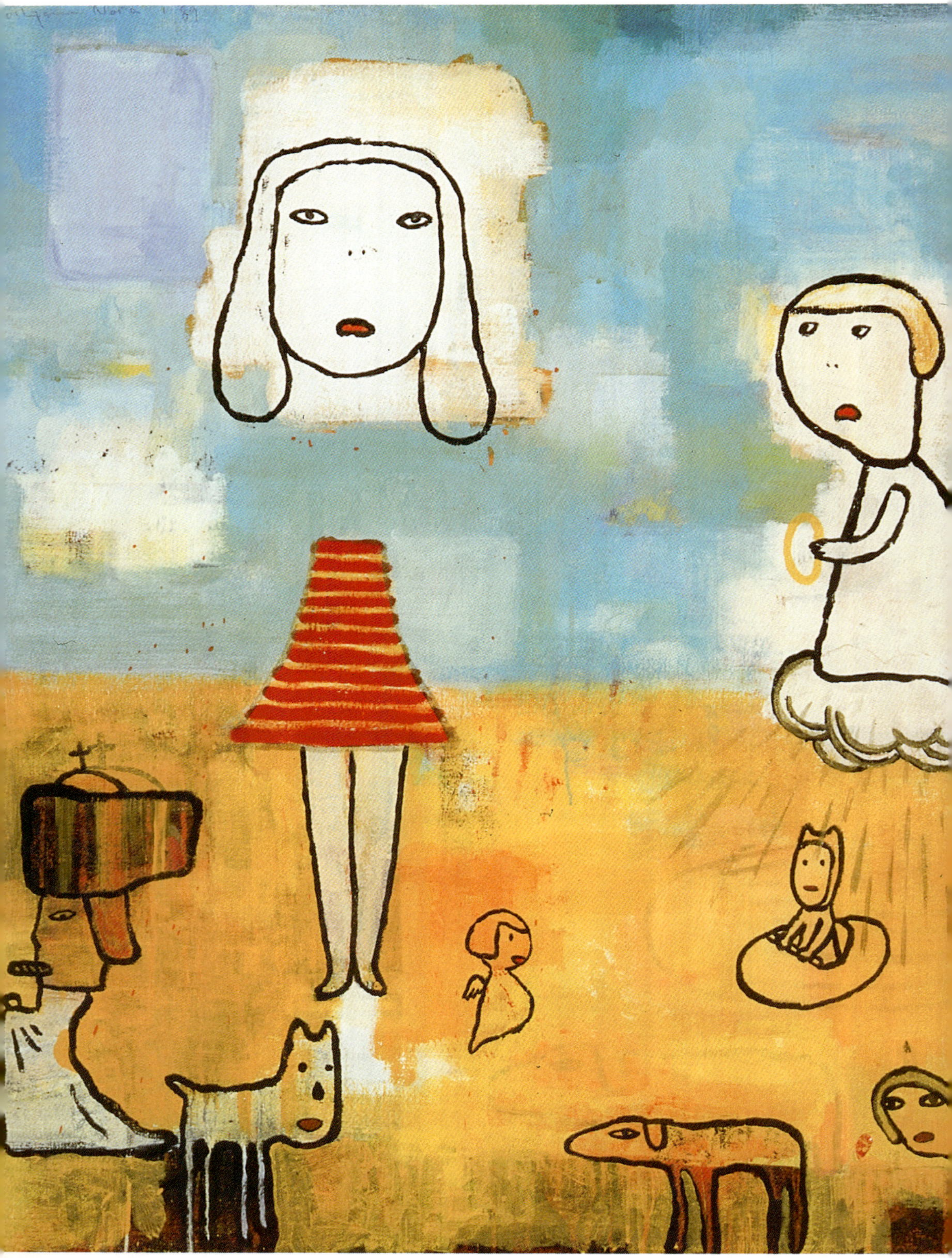

FIG. 9 Yoshitomo Nara **Kumo no ueno minnna** (Friends on clouds) 1989 acrylic on canvas 39 ½ x 39 ½ in. Collection Takashi Hioki; Courtesy Hakutosha, Nagoya

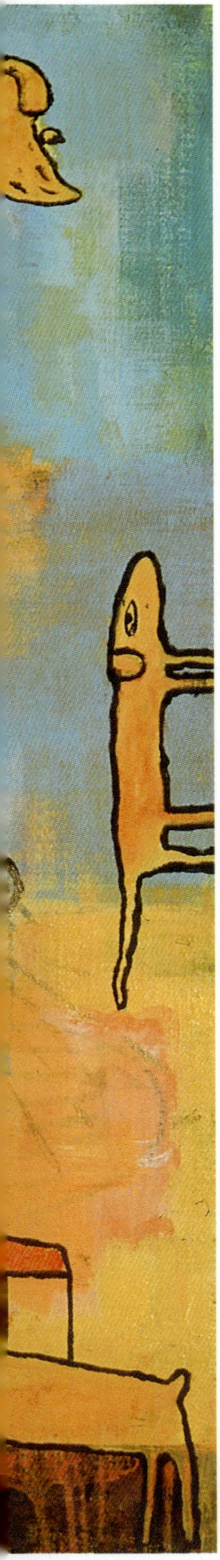

The powerful popular appeal of Nara's paintings, especially to adolescent girls who are the most marginalized sector of Japanese society, makes them susceptible to the reactionary discourse of celebrating emotion in order to jettison conceptual creation and critical thinking, as demonstrated by the Japanese defenders of New Painting in the 1980s. Having studied under Arnold Penck at the Düsseldorf Academy of Painting during the late 1980s and early 1990s, Nara is not unfamiliar with New Painting's exploration of the primary power of images. Nevertheless, his paintings escape becoming hieratic; recapitulating the freedom of popular imagination that prevailed before the consolidation of modern institutions, it reveals the taste that has been present since the participation of people in modern culture, but which was repressed by the progressivist theories of modernism. In that sense, Nara creates his own category of Pop and redefines "minority" as a radical aesthetic of the "adolescent."

Thin Lines of Escape—Hiroshi Sugito and Tam Ochiai
If Nara resonated with the spirit of the late 1990s, in which many artists turned to the search for their lost inner child, by asserting the "minor" sentiment against the confrontational strategy of Murakami, then Hiroshi Sugito and Tam Ochiai marked yet another change of emphasis. Their works suppress visceral emotion in favor of a lyrical perception that results from the radical estrangement of our sense of knowing.

Among many favorable writings on Sugito's practice, Jerry Saltz's commentary reveals the radicalness of Sugito's work by pointing out how his images function as constructive elements of his pictorial plane—a sort of "Cy Twombly meets Color Field" (fig. 14):

> **Everything turns into something else. This trapezoid is a stage; those little smudges with white lines are tugboats pulling a house. . . . The outbreaks and episodes of line and color become tiny, toylike battleships, rockets, and war machines.[39]**

Saltz's explication brilliantly captures the fluctuation of Sugito's pictorial language between figurative enunciation and formal play; the function corresponds to Deleuze's and Guattari's category of "deterritorialization."

There may be an objection to my application of Deleuze's and Guattari's theory of "minor literature" and the deterritorializing function of its language to the analysis of painting. Nonetheless, I find a deep relevance in their categories since they provide, like Kristeva's, a theory of fiction in which narrative unity is constantly destabilized by the poetic—performative—functions of language; it provides a model for a brand of figurative painting in which physical, or ornamental, elements perpetually disrupt the representational illusion while asserting their materiality more powerfully than in directly "abstract" painting. The "deterritorializing" language in "minor" literature provides a fine analogy to the ways in which Sugito's tiny "color fields" override their outlines to assert themselves as individual patterns:

> **[The] warbling [of] blurred words, the whistling of the mouse, the cough of an ape. . . . Everywhere, organized music is traversed by a line of escape—in order to liberate a living and expressive material that speaks for itself and has no need of being put into a form.[40]**

That description seems particularly applicable to the interplay between thin, discontinuous outlines and bright color dots demonstrated by the series of quizzical portraits of imaginary monsters that Sugito has been producing consistently since 1998. In *lobsterman* (1999), for example, a hybrid creature vaguely resembling man, bird, and lobster looms sinisterly on the canvas before a vacant background. Its contours, in thin pencil line, nearly disappear within the glitter of jewel-like dots and candy-colored grids applied to such peripheral details as ears or clothing patterns; or, one could say, its disembodied figure is barely sustained by the tonal accentuation of tiny bright color dots (fields) (fig. 15). Sugito repeatedly creates this anxious but strangely beautiful state of in-betweenness in his

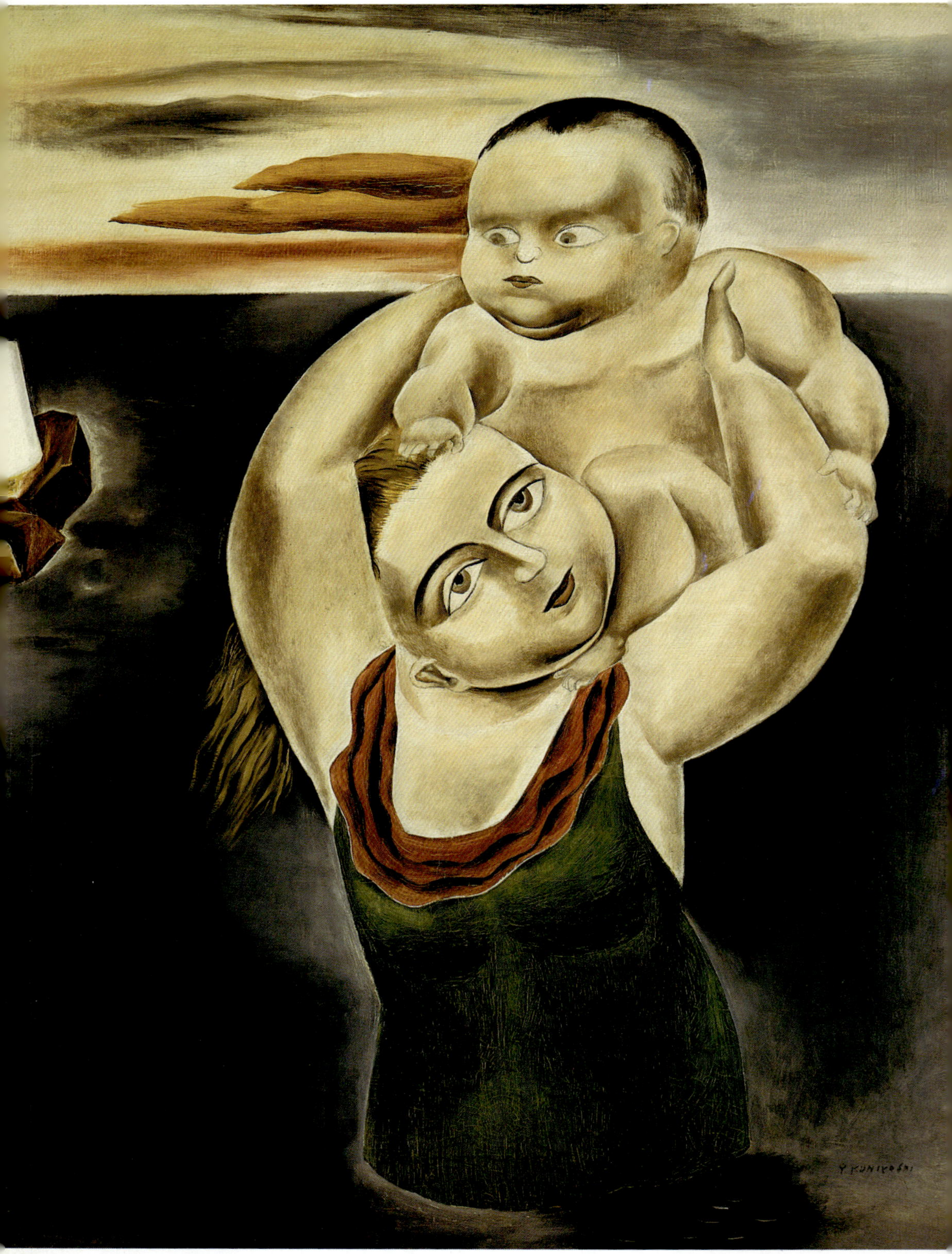

FIG. 10 Yasuo Kuniyoshi **Child Frightened by Water** 1924 oil on canvas 30 ⅛ x 24 ⅛ in. Collection Hirshhorn Museum and Sculpture Garden, Smithsonian Institution, Washington, D.C.; Gift of Joseph H. Hirshhorn, 1966

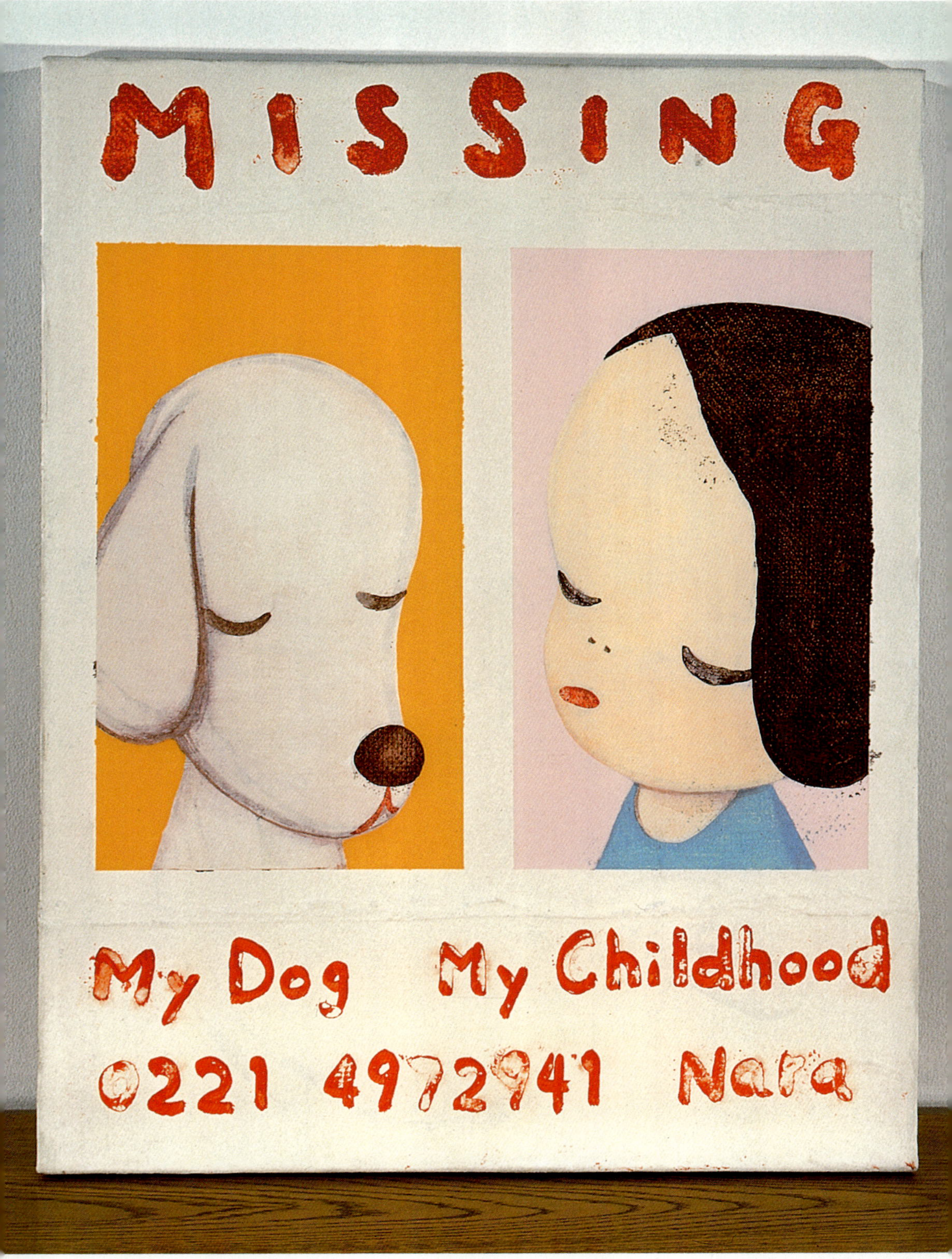

FIG. 11 Yoshitomo Nara **Missing** 1995 acrylic on canvas 21 ¾ x 17 ¾ in. Collection Sueo Miura; Courtesy Tomio Koyama Gallery, Tokyo

FIG. 12 Hiroshi Sugito **stars** 1995 acrylic, pastel on cotton 50 ¼ x 43 ¼ in. Courtesy the artist and Tomio Koyama Gallery, Tokyo
FIG. 13 Hiroshi Sugito **the day of going** 1996 pigment, crayon on cotton 40 ½ x 36 ¼ in. Courtesy the artist and Tomio Koyama Gallery, Tokyo

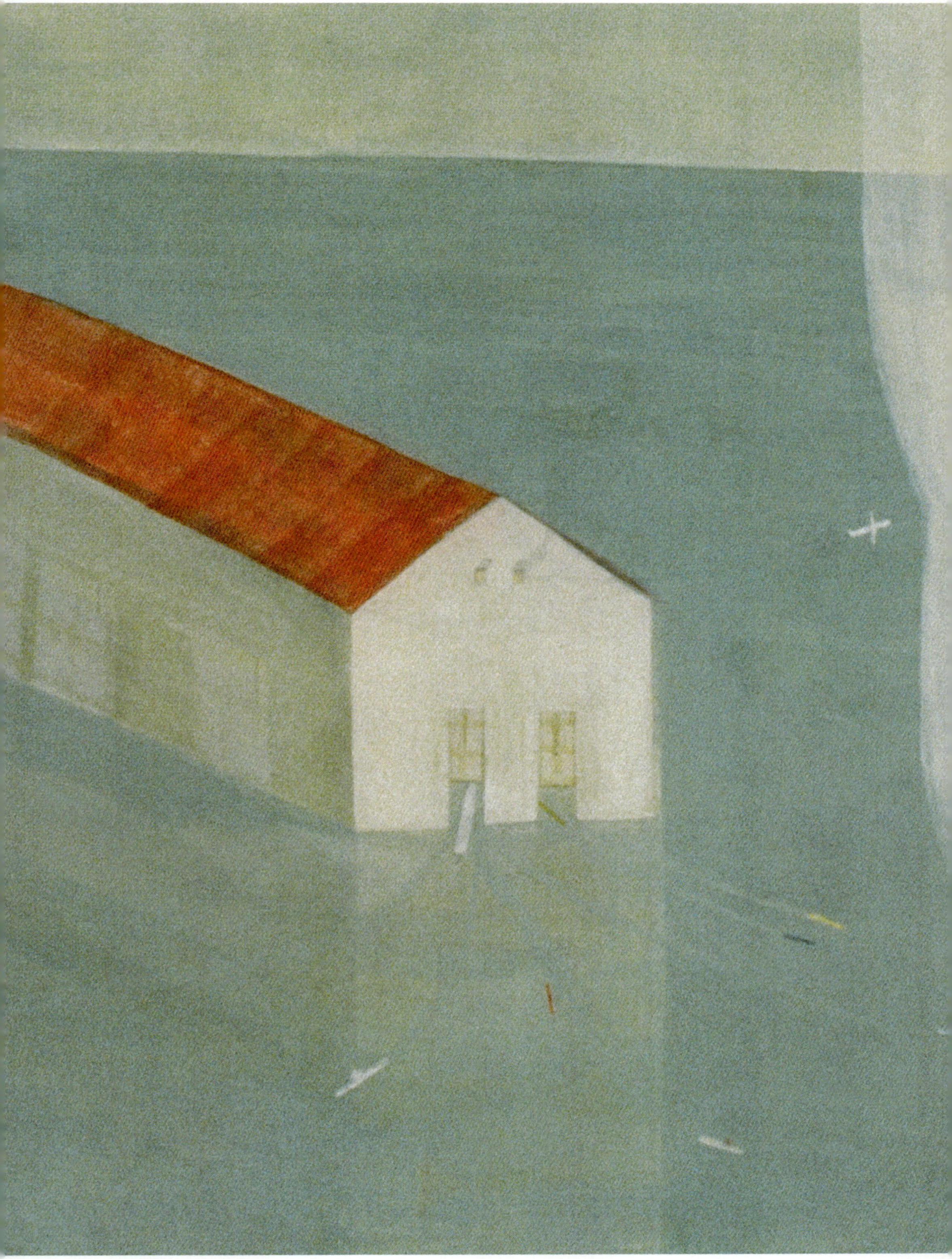

FIG. 14 Hiroshi Sugito **flood** 1996 acrylic on canvas 60 x 72 in. Courtesy the artist and Tomio Koyama Gallery, Tokyo

animal study (1999) and *elephant and buckle* diptych (1999), whose effects are nothing but "deterritorializing" (fig. 16):

> **[The image] has become becoming—the becoming-dog of the man and the becoming-man of the dog, the becoming-ape or the becoming-beetle of the man and vice versa. We are no longer in the situation of an ordinary, rich language where dog, for example, would directly designate an animal and would apply metaphorically to others.[41]**

Sugito's application of figurative shapes as formal structural elements exploits, no doubt, the decorative aesthetic of Nihonga painting in which he was trained. But unlike Murakami, who consciously inscribes Nihonga's national character into his own smoothly mastered flat planes, Sugito neutralizes explicit traces of nationality. His engagement of the "ornamental" vocabulary is individual yet devoid of identity assertion; experimenting with grids and color fields, which evoke both the modernist picture plane and traditional Japanese ornamental patterns, Sugito recapitulates the "modernity" inherent in Nihonga's spatial composition, while also inviting comparison to Robert Ryman and Agnes Martin.[42] At the same time, minuscule figures playing hide-and-seek between his grids, or the incorporation of grids as parts of a portrait embody the process whereby figurative painting is transformed into the abstract (fig. 13).

Sugito's attainment of the legitimacy of modernist painting without turning to any one school finds a precedent in Paul Klee. Surprisingly, it was Clement Greenberg who captured with amazing precision the merits of Klee's lines, colors, and decoration, and Greenberg's comments could easily apply to Sugito. After his important observation that Klee's painting style has "a temporal or musical quality," Greenberg remarks that Klee's line is "not a line along which the eye feels its way, but rather a definition of relations—relations of points," indicating how its disadvantageous ephemerality and decorativeness can lead to innovation:

> **[P]recisely because line—and color too—are disembodied elements [that] do not adhere to bodies and surfaces, because there is an absence of weight and mass, . . . Klee's pictures have a tendency . . . to close up on themselves and become too decorative . . . Yet Klee produced some of his best work when he most consciously and deliberately incurred the dangers of decoration; as in the picture *Pastoral*, which is composed only of horizontal bands of uniformly spaced linear motifs repeated symmetrically from left to right.[43]**

Even while criticizing how Klee's colors "hardly define and describe"—color "intensifies and fades like light itself, translucent, vaporous, porous"—Greenberg identifies Klee's aesthetic of "escape."[44] Sugito's own colors, described by Saltz as "tissue-thin, sherbet-colored," with their "jewel-like" hues being "infused with a shimmering aurora borealis light," join in Klee's type of nondescriptive performance.

Compared with Sugito's masterful works, Tam Ochiai's conceptual canvases seem too eccentric to be called "painting." Yet they are products of his sustained attempt to explore painting in different forms; since his artistic apprenticeship in New York, Ochiai has been consistently engaged in a radical, albeit self-denigrating, act of deterritorialization. The first such attempt was the creation of mock painting canvases made of plastic shopping bags bearing brand-name logos such as agnès b. or Commes des Garçons, pitched over handmade frames with a slight aperture in the side, garnishing the canvases with tiny brush strokes and single-color squares that ludicrously evoke Abstract Expressionist brush strokes and Color-Field pictorial planes. Placing such metonyms on the edges of the paintings, or dwarfing their size, Ochiai diminished his anxiety of influence, while clownishly commenting on his own marginality and belatedness in the modernist painting tradition. After producing a Warholian film that dissolved a figure of a girl into pink drips and color fields, Ochiai turned, around 1997, to the more straightforward task of drawing a waiflike girl in pencil against a white background, painting her dress as bright rectangles. The

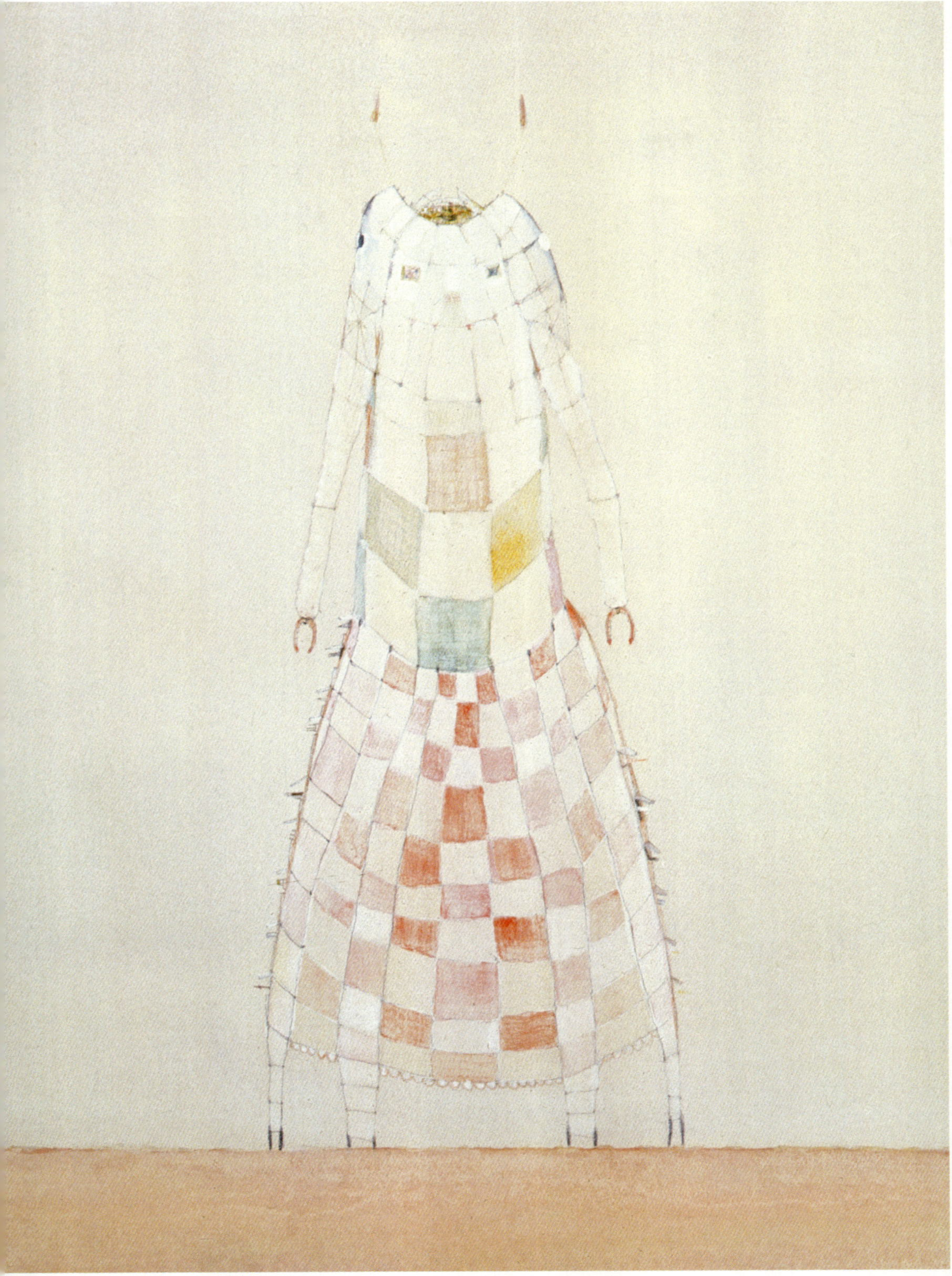

FIG. 15 Hiroshi Sugito **lobsterman** 1999 acrylic, pigment, graphite on canvas 35 ¾ x 28 ¼ in. Courtesy the artist and Tomio Koyama Gallery, Tokyo

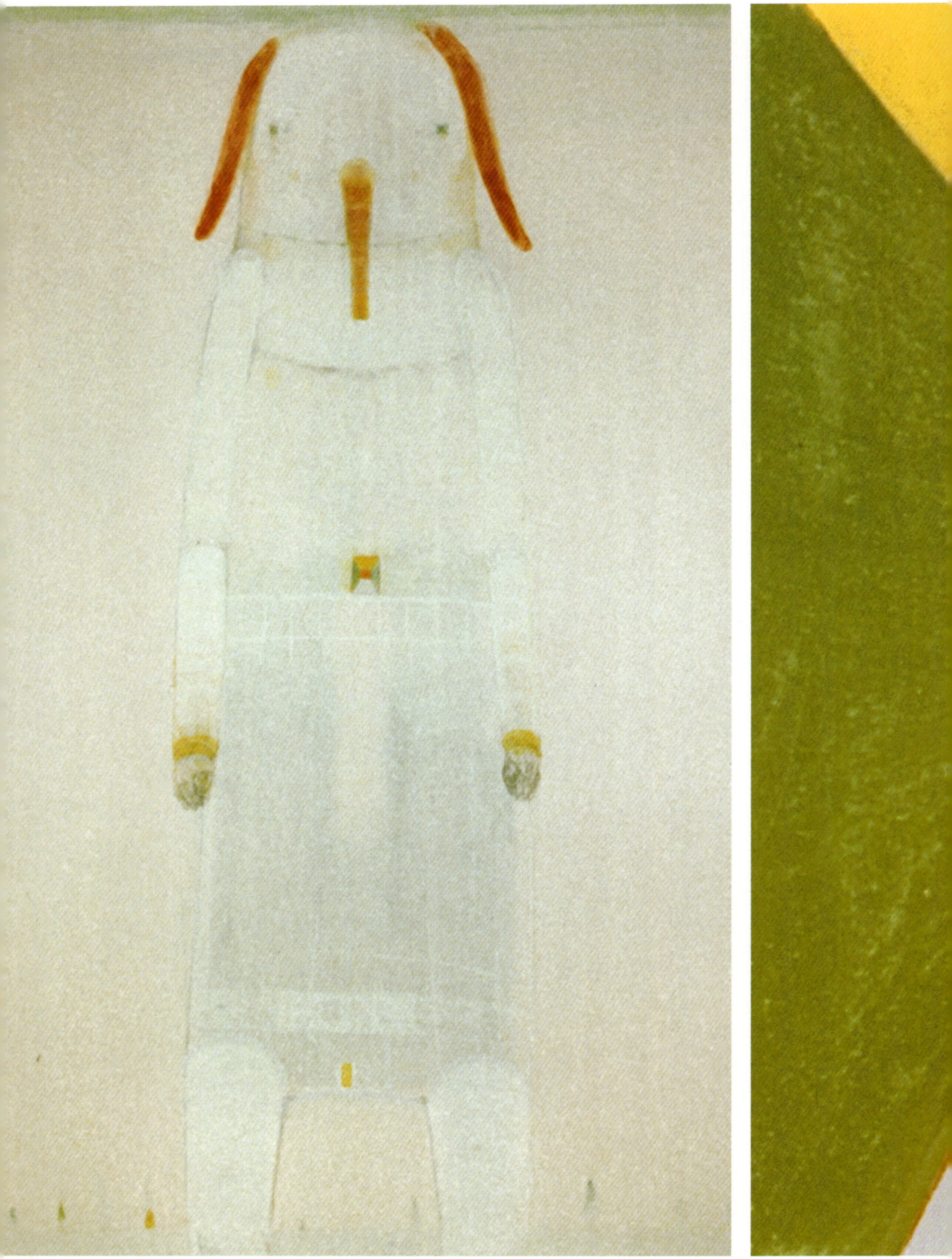

FIG. 16 Hiroshi Sugito **elephant and buckle** 1999 acrylic, pigment, graphite on paper and cotton diptych, 106 ¼ x 70 ¾ in. and 13 x 13 ¾ in. Courtesy the artist and Tomio Koyama Gallery, Tokyo

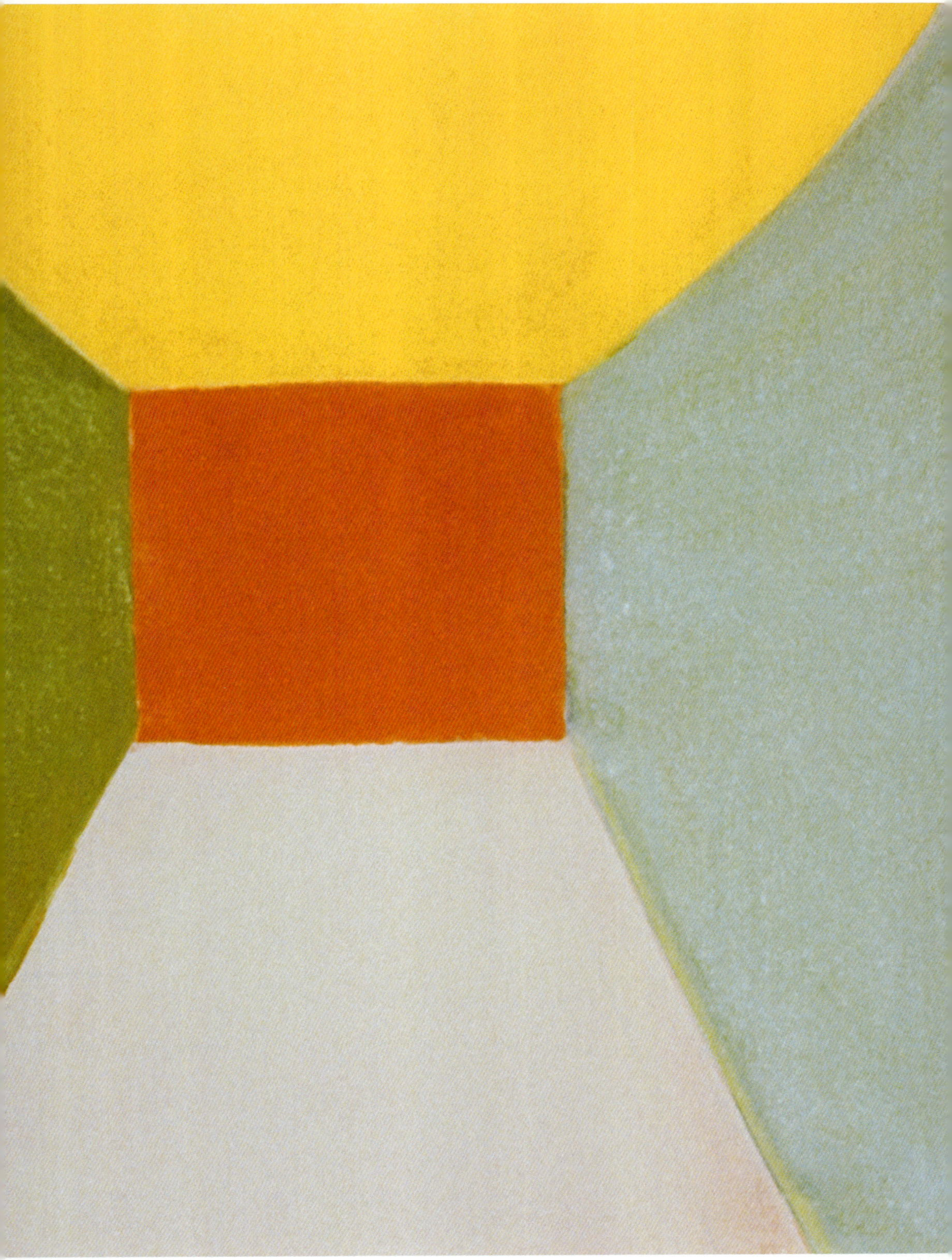

literal subject—the girl in the dress—is made equivocal due to the reversed intensities between the body and the dress, foregrounded as a mock color field. This fluctuation of the figure between theme and formal pattern—the becoming-square of a girl and the becoming-girl of the square—marks a line of "escape," as described by Deleuze and Guattari. With deliberately rough application of paint and the projection of urban pleasure through the depiction of a flat, cartoonish figure of a girl juxtaposed with names such as Madeleine and Cloudine, or film titles such as *Never on Sunday*, Ochiai frees color and shape within a field of arbitrary association (figs. 17 and 18). In that field of metonymical reference, even the smearing of tiny brush strokes—normally considered a blemish—functions as a "painterly" gesture. Despite their apparent flimsiness, Ochiai's canvases are never merely cynical; by undermining every grandiose claim to "painting," Ochiai builds a stage on which marginalized and negative elements are transformed into vibrant "accents" or "acts" as colors and shapes, as if to realize Deleuze's and Guattari's dictum "to use syntax in order to cry, to give a syntax to the cry" (fig. 19).[45]

Although they work in relative ignorance of each other, Sugito and Ochiai have recently created paintings that share many characteristics. Apart from the strong tendency to reverse the relationship between the center and the periphery, and the positive (appearing) and the negative (disappearing), they deterritorialize the boundaries of painting by drawing the central figure in pencil against a vacant white background in order to emphasize the "color fields" that actually constitute the figure, incorporating writing and inserting bright dots (Sugito sometimes collages on painted pieces of gold-streaked Japanese rice paper) or smearing colors as accentuations (fig. 12). They thus achieve the "discontinuity of a pictorial plane," offering a visual experience that is evocative of music.

Painting in Transition—Three Phases of Minor-ity

Through the discussion of these four painters, I have traced the most innovative currents in contemporary Japanese painting. Hardly forming a conscious group, they are united in contesting the ineffectual academicism of domesticated "modernism." At the same time, their three modes of radical "minority" indicate three different areas of excellence—rationality, emotion, and indeterminacy—subtly corresponding to the changing cultural milieus of the early to late 1990s. "Cuteness" has different valences in the works of Murakami, Nara, Sugito, and Ochiai. While Murakami's "dangerously cute" images reveal the incipience of mainstream Japanese culture, and Nara's angelic-demonic children embody the coexistence of violence and innocence, Sugito and Ochiai use cuteness as a pretext for indicating a new beauty through the play between the appearing and the disappearing.

Their differences can also be perceived in their respective negotiations with global postmodernism, the standardizing of temporal and spatial experience, and the dispersal of the power of modern Western rationalism. Murakami consciously plays off his "Japaneseness" by constantly staging his artistic struggle as simultaneously a transcendence of the modern Japanese "colonial" mentality and an articulation of his identity as opposed to Western modernism; ironically, his application of infantile motifs and ornamentation in his apparently nationalistic Super Flat campaign betrays its Enlightening character, with Japan functioning as an emblem both of negativity—a nowhere of art history—and of salvation—a rich reservoir of eccentric figuration. Nara, sharing many characteristics with American and European purveyors of "the adolescent aesthetic," narrowly escapes complying with the Japanese uncritical obsession with cuteness. Sugito and Ochiai experiment in the emergent third area of migrant creation. Accepting the burden of being latecomers to the traditions of modernist and classical Japanese painting, they produce intelligent works that are free of discursive ostentation, perceptual without appealing to the unconscious depth, thus making their fragility a condition of their freedom. Their deterritorializing imagination is not a product of cultural conflict, but of their fuller participation in the processes of globalization—a fact testified to by their critical recognition in New York earlier than in Japan.

Kiyoteru Hanada, a prominent cultural critic of the 1960s, once remarked that "modernism" is a response of original thinkers to a period of intense cultural transformation, in which

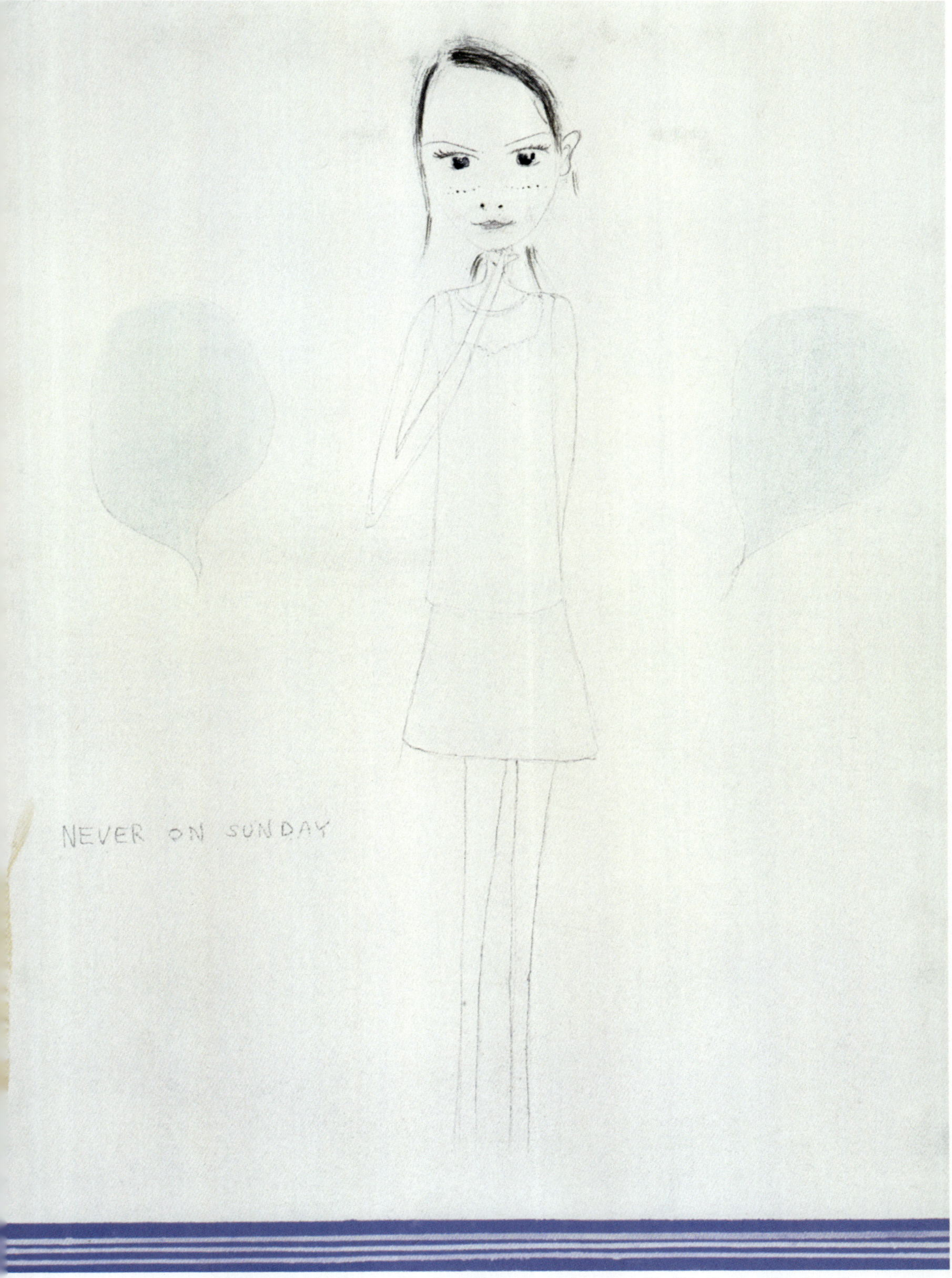

FIG. 17 Tam Ochiai **Never on Sunday** 1997 acrylic, pencil on canvas 30 x 24 in. Courtesy the artist and Tomio Koyama Gallery, Tokyo

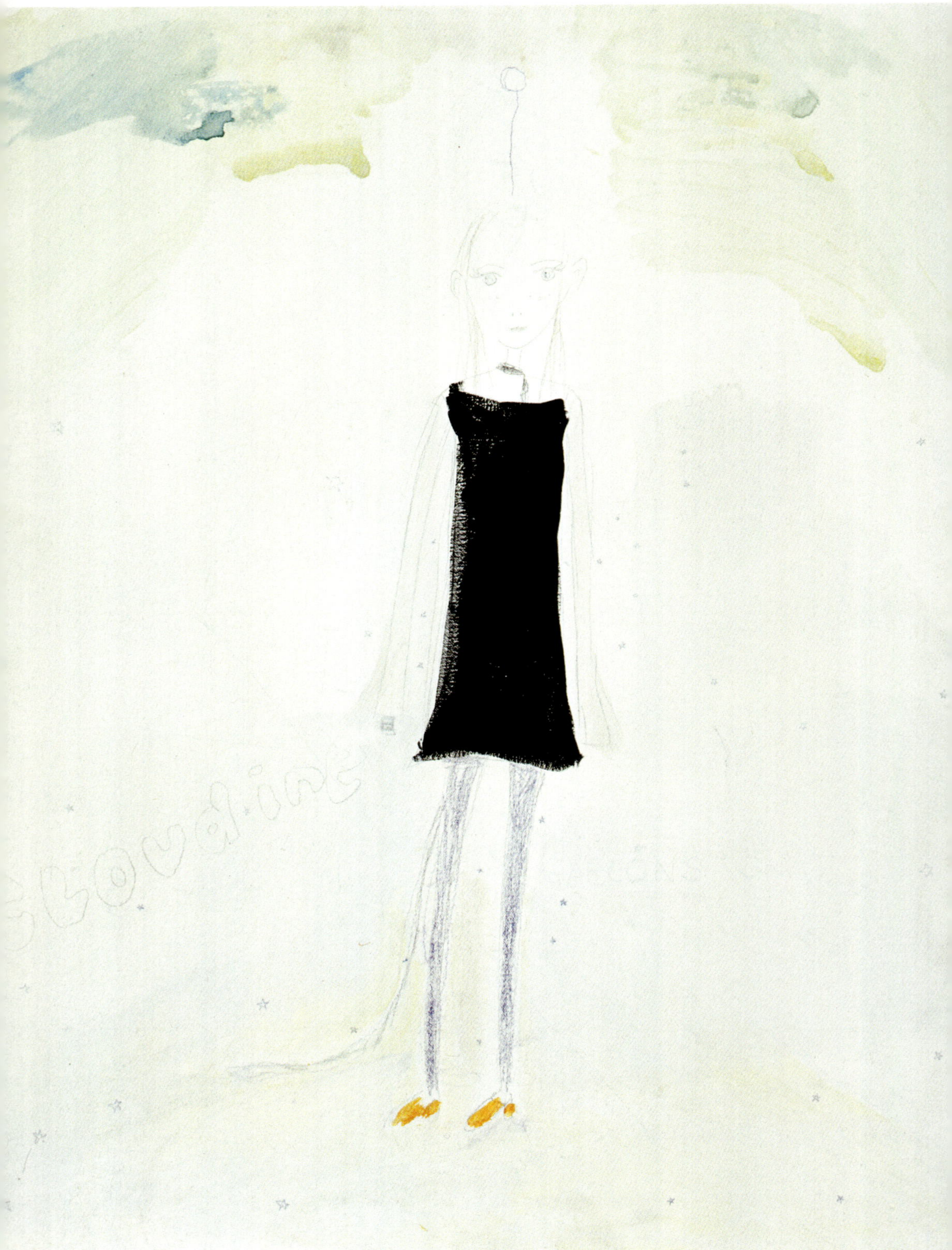

FIG. 18 Tam Ochiai **Cloudine** 1999 acrylic, pencil on canvas 34 x 24 in. Courtesy the artist and Tomio Koyama Gallery, Tokyo

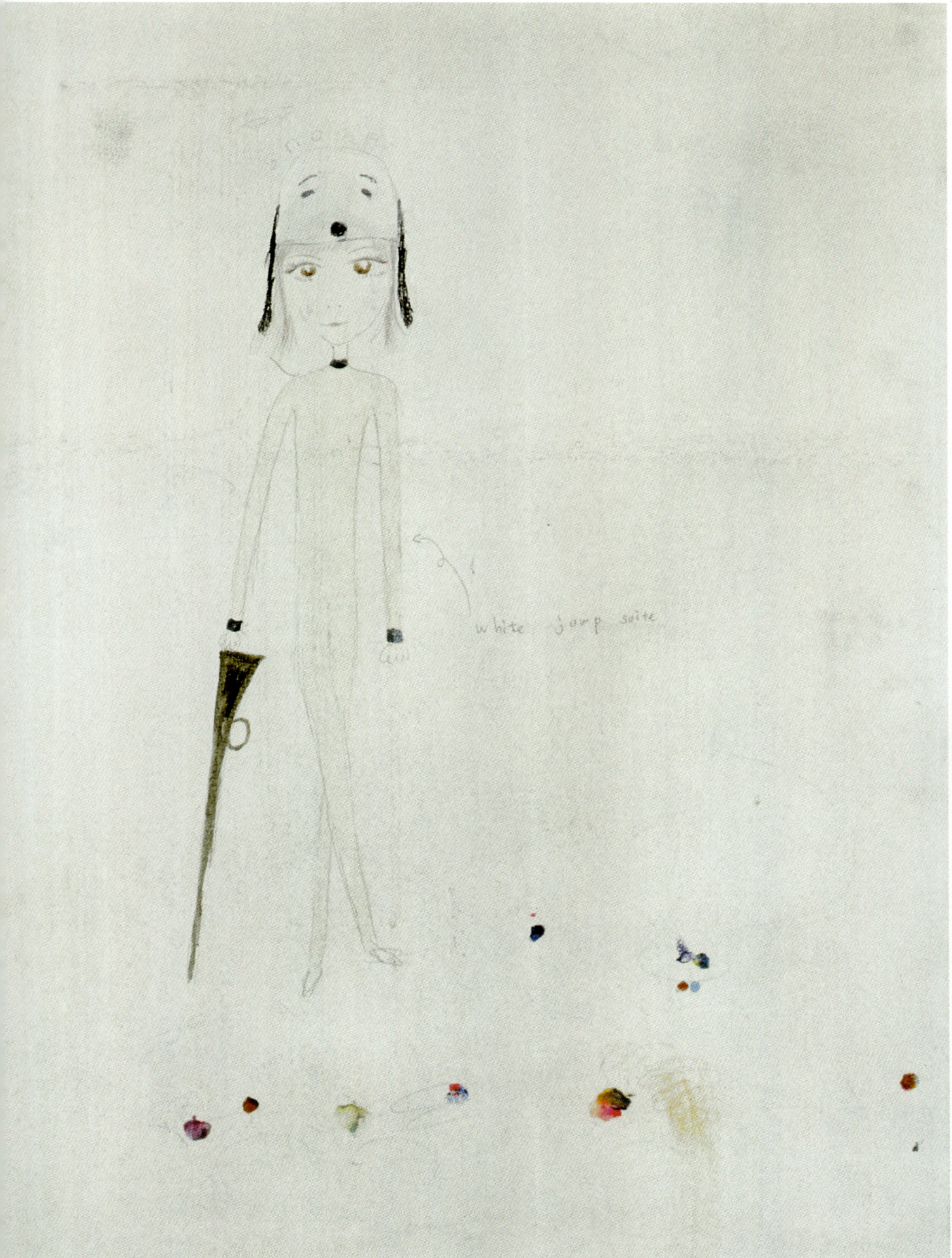

FIG. 19 Tam Ochiai **Niki de Saint Phalle** 1997 acrylic, pencil on canvas 34 x 24 in. Courtesy the artist and Tomio Koyama Gallery, Tokyo

their efforts to create new rules in radical modification of the past give their work aspects of contradiction, vulgarity, and excess, as well as a strange beauty.[46] The artists discussed here perhaps embody this spirit of *tenkeiki*, the period of turbulent transformation. The peripheral relationship to modernity and modernism that once afflicted Japanese painters now provides them with the resources of cultural hybridity: neither conforming to historically sanctioned styles of modernist invention, nor forming a tight-knit group, these artists pursue their individual paths of innovation. In spite of their steadily increasing recognition, their nonconformity keeps them adrift in art history. Their eccentricity, or "minority," imbues their work with transitional character and marks their commitment to an age without definitive criteria. Their ability to live in fluidity has sustained them, and will sustain them always, through contemporary turmoil.

NOTES

1 See Noriaki Kitazawa, "Nihonga no gainen no keisei ni kansuru shiron" (A preliminary argument about the formation of the idea of Nihonga), in *Meiji Nihonga shiryō* (Documents on Nihonga in the Meiji Period), ed. Shigeru Aoki (Tokyo: Chuo kōron bijutsu shuppan, 1991), p. 483.

2 Ibid., pp. 508–509. Kōbu bijutsu gakkō was established in 1873; Tokyo bijutsu gakkō in 1876; the old-fashioned aspects of Nihonga were represented by the educational approach of Nihon bijutsu kyōkai.

3 See Michiaki Kawakita, *Kawakita Michiaki bijutsu ronshū* (Collected essays on art by Michiaki Kawakita), vol. 2 (Tokyo: Kōdansha, 1978), p. 48.

4 See also Kitazawa, "Nihonga no gainen no keisei ni kansuru shiron," pp. 486–487; and Kawakita, *Kawakita Michiaki bijutsu ronshū*, vol. 4, p. 23.

5 See Noriaki Kitazawa, *Kishida Ryūsei and Taisho Avant-Garde* (Tokyo: Iwanami, 1993), pp. 194–195.

6 The acclaim bestowed on Gutai in 1954 by Michel Tapier, a leading critic of French Art Informel, fueled Japanese enthusiasm for painting in the Art Informel style, repressing Gutai's primarily performative potentials, as demonstrated by the artists' frequent use of their bodies as brushes; see Shigeo Chiba, *Gendai bijutsu itsudatsu-shi* (The history of Japanese contemporary art as deviation) (Tokyo: Shobunsha, 1986), p. 54. Hi Red Center consisted of Jiro Takamatsu, Genpei Akasegawa, and Natsuyuki Nakanishi; between 1963 and 1964, they performed happenings and conceptual events including *Shelter Project*, in which they occupied a room at Tokyo Imperial Hotel, measuring and photographing the guests who reserved rooms in their shelter. Bi-kyoto (Revolution) was a short-lived struggle of art-school students who declared the impossibility of artistic production in the gap between Japanese and international artistic practice created by the practices of Mono-ha and previous generations of conceptual artists. Mono-ha, which remained influential for nearly a decade after its peak in 1969 and 1970, was theoretically buttressed by Ri-Uhan, who interpreted the open-air work of Nobuo Sekine, *Isō-Daichi* (Dimension: Earth)—a juxtaposition of a hole dug in the ground and a mud column of exactly the same size—as a "mere thing that transmits the fresh presence of the pristine world"; see Chiba, pp. 87–97, 118–182.

7 Fujieda curated *Kaiga no mondai* (Problems of painting) for the Seibu Museum of Art and *Kanjō to kōsei* (Emotion and composition) for the Yokohama Citizen's Gallery, while Minemura's *Kaiga no yutakasa* (Beyond the planes) was held in 1977 at the Yokohama Citizen's Gallery.

8 See Teruo Fujieda, "Aratana seisei e: kaiga no bāi" (Toward a new formation: A case for painting), *Bijutsu Techo* 33, no. 475 (January 1981), pp. 77–85; and Toshiaki Minemura, "'Watashitachi no kaiga' to 'tōmaki no chōkoku'" (Our painting and environmental sculpture), ibid., pp. 86–95.

9 Fujieda and Minemura respectively commended the formal quality of painters Toeko Tatsuno and Naoki Suwa in *Bijutsu Techo* 30, no. 432 (May 1978), pp. 76–80 and 96–100.

10 *Bijutsu Techo* repeatedly featured the trend through special issues on New Painting (January 1983; January 1984; November 1985), Illustration (January 1987), and New Image (July 1984).

11 Koichi Tanikawa, "Yatterarenai saisentan" (Getting out of the avant-garde), *Bijutsu Techo* 36, no. 520 (January 1984), p. 59; Koji Tagi, "Gendai no rabirinsu" (Contemporary labyrinth), ibid., p. 64.

12 See Arata Isozaki and Takaaki Yoshimoto, "'Ima' to iu muishiki no yukue" (A direction of the unconscious called 'Now') *Bijutsu Techo* 37, no. 532 (January 1985), pp. 27, 31–33; and Naoyoshi Hikosaka and Tadanori Yokoo, "Egokoro no kokoroe: tōsei gaka kishitsu" (Resolutions to paint: Temperament of contemporary painters) *Bijutsu Techo* 37, no. 547 (November 1985), pp. 59–77.

13 Masao Maruyama, *Nihon no shisō* (The Japanese mind) (Tokyo: Iwanami shinsho, 1961), pp. 11–14.

14 Noi Sawaragi, *Nihon, gendai, bijutsu* (Japan, contemporary, art) (Tokyo: Shinchosha, 1998), pp. 15–17.

15 See Noi Sawaragi, "Rorripoppu—sono saishogen no seimei" (Lollipop—Its smallest form of life), *Bijutsu Techo* 44, no. 651 (March 1992), pp. 86–92; and "Dangerously Cute," a talk with Fumio Nanjo, *Flash Art* 25, no. 163 (March–April 1992), pp. 77–79.

16 See Teruo Fujieda, Kunio Motoe, and Akira Tatehata, "Kaiga no tenkai: 80nendai no chihei" (Openings of painting: The horizon of the 1980s), *Bijutsu Techo* 43, no. 645 (October 1991), pp. 95–111; and Shin-ichiro Ozaki, "Kaigaron iko no kaiga" (Painting after the theory of painting), ibid., pp. 81–92. Ozaki claims that determining tendencies in contemporary painting constitute "a paradigm shift from the theory of form to that of function," "an increased referentiality," and a "thematization of the institution of painting" (p. 92).

17 See Jennifer Daryl Slack, "The Theory and Method of Articulation," in *Stuart Hall: Critical Dialogues in Cultural Studies*, eds. David Morley and Kuang-Hsing Chen (New York: Routledge, 1996), pp. 112–127.

18 Stuart Hall, "On Postmodernism and Articulation: An Interview with Stuart Hall" (1986), reprinted in *Stuart Hall: Critical Dialogues in Cultural Studies*, pp. 131–150; "An articulation is thus the form of the connection that *can* make a unity of two different elements, under certain conditions. It is a linkage which is not necessary, determined, absolute, and essential for all time. You have to ask: under what circumstances *can* a connection be forged or made? So the so-called 'unity' of a discourse is the articulation of different, distinct elements which can be

rearticulated in different ways because they have no necessary 'belongingness.' The 'unity' which matters is a linkage between that articulated discourse and the social forces with which it can, under certain historical conditions, but need not necessarily, be connected" (p. 141).

19 See Gilles Deleuze and Felix Guattari, *Kafka: Toward a Minor Literature*, trans. Dana Polan (Minneapolis: University of Minnesota Press, 1986), p. 16.

20 Ibid., pp. 18, 21.

21 Murakami's earliest statements on the significance of *anime* and Nobuo Tsuji's interpretation of Japanese art in terms of eccentric style or mannerism can be found in "Fax Letter from Takashi Murakami to Midori Matsui," in *Takashi Murakami*, the catalogue for *Which is Tomorrow?—Fall in Love*, his solo exhibition at SCAI the Bathhouse, June 17–July 16, 1994, pp. 48–51; I have also elaborated on the influences of Tsuji's ideas, as well as those of Noi Sawaragi, on Murakami in "Towards a Definition of Tokyo Pop: The Classical Transgressions of Takashi Murakami," in *Takashi Murakami: The Meaning of the Nonsense of the Meaning*, the catalogue for Murakami's solo exhibition at Center for Curatorial Studies Museum, Bard College, Annandale-on-Hudson, New York, June 27–September 12, 1999 (New York: The Center for Curatorial Studies, 1999), pp. 20–29.

22 Takashi Murakami, "A Theory of Super Flat Japanese Art," in *Super Flat* (Tokyo: Madra Publishing, 2000), pp. 8–25.

23 See Noi Sawaragi, "Tokyo poppu to wa nani ka" (What is Tokyo Pop?), *Kōkoku hihyō* 226 (April 1999), pp. 77–78.

24 Takashi Murakami, "Art to āto no aida de nihon no bijutsu wa yurete iru" (Japanese contemporary art fluctuates between Western and Japanese ideas), *Kōkoku hihyō* 226 (April 1999), pp. 86–102.

25 See Takashi Murakami, in conversation with Kenji Yanobe and Kodai Nakahara, "Post-Hobby Art in Japan," *Bijutsu Techo* 44, no. 651 (March 1992), pp. 68–81; Murakami remarks that "maniac *anime* fans are attracted to art because art gives them a deep pleasure unattainable in the everyday world," " I cannot be satisfied with the existing art; I want to create something absolutely amazing" (p. 75).

26 Murakami, *Super Flat*, p. 19.

27 See Tenshin's essay "Kindai bijutsu no mondai" (The problem of modern art), as quoted in Kawakita, *Bijutsu ronshū*, pp. 4, 23.

28 Kakuzo (Tenshin) Okakura, *The Ideals of the East with Special Reference to the Art of Japan* (1903; reprint, Tokyo: Charles Tuttle, Co., 1970), p. 217.

29 See Michiaki Kawakita, *Nihon no bijutsu—sono dentō to genzai* (Japanese art: Its tradition and the present age) (Tokyo: Pelicansha, 1982), pp. 55–65.

30 See Noriaki Kitazawa, *Meiji Nihonga shiryō*, pp. 489–491.

31 See Noriaki Kitazawa, *Me no shinden* (The sanctuary of the eye) (Tokyo: Bijutsu Shuppansha, 1989), pp. 235–238.

32 There is a technical confusion in Minemura's sanctioning of *Shōrinzu* (Pine trees) by Hasegawa Tōhaku as the model of Bunjinga. Tōhaku was a sixteenth-century master of wall painting called Shōheiga, while Bunjinga, originally painted by wealthy Chinese intellectuals (landowners and high officials) and culminating in the twelfth century, is not exactly a stylistic category; its stylistic heir, called Nanshōga, was imported to Japan in the seventeenth century from Ming Dynasty China and transformed in the eighteenth century by the painters who were revolting against the then-institutionalized tradition of Shōheiga into an eclectic style called Nanga. Nowadays, the expression Bunjinga is synonymous with Nanga.

33 See Kazuo Amano, "Nihonga and Yōga," in *Bijutsushi no yukue, bijutsushi no gendai* (The direction of art history and the present moment of Bijutsushi), eds. Nagahiro Kinoshita et al. (Tokyo: Heibobsha, 1999), pp. 92–93.

34 See Midori Matsui, "A Gold Rain Falls on the Deepest Puddle—The Immanence of Good and Evil Presented by Yoshitomo Nara's Paintings," in *Hothouse Fresh*, the catalogue for Nara's solo exhibition at Hakutosho, January 20–February 24, 1996 (Nagoya: Hakutosha, 1996), pp. 2–7.

35 Julia Kristeva, "The Adolescent Novel," in *Abjection, Melancholia, and Love: The Works of Julia Kristeva*, eds. John Fletcher and Andrew Benjamin (London and New York: Routledge, 1990), pp. 8–23.

36 Ibid., p. 8.

37 Ibid., p. 9.

38 Walter Benjamin points out the significance of kitsch as a reservoir of popular imagination, whose power was released by early Surrealist experiments; see "Dream Kitsch: Gloss on Surrealism" (1927), reprinted in *Walter Benjamin Selected Essays*, vol. 2, trans. Rodney Livingstone and others, eds. Michael W. Jennings, Howard Eiland, and Gary Smith (London and Cambridge, Mass.: The Belknap Press, 1999), pp. 3–5.

39 Jerry Saltz, "War and Peace," *Village Voice*, December 8, 1998, p. 43.

40 Deleuze and Guattari, *Kafka: Toward a Minor Literature*, p. 21.

41 Ibid., p. 22.

42 From the press release for Sugito's solo show at Nicole Klagsbrun Gallery, February 22–March 22, 1997.

43 Clement Greenberg, "Art Chronicle: On Paul Klee (1870–1949)" (1941), reprinted in *The Collected Essays of Clement Greenberg*, vol. 1, ed. John O'Brian (Chicago and London: University of Chicago Press, 1986), p. 68.

44 Ibid., p. 69.

45 Deleuze and Guattari, *Kafka: Toward a Minor Literature*, p. 26.

46 See Kiyoteru Hanada, *Hanada Kiyoteru zenshū* (Collected works), vol. 2 (Tokyo: Kodansha, 1977), p. 23.

Daniel Birnbaum has published numerous books on art and philosophy, most recently *The Hospitality of Presence: Problems of Otherness in Husserl's Phenomenology* (1998) and, with artist Carsten Höller, *Production* (2000). He is a contributing editor of *Artforum* and a frequent contributor to journals such as *Parkett* and *frieze*. From 1998 to 2000, Birnbaum was Director of IASPIS, an artist-in-residence program based in Stockholm, and he was recently appointed Director of the Städelschule and of Portikus in Frankfurt am Main.

Late Arrivals
Daniel Birnbaum

"Use 'delay' instead of picture or painting; picture on glass becomes delay in glass." — Marcel Duchamp, "The Green Box"

"It is thus the delay that is in the beginning." — Jacques Derrida, "Freud and the Scene of Writing"

Beethoven's C Minor Sonata, Opus 111—famously commented on by Thomas Mann—has a peculiar feature that remained hidden to the composer's contemporaries and, one must assume, also to the creator of the piece himself. What is so intriguing about the composition is a short passage that inexplicably sounds like ragtime music. Thus it would appear that a few notes by a nineteenth-century genius realize their full significance only retroactively, when the industrial mechanization that emerged during the composer's lifetime finally gained a full grip on artistic creativity. When the ear got used to the machinery of ragtime, unexpected qualities seemed to spring forth. Had they been there all the time, as part of a dormant stratum, in a secret pool of potentialities?

What is the temporality of a work of art? It is brought into existence—sometimes over years of hard labor, sometimes in a sudden moment of inspiration. But once it is there, how is its continuous existence to be grasped in temporal terms? Recent meditations on the concepts of tradition, influence, and the historicity of art—from Harold Bloom's Kabbalistic map of misreadings to Hal Foster's theory of the neo-avant-garde—have emphasized the crucial function of repetitions and returns. An artwork—be it a poem, painting, or musical composition—continues to *be* because it is continuously viewed, heard, and read anew. It is read, re-read, misread, and thus given birth to retroactively over and over again. This retroactive rewriting is sometimes so powerful that the original meaning—if such a concept still has any validity—disappears in favor of the new rendering. When we reach that critical passage in Opus 111, all we can hear today is a ragtime piano. Was there ever such a thing as an "original" sense, or is it rather a question of continuous rewritings, each one contributing to the retroactive production of an "origin" that appears as such only belatedly? A work of art would thus exist as a series of deferments, and the concept of an original presence would need to be replaced by something more primary: an originary delay.

Freud's notion of *Nachträglichkeit*—deferred action—seems to signify a comparable temporal structure. The most well-known context in which the concept operates is the analysis of traumatic childhood events, which acquire their full significance only postfactually, in such a way that one may even claim that they have never been experienced as present, but only in a deferred manner.[1] It appears that this notion of belatedness can be extended into a psychoanalytic theory of delay, characterizing the temporality of experience in general. The concepts of *Nachträglichkeit* (deferred action) and *Verspätung* (delay), claims Jacques Derrida, "govern the whole of Freud's thought and determine all his other concepts." He continues, "The irreducibility of the 'effect of deferral'—such no doubt was Freud's discovery."[2] In Derrida's reading, this temporal syncopation cuts right through the very core of consciousness. It is always too late, never now. Freud's theory, of course, applies to the individual psyche rather than to such collective phenomena as the formation of art movements and the reappropriation of earlier aesthetical models, even if those are the issues to which these concepts most recently have been applied.[3] What then are the implications of the principle of *Nachträglichkeit* for the individual subject? To sum it up in a simple formula, *the present is never present*. Or rather, the *consciousness* of what is present is never *self*-present, but always delayed. Which means that the subject lacks the capacity of coinciding with itself in an instant of immediate self-presence. Thus, the "I" appears to itself always as another.

Transplanted to the stage of cultural history, this logic of psychic temporality could be taken to imply the following: the traumas of the "original" avant-garde—the monochrome and the readymade, say—are acted out only in works of art by later generations. Hal Foster, whose book *The Return of the Real* is an attempt to present some of these historical repetitions—a hysterical acting out as well as a laborious working through—contends, "One event is only registered through another that recodes it; we come to be who we are only in deferred action (*Nachträglich*). It is this analogy that I want to enlist for modernist studies at the end of the century: historical and neo-avant-gardes are constituted in a similar way, as a continual process of protension and retention, a complex relay of anticipated futures and reconstructed pasts—in short, in a deferred action that throws over any simple scheme of before and after, cause and effect, origin and repetition."[4] The main prob-

lem of such an approach is, of course, that it applies concepts developed to study the pathology of the single psyche to developments in art history. Foster, who is by no means naive in this respect, observes the difficulties and states them explicitly. If one is to (mis)use a theory of the individual mind to grasp cultural history, then one should at least make sure that it is the most sophisticated theory around; which, according to Foster, implies that one is to employ the Freudian conception of psychic temporality (as emphasized by Lacan).

Before moving to the realm of art history and to certain issues concerning the concept of modernity, let us for a moment contemplate the temporal aspects of self-representation and of the identity/alterity dialectic of subjectivity. In other words: the state of appearing to oneself as another.

Such is the predicament of the painter who tries to capture his/her own image; or for that matter of anyone who, looking into the mirror, ponders the problems of self-awareness. The recent painterly practice of Swedish artist Cecilia Edefalk is a case in point (figs. 1 and 2). Her itinerary, characterized by delays, detours, and temporal loops, is far removed from the expectations of the media or the art market. She works in slow motion, and it seems to me that her paintings rely upon the considerable time span that separates them. A painting by Edefalk is a rare thing, and the scarcity of the output seems intrinsic to her way of working. "A sense of loss pervades these wordless ruminations on the limits of personal identity," writes Okwui Enwezor about Edefalk's series of paintings, *Mirror* (1992–1993) and *Echo* (1993–1994), in the collection of the Museum für Moderne Kunst in Frankfurt. He elucidates, "Edefalk's painting projects in which she represents 'herself' cannot be classified as self-portraits per se; they can be approached by calling them *anti-portraits*, always the same and other. They are anti-portraits because they do not begin by aiming at verisimilitude, to inscribe a consistently durable and stable self."[5] While Edefalk's strength does not lie in some magical uniqueness of painterly expression, her projects do seem to deal with the tension between an evaporating sense of self and a cautious reinscription of the personal into the very medium of its dissipation: repetition. The personal appears not in the form of a confident assertion of a unique ego, but rather in those marginal, sometimes hardly detectable deviations that produce difference in repetition. This is as far as you can get from self-assured expressionism: the subjective functions not as a starting point, but rather as a barely visible trace on the outskirts of the intentional.

The series of self-portraits all refer back to a photograph taken by the artist showing herself in three-quarter profile. The twelve paintings were developed in the following manner: the first painting is reproduced by the second, the second by the third, the third by the fourth, and so on. The photograph, itself already a reproduction, is absent from the series. The canvases differ in size, and a number of alterations give the series a quality quite different from that produced by strict repetition: one painting is painted upside down (not just hung upside down), another is inverted as if seen in a mirror, a third has been diluted to such a degree that it appears to be a gray monochrome. It is an attentive face, one that listens rather than speaks. To enter the room where the paintings are installed is like entering an echo chamber. The full voice will never be heard; here there is nothing but delay. These faces listen to one another listening. Without motion they communicate, in silence.

Once again: Is there such a thing as a *Nachträglichkeit* of collective processes, i.e., can the Freudian model, developed to explain the curious life of the mind, be applied to history? Such endeavors have certainly been made, especially in relation to the concept of the avant-garde. Whereas some writers, notably Peter Bürger, have claimed that the neo-avant-garde represents nothing but a bleak afterimage of the original avant-garde, a repetition devoid of real significance and without critical and artistic efficacy, others—most convincingly Benjamin Buchloh and Hal Foster—have formulated an alternative understanding, questioning the status of an "original avant-garde." The origin is nothing without its repetitions. To be an origin, the Freudian model teaches us, is to be repeated and "produced" retroactively as a point of departure. There is already a plethora of analyses of the art of the 1960s as just such a "productive" repetition of the "original" avant-garde. Must we not assume that such repetitions occur as well today?

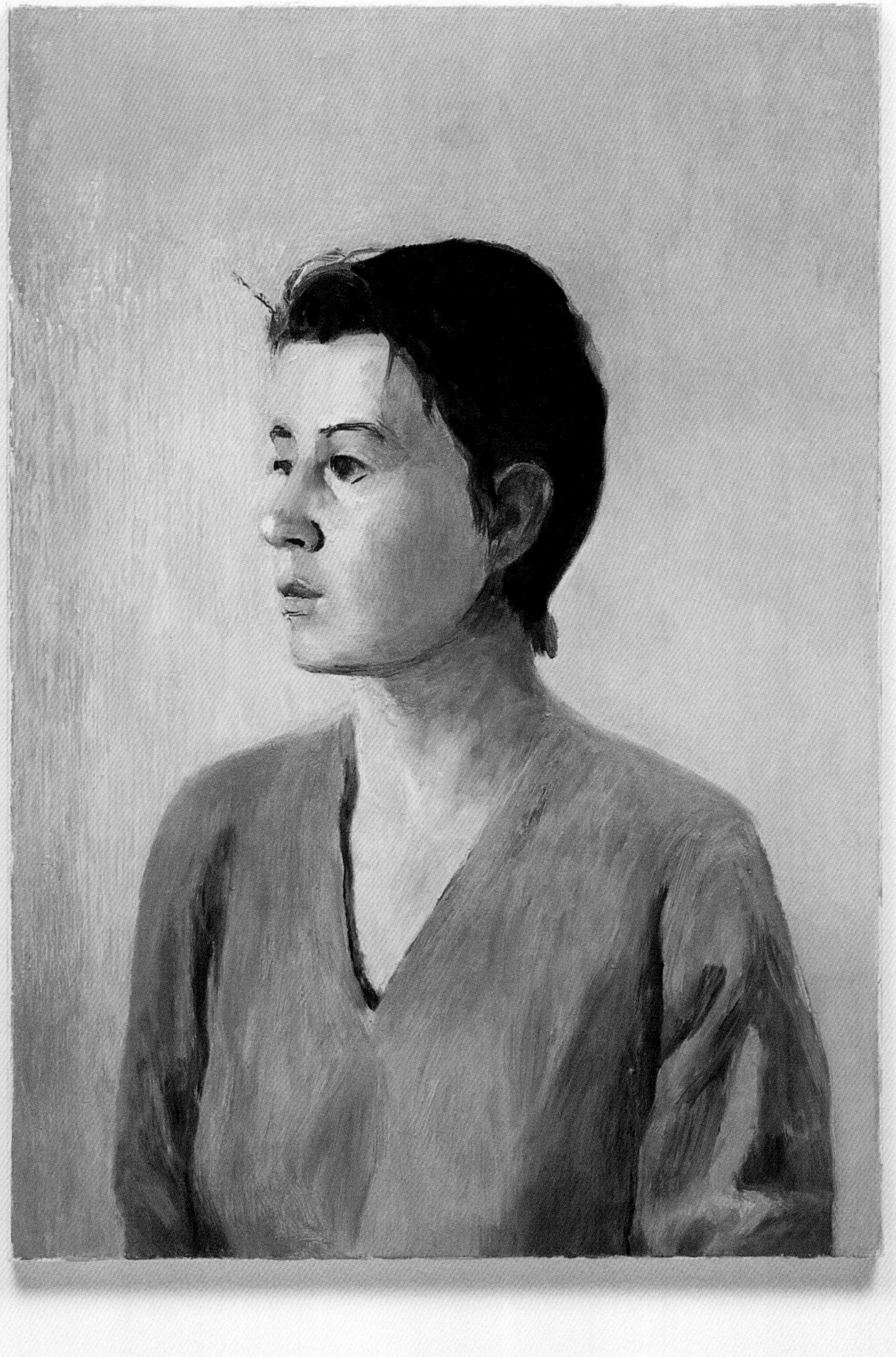

FIG. 1 Cecilia Edefalk detail of **Echo** 1993–1994 oil on linen one of three panels, 23 ¾ x 16 ½ in. Courtesy Museum für Moderne Kunst, Frankfurt am Main; Dauerleihgabe der Freunde des Museums für Moderne Kunst, Frankfurt am Main e.V. photo: Axel Schneider

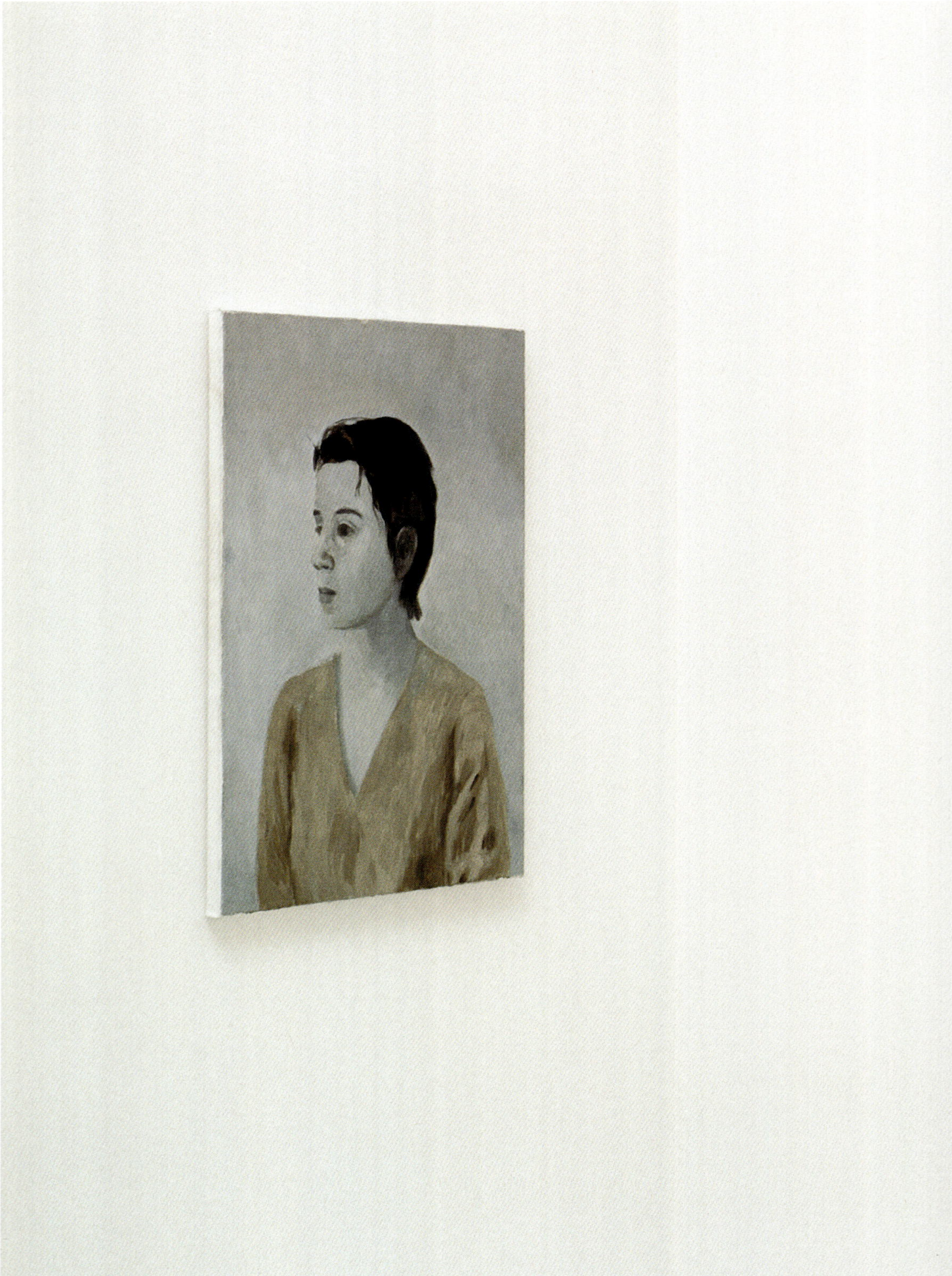

FIG. 2 Cecilia Edefalk **Kammerspiel (Mirror)** 1992–1993 oil on linen three panels, 23 ¾ x 16 ½ in. each Courtesy Museum für Moderne Kunst, Frankfurt am Main; Dauerleihgabe der Freunde des Museums für Moderne Kunst, Frankfurt am Main e.V. photo: Axel Schneider

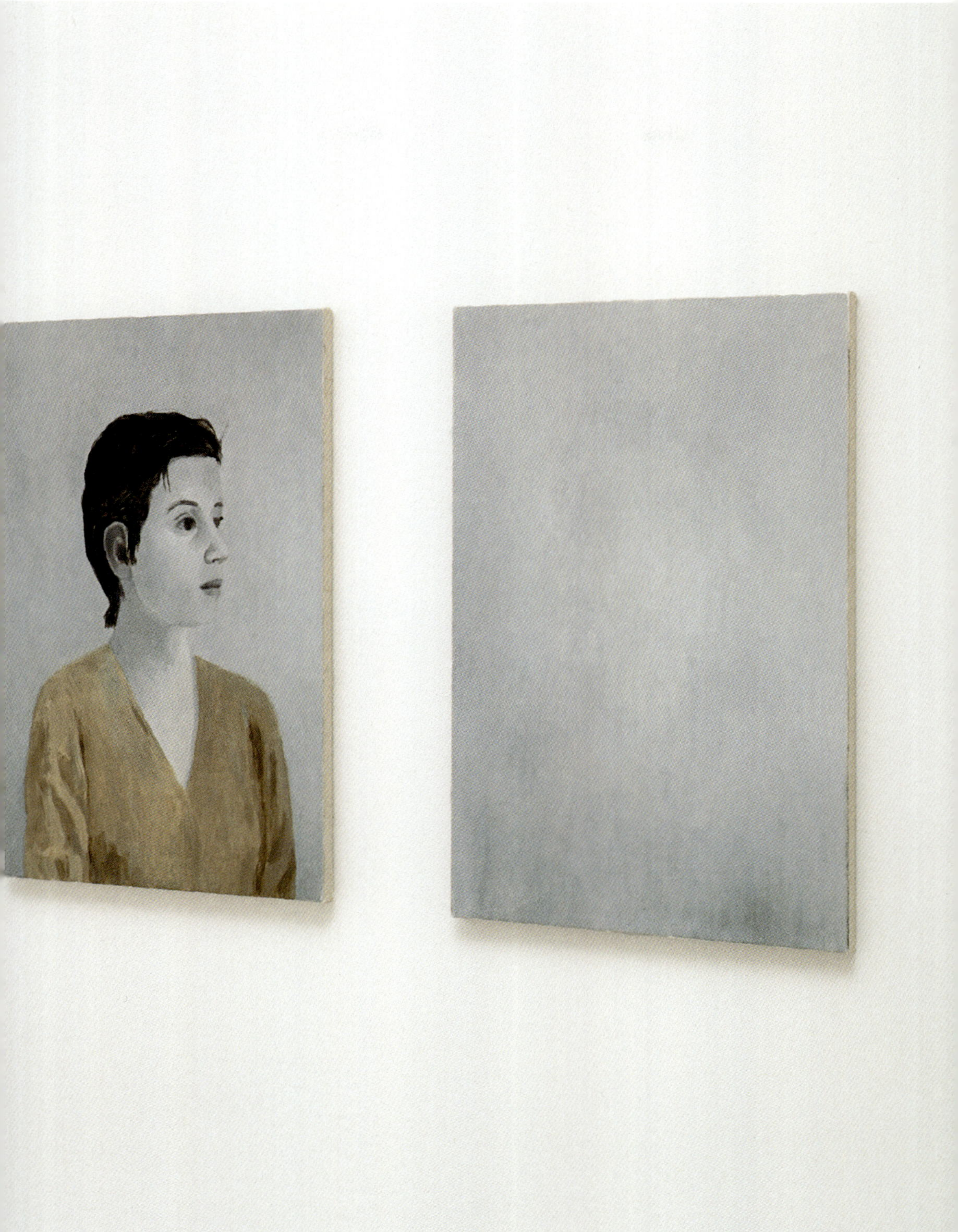

EXCURSUS 1. If we apply a theory of subjectivity to processes of art history, which is clearly a problematic endeavor, then we should at least make sure we employ the most sophisticated theory around, says Foster. The fundamental question he simply leaves aside: Is such an expansion at all possible? The first steps of such a widening can, I believe, be traced with the help of a phenomenology of intersubjectivity, such as it was developed in Edmund Husserl's writings of the 1920s and 1930s. The fact that Husserl's theory of time-consciousness bears an interesting resemblance to the Freudian *Nachträglichkeit* has been analyzed by Jacques Derrida and Rudolf Bernet.[6] In Husserl's view, the transcendental ego's relation to itself is a kind of temporal awareness, but this self-consciousness never takes place in a pointlike "now," but rather through a temporal delay. The living present of self-consciousness is never fully present: it is the delay that is at the beginning. In his writings on intersubjectivity, Husserl repeatedly points to an analogy between the ego's relation to the Other and to its own past, i.e., between inter-subjectivity and temporality. The entire "Fifth Meditation" of the *Cartesian Meditations* (1929) is devoted to a sophisticated understanding of intersubjectivity and the collective. If collective formations and cultural traditions can be said to have their proper modes of temporality, then why not also their own pathologies? Do collective "traumas" make themselves known belatedly (*nachträglich*)?

Repetition, appropriation, revival. It would seem that the rhythm of these artistic returns has become increasingly rapid. Can today's repetitions be interpreted as critical appropriations of previous aesthetical models in the name of a genuine avant-garde tradition, or has today's art finally succumbed to the ongoing recycling of fashions and style? When the abstract surfaces of high modernism today reappear in lifestyle magazines as well as in the art world, one clearly wants an answer to Hal Foster's query: "How to tell the difference between a return of an archaic form of art that bolsters conservative tendencies in the present and a return to a lost model of art made in order to displace customary ways of working?"[7] A relevant case study: German artist Tobias Rehberger's recent return to high-modernist aesthetics and, more precisely, to utopian Swedish painter Olle Bærtling's (1911–1981) hard-edge abstraction. In Rehberger's piece, *Stockholm Summer* (1999), the 14 x 4-meter window on the ground floor of the Leipzig Galerie für zeitgenössische Kunst has been covered with a curtain (fig. 4). Anyone who has spent some time in central Stockholm immediately recognizes the colors; they are from Bærtling's famous drapery for the huge windows of the Stockholm Culture Center lecture hall, first displayed in 1974 and still in use today (fig. 3). *Stockholm Summer* is best viewed from the inside, since it is illuminated by daylight. The installation is not only a copy of Bærtling's work, but Rehberger has actually taken into consideration the geographical—and possibly the cultural—differences. Four of the five sections that divide the window let in normal German sunlight. The last one has artificial light, produced by a lamp in the garden, that reproduces the average light one finds in Stockholm during the months of June, July, and August.

In "Prologue to a Manifesto of Open Form" (1979), Bærtling gave expression to his vision: "We have experienced the transformation of art from figurative into nonfigurative, from static to kinetic and dynamic—from kinetism to open form. For me the central problem has been the open form: in diagonal dynamics—open angles. This new form of art is spatial, expressing itself though forces. The painting becomes a part of the universe, a sun, a power center broadcasting its poetic message. . . . Open formations of organized light irradiate at extreme velocities in unprecedented dimensions, infinite spaces of light travel with incredible swiftness to create the liberation of infinity."[8] What happens when such a high-strung vision becomes part of a society's official image of itself?

The lobby of the first skyscraper at Sergels Torg in central Stockholm, Bærtling's first monumental commission, was carried out in close cooperation with architect David Helldén between 1959 and 1960 (fig. 5). Apart from the entrance to the skyscraper, Bærtling was also working on a huge sculptural piece for the square outside, a project that was never realized. Bærtling speculated about how his creation was to function: "Monumental art is meant to fill the architectural void." He was convinced that his assignment was unique. When this interplay between urbanity, architecture, and painting was completed, the "idea of an esthetical space would be fully realized."[9] Yellow, red, and white dominate the lobby: six elevator doors, three columns, mirrors that create an illusion of a larger space. Here, painting merges with architecture, architecture with painting. In an essay on Bærtling in the magazine *Art d'aujourd'hui*, French critic Léon Degond—one of the more influential of the 1950s—had posed the question: "Where is the architecture?" It was meant as a serious critique of Bærtling's art: his paintings demand a completely different kind of space if they are to work at all. Here came the artist's reply: the architecture had arrived, to a greater degree—and on a much grander scale—than the critic had ever imagined.

Times change, utopia becomes fashionable design. *Wallpaper**, in its last issue of the 1990s, informs us that its average reader is 28.9 years old and travels in business class. Ever since the magazine launched its new "urban modernism" and devoted an entire issue to the city of Stockholm, I have been waiting for the definitive tribute to the Bærtling/Helldén collaboration. This was the peak of Scandinavian Modernism. The area surrounding Sergels Torg seems completely up to date. Others have realized this as well. The video for British techno musician and producer Moby's "James Bond Theme" (1998) takes place in a modern urban setting which proves, on closer examination, to be the steps of the Stockholm Culture Center—Kulturhuset—and the fountain in the square outside. And Victor Vasarely, the Op artist responsible for the patterns on the square itself, is experiencing an international revival in the music world (fig. 6).[10] What does this return to a specific look signify? That the utopian spirit is gone and everything is transformed to mere details in a business-class lounge?

Exaggerated opinions about the importance of one's own works are not rare, but Bærtling's understanding of his commission as unique in the world is perhaps not so far from the mark. The context in which this project took place—the design of the buildings at Sergels Torg and the environs—was in many ways unique. Stockholm at this point in time (1960, the absolute zenith of Swedish Modernism) was peerless with regards to city planning. As an urban project, modern Stockholm was an extreme construction, designed by a political elite that had, for a democratic society, an unusual amount of power.

> **EXCURSUS 2:** Is the Bærtling/Helldén collaboration an example of a modernist *Gesamtkunstwerk* in which architecture, painting, sculpture, design, and city planning produce a whole that is larger than the sum of its parts? Perhaps the role model is to be found in an earlier chapter of European history, a time when Sweden was a European superpower: the Baroque. Describing the interaction between the various forms of art in the perfect baroque city, Gilles Deleuze writes, "If the Baroque establishes a total art or a unity of the arts, it does so first of all in extension, each art tending to be prolonged and even to be prolonged into the next art, which exceeds the one before. We have remarked that the Baroque often confines painting to retables, but it does so because the painting exceeds its frame and is realized in polychrome marble sculpture; and sculpture goes beyond itself by being achieved in architecture; and in turn, architecture discovers a frame in the facade, but the frame itself becomes detached from the inside, and establishes relations with the surroundings so as to realize architecture in city planning. From one end of the chain to the other, the painter has become an urban designer. . . . The sum of the arts becomes the Socius, the public social space inhabited by Baroque dancers."[11] The recent discussion of painting in the extended field has centered around the idea that painting no longer appears as a strictly circumscribed mode of expression, but as a zone of contagion, constantly branching out and widening its scope. Painterly practices emerge in other genres, such as photography, video, sculpture, printmaking, and installation. Bærtling, one could claim, already pushed this much further, when involving architecture, city planning, and the public space as such. Should one see him as a modern Bernini from the North?

It is certainly not easy to get a comprehensive view of the philosophical, political, and aesthetical discussions concerning the evasive category of modernism. In Sweden, however, an unusually clear view can be obtained, because Swedish Modernism was not primarily concerned with novels or philosophical works. Such things did of course exist,

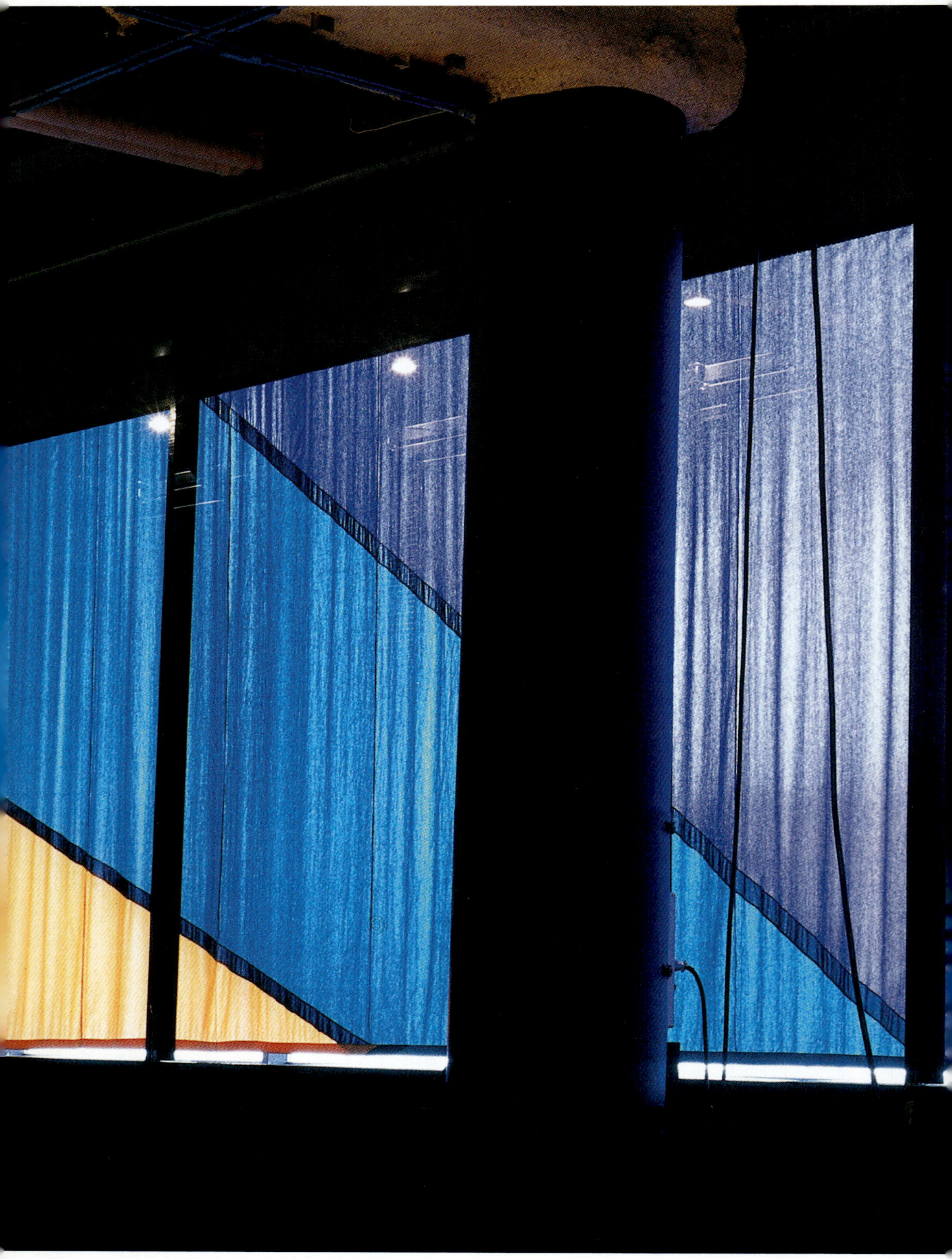

FIG. 3 Detail of draperies by Olle Bærtling in the Stockholm Culture Center, a building designed by Peter Celsing, first displayed 1974
photo: Ann-Katrin Blomqvist

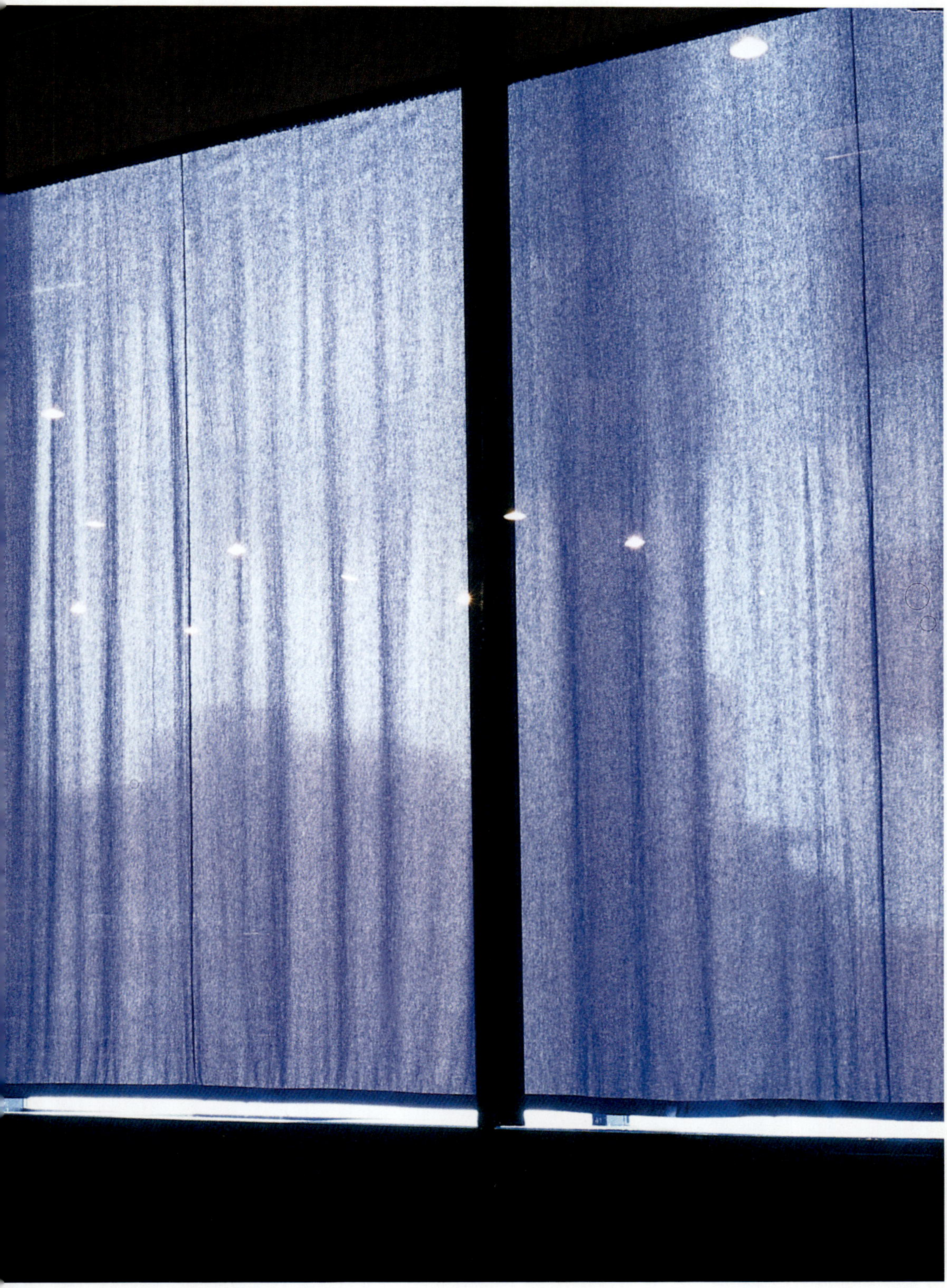

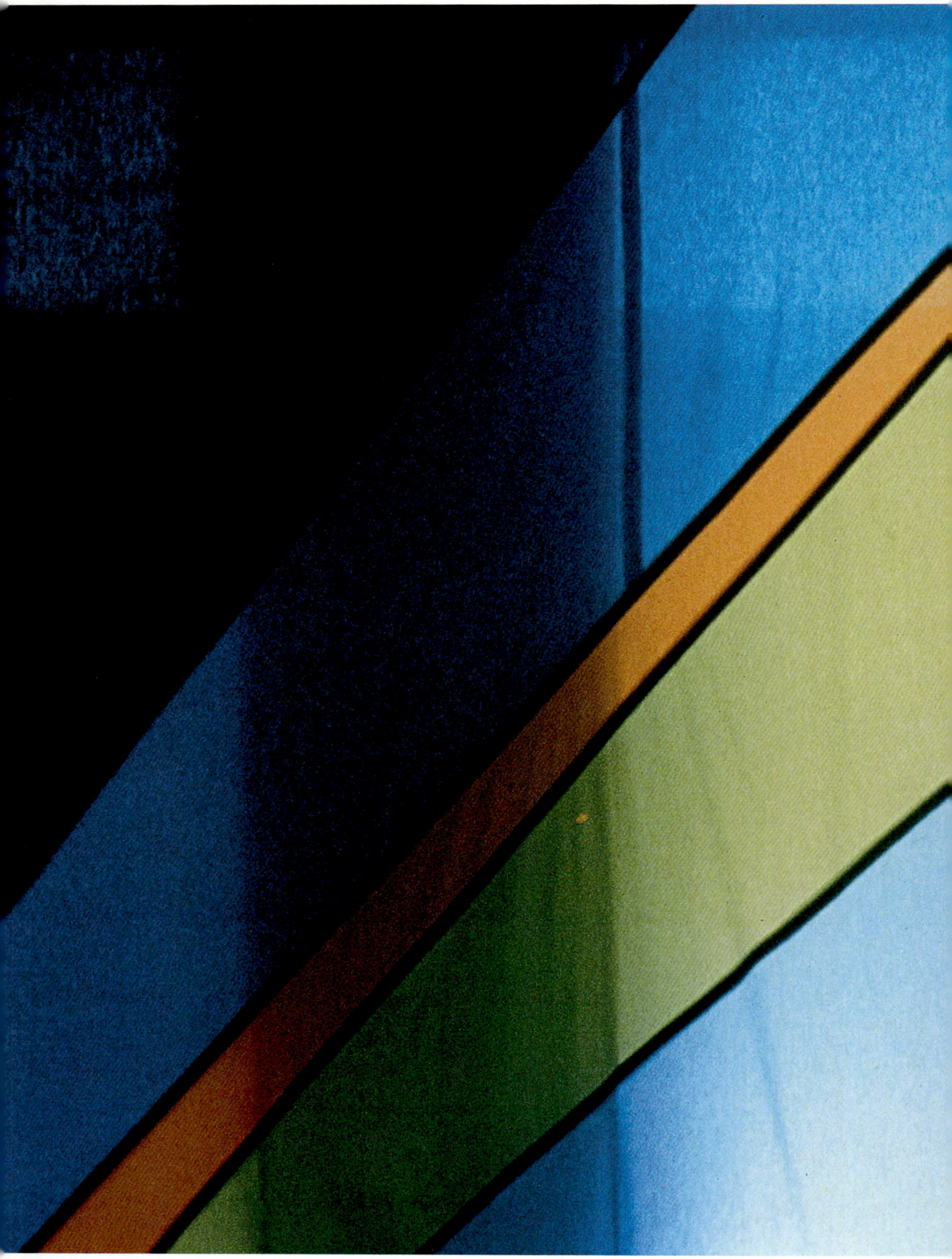

FIG. 4 Tobias Rehberger installation view of **Stockholm Summer** at Galerie für Zeitgenössische Kunst, Leipzig 1999 fabric dimensions variable
Courtesy the artist and Friedrich Petzel Gallery, New York

but far more conspicuous was the construction of society itself, carried out with a level of consistency unmatched in the West—a construction that affected all inhabitants and virtually all aspects of life. The latest to emphasize the exceptional nature of the Swedish model—and the consequences it had for architecture and city planning—is Peter Hall. In *Cities in Civilization* he contends, "But Sweden went further and more consistently down that road than any other country; and, not only was the system forged in the national institutions located in the country's capital, but the city itself came to be seen as the living embodiment, the showcase, of a society they sought proudly to create as a model for the world. Though it had competitors, in the late 1950s and early 1960s it became known worldwide as the quintessence of a social philosophy, realized on the ground. Its apartment towers, grouped around its new subway stations and shopping centers, impeccably designed and landscaped, became an object of pilgrimage for informed visitors from all over the world."[12]

When Hall includes Sweden's capital in his comprehensive exposé of exemplary cities—alongside Athens, Florence, London, New York, Tokyo, and Los Angeles—it is not because Stockholm, relatively modest in size, is a true metropolis, but clearly for other, ideological reasons. This city is an extreme creation, which realizes a clear political vision. With brand new satellite suburbs and a new-fashioned city center, 1960s Stockholm more than any other city embodies the European welfare state as a modern utopia. The artistic collaboration between Helldén and Bærtling represents a paradigm of the ideological vision. No one in this part of the world needed to be in doubt as to the meaning of modernity. The world's most developed welfare state was not an evasive phenomenon.

"The great experiment did not quite work out as planned," concludes Hall laconically toward the end of his exposé. We should not be surprised when the icons of Scandinavian Modernism—the black-and-white pattern of Sergels Torg or Bærtling's hard-edge abstraction—reappear as fragments in art and in popular culture. But what do quotes like that imply? "Now that hard-edge abstraction and what was once called Op Art have been firmly absorbed into the vocabularies of graphic and lifestyle design, what's left for painting?" inquires James Roberts in a thematic issue of the magazine *frieze* that endeavors to come to grips with the continuous—often ironic—recurrence of abstraction at the turn of the century. He continues, "It somehow seems pointless to attempt to reach a kind of Platonic ideal of pure form and color using ground-up stone and animal hair when those nice people at Adobe make things much easier and offer results with a far greater degree of precision."[13]

To quote a segment from a high-strung modernist context and present it today, to a world that no longer believes in heroic utopias, is by no means an unequivocal maneuver. Rehberger's *Stockholm Summer* relies on exactly such a move. No matter how carefully crafted a replica, the act of re-creating a work such as this will have a different meaning from the "original" act, as Jorge Luis Borges was probably the first to demonstrate in his short story "Pierre Menard: Author of the *Quixote*." He describes two fragments of literary works, the first of which is a few lines from *Don Quixote* by Cervantes:

> **. . . truth, whose mother is history, rival of time, depository of deeds, witness of the past, exemplar and adviser to the present, and the future's counselor.**

The second fragment, written not by Cervantes, but several centuries later by Borges' Pierre Menard, reads:

> **. . . truth, whose mother is history, rival of time, depository of deeds, witness of the past, exemplar and adviser to the present, and the future's counselor.**

In the story, Menard, a symbolist in Nîmes and a contemporary of Valéry, has thus produced a fragment exactly like the citation from Cervantes, like it in every graphic respect, but nonetheless he sees the passage as *his*. This act of appropriation—Menard is, of course, fully aware of the likeness—opens up all the familiar issues of authenticity and uniqueness. How do the two fragments stand in relation to each other? Borges comments

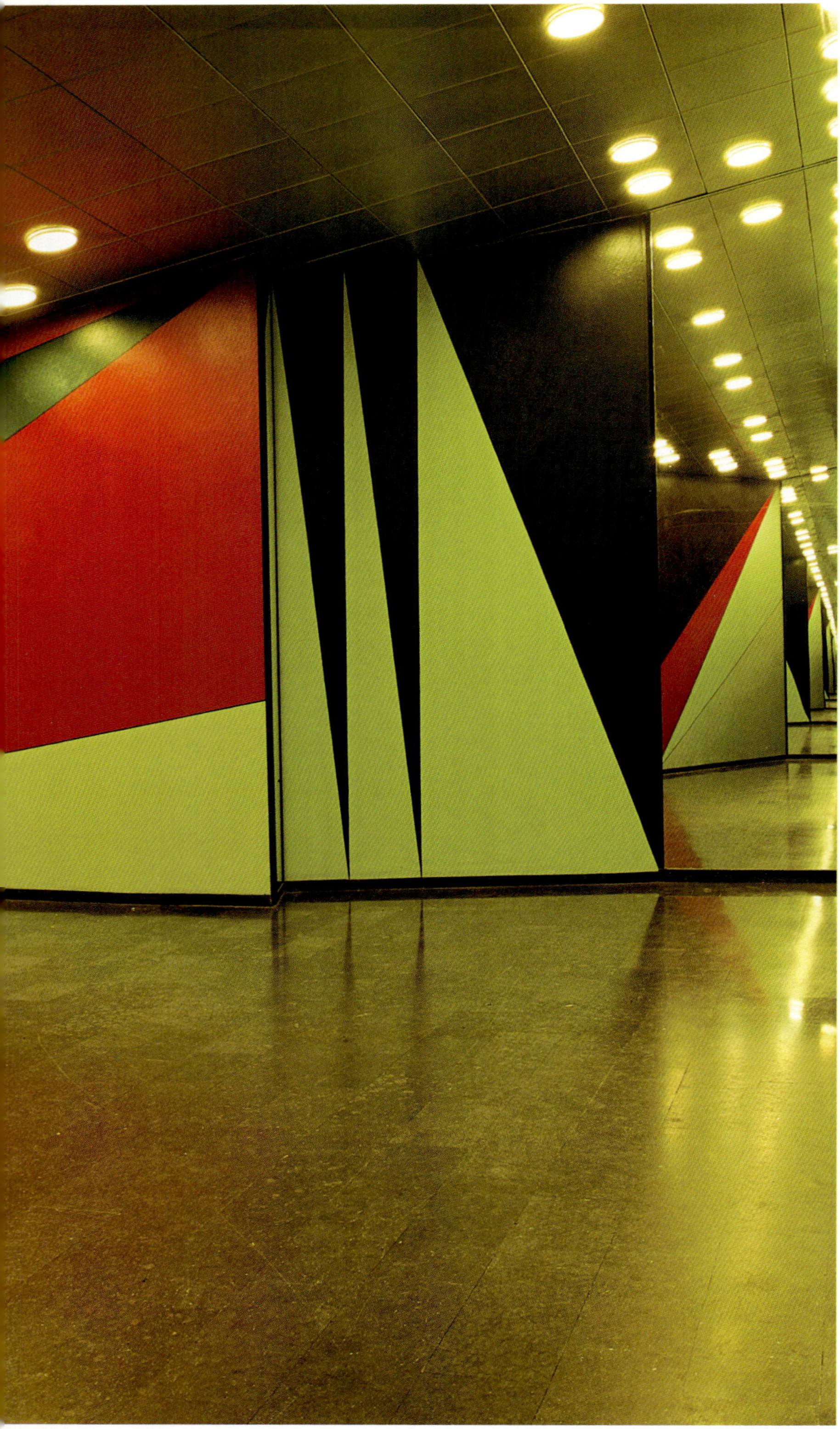

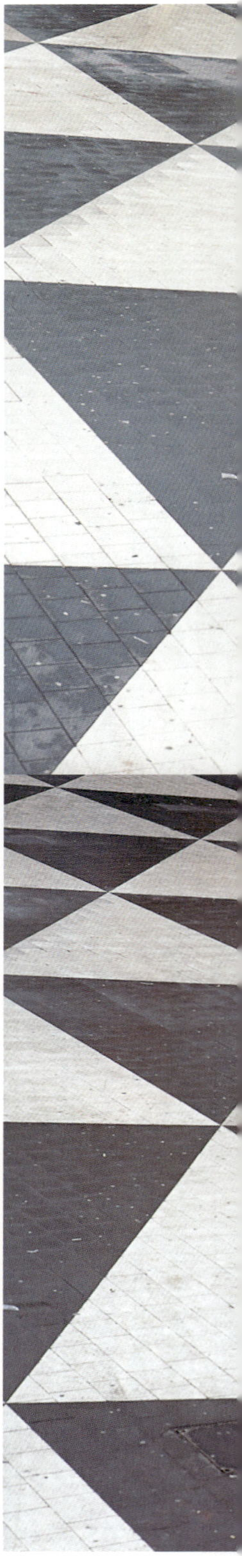

FIG. 5 view of lobby installation by Olle Bærtling in the Haymarket skyscraper at Sergels Torg, Stockholm, in collaboration with David Helldén 1959–1960 photo: Ann-Katrin Blomqvist

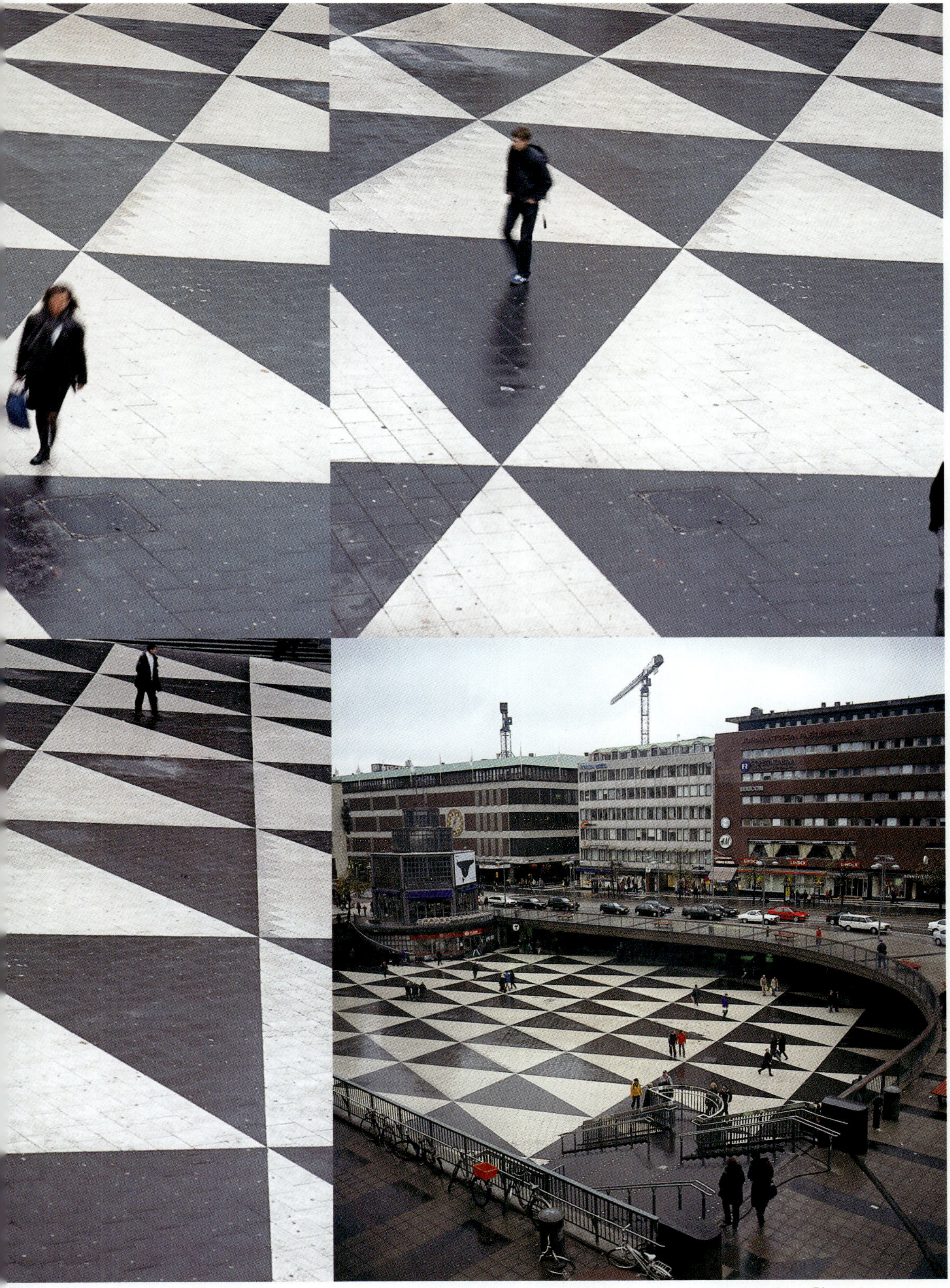

FIG. 6 view of courtyard design by Victor Vasarely at Sergels Torg, Stockholm photo: Ann-Katrin Blomqvist

on the discrepancies: "The difference in style is also vivid." How can he claim that about two completely identical textual fragments? He expounds upon the differences: "The archaic style of Menard—quite foreign, after all—suffers from a certain affectation. Not so that of his forerunner, who handles with ease the current Spanish of his time." In spite of this affectation, Borges judges the *Quixote* of Menard "infinitely more subtle" than that of Cervantes. Menard's endeavor is in fact heroic: "To compose the *Quixote* at the beginning of the seventeenth century was a reasonable undertaking, necessary and perhaps even unavoidable; at the beginning of the twentieth, it is almost impossible."[14]

Less than three decades separate Bærtling's drapery at the Stockholm Culture Center from Rehberger's Leipzig project, a short time span compared to the three centuries in Borges' story. But one may venture that the ideological distance between the two works here in question is just as considerable. The bright colors of Bærtling's gigantic drapery, produced for windows overlooking a square that more than any other place embodied the utopia, give expression to a triumphant sense of history. The geometrical fields of color display full confidence in the future of a rational society. The question, then, is what Rehberger's drapery, parading the same bright colors, gives expression to, displayed as it is in a part of Germany—the former East—where utopian ideas of history and society for most people indicate little but suffering. Is it ironic and poking fun at the confidence of high-modernist aesthetics? Or is it rather affirmative in a somewhat naive way, simply indulging in the splendor of Bærtling's great sense for the combination of colors?

Perhaps there is a third alternative. Rehberger's abstract fields of color certainly represent a late arrival, but a fully self-conscious one—conscious both of its own problematic status and of its heroic genealogy. The fact that this heroism—defined in terms of progressive politics—so easily becomes dated and then returns as style, perhaps sheds some light not only on today's art but on the relationship of radicality to aesthetical packaging in general. Retroactively, it may have something to say about the aesthetics of being progressive. Bærtling's goal, like that of his friend Vasarely, was the artist-as-engineer, creating for the masses. What does it mean to make such a program one's own today? Some thirty years ago, a utopian drapery of this kind—attempting to merge abstract art with visionary architecture—was, to quote Borges, "a reasonable undertaking, necessary and perhaps even unavoidable." At the dawn of the twenty-first century, when the language of abstraction is no longer in use, the venture is "almost impossible." The production of such a piece as this, in spite of this impossibility, also presents a great task for the viewer. To really *see* this object for what it is, means to view it as a monster. It also means understanding something about the life of monsters in general. Thus interpreted, one would have to conclude that Rehberger's drapery, compared to Bærtling's, is "infinitely more subtle."

NOTES

1 For an interpretation of the concept of *Nachträglichkeit* and the various temporal models at work in Freud's texts, see Jean Laplanche, *New Foundations of Psychoanalysis*, trans. David Macey (London: Basic Blackwell, 1989).
2 Jacques Derrida, *Writing and Difference*, trans. Alan Bass (Chicago: University of Chicago Press, 1978) p. 203.
3 See Hal Foster, "What's Neo about the Neo-Avant-Garde?" in *The Duchamp Effect*, eds. Martha Buskirk and Mignon Nixon (Cambridge, Mass.: MIT Press, 1996).
4 Hal Foster, *The Return of the Real* (Cambridge, Mass.: MIT Press, 1996), p. 29.
5 Okwui Enwezor, *Mirror's Edge* (Umeå, Sweden: Bildmuseet, 1999), p. 14.
6 See Jacques Derrida, *Speech and Phenomena: And Other Essays on Husserl's Theory of Signs*, trans D. B. Allison (Evanston: Northwestern University Press, 1978) and Rudolf Bernet, *Differenz und Anwesenheit. Derridas und Husserls Phänomenologie der Sprache, der Zeit, der Geschichte, der wissenschaftlichen Rationalität*, Phänomenologische Forschungen 18 (Freiburg and Munich: Alber, 1986), pp. 51–122.
7 Foster, "What's Neo about the Neo-Avant-Garde?" p. 5.
8 Olle Bærtling,"Prologue to a Manifesto of Open Form"(1979)(Stockholm: Malmö Konshall/Moderna Museet,1981), p. 50.
9 Cited in Teddy Brunius, *Bærtling* (Stockholm: SAK, 1990), p. 131.
10 See Jörg Heiser, "Planetary Folklore," *frieze* 41 (summer 1998), pp. 62–67.
11 Gilles Deleuze, *The Fold: Leibniz and the Baroque*, trans. Tom Conley (Minneapolis: University of Minnesota Press, 1993), p. 123.
12 Peter Hall, *Cities in Civilization* (London: Phoenix, 1999), p. 842ff.
13 James Roberts, "Be There or Be Square," *frieze* 41 (summer 1998), p. 69.
14 Jorge Luis Borges, *Labyrinths* (London: Penguin, 1970), pp. 62–71.

Paulo Herkenhoff is an independent curator and critic who also serves as Adjunct Curator in the Department of Painting and Sculpture at the Museum of Modern Art, New York. He has published extensively, including texts for the exhibition catalogues *Encounters/Displacements: Luis Camnitzer, Alfredo Jaar, Cildo Meireles* (1992), *Ultramodern: The Art of Contemporary Brazil* (1993), and *Louise Bourgeois: Blue Days and Pink Days* (1997), as well as for the recent *Cildo Meireles* monograph (1999). The former director of Rio de Janeiro's Museum of Modern Art, Herkenhoff was selected as the curator for the XXIV Bienal de São Paulo, *Núcleo Histórico: Antropofagia e Histórias de Canibalismos* (1998), the catalogue of which included the original version of the following essay.

Monochromes, the Autonomy of Color, and the Centerless World

Paulo Herkenhoff

"White is tamed light: the dynamic of our contemplation." — Murilo Mendes[1]

"If art has known harmony, rhythm, beauty, it has known zero." — Kasimir Malevich[2]

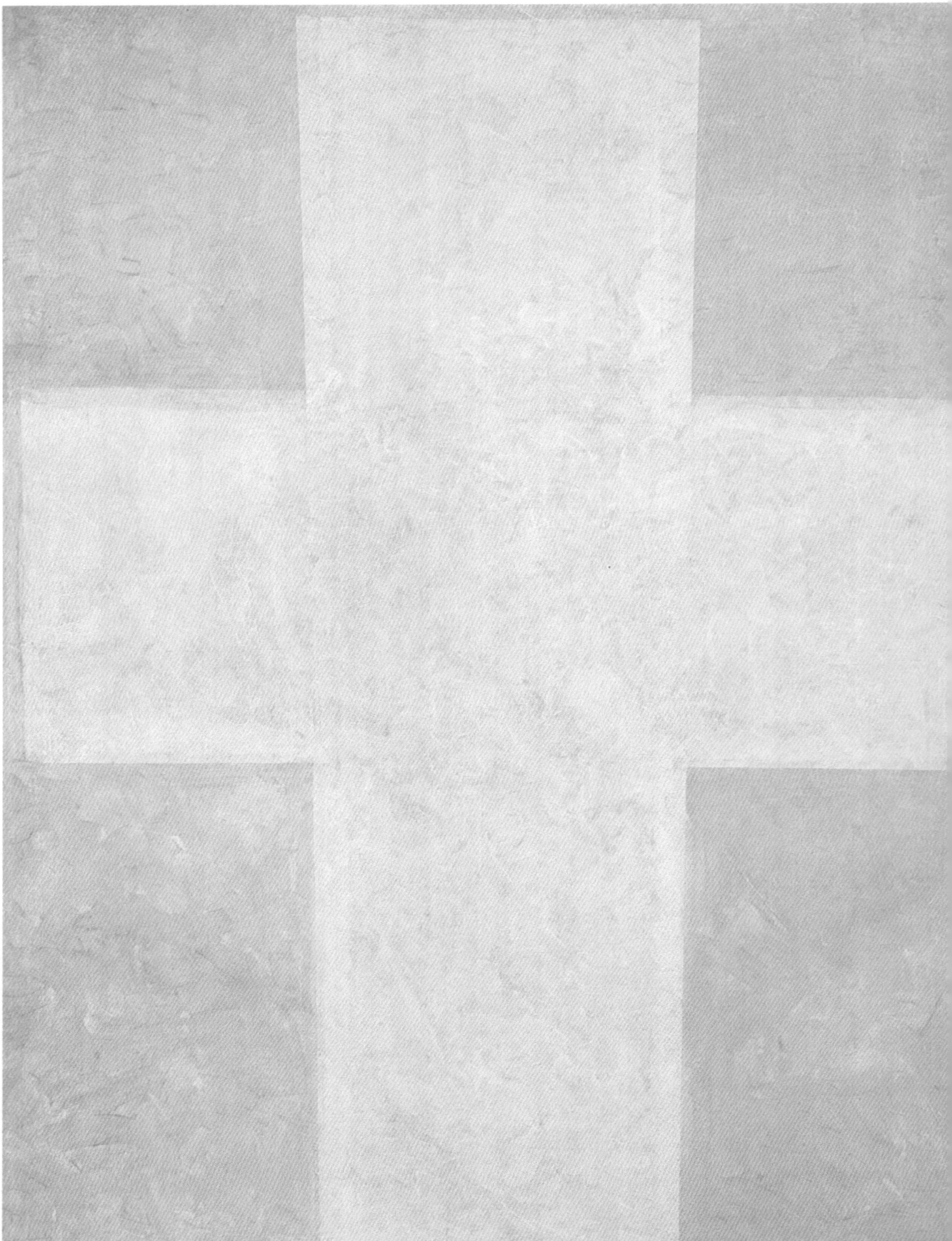

FIG. 1 Kasimir Malevich **Suprematism** after 1920 oil on canvas 34 ½ x 30 in. Collection Stedelijk Museum, Amsterdam

The following text was originally published in the catalogue for the XXIV Bienal de São Paulo, *Núcleo Histórico: Antropofagia e Histórias de Canibalismos* (1998). Therefore, it was written with the perspective of *antropofagia*, the cultural project developed by poet Oswald de Andrade in 1928 that understood Brazilian culture as a process of absorbing multiple inputs and processing them into an autonomous hybrid language. Artists in the postwar period in countries such as Brazil or Venezuela no longer needed to prove their national identity, but wanted rather to construct an emancipated language to inscribe on Western art history. The dilemma was to understand the political possibilities for the emergence of such an autonomous artistic language in third-world societies, as was discussed by Mário Pedrosa, Ferreira Gullar, and Haroldo de Campos.[3] This emancipation also belied a belief in the possibility of a centerless world, in which economic hegemony would not guarantee a monopoly in the production of autonomous artistic languages of historical significance. In this context, the issue of the white monochrome becomes a rich field of parallels, differences, divergence, and convergence around the ground zero of visual language.

Artistic practices in South and North America, Europe, and Asia have witnessed simultaneous elaborations on the white monochrome by distinct artists aligned with diverse artistic movements. After the Second World War, the creation of white monochromes prompted a discussion of the constitutive process of autonomy of cultures from peripheral economies in the face of eurocentrism. As a consequence, one can now consider the dispersion of the idea of a center in art history and of the eurocentric model (even if geographically displaced to New York!). This text has been revised and adapted for the current exhibition and publication.

There are no more models to follow. Some Latin American artists have abandoned the understanding of art history as a flow of styles to be followed. Knowledge of modern art history became imperative primarily for choosing points of insertion and rupture in the common ground of Western culture. Articulating this consciousness, the theorist of Neo-Concretism, Ferreira Gullar, discusses the death of painting in "Teoria do não-objeto" (Theory of the non-object): "It is with Mondrian and Malevich that the elimination of the object continues. . . . After all, it is painting that lies there inarticulate in search of a new structure, of a new way of being, of a new signification."[4] Despite possible correlations with the Baroque, the so-called Latin American postwar vanguards maintained a certain historicism and essentialism, as in De Stijl.[5]

"I have metamorphosed myself in zero forms," Malevich said.[6] The "unfigurable" in Malevich's work and in Suprematist etymology has been discussed by Bruno Duborgel. Nonexistent in Russian, the original word was forged from Latin and Polish to designate an ontological function: "to disclose," "to reveal," "to manifest," "to present" the Absolute as objectless, the Void, the abyssal being, the universal excitement, the "essence of diversities," the nonfigurative being, the objectless world.[7] In the economy of modernity, white has been the essential color and, at the same time, the presence of all colors. Concerning his Suprematist work, Malevich stated, "The free white abyss, infinity are before us" (fig. 1).[8] Arp's white reliefs presented the modern hybrid between painting and sculpture.[9] The North American artist Robert Rauschenberg explained the genesis of the structural simplicity of his *White Paintings* (1951): whereas Albers had pointed out the equivalence of colors, Rauschenberg hesitated before the arbitrariness of their selection. One of the motivations for his *White Paintings* was to not employ color for his personal service.[10]

The monochrome in the postwar years is an extraordinary paradigm. The singularity emerges as extreme at precisely the moment when there seems to have been the greatest similitude in its use. Commenting on the monochromatic inventions of Yves Klein, Rauschenberg, and Ellsworth Kelly, Benjamin Buchloh observes how "the coincidence, as well as the simultaneity and repetitions of other avant-garde paradigms, substantiates the hypothesis that the discursive formation of modernism generated its own historical and evolutionary dynamic. If we assume that the visual paradigms operate analogously to

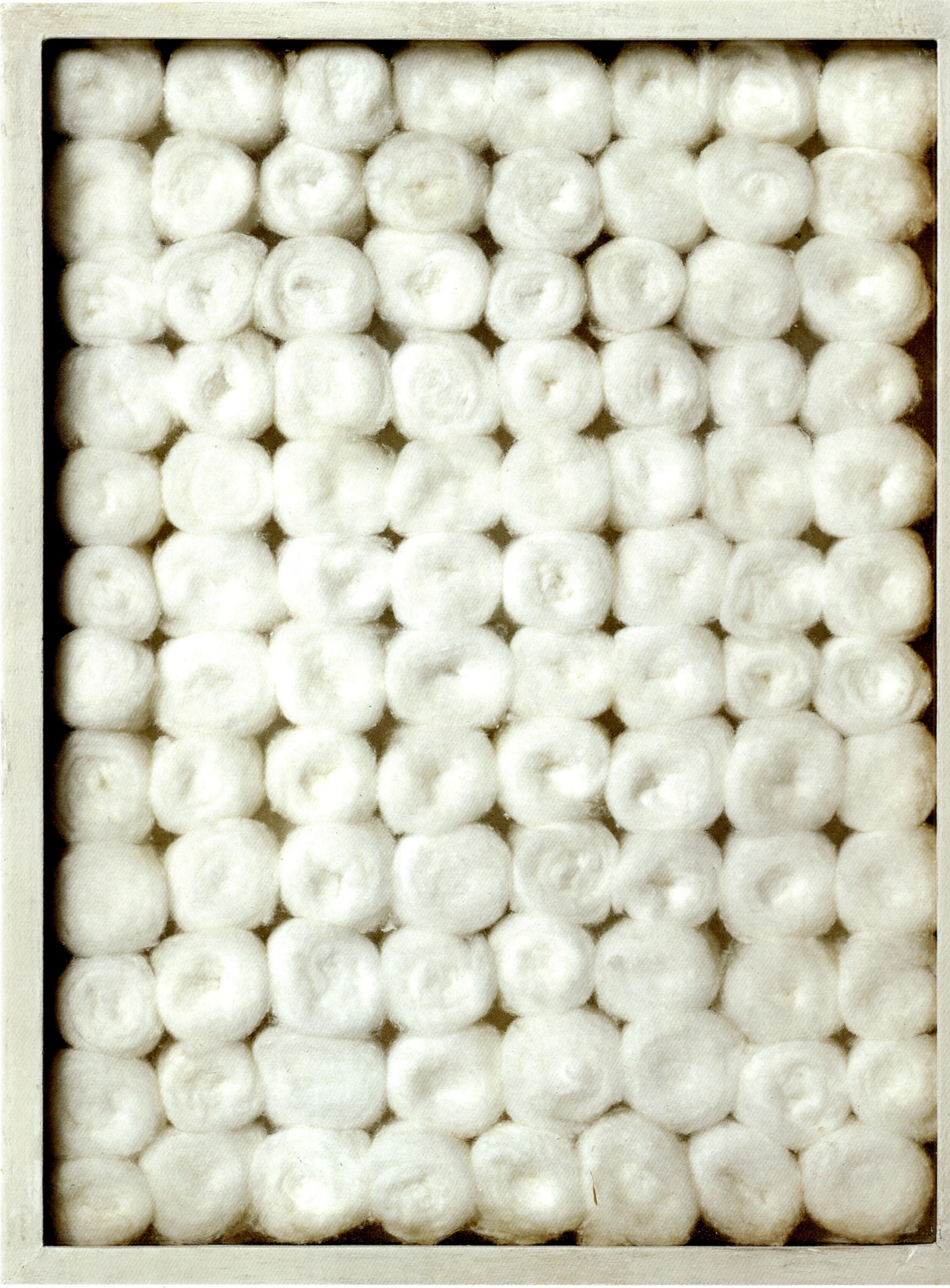

FIG. 2 Piero Manzoni **Achrome** 1961 cotton balls 17 x 12 ¼ in. Collection Galerie Karsten Greve, Cologne, Paris, Milan, St. Moritz

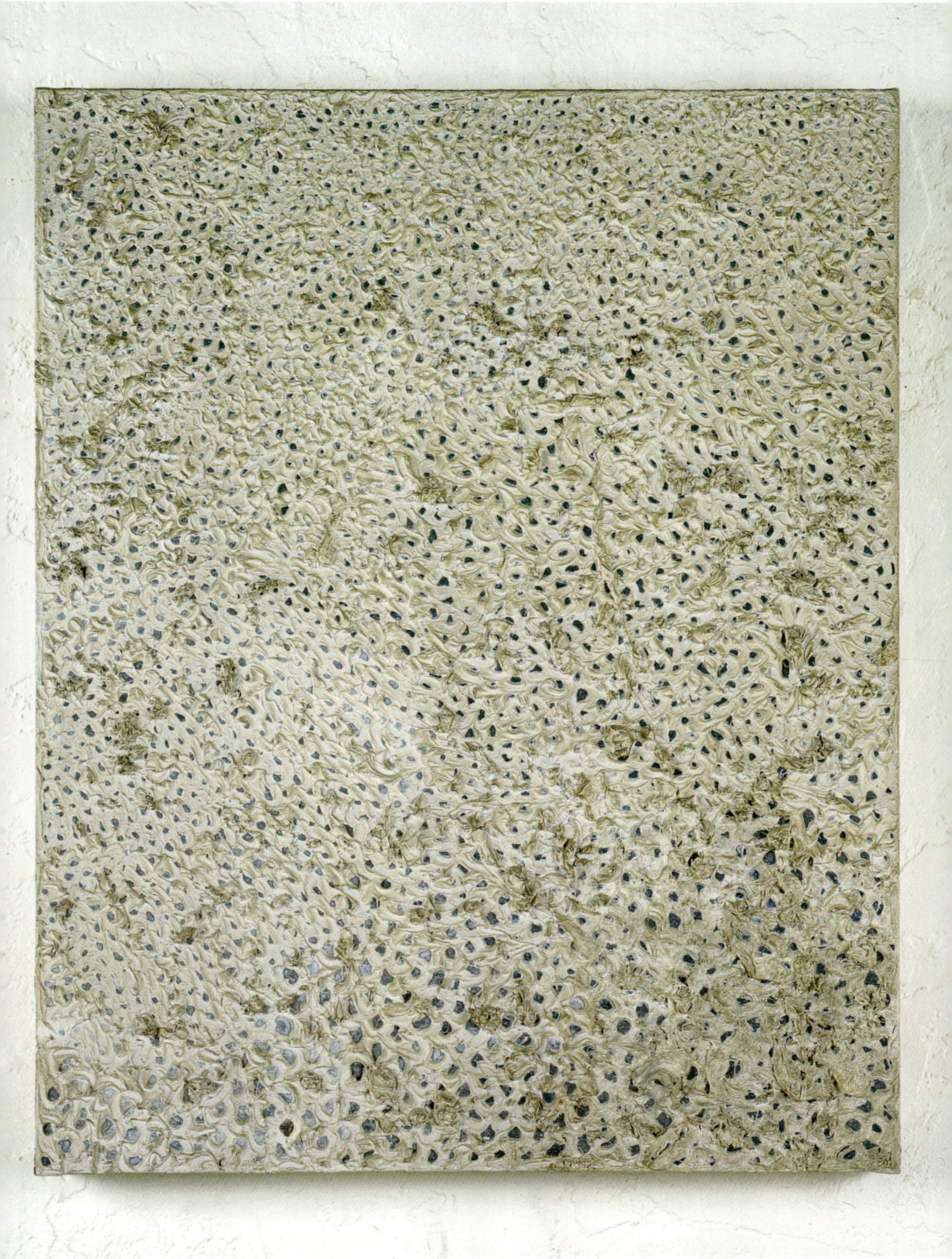

FIG. 3 Yayoi Kusama **No. D** 1959 oil on canvas 35 ½ x 28 ½ in. Collection Donald Judd Estate

FIG 4 Lucio Fontana **Concetto Spaziale-Attesa** (Spatial concept-expectation) 1964–1965 tempera on canvas, lacquered wood 57 ½ x 45 in. Collection Walker Art Center, Minneapolis; T. B. Walker Acquisition Fund, 1998

linguistic paradigms, then the 'langue' of modernism would constitute the neo-avant-garde 'speakers' and continuously replicate and modify their 'paroles.'"[11] White monochromes created in just more than a decade by artists from all over the world point to the dispersion of the idea of center in art history. This occurs when there is an artist who questions the gaze, whether in Brazil, Venezuela, Italy, France, the United States, or Japan.[12] Yves Klein and Piero Manzoni mark Europe in the 1950s. In manifesting the idea of the monochrome, Klein became the owner of IKB blue (International Klein Blue) and of color itself.[13] According to Pierre Restany, blue for Klein is "a tangible figuration of the infinite space," identifying the pictorial and existential phenomena.[14] His methodological project aimed at the brilliancy of the materials and the intensity of "color in freedom." Ideas of color impregnation and incorporation refer us to Manzoni. His first *achromes* date to 1957 (fig. 2). In order to operate the corporeality of the monochromes, Manzoni used hydrophilic materials, as well as hairy and stony ones, to explore the surface, declaring, "My aim is to create an entirely white surface (completely colorless, neutral) that no longer refers in any way to a phenomenon or pictorial element unfamiliar to the nature of the surface."[15]

Ferreira Gullar's article "Arte neoconcreta, uma contribuição brasileira" (Neo-Concrete art, a Brazilian contribution),[16] demarcates the genesis of this Brazilian movement and its references to Malevich and to Mondrian's foreboding of the end of the painting.[17] Following *Gestalttheorie*, Susanne Langer and Maurice Merleau-Ponty's phenomenology split Brazilian concretism, which was then caught in a dogmatic objectivity guided by the theories of Norbert Wiener, Charles Pierce, Max Bill, and Swiss concrete art. Neo-Concretism reestablished distinct levels of subjectivity within the excessively objective concretist art. It relied on the investment of desire, by either the artist or the spectator, for the realization of the visual fact. For example, Hércules Barsotti explores the proportions between light and darkness in his work. A slight movement of the viewer's head gives way to the visual fact of meeting other brightness or light. His delicate Neo-Concrete operation lies in accepting any minor action of the gaze. *Branco branco* (White white) announces the exact point of constitution of the nature of space: the borderline between white planes. As luminosity emerges, tension settles in and difference erupts. The very existence of difference is, of course, what constitutes the birth of language, what makes language necessary and possible. In the case of white monochromes, even the slightest difference is enough to allow language to be created.

Lygia Clark's work is about the adventure of the plane. Toward the end of the 1950s, the artist realized that space emerges from the articulation of independent planes, as in *Planos em superfície modulada n.1* (Planes in modulated surface #1) (1957).[18] In the junction lines of these wooden planes there remain breaches that the artist incorporates into the visual discourse like an "organic line." They are veins through which slip shadows and air. Air invades the white monochrome. In contrast, Hélio Oiticica lives the adventure of color (see pp. 315–317). In the Neo-Concrete period, Oiticica argued that, for the sense of color, white is the "most static that favors silent, dense, and metaphysic duration. The encounter of two different whites occurs deafly, one being more pure whilst the other is naturally more opaque."[19] In order to counterbalance the difference, Oiticica would change the brush stroke's direction.[20] He searches for the color's place, the "organic relation of shape-color," and displaces the plane to become concrete space, until it turns into penetrable architecture. Color's corporeality is the path that directs the experience of art to the complete sensorial potentiality of the individual.

Emigrating from Japan to New York in 1958, Yayoi Kusama created the *Infinity Nets* through pattern repetition, as in *No. D* (1959) (fig. 3). Donald Judd compared such paintings to a "large, fragile, but vigorously carved grill or to a massive, solid lace."[21] The network gives the artist a sense of control in the face of her mental illness.[22] In these "quasi-monochromes," as Lynn Zelevansky designates them, white finalizes the history of the picture, superimposed on all possible and visible color nuances. White does not refute rhetoric, excess, or the misleading traces of the gestural as it comes to live an unexpected crisis of rationality and measure.[23] Tomie Ohtake, a Brazilian artist born in Japan, covers surfaces with white like a film of light. Through it filter other pictorial layers of the painting, revealing

FIG. 5 Alejandro Otero **Monocromo** 1961 oil on canvas 28 ¾ x 23 ¾ in. Courtesy Museo Alejandro Otero, Caracas

the history of color and manifesting the plurality of colors present in white. "According to Zen, the color white knows who lies distant from it," recalls Murilo Mendes. Manabu Mabe, another Japanese-Brazilian, departs from the excess of paint by inscribing calligraphic signs on the monochrome surface. Earlier, Mário Pedrosa had noted Mabe's "gluttonous love of substance."[24]

Neo-Concrete space leads Gullar to argue in "Teoria do não-objeto" that Fontana's canvases are "a retarded attempt at destroying the fictitious quality of pictorial space by introducing in it a real cut."[25] In the Argentinean "Manifiesto Blanco" (White manifesto) (1946), which spuriously bears Fontana's name, color is given as a space-element for an art devoid of artifice that would involve sound, time, and matter. For Murilo Mendes, Fontana's knife represents the "art of dividing the space in harmony with its internal cohesion" (fig. 4).[26] Space springs from perforating and cutting acts, violent on the color-support and arbitrary, yet with its own logic. The blade mutilates the body and creates shadows on the white.[27] In *Vibración en blanco* (Vibration in white) (1960), Venezuelan artist Jesus Rafael Soto displays the logic of the support's thread and texture, in contrast to Fontana's gesturality. The artist directs the openings toward dissolution, strictly following the logic of the support's structure. Thus the support maintains its basic cohesion, despite still being fragile, in order to simultaneously disperse and retain the density of the white as well as light. Soto recalls that as a youngster he discovered the phenomenology of light while reading Dante: "*A quella luce cotal si diventa, che volgersi da lei per altro aspetto è impossibil che mai si consenta*" (In that light one becomes such that it is impossible that he should ever consent to turn himself from it for other sight; *Paradiso*, Canto XXXIII, 100–102). Soto's whiteness has the same quality as Armando Reverón's all-white depictions of the Venezuelan landscape. In *Untitled* (1964), Mira Schendel cuts rectangles in the white plywood surface. The artist manages to introduce, as a calculating device, the void where the degree zero of the gaze was established. The rectangular planes cut space like the negative planes of painting.

"White on white: Absolute white in activity," sang Mendes. Going back to oil painting, Venezuelan artist Alejandro Otero adopts the monochromatic predominance that imposed itself on the formation of color (fig. 5). He develops a deaf game of concealment and veiling. White becomes laconism in a plane of regression toward the utopia of the *White canvas* painting (1961).[28] White is the experience of chords. "Color has to be structured as sound in music," expressed Oiticica.[29] "What I do is music," he once concluded. Robert Ryman's absolute choice of white included the offering of "an experience of delight, and well-being, and rightness. It is like listening to music," to clarify the density of white.[30] *Winsor* (1966) (fig. 6) denotes the procedure of painting in series and giving titles that are not associated with objects, people, and places.[31] It refers to the brand of paints Winsor & Newton. Ryman explores the construction of painting, loading the paintbrush with paint and creating horizontal strips from left to right until the paint dries up. He repeats this procedure, making a new strip below. Robert Storr has written that, like "Inuit who can read with precision a comparably narrow spectrum of snow and ice, Ryman has catalogued white's actual variety, thus ironically demonstrating its latent *non*-neutrality when seen in relation to itself."[32] For Ryman, white "makes other aspects of painting visible that would not be so clear with the use of other colors."[33]

White monochromes reveal the world marked by solitary differences. The monochrome is imbued with symbolic significance, introducing issues such as difference, desire, power, racism, or art. This can be seen in the work of Felix Gonzalez-Torres and in Andres Serrano's blood photography. It can be found in the fusion of symbols in Anish Kapoor's sculpture and it prompts the dissolution of the idea of authorship in Gerhard Richter's painting. It is concept and its reification. Yves Klein restored the monochrome and other colors in the discussion of cannibalism. Political violence compares to cannibalism. Montaigne notes in his *Essays* (I, XXXI) that "[Europeans] exceed them [the cannibal Tupinambás Indians] in all forms of barbarity." Religious wars, ethnic conflicts, civil fights, and fascism demonstrate how society itself devours its children. Glenn Ligon's paintings interrogate. One of his black monochromes is called *White*. The work done in conjunction

FIG. 6 Robert Ryman **Winsor** 1966 oil on canvas 76 x 76 in. Courtesy Doris Ammann, Zürich

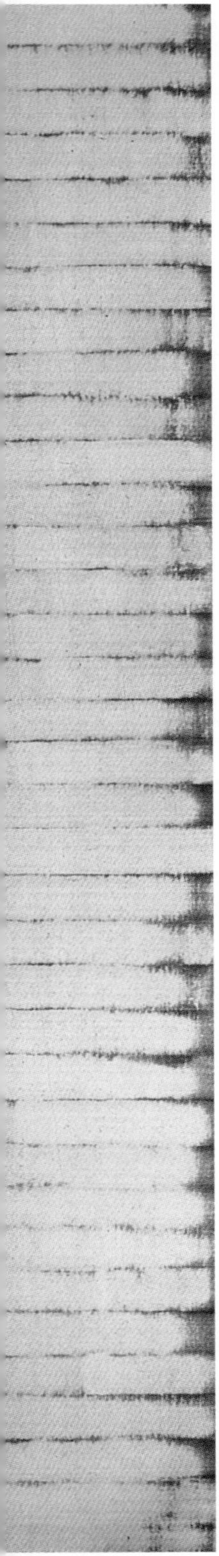

with Byron Kim, *Black and White, Version #1* (1993), consists of a series of monochromes that ironically explore the color-ethnicity relationship, presented like a commercial showcase of paints (fig. 7). As Ligon has noted, "The work of artists of color is often reduced to being simply about race and nothing else, as if our gender, sexual, class, and other identities didn't complicate any discussion of race as a subject matter, or as if race was our 'natural' subject matter."[34] In a subtle way, the artist paints black-lettered texts over a black ground to discuss how the use of color names to designate ethnicities can result in racism when the discourse on ethnic identity denies the discourse of subjectivity. In support of Nelson Mandela, Nigel Rolfe created *Hand on Face* (1988–1996) (fig. 8). Differences of projection—whether on a large screen in Wembley or on a small monitor—discuss social space. Rolfe's anti-Malevich video charges the image with meaning. In real time, the artist's face suffers repeated attacks by a black-painted hand. The subtext refers to the political violence of censorship, torture, and individual identity closely linked to the physical condition. The individual's encounter with the plasticity of power is made evident. In Abdoulaye Konaté's installation *Genocide*, the cutouts of red fabric—monochromes—repair the canvas. These are wounds and sutures on a body that wanes in hunger and mutilates in war under the gaze mediated by the means of communication. Konaté belongs to a generation of artists who incorporate ancestral values into contemporary adversity; thus Africa acknowledges itself as a critical subject of its own political processes. Of Palestinian origin, Mona Hatoum has worked within the tradition of visual symbolization in Islamic culture and its interdict on representation. Ornaments, arabesques, calligraphy, and colors articulate meaning without representing. *Prayer Mat* (1995) consists of thousands of safety-pins. A compass, a "kitsch" inscription, allows one to know the direction of Mecca. The abstract surface of *Prayer Mat* contrasts with *Entrails Carpet*, a repulsive territory, and *Marble Carpet*, in which thousands of glass balls destabilize the space. The sensuality of the materials exacerbates certain territorial frailties. Some of Katie van Scherpenberg's paintings have a surface color that resembles nail polish. The color allows us to see the brush strokes, which look like fingerprints, as if pointing out the artist's identity and profession. Scherpenberg takes bed sheets from her "trousseau"—exactly the kind of material that indicates how women were ascribed to the domestic space—and uses them as canvases. This operation both denounces and abolishes the exclusion of women from art history.

In his anthropometries, Yves Klein used people for printing pigments—"appropriative urgency," says Pierre Restany, applying a term linked to anthropophagy to this kind of shroud.[35] Klein printed "battles" restrained by bodies in turbulent movements—"a battle with the aura of unrestrained exuberance, orgasmic ecstasy, orgiastic chaos, and savage violence."[36] In *Grande antropophagie bleue—Hommage à Tennessee Williams* (Great blue anthropophagy—Homage to Tennessee Williams) (1960), Klein ratifies cannibalism as a symbolic practice, a metaphor of violence, and a phantasmagoric dimension of desire. Williams had approached the theme in his play *Suddenly Last Summer*, in which the character Sebastian, in search of sensory realization, ends up consumed by a gang—a brutal index of social decadence. Like Montaigne, Klein saw that Europe, with its wars, was "pure 'flesh' . . . We will rapidly become anthropophagites."[37] Further still, he saw the Eucharist as an anthropophagic rite. Preceding the edenic "blue era," cannibalism would be the phase of man's redemption. Klein commented that "We are coming into an anthropophagous era. . . . It will be the peaceful realization on a universal scale of the famous words: He who eats of my flesh and drinks of my blood will live in me and I in him."[38] Klein's religious ancestral cannibalism would be the destiny of a last judgment.

In *Project for an Artistic Attitude* (1970) (fig. 9), Antonio Dias inverts the writing of the word REALITY. The relationship between visual sign and verbal sign places the word in suspension on the black ground. The nonverbal space functions as an immense monochrome and alludes to Malevich and his non-objectivity, or to other models of the reduction of painting and its recording in society. Dias' *The Electrician* (1986) is a gray monochrome made of carbon (graphite), which is an electric conductor. The whole surface of the canvas can be electrified. A bone and electric wire hang in front of the painting, which offers the possibility of spreading energy by the same physical fact and with the same elements as those used in political torture. Another of Dias' gray monochromes, *Tango* (1985), uses bones for a

FIG. 7 Glenn Ligon and Byron Kim **Black and White, Version #1** 1993 commercially prepared flesh-colored oil paint and black oil paint on wood panels thirty-two panels, 18 x 10 in. each Courtesy the artists

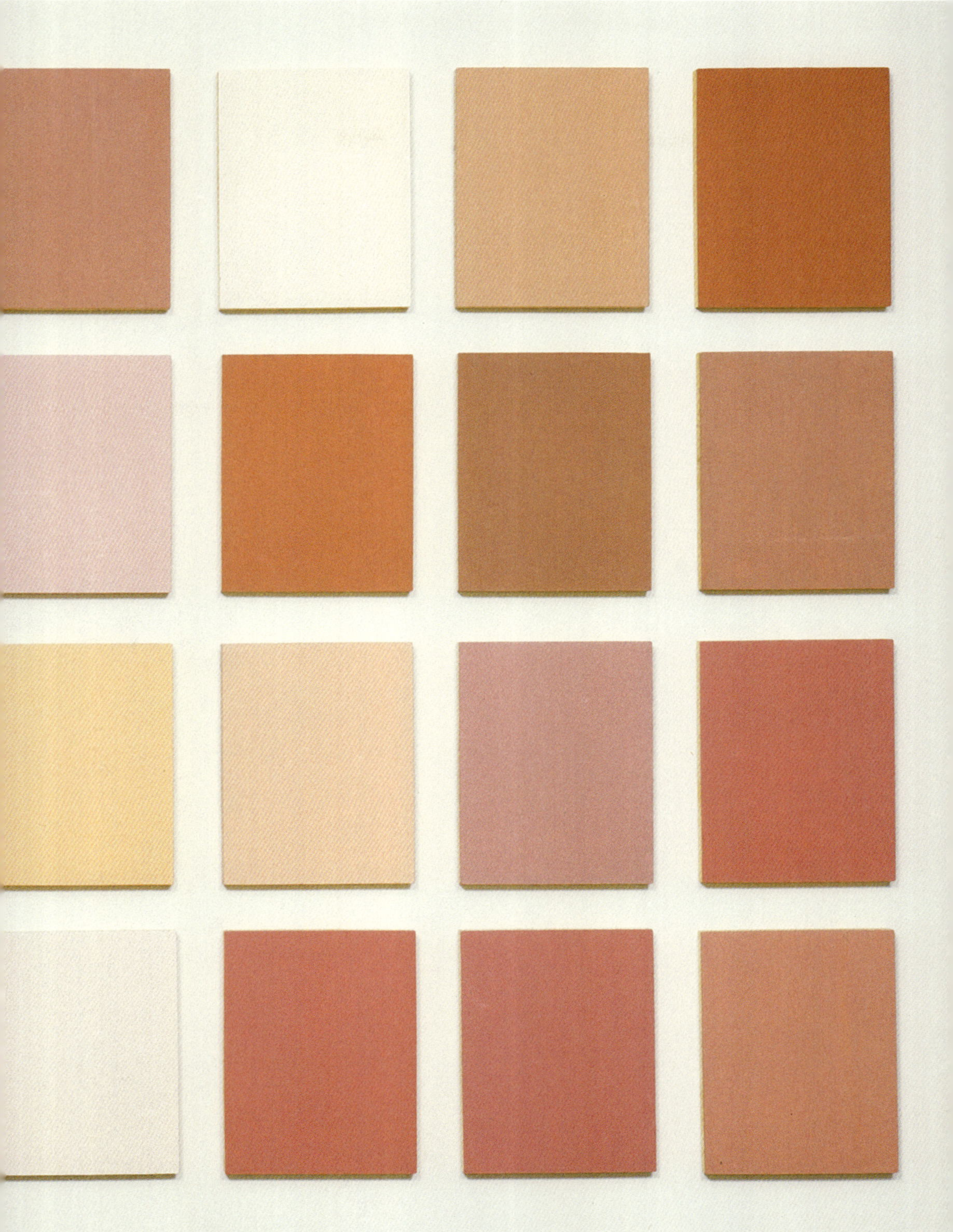

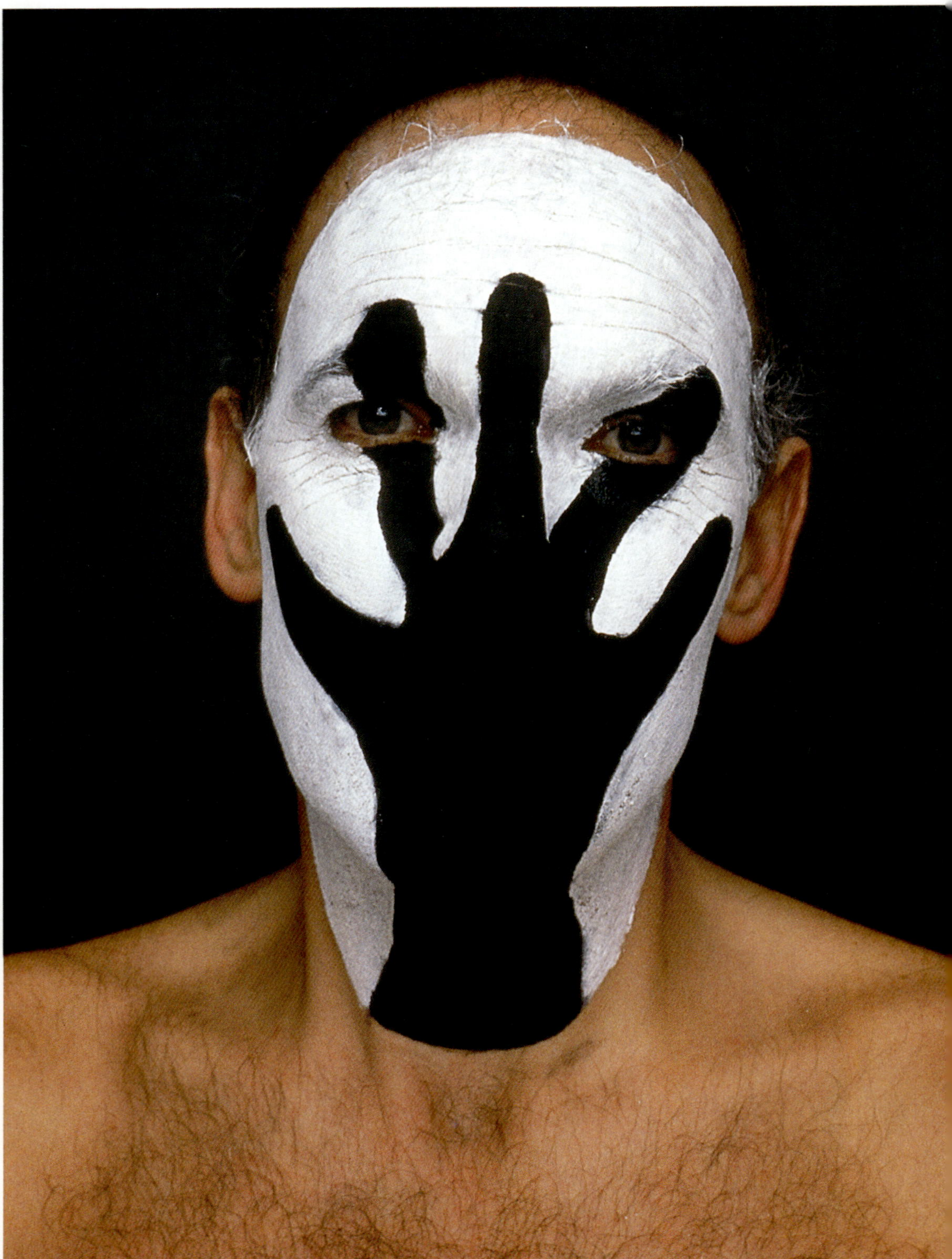

FIG. 8 Nigel Rolfe still from **Hand on Face** 1988–1996 video 3 min. Courtesy the artist

macabre dance, alluding to State terrorism in Argentina. These paintings could be related to Bruce Nauman's *South American Triangle* (1981), which in turn relates to Foucault's pendulum and also to the isolated prison cell of Argentinean journalist Jacobo Timmerman, whose memoirs the artist was reading at the time. Another form of the death instinct appears in numerous artists' works. Katie van Scherpenberg has created monochromes that are lethal paintings, as they were done using poisonous pigments such as vert gris. Sigmar Polke has painted *Negativwerte* (Negative values) (1982) using red Saturn, also a poisonous pigment. These are death acts in art. They tell us that painting can devour painters just as Saturn devoured his own children.

Scherpenberg's inscription of pure pigment, like natural monochromes, onto gardens and beaches is related to her experience of living on an island in the Amazon delta, where, as the artist recalls, the flow of water was like a moving painting. The difference inscribed in nature is here completely harmonious. In the XXIV Bienal de São Paulo, two installations were actual white monochromes: General Idea's *Fin de siècle*, made with styrofoam "ice," and Olafur Eliasson's space in actual ice, like a frozen water mirror, which extended to the outside of the building, bringing "freezing" temperatures to the tropics. The sense of a place is extremely important for such artists. In the field of contemporary thought, "art is the critical model of art" that questions society as one of its contents, and, implicitly, as lack. The artist's attitude model is to create knowledge in the friction field between art and society. Departing from the fact that the monochrome is a reduction to the essential, Cildo Meireles shifts toward the excess of color in *Desvio para o vermelho* (Red shift) (1967–1984).[39] *Impregnação* (Impregnation) (fig. 10), the installation's first setting, apparently draws Meireles closer to Yves Klein's economy. However, Meireles approaches the maneuvers of capital, the encounter between exchange value and utility value, symbolic value and real value. As an inflationary economic operation, color devours and neutralizes ideas of value. The monochrome takes an opposite course: from the notion of zero to the critical recording of history.

TRANSLATED BY VERONICA CORDEIRO

NOTES

1 Murilo Mendes, "Texto branco," in *Transístor* (Rio de Janeiro: Editora Nova Fronteira, 1980), pp. 371–372.
2 Kasimir Malevich, *Le miroir suprématiste* (Lausanne: L'Âge de l'Homme, 1997), vol. 2, pp. 97–98.
3 See Mário Pedrosa, "Vicissitudes do artista soviético," *Correio de Manhã* (Rio de Janeiro), August 28, 1966; Ferreira Gullar, *Vanguarda e Subdesenvolvimento, Ensaios sobre a Arte* (Rio de Janeiro: Civilização Brasileira, 1969); and Haroldo de Campos, "A Poesia Concreta e a Realidade Nacional," *Tendências*, no. 4, Belo Horizonte, 1962, and "Da razão antropofágica: diálogo e diferença na cultura brasileira," in *Colóquio/Letras* (Fundação Calouste Gulbenkian, Lisbon), no. 62 (July 1981).
4 Ferreira Gullar, "Teoria do não-objeto," in *Jornal do Brasil*, Suplemento dominical (Rio de Janeiro), 1960, p. 4.
5 See Yve-Alain Bois, *Painting as Model* (Cambridge, Mass.: MIT Press, 1990), p. 104.
6 Kasimir Malevich, "Du cubisme et du futurisme au suprématisme. Le nouveau réalisme picturial" (1916), in *Malévitch écrits* (Paris: Champ Libre, 1975), p. 185.
7 Bruno Duborgel, *Malévitch, la question de l'icône* (Saint-Étienne: Cierec, 1997), p. 70. He quotes A. Nakov and also analyses the relationship of Malevich's work to the transfigurative art of icons.
8 Malevich, "Le suprématisme," in *Le miroir suprématiste*, vol. 2, p. 84.
9 See Thierry de Duve, *Kant After Duchamp* (Cambridge, Mass.: MIT Press, 1996), p. 229.
10 Robert Rauschenberg and Calvin Tomkins, *The Bride and the Bachelor* (New York: Viking Press, 1974), pp. 199–200.
11 Benjamin Buchloh, "The Primary Colors for the Second Time: A Paradigm Repetition of the Neo-avant-garde," *October*, no. 37 (summer 1986), p. 45.
12 Other painters could be included in the debate. Rodchenko developed his monochromes in the 1920s. Among the white monochromes we should mention are those by Strzeminski, and, more recently, those by Ellsworth Kelly, Jasper Johns, Burri, Megert, Goepfert, Castellani, Colombo, de Vries, Girke, Bartels, Piene, Uecker, Morellet, and Milton Dacosta, as well as Opalka, in whose works the zero degree is reached. We do not include in this discussion the painted reliefs by Schoonhoven, von Graevenitz, Sérgio Camargo, and Simetti, among others.
13 See Buchloh, "The Primary Colors for the Second Time," *October*, no. 37; Thierry de Duve, "Yves Klein, or the Dead Dealer," *October*, no. 49 (1998); and de Duve, *Kant After Duchamp*.
14 Pierre Restany, "Yves Klein, le monochrome," in *La couleur seule* (Lyons, 1988), pp. 73–81.
15 Piero Manzoni, in *Azimuth 2* (1960), cited in Ursula Perucchi-Petri, *La couleur seule*, p. 88.
16 See Ferreira Gullar, *Revista crítica de arte* (Rio de Janeiro), no. 1 (1962).
17 See, for example, Hélio Oiticica's text "16 de fevereiro de 1961," in *Aspiro ae grande labirinto* (Rio de Janeiro: Rocco, 1986), p. 27.
18 Some of Clark's works using this organic line consist of planes cut out in wood and reassembled, while others have the line cut into the wood.
19 Hélio Oiticica, "Colour, Time, and Structure," *Jornal do Brasil*, Suplemento dominical (Rio de Janeiro), November 26, 1960.

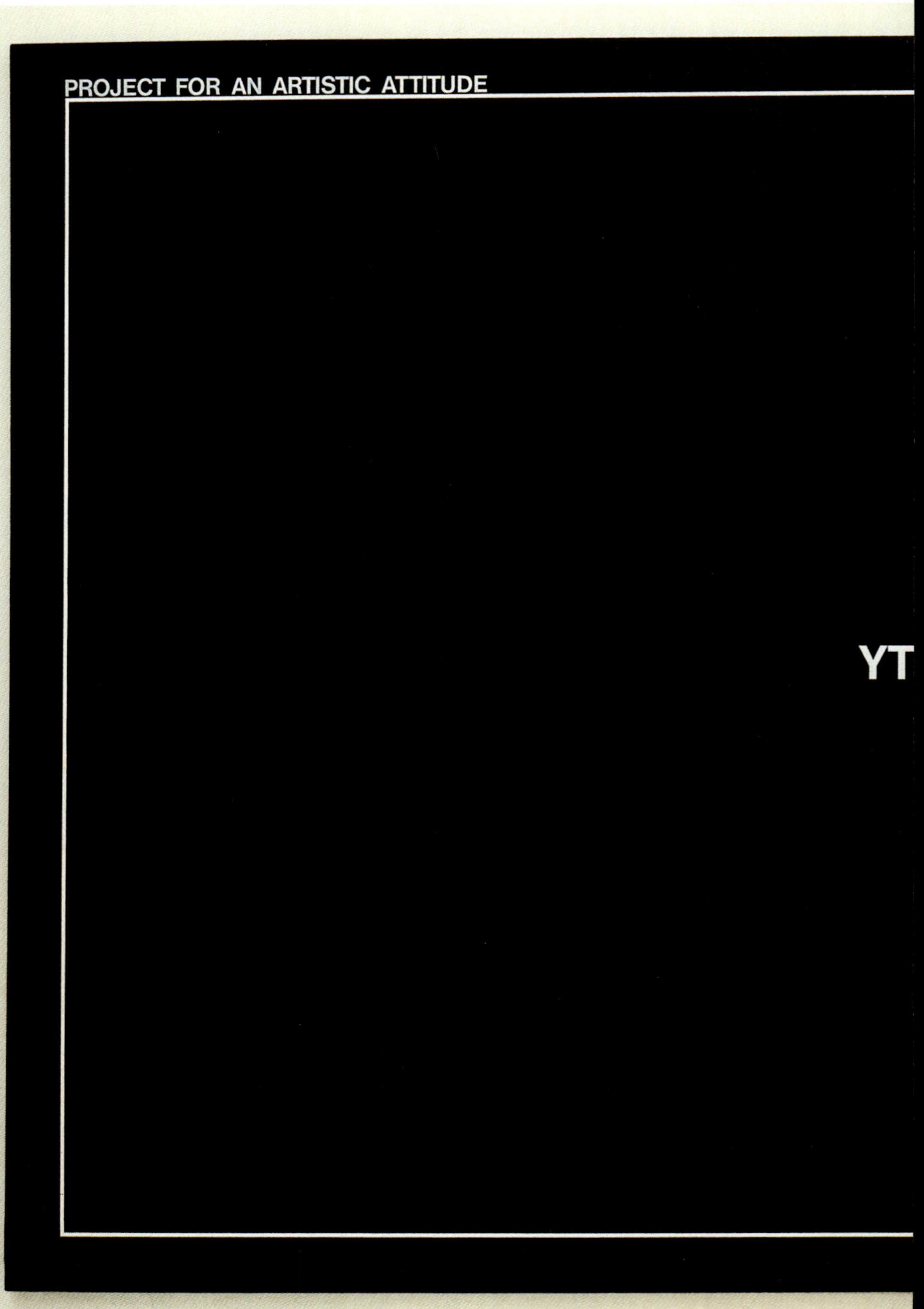

FIG. 9 Antonio Dias **Project for an Artistic Attitude** 1970 acrylic on canvas 78 ¾ x 118 ⅛ in. Courtesy the artist photo: Roberto Cecato

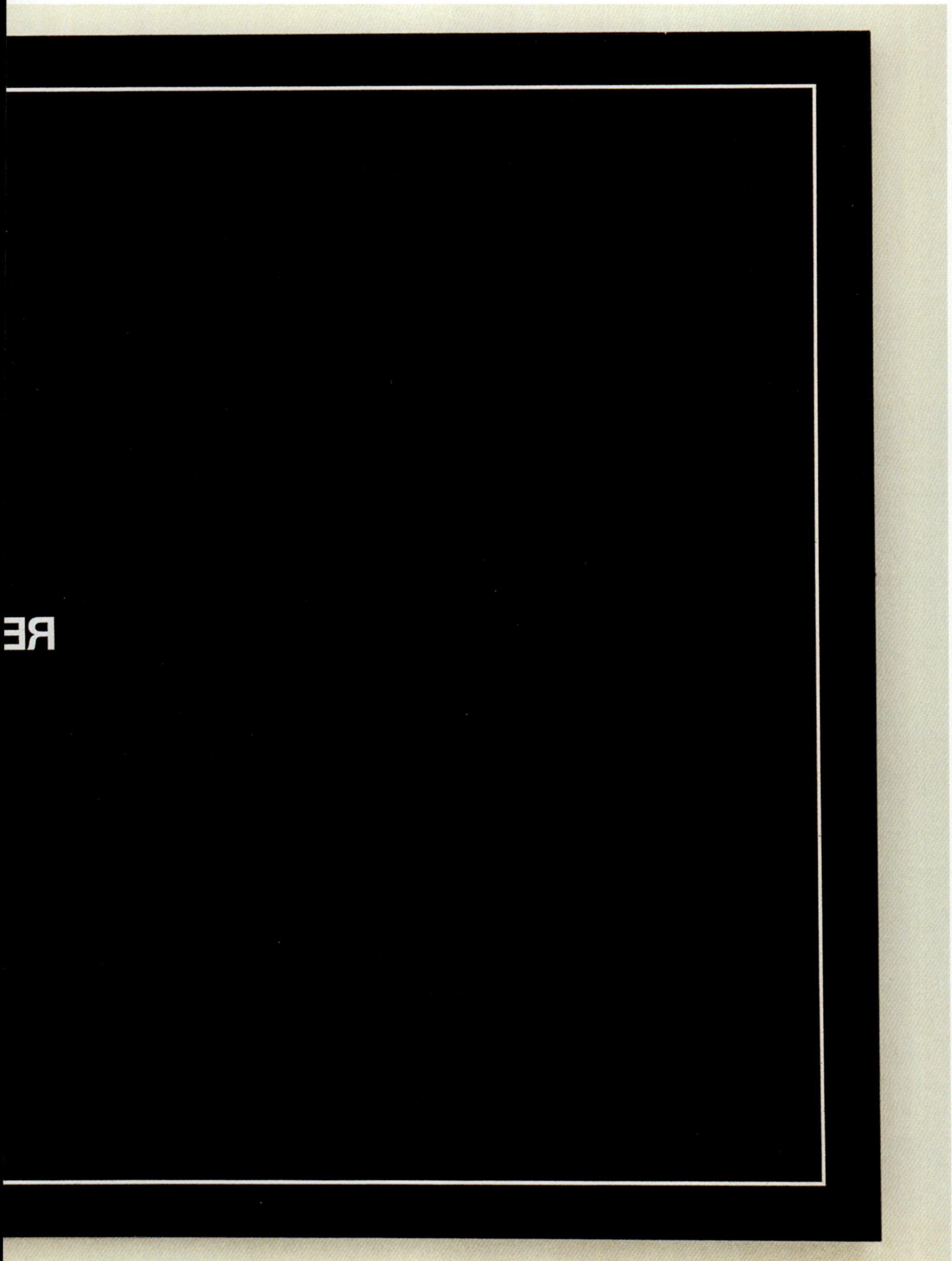

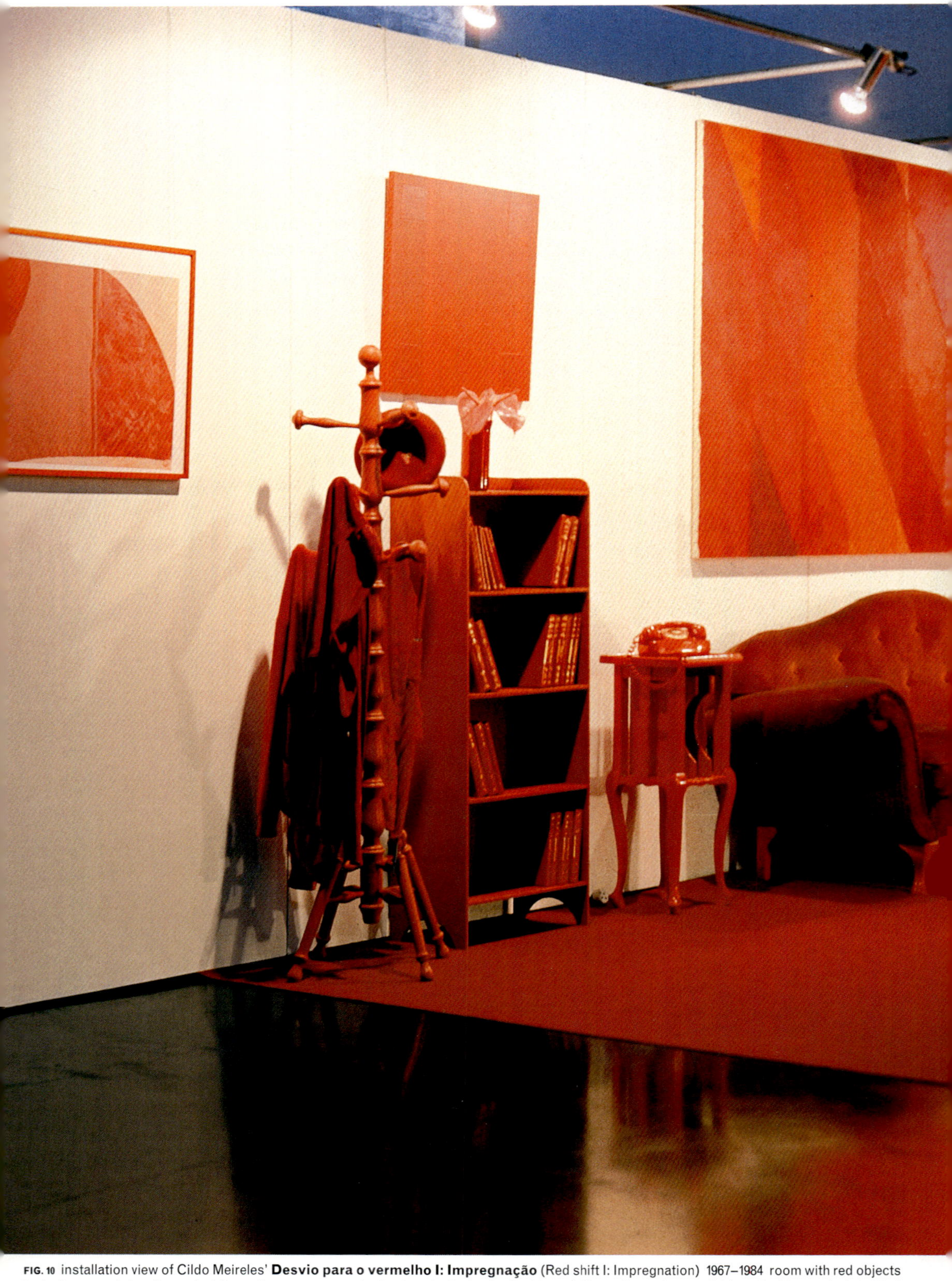

FIG. 10 installation view of Cildo Meireles' **Desvio para o vermelho I: Impregnação** (Red shift I: Impregnation) 1967–1984 room with red objects including carpet, furniture, electric appliances, ornaments, books, plants, foods, liquids, paintings dimensions variable at the Museu de Arte Moderna, Rio de Janeiro Courtesy the artist and Galerie Lelong, New York

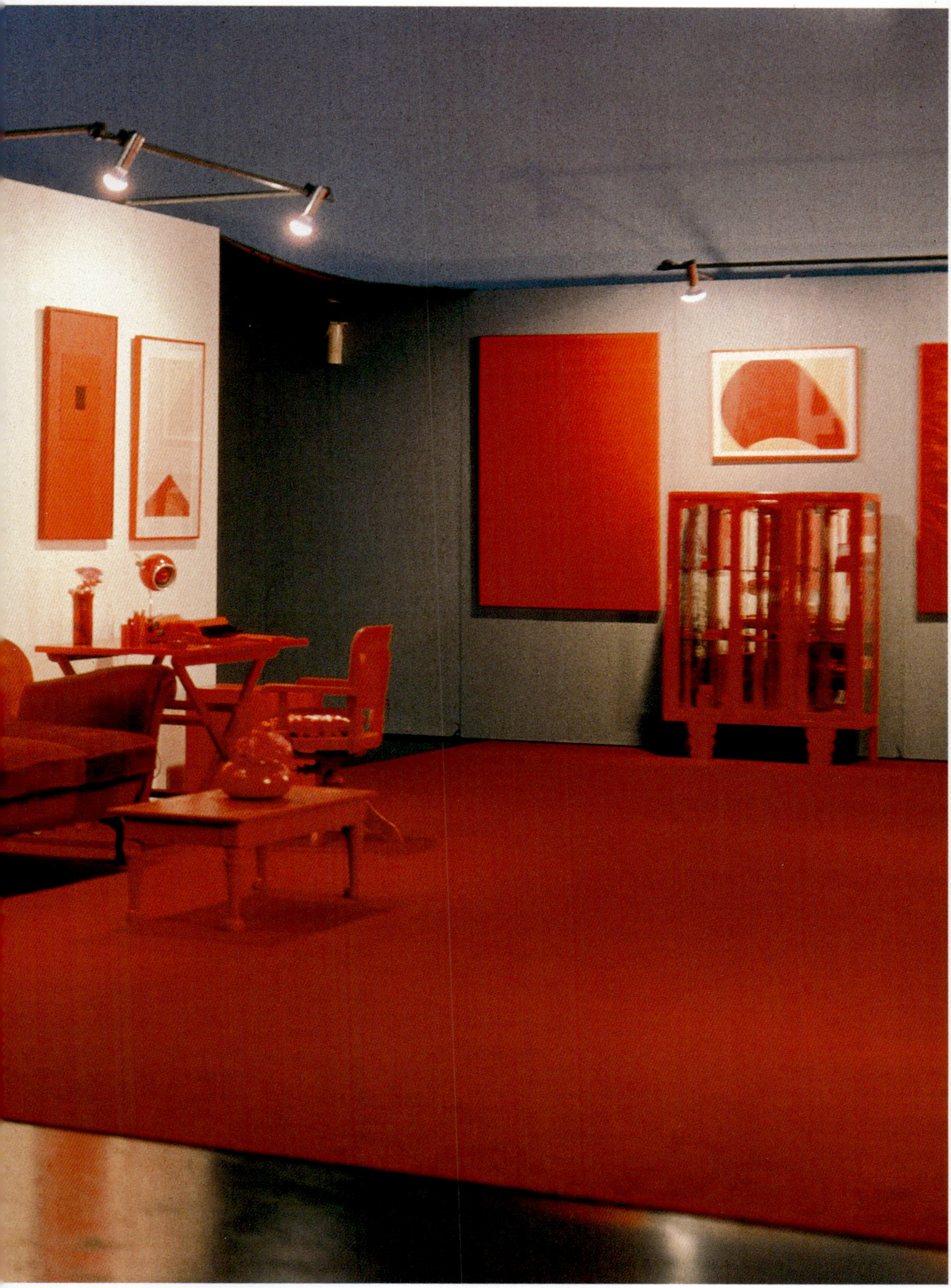

20 Hélio Oiticica, "Dezembro de 1959," in *Aspiro ae grande labirinto*, p. 16.
21 Cited in Lynn Zelevansky, "Driving Image: Yayoi Kusama in New York," *Yayoi Kusama 1959–1968* (Los Angeles: Los Angeles County Museum of Art, 1998), p. 12.
22 Ibid., p. 14.
23 Here, Murilo Mendes' *Texto branco* is parodied (see note 1 above).
24 Mário Pedrosa, "Manabu Mabe," *Jornal do Brasil* (Rio de Janeiro), October 28, 1959.
25 Ferreira Gullar, *Jornal do Brasil*, Suplemento dominical (Rio de Janeiro), 1960, p. 4.
26 Murilo Mendes, "Fontana," in *Transístor* (Rio de Janeiro: Editora Nova Fronteira, 1980), p. 376.
27 See Rosa Olivares' essay in the catalogue for the XXIV Bienal de São Paulo, *Núcleo Histórico: Antropofagia e Histórias de Canibalismos* (São Paulo: Fundação Bienal de São Paulo, 1998), pp. 508–517.
28 These interpretations by Luis Pérez Oramas were extracted from a letter to the author on August 25, 1998.
29 See Oiticica, *Aspiro ae grande labirinto*, p. 25.
30 Robert Storr, *Robert Ryman* (London: Tate Gallery and New York: The Museum of Modern Art, 1993).
31 Robert Ryman interviewed by Lynn Zelevansky on July 7, 1992, in Storr, *Robert Ryman*, p. 118.
32 Storr, *Robert Ryman*, p. 16.
33 Robert Ryman interviewed by Lynn Zelevansky, p. 118.
34 "An Interview with Byron Kim," *Glenn Ligon un/becoming* (Philadelphia: Institute of Contemporary Art, 1997), p. 54.
35 Pierre Restany, *Yves Klein, le monochrome* (Paris: Hachette, 1974), p. 98.
36 Sidra Stich, *Yves Klein* (Stuttgart: Cantz, 1994), p. 180.
37 Yves Klein, note in his journal (1957), cited in Stich, *Yves Klein*, p. 180.
38 Yves Klein, *Zéro* (1973), p. 88.
39 *Desvio para o vermelho* was exhibited in the XXIV Bienal de São Paulo. Previous monochromatic red installations created in Brazil include *Rio Vermelho* (1983) and *Caveat* (1984) by Scherpenberg. Meireles has created monochromatic installations using the other two primary colors: *Fontes* (Yellow), shown at *documenta IX*, Kassel (1992), and *Marulhos* (Blue), exhibited at the Second Johannesburg Biennial (1997).

Hélio Oiticica (1937–1980) was an artist and philosopher central to the Brazilian avant-garde in the 1960s and 1970s and his work is included in *Painting at the Edge of the World*. Oiticica's critical writings played a major role in the development and theory of the Neo-Concretist movement. The following piece, originally published in the *Jornal do Brasil* (Rio de Janeiro), November 26, 1960, was translated for the catalogue accompanying the exhibition *Hélio Oiticica*, organized by the Galerie nationale du Jeu de Paume, Paris, and the Witte de With Center for Contemporary Art, Rotterdam (1992) and is used with the permission of Projeto Hélio Oiticica.

Hélio Oiticica
Colour, Time, and Structure
1960

With the sense of colour-time, the transformation of structure became essential. Already, it was no longer possible to use the plane, that old-fashioned element of representation, even when virtualized, because of its "a priori" connotation of a surface to be painted. Structure rotates, then, in space, becoming itself also temporal: "structure time." Structure and colour are inseparable here, as are time and space, and the fusion of these four elements, which I consider dimensions of a single phenomenon, comes about in the work.

Dimensions: Colour, Structure, Space, Time
It is not an "interlocking" of these elements which takes place here, but a fusion, which exists already from the first creative moment; fusion, not juxtaposition. "Fusion" is organic, whereas juxtaposition implies a profoundly analytical dispersal of elements.

Colour
To pigment-based colour, material and opaque by itself, I attempt to give the sense of light. The sense of light can be given to every primary colour, and other colours derived from them, as well as to white and to grey; however, for this experience one must give pre-eminence to those colours most open to light: colour-light: white, yellow, orange, red-light.

White is the ideal colour-light, the synthesis-light of all colours. It is the most static, favouring silent, dense, metaphysical duration. The meeting of two different whites occurs in a muffled way, one having more whiteness, and the other, naturally, more opaqueness, tending to a greyish tone. Grey is, therefore, little used, because it is already born from this unevenness of luminosity between one white and another. White, however, does not lose its sense in this unevenness and, for this reason, there remains for grey a role in another sense, which I will speak of when I come to this colour. The whites which confront each other are pure, without mixture, hence also their difference from a grey neutrality.

Yellow, contrary to white, is the least synthetic, possessing a strong optical pulsation and tending toward real space, detaching itself from the material structure, and expanding itself. Its tendency is toward the sign, in a deeper sense, and toward the optical signal, in a superficial sense. It is necessary to note that the meaning of the signal does not matter here, since coloured structures function organically, in a fusion of elements, and are a separate organism from the physical world, from the surrounding space-world. The meaning of the signal would be that of a return to the real world, being, thus, a trivial experience, consisting only of the signalizing and virtualizing of real space. The meaning of the signal, here, is one of the internal direction, for the structure and in relation to its elements, the sign being its profound, non-optical, temporal expression. Contrary to white, yellow also resembles a more physical light, more closely related to earthly light. The important thing here is the temporal light sense of colour; otherwise it would still be a representation of light.

Orange is a median colour par excellence, not only in relation to yellow and red, but in the spectrum of colours: its spectrum is grey. It possesses its own characteristics which distinguish it from dark-yolk-yellow and red-light. Its possibilities still remain to be explored within this experiment. Red-light distinguishes itself from blood-red, which is darker, and possesses special characteristics within this experiment. It is neither light-red nor sanguineous vibrant-red, but a more purified red, luminous without arriving at orange since it possesses qualities of red. For this very reason, in the spectrum, it is found in the category of dark colours; but pigmentarily it is hot and open to light. It possesses a grave, cavernous sense of dense light.

The other derivative and primary colours: blue, green, violet, purple, and grey, can be intensified toward light, but are by nature opaque colours, closed to light, except grey, which is characterized by its neutrality in relation to light. I will not deal with these colours now, since they harbour more complex relations, yet to be explored. Up to now, we have only looked at the relation between colours of the same quality, in the sense of light. The colour-light of various qualities has not been jointly explored, since this will depend on a slow development of colour and structure.

Structure

The development of structure occurs to the extent to which colour, transformed into colour-light and having found its own time, reveals structure in its interior, leaving it bare. Since colour is colour-time, it would be consistent for structure to be equivalent, to become "structure time." Space is indispensable as a dimension of the work, but, by the fact of already existing in itself, it does not pose a problem; the problem, here, is the inclusion of time in the structural genesis of the work. The secular surface of the plane, upon which a space of representation was built, is shorn of all representational reference by the fact that the colour planes enter from the outside until they meet at a certain line. Thus, the plane is broken virtually, but continues to exist as an "a priori" support. Afterwards, the rectangle is broken, since the planes which before adjoined one another now begin to slide organically. The wall does not serve here as background, but as extraneous, unlimited space, though necessary to the vision of the work. The work is closed within itself as an organic whole, instead of sliding over the wall, or superimposing itself upon it. Structure is then carried into space, rotating 180 degrees about itself, this being the definitive step toward the meeting of its temporality with that of colour; here the spectator does not see only one side, in static contemplation, but tends toward action going around, completing its orbit, in a pluridimensional perception of the work. From then on, development occurs in the direction of appreciating all positions of vision and the research into the dimensions of the work: colour, structure, space, and time.

Time

Colour and structure having arrived at purity, at the primary creative state—static par excellence—of non-representation, it was necessary for them to become independent, possessing their own laws. Then the concept of time emerges as the primordial factor of the work. But time, here, is an active element: duration. In representational painting, the sense of space was contemplative, and that of time, mechanical. Space was of a kind which represented fictional space on the canvas, the canvas worked as a window, a field of representation of real space. Time, then, was simply mechanical: the time interval between one figure and another, or of the relation between the figure and perspectival space; in any case, it was the time of figures in a three-dimensional space, which was made two-dimensional on the canvas. Well, from the moment that the plane of the canvas began to function actively, the sense of time necessarily entered as the principal new factor of non-representation.

There then emerges the concept of the "non-object"—a term invented and theorized by Ferreira Gullar,[1] a more appropriate term than "picture"—since the structure is no longer one-sided like a picture, but pluridimensional. In the work of art, however, time takes on a special meaning, different from the meanings which it has in other branches of knowledge; it has close ties with philosophy and the laws of perception, but what characterizes time in the work of art is its symbolic signification of man's inner relation to the world, an existential relation.

Faced with the non-object, man no longer meditates through static contemplation, but finds his living time as he becomes involved, in a univocal relationship, with the time of the work. Here he is, even closer to "pure vitality" than Mondrian envisaged. Man lives the polarities of his own cosmic destiny. He is not only metaphysical, but rather, cosmic, the beginning and the end.

Space

As we already saw, the concept of space also changes with the development of painting, and it would be tedious to trace this development here. Let us start with Mondrian, for whom space was static; not symmetrically static, but static relative to representational space. In opposition to the "dynamism" of futurism, which was an "inside-the-canvas" dynamism, Mondrian's static-dynamic is the immobilization of this inside-the-canvas and the virtual dynamization of its horizontal-vertical structure. Mondrian does not conceive time; his space is still that of representation. The concretists still conceive time as mechanical and in this sense—Ferreira Gullar put it well—they take a step backwards.

In their intellectual and analytic conception, space cannot take on a temporal vitality and retains residues of representation.

However, it is not my intention to conduct a historical overview of concrete art, but to show the difference between the "non-object" and a typical "concrete" work. While the first is dynamic, temporal, the other is static, analytical. To these four elements, which I call dimensions: colour, time, structure, and space, I would add one more which, without being a fundamental dimension, is a global expression, born of the unity of the work and of its significance: infinite dimension, not in the sense that the work could dissolve to infinitude, but in the sense of unlimitedness, of "non-particularity," which exists in the relation between full and empty, different colour levels, spatial direction, temporal duration, etc. At present, I am pondering on two parallel directions, which are taken in the work and which complement each other: one, of an architectural kind, and the other of a musical kind, and the relations between them. The architectural sense appears most accentuated in the "maquettes" and in the "large paintings." The musical sense, in the *Equali* or in the *Nuclei*. The first *Equali* is composed of five pieces in space (equal squares), but their relationship is not "sculptural" because of the fact of being in space; it is more like an architectural relationship. But where this truly manifests itself is in the "large paintings" and in the "maquettes." The predominant relationship in the *Equali* is musical, not because the pieces generate counterpoint or eurythmics, akin to music, or have relations of this kind with it: musicality is not "lent" to the work, but rather is born from its essence. In reality, it is very close to the essence of music. In the *Grand Nucleus*, the parts are not equal and the relationship is more complex, in fact unforeseen. Since the idea occurs in three dimensional space, it is tempting to associate it with sculpture, but this association is, upon further analysis, superficial, and can only trivialize the experience. It would be more accurate, though still superficial, to speak of "painting in space." In the "large paintings" and "maquettes," the architectural relation shows itself as predominant and evident, by virtue of the appearance here of the "human scale." The "large paintings" stand on the floor and are 1.70 metres high, enough to envelop us in their life-experience, and the "maquettes" are true pieces of architecture, some in a labyrinthine sense, others with rotating panels. What matters, in these "maquettes," is the "simultaneity" (musical element) of the colours between themselves, as the spectator goes around and becomes involved in its structure. It is then noticeable that, ever since the first "non-object" launched into space, a tendency already showed itself toward a "life-experience of colour," neither totally contemplative, nor totally organic, but cosmic. What matters is not the mathematical or rhythmical relationship of colour, or one measured by physical processes, but colour's value. A pure orange is orange, but if placed in relation to other colours, it will be a light-red or dark-yellow, or another shade of orange; its sense changes according to the structure which contains it, and its value, born of the intuitive dialogue of the artist with the work, in its genesis, varies intimately from work to work. Colour is, therefore, value, as are the other elements of the work: vehicle for "life-experiences," of all kinds (life-experience, here, in an all-encompassing, not vitalist, sense of the word). The genesis of the work of art is to such a degree connected to and experienced by the artist that it is no longer possible to separate matter from spirit, because, as Merleau Ponty points out, matter and spirit are dialectics of a single phenomenon. The artist's guiding and creative element is intuition; as Klee once said, "In the final analysis the work of art is intuition, and intuition cannot be surpassed."

NOTES

1 Ferreira Gullar, Brazilian poet, art critic, and author of the *Manifesto Neoconcreto* (1959).

Andrew Blauvelt is Design Director at the Walker Art Center in Minneapolis. As a practicing graphic designer he has received numerous professional awards and has published and exhibited widely. A critic and historian, Blauvelt has authored essays and guest-edited special issues on design and culture for many publications, including *Emigré*, *Visible Language*, *Design Book Review*, *American Center for Design Journal*, and *Eye*. He is currently preparing an upcoming exhibition on contemporary design and everyday life for the Walker Art Center.

No Visible Means of Support

Andrew Blauvelt

"[A]t root paintings . . . could not possibly exist in their form up to the present without the psychological and physical definition of space given to them by architecture." — Allan Kaprow[1]

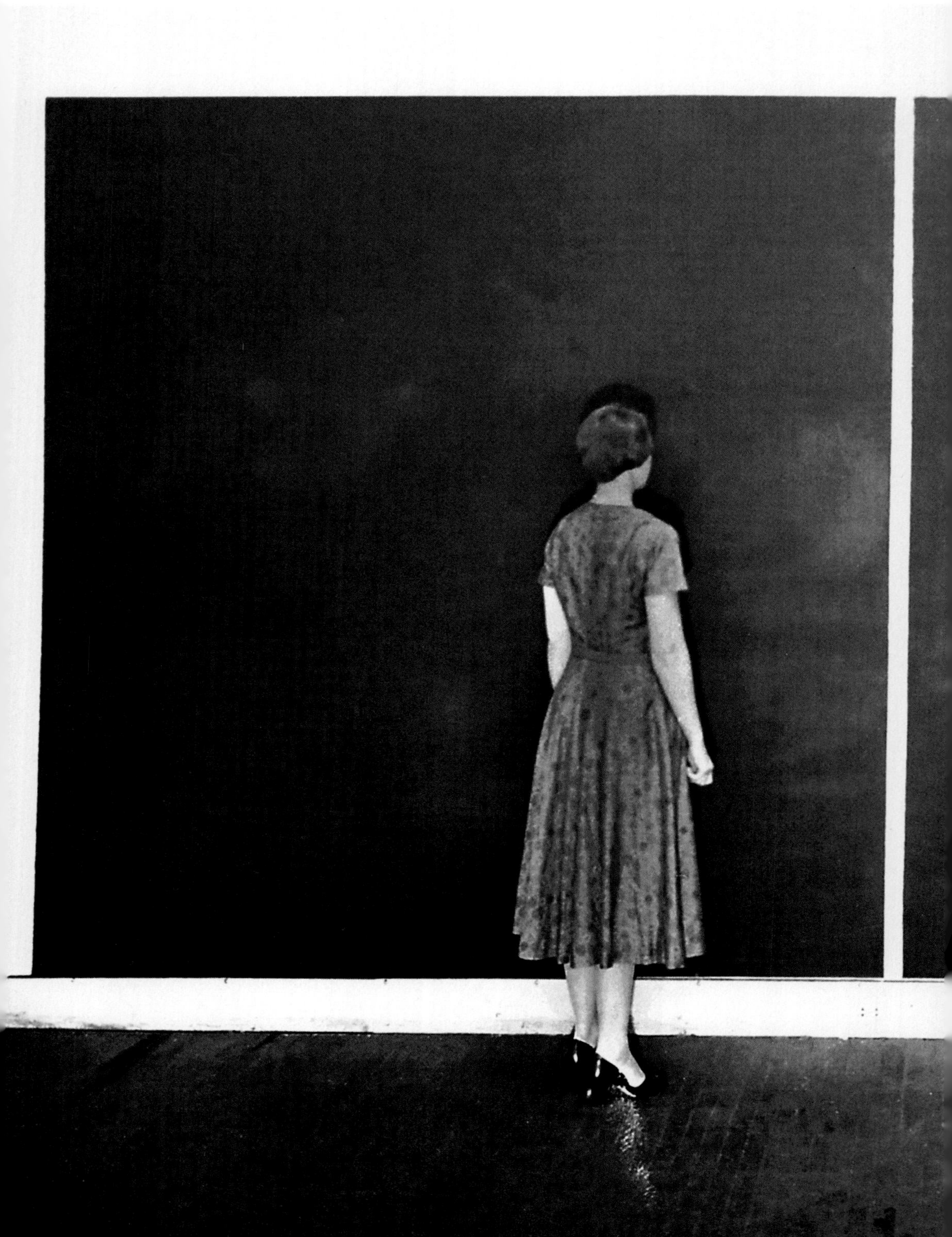

FIG. 1 installation view of Barnett Newman's **Cathedra** (1951) in Newman's studio on Front Street, New York 1958 © Peter A. Juley & Son Collection, National Museum of American Art, Smithsonian Institution, Washington, D.C. © 2001 Barnett Newman Foundation / Artists Rights Society (ARS), New York

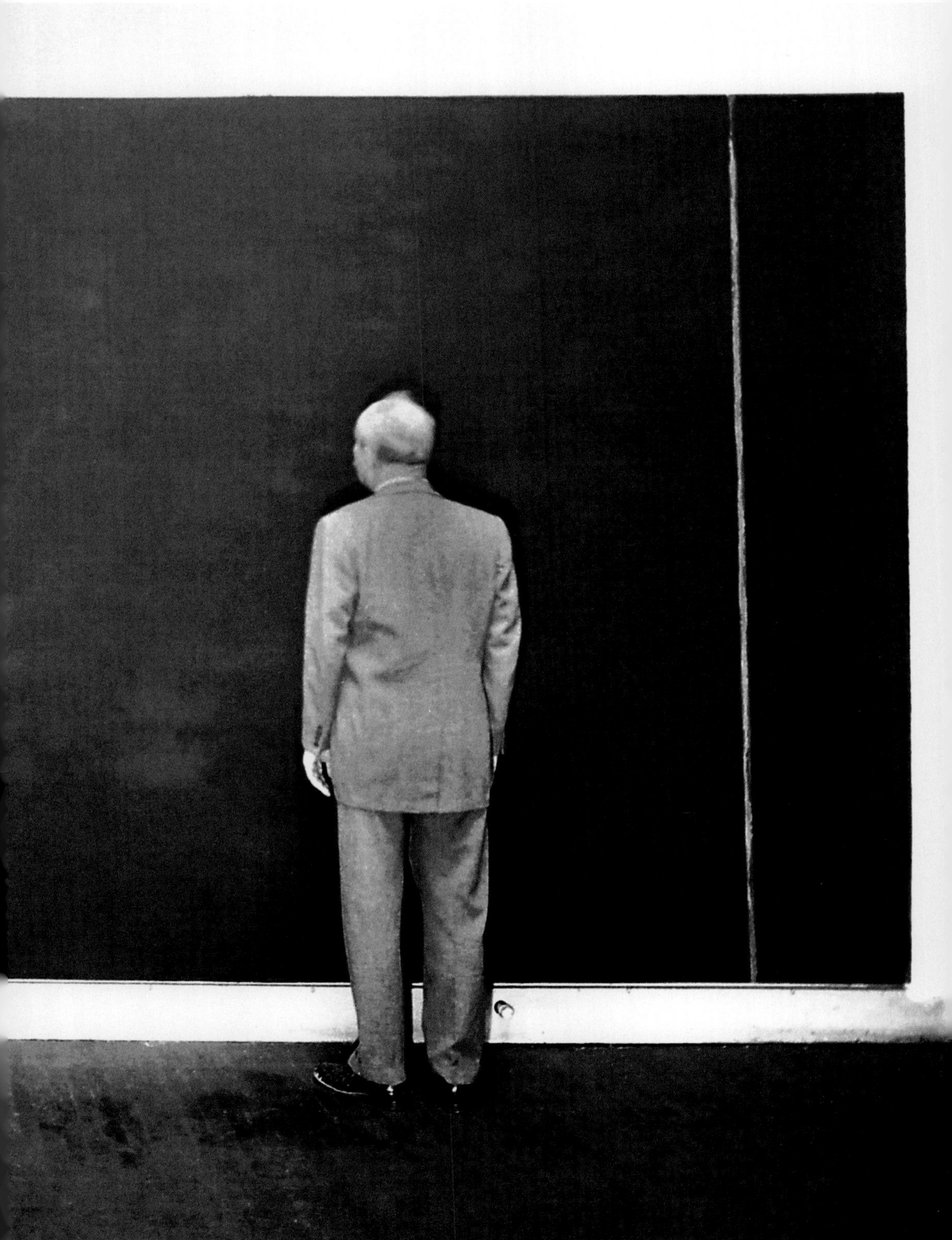

Historically, and at a basic physical level, painting and architecture are joined in the connection to shared surfaces, as in frescoes and murals that adorn walls, floors, and ceilings. In these instances painting acts as a supplement or complement to architecture, providing both decorative ornament and symbolic value to built structures. The overall effect of most murals is to efface the architectural limit of the surfaces they cover. In so doing, the mural—which is created at the human scale of architecture—replaces the perception of actual space with an imagined one. The development of easel painting and its status as an autonomous and therefore portable commodity allowed it to escape its historically subordinate role to architecture and the imposed limits of a specific site. No longer physically connected to architectural space, painting could develop independently. This liberation, however, engendered another kind of dependency: as painting migrated from wall to canvas, it would increasingly take architecture as its subject rather than merely its support.

The Renaissance invention of perspective redefined the space of painting by inscribing an architectural presence. As Victor Burgin explains, "Perspective provided, quite literally, the 'common ground' on which the identification of architectural space with corporeal space could 'take place.' In the Renaissance, the inaugural act in constructing a painting was to lay out the horizontal plane that united the illusory space of the image with the real space of the viewer."[2] The position of the viewer figures prominently in the shift from mural to easel painting. Because the mural conforms to greater architectural limits, its illusionism is dependent on distanced viewing, while easel painting, with its clearly perceived limit of the frame, quickly locates and fixes the viewer in relationship to its image. As Brian O'Doherty (a.k.a. Patrick Ireland) observes in his essay "Inside the White Cube," the miniaturization of the easel painting enhances rather than detracts from the illusion, and while the space implied in a mural is often rather shallow, it rapidly dissolves upon closer examination as the image exceeds the peripheral limits of the viewer's field of vision. The device of the picture frame ensures "that there is no suggestion that the space within the picture is continuous with the space outside it."[3]

Within the Western tradition, late nineteenth- and early twentieth-century developments in painting (Impressionism, Post-Impressionism, Cubism, etc.) mark the disintegration of perspective's "commonsensical" spatial illusionism, and with it painting's classical relationship to architecture. Although the hegemony of perspective was ultimately broken, the continued domination of easel painting remained largely unchallenged. Indeed, it was not until the late 1940s and 1950s that the "crisis" of easel painting was inaugurated through the large-scale canvases of Abstract Expressionism. During this period the size of paintings would increase, occupying first entire walls and eventually whole rooms in galleries and museums (fig. 1). As easel painting approached the scale of architecture, one might expect that the mural would reappear as a means of support. The fact that it did not underscores arguments that late-modernist easel painting is the logical product for late-capitalist consumption: big pictures for big collectors that require bigger spaces for exhibition.[4]

In the wake of modernism, one of the ways in which to speak of architecture and painting was to affirm a new common ground based on the principles of a shared visual language. In his book *Painting Toward Architecture*, Henry-Russell Hitchcock, who co-curated the famous International Style exhibition with Philip Johnson at the Museum of Modern Art in 1932, chronicles the influence of modern painting on architecture at mid-century. Hitchcock concludes that "it is the abstract aspects of various kinds of modern painting which belong to the world of the architect as a visual artist."[5] Hitchcock rereads architecture not as particular and concrete but as abstract, a principle that would allow both disciplines to be understood in relationship to each other through the plasticity of form—by reducing the complexities of each practice to an elemental, yet common, visual vocabulary. Writing in 1948, Hitchcock states, "It was . . . some twenty-five years ago, that abstract painting reached its climax and played a major role in crystallizing the visual character of modern architecture."[6] Exactly twenty-five years earlier it was Piet Mondrian who, in his essay "Is Painting Inferior to Architecture?" adopted purification, not simply abstraction, as an ultimate goal and concluded that:

> **The new aesthetic for architecture is that of the new painting. Architecture that is now purifying itself is prepared to achieve the same consequences that painting realized in Neo-Plasticism after the purifying process of Futurism and Cubism. Through the unity of the new aesthetic, architecture and painting can together form one art and can dissolve into each other.**[7]

This unity and synthesis remained elusive however, with the possible exceptions of Oud's Café de Unie in Rotterdam (1925) and the Rietveld Schroeder House in Utrecht (1924), both of which are cited by Hitchcock. Interestingly, Hitchcock posits the greatest promise of synthesis between the two disciplines in works situated, provocatively, in the borderline fields between painting and sculpture.

It is the dissolution of the specific properties of painting and sculpture that the Spatialists undertook, in particular Lucio Fontana, who in his "Technical Manifesto" of 1951 proclaimed, "Neither painting nor sculpture but forms, color, sound, through space. . . . We conceive synthesis as a sum of the physical elements: color, sound, movement, space, which integrate an ideal and material unity."[8] Importantly, it was Fontana who, in 1949, spatialized painting by piercing the canvas—literally cutting through, and thus undercutting, painting's promise of illusionism (fig. 2). This simple but profound action disrupted the surface of painting, opening it up to real space and at the same time underscoring the objectness of easel painting.

Projects by Hélio Oiticica, such as his *Nuclei*, can be situated in the spaces beyond painting and sculpture. Begun in 1960, the *Nuclei* consist of a series of wooden panels suspended from the ceiling parallel and perpendicular to one another, and often placed above a mirror or gravel on the floor (fig. 3). These painted panels form intricate passages through which viewers can navigate, lending the works temporal, kinesthetic, and spatial properties. In such projects, Oiticica initiates a series of spatial displacements: the dislocation of the mirror from wall to floor not only opens up new viewing possibilities for the work, but it also means that the work can no longer be experienced in the same optical field that had governed painting for centuries. In addition, the multidimensionality of these constructions denies the illusion of flatness that most paintings on canvas achieve in privileging the surface over the edge. Oiticica was careful to disassociate such projects from classification as sculpture, or even as "paintings in space."[9] Reducible neither to painting nor to sculpture, but incorporating aspects of both, the *Nuclei* instantiate the relationship between viewer and artwork in the most immediate of ways. They resist the distanced viewing associated with the sculptural object and instead become perceptual environments that embrace architectonic qualities. Oiticica designated these works as "non-objects," a term that rejects painting's status as a planar object of contemplation, a condition that he sought to transform by placing the artwork and viewer in a more dynamic relationship: "Faced with the non-object, man no longer mediates through static contemplation, but finds his living time as he becomes involved, in a univocal relationship, with the time of the work. Here he is, even closer to 'pure vitality' than Mondrian envisaged."[10]

Mondrian's universalizing synthesis and Oiticica's search for unities notwithstanding, the opening of a new space between sculpture and painting could have been predicated on a mutual refusal of both disciplines, producing an art that would not be reducible to the integration or resolution of their specific properties. However, in the 1960s the transcendent reductivism that Mondrian wrote about was supplanted by an essentialist reductivism—following critic Clement Greenberg—that understood the specificity of painting as a medium both of flatness and of opticality. Indeed, it is Greenberg's argument for an "optical third dimension" that would recuperate a spatial dimension for late-modernist painting. Art historian Rosalind Krauss relates, "No sooner had Greenberg seemed to isolate the essence of painting in flatness than he swung the axis of the field ninety degrees to the actual picture surface to place all the import of painting on the vector that connects viewer to object." Krauss continues: "'Opticality' was thus an entirely abstract, schematized version of the link that traditional perspective had formerly established between viewer and

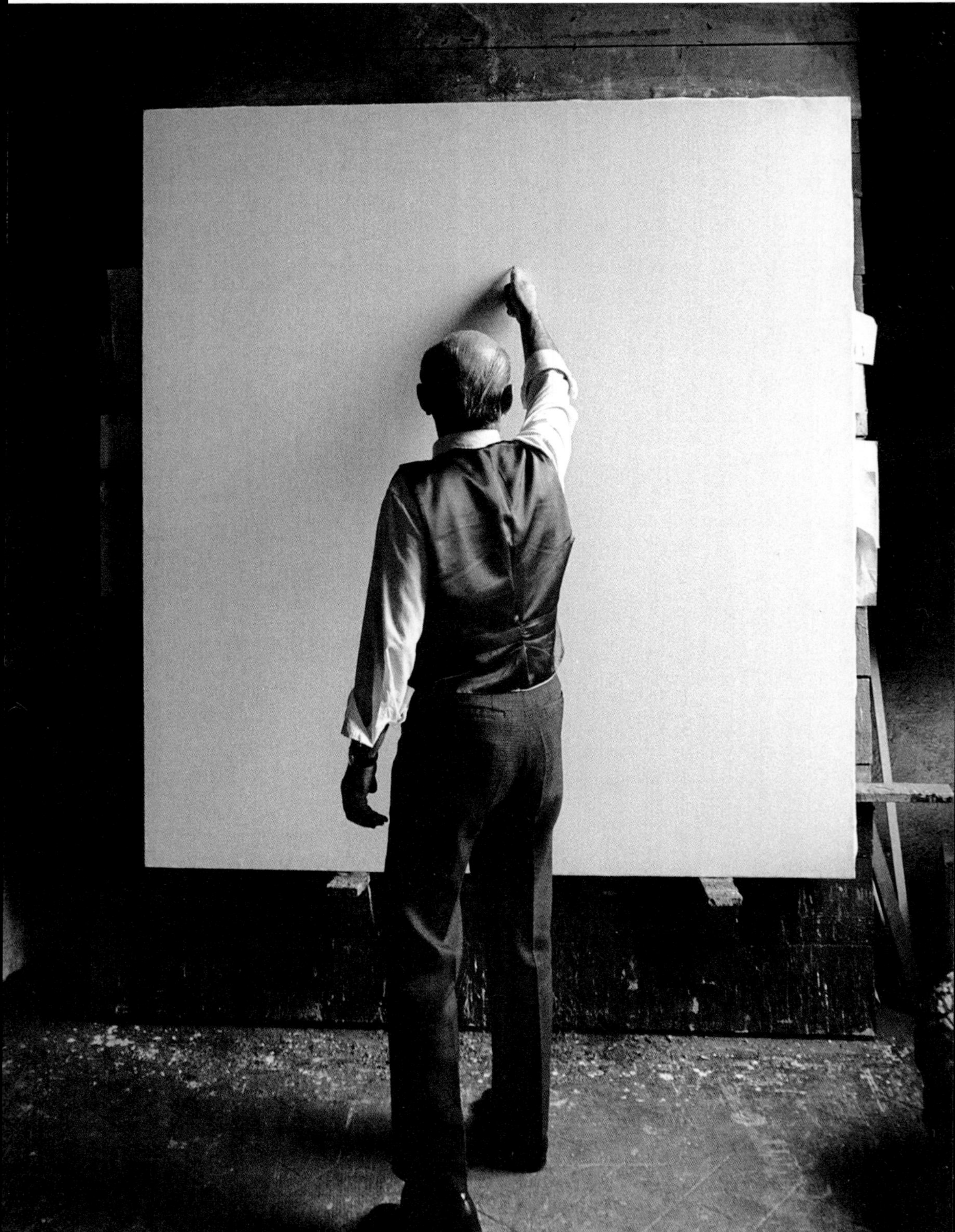

FIG. 2 Lucio Fontana in his studio making a work from the **Concetto Spaziale** (Spatial concept) series 1964 © Archivio Ugo Mulas; photos: Ugo Mulas

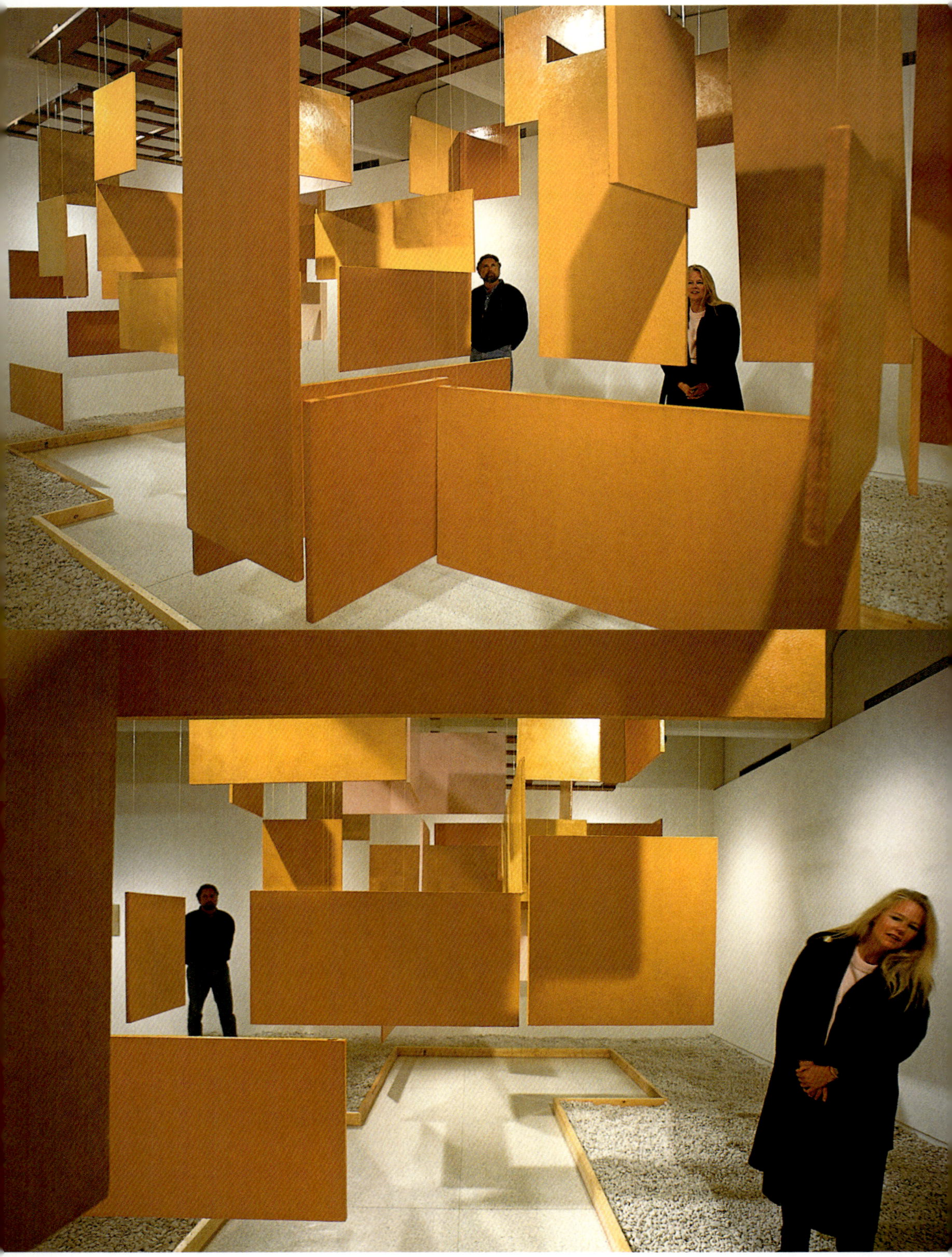

FIG. 3 Hélio Oiticica installation views of **Grand Nucleus NC 3, NC 4, NC 6 "Manifestação Ambiental 2"** 1960–1966 oil on wood dimensions variable from the exhibition **Hélio Oiticica** at the Walker Art Center, Minneapolis 1993–1994

object."[11] Not surprisingly, this drive to reduce the definition of painting to a set of characteristics with which to limit and thus differentiate it as a specific medium would foreclose an understanding of painting as intrinsically plural. To expand notions of painting beyond these delimited essences would be to acknowledge the aggregative and complex conditions that constitute painting's heterogeneity. In other words, it would not be simply enough to ask what makes a painting a painting, but rather to understand the ways in which painting differs from itself.

By the mid-1960s many artists had moved beyond the confines of the autonomous work of art and were active in much broader arenas. For example, sculpture had merged with the landscape in numerous earthwork projects, while other artists dispensed with specific mediums altogether. Donald Judd's treatise "Specific Objects" attempted to define the emergent conditions of the Minimal art object that was "neither painting nor sculpture."[12] Rejecting sculpture's anthropomorphism and painting's illusionism—two "misrecognitions" that transform the work of art into something other than what it is as an actual object—Minimalism instead embraced the existential conditions of the "three dimensional." Judd describes how Minimalism reasserts the presence of the art object in the space of its existence:

> **Three dimensions are real space. That gets rid of the problem of illusionism and of literal space, space in and around marks and colors—which is riddance of one of the most objectionable relics of European art. A work can be as powerful as it can be thought to be. Actual space is intrinsically more powerful and specific than paint on a flat surface. Obviously, anything in three dimensions can be any shape, regular or irregular, and can have any relation to the wall, floor, ceiling, room, rooms, or exterior, or none at all. Any material can be used, as is or painted.**[13]

If the Minimalist art object had shed the painterly problem of illusionism by recasting itself as simply form and material, it was inevitably reframed by the architectural container in which it was placed.

This relationship between the art object and its spatial context was taken up as one of the period's defining themes. Dan Graham, who was one of the first artists to produce reflexive architectural forms, has noted that with Minimalism the sense of composition once internal to the work of art shifted to a frame of reference beyond, and "would appear in relation to the gallery's interior architectural structure."[14] One of Minimalism's most dramatic reappraisals of the art object and the site of its exhibition occurs in Dan Flavin's light projects begun in the 1960s, which used industrially produced and commercially available fluorescent light tubes. Flavin rejected terms such as "sculpture" and "environment" to describe his work, preferring "proposal" and "situation," which were more suggestive both of artistic intentionality and of the provisional nature of his in situ projects.[15] Although Flavin did not produce sculpture or painting as such, his work did render problematic their limits. For example, an untitled work of 1966 (fig. 4) consists of four fluorescent light tubes arranged as a square and installed in the corner of the gallery. Although its form alludes to a painting and its position in a corner utilizes the converging planes of the walls to enframe a deeper space, the effect is dissipated by the intensity of the light. By extending the artwork to its environmental container, Flavin illuminates the larger system of support at work in the institutional apparatus of art.

If the picture frame had once acted as the traditional self-imposed limit for painting, the frame for new works had shifted to the spatial givens of a particular site. In this way the gallery space functions as both frame and support for the work of institutional critique. Indeed, Daniel Buren has written that the gallery is "the inescapable 'support' on which art history is painted."[16] Buren's project *Within and Beyond the Frame*, which took place at the John Weber Gallery in New York in 1973, poignantly underscored this point as its vertical-striped sheets extended out the gallery window and across the street (fig. 5). Many other artists also addressed the issue of institutional enframement: for example, Mel Bochner,

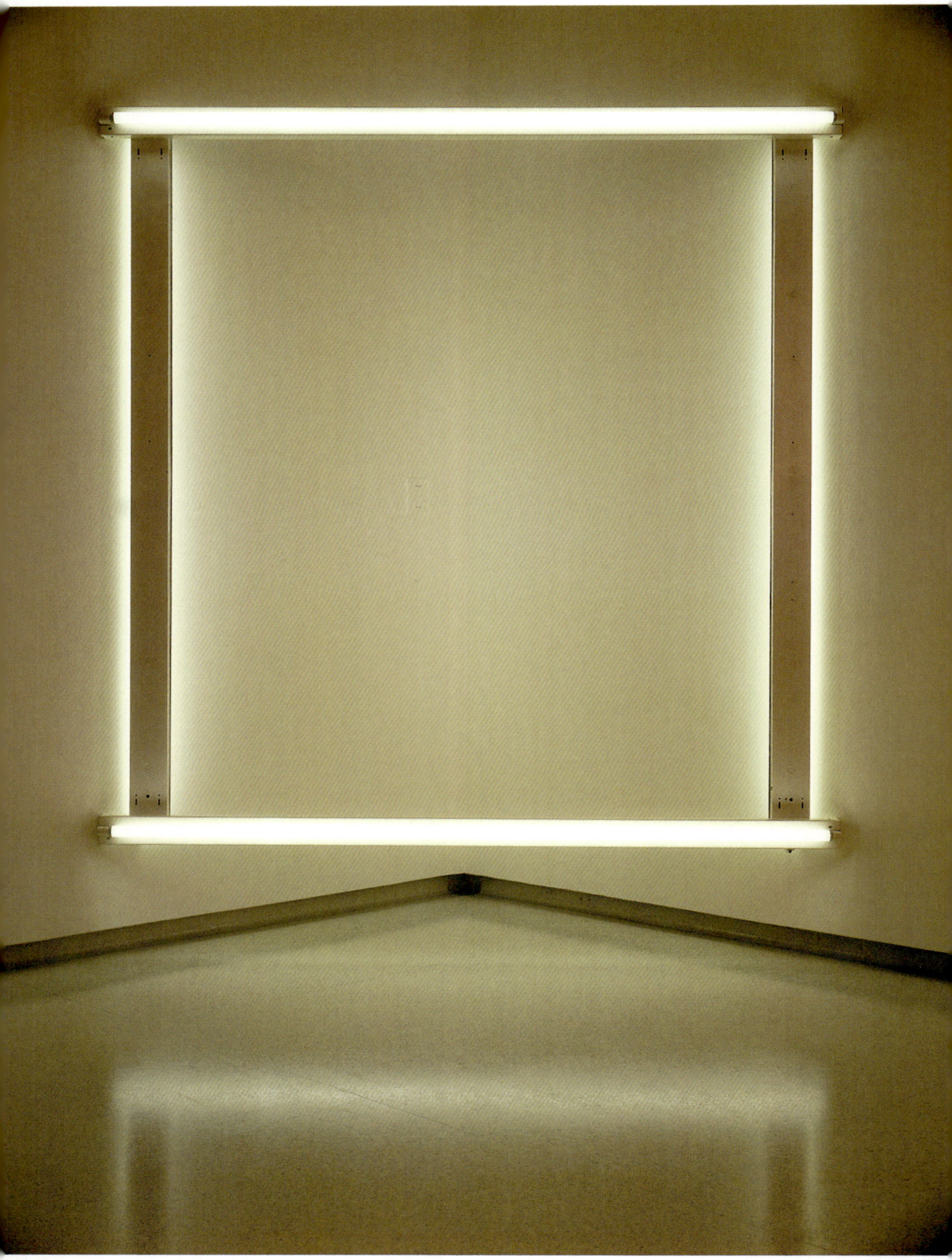

FIG. 4 Dan Flavin **untitled** 1966 fluorescent tubes and fixtures 96 x 96 x 8 in. Collection Walker Art Center, Minneapolis; Gift of the Northern States Power Company, 1969

in his *Measurement* series (1969), notated the dimensions of the gallery directly on its walls, and Lawrence Weiner's wall cutouts (1968)—literally removing portions of the gallery wall—are reminiscent of Fontana's piercing of the painted canvas.

By 1968 Sol LeWitt was also working on the wall, but to different ends. To resolve the contradiction of the easel painting's existence in space (understood as one plane in front of another), LeWitt, with his wall drawings that conformed to the preexisting conditions of the spaces they occupy, problematized the conventional components of painting by eliminating the canvas, the stretcher, and even the paint (fig. 6). LeWitt has stated that he intended to "do a work of art that was as two-dimensional as possible," adding, "it seems more natural to work directly on walls than to make a construction, to work on that, and then put the construction on the wall."[17] While one could read the trajectory of LeWitt's wall drawings as the inevitable consequence of Greenbergian "flatness," these works are notable, among other things, for their reinscription of architectural space within the body of the work. In these projects LeWitt exchanges Greenberg's notion of surface for the specific reality of the varying conditions of different walls, which ensures that each of LeWitt's wall drawings, even if repeated exactly as instructed, is in some way unique.

The wall has reentered contemporary painting, its dramatic scale theorized by some critics as a reaction to today's channels of communication, whether the competitive scale of video projection in art galleries or the building-sized screens of Times Square.[18] Perhaps the use of the wall is painting's response to contemporary art's penchant for site-specific installation art. In this scenario, the portability of easel painting is exchanged for the fixity of wall painting. Yet what remain repeatable are the performative actions of what Miwon Kwon has termed the "itinerant artist": someone who travels the world executing commissions that conform to the unique properties of a specific time and place.[19] Congruent with the logic of deterritorialization, the site has become a nonsite and it is the artist's labor and not his product that is now the portable commodity.[20]

Today, painting and architecture are mediated not through physical proximity but through the image and its technical support, the screen. Contemporary architecture has developed a material concern with "skins" or surfaces with varying degrees of transparency and opacity as well as the capacity for technological "smartness." If the modernist glass-curtain wall functioned as a sign of truthfulness—a material of revelation—the contemporary version represents a fiction, a surface for projection. What was once a window is now a screen. As critic Paul Virilio relates, "After the age of architecture-sculpture we are now in the time of cinematographic factitiousness; literally as well as figuratively, from now on *architecture is only a movie.*"[21]

If architecture is now translatable through the language of cinema, then so too must be the language of painting. Marcel Broodthaers, a progenitor of intermedia art, attempted just such a feat in his *Analyse d'une peinture* (Analysis of a painting) (1973), a 16mm color film composed almost entirely of still images taken of an amateur seascape painting purchased by the artist (see the related project, *Tableau-Bateau*, on pp. 247–249). In this film, the painting becomes the actor and painting its subject. Benjamin Buchloh, in an interview with Broodthaers, notes how the artist uses a cinematic language of painterly techniques as a meditation on the medium of painting: "One detail passes for a romantic English landscape, the other appears in the manner of paintings from the l'École de Paris, finally monochrome structures fill the canvas. It is with a historical eye that the camera makes a review."[22] One painting becomes an allegory for all painting, indeed for a history of art, just as one medium is conflated with another; in the words of Broodthaers, "You have believed to see a painting, but nevertheless you have seen a film."[23] The only action sequence occurs near the end of the film when a man appears and begins rolling up a blank canvas. As Buchloh notes, "The gesture of rolling up a canvas destined to be painted is confounded with the gesture of rolling up the same screen onto which the image has been projected. The painter's canvas and the canvas of the film have become identical."[24]

Virilio provides us with an architectonic history of the window: "The first window is the

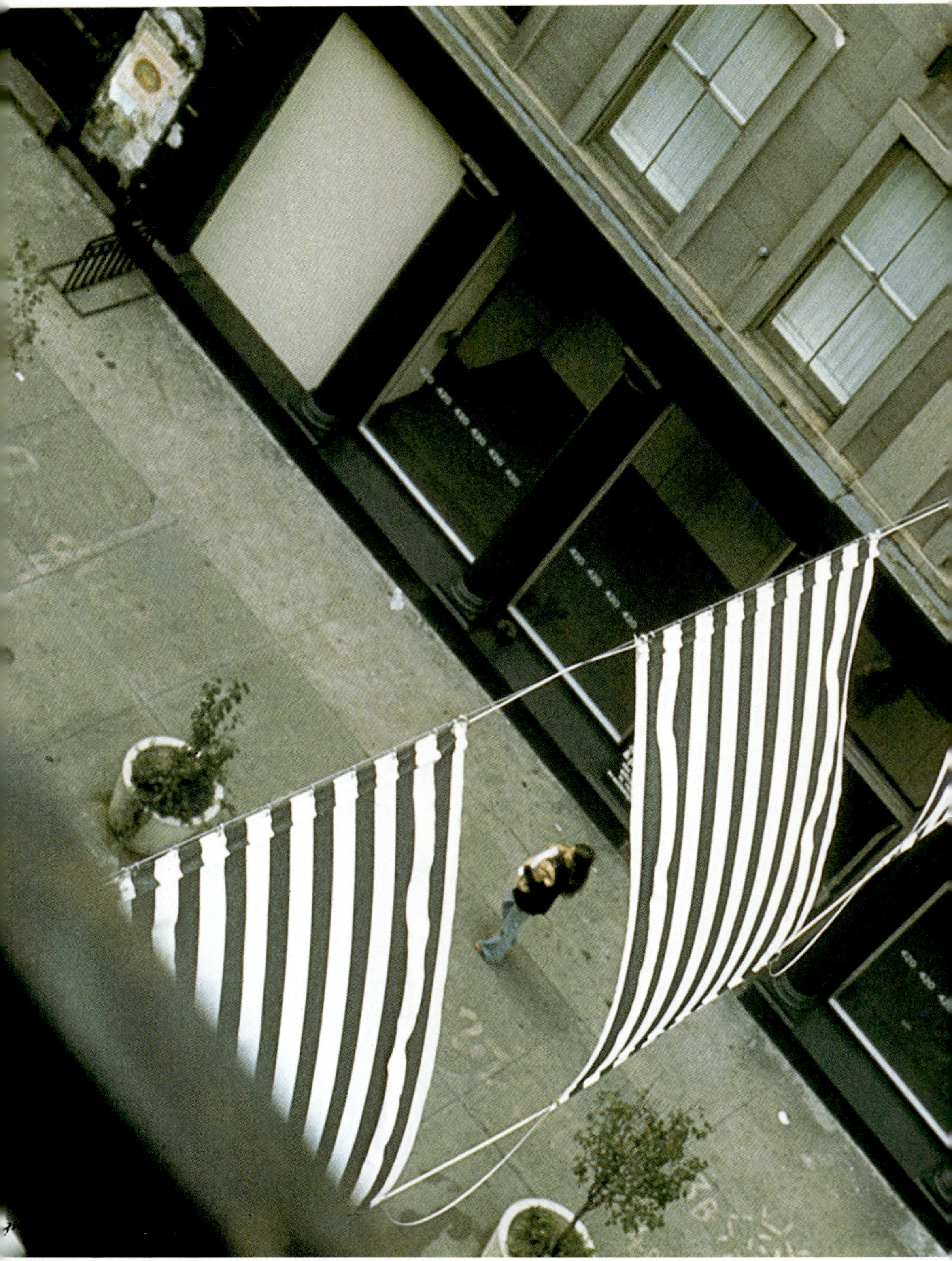

FIG. 5 Daniel Buren Photo-souvenir Daniel Buren "Within and Beyond the Frame," work in situ, October 1973, John Weber Gallery, New York detail

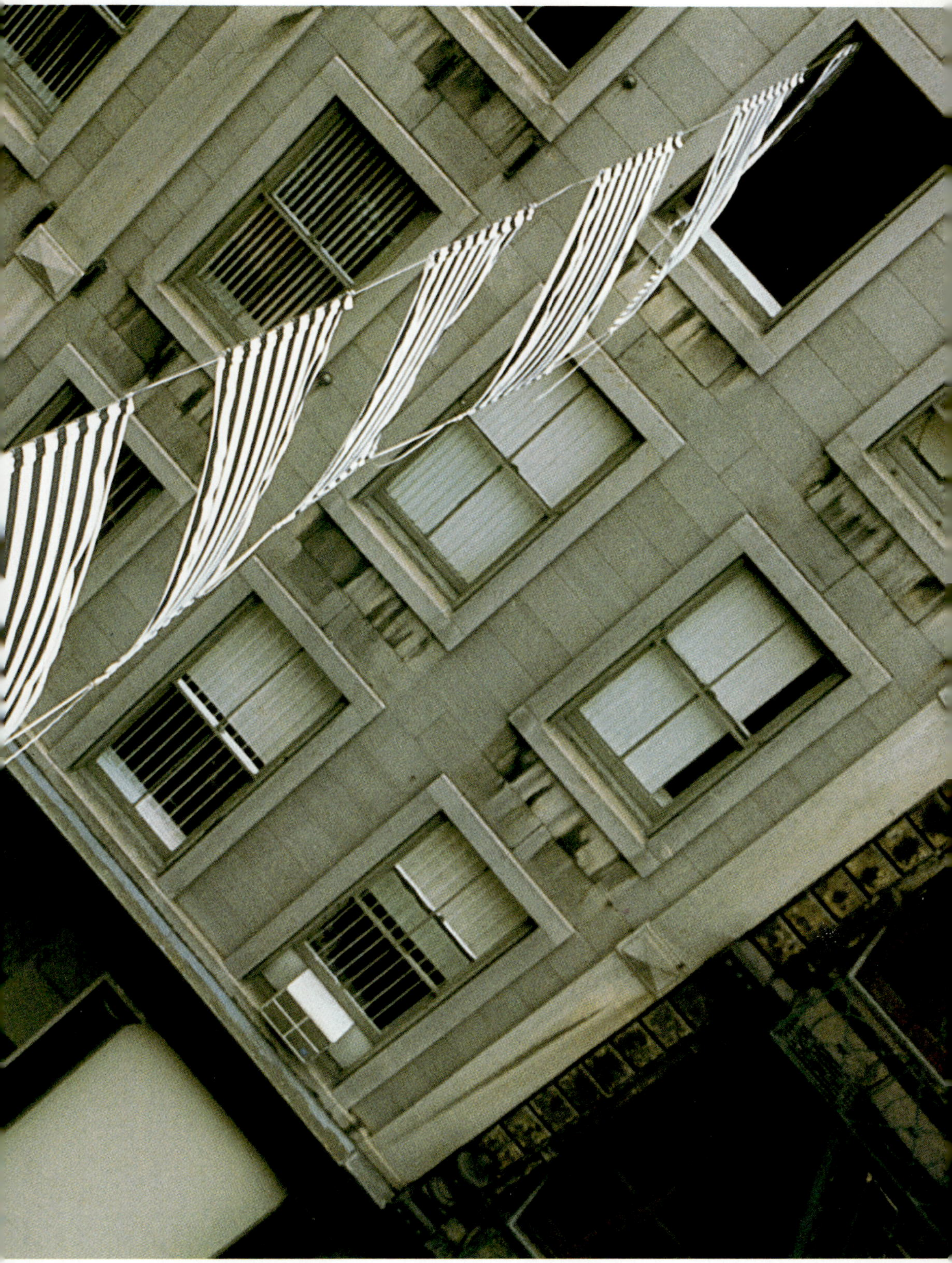

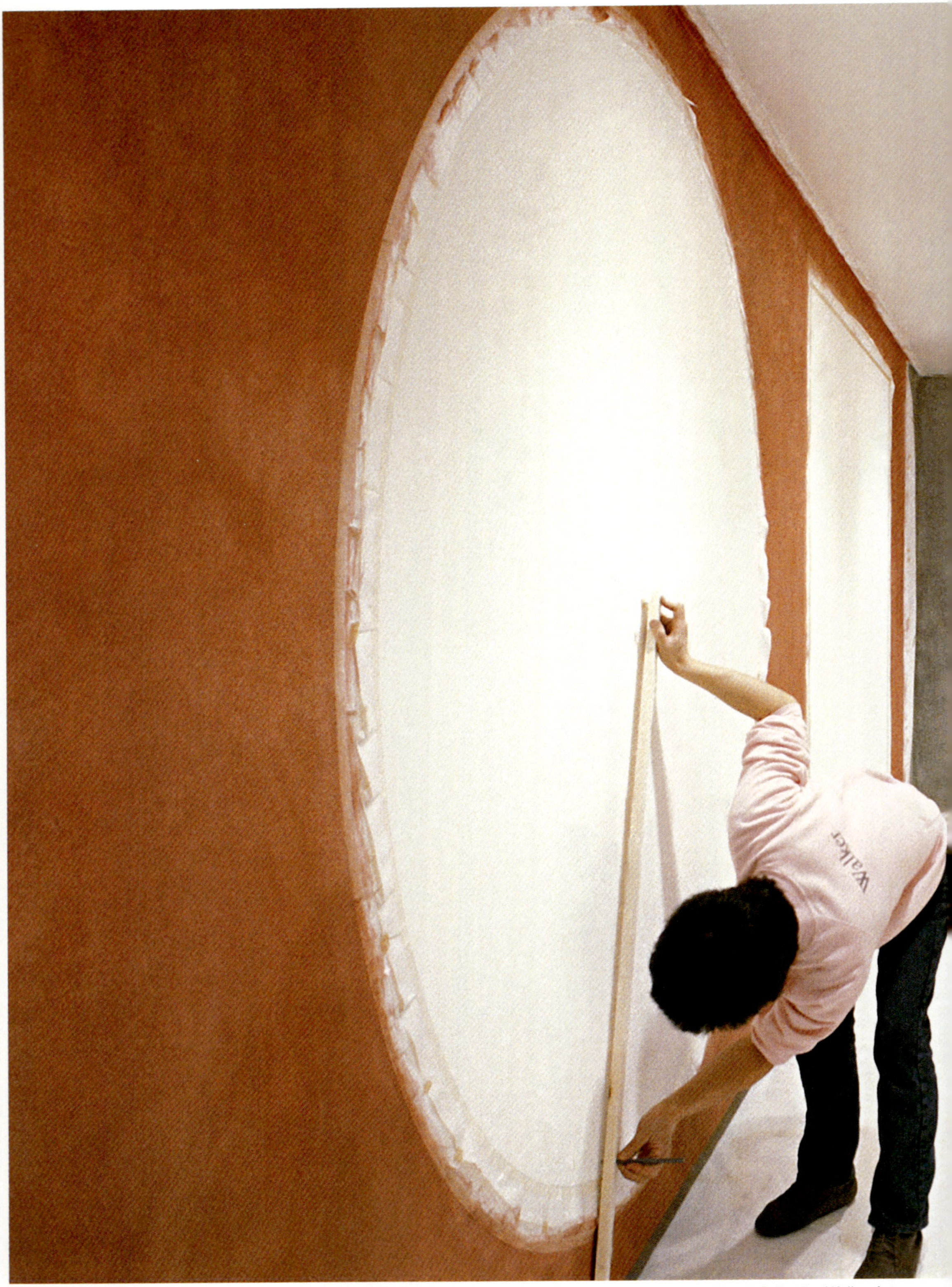

FIG. 6 installation in progress of Sol LeWitt's **Four Geometric Figures in a Room** 1984 ink, latex paint on plaster board Collection Walker Art Center, Minneapolis; Commissioned by the Art Center with funds provided by Mr. and Mrs. Julius E. Davis, 1984

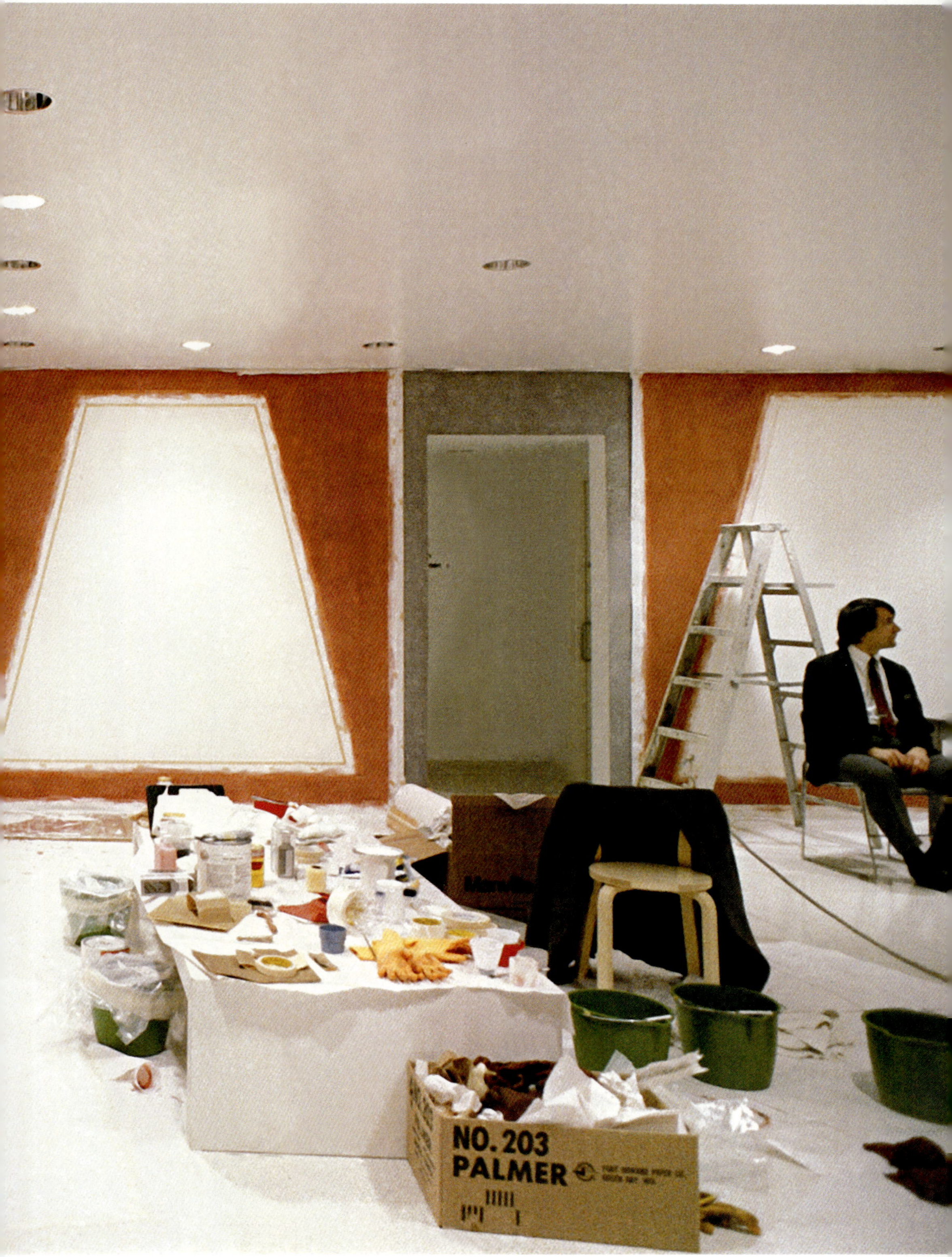
NO. 203
PALMER

door-window: no building exists without a door. By definition, if there is no door, then it's not architecture, it's not a human habitat. . . . The second window, which appears very late, is the window which gives us the day-light only—a window through which one doesn't enter."[25] For Virilio, the third window is the electronic window, which is not tied directly to architectural space, but is a portable window. To amend Virilio's observations, it is painting that stages the first glimpse of remote viewing, and it is the easel painting that becomes a portable architectonic element. It is the screen—whether the immersive silver screen of the cinema, the windshield of the automobile, the flicker of the television set, or the ubiquity and interactivity of the computer monitor—to which architecture and painting now respond.

It is the kind of vision typically associated with television and video—evenness of light and shadow, the flatness of a compressed monocular vision, eccentric viewpoints and dynamic camera angles, including extreme close-ups and the distortions of foreshortening—that can be gleaned in recent painting. For example, Eberhard Havekost's paintings of the repetitious facades of modern apartment buildings, the generic archetype of the pitched-roof house, or the ubiquitous banality of mobile homes frequently employ architectural scenes filtered through the televisual (see pp. 263–264). Havekost's paintings represent the dislocation or dispersal of the architectural into the realm of the virtual. As critic Ulrich Loock, writing in reference to Havekost's work, has noted, "The Renaissance paradigm of painting-as-window is replaced by the paradigm of the infinite availability of images within images: an idea that also appears in the language of electronic image manipulation, where it is denoted by the word 'windows.'"[26] If, in its shattering of spatial illusionism, modernism sought to reassert the primacy of the painted surface, then Havekost's paintings enact another displacement: not opening onto vistas, like a window, but projecting onto the surface, like a screen, a residual image—a kind of architectural afterimage.

There is a corollary, I believe, between the virtualization of the architectural (the building as image) and the disappearance of the architectural from the scene of social reality (the building as afterimage). If contemporary architecture routinely uses the imaging possibilities of the computer in order to produce the "buildable image" (e.g., Frank Gehry's Bilbao), then painting increasingly employs the afterimage of architecture's social presence in order to recuperate the spatial. For instance, the paintings of Michael Raedecker depict scenes of domestic lifelessness: the corner of an empty room, an uninhabited bedroom, or the exterior of an isolated suburban ranch house (see pp. 323–325). Raedecker's use of source material from old issues of magazines such as *Vacation* or *Second Home* imparts a certain incompleteness that is characteristic of the domestic lives such publications depict, namely, spaces devoid of human habitation yet suggestive of its eminent presence. Likewise, the subjects of the mural-size works on paper of Toba Khedoori include auditorium seats, a patch of chain-link fence, park benches, a hallway, a building facade—all anonymous spaces devoid of people and partaking of the aesthetics of an evacuated architecture. Kevin Appel's paintings of domestic space also point to an architectural image world, but one tinged with the postwar optimism of California modernism in the 1950s and 1960s (fig. 7; pp. 243–245). His hard-edged abstractions of interiors have been said to evoke the historic Case Study Houses of Los Angeles, or perhaps the more populist modernist dwellings of Joseph Eichler, but rendered in a style reminiscent of fly-through animation techniques available in today's computer-aided design programs. Just as his work oscillates between an idealized past and a virtualized present, Appel's paintings fluctuate between abstraction and illusionism. Some works cannot be read as literal depictions of Cartesian space, or functionally as architectural renderings: walls do not always meet, sometimes there is no floor or ceiling, and perspectives may not align. The resulting images echo the words of Mondrian, who suggested that the interior of the home must be "a construction of planes in color and noncolor unified with the furniture and household objects, which will be nothing in themselves but which will function as constructive elements of the whole."[27] In these works the disappearance of architecture is restaged and what is remembered reappears as an apparition—a virtualization of the spatial.

To quote Alfred H. Barr, Jr., in his foreword to *Painting Toward Architecture*, "The direct influence of painting upon modern architecture must however not be exaggerated."[28] Yet the relationship between these disciplines is indeed complex and reciprocal. The search for common ground to span them—whether in the development of perspective, the modernist recourse to shared visual form, the dissolution and synthesis of specific mediums, the expansion of the work of art to the site of its display, or the virtualization of spaces and the spatialization of the image—demonstrates the persistent need to connect the two. Architecture and painting, once joined on the basis of a shared physical support, are linked today through the proliferation of images that are governed more by the demands of time than by the constraints of space. In this vanishing act, painting and architecture remain tethered, but increasingly with no visible means of support.

NOTES

1 Allan Kaprow, *Assemblage, Environments, and Happenings* (New York: H. N. Abrams, 1966), p. 153.
2 Victor Burgin, *In/Different Spaces: Place and Memory in Visual Culture* (Berkeley and Los Angeles: University of California Press, 1996), p. 142.
3 Brian O'Doherty, "Inside the White Cube: Notes on the Gallery Space, Part I," *Artforum* 14, no. 7 (March 1976), p. 26.
4 Ibid., p. 29.
5 Henry-Russell Hitchcock, *Painting Toward Architecture* (New York: Duell, Sloan and Pearce, 1948), p. 45.
6 Ibid., p. 14.
7 Harry Holtzman and Martin S. James, trans. and eds., *The New Art—The New Life: The Collected Writings of Piet Mondrian* (Boston: G. K. Hall & Co., 1986), p. 174.
8 Lucio Fontana, "Technical Manifesto" (1951), reprinted in *Arte Povera*, ed. Carolyn Christov-Bakargiev (London: Phaidon Press Ltd., 1999), p. 208.
9 Hélio Oiticica, "Colour, Time, and Structure," (1960), reprinted in *Hélio Oiticica*, exh. cat. (Minneapolis: Walker Art Center and Rotterdam: Witte de With, 1992), p. 37.
10 Ibid., p. 36.
11 Rosalind Krauss, *"A Voyage on the North Sea": Art in the Age of the Post-Medium Condition* (London and New York: Thames & Hudson, 1999), p. 29.
12 Donald Judd, "Specific Objects," in *Donald Judd: Complete Writings 1959–1975* (Halifax, N.S.: Press of the Nova Scotia College of Art and Design, 1975), p. 181.
13 Ibid., p. 184.
14 Dan Graham, "Art in Relationship to Architecture/Architecture in Relationship to Art," *Artforum* 17, no. 6 (February 1976), p. 22.
15 See J. Fiona Ragheb, *Dan Flavin: The Architecture of Light*, exh. cat. (New York: Guggenheim Museum Publications, 1999), p. 85.
16 Quoted in Craig Owens, "From Work to Frame, or, Is There Life After 'The Death of the Author,'" in *Beyond Recognition: Representation, Power, Culture* (Berkeley and Los Angeles: University of California Press, 1992), p. 130.
17 From Sol LeWitt's writings on wall drawings reprinted in *Sol LeWitt: A Retrospective*, exh. cat., ed. Gary Garrels (San Francisco Museum of Modern Art and New Haven and London: Yale University Press, 2000), p. 375.
18 See Christoph Grunenberg, "Up Against the Wall," in *Frieze*, exh. cat. (Boston: The Institute of Contemporary Art, 1999), p. 13.
19 Miwon Kwon, "One Place After Another: Notes on Site Specificity," *October*, no. 80 (spring 1997), pp. 85–110.
20 For a more complete account of the site-specific work of art, see Thierry de Duve, "Ex Situ," in *Art & Design: Installation Art* (London: Academy Group Ltd., 1993), pp. 25–30.
21 Paul Virilio, *The Aesthetics of Disappearance* (New York: Semiotext[e], 1991), p. 65. (Emphasis in original.)
22 Interview transcript reproduced in *Marcel Broodthaers: Cinéma*, exh. cat. (Barcelona: Fundació Antoni Tàpies, 1997), p. 227.
23 Ibid.
24 Ibid.
25 Jonathan Crary, "The Third Window: An Interview with Paul Virilio," reprinted in *Global Television*, eds. Cynthia Schneider and Brian Wallis (New York: Wedge Press and Cambridge, Mass., and London: MIT Press, 1988), p. 191.
26 Ulrich Loock, *Eberhard Havekost/Fenster — Fenster*, exh. cat., trans. David Britt (Lucerne, Switzerland: Kunstmuseum Luzern, 1998), p. 56.
27 Holtzman and James, *The New Art—The New Life*, p. 212.
28 Hitchcock, *Painting Toward Architecture*, p. 9.

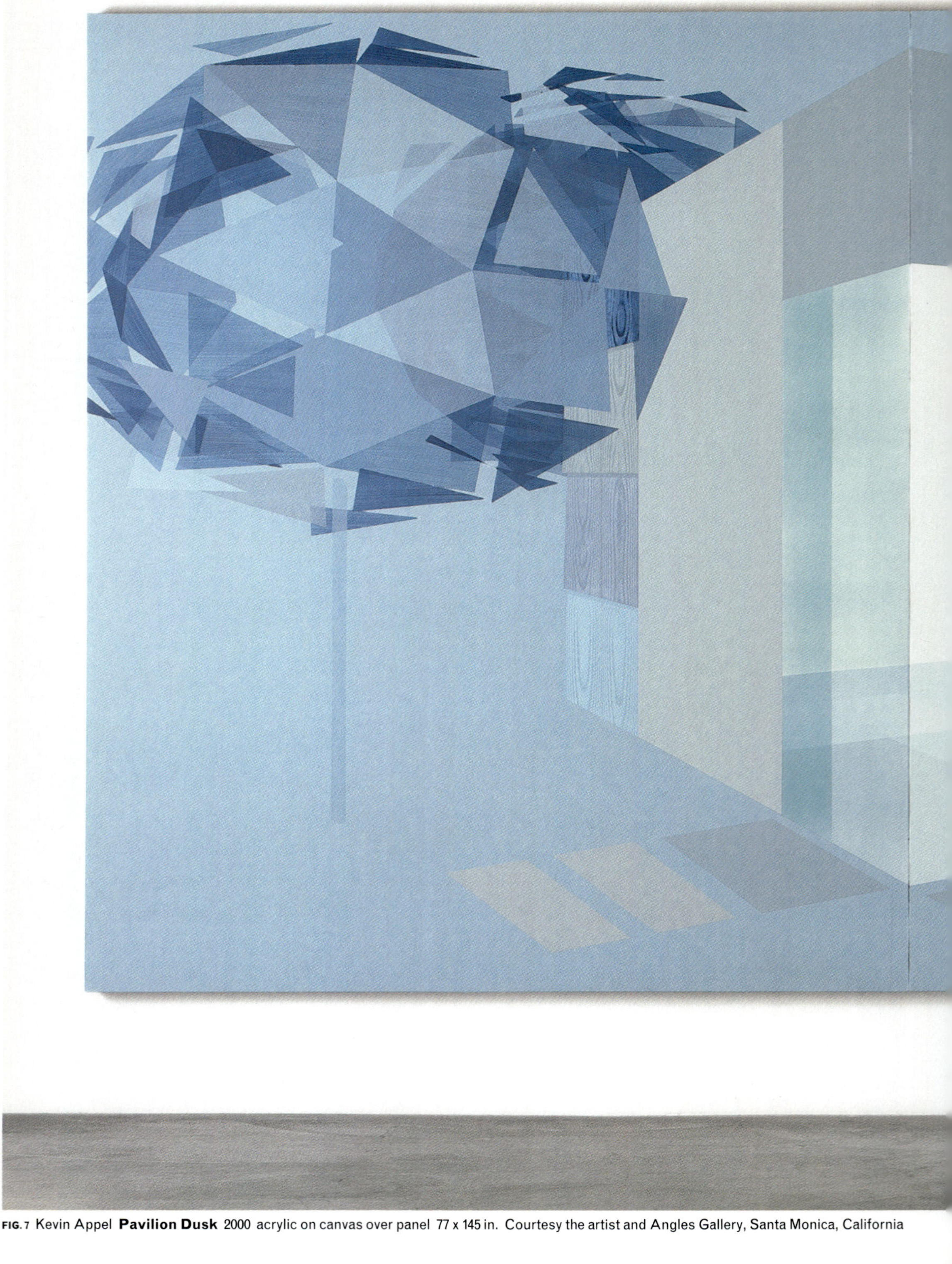

FIG. 7 Kevin Appel **Pavilion Dusk** 2000 acrylic on canvas over panel 77 x 145 in. Courtesy the artist and Angles Gallery, Santa Monica, California

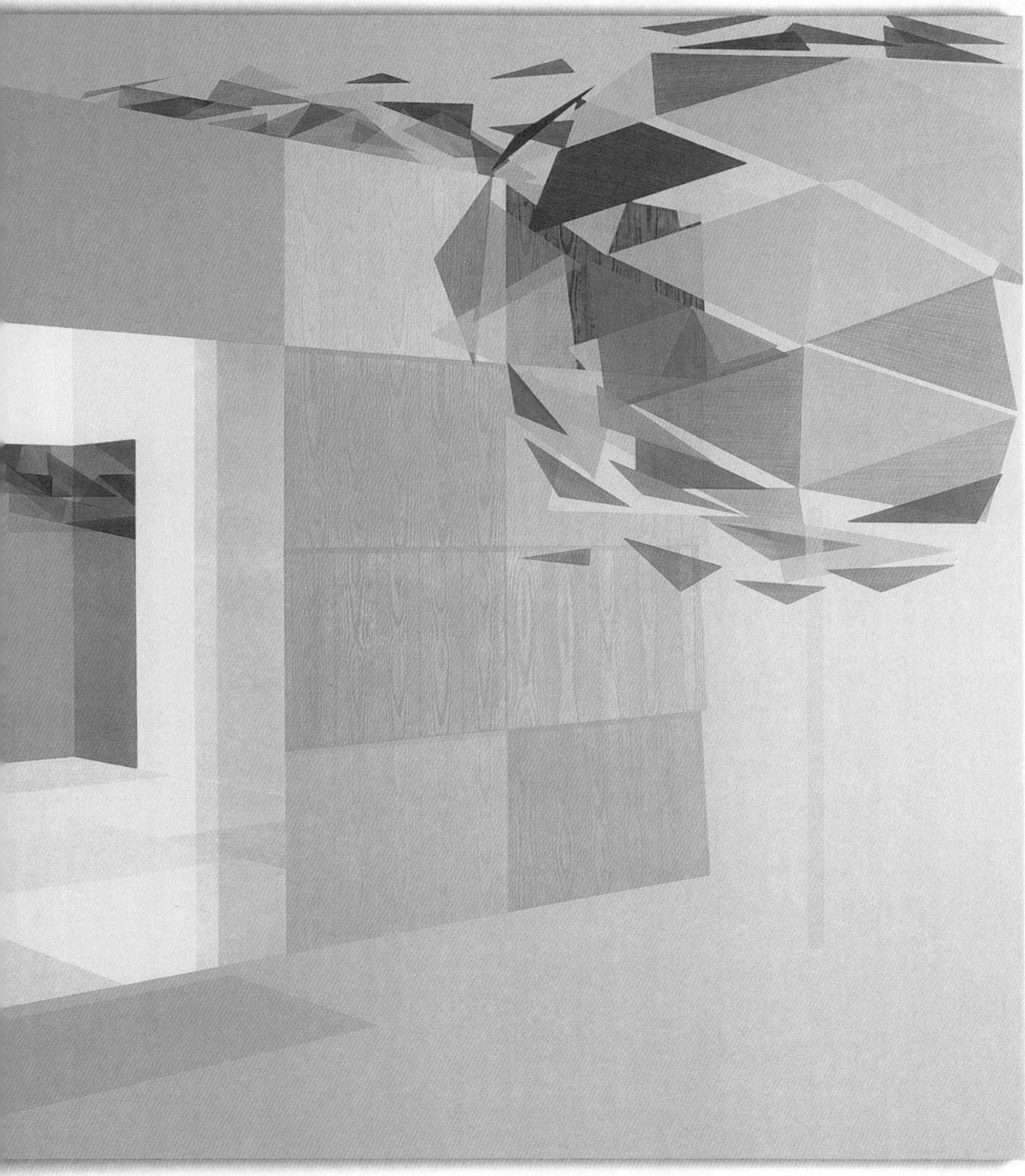

Jörg Heiser is the Associate Editor at *frieze* and a frequent contributor to several German and Swiss newspapers. He has lectured at institutions such as the Camberwell College of Arts, London; the Royal College of Art, London; Merz-Akademie Stuttgart; Kunstakademie Düsseldorf; Konstfack, Stockholm; the Royal College, Stockholm; IASPIS, Stockholm; and Konsthochscholan Umeå, Sweden. He is currently working on a PhD in Art History at Humboldt University, Berlin, where his dissertation addresses shifts of production between art and pop music.

The Odd Couple: Painting, Rock Music, and Their Shared Strategies against Obsolescence in the Digital Age

Jörg Heiser

"Painting is the vast thunderous clash of many worlds . . . the Music of Spheres." — Wassily Kandinsky

"Best of! Most of! / Satiate the need / Slip them into different sleeves! / Buy both, and be deceived / Climber—new entry, re-entry / World tour ('media whore') / 'Please the Press in Belgium!' (This was your life . . .)"

— The Smiths, "Paint a Vulgar Picture"

It was in 1968 when two white, more or less middle-class, heterosexual men sharing an apartment were introduced on the screen: the Odd Couple. Until the mid-1960s, they lived apart, one of them in a so-so happy marriage with his better half, the other a notorious bachelor, only occasionally meeting each other by chance in bars and on the street. Then the newly divorced, anal-retentive Felix (Jack Lemmon) moves in with low-living Oscar (Walter Matthau) at a time of change and turmoil; comic relief ensues as, beyond their factual differences, both would usually deny that they shared anything more than a flat. The longer I have thought about the connection between painting and rock music—traditions long, and in structure still, dominated by the "good old boys"—the more I have come to think of them as an equally odd couple (tellingly, the German title of the film was *Männerwirtschaft*, which translates as "men's housekeeping").

Rock and painting—living clichés. Felix could be the painter, divorced from representation of "reality," making sober decoration for the "rich bastards" (as Rothko once put it), and Oscar the messy rocker, thinking of women as potential threats, in hidden fear of his huge audience. Or you could turn it around and say that Felix is the nice rock-entertainer, divorced from the rebellious impulse of his music, pleasing the record-industry execs, while Oscar is the lonesome cowboy of the canvas.

Either way, painting and rock music started to have more in common from the mid-1960s on. Previously, painting had seemed on a much higher level of sophistication. The more new possibilities turned up for creating fictional worlds of perception and alternative realities—from photography to drugs to electronic environments—the more painting turned to its own parameters to reflect on this. With abstraction and processual thinking—from Mondrian to Pollock to Warhol—it made this its obvious principle and main feature: painting had turned into a system of conscious reflection on its own condition, and a medium with which to reflect on other media's conditions.

Yet when rock lost its "innocence" in regard to its status as an industry and an art form, the seeds for a similar boost of reevaluation were sowed: when the Beach Boys reinvented the pop song on their album *Pet Sounds* and Bob Dylan electrified urban folk-poetics, the world started to look different.

Today, there is an almost uncanny resemblance between the discourses around the status of contemporary painting and rock music. The techno-factions in both art and music have repeatedly buried the canvas and the guitar for good, and time and again both have risen from the grave, claiming that their time had not yet come, that there was still something substantial to say with and about them.

The sophistication of painting and rock music has been in relation to what "threatens" to make each of them obsolete, make them history. Sharing a crisis of legitimacy beyond their mere market value as they compete with electronic media, both have dealt with this crisis by retreating into either a traditionalist refuge or, on the contrary, an ever accelerating buzz of reflecting on their own aesthetic and social history, function, and semiology.

Just as rock came up with postrock—favoring track over song, bass rumble over guitar line, sound over lyrics, as if making electronic music in an analog mode—painting came up with a kind of postpainting that embodies, and reflects upon, other means of producing and copying images, namely digital ones. And just as Apollonian postrock has been in turn contested by a regurgitation of a more Dionysian, noisy, "soulful" kind of metarock songwriting, the insistent, sometimes all too exercised reference of painting to technological means of image-creation has been accompanied by a conscious, self-indulgent libidinization of the entire history of more or less exclusively painterly image-creation.

These parallels may indicate, in a close-up perspective, that there has been an interrelation between art and pop music, painting and rock in particular, that at least contributed to these parallel developments, if not triggered some of them. Being less obliged to the demands of everyday use and large, event-oriented audiences who want to be entertained,

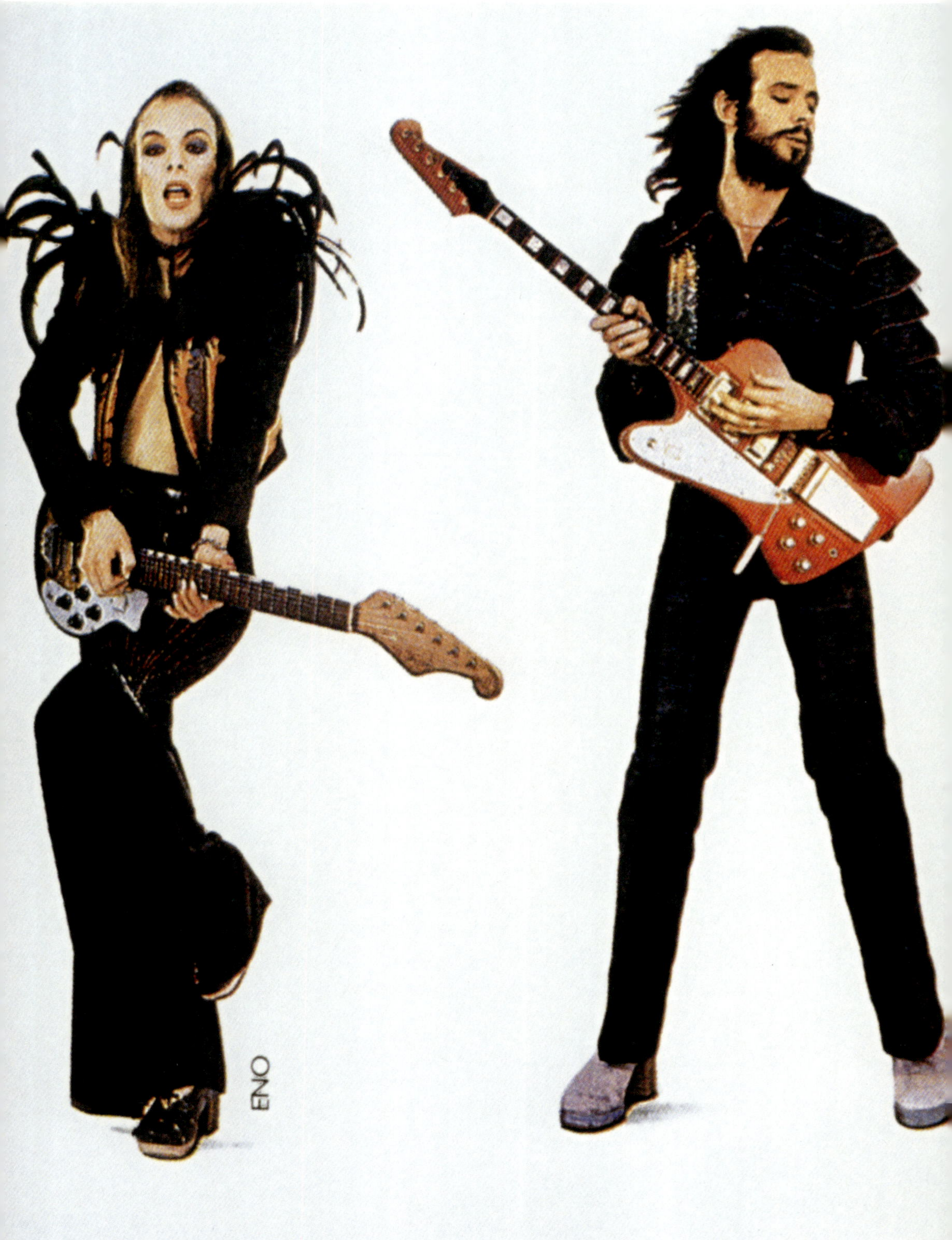

FIG. 1 photograph of the band Roxy Music from the inside cover of their 1973 album **For Your Pleasure**
Courtesy Virgin Records

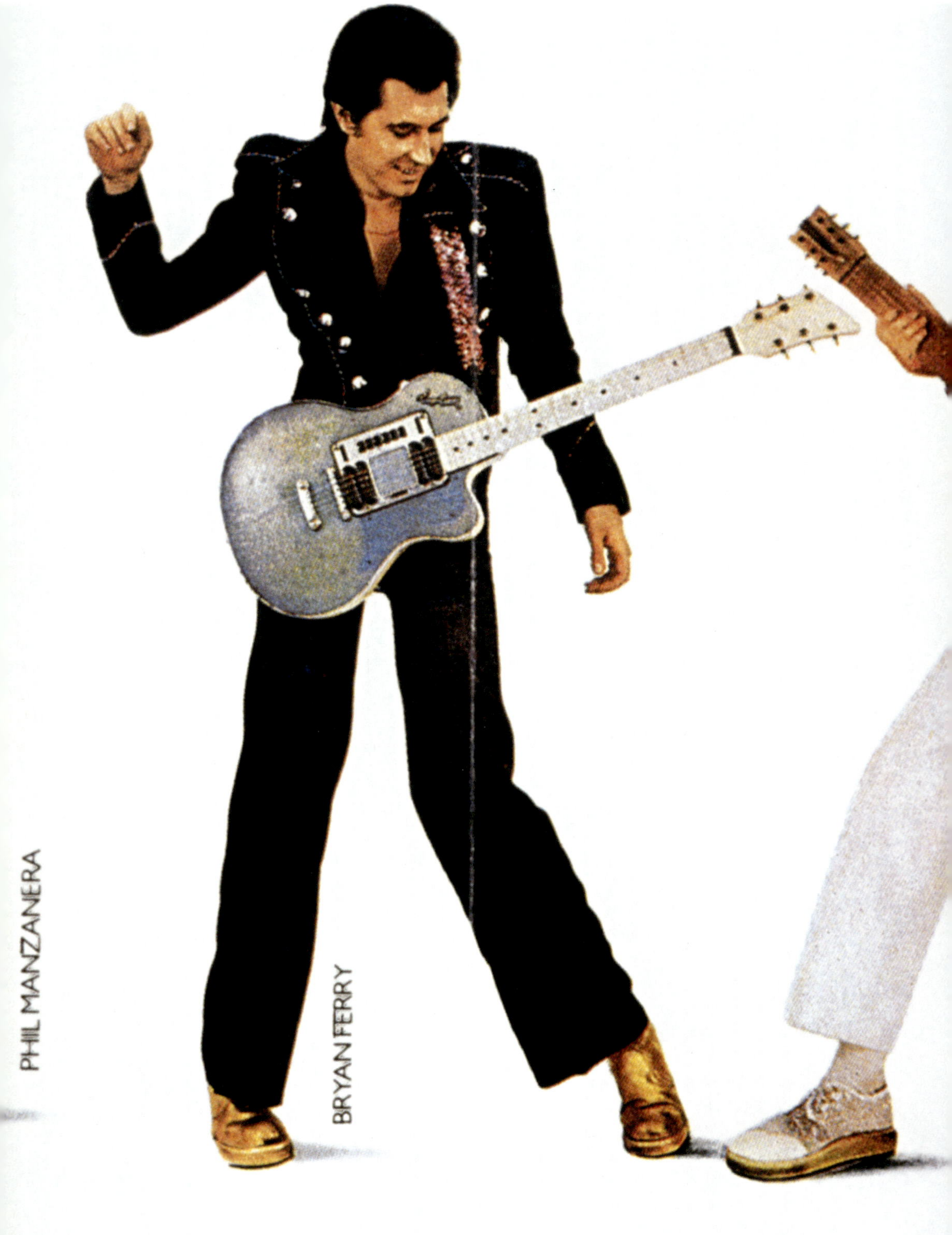
PHIL MANZANERA
BRYAN FERRY

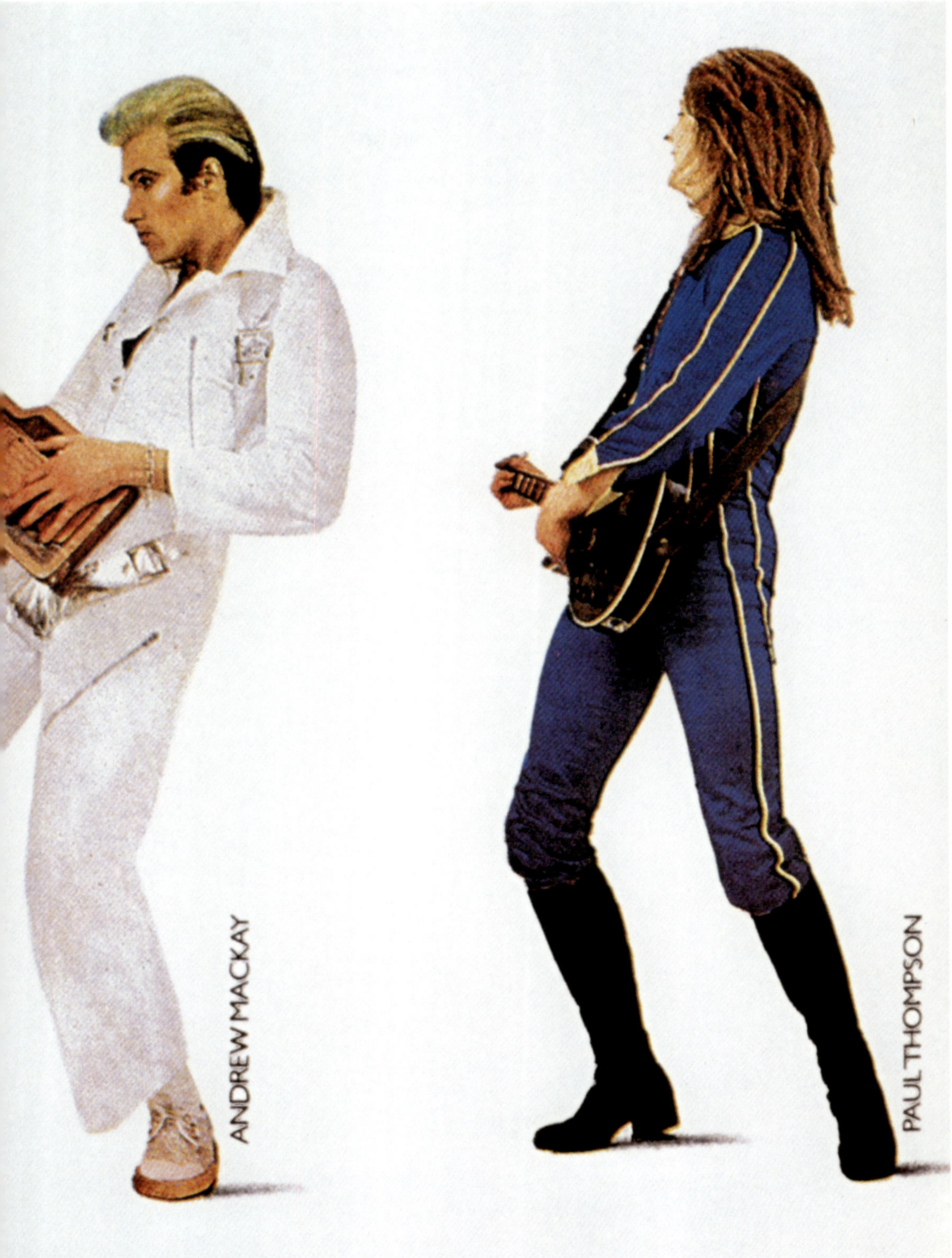
ANDREW MACKAY
PAUL THOMPSON

painting was faster in reconsidering its condition (though it can be argued that jazz and its rhythmic syncopations were as important for Mondrian and Pollock as teenage rock 'n' roll and its repetitive pop format was for Warhol). But by the mid-1970s at the latest, rock had caught up, and, with and against the demands of its audience, it started to publicly think about its own condition.

In July 1972 six exotic, tarted up Teddy Boy–Glam creatures entered the stage of BBC's *Top of the Pops* (fig. 1). Whether the United Kingdom had been waiting for something like this was not yet quite clear. The job of the balding one (Brian Eno) was obviously to make the straight hammering of piano-oboe-drums pulsate by virtue of his huge synthesizer; the camera obsessed on his hand turning the knobs, while the singer with the ducktail (Bryan Ferry) sang in the voice of a befuddled crooner whose restrained agitation vaulted into a howling vibrato. He sang of the American sentiment of Westward-Ho, cruising in the car, before jumping on a plane down to Rio. "Virginia Plain" was Roxy Music's first hit, released on the eve of the great oil crisis, the first major blow to the irresistible dream of unrestrained mobility.

Virginia Plain was also the title of a painting Bryan Ferry had made in 1964. As he recalled in the 1990s, "It was a sort of throwaway watercolor American-dream type of thing. The face of the girl in the painting was based on one of Warhol's Superstars of the time—Baby Jane Holzer—who used to have this amazing huge hairdo. It's about driving down the freeway, passing cigarette ads on vast billboards. And Las Vegas casinos."[1]

Ferry had studied art with Richard Hamilton in Newcastle, undertaking his first musical steps at around the same time—cover versions of soul and R&B standards with his eight-piece band Gas Board. Hamilton was not only among the most important exponents of British Pop Art, but also one of its earliest theoreticians. In 1954 Lawrence Alloway had coined the term "pop" for the first time, referring exclusively to industrially produced cultural products, movies, magazines, music, and posters. Three years later, Hamilton famously declared, in a short analysis and manifesto in one, "Pop Art is: popular (designed for a mass audience); transient (short-term solution); expendable (easily forgotten); low-cost; mass-produced; young (aimed at youth); witty; sexy; gimmicky; glamorous; and, last but not least, Big Business."[2]

Like Warhol, Hamilton had worked in advertising design, and as his definition of Pop Art was completely opposed to the then-ruling Abstract Expressionist movement, this was not about a simple shift in subject matter that would have left the basic condition of painting untouched. Rather, this was about a kind of conscious overaffirmation of the social and economic functions of pop culture, with amplified and duplicated music as its central driving force. Yet, as Warhol, after 1966, went on tour with the Velvet Underground and the Exploding Plastic Inevitable Show, British Pop artists stayed in their studios and left the recording of albums and giving of concerts in the hands of art-school students.

When The Who named their 1967 album *The Who Sell Out*, art-school graduate Pete Townsend appeared on the cover with an oversized roll-on deodorant under his armpit, accompanied by the phrase: "Replacing the stale smell of excess with the sweet smell of success" (fig. 2). This could be read as a sarcastic crowing of the consciously consumerist Mod lifestyle of Pop Art, yet, at the same time, the irony of the title and the photo actually served to forestall possible reproaches of selling out from the more purist, anti-Pop, "male rocker" faction of their audience. Townsend, according to the popular legend put forth by him, took the inspiration for his famous stage act of smashing his guitar from Gustav Metzger. In 1966 Metzger organized the Destruction In Art Symposium in London, during which he painted a picture with acid so that the canvas disintegrated; Townsend had attended another performance-lecture during which Metzger had sawn up an electric guitar.[3]

The Who's adaptation of fine-art strategies of representation remained on the level of integrating them into rock-rebel ideology. But even the Velvet Underground was a piece

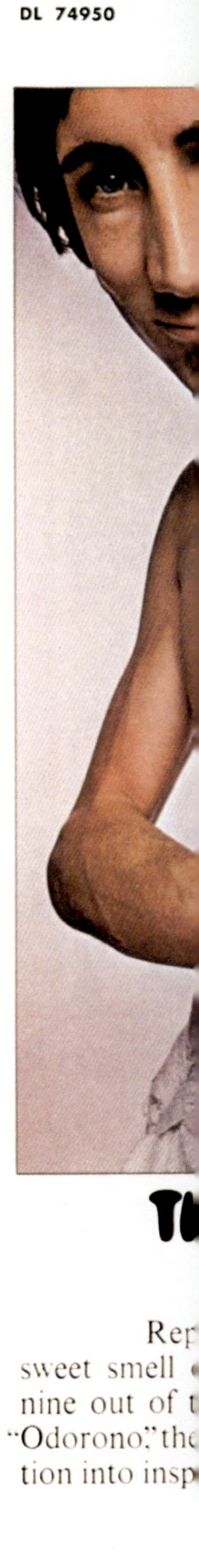

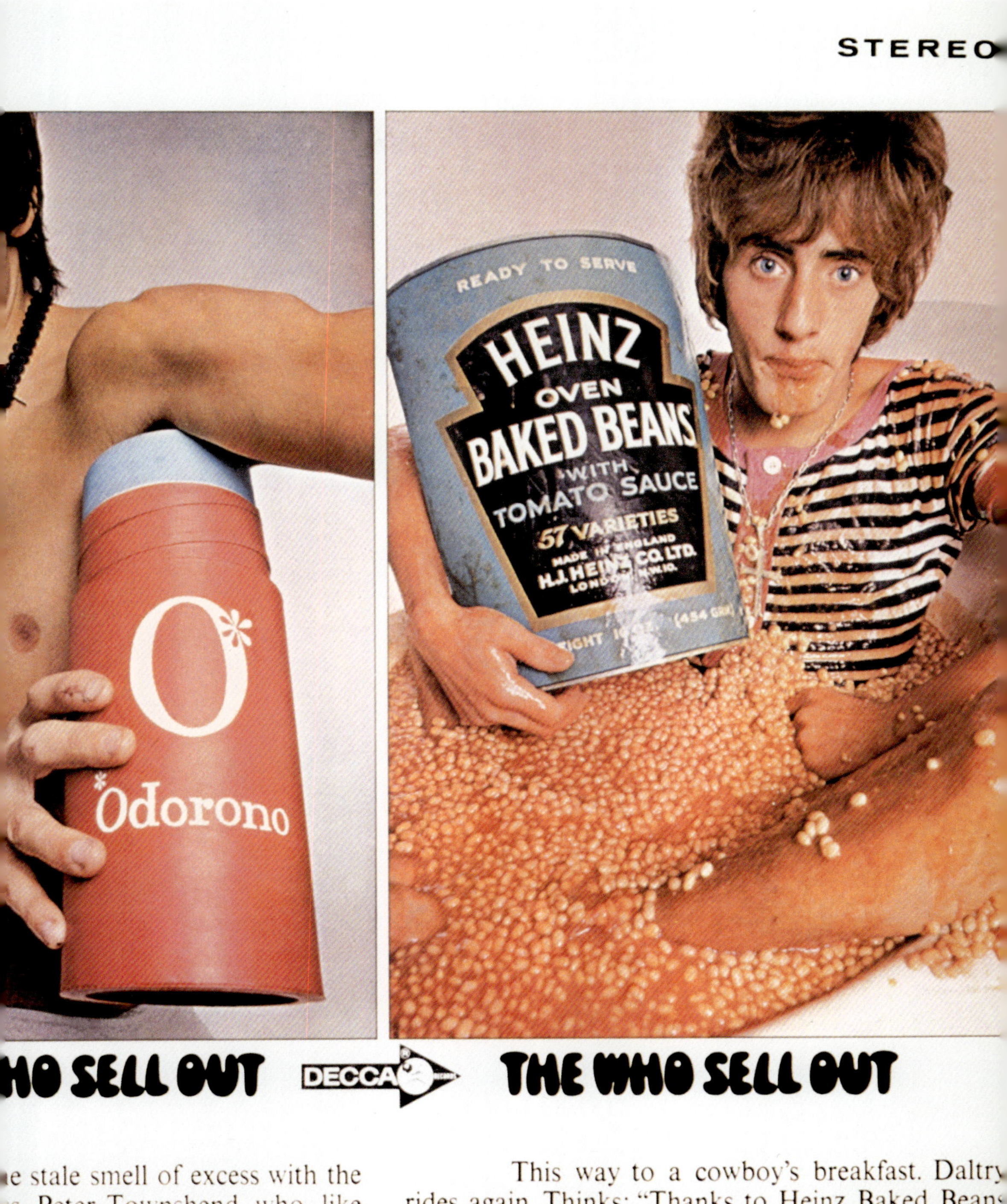

FIG. 2 album cover **The Who Sell Out** 1967 design: David King and Roger Law; photos: David Montgomery
Courtesy the artists and MCA Music Entertainment Group

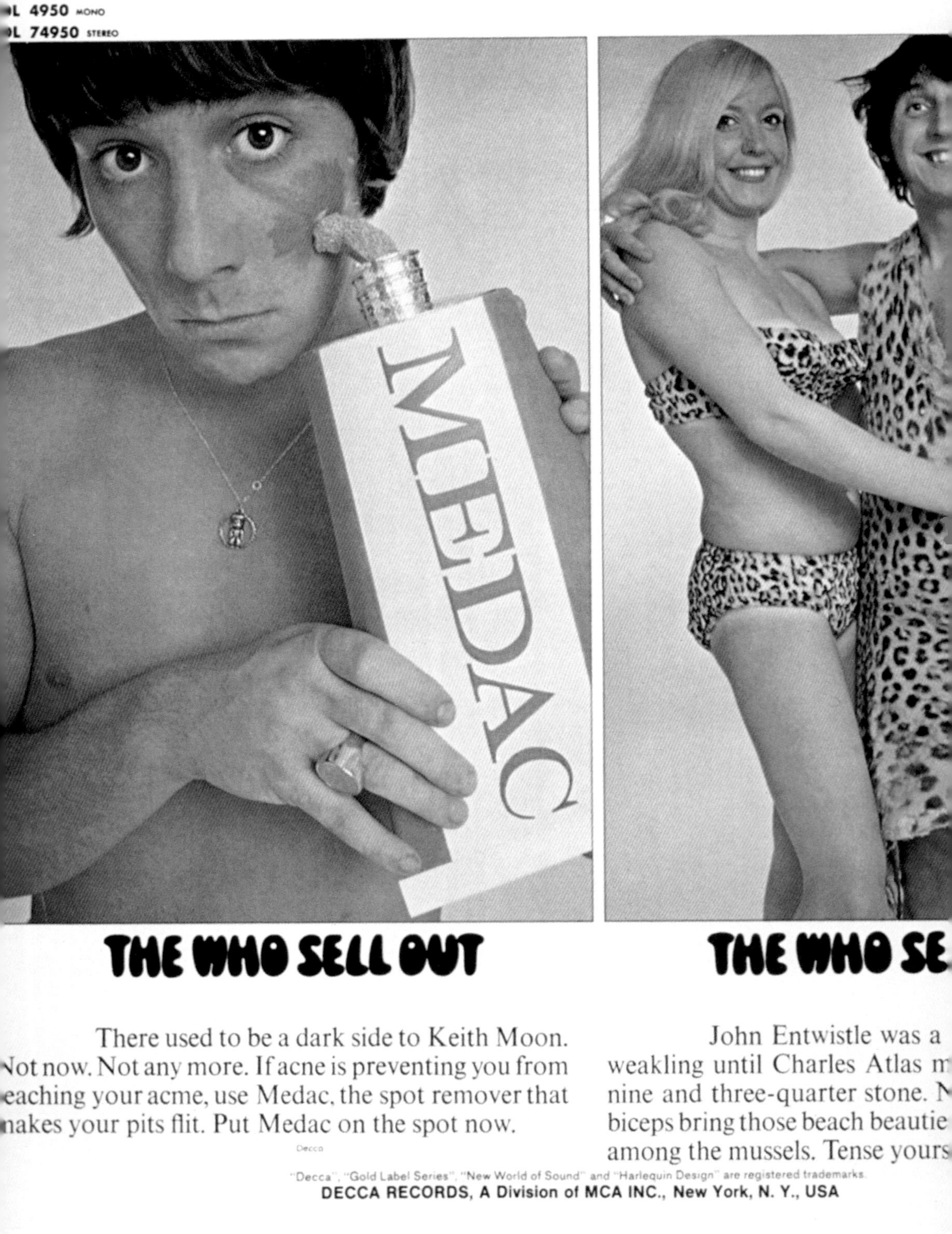
L 4950 MONO
L 74950 STEREO
MEDAC
THE WHO SELL OUT
There used to be a dark side to Keith Moon. Not now. Not any more. If acne is preventing you from eaching your acme, use Medac, the spot remover that nakes your pits flit. Put Medac on the spot now.
Decca
THE WHO SE
John Entwistle was a weakling until Charles Atlas m nine and three-quarter stone. N biceps bring those beach beautie among the mussels. Tense yours
"Decca", "Gold Label Series", "New World of Sound" and "Harlequin Design" are registered trademarks.
DECCA RECORDS, A Division of MCA INC., New York, N. Y., USA

of Pop Art only in the mind of Warhol, who had inducted Nico into the band and created a multimedia spectacle around them. Lou Reed saw himself as a songwriting poet, a dark nihilistic antipode of Bob Dylan, and John Cale still aspired to the field of avant-garde music in the tradition of John Cage and La Monte Young. So five years later, Roxy Music actually was the first band to take rock music to a conscious conceptual level, as if putting Pop Art on stage as a love song that deals with its own nature of being a commodity.

What pop music's process of becoming conceptually self-aware indicates is not so much the disappearance of the "high-low" distinction, but its complication. From the mid-1960s on, pop music started to grow "difficult" branches, with its own (equivocal) "high": most obvious in jazz and in the first crossovers between rock and "serious" avant-garde music, less obvious and more informal in the psychedelic underground. At around the same time, the expansion of education and wealth in Western industrialized countries had enabled a broader access to (predominantly museal) fine art. There was, for example, easily understandable Op Art, which met halfway with popular concepts of the good clean fun of modernity; and there was extremely specialized pop music, such as that by Captain Beefheart, for example, which appealed only to a small audience and ultimately was obliged only to the conflicted needs of its makers.

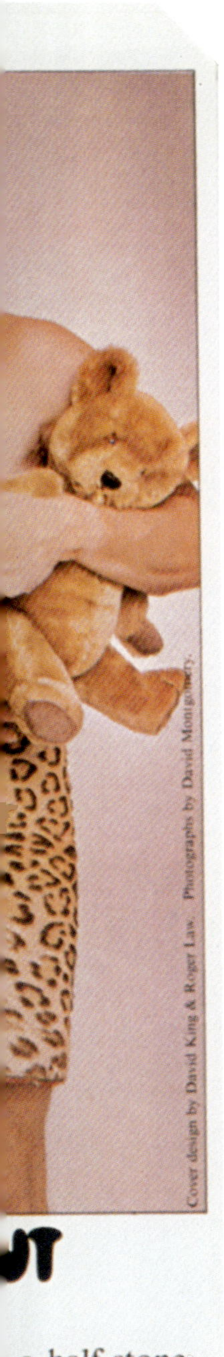

But even a division between "high" and "low" based on the degree of complexity involved in the reception of an artistic utterance has become tricky, if not impossible: generally speaking, audiences have grown more and more self-confident in regard to their own perspective, or usage, of a piece of art or music. And therefore, a complex abstract painting might be turned into a convenient backdrop, while a seemingly simple pop song might trigger an intensely complicated set of feelings, conversations, and social effects. How many respectable, conservative listeners did actually notice that many of the songs by the supposedly all-American jukebox-standard band Steely Dan had homoerotic undertones, and that the band name itself came from a dildo mentioned in a junkie novel by a certain William Burroughs? The achievement of Pop Art, and of pop music with a conceptual edge, was to happily embrace the full scale of possible intensities of reception. The light-hearted gem comes with a bonus pack of cunning referential differentiation.

Today, actual degrees of internal complexity don't seem to function anymore as standards to indicate "high art" in the traditional sense. Instead, any "elitist" cultural segments now seem practically defined by the degree to which the self-confidence of a possible recipient is intended to be discouraged by external codings or restrictions of accessibility, signals that say, "either you don't understand, or you're not allowed to understand." In relation to, for example, a reactionary populist or economically aggressive environment, these signals may help to create a place for marginalized, treasured experiences and simultaneously to preclude their exploitation. But often, when the depth of refined perception or intellectual investigation required by the art are solemnly conjured up (rather than simply practiced), it turns out to be little more than a bluff to secure privileges and stubborn "high-art" habits.

After more than forty years of differentiation and fragmentation, rock music has come up with its own catalogue of codings and access restrictions. And they either serve to secure fossilized privileges of the white male rock rebel, or—quite to the contrary—deal with taking them, or rather him, apart. Hence, at the beginning of the twenty-first century, despite prevailing economic and social differences, rock music and painting are on equal ground in many ways in terms of their modes of distinction.

In regard to their production, an antidistinctive quality still allows them to look attractive: the promise of DIY-immediacy. You plug in a guitar, sing into a microphone, maybe use a slightly outdated four-track home recorder; you manually apply paint to a surface, while perhaps employing some older media, such as an instant camera, a xerox, and an overhead projector to fix visual data. Even if you don't have to rely on a team of engineers, technically more complex processes such as sampling or video-editing have long put a lot more calculating steps, and thus detours and dead ends, between your idea of what you want to get and what you actually get.

This is less and less the case: though you can still run into problems that only a technical expert can fix, working with visual and audio data on a computer has become relatively fast, easy, and cheap, creating a kind of second-order immediacy of real-time processing. And in the big urban centers where rents are high and prices of consumer electronics relatively low, a computer may still cost more than paint material or a guitar amp, but it is ultimately cheaper because a studio, or rehearsal room, is no longer necessary.

So why bother carrying on with the old rubbish? You stain your clothes, rehearsal rooms stink. Instead you can have mobility and flexibility, everything at hand and mouse. And in fact, if art and music were all about practicability, efficiency, and linear technological progress, which they are not, you could end the argument here. Rather, painting's and rock's respective problems of survival can be described by a variation on Adorno's famous introductory sentence to *Negative Dialectics* [4] (commenting on philosophy's status after having failed to establish a directly functional relation to reality): painting and rock music, having once seemed outdated, keep themselves alive because the moment of their fulfillment had been missed.

And what would have been the moment of their fulfillment? When the pleasure and understanding they projected in imagination was equal to the pleasure and understanding they produced in reality. Or, again based on Adorno: after painting and rock music broke the promise that they were at one with pleasure and the unrestrained fight for it, they are now forced to unrelentingly criticize themselves.

From the Rolling Stones fan stabbed at Altamont to the rapes that occurred in the audience of Woodstock II, rock is loaded with enough obvious and incessant sexism, racism, and reactionary conservatism to justify self-criticism. Painting's reasons for self-critique, by the very nature of the discipline, can't be described as easily in the form of events, though, for example, pictures of an intelligent artist such as Yves Klein directing naked women to serve as his brushes or Otto Mühl's sex-dad tyranny over his later commune seem to mark seedy and sad cornerstones of what—in regard to both rock and painting—might be considered long-standing habits of discrimination that reserved the pleasure for the good old boys.

The resolutely fencing brush stroke, or protestant rigor of drawing an exact line; the face of the guitar soloist distorted in strained toilet pathos, or the shoe-gazing stage act of the New Wave wimp: the bodily gestures that have for so long accompanied these "habits" have turned so obviously satirical that painting and rock as disciplines seem to be threatened more by their own history than by techniques that move faster by virtue of intelligent machines (though the latter have already proven to not exactly be free from the customs of stale bonding). And so from the mid-1980s on, the road has been wide open for rock and painting to come up with concepts to counteract their aesthetic and social status as dead horses not even to be flogged anymore.

In both painting and rock, four different, usually mingled, approaches—not always "strategically" chosen as such by their individual makers—have developed from the threat of obsolescence: 1. Remaking and remodeling history by digging up the neglected; 2. Conceptualizing the genre itself; 3. Incorporating other media, thematically and practically, into the genre; and 4. Externalizing and reflecting on elements of the technique from the perspective of another.

1. Looking back on their histories is, of course, a major occupation of cultures, to the delight of "connoisseurs" like us who detect the references. If done merely for its own sake, the redundancy of such retrospection is obvious—closing the system, making it an indifferent pick 'n' mix game: welcome to postmodern retro-hell. But in a feedback coalition that reclaims these references for agents who were not officially entitled to sport them before, they can produce new clusters of meaning. For example, Berlin painter Lukas Duwenhögger's highly crafted imaginary-realist paintings clearly have a conflicted dandyism and pink flamboyance about them that goes back at least to the time of F. Scott

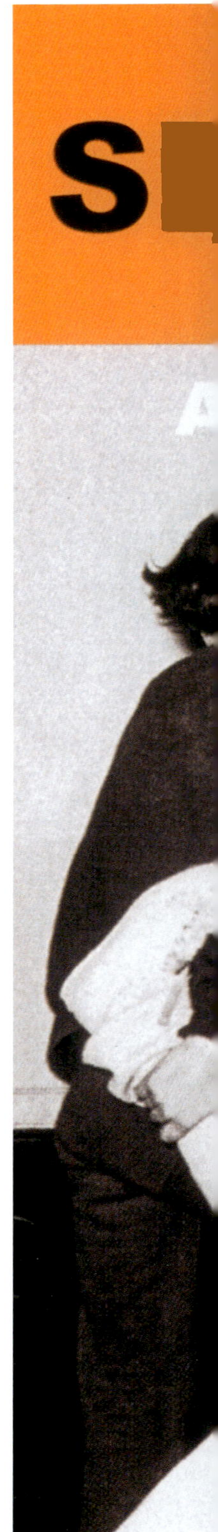

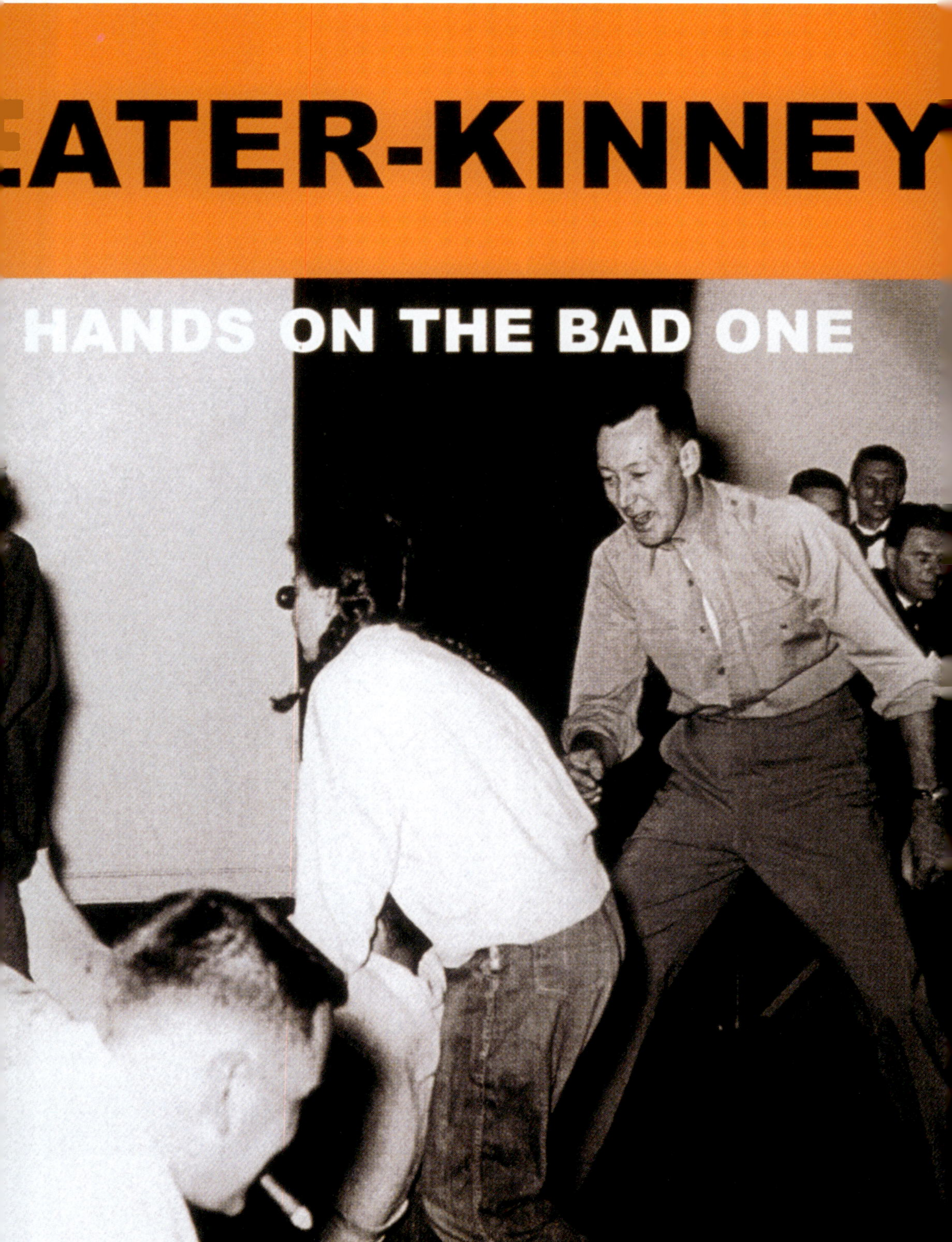

FIG. 3 album cover Sleater Kinney **All Hands on the Bad One** 2000 photos: Marina Chavez, Andrew Auge, and Matt Alcock Courtesy the artists and Kill Rock Stars

Fitzgerald if not to Oscar Wilde; faint allusions to early twentieth-century Neue Sachlichkeit and late nineteenth-century Symbolism collapse into one another; or, one could say, it's a bit like an all-American Norman Rockwell being invaded by an all-amorous Mapplethorpe sensibility on Thomas Mann ground. As Duwenhögger employs installational modes in the hanging of his works, the nostalgia of any single element is subsumed into a scenario that steps out of that time frame and steers privileged mannerism into a queer void.

As for rock, Sleater-Kinney from Portland, Oregon, provide a good example. Singer Corin Tucker's voice is an amalgam of Undertones singer Feargal Sharkey's vibrating falsetto and the snorting exuberance of Poly Styrene, singer of legendary punk outfit X-Ray Spex, and is backed up with twin guitars and drums—no bass—letting the conventional genre of the three-minute punk-rock song come back to life again. Again: punk rock, having come to be seen as outdated, keeps itself alive because the moment of its fulfillment had been missed—namely, its stripped-down sound and initially androgynous, vulnerable look had promised to pension off the handicraft cock-rock daddies, when in fact, in the tales of punk-philology, women again played only supporting roles. And suddenly, an inventive girl-band such as the Slits appeared as nothing more than a groupie support for The Clash. Julian Temple's Sex Pistols documentary *The Filth and the Fury* (2000) does nothing to rewrite the historiography in that respect; Nancy Spungen continues to be projected as the evil woman who finished off the Sex Pistols, as if she had killed Sid, and not the other way around. Sleater-Kinney's "Ballad of a Ladyman" (opener of their latest album *All Hands on the Bad One*) (fig. 3), takes on these persistent castration fears with a melancholic cello accompanying such lines as "I could be demure like girls who are soft for boys who are fearful of getting an earful, but I gotta rock! I'd rather be a ladyman."

2. To some extent the second approach of conceptualization of the genre per se relates directly to the first of redefining its history. American band The Melvins' album *The Crybaby* (2000) concludes their trilogy of albums about "the loser" that began with the aptly titled *The Maggot* (1998), followed by *The Bootlicker* (1999). Yet, this project of the band doesn't simply prolong the rock tradition of the so-called concept album, which normally indicates the ugly habit of thinking that if a story is told across an entire album rather than a single song, it is of greater artistic worth simply because it is more epic. Rather, they offer a set of resignifications that implode on themselves. Kurt Cobain was a great fan of The Melvins, and the fact that a cover version of his "Smells Like Teen Spirit" opens the album makes it crystal clear that the male role model of the crybaby is praised, not mocked, in this setting. Yet the nihilistic euphoria of teen frustration in the original track is frustrated a second time when it is sung by none other than 1970s teen star and crybaby Leif Garrett (!), and played note by note and sound by sound, only with more thud and with some odd minimal entry-delays that exhibit the isolated riffs of the well-known song and detach them from its wall of sound. In Garrett, The Melvins have employed a forgotten hero, a loser, while they themselves continue to make music even after their contract with a major label—which had signed them in the wake of the post-Nirvana grunge hype—was not extended, leaving them "losers" in the market field. As Hank Williams III (grandson of the famous) sings Merle Haggard's redneck song against the anti-Vietnam movement, "Okie From Muskogee," in between noisy experimental hard-core tracks with heavenly flutes and satanic Metal drums, any idea of a "traditional," conservative white-trash rock album is erected and pulverized at the same time.

Today, a conceptualization of painting that is capable of dealing with the realities of itself and the culture around it in a comparable way is not about abstraction and reduction in the early- to late-modernist sense of the terms, as embodied in the works of artists from Malevich to Reinhardt to McCollum. Conceptual paintings in the traditional sense of, say, On Kawara's "date paintings" demonstrate a model-like, linear metonymic signification: the picture *is*, rather than represents, what it signifies. As historically necessary and enriching as that *contraction* of signifier and signified may have been, we have become more demanding as viewers and want pictures to not just contract signifier and signified, but to let them morph into each other, invert onto themselves—a demand that makes about ninety percent of the work that is actively talked about today conceptual painting to some extent. Some of them, however, allow this shift to become more apparent and make it their actual point, as for example, Jim Shaw's *Thrift Store Paintings* (fig. 4). Appropriated artifacts, they are not executed by the artist himself, but by anonymous painters whose hobby endeavors sadly ended up in the musty cardboard boxes of the local Salvation Army shop where Shaw found them. He gives them deadpan descriptive titles, such as *Fast Food Last Supper* (an apocalyptic cityscape vision with Burger King signs rising from the fog and a da-Vincian Last Supper scene up in the clouds above) or *Boy with Duck Toy Peers through the Rusty Gates* (well, just that—a chubby boy, huge gates filling the entire picture). Appearing as part of something they were most certainly not made for (i.e., Jim Shaw's oeuvre) produces a turmoil of signification around these paintings that addresses all contextual factors of producing meaning in painting in general: what they "represent," to what end they were produced, what status as an artwork they can be ascribed, what the "artist's intention" and his/her psychological and social states were at the time, remain ultimately confused. Even without having to relegate them to painterly conventions such as "Naive" or "Bad Painting," we notice that the humor or horror in some of these pictures is not necessarily inadvertent, and that even if so, it has an impact that dwarfs any dubious jokiness of "oh look, these dumb suburban hobby-painter folks": they become U.F.O.s—unknown found objects—that provoke speculation not only about their origin, but about their intrinsic logic as well.

3. The Melvins and Shaw turn the tables on the status, respectively, of rock music and painting precisely by incorporating into their work a tradition or technique that has an even more contested status in terms of its "progressiveness" (grunge, Country/hobby painting). Another, more widespread strategy is, obviously, to go in the opposite direction: to insert *newer* media, thematically and practically, into the production.

Perhaps the seminal monument to this approach is Gerhard Richter's *Atlas*: his collection of small photographic prints that comprises a personalized archive of the visual world. From calm landscapes to 1960s pornography to the prison cells of Red Army Faction members to Holocaust victims, nothing that turns up in media reality is fundamentally excluded from this ordered maelstrom (though it is striking that precisely the images of Auschwitz, it seems, were the only "category" from *Atlas* that Richter decided not to use for his paintings). For the boy in the film *American Beauty* (1999), whose soldier-father collects Nazi paraphernalia, a small digital video camera serves as a prosthesis that enables the boy to both disengage from and keep in touch with his surroundings. Functioning like a Phantom-of-the-Opera mask that doesn't conceal his own ugly side so much as that of the world around him, the camera enables him to deal with parental terror and to fall in love with a girl and the beauty of the visual world (though the mawkish art poetics of a plastic bag dancing in the wind is an unconvincing stand-in).

This uncannily calm push-pull between snail-like retreat and prosthesian engagement, whether coated in post-irony or not, has become a central characteristic of painting today. Richter's pocket camera is replaced mostly by digital devices, as in Eberhard Havekost's accounts of East-German *Plattenbau* suburbias and facial features as seen through the digitally disturbed video-eye (fig. 5; pp. 263–265); or Albert Oehlen's painterly exercises in early computer graphics that recall the days of Commodore 64 and Atari; or Monique Prieto's paintings of flat, shadowless, baggy single color forms entirely composed in a more current computer design program. The "filter" of the technical device is not so much installed between the eye and the mediated world, which includes everything from monoculture trees to mutants in a *manga*, but between your perception of that world and the concept you make of that perception. Accordingly, the painterly act is not a manual mimesis of the mediated world as such, but of the personalized filtering process that is implanted into its perception.

Rock music (what a surprise by now) has come up with strikingly similar filtering tactics of wangling its relevance in the digitized world. The band model of interaction between manually played melodic and percussive instruments is still crucial for Berlin outfit To Rococo Rot, or London's Stereolab (fig. 6), or Air from Paris, or, to name the most notorious of

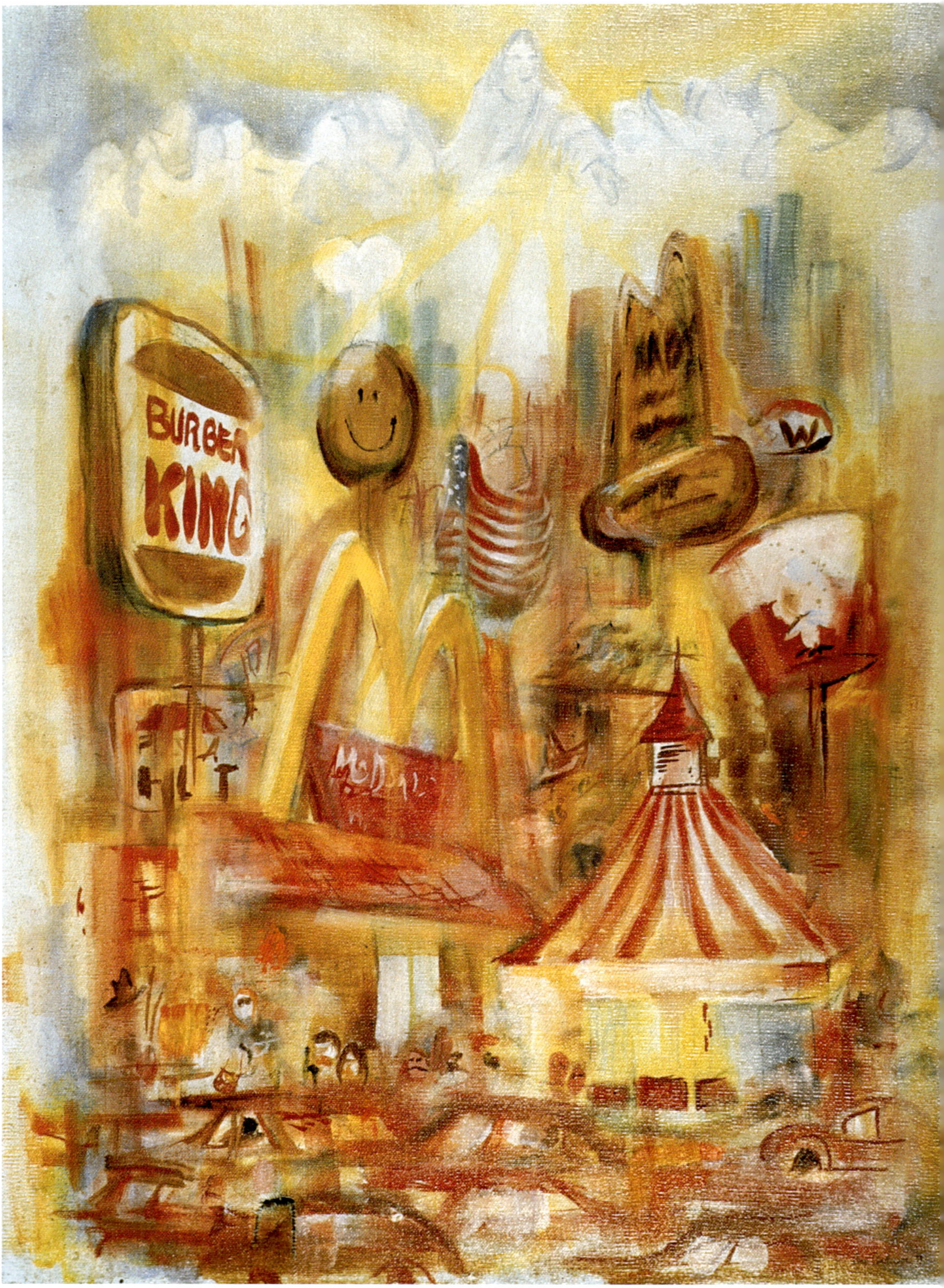

FIG. 4 Jim Shaw **Fast Food Last Supper** by Dan Anderson n.d. from the **Thrift Store Paintings** series acrylic on canvas 24 x 18 in. Courtesy the artist and Patrick Painter Inc., Santa Monica, California

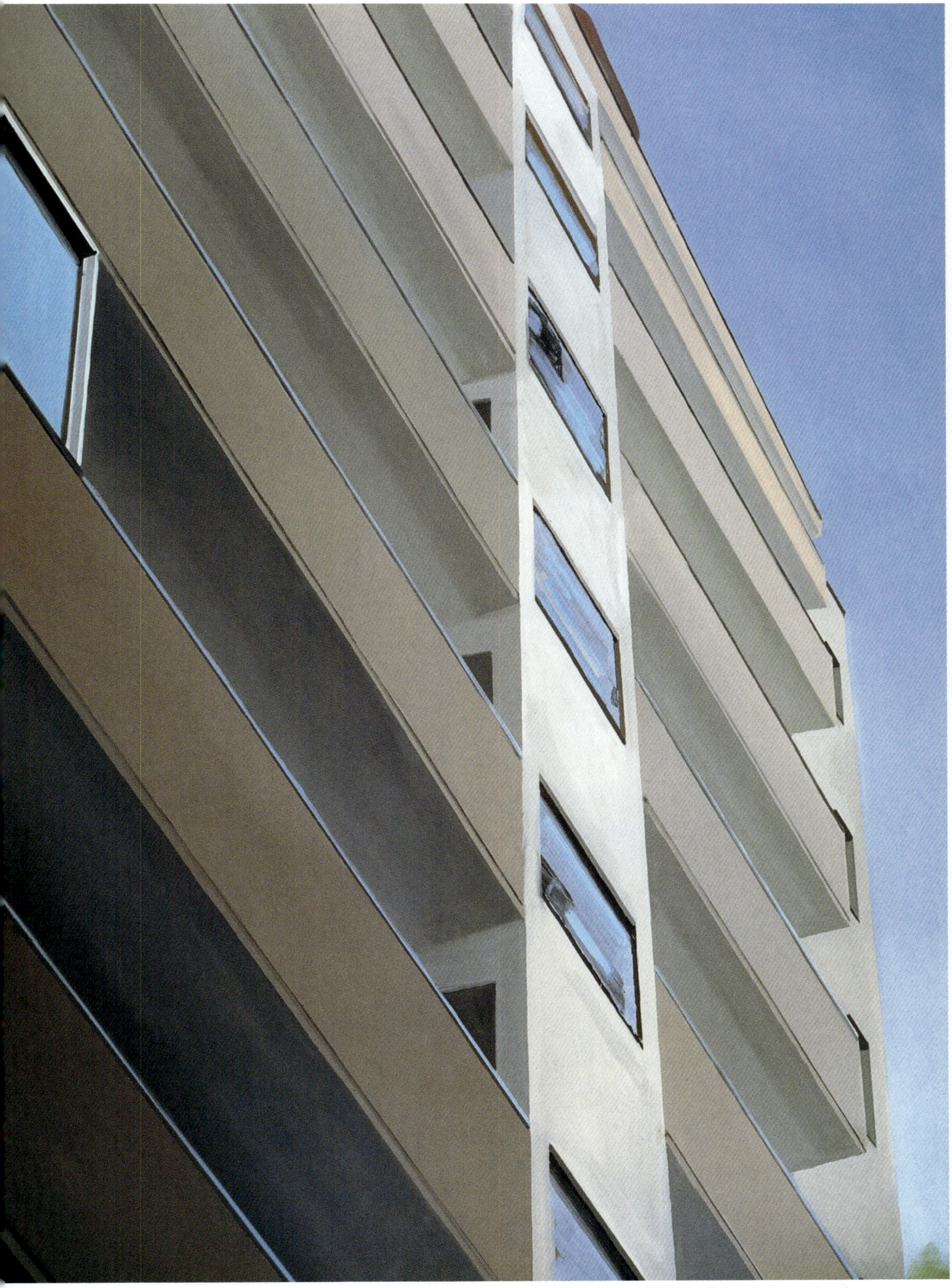

FIG. 5 Eberhard Havekost **G-Kabinen** (G-Cabins) 1998 oil on canvas 71 x 51 in. Courtesy the artist and Anton Kern Gallery, New York

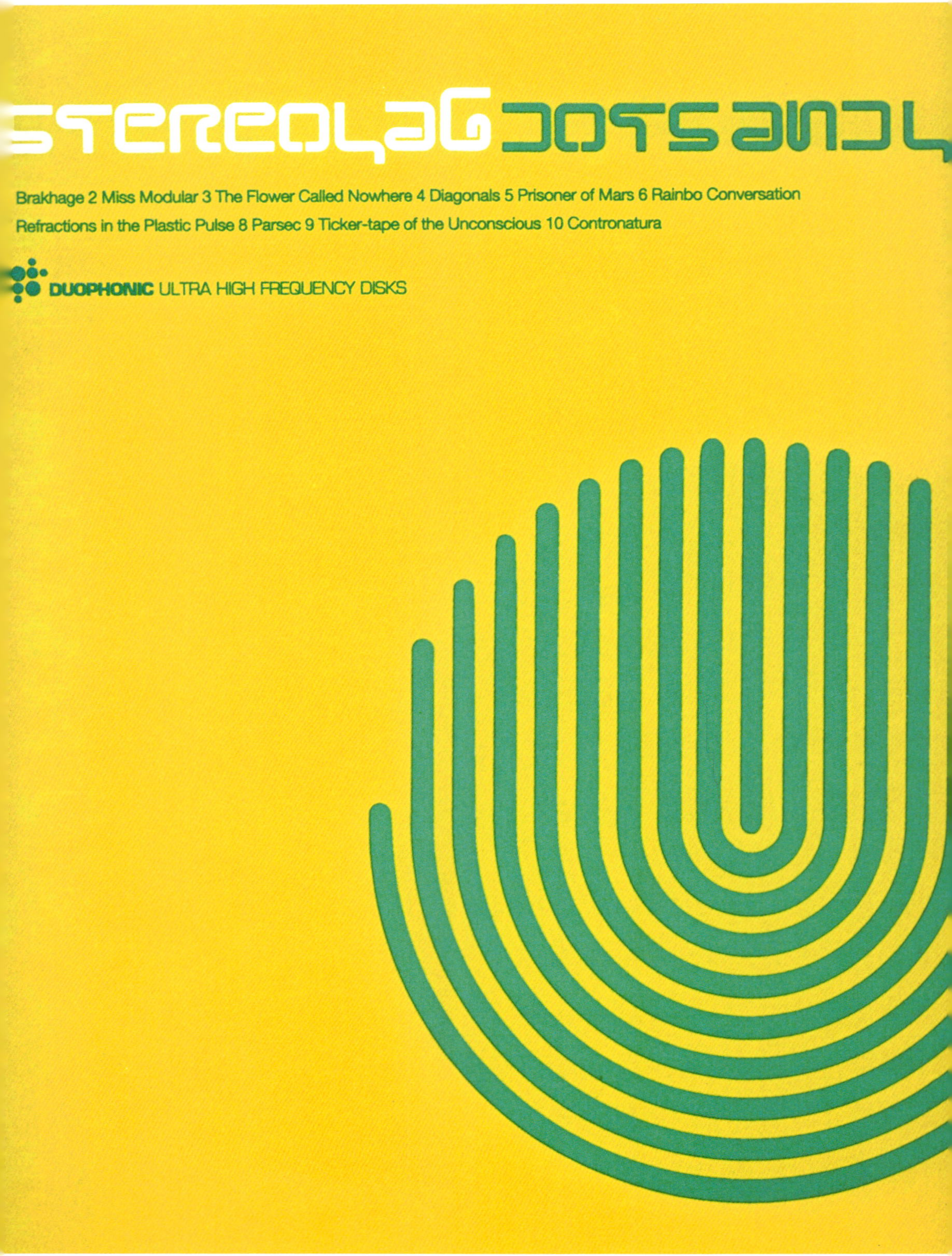

FIG. 6 album cover Stereolab **Dots and Loops** 1997 Courtesy the artists and Elektra Entertainment Group

them all, L.A.'s wunderkind, Beck. But sampling, technical distortion or alteration of voices, and the deconstructive use of studio technology (all of which were pioneered by dub-reggae, hip-hop, and house music) are seamlessly implanted into the musical production process. The extension of the pop-song format to both "track" and "collage" is tested, the guitar's role diminished or erased and replaced by, say, the digital sample illusion of a hand-played vibraphone, or plain E-noise. In the same way that contemporary painting has its soft spots for technologies on the brink of being replaced by more advanced gadgets—slides taken from analog VHS-video freezes projected onto the canvas—these current bands sample sounds from old records that were once produced with 1960s amplifiers, old magnetic tape-recording machines, expensive tube microphones, and recording-engineer expertise; they sometimes even directly use almost prehistoric instruments such as the theremin or the first Moog synthesizers. Whether subsumed under the helpless categories of "postrock" and "postpainting" or not, these practices reflect on the logic of the newest medium—digital rendering technology—by using a recently outdated medium (such as the analog synthesizer or VHS) within an even older production form (playing "live" in a band, manually applying paint). The stubborn rhetoric of the truly handmade has not been answered by an equally stubborn rhetoric of the truly machine-made, but rather by a blurring of the borderline between the two.

4. Having once worked with the newer production form, trading in the older one for it is only a step away. Yet abandoning painting or rock as a practice altogether doesn't necessarily mean you have to erase the fact that you have been socialized into them, and had reasons to turn to these media for a period in your production in the first place. Rather, it should be possible to address these practices from the perspective of the newer production form. Yet it seems that quite a few artists and musicians go to great lengths to play down or even conceal their "regressive" pasts. The rumors about classic conceptual artists cleansing their linear-progressive curricula vitae of early sidesteps into painting are very similar to those about current techno-musicians who project their development as a kind of rebirth or molting, often escorted by a quite shallow rhetoric about the death of the author. To name just two examples from Germany: Markus Popp, a.k.a. Oval, is a brilliant electronic musician, and with albums such as his recent *Ovalprocess* (form & function, 2000), he turns technical interference sounds or CD error clicks into a strangely beautiful soundscape that sometimes bears a resemblance to a very controlled, elegant guitar-feedback orgy; yet, in interviews, he rejects all nonelectronic music as totally regressive, while avoiding to mention his own experience as, for example, former bass-player for acclaimed Berlin punk-rock outfit Surrogat. Very similarly, in interviews, Moritz von Oswald of Basic Channel, influential dub-minimal-techno project from Berlin, neglects to talk about his past as a member of the early 1980s Hamburg New Wave scene around bands such as Palais Schaumburg.

As understandable as a certain desire for anonymity and the irritation of biographical readings may be, to address this personal attachment to an "older" medium without false nostalgia, as a key to understanding the current social and aesthetic structure, would be more fruitful. John Oswald, for example, used the entire collection of dozens of live recordings that exist of the Grateful Dead's epic song "Dark Star" as sampling material to construct a virtual, recombinant two-hour version of the song that lays bare the postrock quality already seeded in the original music (*Greyfolded*, 1998).

Photography, of course, produced legions of Vermeerian portraits, Turnerish landscapes, and Chardinesque still-lifes, as well as more or less conceptually motivated recontextualizations of painting in regard to its display and reception (Louise Lawler or Thomas Struth); likewise, there is already a long history of painting transformed to film, from Len Lye's movies of the 1930s to Stan Brakhage and beyond, setting abstract patterns into motion. The filmic qualities of motion and "immateriality" do not inevitably equal an advance from painting; for example, much of the video work of Bill Viola triggers art historical references not so much to reconsider these "originals" but to borrow heavily on their time-honored patina of authority. More convincing examples of such a transfer are filmic pieces by Douglas Gordon, Sharon Lockhart, and Jeroen de Rijke/Willem de Rooij (fig. 8), which

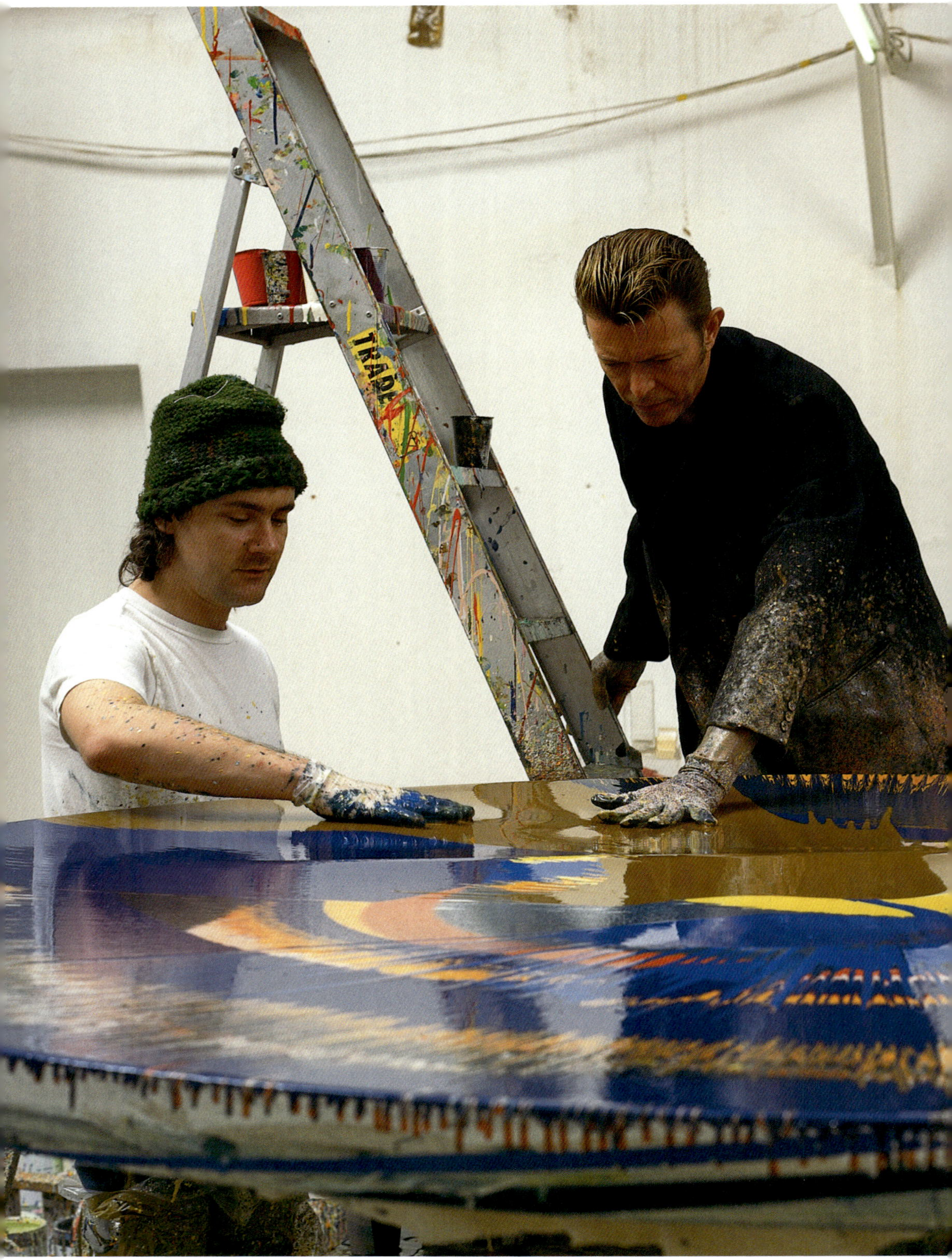

FIG. 7 Damien Hirst and David Bowie making a Spin Painting, April 30, 1995 at Brixton Studio, London
Courtesy Jay Jopling/White Cube, London, and Science, Ltd., London photo: Stephen White

bring the flux and edited speed of cinema to a one-shot, painterly halt, building on a tradition that Warhol introduced in the mid-1960s with *Kiss*, *Sleep*, and *Empire*. Gerwald Rockenschaub updated the emblematic geometry of his early 1980s paintings in his more recent color-foil prints of computer-icon-like vignettes that balance on a brink between pure formalism and allusions to suitcases or door handles—a transformation that was all too natural since the manually executed paintings already had the quality of productlike finish. Sometimes, it seems, painting mutates head-on into the media reality it intended only to mime.

Something makes artists and musicians return not necessarily to the old mode of production, but certainly to what it produced over centuries and decades in terms of a discourse: a robust interplay of repetition and differentiation within the boundaries of its limits, a matured discourse that makes it hard, and challenging, to contribute something new that enriches it. (And with photography, installation, and dance music storming the sales charts, you can't even complain, really, that the return to paint and strum was only for the sake of conservative market value.)

The first two approaches delineated above—remaking and remodeling a genre's history, conceptualizing it—are like two stances of the same tactic: digging one's heels into the materiality of a tradition in order to plough up its conventions. The third and fourth approaches—incorporating other media into the genre, reflecting on it from the perspective of another—blend into each other as well: starting to incorporate, say, computer visuals into painting is only a step away from turning the relationship around.

Seeing how this quadrophonic set of revision-as-progression tactics seems to hold true for both painting and rock music, it is not farfetched to imagine an artist moving between the two. However, the fruits of crossover can be stunningly bitter. A picture in the music magazine *Mojo* (June 1999) shows Paul Simonon, former bassist for The Clash—once visionaries of blending the sensibilities of punk and dub-reggae—standing on a London bridge, painting an embarrassing cityscape in blue, with white seagulls. Paul McCartney is exhibiting his hobby paintings—without really considering it a conceptual act—in a provincial gallery in Germany; Rolling Stone guitarist Ron Wood has released his in a book; David Bowie had Damien Hirst show him how to make spin paintings (fig. 7). There seems to be a severe urge on the part of aging rock musicians, perhaps at a point of crisis in their production, to add the aura of traditional, "serious" painter to their personality.

Conversely, painter Julian Schnabel, after having been left by his young girlfriend, released a CD of rock ballads—*Every Silverlining has a Cloud* (1995)—to ease his pain, sporting black Ray Bans and a sleeveless denim vest over hairy chest in a photo in the CD booklet. In 1999 Damien Hirst turned down the offer to show at the British pavilion in Venice, and instead appeared with Alex James from Blur as the not-so-convincing band Fat Les on *Top of The Pops*. There seems to be a severe urge on the part of some artists, perhaps at a point of crisis in their production, to add the aura of rock star to their personality.

It's easy to ridicule all these attempts at mixing or interchanging the ingredients of popular glamour and supposed artistic seriousness. The odd couple, stuck in the reruns of their sitcom, turns sad couple. Yet an exchange of context between art, not least its traditional medium of painting, and pop music, not least its traditional form of rock 'n' roll, may serve as a kind of litmus test of their respective definitions as fields of production, diffusion, and reception.

This litmus test is brought to a sharp conceptual head in a recent show of paintings by Joni Mitchell curated by young Los Angeles–based artist Amy Adler (LACE, Los Angeles, 2000). Adler (who herself questions the very definition of work on paper by destroying her drawings after photographing them), in her relationship to the show, seems to linger between the Jim Shaw approach of respectfully displaying surreal thrift-store paintings and the role of a fan-as-curator highlighting "the other side" of a legendary songwriter whose music is highly abstracted and deeply emotional at the same time.

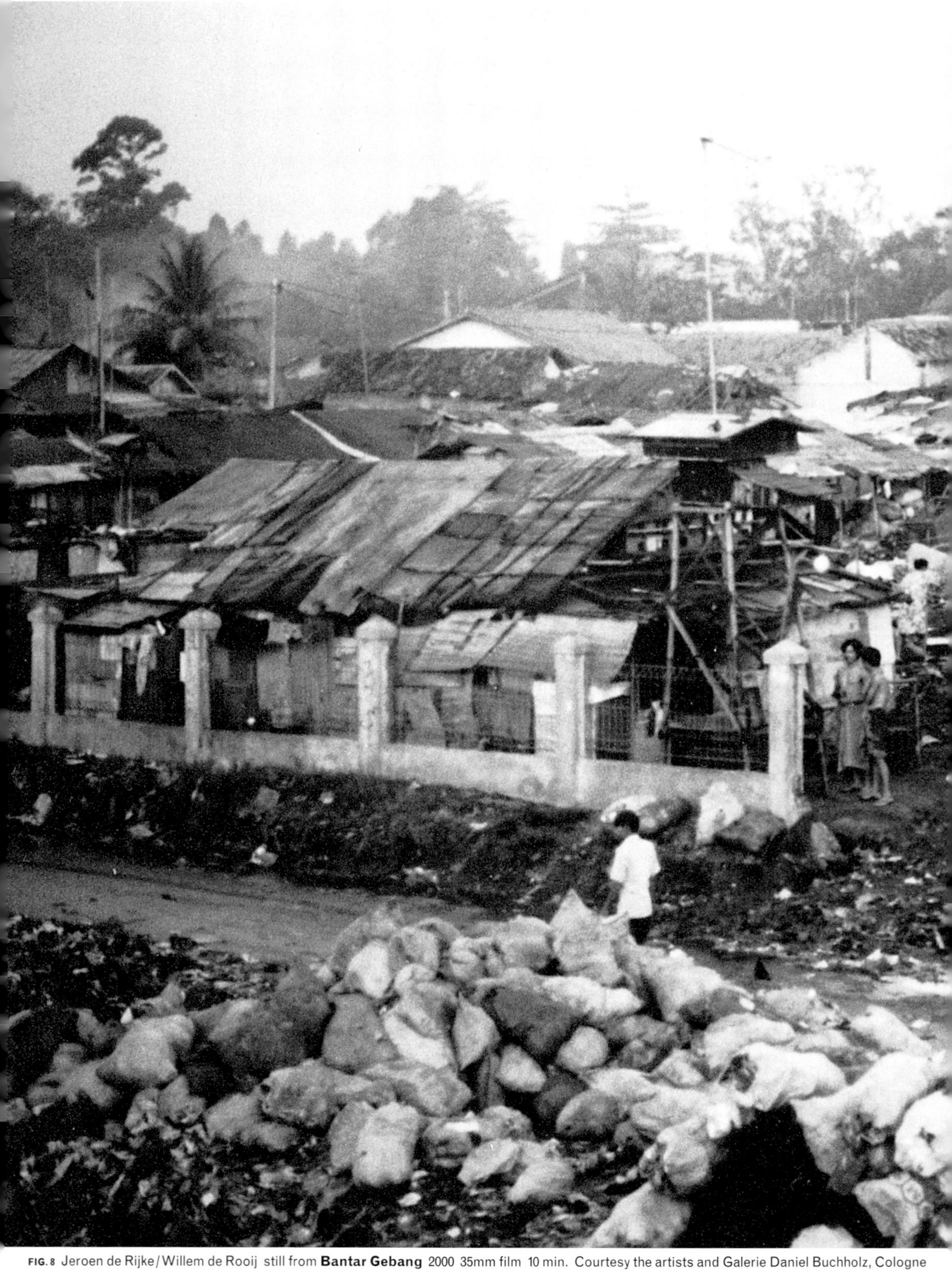

FIG. 8 Jeroen de Rijke/Willem de Rooij still from **Bantar Gebang** 2000 35mm film 10 min. Courtesy the artists and Galerie Daniel Buchholz, Cologne

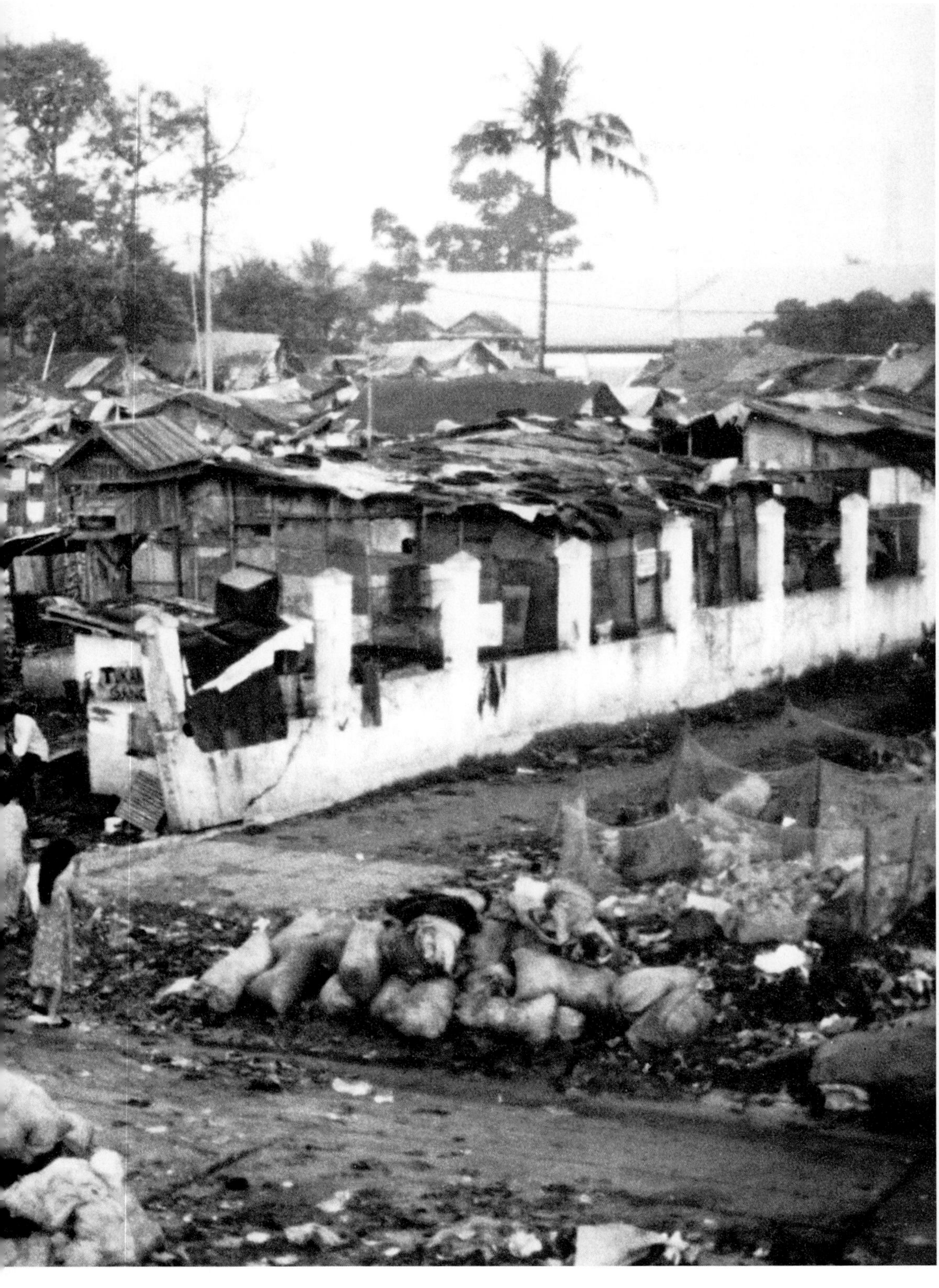

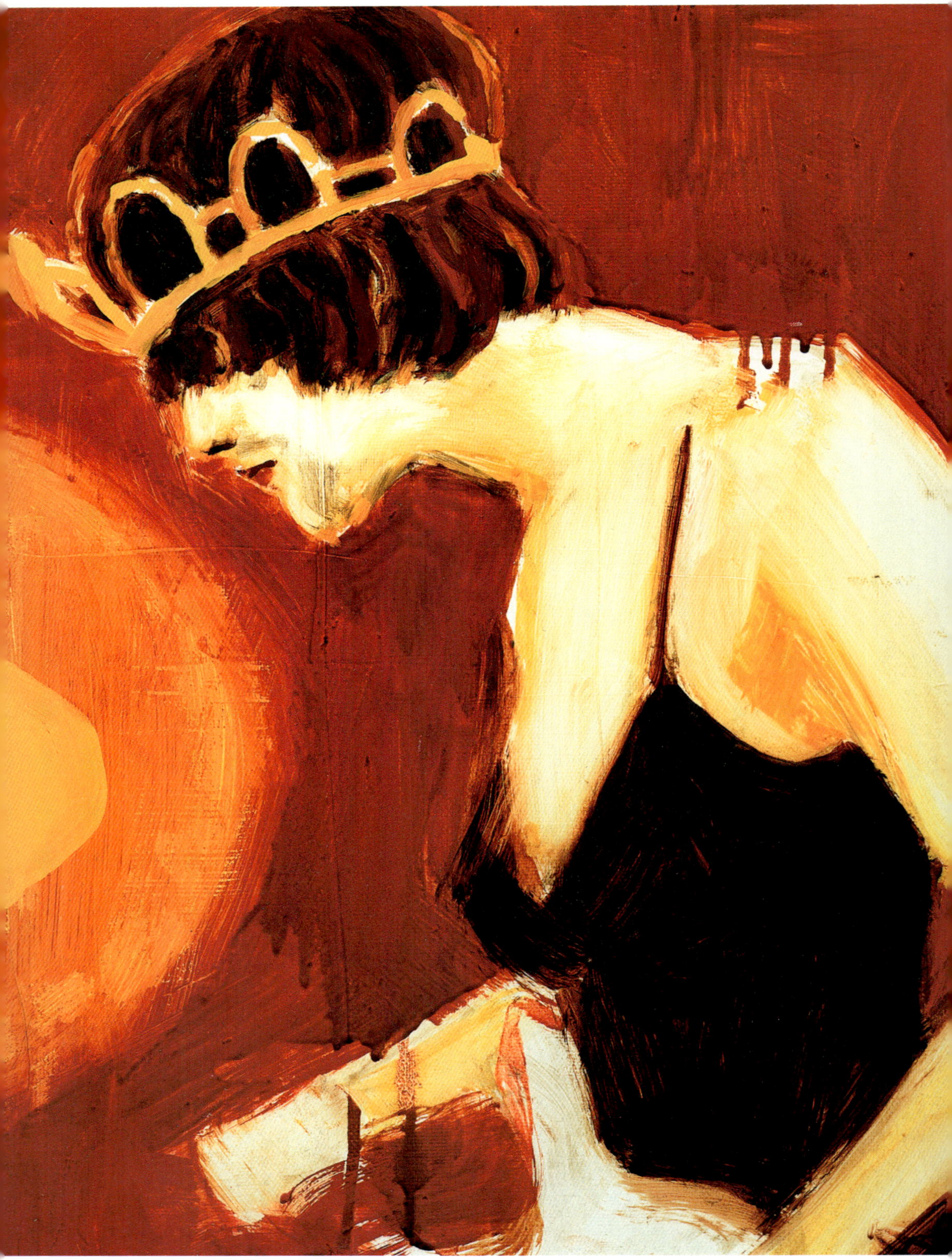

FIG. 9 Elizabeth Peyton **Princess Kurt** 1995 oil on linen 14 x 11 in. Collection Walker Art Center, Minneapolis; T. B. Walker Acquisition Fund, 1995

This scenario left me with a question that is symptomatic of the overall relevance of the relationship between painting and rock music, well beyond merely serving as respective subject matters (as in the rock-star portraits by Elizabeth Peyton [fig. 9] or songs such as Jonathan Richman's "Pablo Picasso Was an Asshole"). If people move from one context to the other, does that indicate a quest or a flight? In regard to her music, Mitchell had certainly been visionary with albums such as *Hissing of Summer Lawns* (1975), inventing a peculiar rhythmic flow of poetry and sound, infusing synthesizers and Burundi drumming, letting any expectation of what a white female folk singer was supposed to be collapse. Yet, at the same time, it seems as if her paintings were meant to level out this leap into the unknown with a reassuring, initially private, traditionalist practice that would stop short of engaging with anything more recent than van Gogh. Thinking of the work of Don Van Vliet, a.k.a. Captain Beefheart, a similar observation can be made: with albums such as *Trout Mask Replica* (1969), Beefheart fused rock music and blues with free-jazzer Ornette Coleman's ideas of "harmolodics," while the paintings he went on to make in the 1970s and 1980s did not really do much more than supplement the means of expression of the New York School with a kind of landscape, California-desert variety.

Perhaps this indicates that it is hard enough to develop a *competence of context* in one field of production, so that even a proper competence of craft in another field cannot make up for a lack of engagement in that other context's discourse. Which makes the myth of a seamless crossover between art forms all the more questionable. As critics paint the picture of the lighthearted, light-handed, tongue-in-cheek young producers who move effortlessly among categories, which are all embraced within a common notion of "good entertainment," the need to eagerly conjure up that sense of naturalness is precisely an indicator of its absence. Yet, competence in *one* context necessarily includes knowledge of *other* contexts (which doesn't necessarily mean you have to produce in or toward them). As composer Hanns Eisler once put it, in regard to his own genre, "If you know only about music, you know nothing about music."

What you often get in electronic production that fetishizes its own technological status is the setting for a leap into the unknown that turns out to harbor the sadly known. The mastery of a complex technical apparatus that can absorb all skills and energies leaves no room for an imaginative way of employing it; high-end engineers are not necessarily the best artists.

Even when a nostalgic futurism is claimed in its name, the conflicted historicity of painting and rock is a good antidote to mindless tabula-rasa bulldozing. They should not be considered as testimonials of some ultimate, time-transcending essence, but rather, their second-hand status should be admitted: they are commodities that offer themselves up continuously for reconsideration in the flea market of vanities. And amidst all that jumble, the odd couple gets reunited and divorced once again.

NOTES

1 Sleeve notes, *Roxy Music: The Thrill of it All*, Virgin Records, 1995. See also Paul Stump, *Unknown Pleasures: A Cultural Biography of Roxy Music* (London: Quartet Books, 1998), p. 59 ff.

2 Quoted in Mario Amaya, *Pop Art and After* (New York: Viking Press, 1965), p. 33.

3 See Simon Frith and Howard Horne, *Art into Pop* (London and New York: Methuen, 1987), pp. 62, 100.

4 "Philosophie, die einmal überholt schien, erhält sich am Leben, weil der Augenblick ihrer Verwirklichung versäumt ward," Theodor W. Adorno, in the introduction to *Negative Dialektik* (Frankfurt a.M.: Suhrkamp, 1966), p. 15.

Mike Kelley is a Los Angeles–based multidisciplinary artist whose series of paintings *The Thirteen Seasons (Heavy on the Winter)* is included in *Painting at the Edge of the World*. Kelley's prolific writings, which range from creative prose to critical texts, have been published widely in magazines and books. Many of these works will be collected in *Mike Kelley: Selected Writings*, forthcoming in 2001 from MIT Press. The following text was originally published in the exhibition catalogue *The Thirteen Seasons (Heavy on the Winter)* (© 1995 Jablonka Galerie, Cologne); reprinted with the permission of the artist and Jablonka Galerie, Cologne.

Mike Kelley
Goin' Home, Goin' Home
1995

Q: How do you know if your Doctor is a man?
A: There's shit on his speculum.

Looking backwards, ass backwards.
This is your life.
Peephole history.
The Wayback Machine.
Porthole to the soul.
Your lemon sheets, hung out the bedroom window to dry.
Lonesome yellowing scrapbook in the sun.
Gilded hair gone white.
Silver mirror.
Golden Boy/White Trash.
Upscale cracker, with caviar on it.
Tommy Roe, Cum Gum, Bun Boy, Love Gun.
This is the oval reflector, solar-framed, exuding light.
The mirror has been painted on, outlining the self.

At the crossroads of life.
At Tross City limits.

Standing, vertical, in front of a mirror, in the dark, with candle in hand, reveals the multi-colored aura.
Caught squatting over a mirror with a flashlight.
"Say, Doc, is there such a thing as an anal speculum? Huh?"
Oh oh! Candle in the sock drawer.
Yes, right below the vaseline drawer, sir.
It's next to Mommy's secret cabinet . . . of . . . of HORRORS.
Body loathing, Mmmmmmmmm good.
Gaze trauma. Wow! And, va va voom!
Keyhole shock. Zzzzzzzzzz.
Electric door knob.
Jane and/or John Doe caught a disease from it.
They all bumped into it and got a hickey. Yeah, sure!
Blame it on the toilet seat, just like everyone else.
What's that a picture of, in there?
I don't know, and if you can't say what it is . . . it must be dirty.
It's bad, and I'm bad, and we're both alike and that's good.
Tee hee! Look at me! I'm naughty.

When painting a painting, there comes the final period when you enter into struggle with it. It taunts you; it dares you to force it to behave, to make it be "right." A painting might be finished, that is, the support may be adequately covered with paint, the handling of the medium may display a proficiency with materials, yet the painting does not seem done. It calls out: "I have yet to conform. That mysterious sense of order and balance has not yet been attained." But when this balance is found you instinctively know it is so. Then the painting becomes placid and ceases to cry out. Only then is it good.

But what are the rules that define this completion? What are these laws that elude utterance? One can speak, but the language that surrounds a true image never conveys its material perfection. An image that sits well defies explanation. Its surrounding landscape has an other-worldly air, divorced from body and soul. It comes off as pedantically technical, emotionally empty. The thing done correctly is the thing that assumes its own naturalness. And the natural is irretrievable through anything but itself. It can only be spoken through itself. The laws that

govern true being must not be questioned. They simply are. To question them is to destroy their naturalism. To pose the question makes the truth into a lie. What are the laws? Shut up, and don't ask. The law is the law. It is buried in you. You operate perfectly well under its domination. And, believe me, you really don't want to know anything anyway.

Pray to the old God, the cruel one.
Pray to the One you struggled to erase your belief in.
Pray to the One who preys on you.
This is the vicious God of the Old School.
He is the maker of the violent universe.
He is the cosmic torturer.
He snorts when you say the Messiah has come.
"No son of mine," the bass intones.
"Slap the Sissy around."
And Helen Girly-boy Brown
Came to town
Sittin' like a girl, crossed legs
Carryin' schoolbooks like a girl, pressed to chest
Sobbin' like a girl, tears rolling down apple cheeks
Gigglin' like a girl, with a gaggle of others
Gettin' beat like a girl, submissive-like
Suckin' Dad's Cock like a girl, etc., etc., etc.

Except maybe it's Mom's Cock. A lot of things aren't what they seem, are they? Take the painting's aura of completion, for instance. Let's call this sense of completion the painting's normalcy. What if this normalcy is only a screen memory: a projected image of comfort, based on social stereotypes, used to mask an unbearable true event that cannot be faced without grave psychic damage? In this scenario the painting's comfort, its sense of naturalness, comes only from repressed indoctrination covering up subjugation and abuse. Your root, your true self, is a false mirror. Who knows what's really there? It's a moot point now, because nothing's been left behind. You are only compliance. Your inability to get to the bottom of your sense of aesthetic pleasure is not a merging with a natural order—akin to not recognizing yourself in the mirror, which is a beautiful humble experience—it is simply repression. Oh, you think you have risen above. You think that your loss of memory is a sign of getting past certain wrong-headed childhood fantasies, of leaving old useless baggage behind. Not true. Your memory loss is successful, planned erasure. You are now living, breathing indoctrination.

You are now "you." Since your true self cannot be confronted you have mystified it. Now that which has been tossed into the mind's garbage can becomes "special." The so-called "finished" artwork is simply the one that presses unlabeled psychic buttons. They switch on the pleasure sign, the one that illuminates your denied, hated self in an admirable light. Every time you feel aesthetic pleasure you unconsciously reenact your abuse at the hands of the law. You live out again the unchanging rule. You don't know you are doing it. Your sense of accomplishment is mysterious. You don't even realize you are in compliance. You don't realize that your very being is a continuous loop playing back your originating abuse.

I am the reincarnation of Hans Hofmann.
Prodigal son.
To Sir with love.
Beachside painting resort disciple.
Old-fashioned acolyte.
Fawning at your lord's feet.
You can go home again.
Teach Me Tonight.
Rebirthing once a week.
Put down in the ship's log.
Hearth and home.
Call me Norman Bates.
Summoned up.
Making the primal scene.
Family-treed by bloodhounds.
Puppet of the ancients.
Unhooded by the Clan.
Outlived by Jim Morrison's dad.
Transfused with Master's blood.
I, Renfield.
The Fall of the House of Maytag.
Still warm stiff.
Blood is thicker that matte medium.
In the shanty foldin' panties.
Ed Gein Memorial Junior High School.
Past sniffer.
Corpseophile.
Not dead, just sleeping.
Awake!

Whenever you "rediscover" your old creations, isn't it funny that you find them so satisfying? You're as engrossed as baby is with his or her own poop. And, to top it off, it seems as if a hiatus from old ways sharpens your skills at those abandoned practices. Then you ask yourself: "Why did I ever stop doing this? How is it that I forgot myself? Why do I have to rediscover what I already know?" And then you cry out: "I want to go home again!" Well, come on back. Your room's just like it was when you left. We've kept it exactly the same, untouched, in anticipation of your return. You're home.

So here I am back at the steps of my old academy. I knock on the wise door with a tear in my eye. Yes, I am the first to admit that my paintings are willful perversions of my training. They are full of ironic inversions and grotesque substitutions. All of these strategies are empty posturings; they are simply flimsy facades hung on a solid framework, but they do not diminish the truth of their interior structure. All my pathetic Oedipal struggles to construct a new aesthetic, one that is solely "mine," cannot hide the fact that all of my later "innovations" are based on unshakable law. Inversion and perversion only serve to reinscribe the law they seek to undermine. Surface meaning is of no consequence. The underlying rule never falters.

I, on the other hand, stumble. Weak-kneed, I totter ahead still deluded that I chart my own course. I live a lie. I believe that I have matured when I have only aged. I fancy that I have constructed my own history. It is all shit. The law is there. And in my last breath, like all lapsed believers, I will whimper and ask for forgiveness. I will die groveling, begging to be reinstated into the ranks I never truly left: the ranks of the law-abiding. Stupid me. I was a believer all along.

Hubert Damisch is Director of Studies at the École des Hautes Études en Sciences Sociales in Paris. He is the author of numerous books on art and philosophy in English translation, including *The Origin of Perspective* (1994), *The Judgment of Paris* (1996), and the forthcoming *Skyline: The Narcissistic City (Cultural Memory in the Present)* (2001) and *A Childhood Memory by Piero della Francesca* (2001). He lectures at institutions internationally, and in 1997 he was a Kress Professor at the Center for Advanced Studies in the Visual Arts at the National Gallery of Art, Washington, D.C. The following essay was first published in *Das Bild nach dem letzten Bild* (The picture after the last picture) edited by Christian Meyer and Peter Weibel (© 1991 Galerie Metropol, Vienna, and Walther König, Cologne); reprinted with the permission of Galerie Meyer Kainer, Vienna.

The Trickery of the Picture

Hubert Damisch

1991

1. The French definition is straightforward: a "tableau" is, first of all, an object, a plane, a flat surface of wood or of canvas mounted on a frame, something like a *table*, but one that is placed vertically, at a level and in such a way as to serve as the base for whatever one may wish to inscribe or display on it. A metonym, then (a word standing for another one, the base representing the work in its entirety), or rather a synecdoche that is the opposite of the one used in English. Where the English language puts emphasis on the object represented (*picture*) and distinguishes clearly between the picture in the active, "progressive" sense of the term, or *painting*, and the base on which the painting takes place (*canvas, panel, picture plane*), French is not adverse to stressing, right from the beginning, the material aspect of what it calls *tableau*, leaving it to the museums to be more specific and display, as the Louvre does, their works in what they call collections, not "de *la* peinture" (of *painting*) but "*des* peintures" (of *paintings*).

Merely a question of terminology, one may say. Yes, but not so harmless or inconsequential as it may appear at first sight. The fact that one and the same word may denote the product of painting and the material base on which it is placed may well make us wonder what relationship exists between what one might call the "operation" of the painting with its external form, its "exterior" and its substrate, if not its very substance. Though formulated, at the beginning of this century, in solely visual and pictorial terms in line with Cézanne's and Seurat's ideas, this question has been with us since the beginning of art, and particularly since the beginning of contemporary art, even though the latter may claim to have "broken with easel painting." As Daniel Buren saw (and said) so clearly, the elimination, the material disappearance, of the "frame," the "base," the "canvas," even of the "painting" as such, is not enough to make these concepts anachronistic: In a way the same holds for the "picture," the standards of which, in the absence of form, continue to be clandestinely respected even in a great many works which seem to have entirely broken with the convention, continue to be *reflected* in them, often in substitutive or indirect ways that do not lend themselves to conscious or deliberate projection, nor to further development or consistent pictorial or intellectual processing.

2. Is it true, then, that the picture is a thing of the past, as is also the painter's perspective, with which it has been so closely linked throughout history as the emergence of the form, if not the object, of the picture itself—coincided in time with the development of the representation technique known as *costruzione legittima*? Conventional art history takes it for a fact that the disappearance of the one inevitably results in the abandonment of the other, though this close relation between the form of the picture and *perspectiva artificialis* has never been critically analysed. According to the epigones of Cubism, the break that gave rise to modern art was first effected by Cézanne, whose work, they say, heralded the end of what has been called "scientific" perspective. The relation or chain of dependence which history suggests might exist between the picture and perspective, or which it demonstrates and throws into relief, urgently calls for thorough theoretical investigation which might shed light on the matter. Still, there remains the question of the standing and operation of both the "picture" form and the paradigm of perspective in the context of modern art, since both of them, though "things of the past," have not entirely lost their significance and authority.

3. The alleged break with the "picture" form is based on diverse lines of reasoning. First of all, there are reasons of an ideological nature, derived as they are not so much from aesthetic or pictorial considerations but rather from criticism of the ideology behind them, be it the ideology of "art" or of the museum. The "picture" in the concrete sense of the term is a product of a history and presents itself as a culturally determined form. The French concept of "tableau," and indeed the term itself, indicates an object that is basically mobile, displaceable, and therefore replaceable. It is an object that lends itself to private ownership and thus is marketable commodity. It follows, too, that it is an object that can be removed, or can escape from, its original context, which will inevitably result in its losing its original content, which loss cannot be made up, strictly speaking, even by the additional meaning that the work acquires when it is incorporated into a series of other works in an art collection or museum.

The determination to do away with "easel painting" is largely due to the desire to give back to the work of the painter something of the necessity, something of the immediacy it had when it was inseparable from the wall, or from the book, from which it derived its contextual value. But the "picture" needs the easel. One certainly cannot simply detach a fresco from the wall and consider it ready to display in a museum as one would display a "picture"; yet the large-scale paintings of Pollock, though they may have been painted on the floor, nevertheless present themselves, in the museum, like "canvases" fixed to a "frame" and then covered with paint, though, by virtue of their sheer size (and this remark holds for most of the adherents of the big canvas), they seem to aspire in a new way to a—perhaps somewhat nostalgic—kind of "mural" quality, which implies a different relation to the museum walls on which they are displayed, and also to their visitors.

4. Is the "picture," then, really a thing of the past? But what picture, or the picture in what sense of the term? The picture as an object? As a form? The picture as a function—and what function could be fulfilled without context, let alone without a frame? The picture as an activity, which would require a new definition of the operation of painting?

The "picture" form corresponds to a particular moment in the history of painting and, more generally, in the history of art. A chronological moment, for the emergence of what is called easel painting can be dated with a fair amount of precision, as can be its alleged end. An historic moment, for the advent of easel painting may be said to have coincided with the development of modern trade, capital accumulation, and the predominance of commodities seen, and idolized, as having intrinsic value. A dialectic moment, too, for the "picture" may be seen as the negation of what had previously formed the base for the picture (it "interrupts" the wall). And, lastly, an ontological moment, for what can become of painting, both when it conforms to the standard of the "tableau" and follows its rules, and when it claims to have liberated itself from its fetters?

5. We are familiar with the contradiction that faced Mondrian and which is borne out by the presence of his works in museums today. For these works are not really *present* on the museum walls, just as the works of Picasso or Matisse are not, nor other paintings regarded as abstract. Paradoxically, it is when the small panels painted by Mondrian present themselves, in the museum, in the guise of tableaux that the question arises most insistently (a theoretical question, and one that is not only historical in nature but again ontological in the strict sense of the word)—the question of what such a form of painting is supposed to mean, what it aims at, and how it is to work. To Mondrian, neoplasticism was the harbinger of the end of the "culture of singular forms," which was to be followed by a culture of relations of equivalence, as he called them, where the "individual oppression of form" would be replaced with the "universal expression of rhythm." As he saw it, painting and sculpture were destined to dissolve themselves as separate objects, to be directly projected—as the painter wrote—"into life." Seen in this light, the picture is doomed insofar as it conforms to the definition of the singular form as it is produced by lines and, as such, is contained within the limits of a contour. If the term *projected* has been used here, if the very idea of projection has arisen, it is not only because "life," as conceived in the ideology of neoplasticism, has taken on the appearance of architecture. Colours, Mondrian said, ought to be applied at the very place where the work was to be seen, as the effect could be precisely calculated only in the context of the relations between the colours and the architecture; but Mondrian was the first to admit that the time had not yet come for a complete unification of the arts under the name of architecture, and that the "new plastic" would still have to manifest itself *in the form of painting,*[1] a kind of painting, however, which was not to seek merely a static form of equilibrium such as can be attained within the limits of a picture, but a dynamic equilibrium, some "composition" that would function like an expanding graph or matrix, the lines of which seem to be continued on the wall thanks to a linear form of projection that progresses in the two dimensions of the picture plane. Merely attaching these panels to the museum wall will not necessarily put an end to this effect. This does not mean, however, that the "cutting off," or rather, the delimitation that gives rise to the form of the "picture" will not prevail in the museum setting over the centrifugal qualities of the graphic and/or colour matrix.

6. The "directions for use" that accompany some of Mondrian's paintings which were made, according to the painter, to be viewed from a certain height and distance necessarily call to mind the principles of painting in perspective, with one little difference, viz., that where a picture designed according to the laws of perspective would have to be seen from a specific point located to the right of the "vanishing-point," the orthogonal grids designed by Mondrian serve—merely optically, at first—to baffle the eye, and thus throw the subject out of balance—in our case the subject of art itself. If a picture actually is the device, the "dispositif" that Lacan called it, this situation, where it is for the subject itself to find its bearings, is one not entirely unknown in the paradigm of perspective, the emergence of which actually preceded the development of the—essentially "modern"—concept of a scientific subject. It was not by accident that the first tableau in the modern sense of the term was, perhaps, the small panel painted by Brunelleschi at the beginning of the quattrocentro to serve him for his experiments in perspective: the *tavoletta* on which he represented the Battistero of Florence such as it could be seen by a person on the inside of the central portal of the Cathedral, and in which he drilled a hole at the very point on which converged the vanishing lines of the painting, so that turning it around and peering through the hole from the *back* of the picture he could study the *obverse* (the painted face) of the picture in a mirror. The first and foremost objective was to demonstrate that the viewing point coincides, by projection, with what has come to be called the vanishing point; and that what the Italians and Germans justly call the "point of the eye" (*punto dell'occhio, Augenpunkt*) is simply the image, in the picture plane but hypothetically removed to infinity, of the point sometimes referred to as the "subject point" (*point du sujet*).

Perspective design is said to have, first and foremost, aimed at producing, in the form of a foreshortened chequered pavement, the setting in which the "story" which, according to Alberti, was the foremost goal of painting, could take place. But what happens when the chequered plane, the "grid," is set upright and presented from the front and when the lines no longer converge on a single point which serves to bring infinity within the limits of a finite organism, the "picture"? What if, at the price of a *diversion* whose aim is to divert the view from what is believed to be the reference point and to shift the subject away from the story which it was supposed to dominate, what if the subject is, though perhaps not completely defeated, at least thrown off balance and *can no longer find its way* through the painting, let alone "read" it, as seemed possible with a traditional picture? In this so-called "terminal" stage, does painting still have resources which one could (or should) call "tabular"?

7. Even the "last picture" is a "picture." Now, does "last picture" mean one that puts an end to painting, or does it suggest that painting comes to an end of its own accord, or is it the ultimate work, one that heralds the possibility of an art freed of the limitations, the tyranny of the conventional "tableau"-type picture? "Ultimate paintings," like perhaps the paradoxically monochrome draughtboards painted by Ad Reinhardt, the squares of which appear as such only thanks to a pronounced difference in colour density, paintings which Reinhardt considered the first of a new era, where the term, in the case in point, included, right from the beginning, the concept of figure?

It is, in fact, the function of what we have called "term" that we have to investigate if we wish to consider, from the angle of today, what might be the destiny of the picture and what we should think of its continued covert presence in today's painting. A *surreptitious* presence, one might say, because it makes its presence felt through some kind of trickery. Piero della Francesca defined the picture as a term (*termine*, from Latin *terminus*: "that which limits meaning") which actually meant a twofold limitation, since a picture painted in perspective should be seen from a distance slightly less than its width, while at the same time the width of the picture should be sufficiently small to avoid any deformation in the plane. There can be no doubt that this rule meant that the picture was to be considered to be more or less the same as a projection plane. But Brunelleschi's experiment, and his instruction to the viewer to put his eye against the hole in the back of the picture and look at it in a mirror, has a lot more to tell us about the relationship between the *obverse* and the *reverse* of a painting in the classic sense of the term than we can learn from an icon of disillusioned modernity—which was soon to adopt the guise of a *cartoon*—a picture that shows the image of a frame painted upon the reserve of the canvas so that what we see is what the picture would look like if it was hung with its face to the wall.

8. Thus, from now on our task will not be to look for the traces of the "picture" form, or for what has replaced it, in contemporary work, but rather to review the various ways in which to "make pictures," including the most recent and most incongruous ones. In other words, to relate the adventures of the picture—its development from a picture-as-a-form to a picture-as-an-activity, or as a process. As a consequence, the effort of *idealisation*, which is a prerequisite for the operation of painting, will appear as what it really is: not a purely negative feature through which is revealed the ideological function that painting may well have (it is high time we understood that the "picture" by its very nature excludes the trompe l'oeil, and that the illusion—the "trap" set for the viewer—only works within strictly defined limits), but—as in the field of mathematics—the most constant, and most fruitful, area in which it can operate.

When we talk about what a "picture" represents, the "tableau" depicts in a way an instantaneous moment of equilibrium at which the action comes to a momentary halt and which is bound to be disrupted. Such is actually the case in the *tableaux vivants* conceived by the past master of sensual pleasure, de Sade ("Truly, friends, it is a pleasure to order pictures from you, as there is no artist in all the world who could execute them better than you"). And such is the case with Hoffmann's story of the orchestra which, frozen into inaction in its pause in the famous picture of Hummel, all of a sudden starts playing again as the conductor lowers his baton too soon. And such is the case for Lessing's reference to the need for the painter to choose that moment of the action which he feels is the most fertile, the moment "which allows the viewer to understand best what happens at the moment immediately preceding and that immediately following."

Even if it were to confine itself to depicting a group of objects or a landscape the very aspect of which, devoid of any action whatsoever, was enough to arouse the viewer's interest, the classic picture would still be the setting in which an operation of an essentially representative nature was taking place: the delimitation from which it starts is intended to provide the basis for constructing a scene and, in contrast to a stubborn prejudice, as such contradicts any idea of "centering" or "framing" other than one inherent in the composition. Eisenstein saw no other way out than to abandon the stage for the cinema, which offered him the means to play on a large scale and with different forms of cutting and montage which do away with the illusion of an object presented in its entirety, which is what the ideal of the painted picture actually boils down to. Cubist and futurist painting may well have paved the way, by giving free reign to part-objects to manifest themselves on their own. But abstract painting was to change all that by passing from the "tableau" as the site of "operation" to a tabular quality which becomes the very area in which the painter's work takes place.

9. The standard of "making pictures" continues to govern a considerable part of contemporary painting even though the products may have the appearance of anything but classic paintings. But for this to happen it was first of all necessary that painting rediscovered "*la table*" beneath "*le tableau*" and revived its intimacy not only with the metonym but the metaphor. From Cézanne to the cubist painters to Dubuffet, the "table"—the "panel"—becomes again that surface set up vertically to serve as the base for the painter's work. It is enough to divide this base, to break it down into compartments in line with some simple rules (such as the one to which Mondrian so strictly obeyed, viz., not to allow even a single oblique line) in order to throw its tabular properties into relief. Just as, in mathematics, a matrix is simply a table composed of columns and lines which delineate the boxes over which are distributed the elements which satisfy a specific law and in respect of which one defines a certain number of operations, "abstract" painting (how appropriate a name!) has come to make use of a similar device for its experiments with, say, the interaction of colours. But even this would amount to nothing if the act of abstracting had not resulted in an even more radical subversion of the standard of the tableau: a number of panels in

different colours placed side by side on a wall will, in turn, form a "picture," while the painter is free to work on the panel itself and, breaking away from the hallowed form of the *quadro*, of the rectangular *tavola*, to concentrate (as Ellsworth Kelly is doing) on the common ground of painting and sculpture within that blurred outline which still *represents* the "picture."

10. Such is the trickery of the picture that, even today, each and every pictorial design of consequence is somehow affected by it. The tableau has not ceased to function as a model and ideal standard, even though the concept as such has been radically transformed. But, as regards turning the terms of the problem around and having the picture, in its turn, *affected* by the painting, the narrow vertical bands which show discreetly in the canvases of Barnett Newman and cause in them something like a transverse shift have a similar effect as Brunelleschi's hole in the middle of his panel, though in a way which relies on a tabular principle of a completely different nature. All differences apart, in either case the painter has to accord the "picture" its full *ideal* value—in the sense of "mathematical idealities" such as a number or a linear function defined in terms of the elements of abstract space, or indeed an "integral." The problem in both cases (the term "abstraction" has, in fact, the same meaning both in mathematics and in painting) is to understand how mathematics and painting *come about*,[2] the difference being, however, that, while the mathematician works with a set of symbols without bothering too much about them, leaving it to epistemology to explore the realm in which they operate, the object of painting is simply to do again and again what is its calling to do, to deal incessantly with the concerns inherently its own in order, by going to the very limits of abstraction (which is fundamentally the same as that assigned to the activity of the "picture"), to demonstrate its paradoxical density.

NOTES

1 Piet Mondrian, "The New Plastic in Painting" (1917), in Harry Holtzman and Martin S. James, trans. and eds., *The New Art—The New Life: The Collected Writings of Piet Mondrian* (Boston; G.K. Hall & Co., 1986), pp. 35–37.

2 See Jean T. Desanti, *Les idéalités mathématiques* (Paris, 1968).

Marlene Dumas is an Amsterdam-based visual artist whose work is included in *Painting at the Edge of the World*. Dumas has written extensively throughout her career and her texts are often reproduced in exhibition catalogues and periodicals in relation to her paintings. Many of her writings, which range from short poetic works to analytical essays, have been collected in *Sweet Nothings: Notes and Texts* (1998). The following text was first published in *Parkett*, no. 37 (1993) and is reprinted with the permission of Parkett Publishers, Zürich/New York.

Marlene Dumas
Women and Painting
1993

I paint because I am a woman.
(It's a logical necessity.)
If painting is female and insanity is a female malady, then all women painters are mad and all male painters are women.

I paint because I am an artificial blonde woman.
(Brunettes have no excuse.)
If all good painting is about color, then bad painting is about having the wrong color. But bad things can be good excuses. As Sharon Stone said, "Being blonde is a great excuse. When you're having a bad day you can say, I can't help it, I'm just feeling very blonde today."

I paint because I am a country girl.
(Clever, talented big-city girls don't paint.)
I grew up on a wine farm in Southern Africa. When I was a child I drew bikini girls for male guests on the back of their cigarette packs. Now I am a mother and I live in another place that reminds me a lot of a farm—Amsterdam. (It's a good place for painters.) Come to think about it, I'm still busy with those types of images and imagination.

I paint because I am a religious woman.
(I believe in eternity.)
Painting doesn't freeze time. It circulates and recycles time like a wheel that turns. Those who were first might well be last. Painting is a very slow art. It doesn't travel with the speed of light. That's why dead painters shine so bright.
It's okay to be the second sex.
It's okay to be second best.
Painting is not a progressive activity.

I paint because I am an old-fashioned woman.
(I believe in witchcraft.)
I don't have Freudian hang-ups. A brush does not remind me of a phallic symbol. If anything, the domestic aspect of a painter's studio (being "locked up" in a room) reminds me a bit of the housewife with her broom. If you're a witch you will still know how to use it. Otherwise it is obvious that you'll prefer the vacuum cleaner.

I paint because I am a dirty woman.
(Painting is a messy business.)
It cannot ever be a pure conceptual medium. The more "conceptual" or cleaner the art, the more the head can be separated from the body, and the more the labor can be done by others. Painting is the only manual labor I do.

I paint because I like to be bought and sold.
Painting is about the trace of the human touch. It is about the skin of a surface. A painting is not a postcard. The content of a painting cannot be separated from the feel of its surface. Therefore, in spite of everything, Cézanne is more than vegetation and Picasso is more than an anus and Matisse is not a pimp.

Reinaldo Laddaga is an Assistant Professor of Latin American Literature in the Department of Romance Languages at the University of Pennsylvania, Philadelphia. He is the author of a collection of essays on contemporary fiction, *Literaturas indigentes y placeres bajos* (2000); a novel, *La euforia de Baltasar Brum* (1999); and several essays on art, film, and literature.

Painting and Trance in Severo Sarduy's *La simulación*

Reinaldo Laddaga

FIG. 1 book cover of Severo Sarduy's **La Simulación** (Simulation), published by Monte Avila Editores, Caracas, Venezuela, 1982

Should we be surprised that the name of the "Franco-Cuban"[1] Severo Sarduy is absent from the network of references underlying recent discussions on the formless, on inscriptions in the image of the real, on "low" art, on the intersection of trace, print, *empreinte*, discussions that have resulted in some of the most fertile recent thinking about painting?[2] Or that his name doesn't arise in discussions about the state of painting today? Yet should it not be otherwise? I believe so, based on, at the least, one book: a more or less systematic collection of essays and fragments of fiction, many of them occasional pieces, written in Spanish and French and published by the author in 1982 under the title *La simulación* (Simulation). And why should Sarduy's work be of interest to us at the present time? What contribution can his reflections on painting make today? For the moment let us leave the answer to these questions pending, while we briefly review the postulates formulated in Sarduy's text.

Who was the Severo Sarduy of 1982? A rapid review of his biography indicates that he was born in 1937 in Camagüey, Cuba, and that he participated briefly in several cultural enterprises during the first months of the Revolution. He went to Paris in 1960 for the purpose of (or under the pretext of) studying at the Louvre. Shortly thereafter, he established himself permanently in France and lived in an intellectual environment that philosopher François Wahl, in a recently published biographical piece, describes as "distinguished by the presence of Roland Barthes, Sollers, Lacan, Derrida, and Alain Badiou."[3] In 1966 Sarduy published his first novel, *Gestos* (Gestures). The writer describes the book as an exercise in "action writing," and states that in it he employs forms and methods analogous to those of a type of painting associated with Jackson Pollock, Willem de Kooning, and especially Franz Kline (as well as Antoni Tàpies, Asger Jorn, and Karel Appel). *Gestos* is one of the central works of an avant-garde literature in Spanish that had interests similar to those of the French avant-garde centered at that time around the magazine *Tel Quel*, which was then publishing various texts that Sarduy had written in French. The author's first masterwork appeared in 1969, the curious and notable comic saga *De donde son los cantantes* (From Cuba with a song), followed by an extraordinary piece of fiction entitled *Cobra* (referring both to the group of painters of that name and to the animal; the relationship between painting and animality is one of the main themes of *La simulación*). *Cobra* was translated into French by Philippe Sollers and received the prestigious Premio Medicis; Roland Barthes' *Le plaisir du texte* calls it one of the most important reference points for a type of modern literature that attempts to definitively problematize the *status* of the written word. It would be worth spending more time examining this novel, which is a celebration—as is the book that is the subject of this essay—of transvestism and painting. But let us simply say here that this celebration continued in the splendid *Maitreya* (1978) and *Colibrí* (1984). In 1982 Sarduy decided to assemble various earlier texts originally commissioned by magazines or catalogues for specific purposes and with them formed his third collection of essays (the first two being *Escrito sobre un cuerpo* [Written on a body] and *Barroco* [Baroque]), which he gave the title of *La simulación*. The remainder of Sarduy's biography includes two additional novels, a number of poetry collections, several pieces for theater or radio, numerous paintings, his illness at the end of the decade, and his death in 1993.

What is *La simulación* about? The book's theme, its subject, its problem, its object of desire is painting—with a capital "P," as Sarduy says. In the book's exordium, he presents it in this manner:

> **Simulation connects and groups together within the same energy—simulation drive—dissimilar phenomena, coming from heterogeneous and seemingly unconnected spaces that range from the organic to the imaginary, from the biological to the baroque: animal (defensive?) mimetics, tattooing, human (sexual?) transvestism, make-up, *Mimikri-Dress-Art*, anamorphosis, trompe l'oeil . . . The space in which this galaxy unfolds is Painting: reflection and tribute. (*OC* II, 1264)[4]**

This forthright description is to the point: the book is a collection of very different texts (the form of which also varies: aphorisms, essays that are developed to greater or lesser

degrees, "autobiographical vignettes," short narratives) on subjects apparently unconnected (as the author himself indicates in the above-quoted passage). Yet in these texts one finds the systematic unfolding of a specific thesis: that of painting as a place where a unique energy expands as a function of "simulation drive." "Simulation" is, of course, a term current in the theoretical culture of which the writer was a part. It plays a fundamental role, for example, in Derrida's *La dissémination* and especially in the *Logique du sens* of Deleuze (who, on his part, employs certain ideas of Pierre Klossowski). Sarduy's book contains numerous echoes of the ideas of Deleuze, Klossowski, and Derrida, but these echoes are modulated ("tuned" as Borges would say) by his passionate interest in other topics, in themselves quite diverse: transvestites, Buddhism, popular Cuban culture, Baroque poetry, eighteenth-century Spanish mysticism, the phenomena of animal mimetics (initially culled from Roger Caillois' texts on the subject). Hence all of the book's concepts are curiously complex: in each he unites layers of motifs, orientations, and issues.

These motifs and issues are modulated, in the context of Sarduy's book, by his idea that the function of art in general is to construct devices designed to induce trance. Very little can be understood of much of the most powerful Latin American art and literature produced between, say, the 1950s and the 1980s (I am thinking not only of Sarduy, but of the likes of José Lezama Lima, Reinaldo Arenas, Clarice Lispector, or Hélio Oiticica) if we do not take into consideration that these writers and artists frequently conceived of their practices as having the power to provoke in those who are exposed to them an escape from the self that manifests itself as pleasure, but which, because it presupposes destruction—however momentarily—of the "I," might at any moment tip the scales toward the realm of horror.

In order to fully understand Sarduy's position regarding painting, one must take into account that in *La simulación*, painting is an ecstatic art—a technique intended to induce in its subjects a trance during which the visible takes on a singularly problematic character, a mechanism set in motion, a galaxy that unfolds because of "simulation drive." What is this "simulation drive?" *La simulación* is not the work of a philosopher or a psychologist, nor is it the work of a critic, and it is pointless to read it in search of precise definitions. In the foreground is always an example, a sample scenario. The first scenario Sarduy uses to explore the dynamics of this drive has as its central figure a transvestite.

What is it that a transvestite seeks, according to Sarduy? To imitate a woman? Not really. His goal is an impossible one: to be something "more-than-woman," which is, strictly speaking, unattainable. If we were to suppose that woman, as she actually exists, is the object which a transvestite sets out to copy, we must then say (according to Sarduy) that the transvestite goes beyond, that he over-imitates, that he carries the unfolding of forms to the point at which the model itself disappears from view. This is the writer's contention: the transvestite is *hypertelic*. For this reason Sarduy maintains that "the transvestite does not copy, he simulates, since there is no norm to motivate and magnetize the transformation, or determine the metaphor; it is rather the nonexistence of the cherished one that constitutes the space, region, and support for the simulation, for the attempted imposture: an appearance dominated by a Goya-esque drive between laughter and death." (*OC* II, 1267) The transvestite, the hypertelic simulator, "hurls himself toward the pursuit of an infinite unreality, accepted as such from the beginning of the game, an unreality more and more fleeting and unattainable," and weaves a web of transformations without end or destination, carried away by a confused emotion that wavers "between laughter and death."

The transvestite, hypertelic, simulates. For what purpose? None, in a certain sense. Because the drive that propels him is unconquerable: to experience the euphoria of his transformations. Or to disappear. "There is no assurance that the cosmetic—or surgical—conversion of a man into a woman will not have as a hidden result a kind of disappearance, of invisibility, of *effacement*, of erasure of the male from the aggressive clan, the brutal horde of males, and, in the measure of his separation, his difference, of his deficiency or excess, likewise from the female sphere; disappearance, nullification, which is the result of the transvestite's lethal drive and his fascination with his fixedness, in turn fascinating."

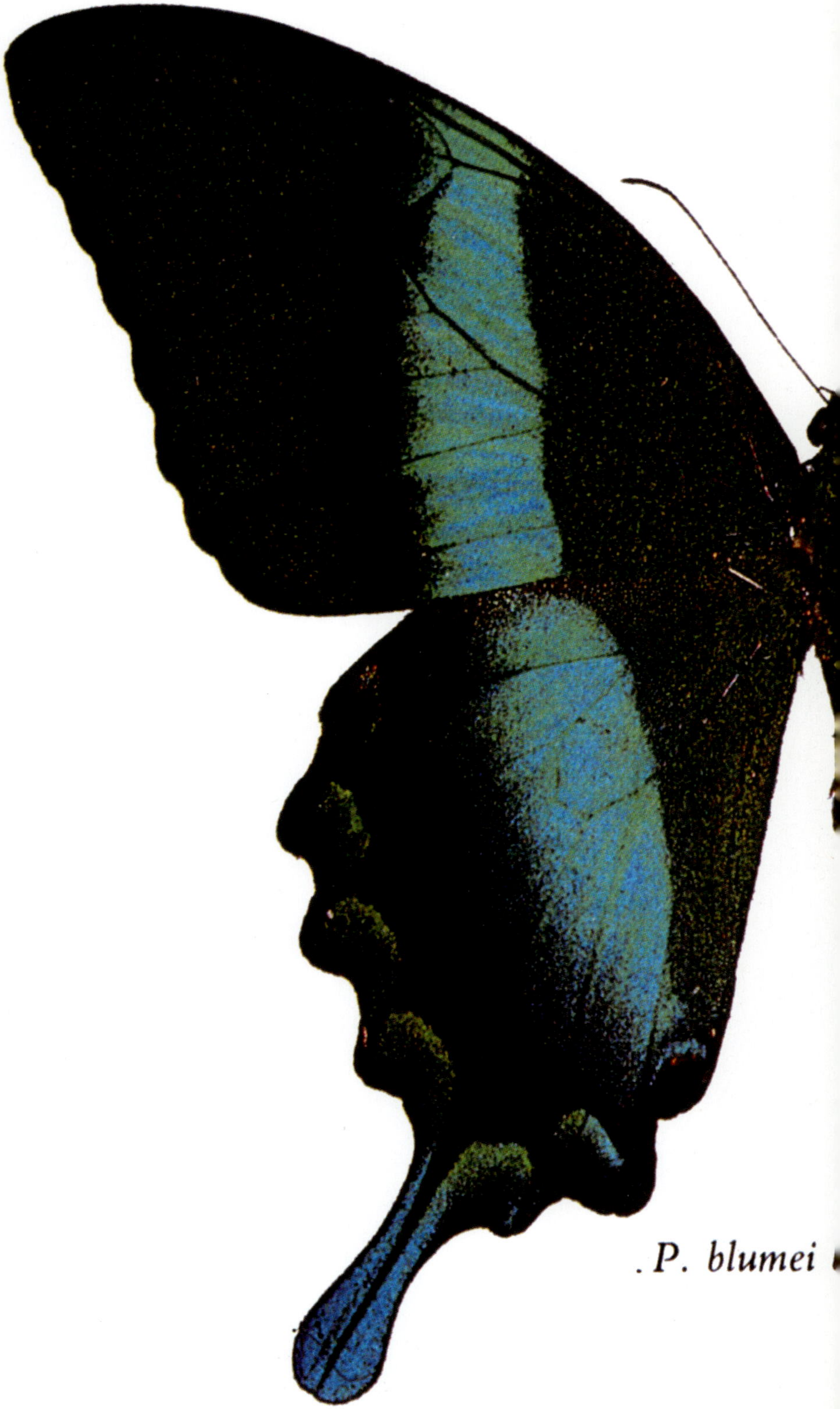

FIG. 2 *Papilio blumei*, a species of Indonesian butterfly

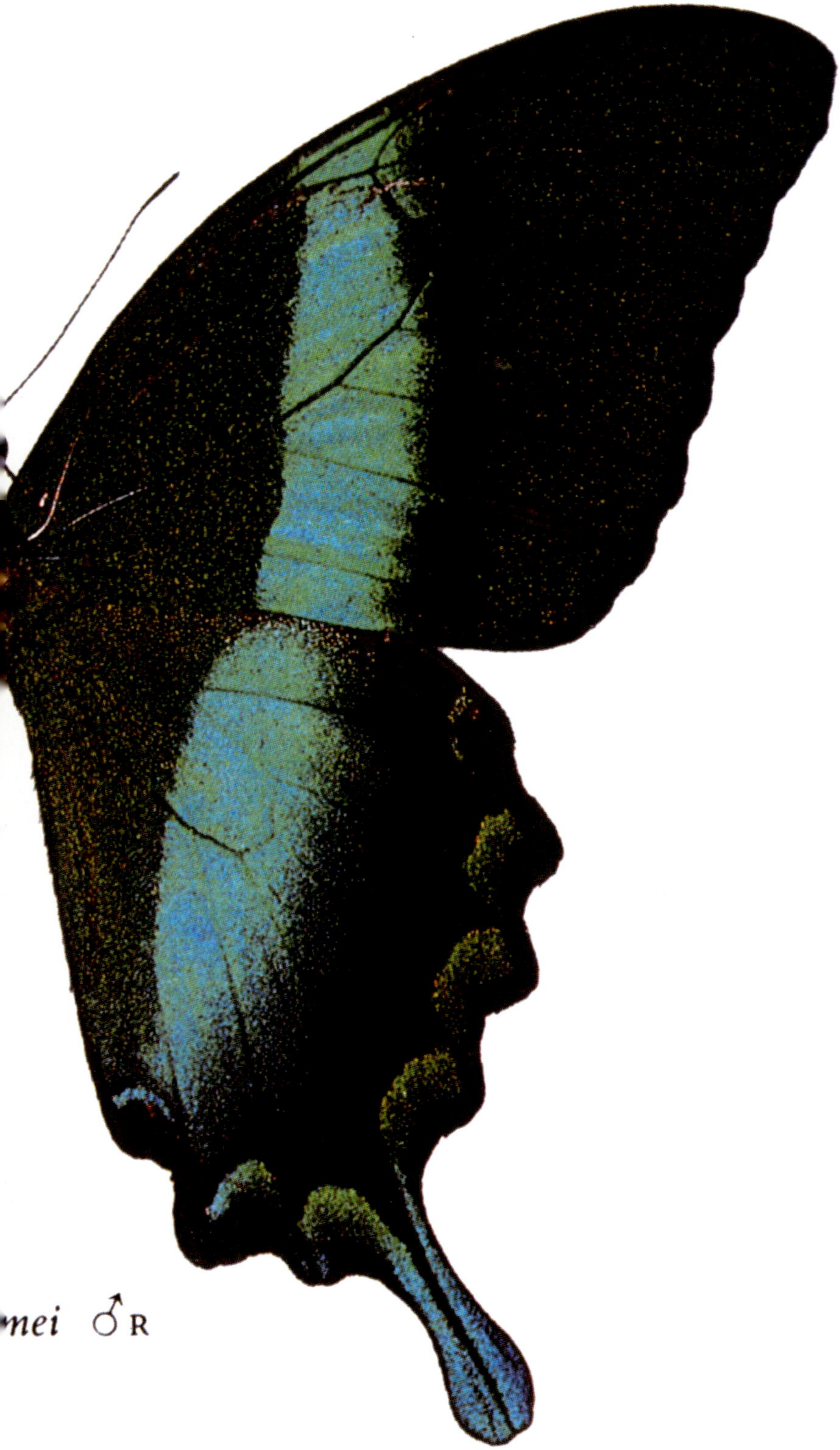
nei ♂ R

(*OC* II, 1268) The transvestite simulates in order to erase himself, to become unrecognizable to others, through an accumulation of forms that, once the limit is exceeded, brings about a distortion, a conversion into an unintelligible image, a blotting out that removes him from the categories (masculine, feminine) which, in common perception, define the human condition. But he also simulates in order to reach the point at which, tangled in the unfolding of forms, he loses sight of himself and surrenders to a kind of ecstasy.

This ecstasy terrorizes, since "the frequent disarranging or disordering of his get-up, the visible signs of artifice, the ill-assembled mask, paralyzes or terrifies." (*OC* II, 1268) This is the third characteristic of the transvestite, according to Sarduy: he is possessed by the hidden desire to terrify. Let us review the three traits that define the transvestite in Sarduy's work: the desire to hurl himself into an unfolding of forms without end until this game becomes lost in a "whirlwind of laughter and horror" (the phrase is Mallarmé's), in an overall collapsing that results in a formless appearance; the desire to become opaque, to erase or blot himself out; and the desire to terrorize by means of a series of manifestations that waver between splendor and disaster. According to *La simulación*, these three characteristics appear obsessively in those modern paintings which in the early 1980s Sarduy identifies as truly significant, those which constitute, in his opinion, the most important and creative paintings of his time.

But what do the practices of transvestites have to do with those of modern painters? A second example, drawn from the animal world, may give us a more precise idea. In Sarduy's scheme, the act of simulation is not exclusively human: the desire to simulate (to transform oneself to the point of stretching form to the limit, to become motionless until one disappears, to disfigure oneself to the point of causing fright) is a primary point of suture between the world of humans and that of animals. The impulse that underlies works by those modern painters who interest the author—from Rothko to Warhol, from Morandi to Twombly or Tàpies—can, in effect, be observed in a species of Indonesian butterfly described in *La simulación* and which becomes, as the text unfolds, an emblem of painting (fig. 2). Here are the first lines of the text:

> **As soon as the Indonesian butterfly alights on its bush—each variety has its own—it begins its conversion: it sprouts appendages instinctively, so as to produce an illusion, affixing them as though they were petioles; its upper wings, now lanceolated, become leaves through which runs a central vein; on both sides of this axis extend scales which are alternatively dark or transparent, shiny or dull, bumpy or smooth. Fixedness. Or, rather, lightly balancing, oscillating, swaying to-and-fro, almost imperceptibly, in the wind. (*OC* II, 1297)**

The butterfly paints. It paints itself, spreads itself out like a painting, and it also paints the leaf on which it has perched; paints it from itself. To what end? In order to attain fixedness and remove itself from the realm of the visible by imitating its support. But once the conversion has begun—the transformations unleashed, the appendages extended, the outer covering arranged—and it has presented "its performance: 'Representation of Invisibility,'" the process continues:

> **The insect's performance goes even further. The leaf, in its present state, is not sufficient. From the wings will sprout—the simulation process speeds up, it mocks the "endurance" of a damp wall—tiny spots, grayish, like those which normally indicate a lichen-like disease on a leaf. Because the insect must imitate to the point of the waste that is death; the leaves are sick, anemic, torn, mossy, erased by the transparent scars left by the devouring insects, which spin a tiny filament of nacre.**
>
> **Still more: black spots arise, imitating the excrement of caterpillars, or white ones: bird-droppings, smeared by the rain. A superfluous addition: holes, orifices in the wing-covers/leaves, holes that cannot be seen except in flight, when the insect has no need to appear to be a leaf. A process of abusing the**

mechanism of simulation—sometimes fatally—"some larvae simulate the buds of a bush so well that gardeners cut them off with scissors; the case of the Filias is even more wretched: they eat each other, thinking they are eating leaves." (*OC* II, 1298)

As I have said, the butterfly acts like a painter; more precisely, like a modern painter. Why? On the one hand, because of its propensity to create manifestations that are often unpleasant: "a lichen-like disease," "leaves that are sick, anemic, torn," the nacreous lines like "transparent scars." But also because, in the process, a certain *artistic* operation takes place: the suppression of the distance between that which constitutes the figure perched on the leaf and its support, i.e., the leaf on which it has perched. A number of years before *La simulación* (at least as early as the 1960s), Sarduy took for granted a theorem common in the culture of modern art, one which is not his own, of course, but to which he gave a surprising twist: the operation of modernity itself, in the realm of the purely plastic, is to suppress distance, on each canvas, between the figures and the background, or between the material and its support. This is precisely what the Indonesian butterfly does. Even to the point of death; because it is no accident that the moment in which the process approaches the point of consummation is the instant of death. In Sarduy's eyes (and here is the twist), there is an essential analogy between a figure's passing on into the background (or of a material into its support) and an individual's passing on into death. This analogy between an artistic device and an existential process, between the vanishing of form and loss of life, structures the development of all of the texts that comprise the book.

If it is possible to say that the Indonesian butterfly behaves like a kind of modern painter, it is because, from the point of view of *La simulación*, in every great modern painting, the image dies. "Death of the image" is a familiar-sounding idea. But it takes on an unusual force in the book's context. This is due to the singular explicitness of a term that, in modern theories on the death of painting or art or literature, generally remains oddly indeterminate, namely, "death." What does "to die" mean? Texts affirming that, in modernity, art (or painting or literature) is dying usually have little to tell us on this point; these texts generally assume that death is a simple concept: the instantaneous passing between, shall we say, being and nothingness. But death, according to Sarduy, is instead a slow dispersion, a corruption that takes place little by little, a parsimonious process, a sort of progression that is in some sense interminable (or at least one whose end is difficult to determine). This death is strangely sweet, even in its horror—unimaginably sweet unless we take into account the intricate constellation of references that underlie the text. In *La simulación*, a vaguely Freudian or Lacanian anthropology (or, perhaps, simply Baroque: Gongorian, Quevedian) is modulated by other influences: that of Georges Bataille, of course, specifically his notion of *dépense*, excessive expenditure, waste (to die would be, with regard to this reference, the greatest waste; hence one speaks of "the waste that is death"); as well as the influence of Buddhism derived from the Indian texts of Octavio Paz (in which death, a good death, the death one ought to desire, is an ecstatic passing into fixedness); and, above all, that of the Spanish mystics of the seventeenth century, Santa Teresa de Jesús and San Juan de la Cruz, in whose texts the figure of death can be read as the resplendent nullification of the ego's passions, but also as a delightful escape from oneself through a kind of bleeding to death.

Figures die in the background, materials die on their supports, the Indonesian butterfly dies on its leaf, through a kind of suicide by exhaustion, the result of an unfolding whirlwind of transformations, an extinction of the form that fixes itself as an incomprehensible image and is no stranger to the realm of terror. This is the dynamic of the galaxy that unfolds in the space of painting. This is what happens each time a portion of the visible is carried away by the "simulation drive." This is what invariably happens, for example, in the modern paintings that interest the author, as well as in certain performances, such as the theater of Tadeusz Kantor or the first period of the work of Gilbert and George, which Sarduy refers to in a section of the book dedicated to trompe l'oeil. On the performances by Gilbert and George, which essentially consisted of the two artists displaying themselves on pedestals, discreetly costumed, Sarduy writes:

> **In the saturation of the inanimate, in the return of the motionless double, the performance of Gilbert and Georges [*sic*] surpasses Kantor's teaching dummy, present on the stage, watching. Gilbert and Georges [*sic*] have negated the model—which might be their own image in wax—they have excluded it from the performance, but as if to incorporate it, to physically internalize it, converting it into something natural, an almost insignificant death that is, however, evidenced by the rigidity of the gestures, the paleness of the sick neon faces, the crude energy of the bodies, less fit to live than to exhibit the English cut of their suits. (*OC* II, 1291)**

Just as the Indonesian butterfly extends itself on a leaf, Gilbert and George, in their performances, spread themselves out into their motionless doubles and disappear into an inert and pale image, that of "sick neon faces," which inscribes a colorless zone in the visible realm. Other paintings discussed in the book do the same. Those of Antoni Tàpies (fig. 3), for example, which are discussed in an essay entitled "Koan," are described by Sarduy as follows:

> **A fall, or, rather, a wavering, inadequate movement, a loss of focus, porosity, fracture, dissolution into the gray of the object gazed upon. Soon, this negation recedes quickly back to the eyes, upriver, ending, closing up the history of the gaze. Tàpies' paintings move on (descend) from this *night of the senses*: this *stopping up of the gaze*, reiterated driving back of the retinal dimension, charring of light, and, at the same time, forgetfulness and marginalization, obscuring of the signified. (*OC* II, 1323)**

The paintings move on, downward, the "retinal dimension" is driven back, light is charred: in the paintings of Tàpies, from Sarduy's perspective, we experience the unfolding of figures that, before firmly establishing themselves on the surface supporting them, move toward the background, wavering, losing focus, dissolving, breaking (and at the same time spreading themselves out just as the Indonesian butterfly spreads itself out when it perches on a leaf)—falling toward that which the writer, paraphrasing San Juan de la Cruz, calls "night of the senses." Sense as in "sensation" (because the image remains on the edge of the visible, just about to leave the world, gray being a metaphor for this location); sense as in "signification." Because the theater of these paintings is inhabited by "marks, prints, incisions, and writing," which "are ceasing to be legible or clear, like remote parietal incisions, charred and bloody, in order to form, mimetically confused with it, material that is blind, unnamed, raw: the series of whole numbers changing into a succession of clumsy and shaky lines, into scribbles: the letters of the alphabet break apart into smudges and marks." (*OC* II, 1324) In these paintings, the signs of language, as if overcome by a deathly impulse, move toward material that, at the same time, tilts toward the realm of signs. The book uses a recurring term to designate this point of oscillation: "suture." The term (which comes from Lacan) designates passing between two dimensions, as well as the union of and dissent between those dimensions. Modern painting, as defined in *La simulación*, is a practice that concentrates the most important of its manifestations, and realizes its most characteristic operations, at points of suture: between animation and stillness, between the figure and its background, between materials and their supports, between material and language. Or between the painting and the structure that houses it.

This is what happens, according to Sarduy, in the work of Andy Warhol. Sarduy refers briefly to the American artist and praises him for his attempt to locate "opacity, the indecipherable, in the foreground: Andy Warhol brings to an end the era of painting that is legible and replaces it with opacity." Opacity that is consummated when the canvases are placed in a museum, a placement in which the "violent clarity" characteristic of his work is turned into "a calm apotheosis": "with equal detachment [Warhol] takes hold of all that comes to hand, thing or person, copy or (included in repetition drive) the copy of a copy, until he arrives at blotting out or at satiety—filling the entire museum with the same image." (*OC* II, 1278) What drives Warhol's work? It is the desire to reach a point at which

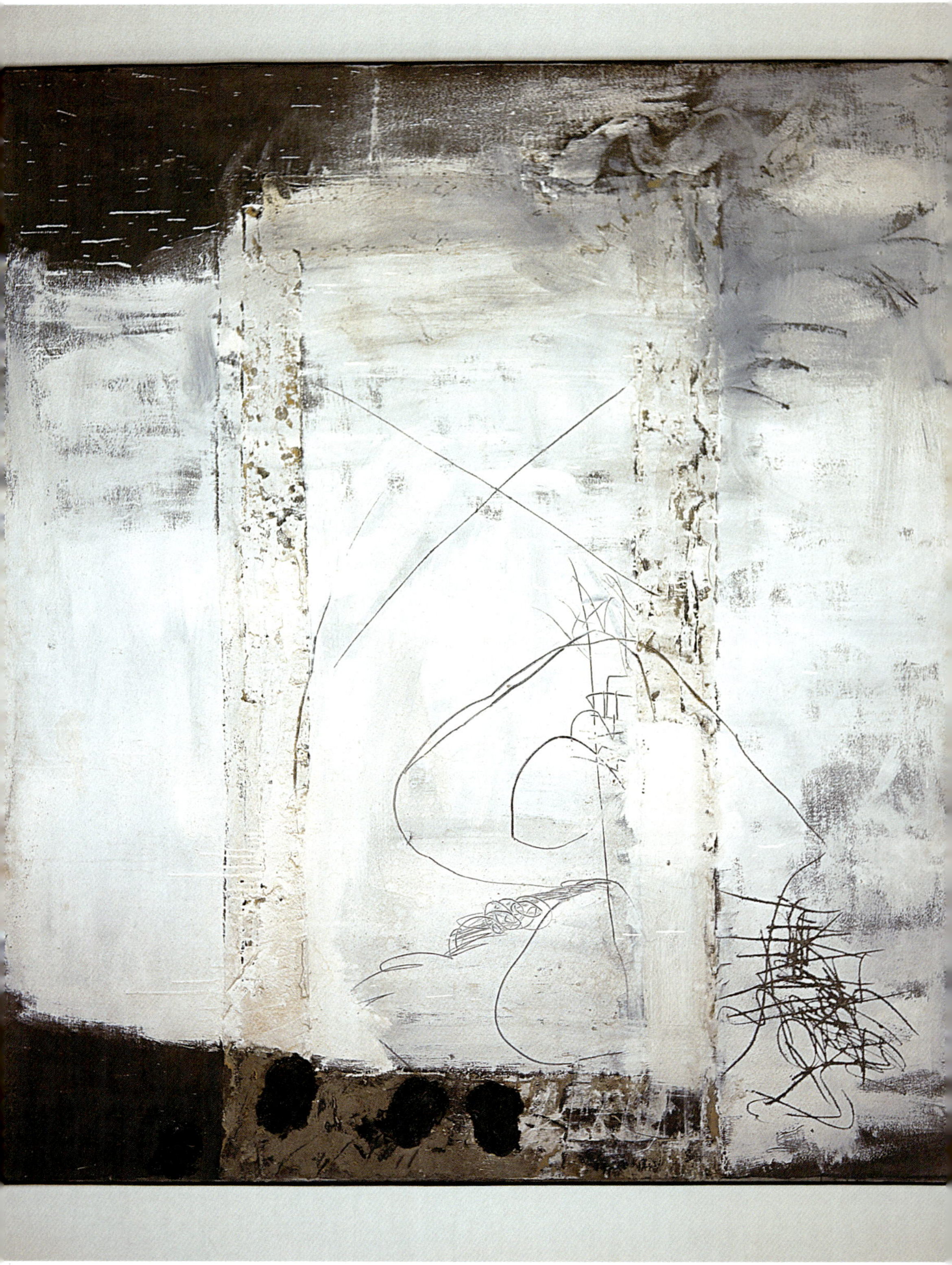

FIG. 3 Antoni Tàpies **Blanco y Grafismos** (White with graphism) 1957 mixed media on canvas 75 ⅞ x 63 ¾ in. Collection Washington University Gallery of Art, St. Louis; Gift of Mr. and Mrs. Richard Weil, 1963 © 2001 Artists Rights Society (ARS), New York/ADAGP, Paris

the image achieves the end of its expansions and ceases, spent—the point at which an image, falling, sweeps with it the environment that houses it, like the Indonesian butterfly, which takes with it, in its slow vertigo, the leaf on which it is perched, or the transvestite, who, with his pile of trappings, demolishes a space the organization of which was determined by gender categories.

Signs that, rushing headlong, end up being blotted out; an image that is destroyed through repetition, but at the same time, like a germ, occupies space: these are the emblems of painting to be found in Sarduy's book. And so it is understandable that, at the time of writing, Sarduy believed that a key scene exists for modern painting, a scene in which its own dynamic would, in a certain sense, culminate. This scene is the suicide of Mark Rothko, a suicide that, in the fable Sarduy weaves around him, is a particularly dramatic manifestation of the "simulation drive." In a 1993 interview, the writer said that if there is an explanation for the suicide, it lies in the following: Rothko "wanted to get the right red; this was his life's obsession. The red of his spilled blood—as well as that other, unnamed blood, alcohol—was to culminate a search that no painting could fulfill." (*OC* II, 1839) This explanation, at first seemingly fanciful, is reasonable if one considers Sarduy's stance: Rothko's act must have been guided by his desire to erase the distance between himself and his materials, and must have been in response to a (hypertelic) desire to be transformed into pure color. The artist's desire to die as a nebulous image, in dissolution, in a flow of blood, inspired a sonnet; it does not appear in *La simulación*, but was written at around the same time and was published in 1985 in a collection of poems entitled *Un testigo fugaz y disfrazado* (A witness fleeting and disguised). Bearing the simple title "Rothko," the sonnet reads:

**Neither colors, nor pure form.
Memory of a shade. Sediment
decanting the light of its pigment
beyond the canvas and its frame.**

**Neither lines, nor shadow or texture,
nor the brief semblance of movement,
only silence: the feeling
of being in his presence. Painting**

**in parallel bands, whose mist
crosses the canvas, untouched, yet stained
with cinnabar, with vanishing wine;**

**purple, vermilion, orange . . .
The red of blood shed
marks his quest. And his life.
(*OC* I, 209)**

What is it that can be seen in Rothko's paintings? A series of crossings that, at the moment we come upon them, are still incomplete, processions continuing on their way. For this reason, his colors do not possess a full presence, but allow themselves to be perceived as a "memory of a shade" (even to the point of being a misty memory, which vanishes). The surfaces that present themselves on the canvas (as if they do not actually touch it—it remains "intact") rather than spreading out as stabile forms, do so as blurred sediments (fig. 4). Images of impregnation recur in the poem: the decanting of a light which it is difficult not to imagine as liquid (the slowness of light—in progressive expansion or contraction—is a constant image in Sarduy's writings on painting), a slow staining of the canvas, and, above all, the painter's passing on into his paintings. The poem discreetly imagines an arresting moment: the moment in which the spilled blood of the painter impregnates his canvases, and his living self, saturating the inanimate painting, hurls itself toward the fixedness of death in a moment of ecstasy.

FIG. 4 Mark Rothko **Number 207 (Red over Dark Blue on Dark Grey)** 1961 oil on canvas 92 ¾ x 81 ⅛ in. Collection University of California, Berkeley Ar
Museum; Gift of Mark Rothko © 2001 Kate Rothko Prizel & Christopher Rothko/Artists Rights Society (ARS), New York

Since to paint implies entering into a trance, Rothko's suicide is a key point in painting's history, the event in which the "simulation drive" unfolds in its most intense manner. But is a trance brought about by painting accessible only to painters? Sarduy would say no: painting can also bring about ecstasy in some viewers, at least under certain conditions and when confronting certain images. This is suggested by one of the book's key texts, "Fixedness," which is dedicated to the work of David Hockney. The text concentrates on his pool series; more precisely, on the splashes at the center of these paintings. Sarduy begins by minutely describing the scenes that these paintings depict, and focuses in on the pools themselves:

> **The water is calm, except under the diving board and in the center: without rough waves, ascending almost vertically, as a compact waterspout, the violent spattering of a splash. Tiny strokes, zinc or titanium white, twisted and nervous like fine string, painted directly with a tube of paint, or with a saturated, dripping brush point. From the diving point in the painting's center arise tight spirals, like withes, tendrils of a vine. (*OC* II, 1331)**

In those "tiny strokes" and "tight spirals" it is easy to see once again the Indonesian butterfly, extending its petioles, its appendages, darkening itself while at the same time displaying itself and succumbing to what is essentially a fatal desire. This fatality is found inscribed in Hockney's splash: because "a second afterward, just following what is shown on the canvas, the rough water falls, beginning its descent, until it disappears in dissolution, erased in the smooth, calm, surface." The splash also circumspectly indicates a tomb, the mark of a fallen body, one that is now "totally absent, buried for a few moments beneath the water, tracing a slow curve, like a trail that has been wiped out, a momentary drowning of the one who is submerged." (*OC* II, 1331) The idea of combining splendor and unpleasantness at each point of the image, the idea of energy which unfolds and inertia which causes it to fall, is obsessively repeated in Sarduy's text and is enunciated in various ways: in statements such as "in the fixedness of the representation, painstaking, minute, intent on the corrosion of the momentary, there death is" and "there, behind the image, or rather in the suture that sews it together and superimposes it on the real, in the welding of its wavering edges, there death is"; when he suggests that "behind the eurythmic sound of the stroke of the swimmer, stagnates a purulent and thick silence; behind the splashing water, that of a still and cunning river" (*OC* II, 1332); and when he writes:

> **In the swimming pools, motionlessness is different** [different from the motionlessness of the figures of classical sculpture, for example, such as the *Discobolos*, which Sarduy has just mentioned]**. An interstice, a fault through which suddenly a fountain or geyser erupts, as if the whole sequence has no other purpose but to stop it up, to contain it, "stopping up" is the goal of every image.**
>
> **I repeat, we are not looking out, as if through a crack, onto a neutral, colorless, meaningless space—stripped of figures and sense—but one that raises up a thin sheet, of the same minute thickness as the image; the protective shield cracks open, it leaps, *il gicle*—with the seminal meaning of this French verb: sperm, upon ejaculation, *gicle*, bursts forth in a spurt. Then, a clotted and pale contagion inundates our gaze: the viscous obscenity of death. (*OC* II, 1334)**

What is it that these paintings do, given the scenario Sarduy weaves around them in *La simulación*? How do they affect their viewers? They present death to their eyes; they cause death to leap into view, not as a figure that can be determined by its outlines, but as a contagion that adheres like a "viscous obscenity," which winds its threads around them like threads of ejaculated sperm. And, thereby stopping up the viewer's sight, "inundating his gaze," it causes a kind of blindness that must be understood as a slow exhaustion of the ability to see. To go blind is, in effect, the death of vision; but in Sarduy's texts, in the same way that death masquerades as an ecstatic escape, a gradual bleeding to death, this blindness is a slow, liquid extinction of figures and lights, an endless "movement that is wavering, uncertain, losing focus," an indeterminate falling away from the consistency of the visible.

From this a corollary follows: the painting, by stopping up the sight of the viewer, has the potential to change the world beyond its frame, if only for a moment. How? In what way? By contagion. By infecting the viewer with the "viscous obscenity of death," and thus impregnating his or her gaze, the painting infects the world. With what? We can well imagine that Sarduy might, after the phrase cited above and beyond the frame of his text, suggest the following: "Turn your gaze away from the painting. Direct it beyond the canvas, toward the world. What do you see? A pale and clotted expanse, fog, silence. And death's handiwork all around." Death's handiwork: creatures exceeding their outlines—their profiles vanishing, their fluids draining, each becoming like a splash, a vertigo of features—who lose themselves in terror and in delight.

One last question, which was posed at the beginning of this essay: why should we recall today the postulates developed in *La simulación*? For a number of reasons. Because certain motifs that have become common in recent criticism appear in Sarduy's book, modulated by ideas from other spheres, from other theoretical, poetic, and cultural traditions: the themes of Georges Bataille come into immediate contact with (are infected by) those of San Juan de la Cruz, those of Gilles Deleuze are examined under the light of certain aspects of Cuban popular culture, so that current theorists of art interested in the formless and in trace, in the contamination of the "high" with the "low," in the question of underlying connections between recent photographic, theatrical, architectural, or cinematic practices and trends in modern painting cannot help but be interested in the ideas of Sarduy. Because, within the constructed space of Sarduy's book, he establishes unexpected links, and Gilbert and George or Tadeusz Kantor are found directly alongside Rothko and Tàpies, and Rothko and Tàpies alongside the transvestite and the Indonesian butterfly, in a way that should not be ignored by a culture of art interested in investigating the state of painting and other arts today, or by those attempting to construct new histories of modern art. And because it is possible that the most relevant painters working today inherit precisely those characteristics that Sarduy identifies in the immediately preceding tradition, i.e., the passion for forms that unfold in a whirlwind until they reach the point of debilitation and fall; the propensity to compose images that are inhabited by a "Goyaesque drive," which oscillate between the realm of horror and the land of laughter; the desire to create images that, impregnating the viewer's gaze, mark out zones where the world's consistency wavers.

TRANSLATED BY DAVID HINKLE

NOTES

1 The (apparently derogatory) phrase is that of Cuban bureaucrat Ambrosio Fornet.

2 I am, of course, referring to discussions conducted in the United States and France by Rosalind Krauss, Hubert Damisch, Yve-Alain Bois, Hal Foster, Georges Didi-Huberman, Leo Bersani, and T. J. Clark, among others.

3 François Wahl, "Severo de la rue Jacob," in Severo Sarduy, *Obra Completa: edición critica*, 2 vols., eds. Gustavo Guerrero and François Wahl (Madrid: Archivos, 1999).

4 Ibid. Quotations from Sarduy's texts are cited from this edition, with the abbreviations *OC* I and *OC* II indicating volume number, followed by page number.

Takashi Murakami is a Tokyo-based artist whose work is included in *Painting at the Edge of the World*. Murakami studied visual art and art history, and self-published his own book on the tendency toward two-dimensionality in the history of Japanese art, *Super Flat* (2000). Murakami organized an accompanying exhibition, originally mounted at the Parco Gallery, Tokyo, in 2000 and presented at the Museum of Contemporary Art, Los Angeles, in 2001. The following text was originally published in *Super Flat* (2000) and is reprinted with the permission of the artist and Madra Publishing, Tokyo.

Takashi Murakami
A Theory of Super Flat Japanese Art
2000

1. "Japan" and "Art"

We want to see the newest things. That is because we want to see the future, even if only momentarily. It is the moment in which, even if we don't completely understand what we have glimpsed, we are nonetheless touched by it. This is what we have come to call "art."

When one tries to express something artistically, that expression's background, motivation, and premises become vital. The more works you produce, the more you have to ponder such premises as the "self" that was born and raised in "Japan" and the nature of the "art" you are producing, if you are going make any progress at all. The reason that I produce works is not a logical one, but is because I want to integrate disparate background elements as preparation for understanding that "miraculous moment" and because I want to store that away in my mind in a highly accurate shape. Unfortunately, I can never give "Japan" a fixed shape. I cannot meet my real "self." Nor can I discern what "art" really is.

Since that is the case, I thought perhaps I could solve the problem by lining up a series of images in a powerful procession that words could not clarify. Let me explain the scene I saw the moment I fused those many windows into one.

2. "Super Flat" in Images

The Japanese art historian, Nobuo Tsuji, in his book *The Lineage of Eccentricity*, produced the concept of "eccentricity," which was a revolutionary concept in the understanding of postwar Japanese art history.[1] This study of "a lineage of artists with expressionistic tendencies from the Edo period whose shared characteristic was the production of eccentric and fantastic images" looks at six artists: Iwasa Matabei, Kanō Sansetsu, Itō Jakuchū, Soga Shohaku, Nagasawa Rosetsu, and Utagawa Kuniyoshi. While praising them as the avant-garde of their day, Tsuji implies a similarity to what he calls contemporary "*manga* and poster art." His work introduces these "eccentric artists" who had not received much critical attention prior to his contextualization of their work. The sequel, *The Categories of Eccentricity*, takes up the works of Katsushika Hokusai and Itō Jakuchū, arguing a theory of "decorative culture."

The strange style of timing structure in Japanese television animation, which I had been interested in for some time, matched perfectly with my interest in the six eccentric artists discussed in *The Lineage of Eccentricity*. In the past I had thought about the logic of that animation by thinking about the movement of the observer's gaze along planes in Japanese art using reproductions of Hokusai and Shohaku made by the German *manga* artist Horst Janssen. I was unsatisfied with the answers I found until I came across the word "eccentricity," which I thought fit perfectly. Having majored in Japanese painting at university, I was surprised to discover that all of the artists I liked fell into this "lineage of eccentricity." At the same time, the book also was a great help in thinking about the formula for composition structure that I am always concerned with as an artist.

I thought that perhaps the way that a picture controls the speed of its observer's gaze, the course of that gaze's scan, and the subsequent control of the information flow might match well with the artists' concepts that Tsuji described in his book. It was from that hypothesis that my theory of "super flat" was born. All of the "eccentric" artists shared a certain structural methodology, in which they created surface images that erased interstices and thus made the observer aware of the images' extreme planarity. I would like to clarify this assertion using works by Jakuchū (fig. 1), Shohaku, and Sansetsu as examples.

In Itō Jakuchū's *A Group of Roosters,* a rooster has its face directly toward us, calling our attention to the rooster and obstructing our line of sight. One thing that is particularly emphasized here is that the other roosters are only shown in profile. Even in terms of composition, the observer's gaze moves from the roosters at the top of the image downward, zigzagging left and right until it arrives at the forward-facing rooster just above the base of the image. There is a mechanism at work in which the rooster's eyes fix the image and make the layers of the zigzagging scan fuse into one.

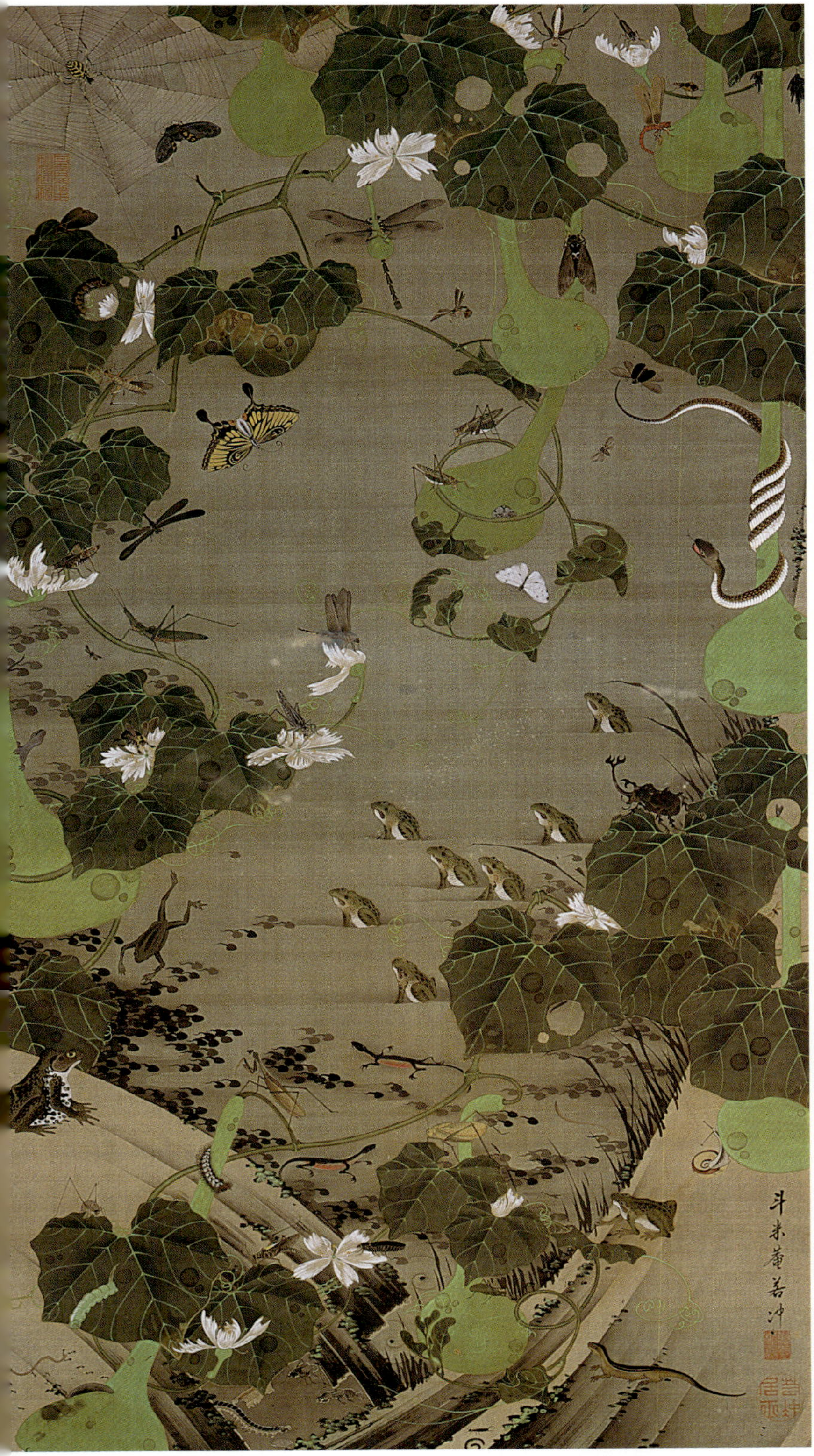

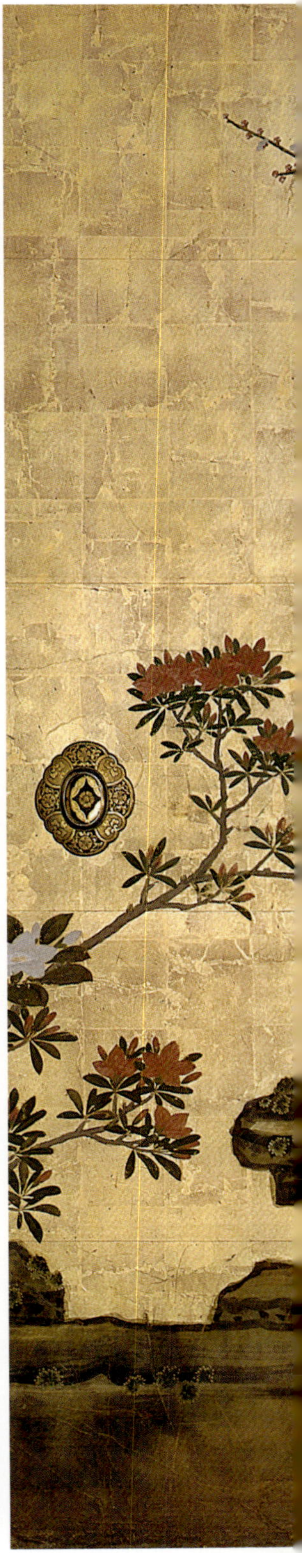

FIG. 1 Itō Jakuchū detail of **Insects and Reptiles at a Pond (Colorful Realm of Living Beings)** Edo period, 18th century ink and color on silk thirty hanging scrolls, 56 x 31¼ in. each Museum of the Imperial Collections, Sannomaru Shozokan, Tokyo © The Imperial Household Agency

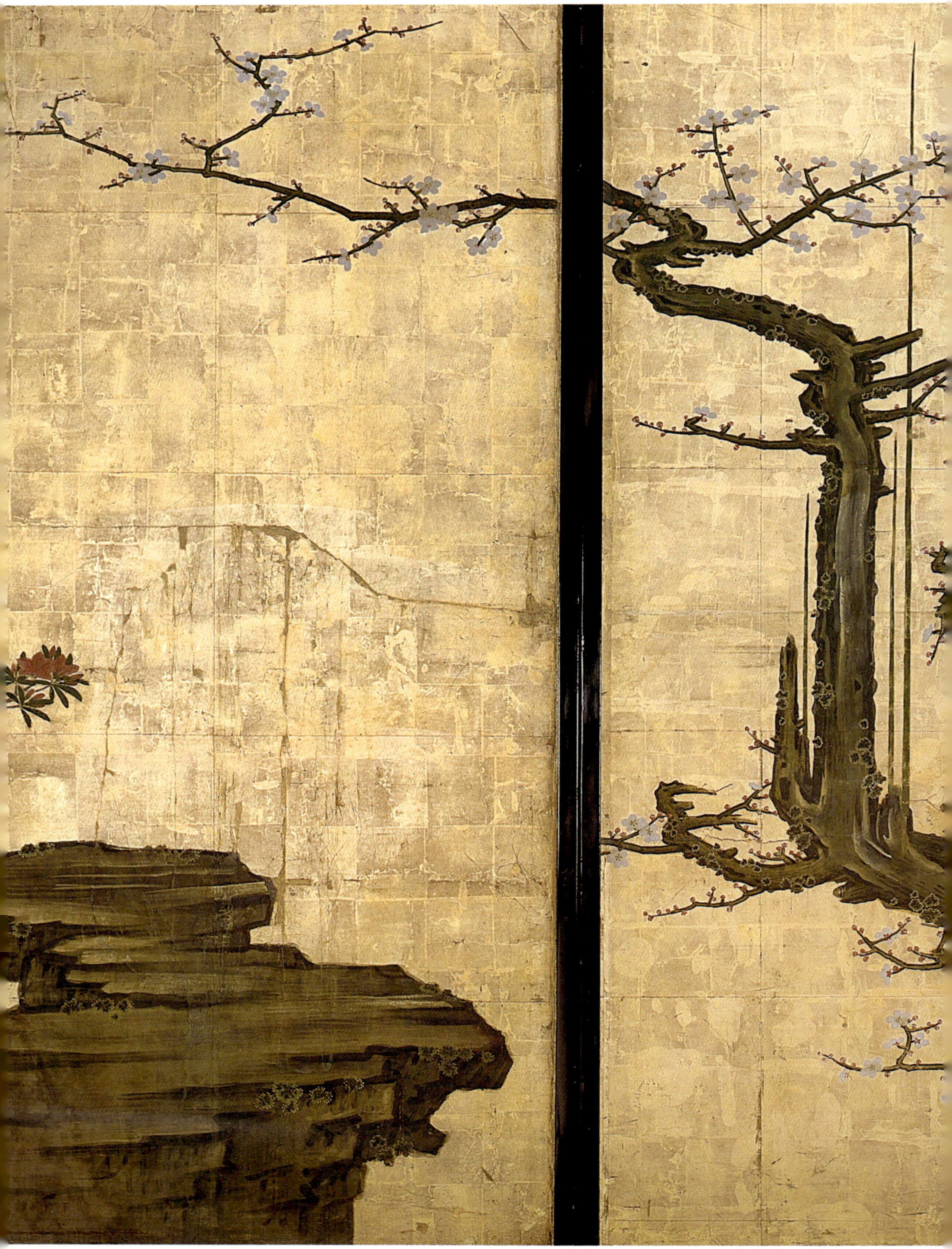

FIG. 2 Attributed to Kanō Sansetsu **The Old Plum** Edo period (1615–1868), 1647 ink, color, gold leaf on paper four sliding door panels, 68 ¾ x 48 in. each Collection The Metropolitan Musem of Art, New York; The Harry G. C. Packard Collection of Asian Art, Gift of Harry G. C. Packard, and Purchase, Fletcher, Rogers, Harris Brisbane Dick, and Louis V. Bell Funds, Joseph Pulitzer Bequest, and The Annenberg Fund Inc. Gift, 1975

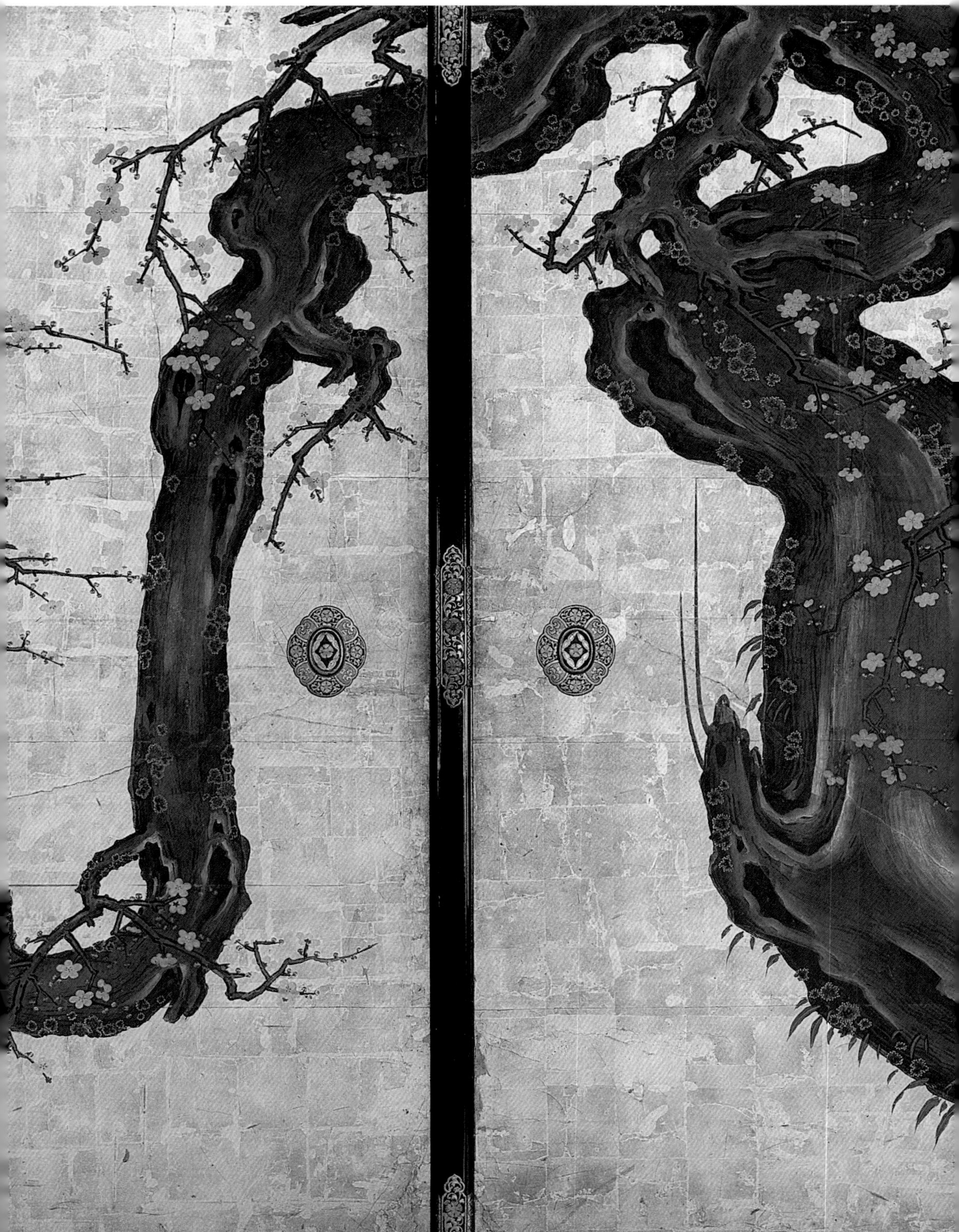

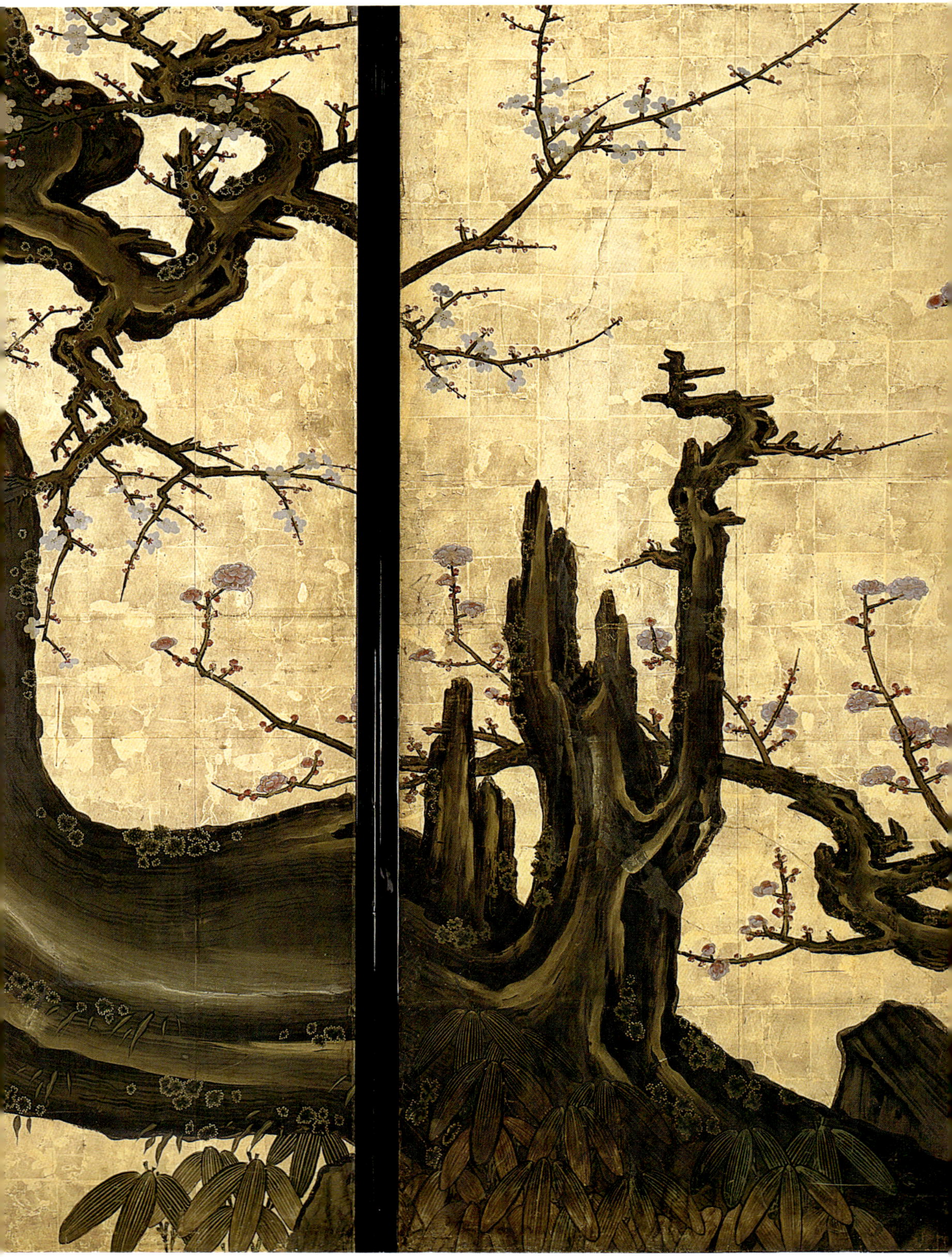

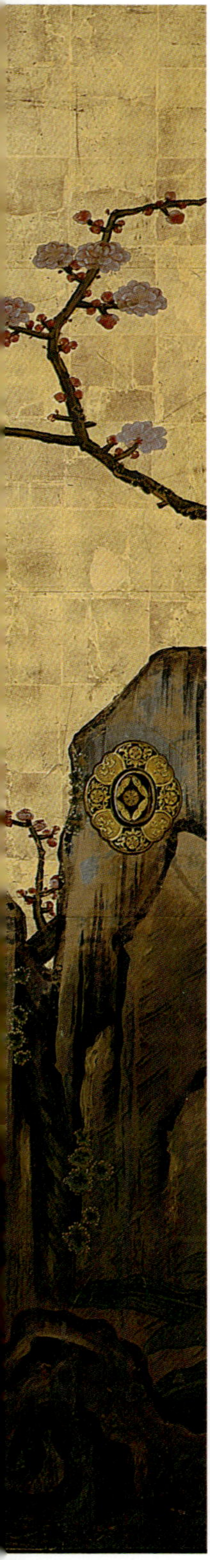

Let us look at *Birds, Animals, and Flowering Plants*. This work, which is distinctive even within Jakuchū's oeuvre, is thought by some to have been based on Western embroidery. Jakuchū must have been interested in embroidery because of its emphasis on planarity. Dripping color into a finely demarcated grid, he produces birds and beasts that crowd the image. The structure of the image's primary subject, a white elephant, is a great success for Jakuchū. Above a white mass facing forward there are two narrow eyes that are oriented toward the observer, riveting the observer's gaze on the elephant. Though the image as a whole initially appears to be made up of a grid of colored squares with rounded corners, on closer inspection one discovers that each block has its own independent shape, making the picture into a kind of optical illusion. In this way a planar work can create a kind of tension by freezing the gaze of the observer. The technique is similar to that used by Chuck Close in his portraits. In Jakuchū's work, however, the absence of humans from this purely planar work is also palpable. In that it is connected to a contemporary Japanese sensibility.

The intention of Kanō Sansetsu's *The Old Plum* (fig. 2) might be to present an odd shape that makes one aware of a sense of speed, bears a certain prestige, overflows with the eccentric desires of the artist, and possesses a luxuriousness in accordance with the wishes of his sponsor. The trunk of the plum tree, which is slightly right of center in the painting, provides a starting point similar to that of Kanō Eitoku's *Cypress Tree* by using an open and stable gaze. Immediately after that is a branch to the left that extends vertically, with small white plum blossoms spreading out in a strange zigzag at the top. These blossoms fix the viewer's gaze. In order to make the blossoms come alive, below and to the left of these blossoms there are a number of rocks that are (rather artificially) distributed along a horizontal axis. Perhaps as an antidote to that artificiality, there are also a number of scattered peony blossoms. The observer's gaze moves above the horizontal axis and to the right, returning to the starting point of the trunk. The horizontal, thick trunk is waiting to lead the observer into the drama's climax. As a conclusion there is a vertical rock placed in the lower right portion of the painting. Following that rock's dynamic leads to a small branch that provides a respite from the linear movement of the viewer's gaze, much as the peony blossoms had previously. Able to relax there for a moment, the viewer's gaze then begins to retrace its path.

Sansetsu's *Pheasant and Plum Tree* is similar. The painting spans four sliding doors. The observer's gaze starts on the main panel, the second door from the left, with a beautiful plum tree that spreads out in a "v" shape. The painting allows one to rest one's gaze here momentarily, but soon it begins its story with the zigzagging, inclined trunk that extends off to the right. Midway there is some withered ivy that shows the Japanese tendency to search only for ephemeral beauty. This brings us to the second door from the right. A plover steals one's attention for an instant, but it can be ignored. One's gaze then follows the trunk further and further down. In order to maintain balance, a number of vertical branches are placed growing up from the left side of the trunk. Allowing one's gaze to slide sideways, there appears a rock that also suggests a zigzag motion. Here some bamboo leaves are thrown in to break up the linear movement. The pheasant is something that is thrown in as a bonus, like dessert. Using that metaphor, the camellia blossoms on the far right are the espresso that pulls together the dessert.

What about Soga Shohaku's *Lions*? The observer's gaze initially fixes on the line of sight of the lion facing forward, but then suddenly moves off both upward and downward. As one's gaze moves upward, it begins to follow the flowing water that moves down and to the left. Continuing to follow the flow of the water, the gaze will move to the right, until it reaches the splash where one's initial downward gaze may have broken off. After a brief rest, one's gaze will move back to the left to the artist's signature, which reads, "Painted by the Wastrel in the Imperial Garden, Soga Kiyū." Shohaku was his pen name and Soga was a name he used despite having no relation to that family. He had taken the name to imply, ironically, that he descended from the famous Soga Family. As a satire on Chinese intellectuals who would take long names, he used a variety of long names, including this one used to sign the painting.

In *Han-shan and Shi-de*, Shohaku composed a relatively gentle picture, by making Han-shan's laughing face the focus and then making his eyes, seen straight on, the focus of his face. The texture of his rough brush is visible on the rock upon which Han-shan sits. The true subject of the picture, however, is Shi-de. The profile of his bald pated head is bumped like a monster, and the lines used to draw his body are drawn unsteadily and lightly, as if to melt away. Though it seems that one's gaze will move to the long nails on his fingers and toes, it instead moves to the fragile bamboo broom he holds. Looking at the picture of this pair, one begins on Shi-de's bald head and then moves quickly to his face. After briefly moving toward his hands and feet, one is drawn to the broom. After looking at the darkened area that seems to be a rock near his back, one is fixated not on Han-shan, whom Shi-de is directing with his outstretched hand, but on Shi-de's strange eyes. Afterwards, having grown accustomed to the image, one realizes that it is a work that violently accelerates and decelerates the gaze as it swings it from side to side.

Only these eccentric artists could capture such directness and gaze movement in a single image.

3. The "Super Flat" Lineage

The people who brought this "eccentric" composition to animation were Yoshinori Kanada and his disciples. That is not to say that they were consciously molding their images after these models from the history of Japanese art. Nonetheless, the compositional dynamic of their works resembles that of the "eccentric" artists to a startling degree. While the earlier artists picked up natural phenomena as the subject matter for many of their works, Kanada's tastes ran more toward explosions, and strange poses and movements for humans and robots. Like the dynamic natural phenomenon of cresting waves used by Hokusai in his *Thirty-six Views of Mt. Fuji*, Kanada was drawn to the human form. Kanada's popularity caused him to have many followers, who assembled in a single studio to produce Kanada-style film animation. Kanada and Masahito Yamashita had a spiritual relationship of mentor and disciple much like that between Kanō Eitoku and Sansetsu. (Though Sansetsu's actual mentor was his foster father, Kanō Sanraku.) If Yasuo Otsuka and Hayao Miyazaki of the Tōei film animation team were the fathers of Japanese *anime* special effects, Yoshinori Kanada was part of the first generation of effect animators for television, in the 1970s. One of the key issues in the history of animated movies was the integration of images made by multiple animators, each of whom had a different style. Under the directorial system, the shapes and lines of drawings would be edited and a system was developed in which color was put on the back of the transparent celluloid in order to eliminate variations. One special characteristic of Kanada's was that he rebelled against this system, allowing each animator to assert his or her individuality. In the field of Japanese television animation, low wages and inferior conditions of employment led to a shortage in workers. This, combined with insufficient budgets and limited time, made it difficult to bring a work together seamlessly. Meeting the deadlines set was always a unique challenge. At the same time, the art form began to draw the attention of maniac fans who were starting to realize that television animation was a special means of expression. The journal *Animage*, for example, was founded after the unprecedented success of "Space Cruiser Yamato." Kanada had distinguished himself as a star animator by that time and had such influence that at one time all explosion scenes were done in the Kanada style.

The special characteristic of his style lay in his ability to produce effects like those of Sansetsu, Shohaku, and Hokusai in images of warships, tanks, robots, and girls. The formula for creating those images was startlingly similar to that used by the "lineage of eccentricity" artists. The climactic battle scene of one representative work, *Galaxy Express 999* (fig. 3), is thought to have influenced the liquid metal motif of the later film, *Terminator 2*. The scene in *Goodbye to Galaxy Express 999* (fig. 4), in which a shape-shifter metamorphoses, and the scene in *Harmageddon*, in which a dragon changes shape, are other examples given. Ironically, the success of the principle of limited animation, created out of the reality of insufficient budgets, brought its strange movements and timing into areas with no such shortages. This timing is similar to Aphex Twin's use of digital audio sound on the second track of their album, *Windowlicker*. When I heard this song, the space before my eyes warped and squirmed like a Kanada effect. Sadly I was unable to analyze the song in the same way I would have a single image. Listening to the song, however, one definitely recognizes Kanada-esque timing.

Despite these many accomplishments, his work was seen as part of a temporary animation boom and has now begun to be buried in history. He should be recognized, however, for being a historic artist whose animation froze time just as Shohaku's direct line of sight in *Lions* had. Because of his work, there was a period in which the special effects created by a succession of special scene animators became the centerpieces of many works. Ichirō Itano, Hideaki Anno, and Masami Obari were a few of the leaders at that time, though Kanada was the pioneer. In contrast to that situation, the famous quote of first generation Tōei animator Yasuo Otsuka, "How about animators who can't draw people, but only draw explosions?" is a kind of praise for "eccentric" artists. Their approach to images is extremely Japanese, with single-perspective painting never crossing their minds. Instead, they constructed their images along vertical and horizontal lines. Rather than balancing the main picture, they establish a minimum balance that reaches out toward each of the four corners of the square. As I mentioned before, they also went in the direction of strange movements for people and animals, and focused the greatest interest on their effects, like explosions. That extreme planarity and distribution of power allowed the viewer to assemble an image in their minds from the fragments they gathered scanning the image. This movement of the gaze over an image is a key concept in my theory of the "super flat."

4. Changes in "Art"

The words "art" and "artist" are tricky. What sort of foundation are they premised upon?

Nariaki Kitazawa defines the Japanese terms *geijutsu* and *bijutsu* (both of which are often used interchangeably with the imported word "art") in his book, *The Temple of the Eyes*.[2] According to Kitazawa, "the word *geijutsu* means technique and learning."[3] At another point he writes, "*Geijutsu*, or the technique of creating beautiful things."[4] *Bijutsu*, on the other hand, was a term developed around the time of the 1872 Vienna Exhibition "as the official government translation for the German term *Schöne Kunste* when Japan participated in the Exhibition."[5] According to another translation authority, it was used as a translation for "fine art." One definition of the term *bijutsu* includes the following: "In the West, music, painting, sculpture, poetry, and the like are called *bijutsu*." As you can see, the definition includes both music and poetry as well. Today, the differences among the terms *geijutsu*, *bijutsu*, and "art" have become very minute. Although I know little about their historical roots, I use the words based on an instinctual understanding of their differences. *Geijutsu*, which has a slightly older feel to me, I use to refer to all forms of art. *Bijutsu*, on the other hand, refers to the visual arts, does not include music or poetry, and is divided into Japanese painting, Western painting, and sculpture. Art, however, seems to me to be the contemporary form of the term *geijutsu*. The concept of "freedom" within these various terms for art in Japan is not freedom in the sense of discovering oneself and then examining one's surroundings from that perspective. In the Japanese context, the term refers to a state like that of a newborn: not bound by limits, not connected to the system, not filled with information. It is a blank slate.

In recent years outsider art has experienced something of a boom in Japan. The reason for that and for the popularity of Picasso's later works is the Japanese view of art, in which a non-discriminating "freedom" equals "art."

On the other hand, what is Japanese society looking for in artists? What sort of structure determines those artists' actions? Let me begin with a review of the different genres in the postwar art world.

Japanese painting, Western painting, sculpture, design, and crafts. These are the names of the departments at the Tokyo School of Fine Arts and Music (now the Tokyo University of Fine Arts and Music) established in 1889 by Okakura Tenshin. These genre divisions formed separate worlds for each type of art, with Japanese painting, Western painting,

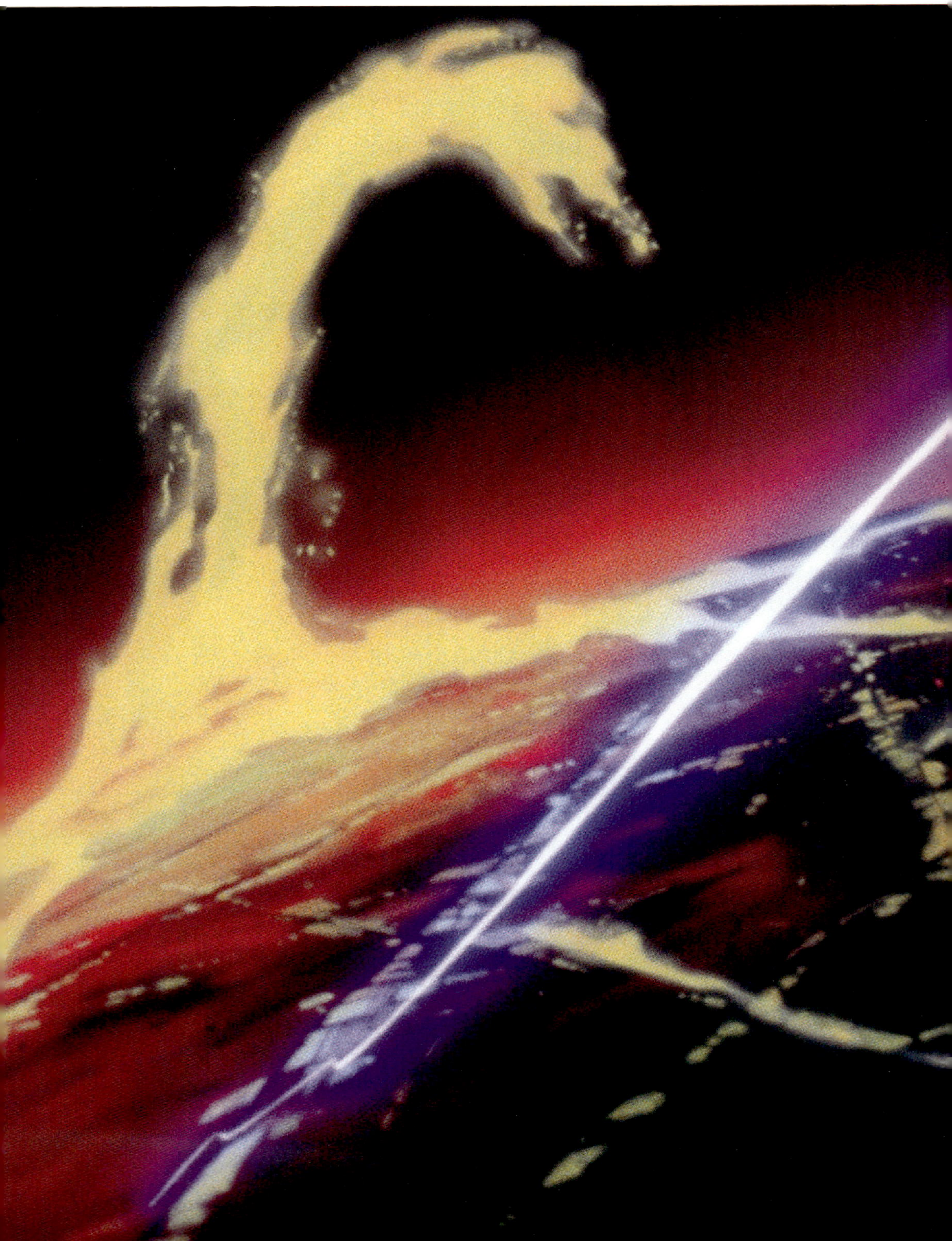

FIG. 3 (ABOVE AND RIGHT) Yoshinori Kanada (Animation Director) stills from **Galaxy Express 999** 1979 animated film 128 min.

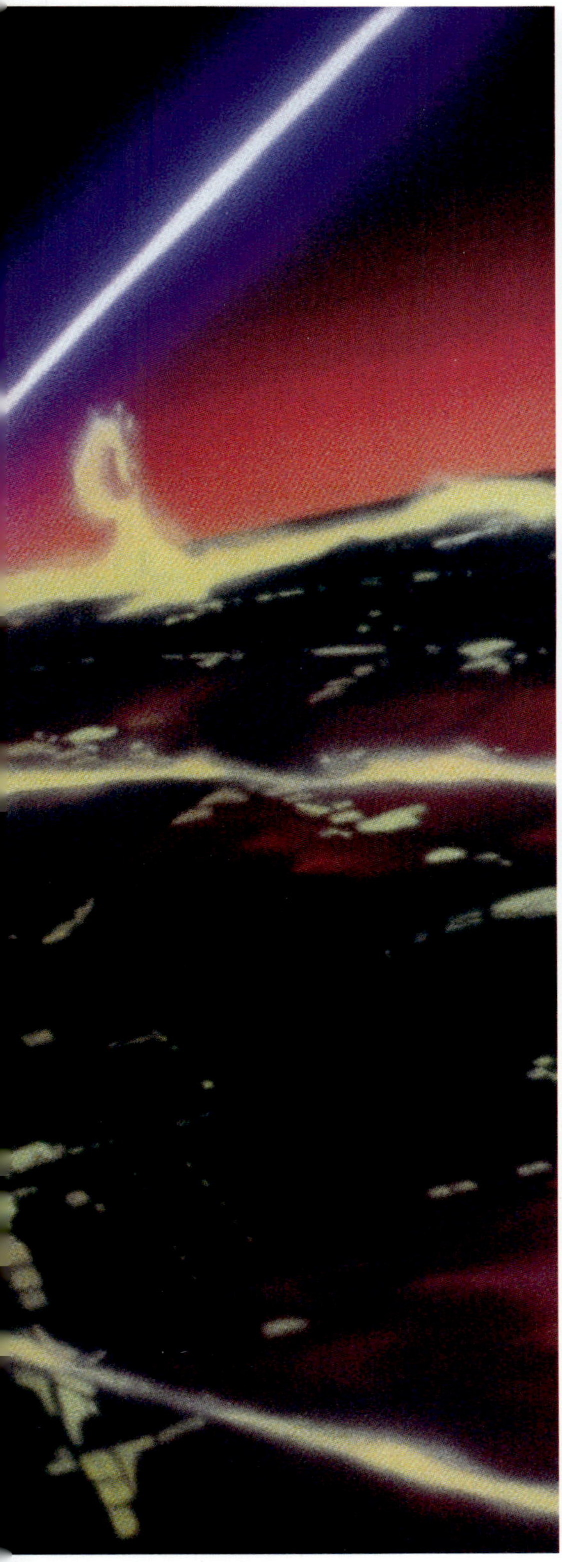

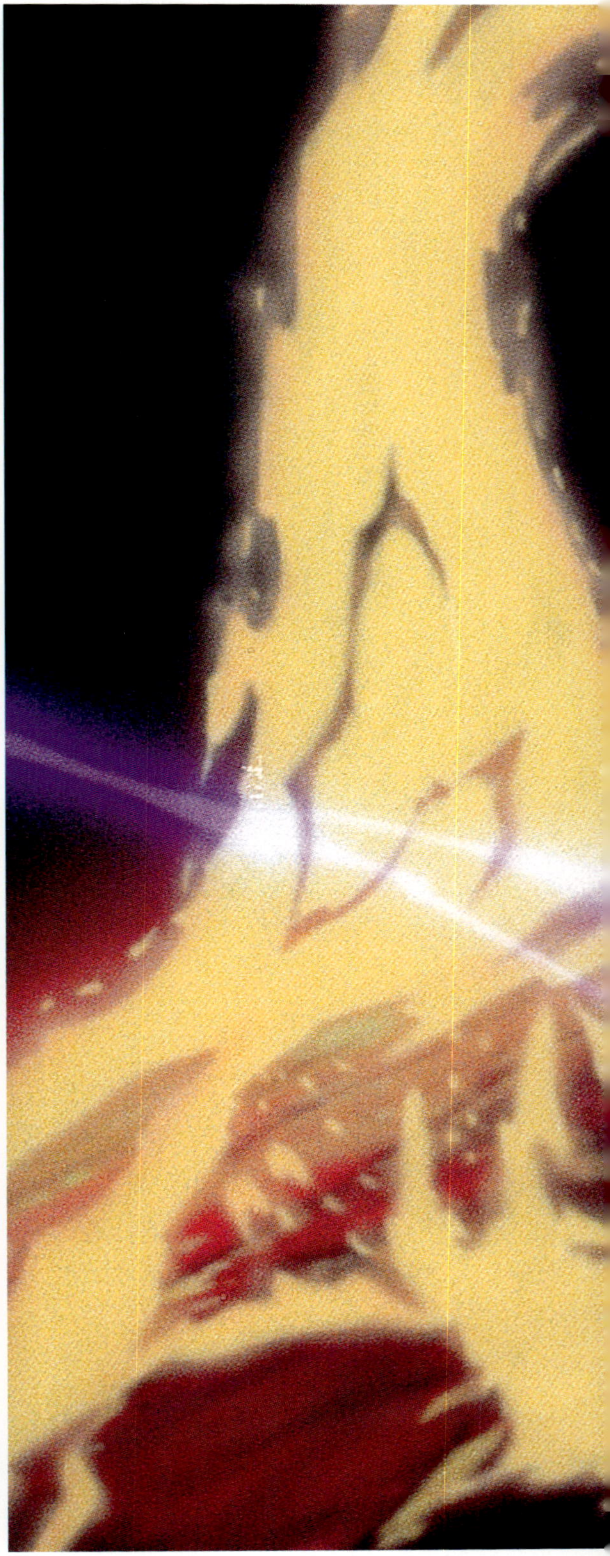

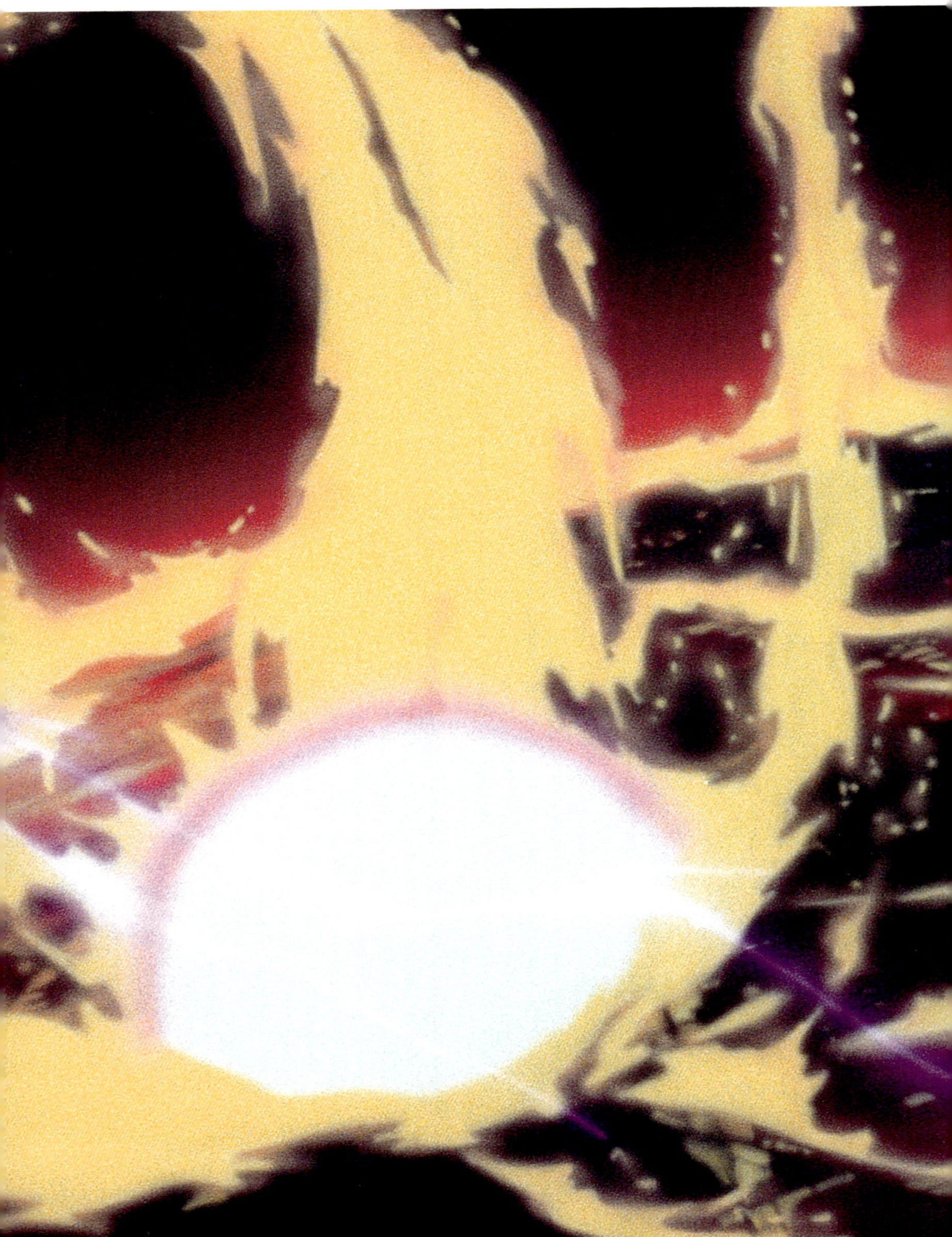

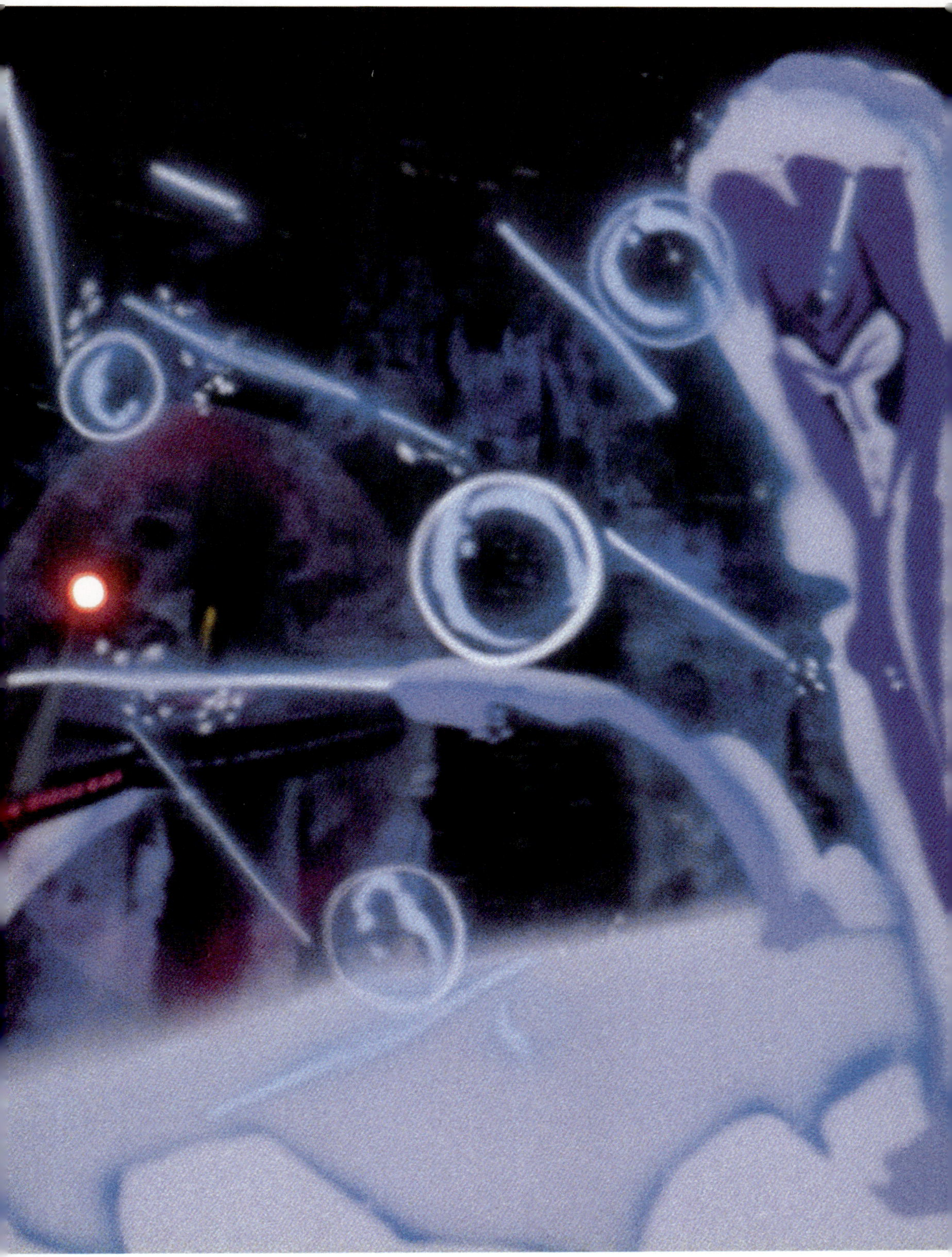

FIG. 4 (ABOVE AND NEXT PAGE) Yoshinori Kanada (Animation Director) stills from **Goodbye to Galaxy Express 999** 1981 animated film 130 min. © Leiji Matsumoto, Tōei Animation

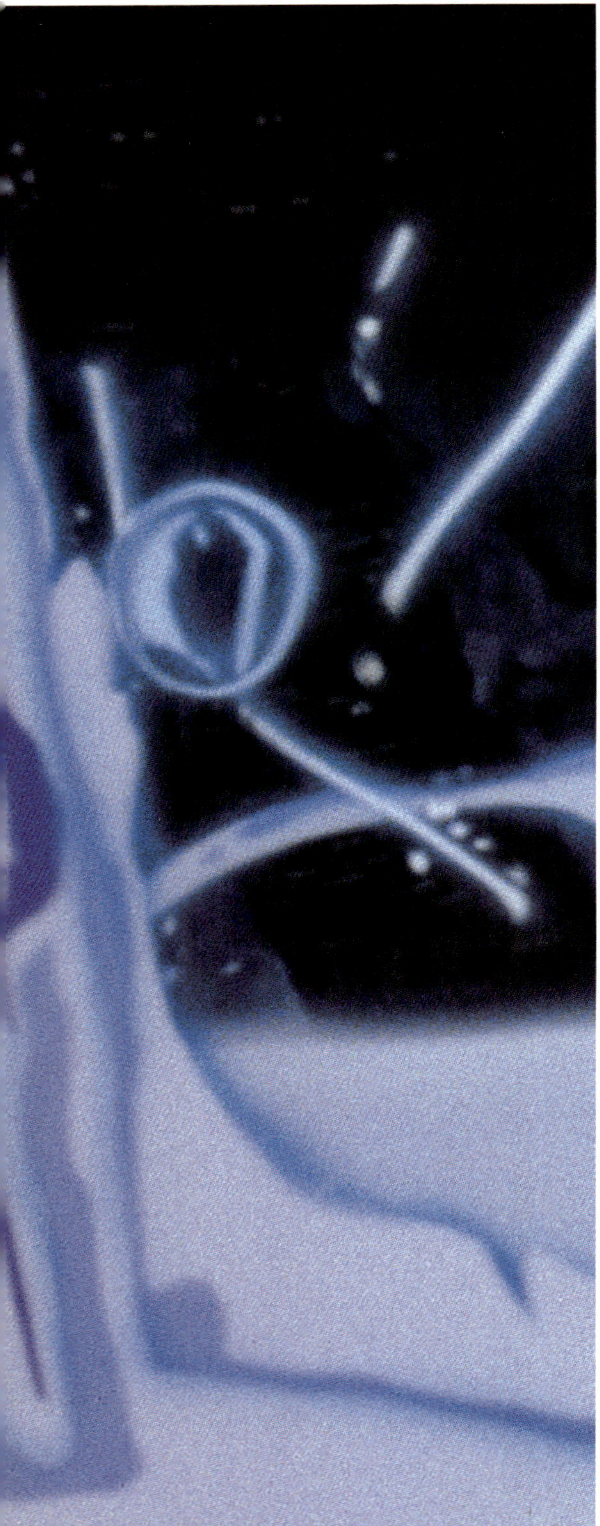

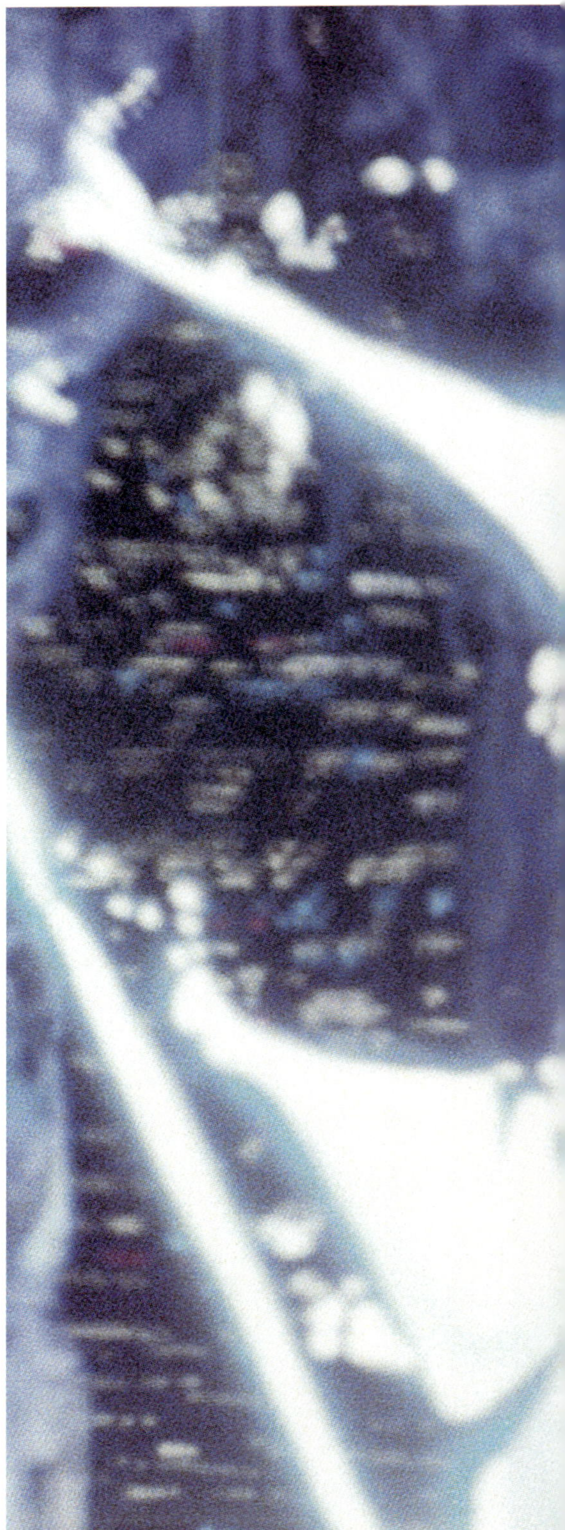

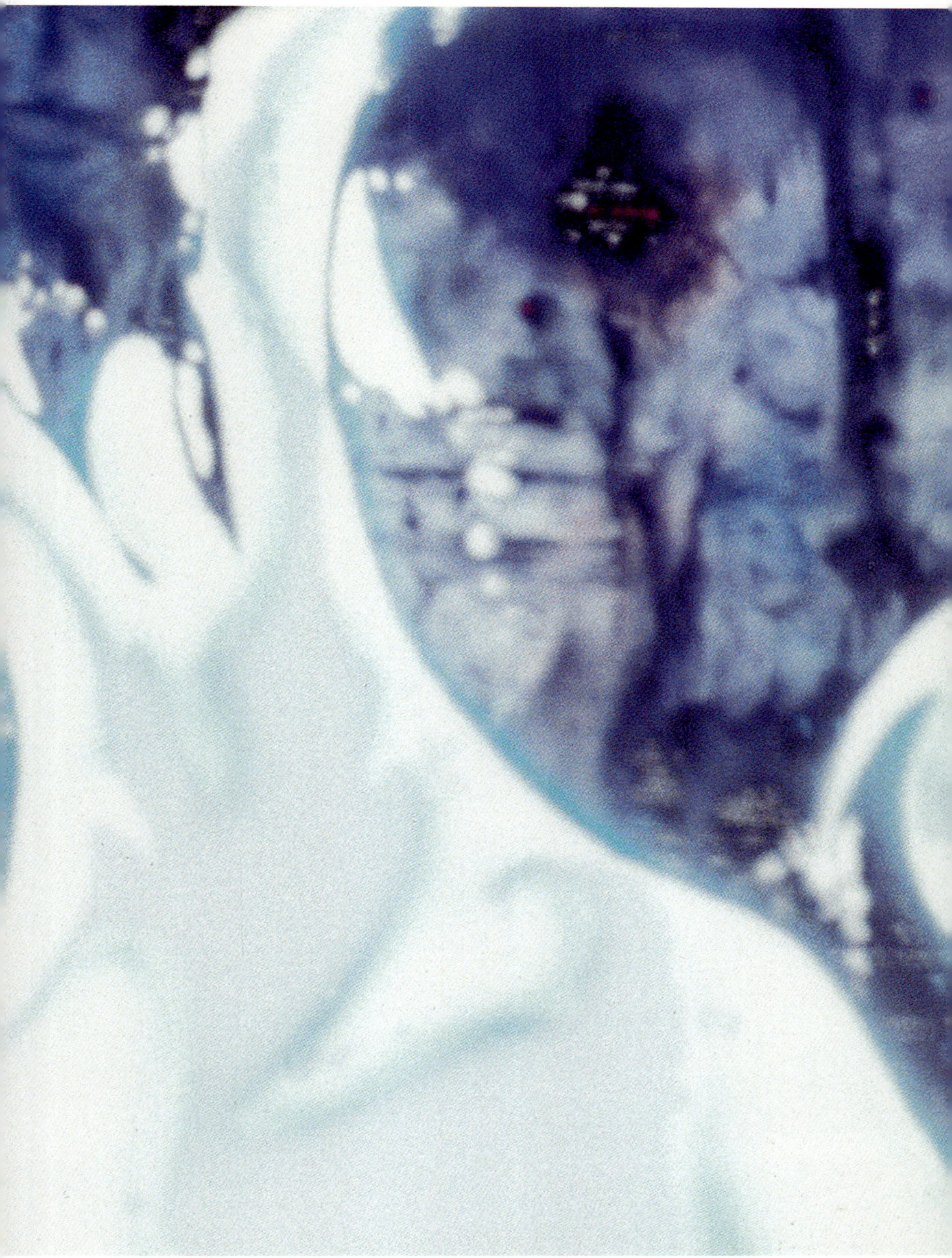

and sculpture becoming the predominant arts after the beginning of public exhibitions in the postwar caused them to gain mass appeal. The art boom in Japan began with the economic growth of the late 1960s. At that time sales of Japanese painting, Western painting, pottery, and craft were growing steadily. Department stores would show (and sell) paintings in their halls and newspaper companies would regularly sponsor shows of famous Western works. At that time, Japanese paintings done in a Western style were falling out of favor due to exhibitions of actual imported Western paintings. Had this occurred later, perhaps Japanese artists would have been glad to see the latest works from another country. Unfortunately, at this stage the appearance of famous Western works showed quite clearly the difference in level of ability, putting the necessity of the Japanese artists in question. What was seen as original Japanese art—ceramics and Japanese painting—began attracting attention at that time. Though Japanese painting had been pushed into near extinction with the importation after World War II of art theories from the West, this generation turned to it in a search for Japanese identity, leading to a great boom. At the same time, within the art establishment a hierarchy was being constructed that attempted to stabilize prices. Similarly, the ceramics world linked with the tea ceremony world to maintain high prices and the status that accompanied them.

Though one effect of the bubble economy of the 1980s was that prices throughout the industry rose too high, another effect was that discount travel brokers such as H.I.S. appeared, lowering the primary hurdle to traveling abroad. As a result, Japanese traveled around the world and were able to see various famous works for themselves. Information about the art market abroad also entered Japan, making Japanese aware of the imbalance between the world price standard and current Japanese prices. Leaving the development of these travelers' tastes aside, the Japanese painting and Western painting industries were only interested in the money game, and were taking great pains to protect the system and its organizations. The creation of a sense of value and vision for the present and future—what people really wanted to see—was completely forgotten. In the end, the existing art industry collapsed with the bursting of the bubble economy. "Art" has begun to disappear. Eroticism and nonsense, which the West looks for in the realm of art, have always been a part of Japanese subculture and *manga*; perhaps excessively so. The majority of youth in search of an identity shifted their interest to music. The latest trend has been the appearance of the genre known as celebrity art (art whose subject matter is a celebrity.) This has been the most recent product of a business that has been exploiting the genre confusion created by the explosive proliferation of media. The "art" produced by this business is made up primarily of lithographs of special effects illustrations with the motifs of celebrities, *anime*, *manga*, and Godzilla. In addition, "happy illustration art" has been very popular since the mid-1990s. Today you can buy it just about anywhere. The reason that "Japanese" contemporary art and photography are getting attention domestically is because even though Japanese tastes have been developed by seeing original works abroad, artists and works have a strong Westernized identity and bearable works have slowly started to be produced. In a sense, seeing the art scene at the height of its confusion was a valuable warning for individual artists and probably acted as encouragement. Nowadays, when the music available in any large record shop contains tremendous amounts of information and distribution networks have been completed that allow us to browse foreign magazines, the material is readily available for a popular art that we can evaluate for ourselves. If we take a close look at the situation we find ourselves in, then the basis of our own lives today should become clear. The future would become visible once again.

5. The Real in Postwar "Art"

Within the meaning of "art" as it was used in Japan in the postwar [period], a clear line was drawn dividing avant-garde art in the Western conception and folk art such as domestic Japanese painting and crafts. As I mentioned before, the latter came to be supported as art by a mass audience. The former, on the other hand, began to develop as part of a movement by the avant-garde artists themselves to find their place in the realm of "art." The artists who burst onto the scene at the Yomiuri Indépendants exhibition were treated as eccentrics by society at large, primarily because of their belief in extreme "freedom."

Still, they did gain popularity, partially as a result of attention from the media. Though their methods of searching for identity disavowed public appeals or systematizing, groups nonetheless did form, dividing into such small factions as the "Neo-Dada Organizers," "[Hi] Red Center," "The Kyushu School," "Concrete," and "The Zero Dimension." The trends of such groups were covered by media such as *Bijutsu Techo* and *Mizue*. They also began to link up with the underground theater and dance scene and became connected to such cultural figures as Shuzo Takiguchi and Tatsuhiko Shibusawa; this began to show the depth of the movement. All of their activities, including "Concrete," Rauschenberg, and Taro Okamoto, were swallowed up into the 1970 Osaka World's Fair. "Art" had become "celebration." It was also around this time that the words *bijutsu* and *geijutsu* started to create confusion. After the World's Fair, the *geijutsu* movement lacked any upsurge and the *bijutsu* media began to lose energy. As a result a number of *geijutsu* artists began to enter directly into mass society as entertainers. Taro Okamoto, famous for his *Tower of the Sun* at the Osaka World's Fair, was a major artist in postwar Japanese society. He gained more fame, however, in the latter half of his life as he assumed the role of "artist as eccentric" within the medium of television, and produced the well-received catch phrase "art is an explosion." At the same time, however, he maintained the position that he would not sell any of his art. By preserving his artistic purity through this rejection of the art market, he preserved the image of a Western-style artist in Japanese society.

Masuo Ikeda, the recipient of the award for printmaking at the 1966 Venice Biennale, received little attention outside of specialist journals until he won the prestigious literary award, the Akutagawa Prize, which gave him a certain degree of social status. The film based on his work, which fell somewhere between art and entertainment, was a very successful promotional clip for the artist himself. Later in his life he continued challenging the center of Japanese culture by throwing himself into creating pottery.

The avant-garde artist Genpei Akasegawa, under the pen name Katsuhiko Otsuji, was another recipient of the Akutagawa Prize. Akasegawa, an artistic acrobat balancing ultra-Japanese and eccentric viewpoints, successfully transferred his unique sensibility to the literary world. Even today he maintains a serious position as an artist in Japan by working as an artist and novelist and refusing to be limited by genre. Avant-garde artists who think seriously about the relationship between Japanese society and "art" have moved their artistic pursuits into the popular media, allowing them to enter Japanese society.

It is easy to forget that it was Japanese painting that most actively crossed cultural boundaries during the postwar. The most popular of these painters were Matazō Kayama, Yasushi Sugiyama, Tatsuo Takayama, Kaii Higashiyama, and Ikuo Hirayama. In particular Hirayama, whose silk road works helped launch the search for Japanese identity, could be reevaluated as an artist who mixed media. Unfortunately, from that time until the present the various genres of contemporary art, including Japanese painting and Western painting, have not been able to cross over, but have developed in parallel without coming into contact with one another. In the world of Japanese painting especially, internal politics have played a large role, setting incredibly high prices domestically. Because of the opacity of the industry formula through which prices are kept at an irrationally high level, the popularity of and respect for the industry are low. Moreover, with the collapse of the bubble economy and the accompanying radical drop in prices for works, the market has come to lack stability. Until the bubble period Japanese painting had come to represent "Japan" and "art," but since the advent of digital production, it has failed to connect with the age and, like Western painting, is beginning to fade. What is contemporary "art"? The social stance of "artist" in "Japan," with the appearance of genres, has remained vague as always. Since the 1980s, designers, musicians, and others have begun calling themselves "artists." The fact that the established art journal, *Bijutsu Techo*, has taken the title *BT*, using roman letters and not the original Japanese characters, is symbolic of the shift from a Japanese conception of art, *bijutsu*, to a Western conception. Artists who copy foreign artists continue to appear, and the vagueness of their position decreases faith in the term *bijutsu*. Weaving through the interstices of the industry, these entertainers have begun to successfully hold "art" shows as a form of enterprise. In another sense, though, the chaos

of this situation is the reality of the Japanese art production scene, in which "art" and "entertainment" are being fused.

6. The Shared Center of "Art" and "Entertainment"
An inhuman power was visible in the techniques employed by professionals, their entertainment, and in magic. The professionals themselves must have felt the power of a god in the background of their own "entertainment." That power is one that works on the border between the "secular" and the "ecclesiastic," acting as a bridge between the limitless power of nature and the society of mankind.

The concepts of "entertainment" and "profession" have existed in Japan since the distant past. The imported term "art,"[6] however, has created confusion between them since the Meiji period. When I talk to the creators of *otaku* figurines whom I consider avant-garde "artists," for example, they just see their "art" as a "profession," albeit one performed with a high degree of technical skill. When I asked students in an oil painting class at the art university preparatory school what "art" was, I also received only unsatisfactory answers. They only have ideas that are based on their teachers' tastes and in the sketching abilities necessary to pass the entrance examination. Art university students today give similar responses. Despite the fact that we are all professional artists, it is hard to see eye to eye on this question.

While it is partially due to the ambiguity of the term "art" in Japan, it is also partially the fault of Japanese art education as it is practiced in elementary, middle, and high schools. The textbooks do not contain concise explanations of the artists presented, and though teachers probably add their own explanations, there is a great danger of distortion. For example, why is Picasso so respected in the world art scene? Textbooks focus more on his drawing ability during the "Blue Period" than they do [on] his avant-garde work. Either that, or they explain that a groundless "freedom" gave birth to cubism, and then from that illogically conclude that they should encourage the students to draw with a similar "freedom," turning art into a form of recreation. If the significance of Picasso in the history of "art" is understood as no more than a question of the superiority of his technique or a simple issue of temperament, an important point has been missed. There are other, more important questions to ask. What was the role of a given artist or movement in the course of history? How did the avant-garde movement shatter the existing conception of that role? What sort of history emerged from this reconsideration? Once the axis of time has been introduced, how can we achieve "freedom"? The approach to that sort of original concept is done through the Western-style view of "art." The respect afforded to originality in that view of art is one great difference from the Japanese view.

In "Japan," where "art" has been recognized by society as a medium in which a groundless freedom can be expressed, the definition of a term such as "art" has remained vague among the masses. The bases of such terms have been preserved up through the present day. On the other hand, a term like "entertainment" has a reality, and is generally understood. Japanese "art" has become attached to an idea of a creative Japanese original "entertainment." The confusion over these two terms is symbolized by the "celebratory" dimension of the Osaka World's Fair. Japanese artists, led by the elite of the Japanese architecture industry, participated in the creation of this sense of "celebration." Japanese "art" became connected to "celebration" and was thus absorbed into "entertainment." For example, there was the *otaku* festival for selling *manga* known as the "Comic Market," in which 450,000 people participated. Its management structure was consciously amateur, being primarily run by volunteers. The willful ignoring of both copyrights and sexuality censorship created an intentional chaos that is representative of the radical nature of contemporary "art" in Japan.

7. The Super Flat Image "Japan"
Like the images created by the "eccentric" painters or the animation timing created by Yoshinori Kanada, I would like to sketch "Japan" in a "super flat" style. Collecting the images in this book [Murakami's *Super Flat* (2000), in which this essay originally

appeared], I will fuse the images together into a pair of four-paneled doors. I will call this work "Japan." At the center of the image is the thick trunk of Japan's eccentric, secular, grotesque "sub-culture." Moving up the trunk to the upper left of the image, you see a small bird representing a meaningless "hierarchy," but you can ignore that. After moving your gaze slowly along a horizontal path to the left, there are "celebrations" and "media frenzies" that produce a sense of speed that zigzags up and down, but when you look at the extreme left you see a small branch growing up. At the end of the branch are two small blossoms, "eroticism" and "grotesquerie." From there your gaze speeds over to the lower center of the image, where there is something crushed beneath the thick trunk that looks a bit like a dog. Your gaze then fixes on the two dark eyes of the creature, which you recognize as an *otaku*. It would not be an exaggeration to say that this is the subject of the image. Alongside this creature are bamboo leaves known as *manga* and *anime*, which have been scattered about to diffuse their power. Returning to the thick trunk of "freedom" and "childlikeness," you see that it slides off to the right before curving down suddenly. Beside the trunk is the rock of "pop," whose upward directionality is emphasized. Running above the trunk is deformed "cheap ticket" moss, which sets the tempo. All along the bottom, the scattered cosmos of "entertainment" are blossoming out of season. At the top of the image are gilded clouds, above which "The West," "History," and "Art" are only partially visible. This image is, as you would imagine, very eccentric, and it is hard to say that it is beautiful. As it is done in a "super flat" style, though, it is also extremely "avant-garde" and "original." Perhaps in the future, in some distant country, a researcher will give it some unusual title and an entirely new interpretation, but that is only a nonsensical fantasy. It seems meaningless for the search for the self known as "art" to develop in a country that does not possess the foundation for "art." Still, if it is possible to look over an image created by a gadget that constructs "Japan" as if it were a "super flat" picture, then perhaps that can become one kind of art history.

8. The Birth of "Super Flat"-ism

The chaos surrounding "art" in Japan has continued to be the source of energy for its production. The "avant-garde" lineage that I selected from that chaotic history was the lineage of "eccentricity" embodied in the animation form of Yoshinori Kanada. From that lineage I extracted the concept of "super flat," a term that integrates artists and works possessing that unique Japanese sensibility. In addition, I examined the site that gave birth to that original expression, Japan.

It is a pioneer, an epoch, and the creation of heretofore-unseen images. "Super flat," one form of "Japanese" "avant-garde" "art," is an "-ism"—like Cubism, Surrealism, Minimalism, and Simulationism before it—only this is one we have created. Though the Japanese "avant-garde" has always been alternative and underground and has not yet made its appearance on the main stage, as the DNA that formed Japanese culture, "super flatness" has been continually producing the "avant-garde" up until the present day.

It is the art at the center of a Japanese culture that lacks prestige, authority, celebration, and cost. In it, however, one can see the budding saplings of a new future. For example, no one has yet taken a serious look at the image resulting from the integration of the layers of entertainment and art. But that integration is already occurring. Much integration is still underway. That integration is producing yet another "super flat" image: us.

NOTES

1 *Kiso no keifu*. Perikan-sha, 1988. Second printing, 1993.
2 Nariaki Kitazawa, *Me no shinden*. Bijutsu Shuppan-sha, 1989.
3 Ibid., p. 146.
4 Ibid., p. 148.
5 Ibid., p. 145.
6 Yoshihiko Okano, *Chusei no hinin to yūjo*. Akashki Shoten, 1994. This quote comes from the fourth printing, 1997, p.11.

Frances Stark is a Los Angeles–based artist whose work addresses the architecture of language and is often accompanied by related personal texts. Her work has been shown extensively, including group exhibitions at the San Francisco Museum of Modern Art; the Museum of Contemporary Art, Los Angeles; and the Gesellschaft für Aktuelle Kunst, Bremen, Germany. Stark has published her writings, including essays and book reviews, in *Artforum* and *Art & Text*; her artist's book *The Architect and the Housewife* was published in 1999.

Scared to Death

Frances Stark

"Speech is a symptom of affection."
— Emily Dickinson

Some people get up in front of a group of people and the first thing they have to get out of their mouth is how nervous they are. Once they do so, they begin to calm down; some may even ease into eloquence. Most audiences probably don't mind this sort of admission of fear, since most people—according to an oft-repeated but dubious statistic—fear public speaking more than death itself. I assume the horrifying part is in the speech act, the saying of something, rather than in facing a public. If you had to sit on a chair in front of an audience and say absolutely nothing, perhaps that wouldn't be so scary. Everyone knows death is mandatory and addressing an audience is not; however, doing something with your scared-of-death self that would necessitate an audience, before and/or after your death, could very well deliver immortality. In any case, I want to start by saying, ladies and gentleman, I'm a little nervous. But it's not out of fear of having to say something, and it's not you (I don't think); it's our big topic, "painting," that has me a bit on edge. I think the reason I'm even here addressing the topic is because of another monologue I delivered called *The Architect and the Housewife*. That began with a cute but mildly macabre rhyme prompted by a housewife's hunger. After searching her cupboards and finding nothing to spread between her bread, she's forced to poke a knife into "her hungry head." She tries to make a sandwich with nothing but her brain, which she claims is "something like smoked ham." "My eyes can serve as olives," she concludes, "to garnish the sandwich I am."

Have you ever noticed how some people, when they attempt to talk in front of a painting, try to prove that they are smart or that they have at least considered some of the possible trajectories of a discussion about painting, and later let it slip that they would rather just paint, period. I admit this statement applies to me, although instead of *just paint*, I'd rather tell some jokes. The problem is, I don't know that many jokes. The problem with the other thing, the wanting to be smart part, is that it makes it hard for people to put anything on the table. So far we have on our table a brain sandwich garnished with eyes, a weird way of announcing, perhaps, that what we are dealing with here is a light lunch, a dialectic between language—written or spoken—and painting. It would be very different to say between music and painting, because when we see paintings we like to talk about them. It is less likely, although certainly not unheard of, that we sit down at the piano or pick up a guitar upon seeing or painting a painting. If you decided to break into song in front of a painting, say in a museum, a guard might have to tell you, *Quiet please*, because that is only allowed (aloud) under very special circumstances. We are accustomed to reading about paintings and so we like to read or hear what painters have to say about their painting and/or the act of painting their paintings. Anything the painter might possibly say is something we want to hear or read so we can say *yes, yes* or *no, no* or quote the painter later. In school someone makes a painting and another person, a teacher or a fellow student, comes along and demands that the painter speak. If they aren't demanding the painter to speak, chances are the painter is imagining being demanded to speak, so he or she starts speaking and leading that person in a certain direction, sometimes toward, sometimes away from, the painting that precipitated the speaking. If someone makes what appears to be an inane painting but interesting things come out of the artist's mouth, you think *yes, yes* and cross your fingers. If someone makes an interesting painting but he or she says something inane, you are obliged to ignore the inane and concentrate on the interesting, or you dismiss the promising, interesting thing, since it is negated by the inanity. And if you say, *Be more specific than inane and interesting*, I have to say *Sorry, no*. For at any given time it's going to be a different attribute that—to you—announces inanity, a different attribute that captures your interest. You don't have to be a historian to know, though you may *know better*, about the imaginary time line that serves as an index of things one can no longer do. One of those things, on again, off again, has been painting. The rules get trickier when there's "a painter," which to nonpainters suggests the person painting is some kind of alchemist, or the painter has done some unknown thing in order to earn a license to paint. As for not having a license, I don't even have a license to drive, but I drive anyway. Well, the truth of the situation is that I did have a driver's license, only foolishly I let it expire.

But, you may say, we asked you to write about painting—what has that got to do with speaking about speaking? I will try to explain. If, in the sentence above, you replace "write about painting" with "speak about women and fiction" and "speaking about speaking" with

"*A Room of One's Own*," then what you have—exactly—is the opening of Virginia Woolf's famous address to the Arts Society. Don't ask which arts society. Most times, whenever I stand up, as an artist, in front of any arts society (art school!), I am just winging it, as they say. I never have a paper in my hand unless I am reciting a piece of my own fiction. Conversely, whenever I have been in the audience on the receiving end of a visiting artist's talk, I could see that it was a winged business for them as well. Even so, formal or not, because you can watch the words come out of the artist's mouth, a mouth in the vicinity of a projected image of something the artist has done, you can get a really strong sense of the degree to which the speaking artist believes in what he or she is saying or reading from. It's worth noting that there doesn't seem to be a prominent, formal paper-delivery system for artists these days. Even *Artforum*, the publication that brought you many of the artist texts found in anthologies today, presents mere pseudo-texts by artists with its new "1,000 Words" column. This is where a writer and an artist get together and the writer turns what the artist says into writing that reads as if the artist wrote it, with nothing to indicate otherwise. Could it be that language is losing its hold? Has a fear of speaking publicly washed over those who know that a certain loquaciousness is expected of them? What originally changed things drastically for the artist and the work of art was (and I like the way Howard Singerman puts it) "the spread of language—indeed language as spread [in my case, sandwich-spread] . . . a spreading thin of time and energy and commitment to craft."[1] In a sense, some might go so far as to say that the tongue began to bully the eyes and hands and, as you know, led to what Singerman succinctly refers to as "the production of ever clearer and more knowing works of art and the development of ever more effective methodologies to place and determine them."

Knowing I was supposed to speak to you about painting today, I decided to go see some artists who recently began painting in addition to doing what it is they usually do, that is, the thing they are recognized for doing. One of those artists is known for his sculptures, one for his collages, and one for his films—all bricoleurs of sorts, and all artists I initially encountered in a visiting-artist scenario. Jason Meadows came out of school several years after me, Richard Hawkins was out of school several years before me, and Morgan Fisher came along way before Richard. Jason showed me a painting of a chair, which looked just like the one he sat on while we talked about it. The painting was really worked at the edges where the negative space met the object—where you perhaps shouldn't fool around so as not to muck up the perspective. The chair looked like an excuse to dabble in the area around it. It was rather nice and immediately exciting to look at and made sense in relation to his sculptures. It reminded me of Richard Hawkins' Post-it-sized billboard shapes that echoed the actual Post-its that appeared in his collages, on which were scrawled curt Proustian sentiments; only in the paintings there wasn't any writing anywhere. Both Jason's chair and Richard's mini-billboards seemed to be jumping-off points for abstract abandon, easy givens, the meaning-free area around which one could then indulge.

Richard said one of the things that prompted him to work with actual paint on canvas was all the time he spent, on account of teaching, listening to students lamely attempt to defend their painting efforts. Jason told me he was inspired by the Tintorettos he saw in Venice. I instantly pictured Tintoretto's *White-Bearded Man*, as it is reproduced on the cover of at least one edition of Thomas Bernhard's *Old Masters*.[2] Bernhard's novel, a comedy, takes place in the Kunsthistorisches Museum in Vienna. It begins as the storyteller prepares to meet his friend, Reger, in their usual spot, a settee in front of *White-Bearded Man*. There Reger, a music critic, sits and lectures the storyteller on topics such as the art of the fugue. Then there's Irrsigler, a museum guard, who for more than thirty years has been every bit the regular as the storyteller and Reger. Irrsigler, who was turned down for police duty on account of his weakness, took a job as a museum guard—which made little difference to him since all he wanted was to wear the same uniform day in and day out. After years of guard duty in the museum, Irrsigler had acquired an understanding of art. "*For decades the museum guides have always been saying the same thing, and of course a great deal of nonsense, as Herr Reger says*," Bernhard's Irrsigler says. "*The art historians only swamp the visitors with their twaddle*, says Irrsigler, who has, over the years, appropriated verbatim many, if not all, of Reger's sentences." As a museum guard, Irrsigler could stand around and look at paintings all day. Robert Ryman was a museum guard, too, only in real life, and in New York, not Vienna, and he could do the same. Unlike Irrsigler, his first ambition was not to be a cop but a musician, and now, of course, he is known for his paintings not for his style of guarding them or his saxophone playing. Jason mentioned Ryman and said, *You can't do that anymore*, and Richard mentioned Ryman, and Morgan mentioned Ryman, also intimating that one can no longer paint that way, and all without any prompting from me. All were enamored of Ryman's paintings, and I, too, am enamored of Ryman's paintings. I struggled to speak of this fascination with Ryman's work, and, embarrassingly enough, found myself asking, *Is this some kind of mysticism*? Surely mysticism is the wrong word, but I said it anyway, since fresh in my mind was this passage from the book *Wittgenstein's Vienna*: "[A] certain type of language mysticism . . . assigns a central importance in human life to art, on the ground that art alone can express the meaning of life. Only art can express moral truth, and only the artist can teach the things that matter most in life. Art is a mission."[3] It wasn't sitting there in my head just like that, word for word, but the gist of it was lingering. You have to understand that Wittgenstein was one of my housewives who felt philosophy was less like building buildings and more like tidying up rooms.

I traced a painting called *A Private Conversation* by Félix Vallotton to decorate my *Architect and the Housewife*, which was actually a book, not just a monologue. I also borrowed from his *Woman Searching Through a Cupboard* and another painting of his that features a baby tearing up a piece of paper. Vallotton is not well known for his paintings, but rather for his cartoonlike woodcuts, mostly of crowd scenes and stark even cynical couplings of men and women. When he married the daughter of an important art dealer, he settled down into bourgeois domesticity and comfort, and he moved away from the crowds and the medium that had made his name and returned primarily to the privileged medium of paint. Supposedly he wasn't concerned with originality; he said he didn't think art ever took new directions and that art's goals were "immutable, perpetual."[4] That sounds so unacceptable, so undefendable, so unimportant, so, so romantic. *I guess I'm just a romantic* is not at all an uncommon exclamation for me. Unfortunately, it's such a misleading thing to say. "The entire Romantic ethic and body of art rests upon the assumption of insecurity, an insecurity which begins at the personal level of immortality and extends into all the intellectual fields where insecurity is least tolerable."[5] I read this on an airplane the other day in an essay by the recently deceased Alex Comfort. He wrote it in 1942, but I was reading a reprint of it in a handsome new journal ("of art, context, and enquiry") that had an image of airplane windows reproduced on the cover. I should also mention that I was sitting next to a woman my mother's age who was clutching a white stuffed animal, the wear and tear of which made me cry, but just for a minute. I remember Morgan Fisher saying, *What do you mean by romantic*? His father was an architect from Chicago in the beaux-arts tradition but made his living building flat-roof houses. Morgan is making paintings inspired by books on panels built up more like furniture than stretcher bars. Utilizing an orthographic method, borrowed from the practice of architectural rendering, he arrives at an irregularly shaped canvas, onto which he applies an even coat of gray house paint, the exact tone of the photographer's gray card. It's hard to explain, because it's all very complicated, and all the complicated explanations seem like justifications, but they're actually inspiration, easily mistaken for justification. Morgan told me I should read the essay by Yve-Alain Bois, "Painting: The Task of Mourning." I was surprised to find that Bois concluded his essay by paraphrasing the novelist Robert Musil: "If some painting is still to come, if painters are still to come, they will not come from where we expect them to."[6]

It's funny that it didn't occur to me until after the fact that two of the painters I sought out for conversation collaborated with the artist Jorge Pardo, who figured quite prominently in my architect and housewife metaphor. I saw a Pardo painting the other day that looked like a heap of melted indigo iMacs. It, or something like it, may be hanging in my home soon, as I live with gallerist Steve Hanson, to whom Jorge has made an unusual offer. When asked for a description of his gallery to be printed in an art-fair catalogue, Steve submitted the following sentence: "We're having a great time here in L.A. because of our importance." Jorge liked the sentence so much he offered to trade a painting for it.

Not all of us have always been having a great time in L.A. because of our importance. I was employed as a house painter to do faux-painting in Mel Gibson's home. This is when I first had a strong urge to try to make paintings. It was several years ago, the same year the O. J. trial was blanketing the airwaves. We listened to the radio while we worked and I distinctly remember being agitated to the point of not being able to concentrate when a woman scientist's academic prestige and knowledge were being debunked on the basis that it was untranslatable to a jury of science illiterates. At that point we had to change to a station that would allow more freedom for our minds to wander. One possible trajectory may have been: does Mel Gibson's wife know that most of her professional painters aren't actually painters but professional artists of a different brand entirely? You see, I was painting every day with three other nonpainting women artists—Marnie Weber, Sarah Seager, and Sharon Lockhart—all of us brought together not because of our relationship to painting but because of our relationship to money. I believe it was *Braveheart* that was making Mel Gibson a ton of money at that time, which for us meant we could dedicate entire days to making a new door look old. Working with a large variety of media on a window pane in the closet of the guardhouse, I got to thinking that someone could have a nervous breakdown in there someday. Such a breakdown could prompt the afflicted individual to spend a lot of time staring at some small insignificant portion of paint, eyes glued to a random set of details. For faux painting to sustain its effect, a viewer must not partake in any isolated or protracted viewing; it is meant for glancing, not looking. I like to believe someone could inevitably break out of the glance mode and start to pay attention, at which point all hell could very well break loose.

I just made the huge mistake of looking at a fragment of turgid yet thorough theoretical text that happened to pass across my table and now I feel myself falling apart as I begin to worry that I've made a mistake with all this candid chatter, this quasi-populist routine. But I don't want not to talk, I don't want to sit on a chair on a stage and face a crowd and be mute just because I can't talk the way I think I'm supposed to. Bernhard's Herr Reger tells the storyteller that "*the world and mankind have arrived at a state of hell, such as the world and mankind have never before arrived at throughout history . . .*" and he goes on and on, as is his fashion. And after a fashion, "*You sneaked off into philosophy and authorship*, Reger said, *but you are neither a philosopher nor an author, that is what is simultaneously so interesting and so unfortunate about you and in you, because you are not really a philosopher and not really an author either, because for a philosopher you lack everything that is characteristic of a philosopher, and for an author similarly everything, even though you are exactly what I call the philosophical writer, your philosophy is no real philosophy and your writing is no real writing*, he repeated. *And a writer who does not publish anything is, basically, not really a writer*."[7] I know I should've paraphrased that! If I had, I could've paralleled Bois' essay on mourning by giving the last (albeit not exact) word to an Austrian literary figure. Except, of course, my comedic nonparaphrased excerpt lacks the optimism of the Musil/Bois suggestion that painting will come from where we least expect it to, although I did attempt to suggest that myself, before finally sneaking off into romantic insecurity or less intellectual fields. *You've been a great crowd.*

NOTES

1 Howard Singerman, *Art Subjects: Making Artists in the American University* (Berkeley and Los Angeles: University of California Press, 1999), p. 155.
2 Thomas Bernhard, *Old Masters: A Comedy*, trans. Ewald Osers (Chicago: University of Chicago Press, 1989); following quote, p. 4.
3 Allan Janik and Stephen Toulmin, *Wittgenstein's Vienna* (New York: Simon & Schuster, 1973), p. 197.
4 See Sasha M. Newman, *Félix Vallotton* (New Haven: Yale University Art Gallery and New York: Abbeville Press, 1991).
5 Alex Comfort, "Art and Social Responsibility: The Ideology of Romanticism," reprinted in *Afterall*, no. 2 (2000), p. 46; cover image by Isa Genzken.
6 Yve-Alain Bois, "Painting: The Task of Mourning," in *Endgame: Reference and Simulation in Recent Painting and Sculpture* (Cambridge, Mass.: MIT Press and Boston: Institute of Contemporary Art, 1986), p. 47.
7 Thomas Bernhard, *Old Masters*, pp. 105 and 95.

Rudolf Stingel is a New York–based artist whose work is included in *Painting at the Edge of the World*. In 1989 Stingel published an artist's book, *Instructions*, which is excerpted here. In addition to this English-language section, the original book included identical sections written in Italian, German, French, Spanish, and Japanese.

Rudolf Stingel
Instructions
1989

INSTRUCTIONS

213

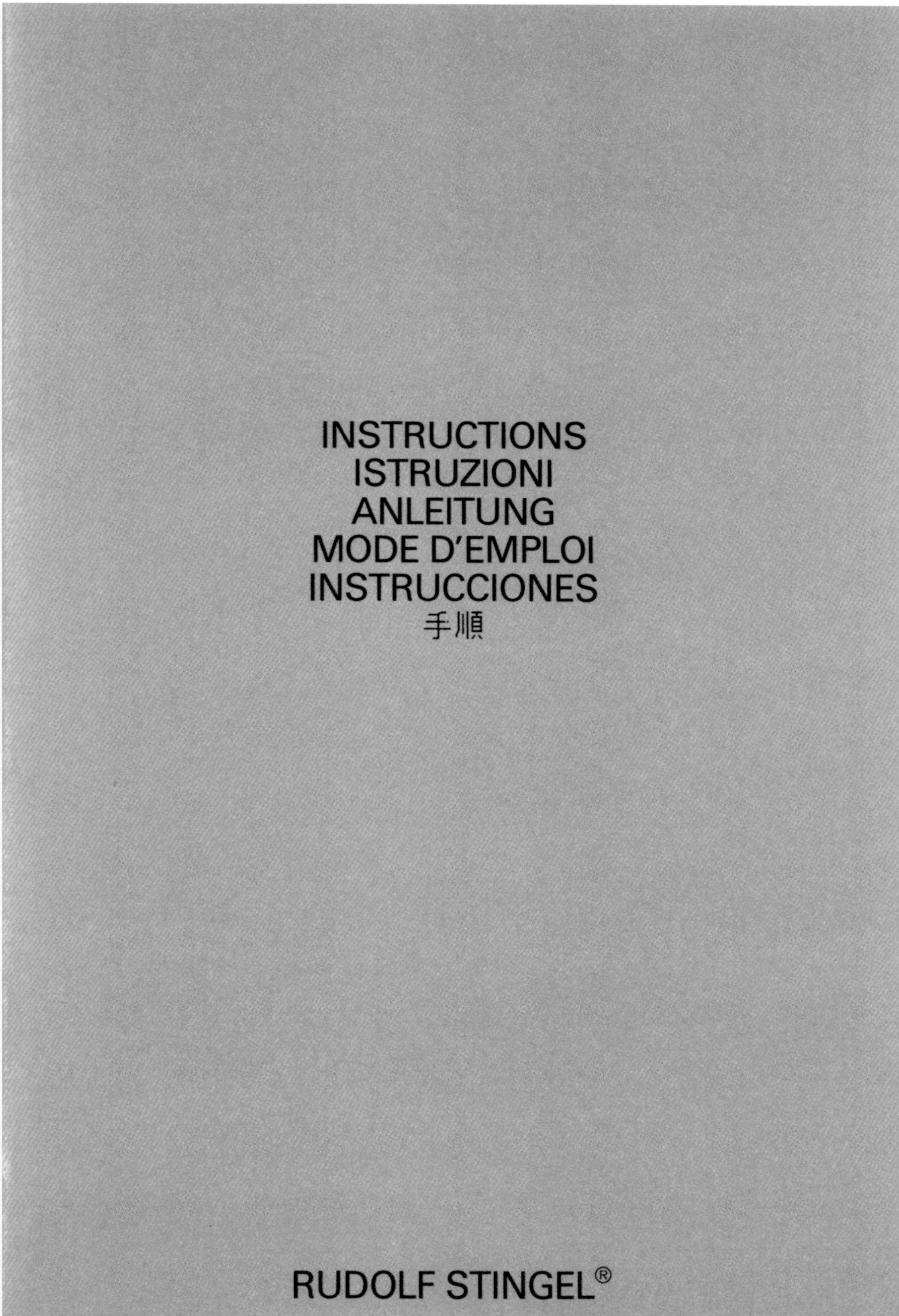
INSTRUCTIONS
ISTRUZIONI
ANLEITUNG
MODE D'EMPLOI
INSTRUCCIONES
手順

RUDOLF STINGEL®

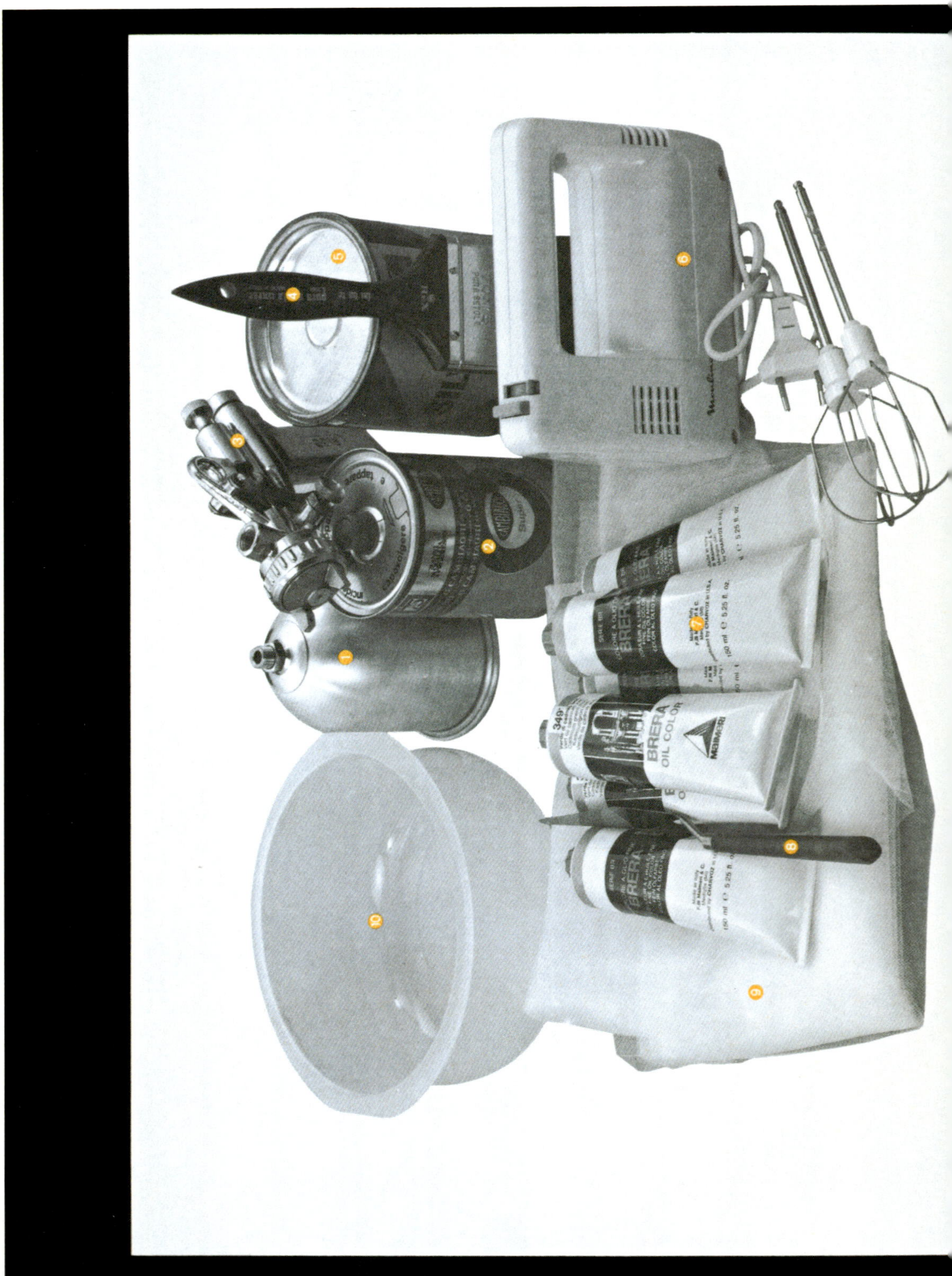
1
2
3
4
5
6
7
8
9
10
349
BRERA
OIL COLOR

PARTS IDENTIFICATION

1 Paint tank
2 Nitrate thinner
3 Compressed air gun
4 Pure horse-hair paintbrush
5 Silver paint
6 Electric mixer
7 Oil paints
8 Spatula
9 Gauze fabric
10 Plastic bowl

OPERATION

A) Take several tubes of oil paint 7 chosen at random (the number of tubes will vary according to the size of the painting), and squeeze their content into the bowl 10.

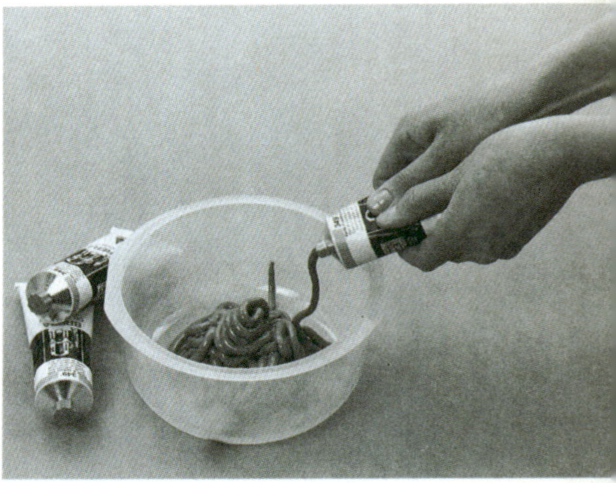

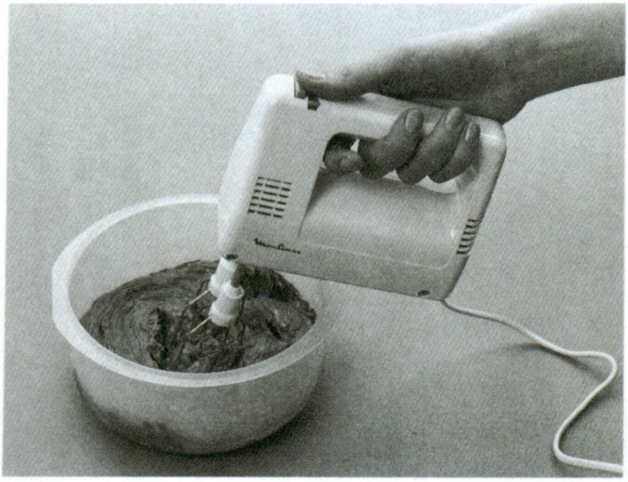

B) Mix the paint well using th mixer 6, until you get a unifor consistency. If desired, the mi ture can be diluted with turpe tine.

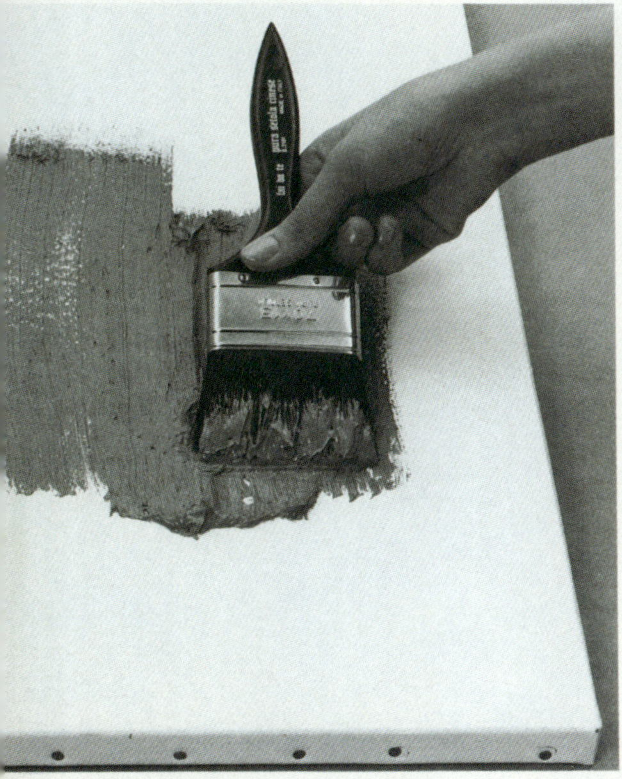

C) Using the paintbrush 4 spread an even layer of paint over all of the surface of the canvas.

D) Prepare a piece of gauze 9 bigger than the canvas.

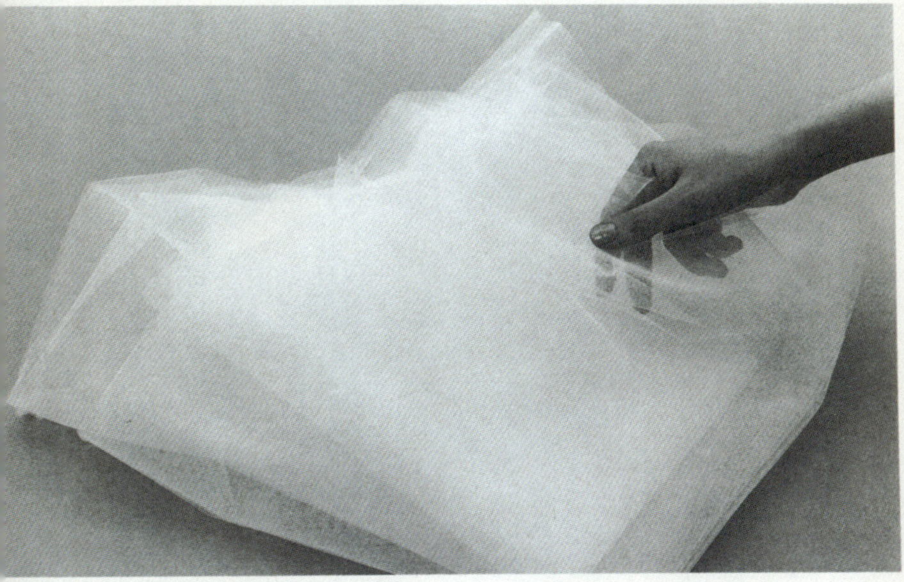

E) Lay the pre-cut gauze cloth over the painted canvas.

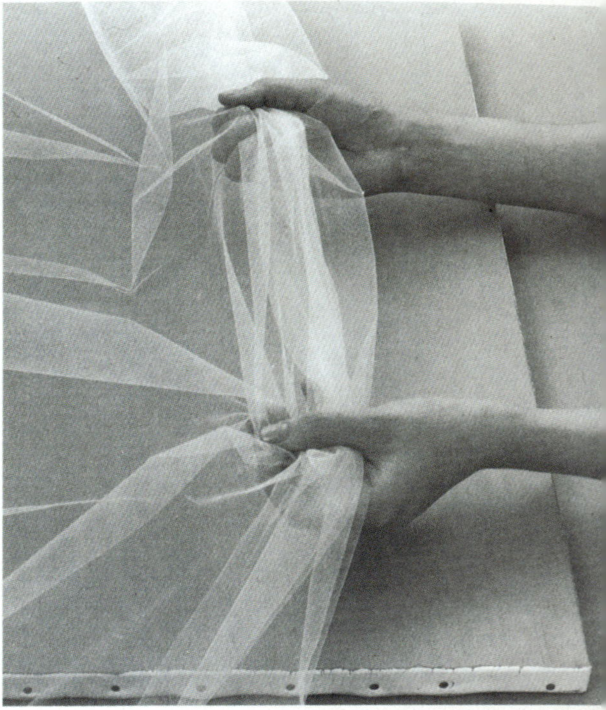

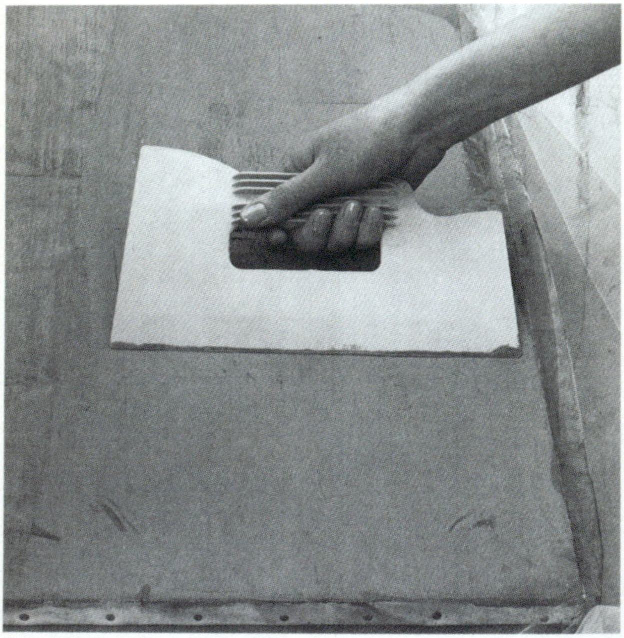

F) Pass a spatula over the gau
to make it adhere perfectly to t
layer of fresh oil paint.

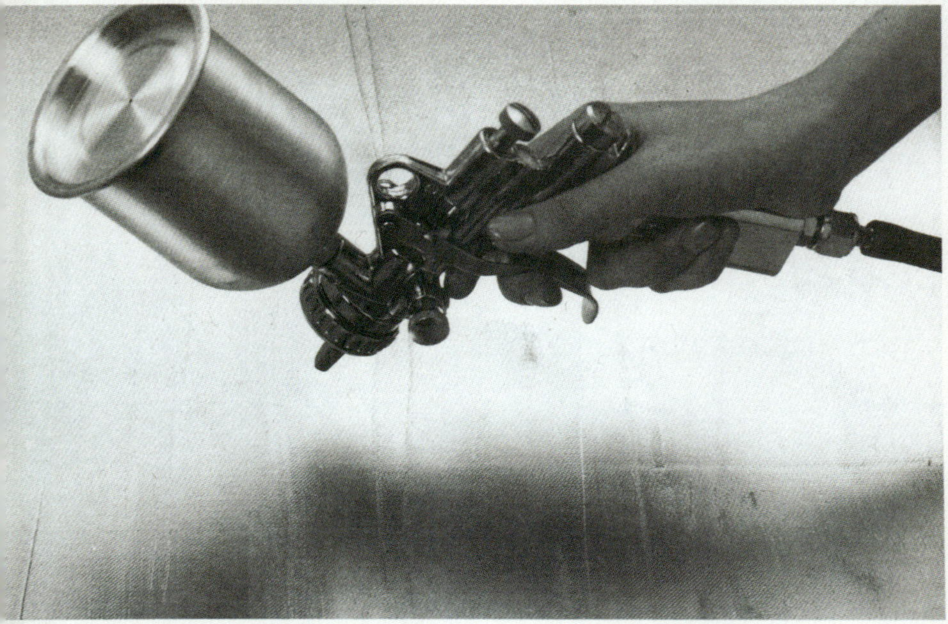

G) Take the compressed air gun 3, which has been filled with silver paint 5, and spray the surface of the canvas evenly from right to left, and left to right, working down towards the bottom.

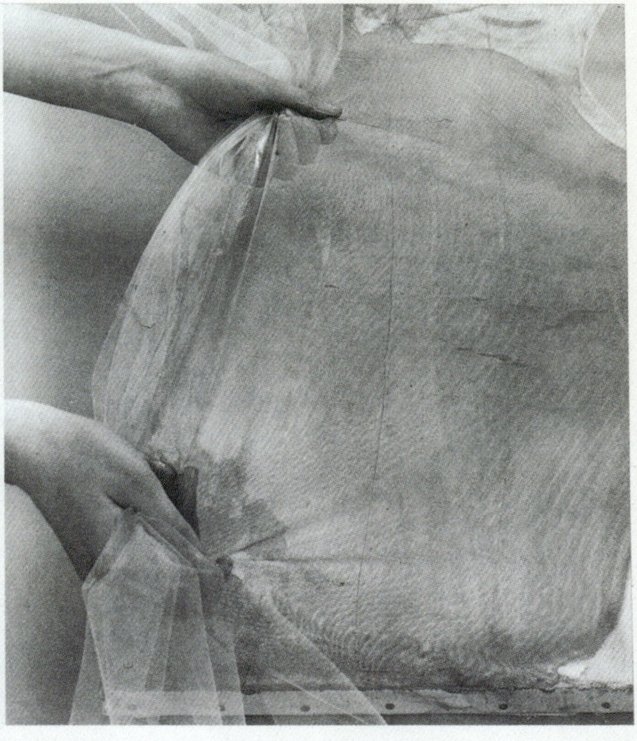

H) Taking hold of a corner of the gauze cloth which sticks out from the canvas, gently lift it up until you have completely removed it from the canvas.

Page numbers in *italics* refer to illustrations.

Paul Thek **The Eighties** 1979 oil on canvas with artist's frame and picture light 9 x 12 in. Courtesy Estate of George Paul Thek and Alexander and Bonin, New York

Paul Thek **Bambi Growing** 1979–1980 acrylic on canvas with artist's frame and picture light 10 ½ x 13 ½ in. Courtesy Estate of George Paul Thek and Alexander and Bonin, New York

Paul Thek **Boy Flipping** 1979–1980 acrylic on canvas with artist's frame and picture light 9 x 12 in. Collection Sabbag, Beirut, Lebanon; Courtesy Galerie Samy Kinge, Paris

Paul Thek **Bread and Buttocks** 1979–1980 oil on canvas with artist's frame and picture light 10 ½ x 13 ½ in. Courtesy Alexander and Bonin, New York

Paul Thek **Eighty Six** c. 1979–1980 acrylic on canvas with artist's frame and picture light 9 x 12 in. Courtesy Estate of George Paul Thek and Alexander and Bonin, New York

Paul Thek **Jack Rabbit** 1979–1980 acrylic on canvas with artist's frame and picture light 13 x 17 ½ in. Collection Dona Nelson, New York

Paul Thek **Jesus in the Arms of Krishna** 1979–1980 acrylic on canvas with artist's frame and picture light 10 ½ x 13 ½ in. Courtesy Estate of George Paul Thek and Alexander and Bonin, New York

Paul Thek **Mary in the Arms of Jesus** 1979–1980 acrylic on canvas with artist's frame and picture light 10 ½ x 13 ½ in. Collection Kenny Schachter, New York

Paul Thek **Neolithic Porno** 1979–1980 oil on canvas with artist's frame and picture light 9 x 12 in. Courtesy Galerie Samy Kinge, Paris

Paul Thek **Periscope** 1979–1980 oil on canvas with artist's frame and picture light 9 x 13 ¾ in. Courtesy Galerie Peyroulet, Paris

Paul Thek **Planks of a Roman Vessel** 1979–1980 acrylic on canvas with artist's frame and picture light 10 ½ x 13 ½ in. Courtesy Estate of George Paul Thek and Alexander and Bonin, New York

Paul Thek **Seeds** 1979–1980 oil on canvas with artist's frame and picture light 9 x 12 in. Collection Dan and Jennie Dietrich, Chester Springs, Pennsylvania

Paul Thek **Thirteen** 1979–1980 acrylic on canvas with artist's frame and picture light 10 ½ x 13 ½ in. Collection Kenny Schachter, New York

Paul Thek **This Won't Take a Minute** 1979–1980 oil on canvas with artist's frame and picture light 9 x 12 in. Collection Sabbag, Beirut, Lebanon; Courtesy Galerie Samy Kinge, Paris

Paul Thek **Twelve** 1979–1980 acrylic on canvas with artist's frame and picture light 9 x 12 in. Courtesy Galerie Samy Kinge, Paris

Paul Thek **Two Men Throwing Words at Each Other** 1979–1980 acrylic on canvas with artist's frame and picture light 9 x 12 in. Collection Sabbag, Beirut, Lebanon; Courtesy Galerie Samy Kinge, Paris

Paul Thek **Untitled (Abstract Yellow Landscape)** c. 1979–1980 acrylic on canvas with artist's frame and picture light 9 x 12 in. Courtesy Estate of George Paul Thek and Alexander and Bonin, New York

Paul Thek **Where It's At** 1979–1980 oil on canvas with artist's frame and picture light 15 ¾ x 18 ¾ in. Collection Robert Wilson, New York

Paul Thek **Wild Irish Rose** 1979–1980 acrylic on canvas with artist's frame and picture light 11 x 14 in. Private collection; Courtesy Galerie am Lindenplatz AG, Vaduz, Principality of Liechtenstein

Paul Thek **Abstract Pattern on a Cave Wall** 1980 oil on canvas with artist's frame and picture light 13 x 16 in. Courtesy Galerie Samy Kinge, Paris

Paul Thek **Fireflies** 1980 acrylic on canvas with artist's frame and picture light 13 x 17 ½ in. Collection GE Capital Fleet Services, Eden Prairie, Minnesota

Paul Thek **Me—You** 1980 oil on canvas with artist's frame and picture light 10 ½ x 13 ½ in. Collection Sabbag, Beirut, Lebanon; Courtesy Galerie Samy Kinge, Paris

Paul Thek **MM (Roman 2000)** 1980 oil on canvas with artist's frame and picture light 26 x 26 in. Collection Greenville County Museum of Art, Greenville, South Carolina; Gift of Buck A. Mickel and museum purchase

Paul Thek **Purple** 1980 acrylic on canvas with artist's frame and picture light 9 x 12 in. Courtesy Galerie Samy Kinge, Paris

Paul Thek **Space Age Pattern Painting** 1980 acrylic on canvas with artist's frame and picture light 13 x 16 in. Courtesy Estate of George Paul Thek and Alexander and Bonin, New York

Paul Thek **Towards an Abstract Icon** 1980 acrylic on canvas with artist's frame and picture light 9 x 12 in. Courtesy Galerie Samy Kinge, Paris

Richard Wright no title 2001 site-specific wall painting dimensions variable Courtesy the artist, Glasgow; BQ, Cologne; The Modern Institute, Glasgow; and Gagosian Gallery, New York

Paul McCarthy **Whipping a Wall and a Window with Paint** 1974 performance videotape transferred to laserdisc Courtesy the artist, Altadena, California, and Luhring Augustine Gallery, New York

Paul McCarthy **Painter** 1995 videotape transferred to laserdisc Courtesy the artist, Altadena, California, and Luhring Augustine Gallery, New York

Lucy McKenzie **Curious** 1998 oil on canvas 31 x 19 in. Collection Georg Geyer, Vienna; Courtesy Cabinet, London

Lucy McKenzie **Fan Treffen** 1998 acrylic on found canvas 48 1/2 x 36 1/2 in. Courtesy the artist, Glasgow, and Cabinet, London

Lucy McKenzie **Festival** 1998 acrylic on canvas 48 1/2 x 36 1/2 in. Courtesy the artist, Glasgow, and Cabinet, London

Lucy McKenzie **Olympians** 1998 oil on canvas 33 x 24 in. Collection Jane Lombard, New York; Courtesy Cabinet, London

Lucy McKenzie **Music From the Death Factory** 1999 acrylic on found canvas 29 15/16 x 20 1/16 in. Courtesy the artist, Glasgow, and Cabinet, London

Lucy McKenzie **Medal** 2000 acrylic on canvas 31 1/2 in. diameter Private collection, London; Courtesy Cabinet, London

Lucy McKenzie **Sport March** 2000 acrylic on canvas 15 x 12 in. Collection Nicholas Lawson, London; Courtesy Cabinet, London

Lucy McKenzie **Subventionieren** 2000 oil on canvas 72 x 48 in. Collection Ken Rowe, London; Courtesy Cabinet, London

Lucy McKenzie **Three Years to Go** 2000 oil on canvas 42 x 83 in. de Botton/Green Collection, London; Courtesy Cabinet, London

Lucy McKenzie **Window (1980)** 2000 acrylic on canvas 12 1/4 x 10 1/4 in.Courtesy the artist, Glasgow, and Cabinet, London

Julie Mehretu **Babel Unleashed** 2000 ink, acrylic on canvas 60 x 84 in. Courtesy the artist and The Project, New York

Julie Mehretu **Bombing Babylon** 2000 ink, acrylic on canvas 60 x 84 in. Courtesy the artist and The Project, New York

Takashi Murakami **727** 1996 acrylic on canvas on board 118 x 177 in. Private collection; Courtesy Blum & Poe, Santa Monica, California

Takashi Murakami **The Castle of Tin Tin** 1998 acrylic on canvas on board 120 x 120 in. Collection Ruth and Jake Bloom, Los Angeles; Courtesy Blum & Poe, Santa Monica, California

Nader **Die Vergewaltigung der Ontologie durch die Logik** (The rape of ontology by logic) 2000 acrylic on canvas 51 x 78 3/4 in. Courtesy the artist and Klosterfelde, Berlin

Nader **For Ezra Pound** 2000 oil on canvas 51 x 78 3/4 in. Collection Thomas Dane, London; Courtesy Klosterfelde, Berlin

Chris Ofili **He** 1999 acrylic, collage, glitter, resin, map pins, elephant dung on canvas 96 x 72 x 6 in. Collection Warren and Victoria Miro, London

Chris Ofili **Third Eye Vision** 1999 acrylic, collage, glitter, resin, map pins, elephant dung on canvas 96 x 72 3/8 x 6 in. Collection Walker Art Center, Minneapolis; T. B. Walker Acquisition Fund, 2000

Chris Ofili **The Naked Spirit of Captain Shit and the Legend of the Black Stars** 2000–2001 acrylic, collage, glitter, resin, map pins, elephant dung on canvas 96 x 72 x 6 in. Courtesy the artist, London, and Gavin Brown's enterprise, New York

Hélio Oiticica **Nucleus NC 1** 1960 oil on wood, mirror dimensions variable Courtesy Projeto Hélio Oiticica, Rio de Janeiro

Laura Owens **Untitled** 2000 acrylic on canvas 72 1/4 x 66 1/4 in. Courtesy the artist, Los Angeles, and Studio Guenzani, Milan

Laura Owens **Untitled** 2000 oil, acrylic on canvas 111 x 72 in. Goetz Collection, Munich

Michael Raedecker **kismet** 1999 acrylic, thread on canvas 80 3/4 x 98 7/16 in. Collection Van Abbemuseum, Eindhoven

Michael Raedecker **100,000 years** 2000 oil, acrylic, thread on canvas 80 15/16 x 124 in. Courtesy the artist and The approach, London

Michael Raedecker **sensoria** 2000 acrylic, thread on canvas 28 x 35 3/4 in. Courtesy the artist and The approach, London

Thomas Scheibitz **Untitled** 1999 oil on canvas 56 x 42 in. Collection Kenneth L. Freed, Boston; Courtesy Bonakdar Jancou Gallery, New York

Thomas Scheibitz **Greeting Card** 2000 oil on canvas 72 x 64 in. Collection Cecile and Steven Biltekoff, Buffalo, New York; Courtesy Bonakdar Jancou Gallery, New York

Thomas Scheibitz **Schriftbild (Writing Picture)** 2000 oil on canvas 63 x 100 3/8 in. Courtesy Galerie Gebr. Lehmann, Dresden

Thomas Schütte **Ringe (Rings)** 1977/1994 oil on wood, nails dimensions variable Artesia Contemporary Art Collection, Brussels

Rudolf Stingel **Instructions** 1989 screenprints on paper four panels, 42 1/2 x 30 5/8 in. each Edition 1/5 Courtesy the artist and Paula Cooper Gallery, New York

Rudolf Stingel **Untitled** 1998 oil, enamel on canvas 32 x 32 in. Courtesy the artist and Paula Cooper Gallery, New York

Hiroshi Sugito **the pink floor** 1998 acrylic, pigment, graphite, colored pencil on cotton duck 80 x 96 in. Collection Dean Valentine and Amy Adelson, Los Angeles

Hiroshi Sugito **changing rooms** 2000 acrylic, pigment on canvas 74 x 96 in. Courtesy the artist, Nagoya, Japan, and Marc Foxx Gallery, Los Angeles

Hiroshi Sugito **time** 2000 acrylic, pigment on canvas 11 x 11 in. Courtesy the artist, Nagoya, Japan, and Marc Foxx Gallery, Los Angeles

Paul Thek **Ponza Agave** 1975 oil on canvas with artist's frame and picture light 20 x 20 in. Courtesy Estate of George Paul Thek and Alexander and Bonin, New York

Paul Thek **Ponza Agave Dawn** 1975 oil on canvas with artist's frame and picture light 20 x 20 in. Courtesy Estate of George Paul Thek and Alexander and Bonin, New York

Paul Thek **Ponza/Seascape, Boats** 1975 oil on canvas with artist's frame and picture light 20 x 20 in. Courtesy Estate of George Paul Thek and Alexander and Bonin, New York

Paul Thek **Untitled (Prunes)** c. 1975 oil on canvas with artist's frame and picture light 9 1/2 x 11 3/4 in. Collection Dan and Jennie Dietrich, Chester Springs, Pennsylvania

Paul Thek **Untitled (Seascape With Rocks)** c. 1975 oil on canvas with artist's frame and picture light 9 1/2 x 11 3/4 in. Collection Molly and Walter Bareiss, Stamford, Connecticut

Paul Thek **Pink Cross and Green Buds** 1975–1980 acrylic on canvasboard with artist's frame and picture light 12 x 16 in. Collection Carolyn Alexander, New York

Dimensions of works are given in inches; height precedes width precedes depth.

Franz Ackermann **Abschied auf See** (Farewell on the sea) 2000 oil on canvas 105 ¾ x 212 ¹³⁄₁₆ in. Private collection, Berlin; Courtesy neugerriemschneider, Berlin

Franz Ackermann **Helicopter XIII** 2000 oil on canvas 109 ⅜ x 113 ⁹⁄₁₆ in. Collection Susan and Michael Hort, New York; Courtesy Gavin Brown's enterprise, New York

Franz Ackermann **Helicopter No. 15 (News)** 2001 site-specific wall painting; acrylic on wall 280 ½ x 355 in. (dimensions vary) Collection the artist, Berlin, and Gavin Brown's enterprise, New York

Haluk Akakçe **Sweethearts (beneath the water's spate)** 2001 site-specific wall painting; latex enamel paint, wood on wall approximately 120 x 360 in. Courtesy the artist and Deitch Projects, New York

Francis Alÿs **The Leak** 1995–2001 walk with enamel paint, paint can dimensions variable Courtesy the artist, Mexico City

Francis Alÿs **le temps du sommeil** 1997–2001 oil, mixed media on panel fifty paintings from an ongoing series, 4 ¼ x 6 in. each Courtesy the artist, Mexico City

Kevin Appel **House: East View (Vista)** 1999 acrylic on canvas over panel 80 x 180 in. Collection Michael and Judy Ovitz, Los Angeles; Courtesy Angles Gallery, Santa Monica, California

Kevin Appel **House: Northwest View** 1999 acrylic on canvas over panel 80 x 90 in. Collection Marcia Goldenfeld Maiten and Barry David Maiten, Los Angeles; Courtesy Angles Gallery, Santa Monica, California

Marcel Broodthaers **Tableau-Bateau** 1973 projection of eighty 35mm slides dimensions variable Collection Walker Art Center, Minneapolis; T. B. Walker Acquisition Fund, 1997

John Currin **Minerva** 2000 oil on canvas 28 x 22 in. Courtesy Galerie Monica Sprüth, Cologne

John Currin **Park City Grill** 2000 oil on canvas 38 x 30 in. Collection Walker Art Center, Minneapolis; Justin Smith Purchase Fund, 2000

John Currin **The Cuddler** 2000 oil on canvas 38 x 24 ½ in. Collection Frances and John Bowes, San Francisco; Courtesy Sadie Coles HQ, London

Marlene Dumas **Young Boys** 1993–1994 oil on canvas 39 ⅜ x 118 ⅛ in. Collection Lois Plehn, New York; Courtesy Jack Tilton/Anna Kustera Gallery, New York

Marlene Dumas **The Painter** 1994 oil on canvas 78 x 39 in. Collection Martin Eisenberg, Scarsdale, New York; Courtesy Jack Tilton/Anna Kustera Gallery, New York

Andreas Gursky **Untitled VI** 1997 C-print 73 ¼ x 94 ¹⁄₁₆ in. Edition 2/6 Courtesy Matthew Marks Gallery, New York

Eberhard Havekost **Scharfschütze (Sniper) 1–3** 1998 oil on canvas triptych, 12 x 16 in. each Collection Susan and Michael Hort, New York; Courtesy Anton Kern Gallery, New York

Eberhard Havekost **Mobil 3** 2000 oil on canvas 55 ⅛ x 78 ¾ in. Courtesy the artist, Dresden; Anton Kern Gallery, New York; and Galerie Gebr. Lehmann, Dresden

Eberhard Havekost **Orange** 2000 oil on canvas 55 ⅛ x 78 ¾ in. Courtesy Anton Kern Gallery, New York, and Galerie Gebr. Lehmann, Dresden

Arturo Herrera **All I Ask** 1999/2001 site-specific wall painting; latex on wall dimensions variable Courtesy the artist and Brent Sikkema, New York

Mike Kelley **The Thirteen Seasons (Heavy on the Winter)** 1994 acrylic on board thirteen paintings, 62 ½ x 40 in. each Courtesy Jablonka Galerie, Cologne

#1 The Birth of the New Year Fondazione Sandretto Re Rebaudegno per l'Arte, Turin
#2 Fecundity Collection Drs. Michael and Eleonore Stoffel, Cologne
#3 What's Limp in 3D Is Erect in 2D Collection Brandhorst, Cologne
#4 The Dawning of Sexuality Private collection, Cologne
#5 Summer's Rage Collection Magali, T
#6 Fall Peter Stuyvesant Foundation, Amsterdam
#7 The Descent Peter Stuyvesant Foundation, Amsterdam
#9 Snow on the Temples Collection Drs. Michael and Eleonore Stoffel, Cologne
#10 The Decay of Year-End Private collection, Essen
#11 The Giving Old Man Collection Hans Böhning, Cologne
#12 Death Collection Drs. Michael and Eleonore Stoffel, Cologne
#13 Art Private collection; Courtesy B.F.A.S., Blondeau Fine Art Services, SA

Martin Kippenberger **Untitled** 1991 rubber, acrylic on canvas 70 ¾ x 59 x 4 ⅝ in. Private collection; Courtesy Barbara Gladstone Gallery, New York

Martin Kippenberger **Untitled** 1991 latex, acrylic, pigments, foam on canvas 70 ¾ x 59 x 15 ¾ in. Courtesy Estate of Martin Kippenberger and Galerie Gisela Capitain, Cologne

Martin Kippenberger **Untitled** 1991 latex, acrylic, pigments, foam on canvas 70 ¾ x 59 x 15 ¾ in. Courtesy Estate of Martin Kippenberger and Galerie Gisela Capitain, Cologne

Udomsak Krisanamis **Avalanche** 2000 collage, acrylic, felt-tip pen ink, noodles on cotton fabric 72 x 48 in. Collection Bernardo and Laura Nadal-Ginard, Chestnut Hill, Massachusetts; Courtesy Gavin Brown's enterprise, New York

Udomsak Krisanamis **Candy Apple** 2000 collage, acrylic, felt-tip pen ink, noodles on burlap 72 x 48 in. Collection William Goldiner, Pikesville, Maryland; Courtesy Gavin Brown's enterprise, New York

Udomsak Krisanamis **Heineken** 2000 collage, noodles, acrylic, felt-tip pen ink on canvas 72 x 48 in. Collection Albright-Knox Art Gallery, Buffalo, New York; Sarah Norton Goodyear Fund, 2000

Udomsak Krisanamis **Road Hole** 2000 collage, acrylic, felt-tip pen ink on blanket 72 x 48 in. Collection Michael Lynne, New York; Courtesy Gavin Brown's enterprise, New York

Jim Lambie **Psychedelic Soul Stick** 2001 mixed media dimensions variable Courtesy the artist and The Modern Institute, Glasgow

Jim Lambie **ZOBOP** 2001 colored vinyl tape dimensions variable Courtesy the artist and The Modern Institute, Glasgow

Margherita Manzelli **Binaural** 2000 oil on canvas 71 x 145 ½ in. Private collection; Courtesy Studio Guenzani, Milan

Margherita Manzelli **Nottem** 2000 oil on canvas 98 ½ x 78 ¾ in. Courtesy the artist and Studio Guenzani, Milan

Paul McCarthy **Face Painting—Floor, White Line** 1972 performance videotape transferred to laserdisc Courtesy the artist, Altadena, California, and Luhring Augustine Gallery, New York

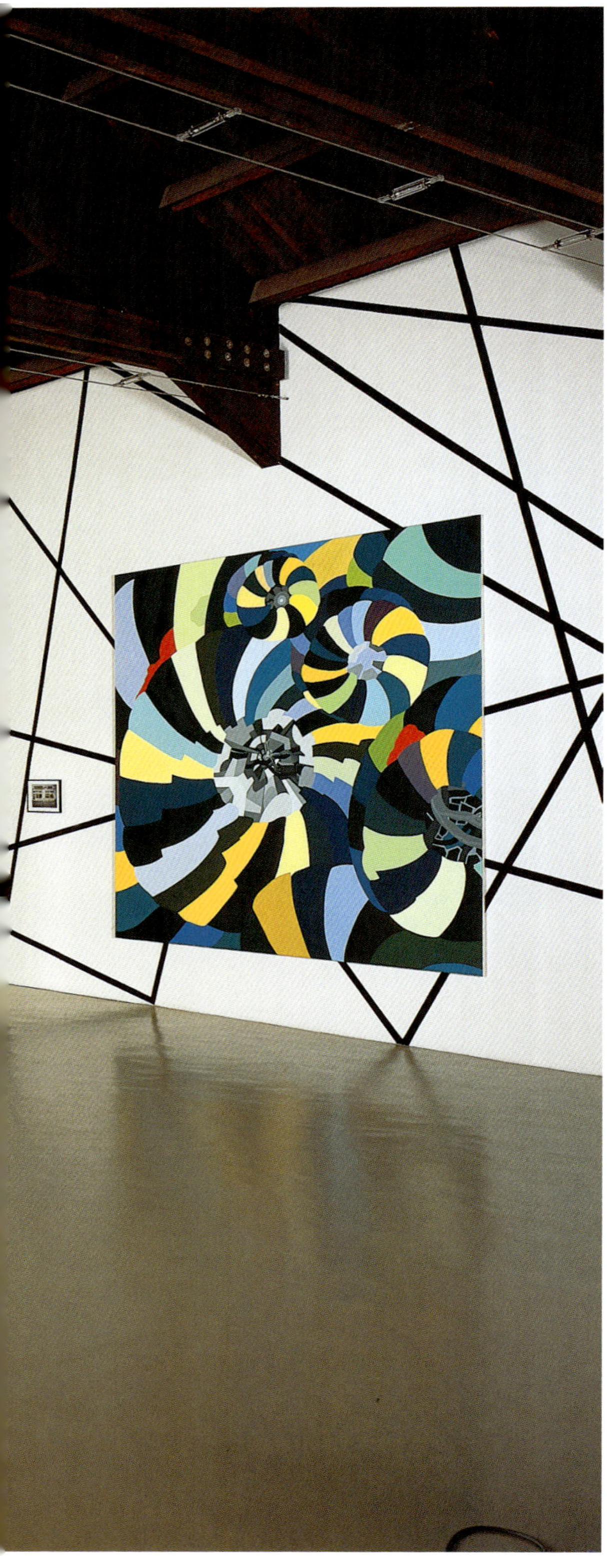

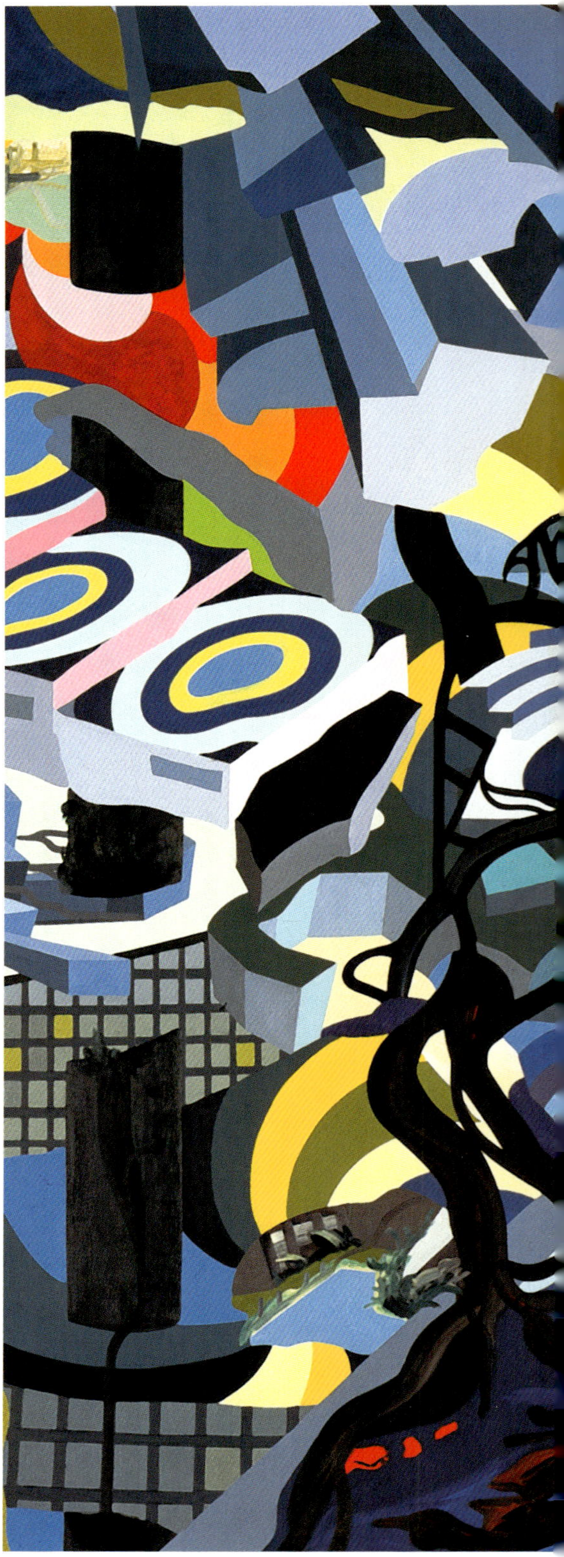

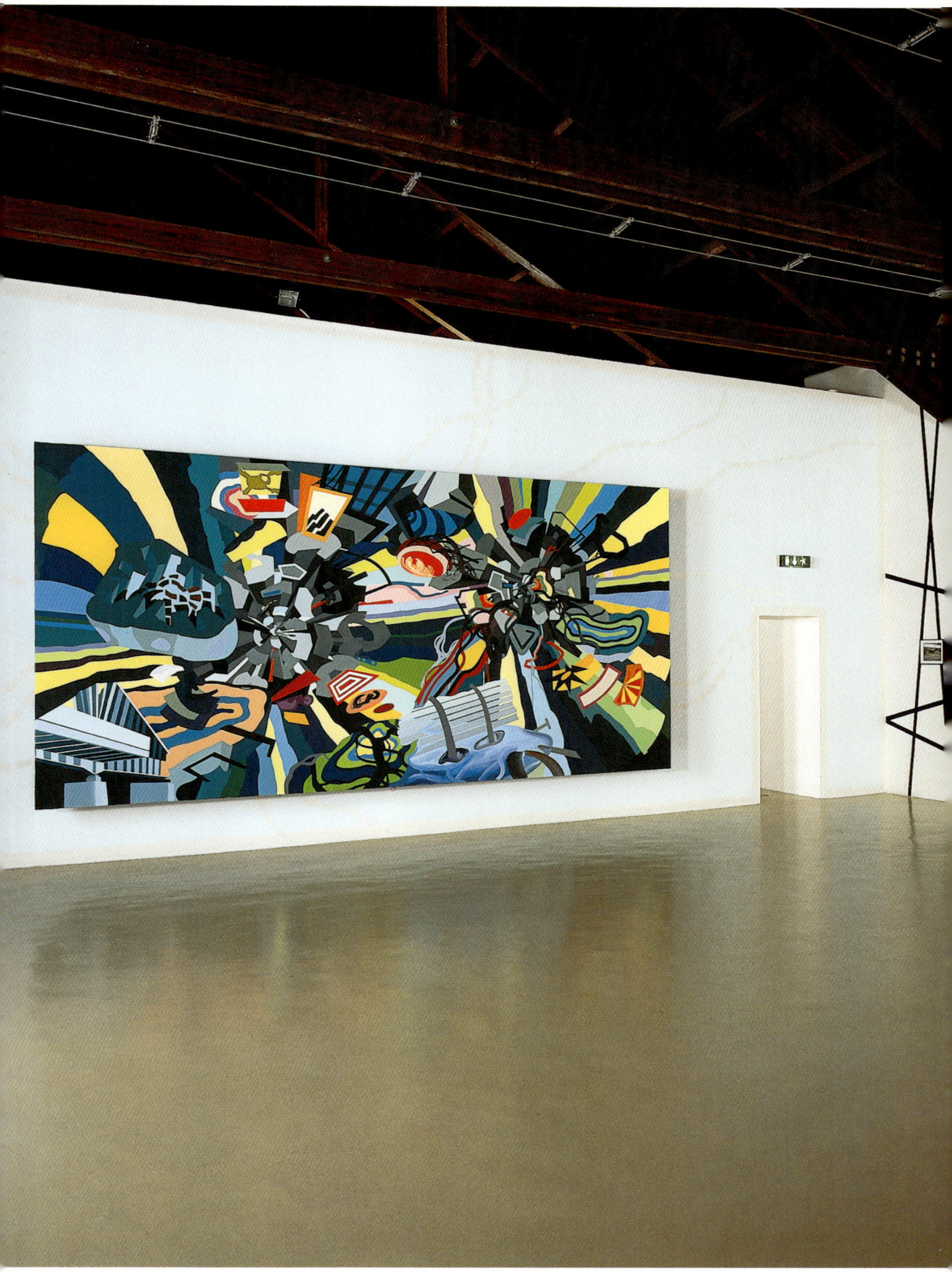

ABOVE installation view of **Abschied auf see** (Farewell on the sea) 2000 (left) and **Helicopter XIII** 2000 (right) from the exhibition **B.I.T.** at Castello di Rivoli 2000 **OPPOSITE** detail of **Naherholungsgebiet** (Public park) 2000

Franz Ackermann

Born 1963 Germany; lives and works in Berlin

Franz Ackermann's densely packed, vividly colored wall paintings interpose our physical relationship to the built environment with an investigation into the personal experience of contemporary urban space. Verging on abstraction, the brash patterns of circles, bands, and other geometric shapes evolve out of a collision between architectural drafting and spatial mapping. In consonance with these large-scale works, Ackermann charts his own spontaneous "mental maps" of his travels through the metropolitan landscapes of Europe, Southeast Asia, South America, and elsewhere. Taking the form of portable drawings, these Situationist-influenced meditations are concerned with both the physical structures of a location and the political and cultural context of a site. They signal the fluidity of contemporary urban spaces and the cosmopolitanism that now links so many of the world's cities under the aegis of globalization. Since 1989 Ackermann's work has been presented in numerous exhibitions, including the *Carnegie International*, Pittsburgh (1999), and at major venues such as the Castello di Rivoli Museo d'Arte Contemporanea, Rivoli-Torino (2000), the Kunstverein Kassel (1999), the Institute of Contemporary Art, Boston (1999), the Royal College of Art, London (1999), Portikus, Frankfurt am Main (1997), and P.S.1 Contemporary Art Center, New York (1997).

OPPOSITE Franz Ackermann detail of **Naherholungsgebiet** (Public park) 2000 oil on canvas 110 x 145 in. Image courtesy Castello di Rivoli, Museo d'Arte Contemporanea, Rivoli-Torino; photo: Paolo Pellion, Torino

FOLDOUT Franz Ackermann installation view of **Abschied auf see** (Farewell on the sea) 2000 and **Helicopter XIII** 2000 from the exhibition **B.I.T.** at Castello di Rivoli 2000 Image courtesy Castello di Rivoli, Museo d'Arte Contemporanea, Rivoli-Torino; photo: Paolo Pellion, Torino (checklist)

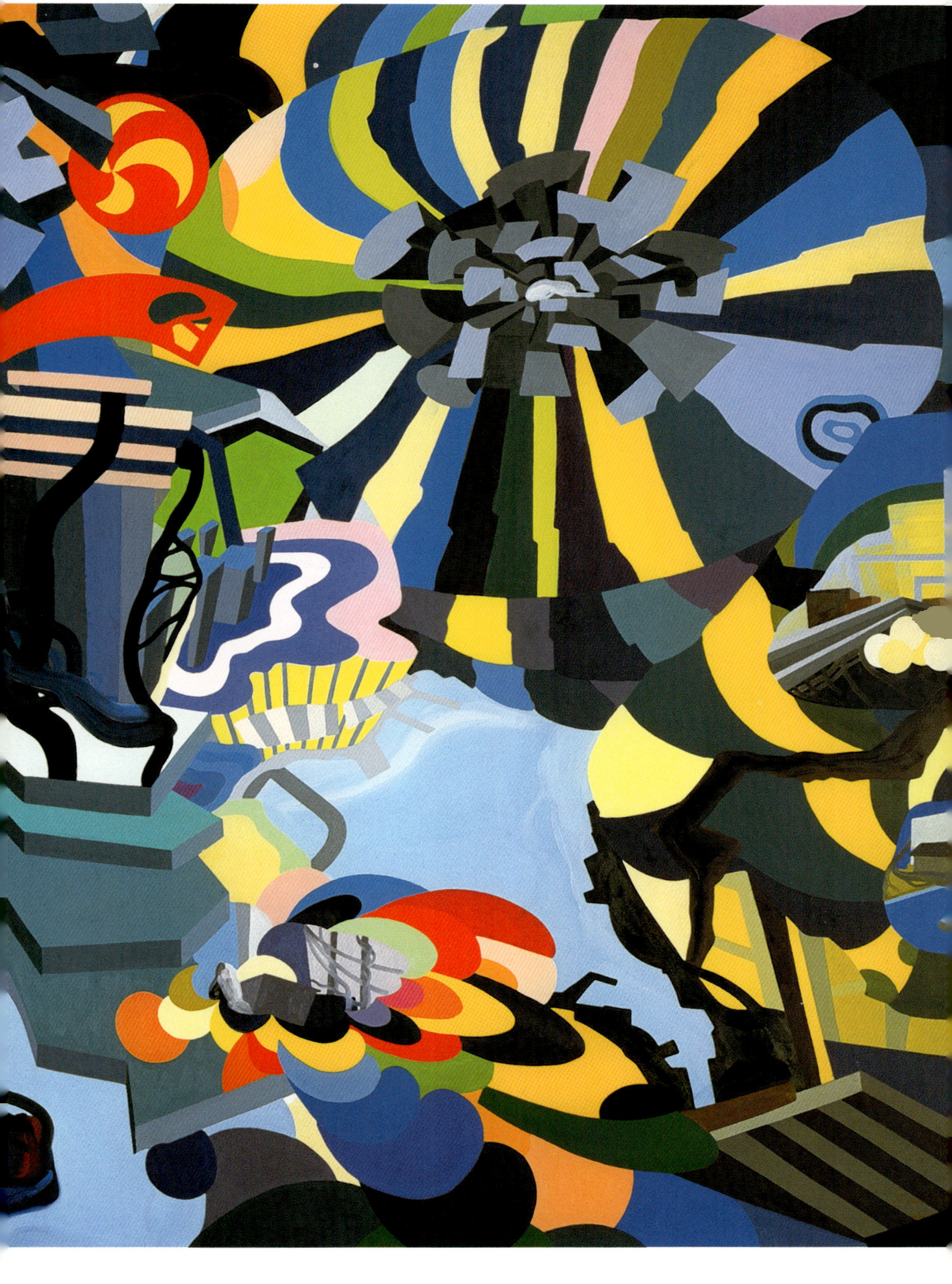

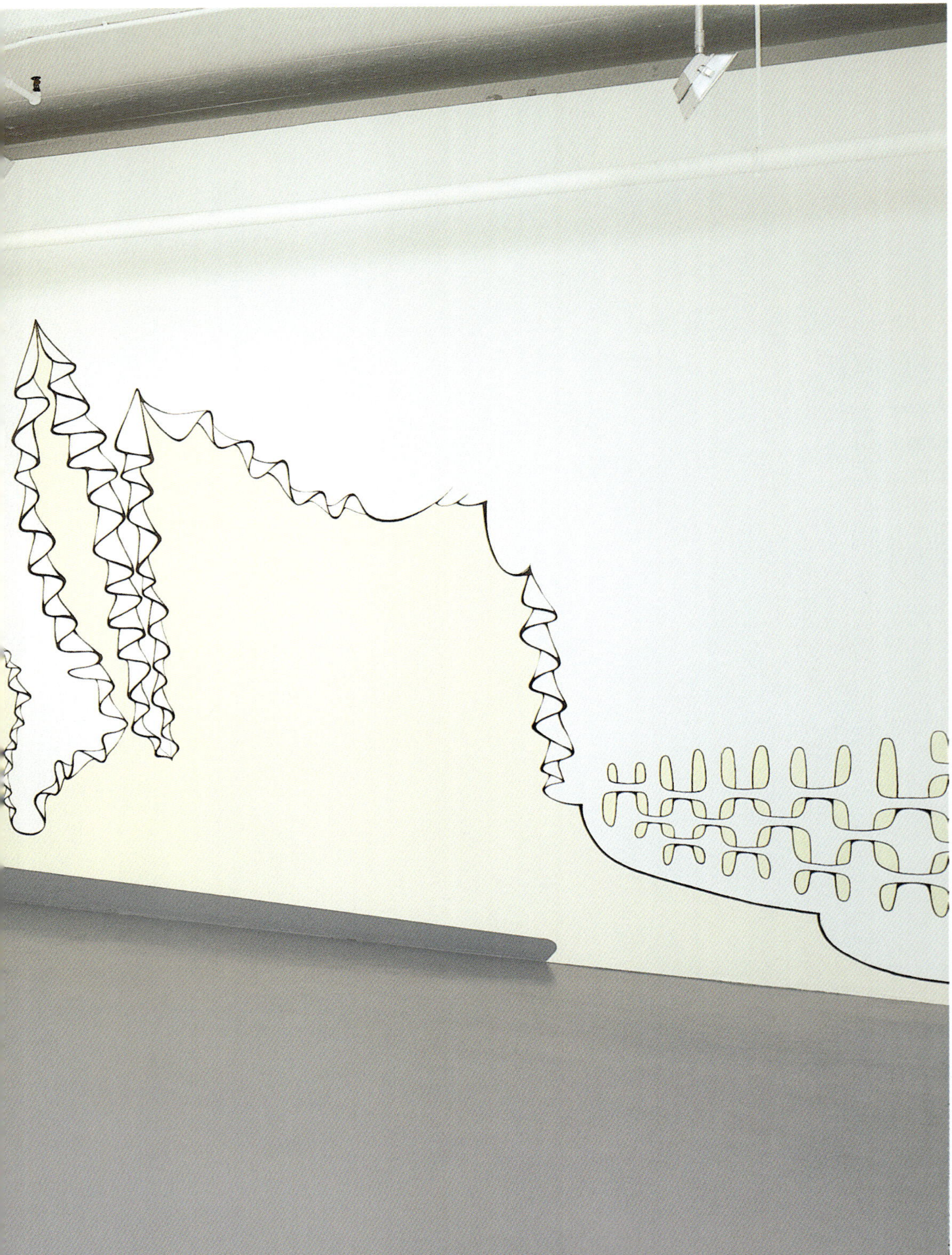

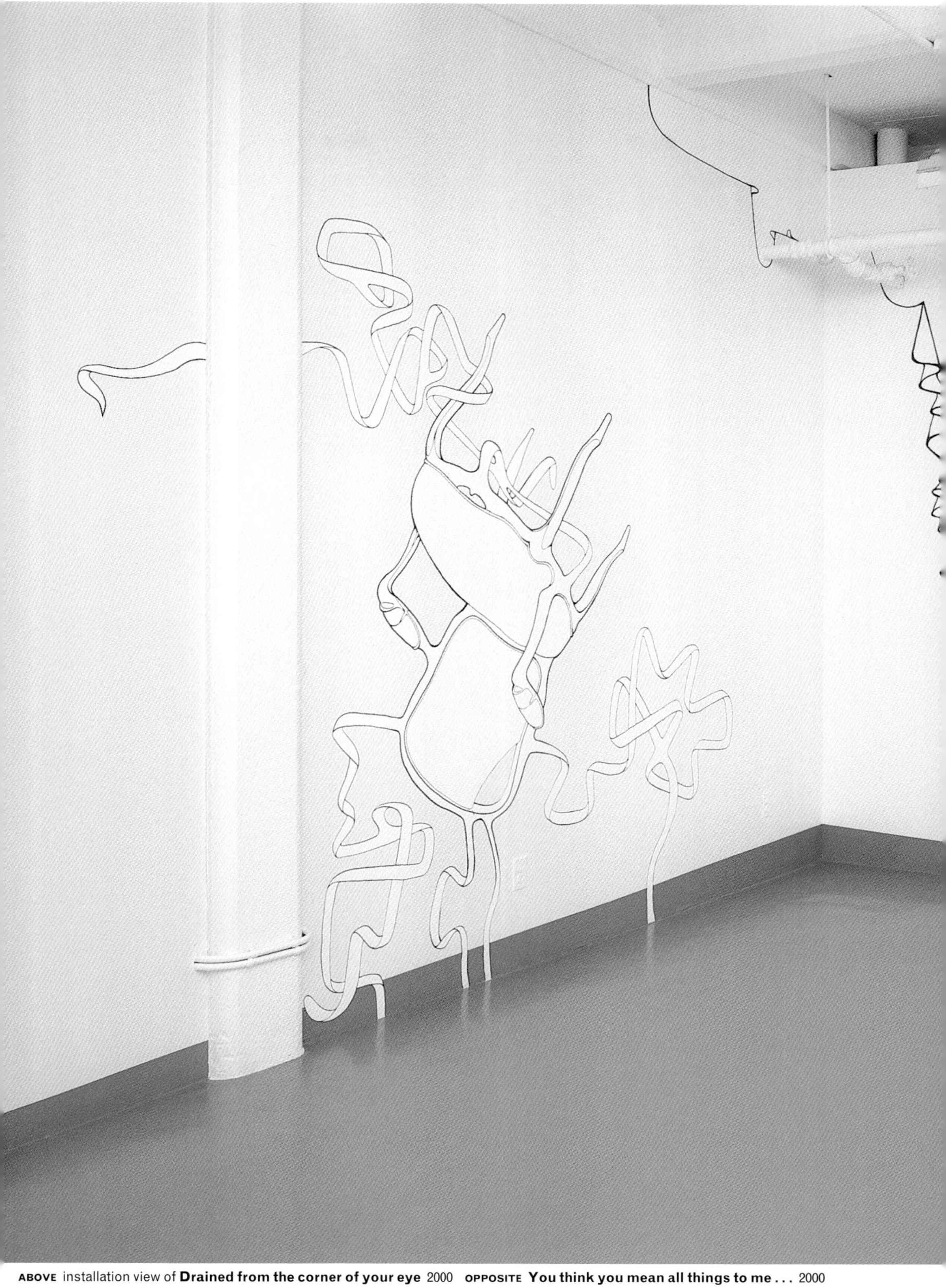

ABOVE installation view of **Drained from the corner of your eye** 2000 **OPPOSITE** **You think you mean all things to me . . .** 2000

Haluk Akakçe

Born 1970 Turkey; lives and works in New York City

Haluk Akakçe's drawings and site-specific installations are preoccupied with mutation; in an ambiguous conflation of pictorial styles he creates "a resonant space where transformations become forms in themselves." These large-scale works chart a self-contained reality, another universe born of eccentric imagination and the assimilation of science-fiction fantasies, decorative illustration, and computer-generated animation. Although the collapsing of so many styles might suggest the potential of digital manipulation, Akakçe's morphing images are in fact generated by hand. In paint he is able to achieve effects of impossible, vacillating perspectives and of space that slips in and out of three dimensions—an abstracted world populated with intricately rendered hybrids of technology and biology. His work responds to the shifting landscape of postglobalization—or, as the artist suggests, "the disappearance of coordinates, caused by shifting cultural regimes and the fragmentation of social structures." Akakçe has been exhibiting since 1995 and was the subject of a solo exhibition at P.S.1 Contemporary Art Center, New York (2000). His work has been included in numerous group exhibitions at such venues as the Casino Luxembourg—Forum d'art contemporain (2000), the Istanbul Biennial (1999), and the Drawing Center, New York (1998).

OPPOSITE Haluk Akakçe **You think you mean all things to me . . .** 2000 ink, enamel paint on wood diptych, 16 x 20 in. each Image courtesy Deitch Projects, New York

FOLDOUT Haluk Akakçe installation view of **Drained from the corner of your eye** 2000 enamel paint on wall dimensions variable at Henry Urbach Architecture, New York Image courtesy Henry Urbach Architecture, New York

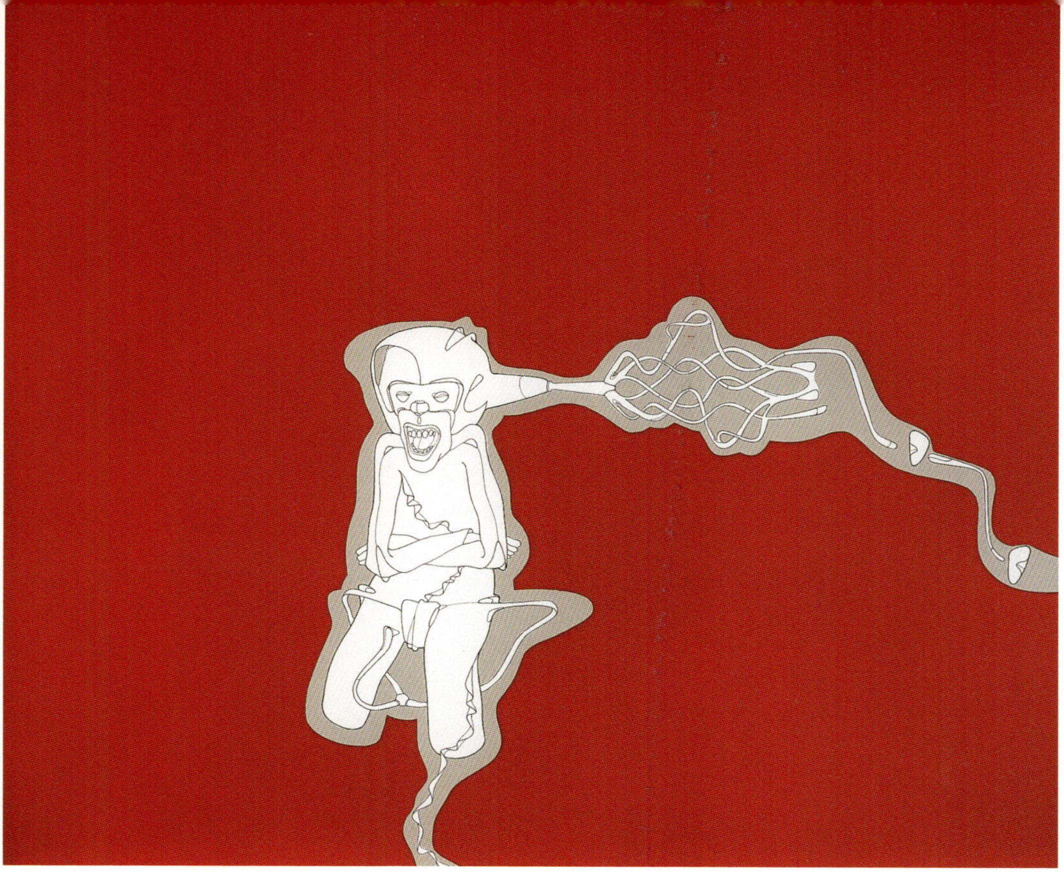

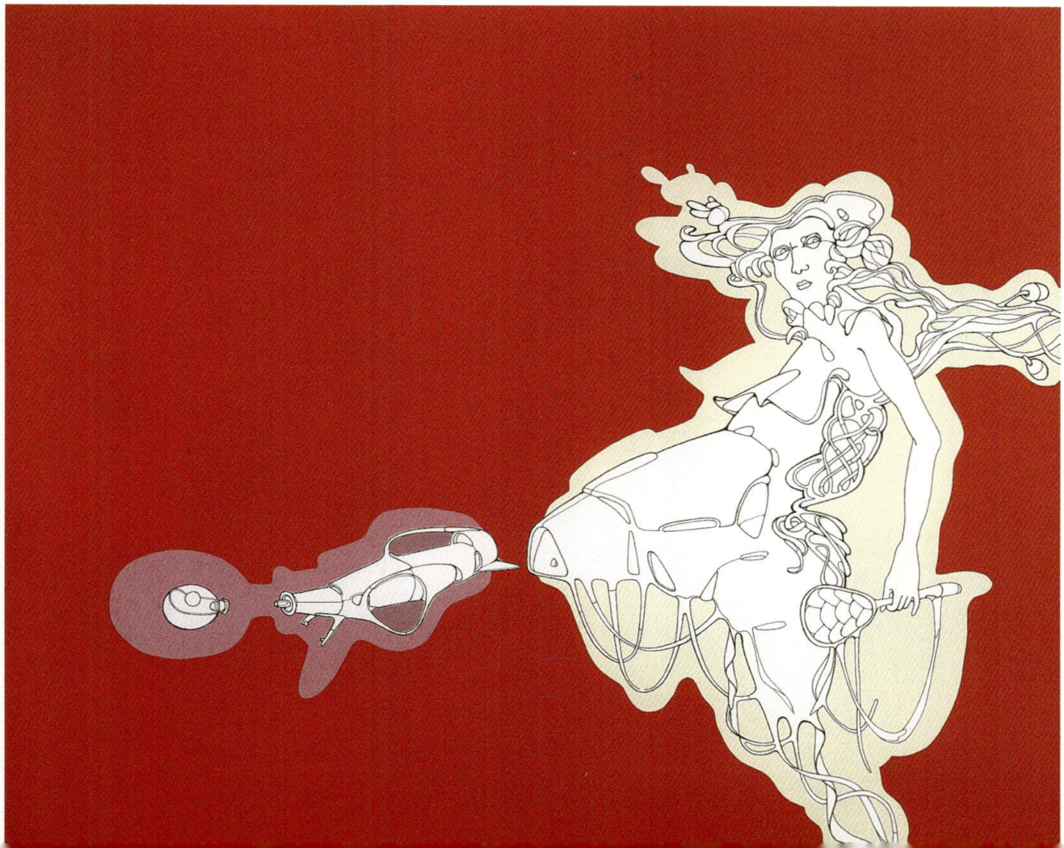

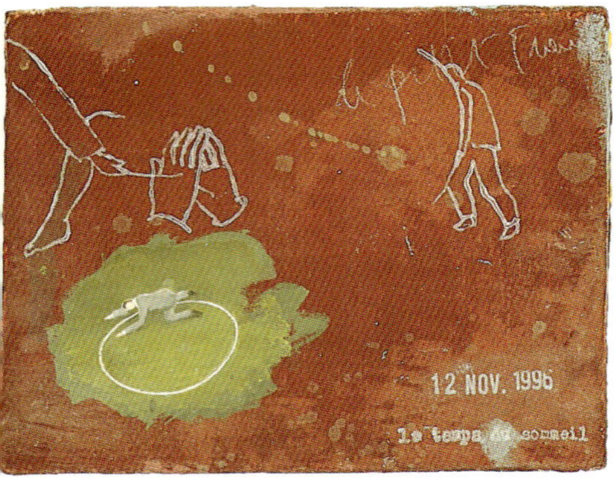
12 NOV. 1996
le temps du sommeil

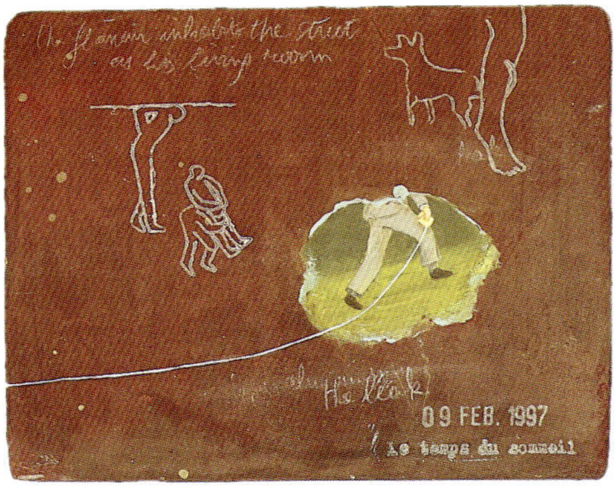
09 FEB. 1997
le temps du sommeil

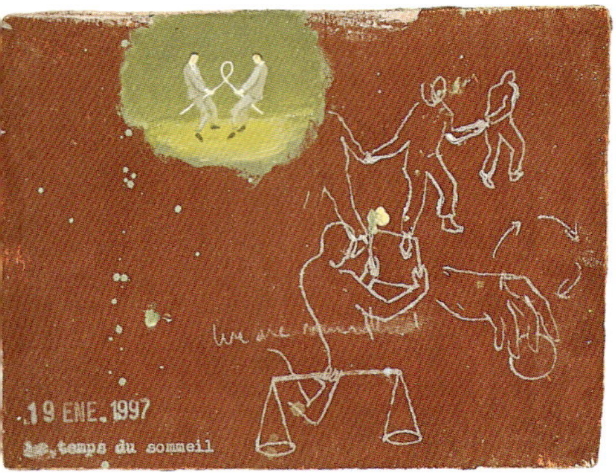
19 ENE. 1997
le temps du sommeil

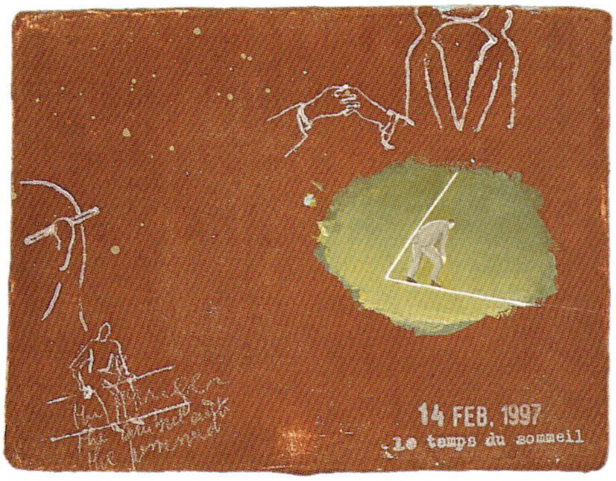
14 FEB. 1997
le temps du sommeil

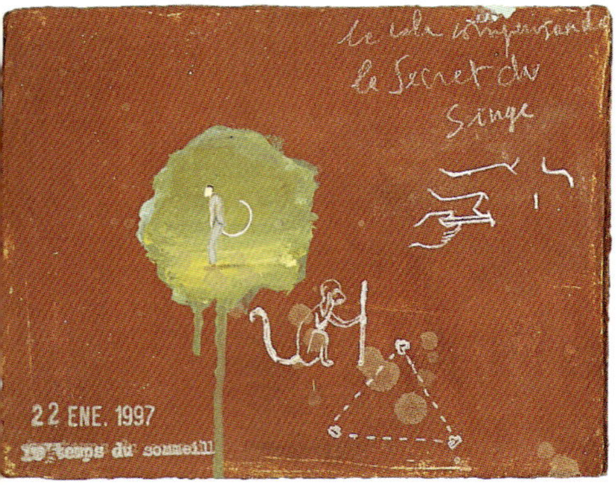
le Secret du
Singe
22 ENE. 1997
le temps du sommeil

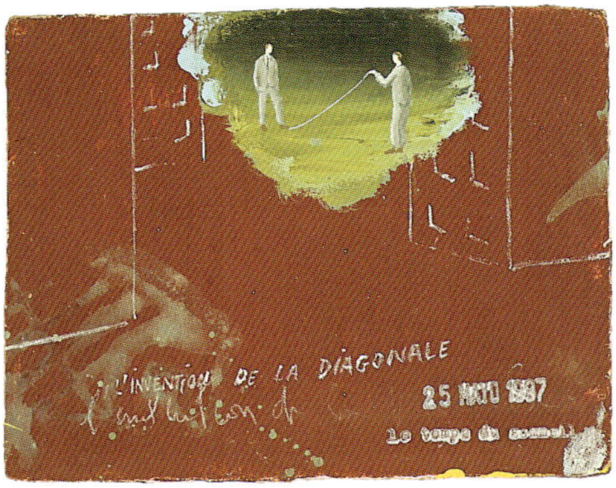
L'INVENTION DE LA DIAGONALE
25 MAYO 1997
le temps du sommeil

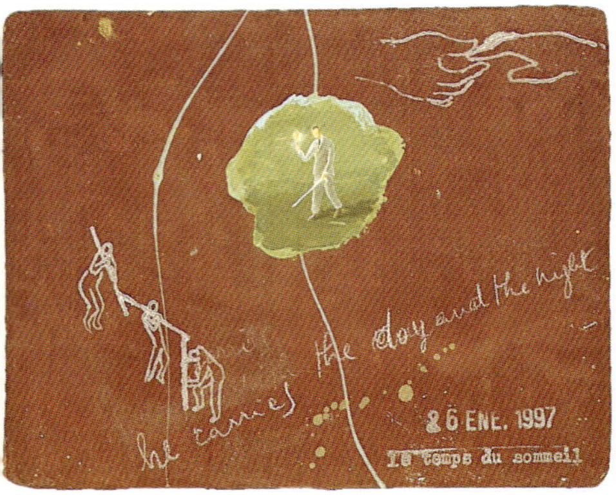
he carries the day and the night
26 ENE. 1997
le temps du sommeil

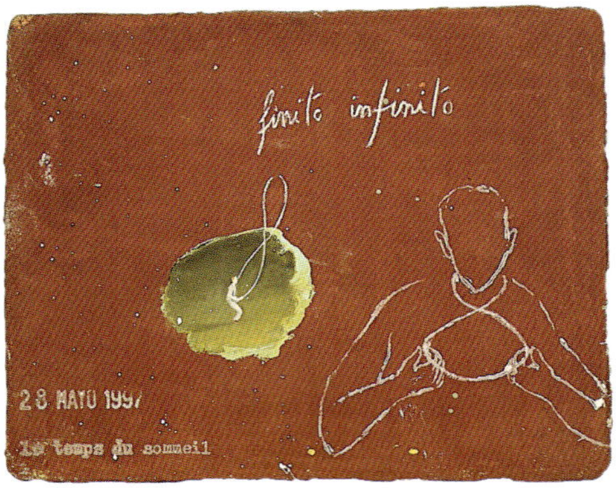
finito infinito
28 MAYO 1997
le temps du sommeil

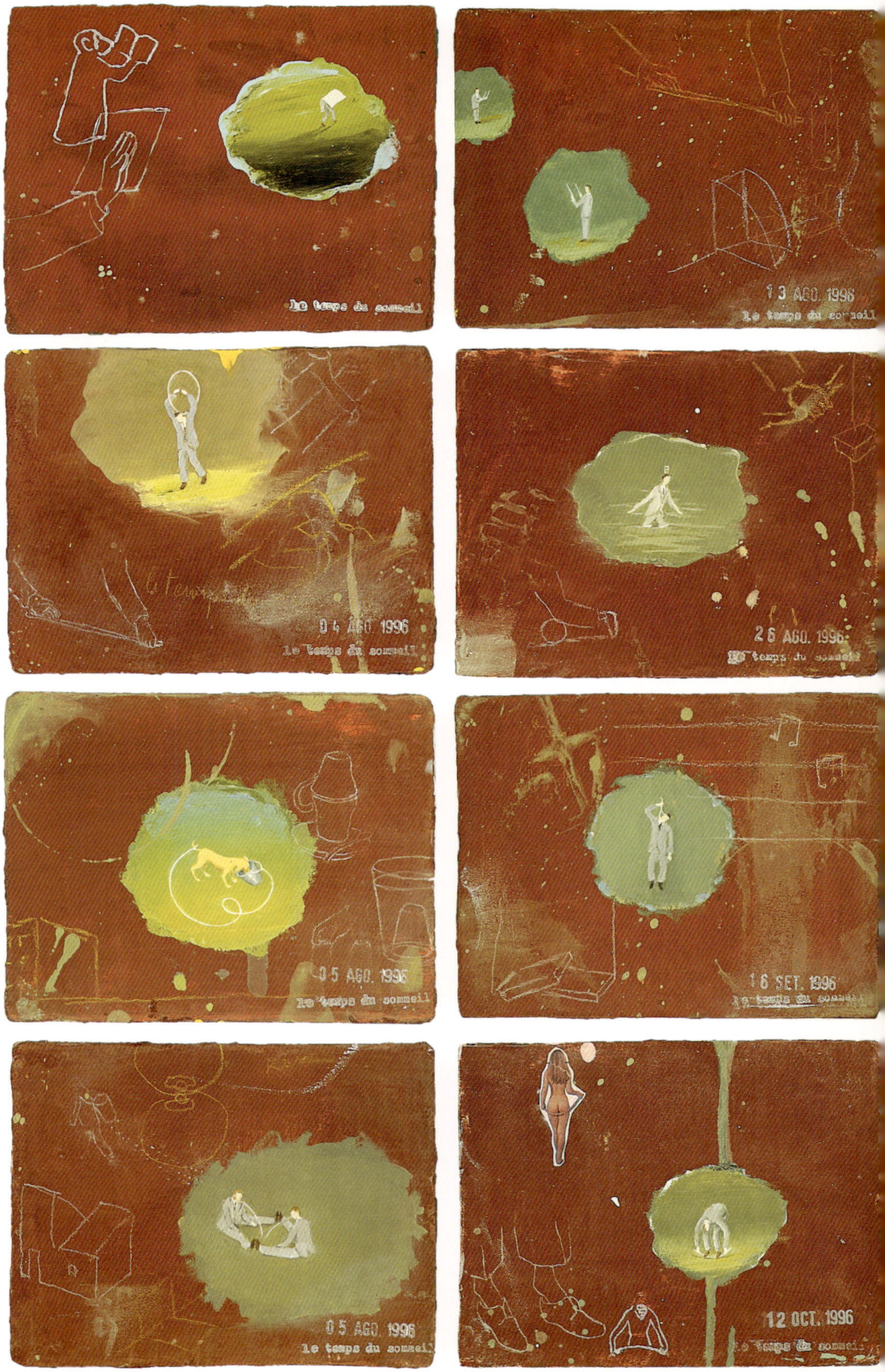

ABOVE **le temps du sommeil** 1997–2001 **OPPOSITE** **The Leak** 1995

Francis Alÿs

Born 1956 Belgium; lives and works in Mexico City
Originally trained as an architect, Francis Alÿs' artistic practice emphasizes an engagement with the performance of quotidian activities inspired by Situationism: "My paintings, my images, are only attempting to illustrate the situations I confront, provoke, or perform on a more public, usually urban, and ephemeral level." For Alÿs, the action of walking serves as a potent aesthetic and cultural metaphor as well as a strategy for inscribing the body into social space. For example, in *The Leak* (first performed in São Paulo in 1995), the artist began a walk from inside a gallery out into the urban landscape, leaking a trail of paint behind him as he meandered throughout the city, conceptually reinventing Jackson Pollock's drip gesture and using the topography of the neighborhoods he traversed as his canvas. He engages in diverse artistic modes—from performance and video to painting and photography; his work both documents and extends the vocabulary of an itinerant practice that radically redefines art-making in the context of everyday experience. Alÿs has participated in numerous international exhibitions, including the Venice Biennale (1999), the Bienal de São Paulo (1998), and the Bienal de la Habana (1997, 1994). Solo exhibitions of his work have been presented at La Caixa Foundation, Barcelona (2000), the Contemporary Art Gallery, Vancouver (1998), and the Museum of Modern Art, Mexico City (1997).

OPPOSITE Francis Alÿs **The Leak** 1995 performed in São Paulo walk with enamel paint, paint can Images courtesy the artist, Mexico City (checklist)

FOLDOUT Francis Alÿs **le temps du sommeil** 1997–2001 oil, mixed media on panel sixteen paintings from an ongoing series, 4 ¼ x 6 in. each Images courtesy the artist, Mexico City (checklist)

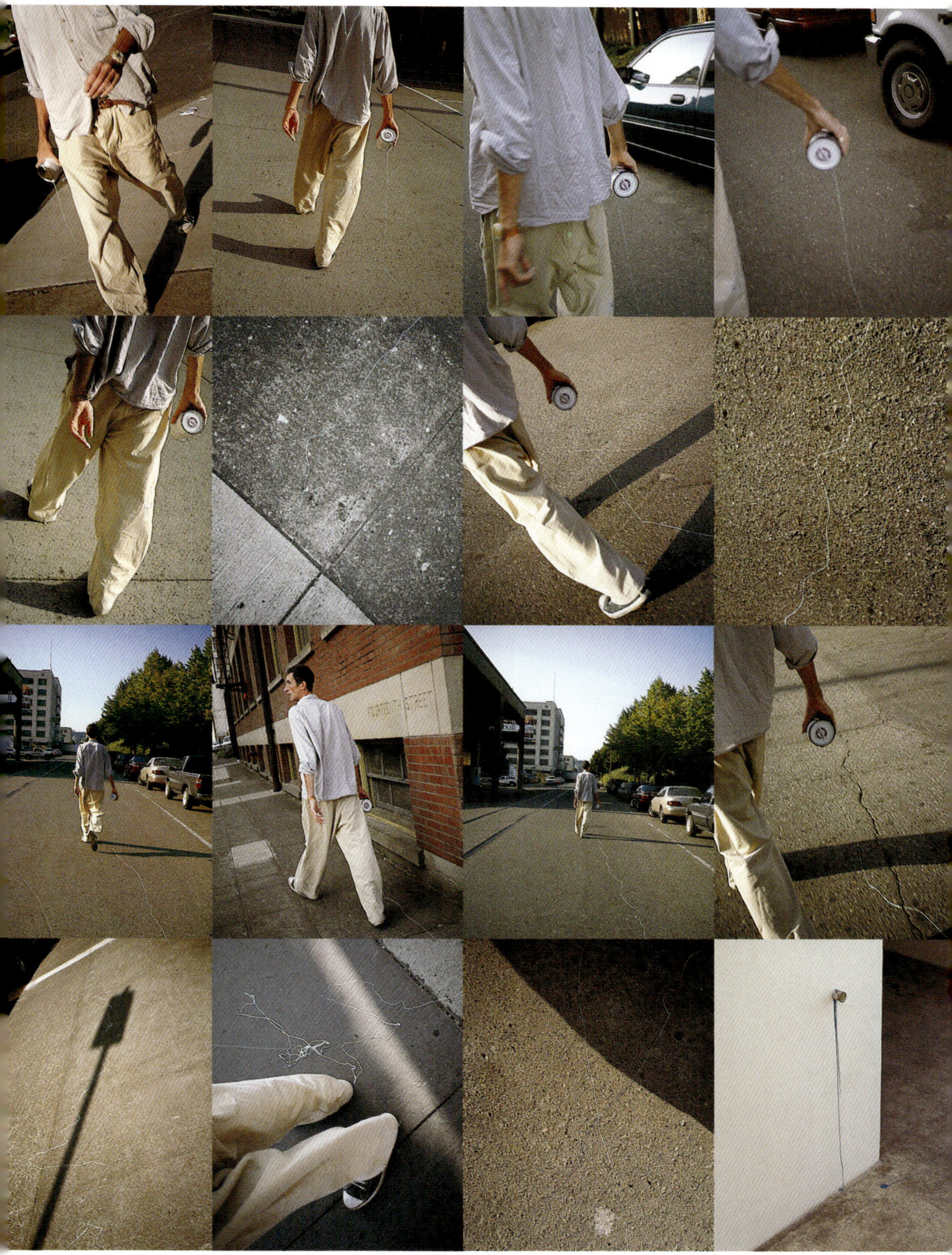

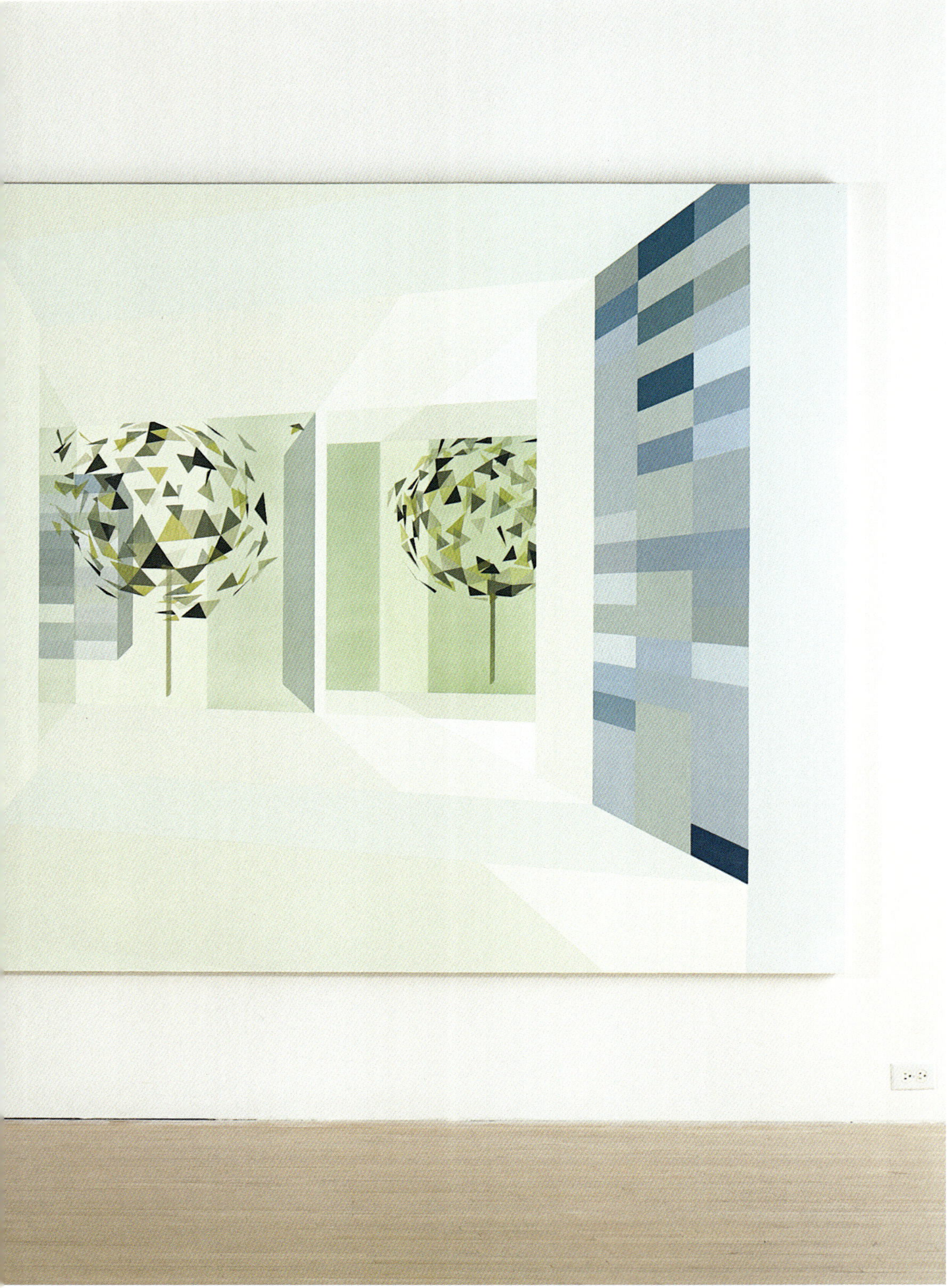

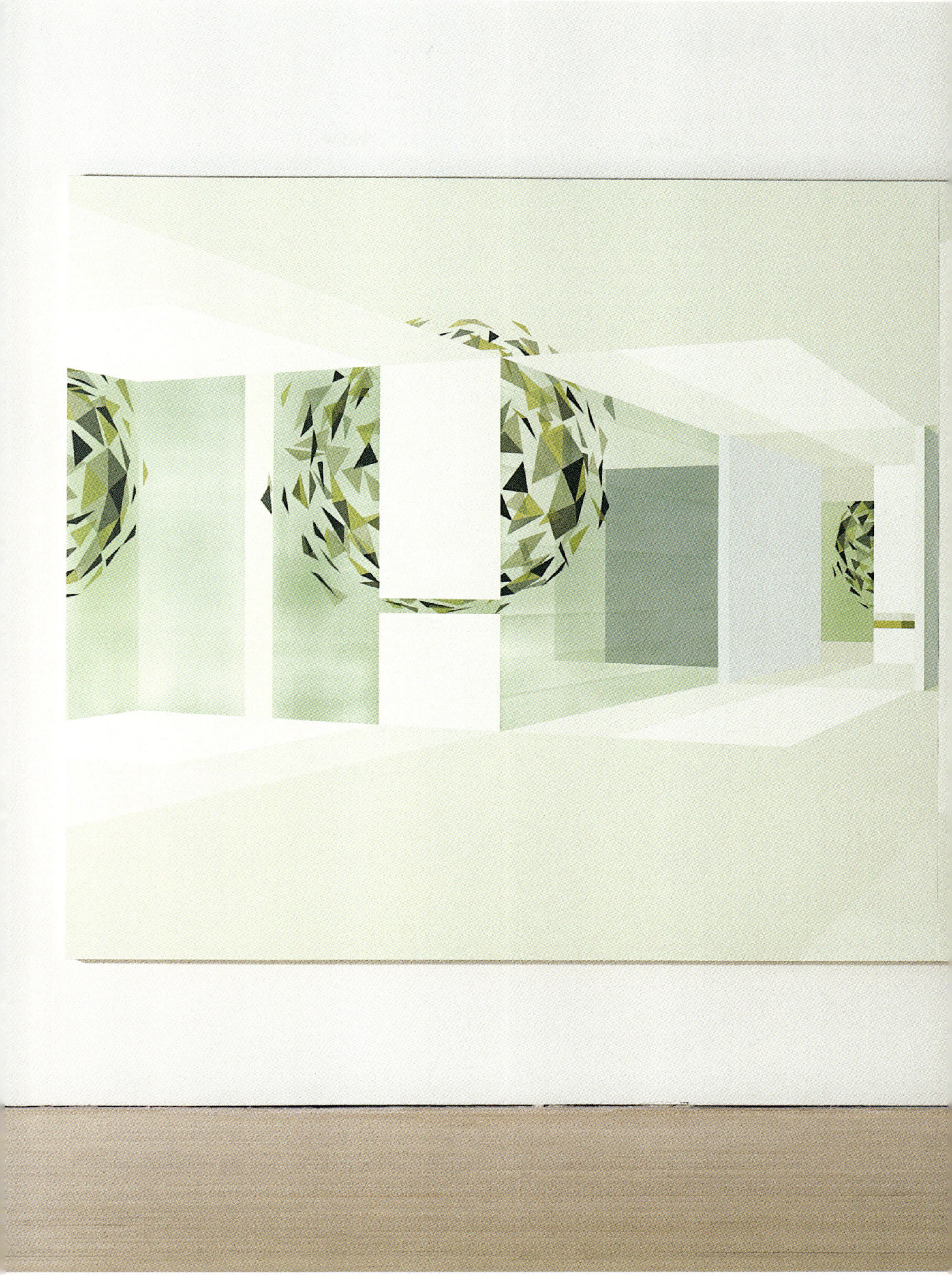

ABOVE **House: East View (Vista)** 1999 OPPOSITE **House: Northwest View** 1999

Kevin Appel

Born 1967 United States; lives and works in Los Angeles
Kevin Appel draws inspiration from computer-modified images of 1950s and 1960s modernist interiors. Originally appropriated from actual structures, Appel has recently begun to design his own interiors as material for reinterpretation in his paintings. Their style envisions a particular design aesthetic that is consistent with prevalent nostalgic revisitations of modernism such as *Wallpaper** magazine. But underlying this series is a conceptual investigation of artifice that both dispels the utopian vision of modernist architecture and renegotiates the practice of painting itself. His flat, hard-edged style underscores the simultaneous realities of painting as an abstracted series of colored shapes and as an illusionistic enterprise. Devoid of human presence, his paintings empty modernist architecture's promise of livability in their depictions of vacant, uncannily dysfunctional spaces. Appel was the subject of a solo exhibition at the Museum of Contemporary Art, Los Angeles (1999) and his work has been included in group exhibitions at the San Francisco Museum of Modern Art (2001), the Henry Art Gallery, Seattle (2000), and the South London Gallery (1999).

OPPOSITE Kevin Appel **House: Northwest View** 1999 acrylic on canvas over panel 80 x 90 in. Collection Marcia Goldenfeld Maiten and Barry David Maiten, Los Angeles Image courtesy Angles Gallery, Santa Monica, California; photo: Brian Forrest (checklist)

FOLDOUT Kevin Appel **House: East View (Vista)** 1999 acrylic on canvas over panel 80 x 180 in. Collection Michael and Judy Ovitz, Los Angeles Image courtesy Angles Gallery, Santa Monica, California; photo: Brian Forrest (checklist)

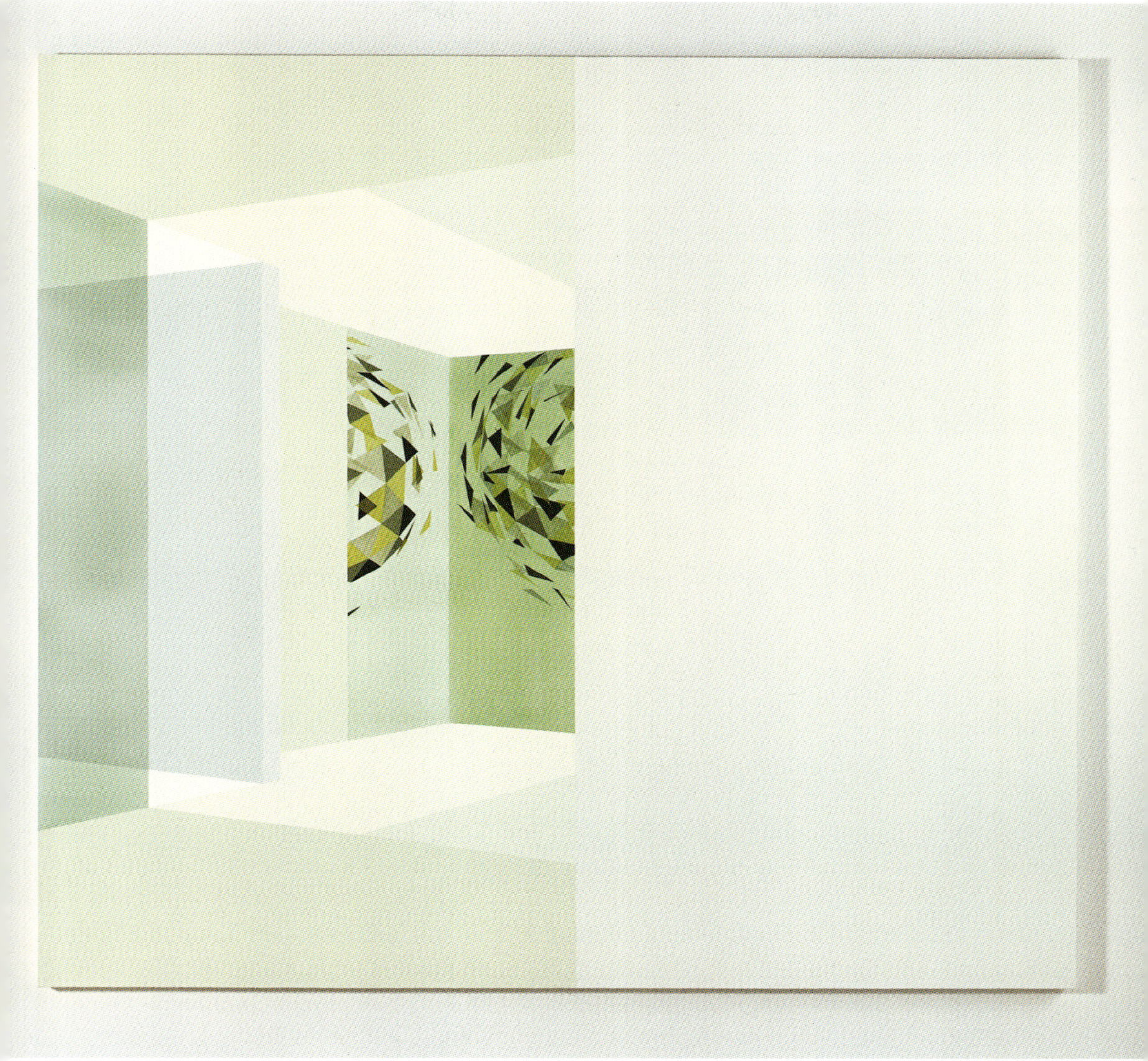

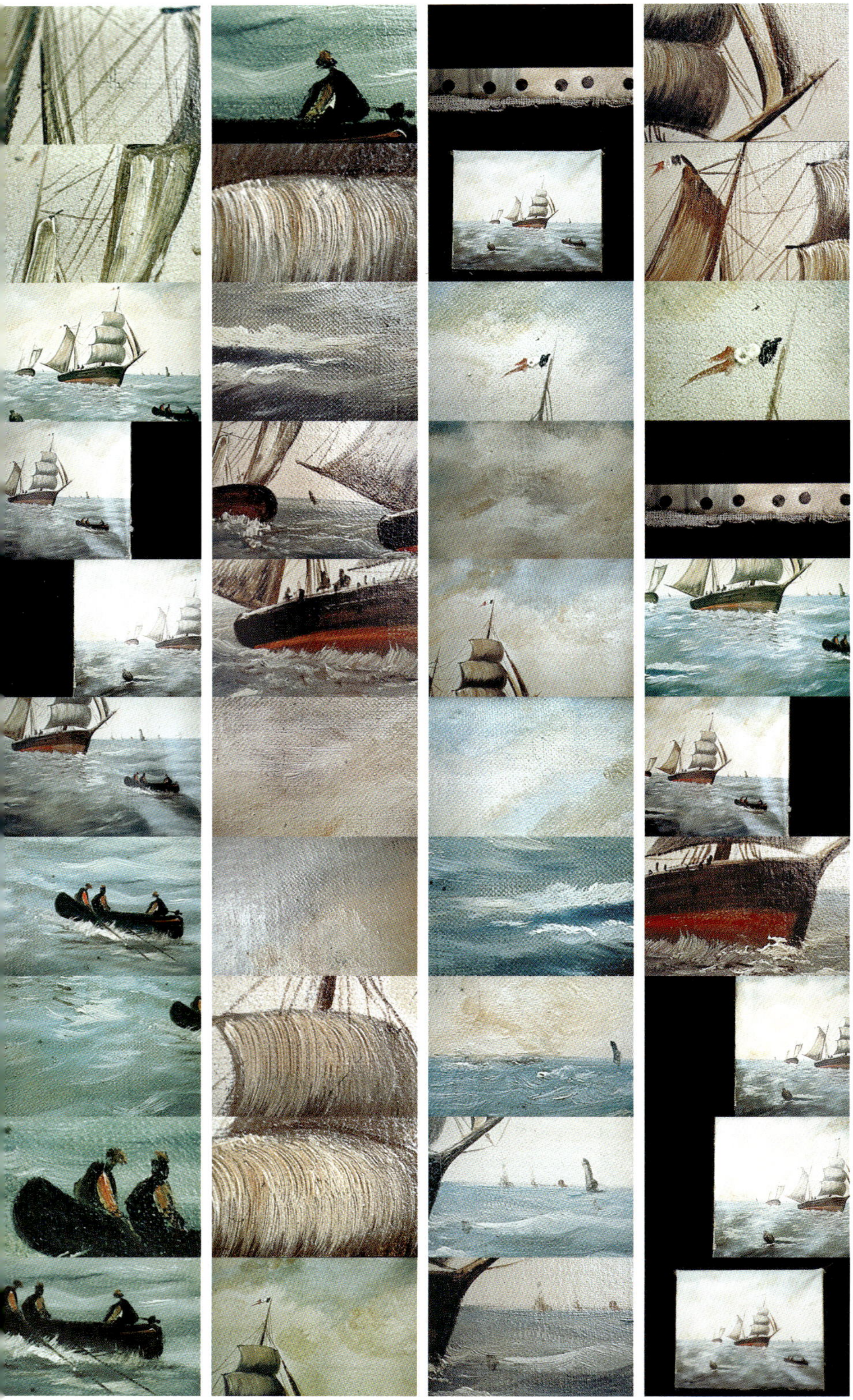

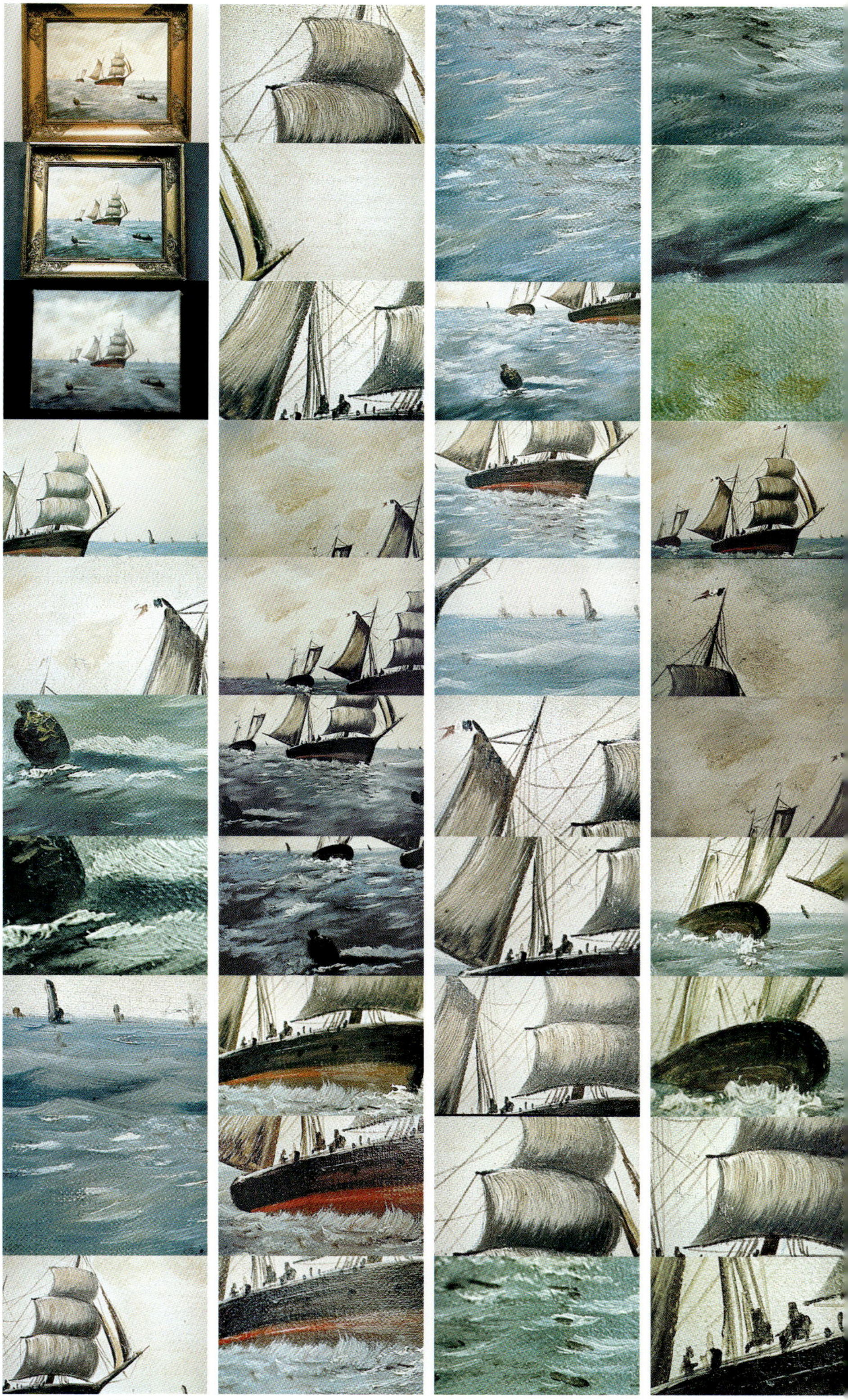

ABOVE AND OPPOSITE **Tableau–Bateau** 1973

Marcel Broodthaers

Born 1924 Belgium; died 1976
Marcel Broodthaers became a visual artist after working as a poet and writer. Language, whether in the form of creative writing or analysis, remained a strong influence throughout his artistic career. He created a diverse body of work, including assemblages, film and slide projections, paintings and prints, photographs, artist's books, and installations, in order to investigate the fundamental nature of the artwork and its status as both a cultural and commercial product. Widely influential, Broodthaers anticipated major shifts in artistic practice and institutional critique as he examined the systems of production, reception, and commodification in the art world. A work such as *Tableau–Bateau* (1973) exemplifies his conceptual approach and inhabits an ambiguous position between media. The piece involves the projection of eighty slides, each of which excerpts and dissects an anonymous amateur painting from the late nineteenth century and transforms it from its original form and context: a painting becomes a projection, a static composition becomes a dynamic presentation, a frozen moment is imbued with temporal progression, a nineteenth-century artifact is recast in a twentieth-century medium. Broodthaers has been the subject of major solo exhibitions at the Centro Galego de Arte Contemporánea, Galicia, Spain (1997), the Van Abbemuseum, Eindhoven (1994), and the Walker Art Center, Minneapolis (1989).

OPPOSITE (DETAILS) AND FOLDOUT Marcel Broodthaers **Tableau–Bateau** 1973 projection of eighty 35mm slides dimensions variable Collection Walker Art Center, Minneapolis; T. B. Walker Acquisition Fund, 1997 (checklist)

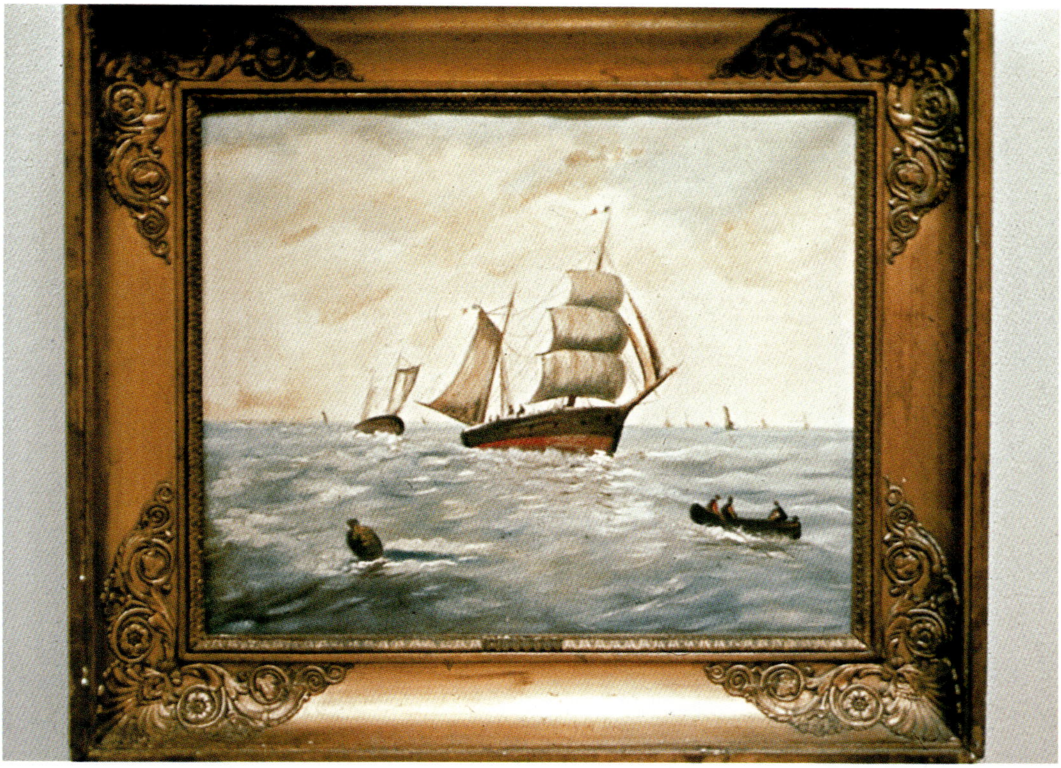

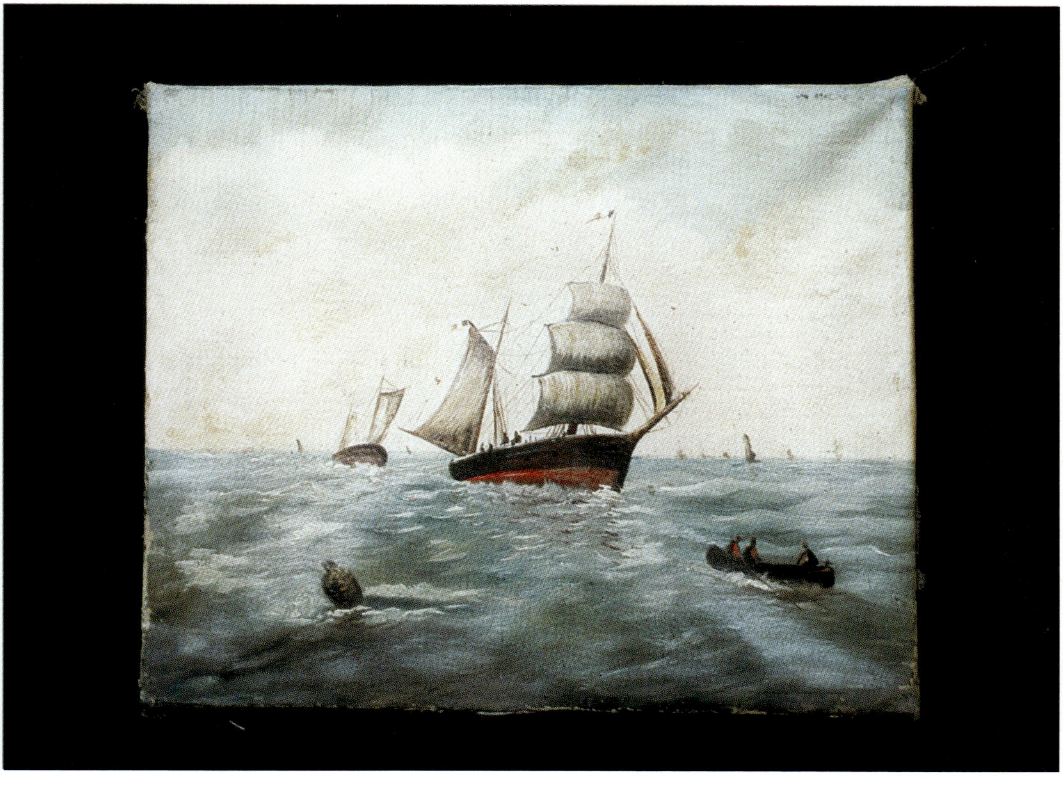

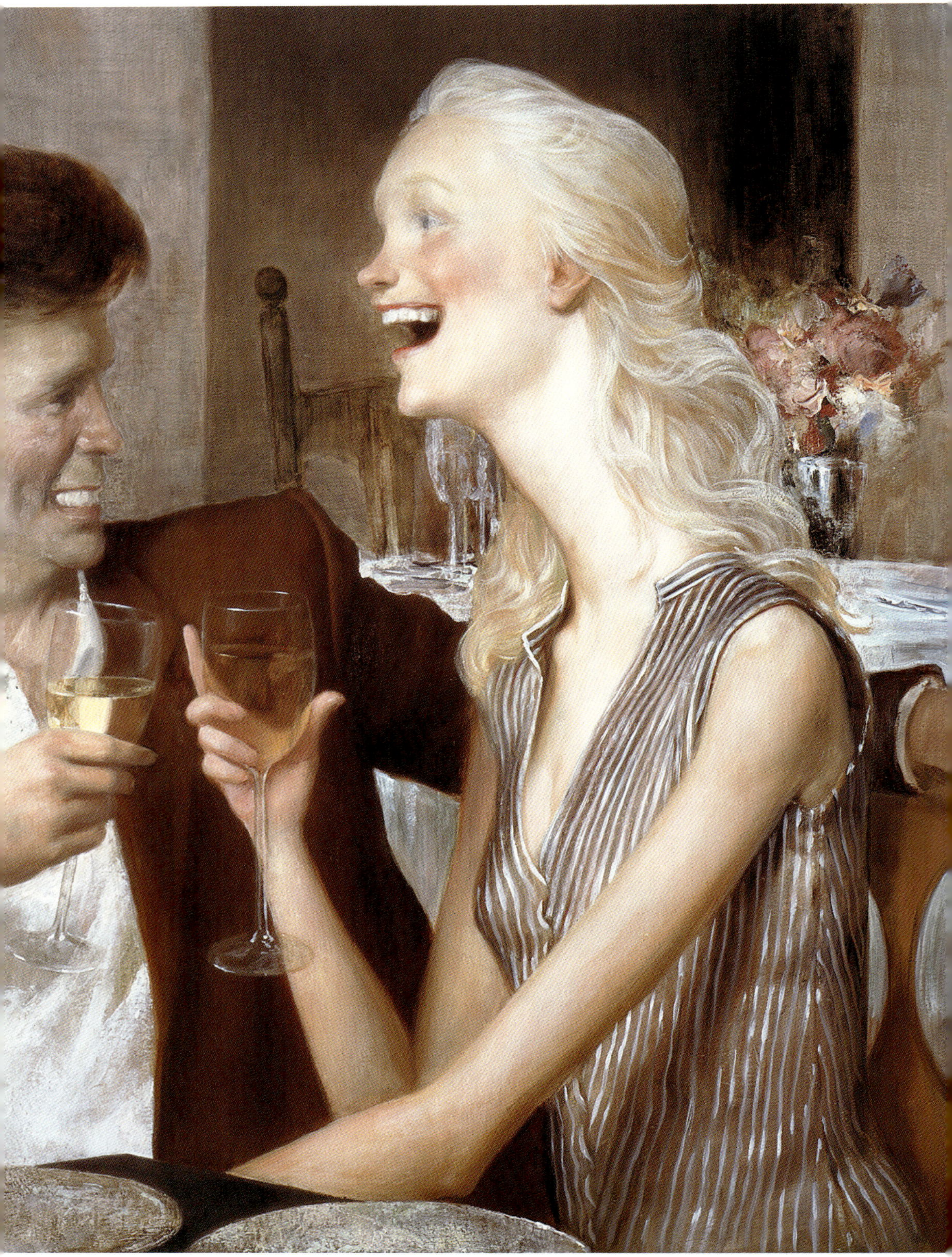

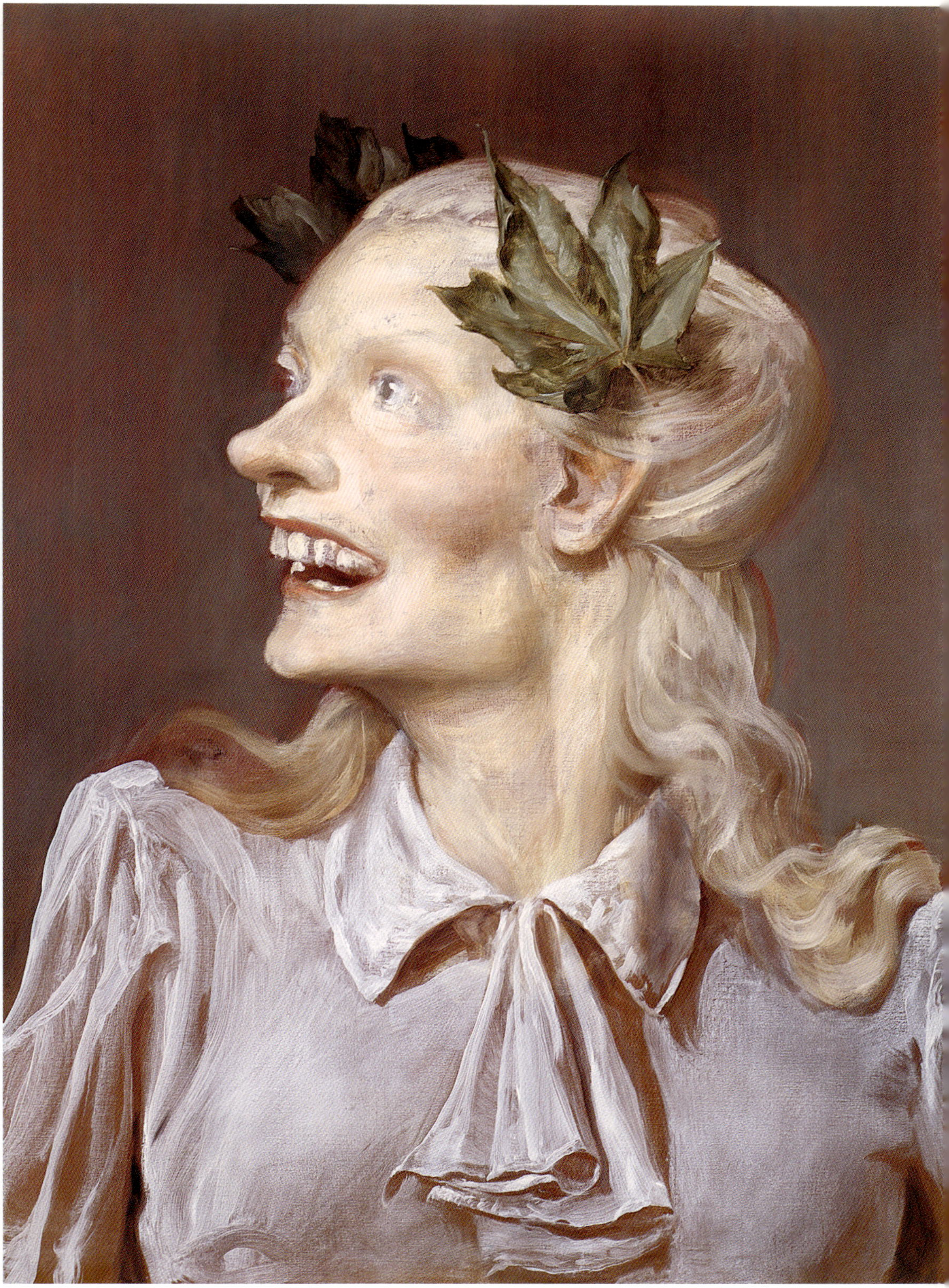

ABOVE **Minerva** 2000 CENTER **Park City Grill** 2000 OPPOSITE **The Cuddler** 2000

John Currin

Born 1962 United States; lives and works in New York City
John Currin synthesizes historical and contemporary styles, invoking the classical traditions of figurative painting and filtering them through the lens of modernist practice. One of many young painters who marked a return to the figure in the early 1990s, he deliberately quotes various art-historical references—from Lucas Cranach to Vincent van Gogh to Alessandro Botticelli—in the style and composition of his evolving body of work. Although he paints both male and female figures, Currin has received great attention for his paintings of women—whether showing the strain of age or flaunting model-like beauty and youth—that eschew idealization or easy classification. He pushes his figures to the limits of representation through the exaggeration of character and the overstatement of physical traits to the point of near deformity. His often unsettling scenarios further a psychological investigation of representation and human relationships. A technically accomplished painter, Currin's work often combines incompatible visual languages, mixing grotesquely impastoed figures with delicately worked illusionistic sections. Currin recently participated in the Whitney Biennial, New York (2000) and the *Carnegie International*, Pittsburgh (1999). His work has been included in group exhibitions at the Whitechapel Art Gallery, London (1999), the Museum of Modern Art, New York (1997), the Stedelijk Museum, Amsterdam (1995), and the Institute of Contemporary Arts, London (1995).

OPPOSITE John Currin **The Cuddler** 2000 oil on canvas 38 x 24 ½ in. Collection Frances and John Bowes, San Francisco Image courtesy Sadie Coles HQ, London; photo: Andy Keate (checklist)

FOLDOUT (LEFT) John Currin **Minerva** 2000 oil on canvas 28 x 22 in. Courtesy Gallerie Monica Sprüth, Cologne Image courtesy Andrea Rosen Gallery, New York; photo: Fred Scruton (checklist)
(RIGHT) John Currin **Park City Grill** 2000 oil on canvas 38 x 30 in. Collection Walker Art Center, Minneapolis; Justin Smith Purchase Fund, 2000; photo: Andy Keate (checklist)

JOHN CURRIN
253

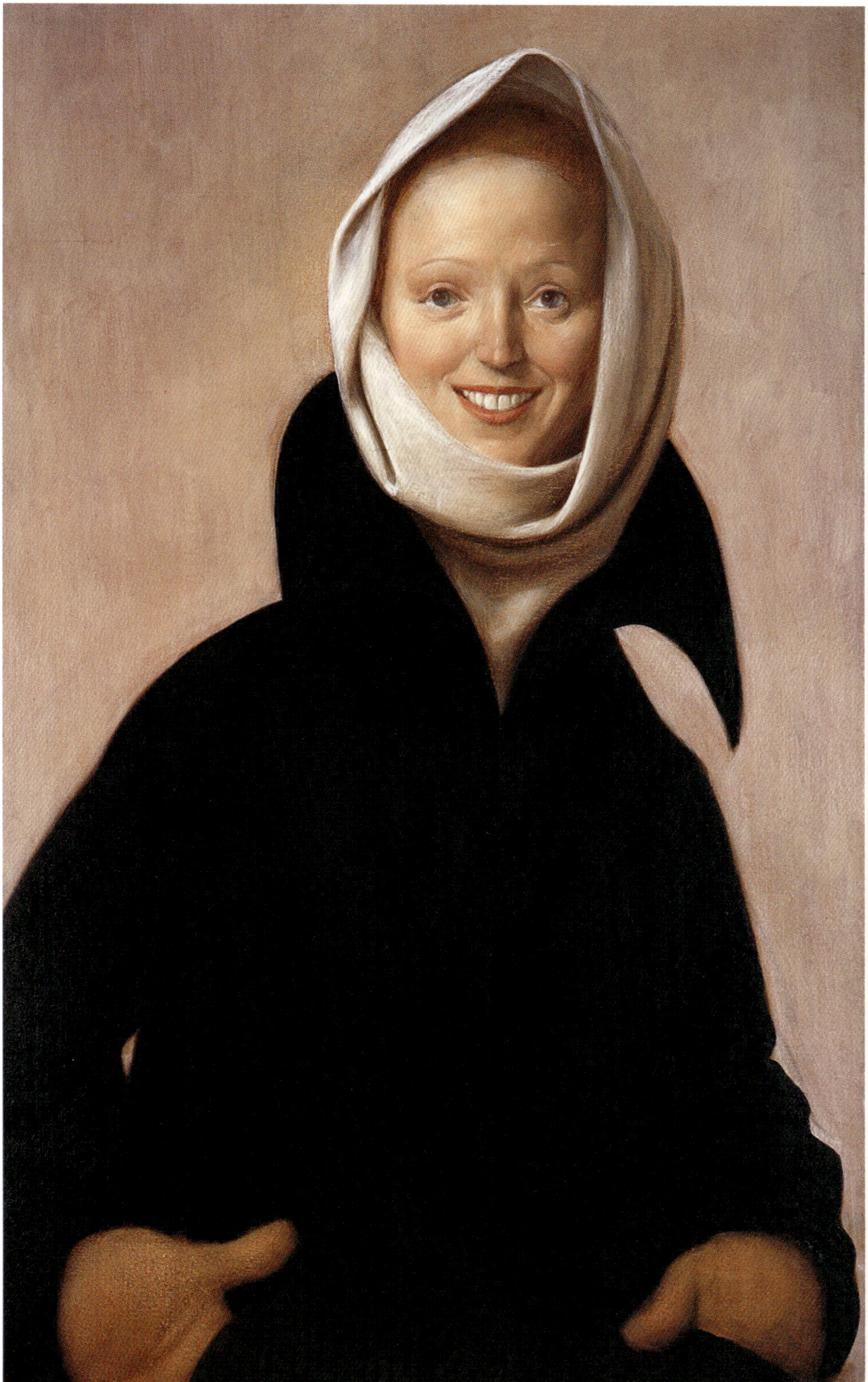

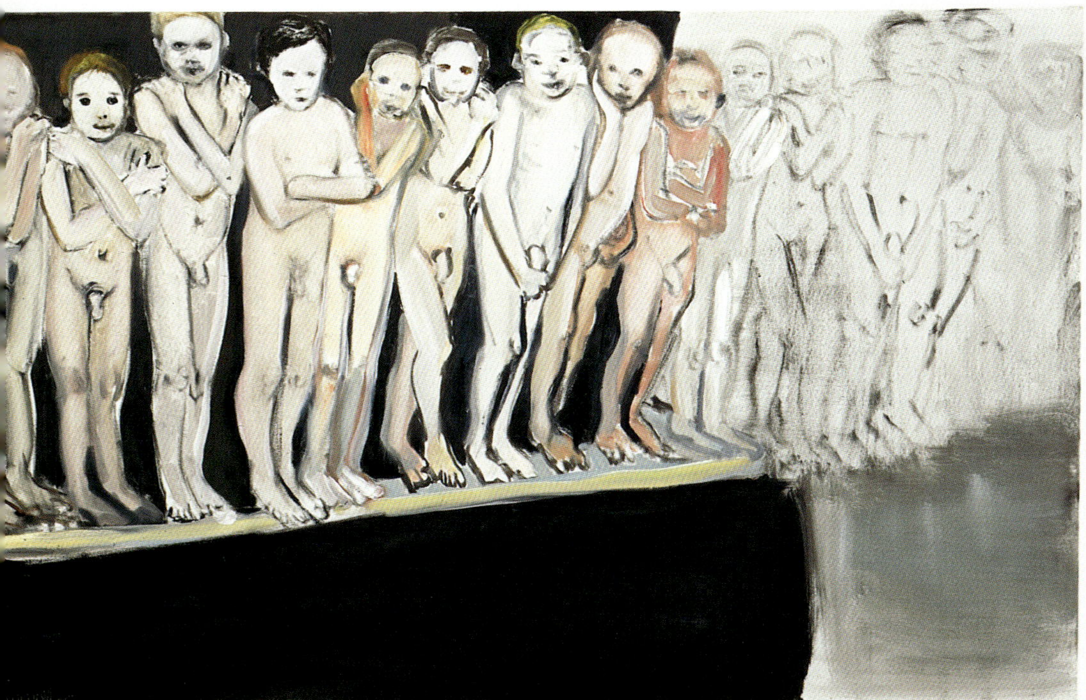

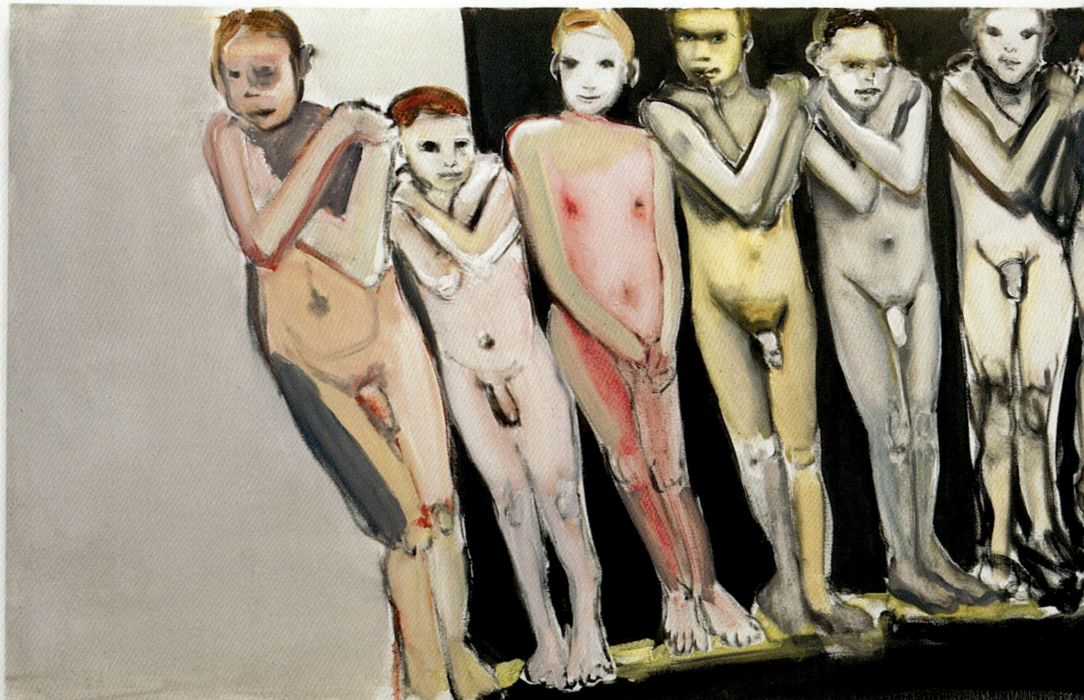

ABOVE **Young Boys** 1993–1994 OPPOSITE **The Painter** 1994

Marlene Dumas

Born 1953 South Africa; lives and works in Amsterdam
Marlene Dumas' career is marked by a consistent preoccupation with the figure and the potential for bringing to the surface what lies deep inside a subject. A student of psychology as well as art, she bears witness to painful histories and raw emotions in her paintings, which seek to convey universally recognizable situations without relying on literal representation. As she has said, "I want to portray people in all their complexity and never [as a] completely definable identity." Drawing her subjects from a variety of photographic sources of famous and anonymous individuals, Dumas renegotiates ideas of beauty in confrontational and instinctive portrayals. Her expressive paintings mix beauty with ugliness, revelation with obliteration, the body with the senses. Both an artist and a writer, Dumas is very conscious of her art-historical position as a painter of female nudes and she often writes personal or critical texts that address the complexity of imaging the human body. She has exhibited internationally for twenty years, with recent solo exhibitions at the Museum of Contemporary Art, Antwerp (1999), CAPC Musée d'art contemporain, Bordeaux (1999), and the Tate Gallery, London (1996). She participated in the Sydney Biennial (2000) and has been included in recent group exhibitions at the Hirshhorn Museum and Sculpture Garden, Washington, D.C. (2000) and the Moderna Museet, Stockholm (1998).

OPPOSITE Marlene Dumas **The Painter** 1994 oil on canvas 78 x 39 in. Collection Martin Eisenberg, Scarsdale, New York Image courtesy Jack Tilton / Anna Kustera Gallery, New York (checklist)

FOLDOUT Marlene Dumas **Young Boys** 1993–1994 oil on canvas 39 ⅜ x 118 ⅛ in. Collection Lois Plehn, New York Image courtesy Jack Tilton / Anna Kustera Gallery, New York (checklist)

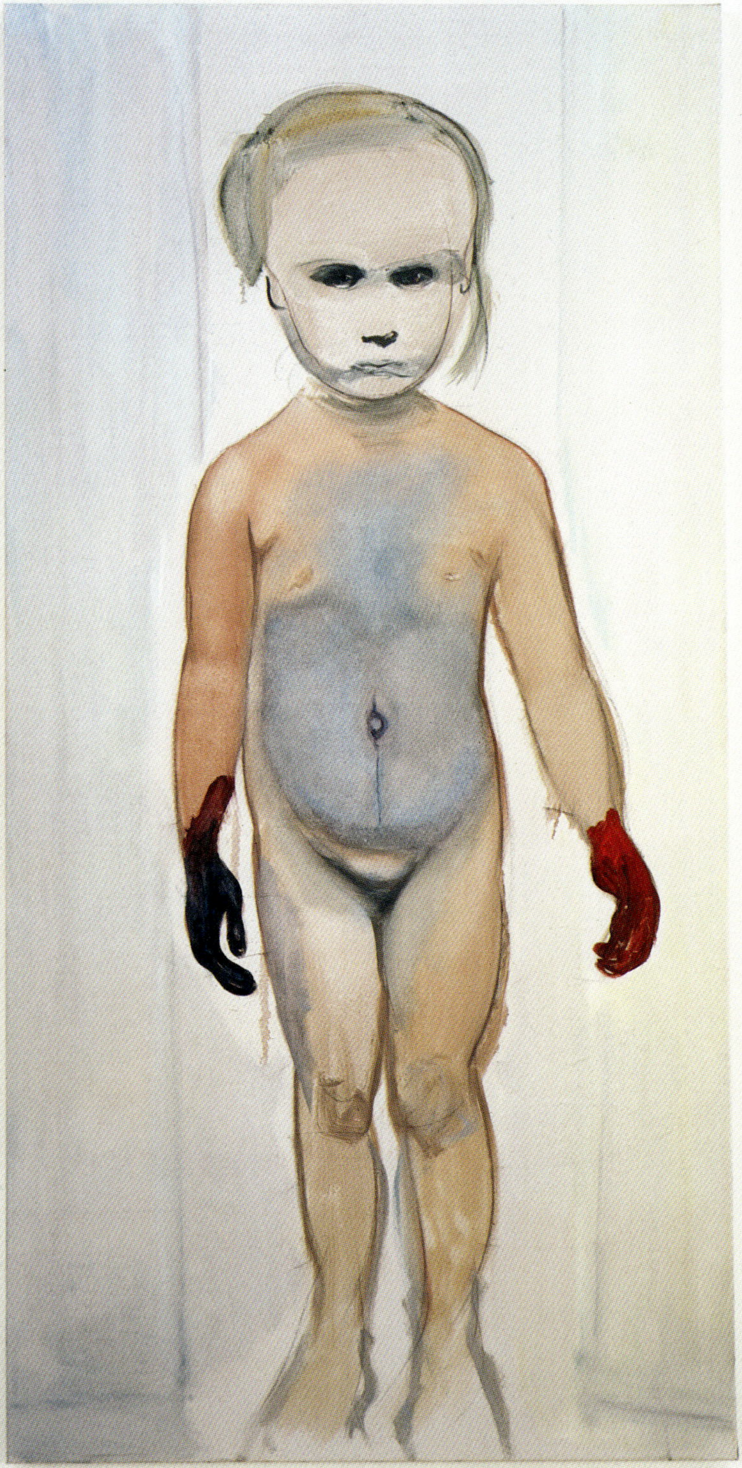

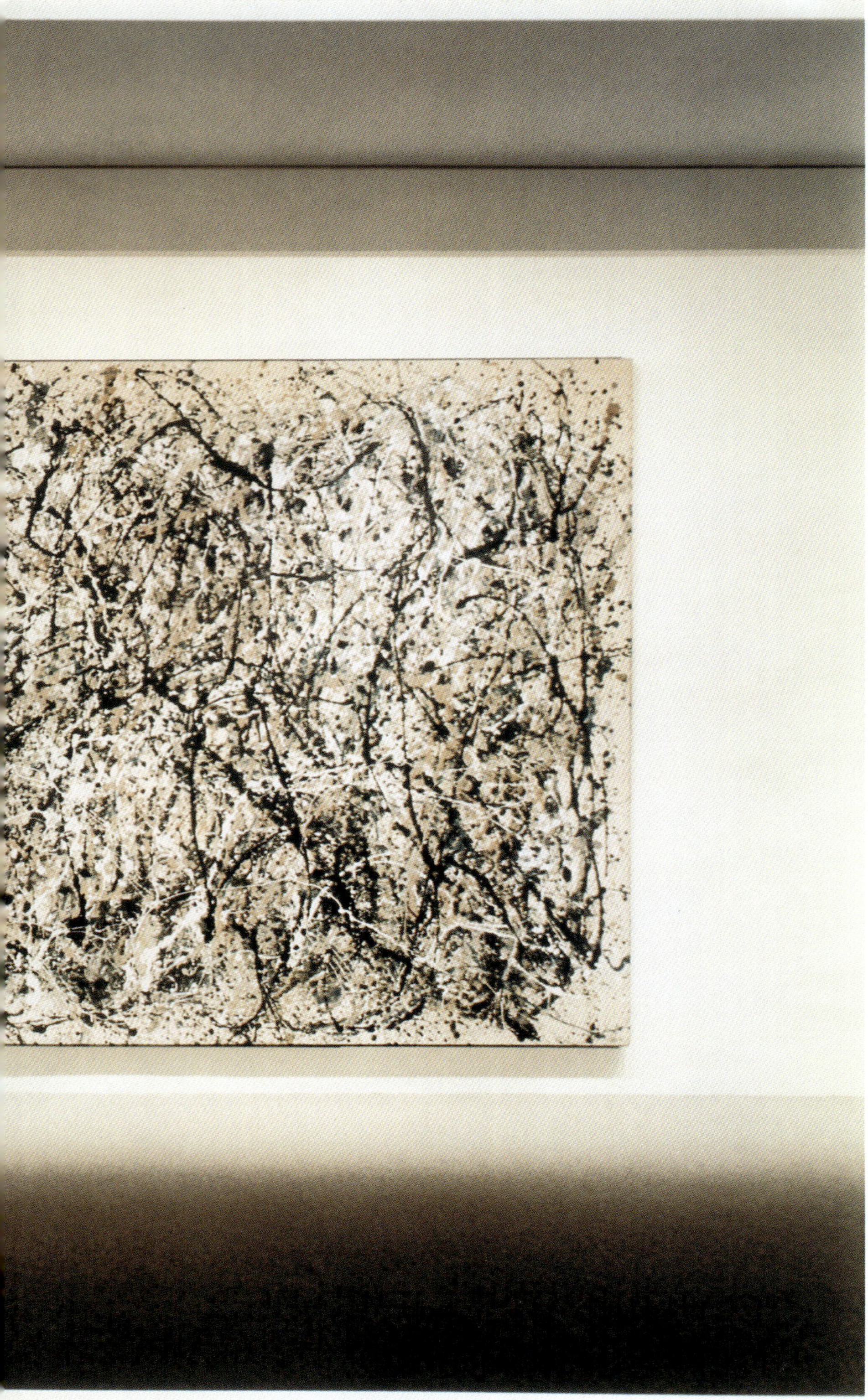

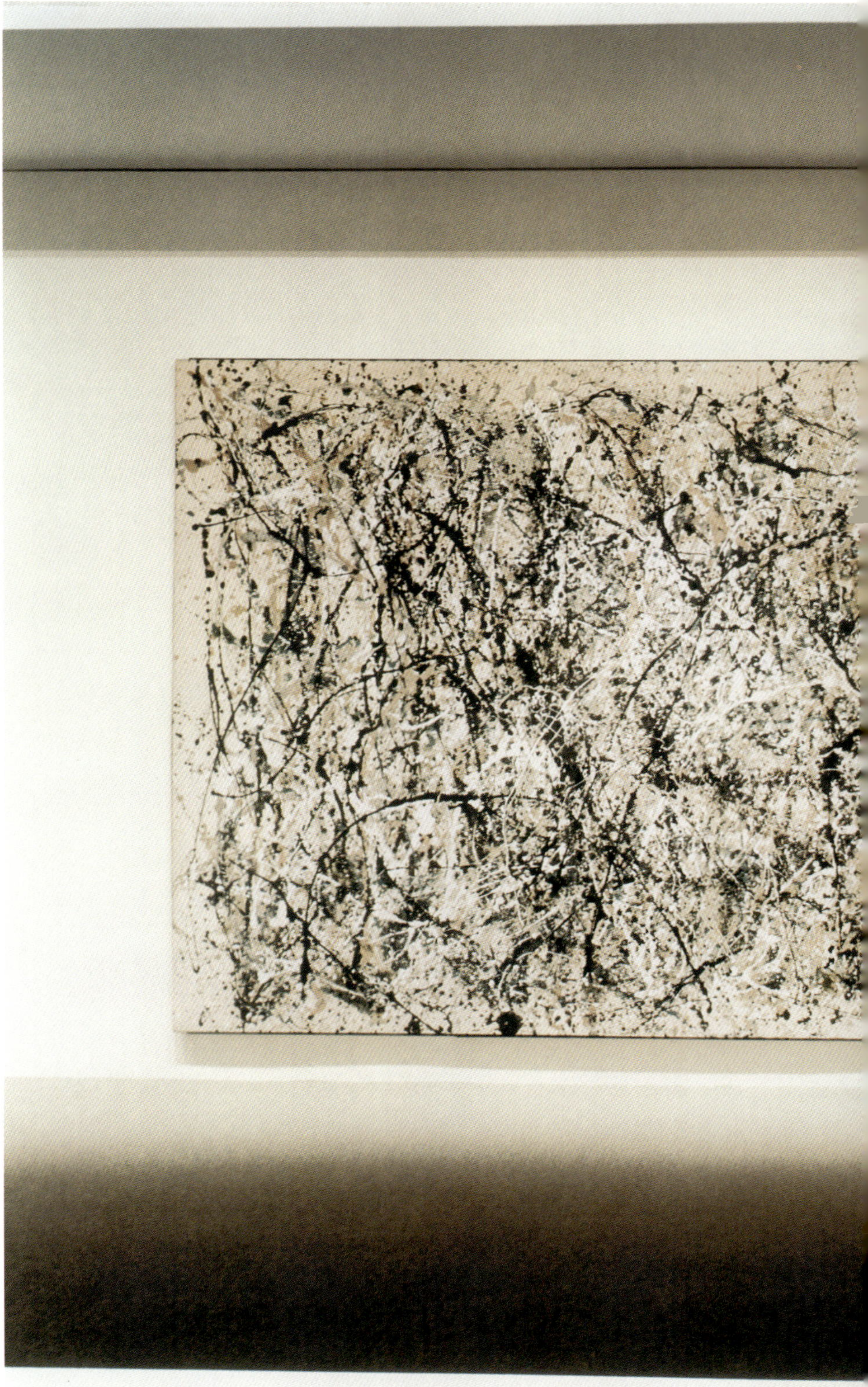

ABOVE **Untitled VI** 1997 OPPOSITE **Untitled X (Constable)** 1999

Andreas Gursky

Born 1955 Germany; lives and works in Düsseldorf

Andreas Gursky's large-scale, saturated photographs inhabit a space between painting and photography, landscape and human concern, the animate and inanimate. His careful photographic compositions reflect an underlying painterly structure. Gursky positions his camera at a high-angled distance from his subjects, which include anonymous corporate buildings, crowds engaged in mass spectacle, and complexly patterned natural environments. The resulting flattened images are often further manipulated in order to intensify and underscore the inherent abstraction and repetition of elements found both in the natural world and in the built environment. The resolute flatness of his compositions references the geometric forms of minimalist art and the all-over quality of Jackson Pollock's paintings, as the viewer's eye surveys the photographs without ever resolving a single point of perspective. Gursky has exhibited widely since 1987, with solo exhibitions at the Kunstmuseum Wolfsburg (1998), the Milwaukee Art Museum (1998), and the Rooseum Center for Contemporary Art, Malmö, Sweden (1995). He has also participated in group exhibitions at the Van Abbemuseum, Eindhoven (2000), the *Carnegie International*, Pittsburgh (1999), and the Photographers' Gallery, London (1998).

OPPOSITE Andreas Gursky **Untitled X (Constable)** 1999 C-print 111 ¾ x 81 ½ in. Image courtesy Matthew Marks Gallery, New York

FOLDOUT Andreas Gursky **Untitled VI** 1997 C-print 73 ¼ x 94 1/16 in. Edition 2/6 Image courtesy Matthew Marks Gallery, New York (checklist)

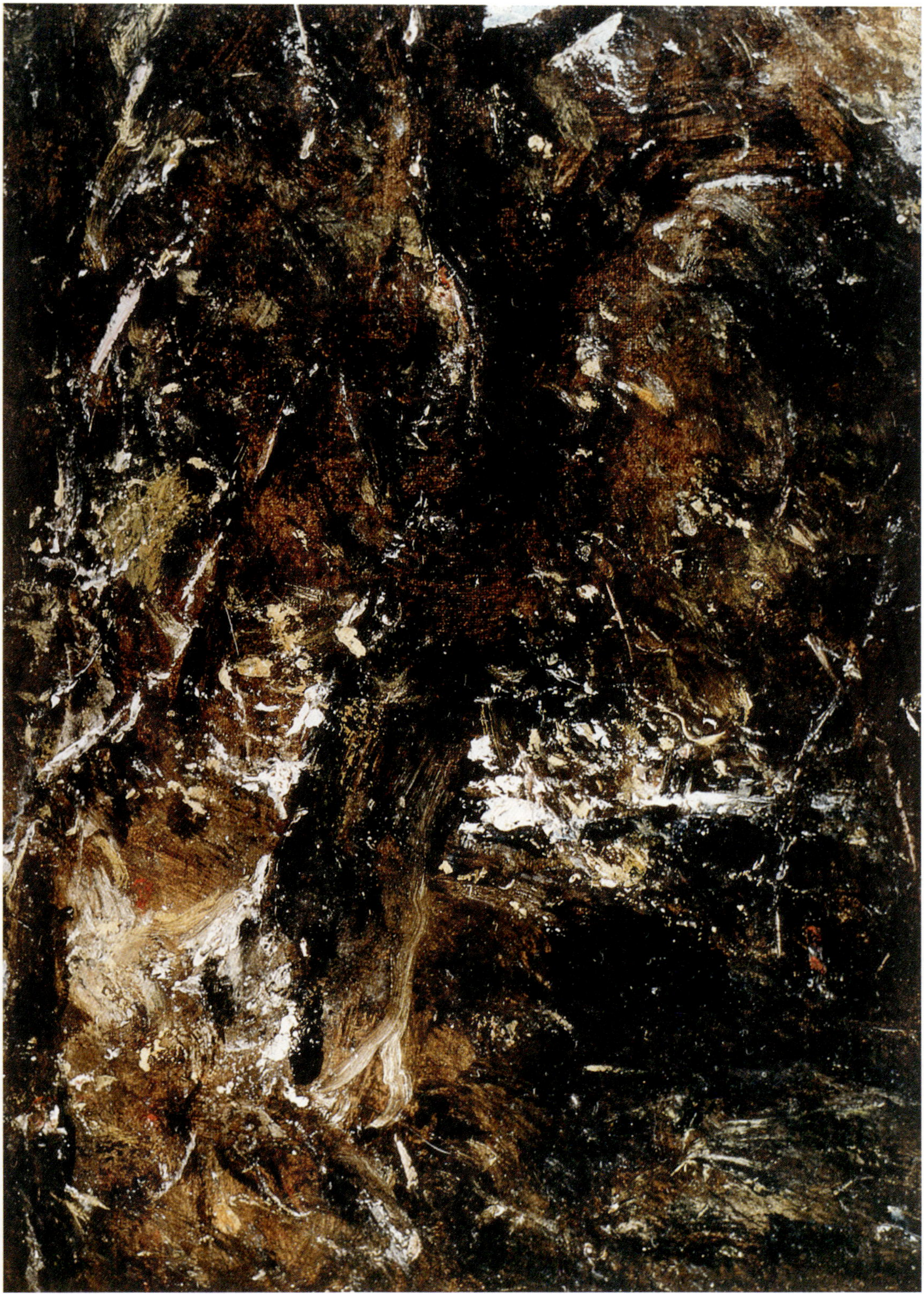

ABOVE **Mobil 3** 2000 OPPOSITE **Scharfschütze (Sniper) 1–3** 1998

Eberhard Havekost

Born 1967 Germany; lives and works in Dresden

Eberhard Havekost's meticulously painted canvases reflect the intrusion of other media into the field of painting. The architectural and figurative sources of his work are derived primarily from media such as video, television, and found photographic reproductions, though he often uses his own photographs. Havekost exposes the visual imprint of moving images in terms of the atmospheric quality of light and artificial coloring in his work, but he does not attempt to imitate the visual effects of a televisual or photographic image in paint. Rather, he assimilates the modes of their production and manipulation into his painterly vocabulary. Employing filmic compositional strategies such as close-ups, cropping, and exaggerated camera angles, Havekost creates a pictorial space that breaks with the logical construction of perspective in the history of painting. His work also investigates the conventions of narrative sequence by exploring the possibilities for rupturing or reconfiguring them. Havekost has been showing his work internationally since 1995, including solo exhibitions at the Galerie für Zeitgenössische Kunst, Leipzig (1999) and the Kunstmuseum Luzern (1998). He has participated in group exhibitions at the Kunsthaus Hamburg (2000), the Arnolfini Gallery, Bristol (1999), and the Sydney College of the Arts Gallery (1998).

OPPOSITE Eberhard Havekost **Scharfschütze (Sniper) 1–3** 1998 oil on canvas triptych, 12 x 16 in. each Collection Susan and Michael Hort, New York Image courtesy Anton Kern Gallery, New York (checklist)

FOLDOUT Eberhard Havekost **Mobil 3** 2000 oil on canvas 55 ⅛ x 78 ¾ in. Image courtesy Galerie Gebr. Lehmann, Dresden; photo: Werner Lieberknecht (checklist)

EBERHARD HAVEKOST

265

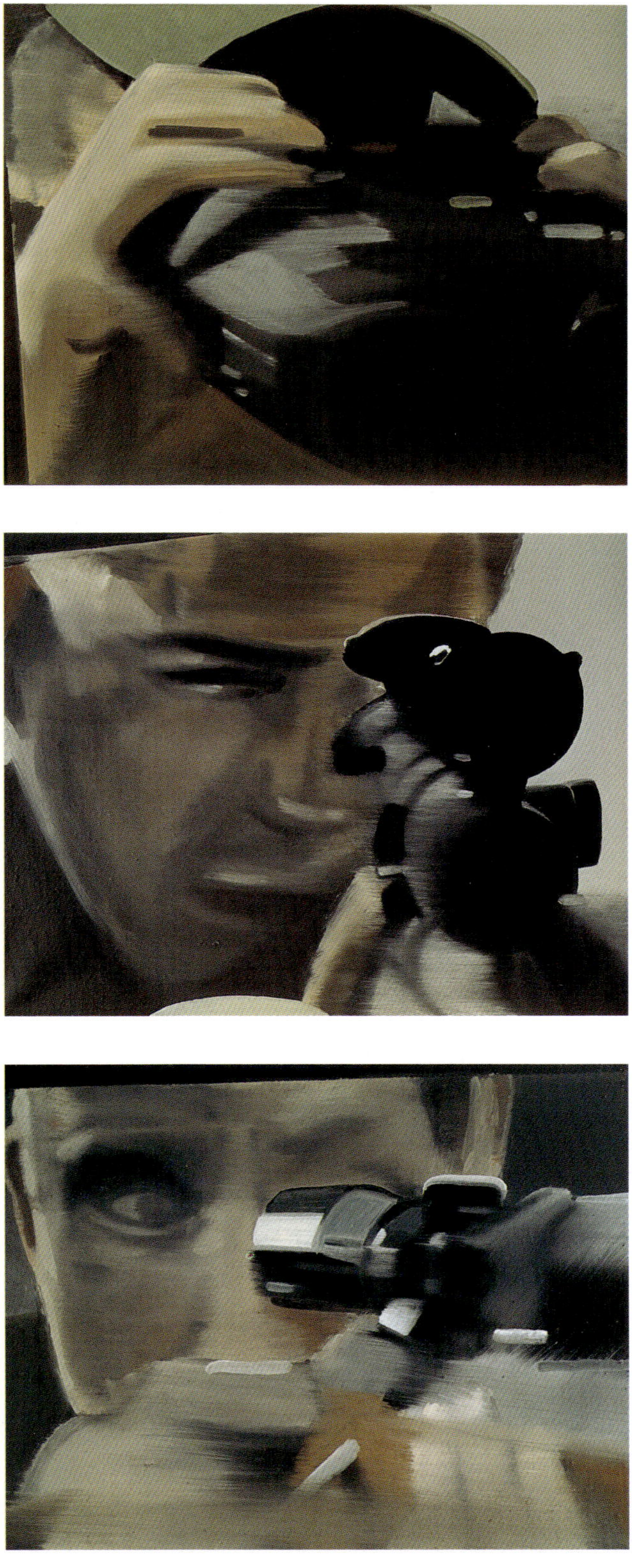

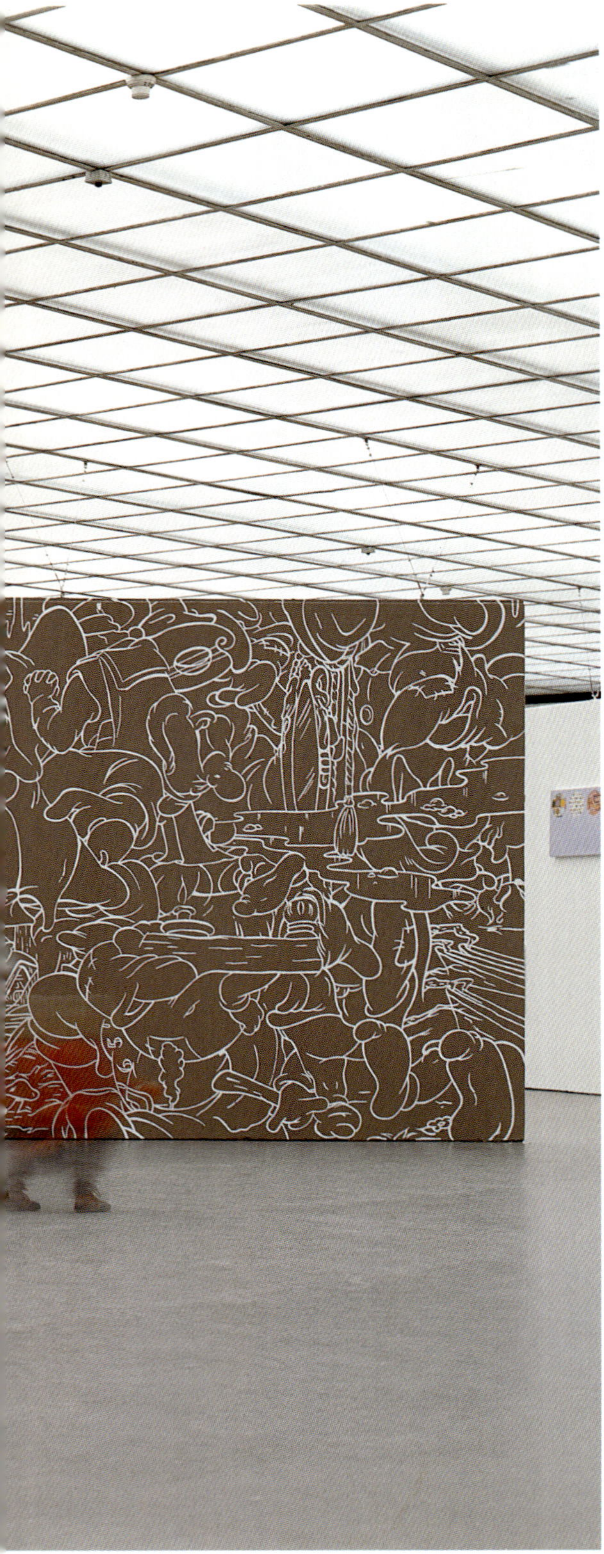

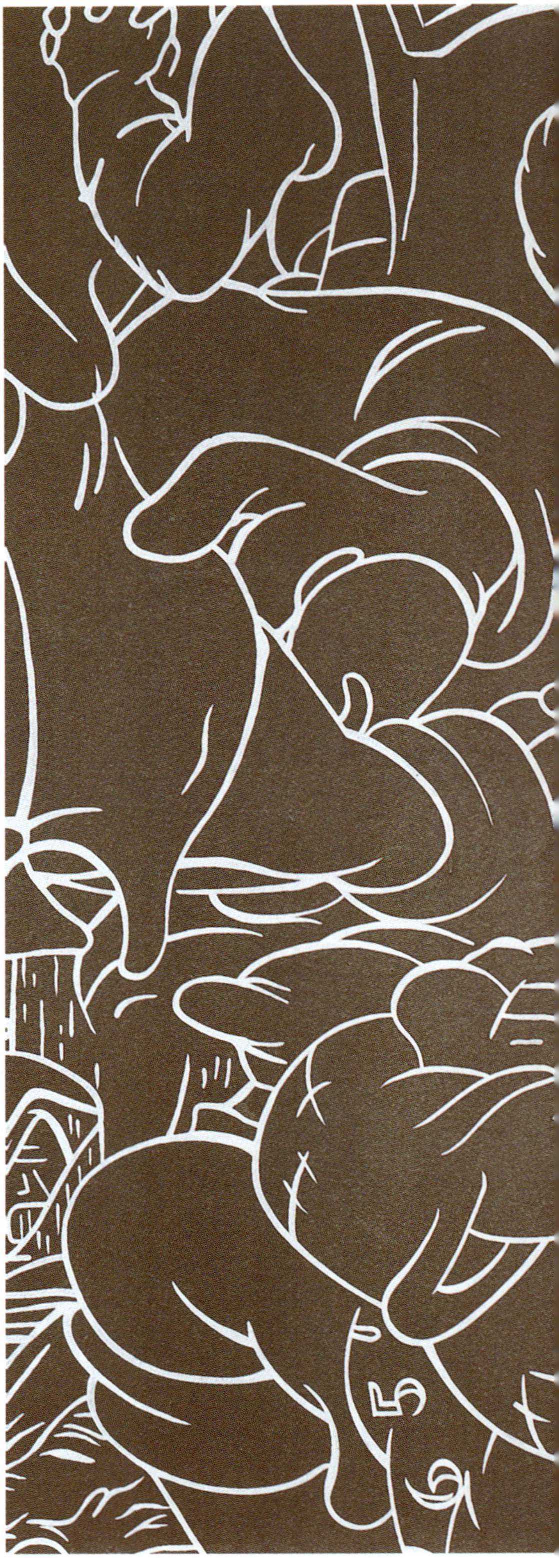

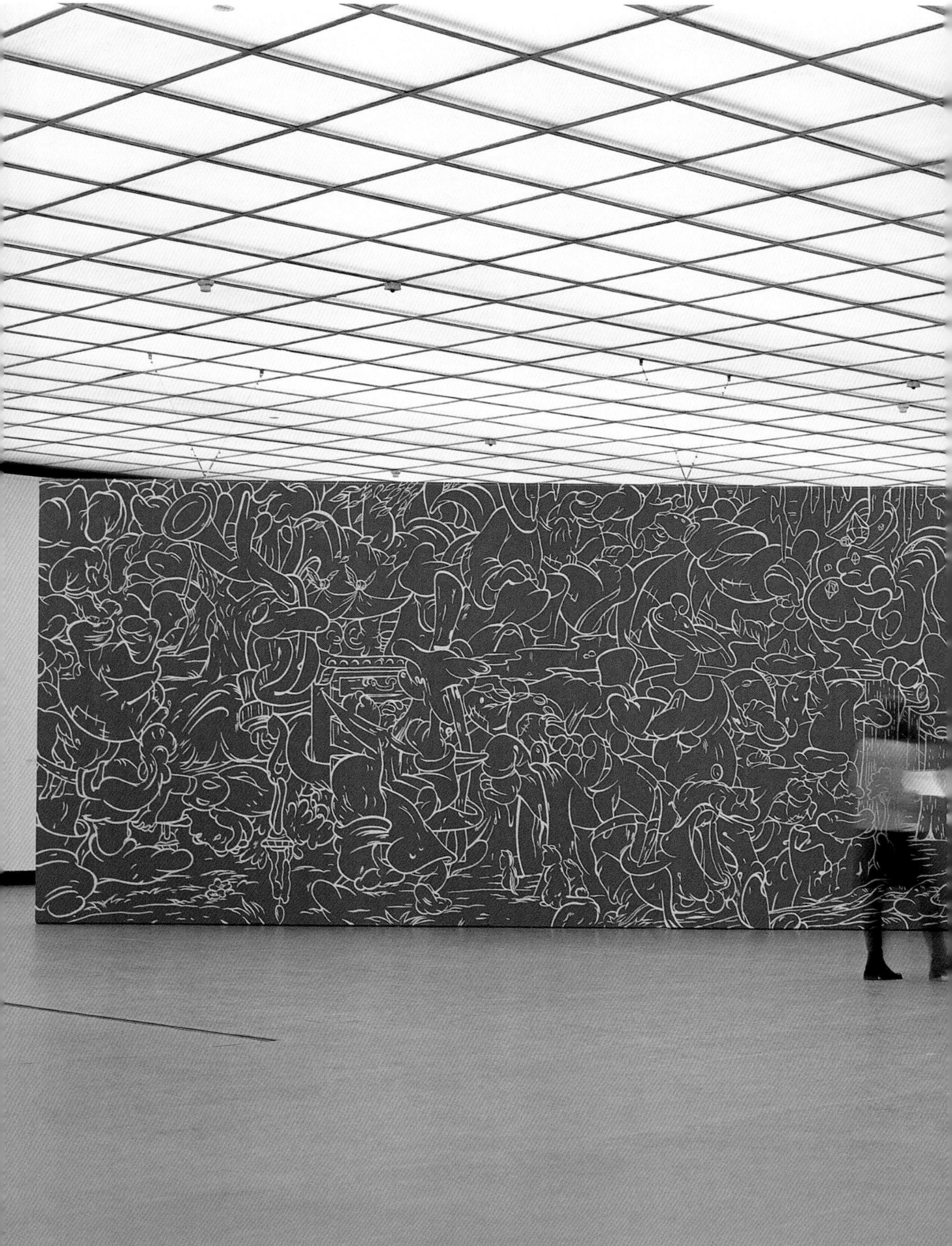

ABOVE installation view of **All I Ask** at Württembergischer Kunstverein, Stuttgart 1999 **OPPOSITE** detail of **All I Ask** 1999

Arturo Herrera

Born 1959 Venezuela; lives and works in New York City
Arturo Herrera's work in collage, photography, painting, and sculpture exploits the possibilities of juxtaposition, cropping, and exposure in the investigation of both formal and narrative conventions. He excerpts and recombines psychologically charged imagery from popular culture, specifically from comic strips, children's books, and Disney iconography. These large-scale wall paintings, often executed in off-key colors, extract and rearrange the ballooning gestures of cartoonish line drawings into massive conglomerates of fragmented images. The mutability of his forms—the balancing act between abstraction and representation, the Surrealist-inspired fusion of appropriated images, the dramatic shifting of scale—is central to the viewer's subjective experience: "I am interested in the effect of nonlinear and associative readings . . . and the potential of painted space to be an intimate receptacle for the imagination and an aesthetic experience." Herrera was recently artist-in-residence at ArtPace, San Antonio (1999–2000) and has had solo exhibitions at the Centre d'Art Contemporain, Geneva, Switzerland (2000), the Renaissance Society, University of Chicago (1998), and the Museum of Contemporary Art, Chicago (1995). His work was included in *Greater New York* at P.S.1 Contemporary Art Center, New York (2000), *Colour Me Blind!* at the Württembergischer Kunstverein, Stuttgart (1999), and the Istanbul Biennial (1999).

OPPOSITE Arturo Herrera detail of **All I Ask** 1999 latex on wall dimensions variable Image courtesy Brent Sikkema, New York; photo: Uwe Seyl, Stuttgart (checklist)

FOLDOUT installation view of **All I Ask** at Württembergischer Kunstverein, Stuttgart 1999 Image courtesy Brent Sikkema, New York; photo: Uwe Seyl, Stuttgart

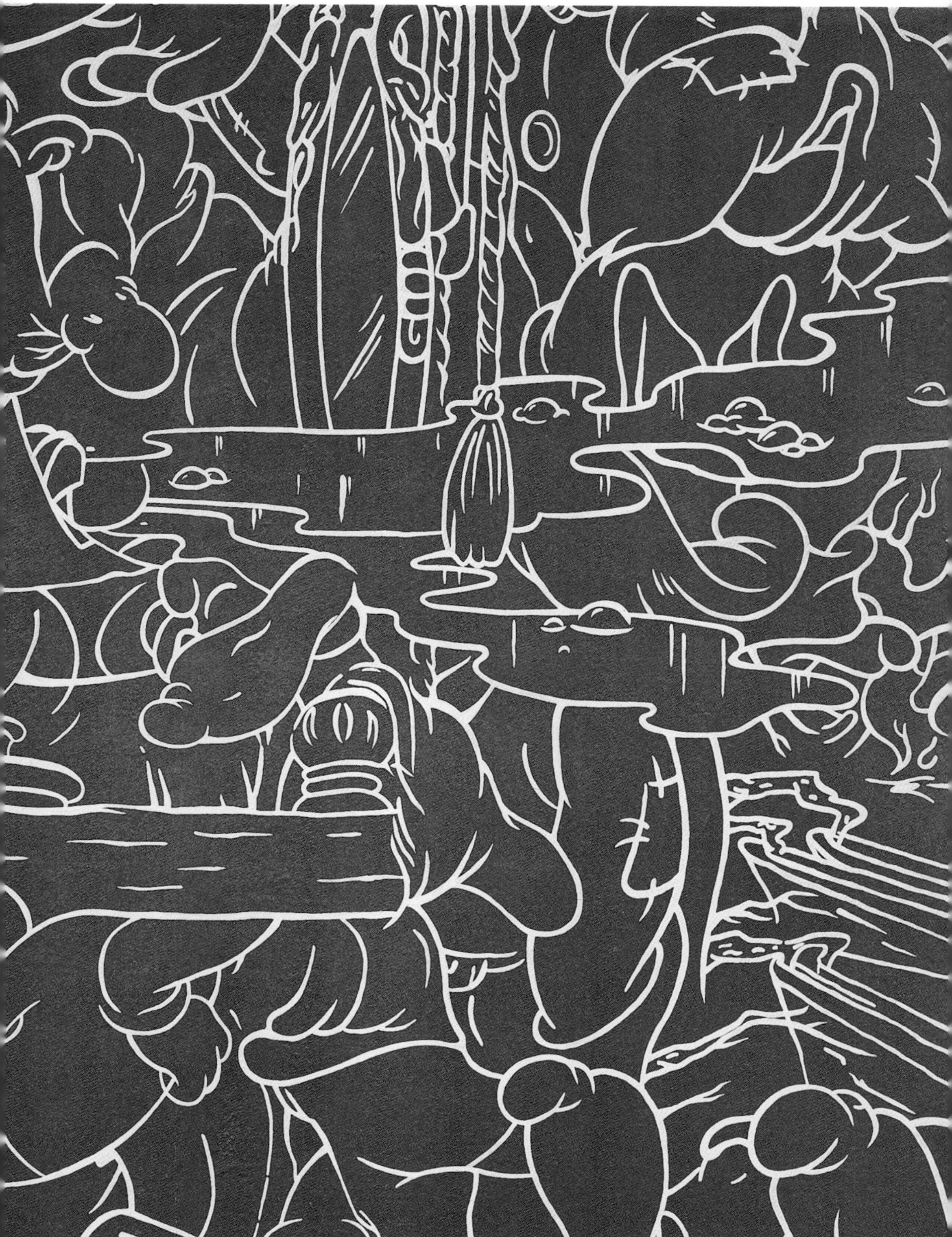

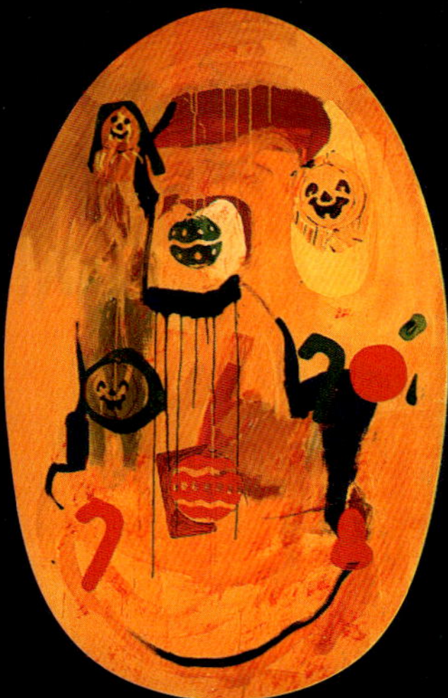
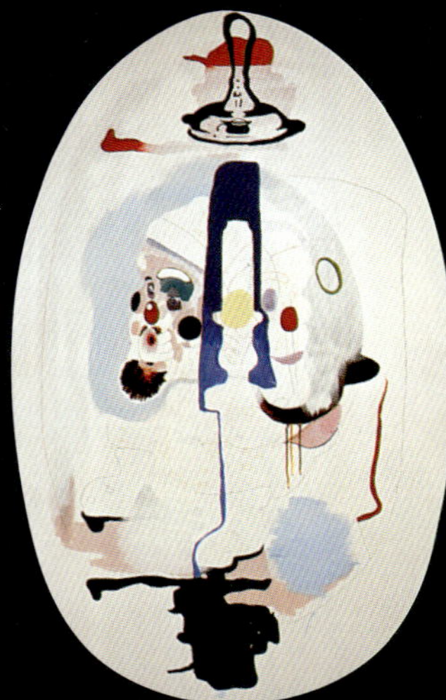
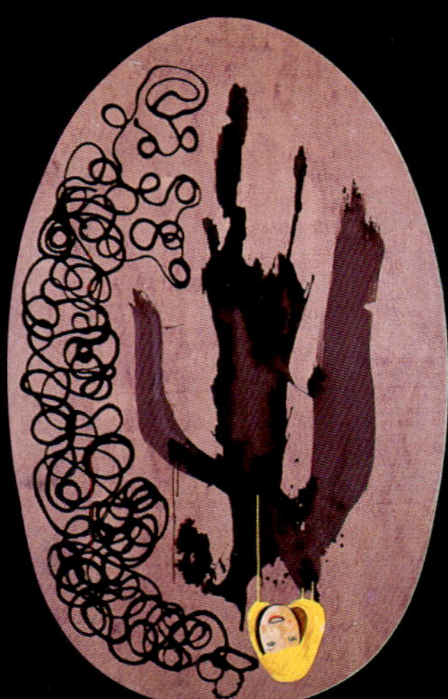
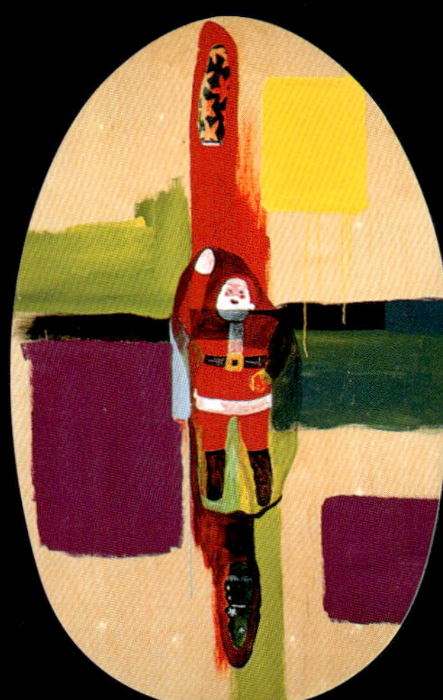
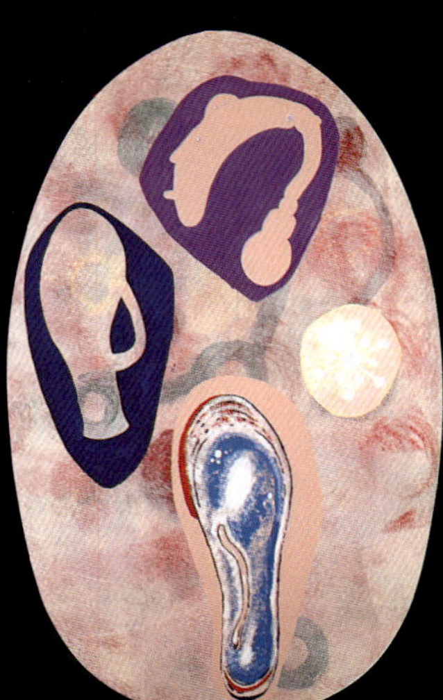
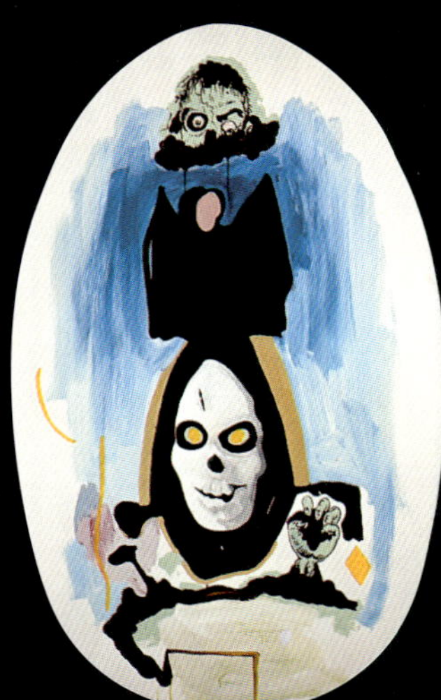

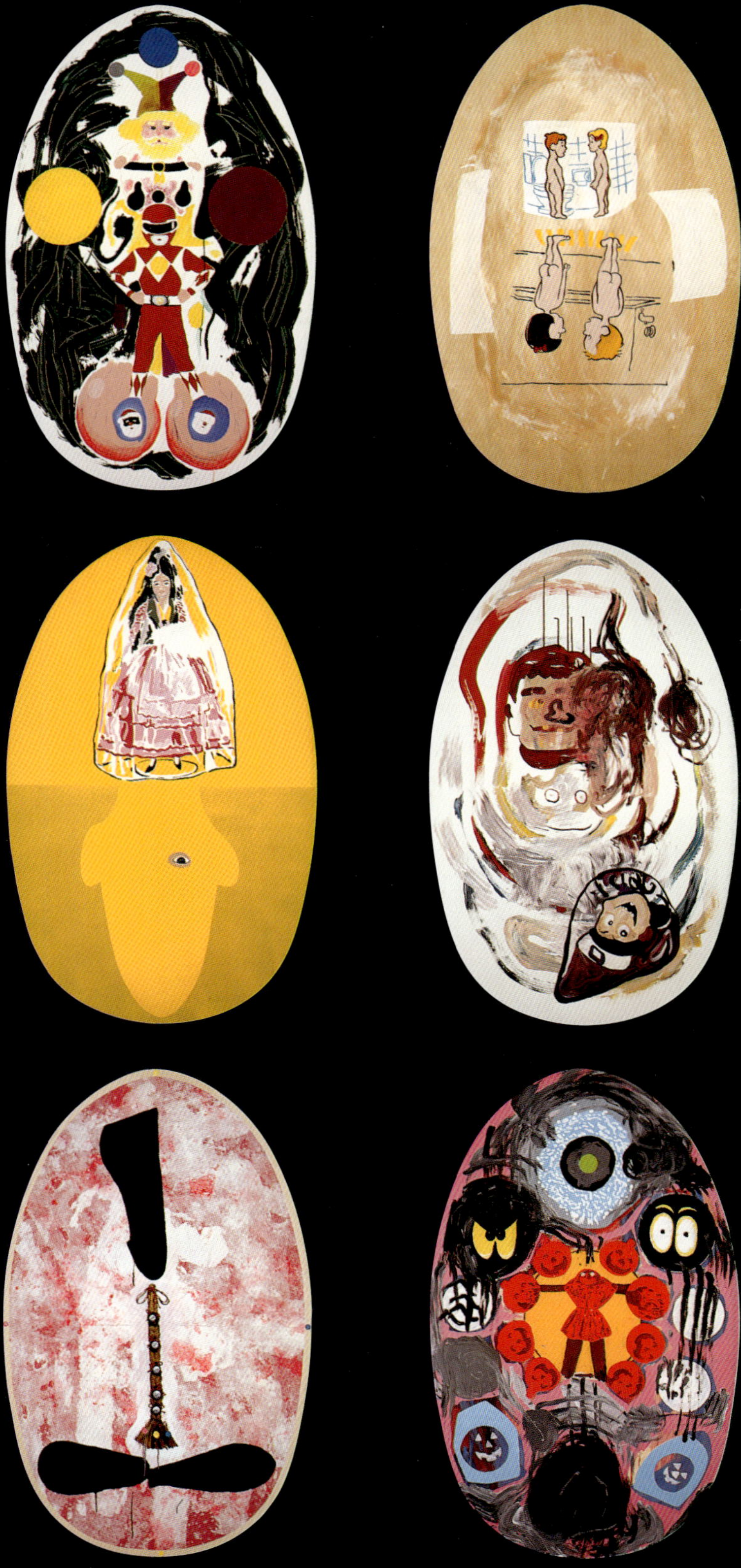

TOP TO BOTTOM, LEFT TO RIGHT
#1 The Birth of the New Year
#2 Fecundity
#3 What's Limp in 3D Is Erect in 2D
#4 The Dawning of Sexuality
#5 Summer's Rage
#6 Fall
#7 The Descent
#8 Cactus Flower
(The Purple Twilight of Middle Age)
#9 Snow on the Temples
#10 The Decay of the Year-End
#11 The Giving Old Man
#12 Death
#13 Art

Mike Kelley

Born 1954 United States; lives and works in Los Angeles
Since the 1970s Mike Kelley has mined the highly charged terrain of desire, repression, and dysfunction in everyday America through an inventive body of work that challenges prevailing notions of taste, authenticity, moral authority, and the transcendent function of art. Kelley trained with a disciple of Hans Hofmann, but rebuffed high-modernist convention, saying he'd "rather make adolescent art." He also sought to liberate ideas and objects that were repressed by the dominant discourse of Conceptual Art and Minimalism in the late 1960s and early 1970s. His discordant approach to art-making—which includes painting, performance, music, and installation—often eerily recontextualizes childhood imagery and craft objects, adopting the vocabulary of these banal artifacts to subversive ends. A prolific writer, Kelley often employs text in his work and drafts companion writings that mirror the aesthetics of his installations. Kelley has been the subject of major solo exhibitions at the Kunstverein Braunschweig (1999), Wiener Secession, Vienna (1998), the Museu d'Art Contemporani, Barcelona (1997), and the Whitney Museum of American Art, New York (1993). His work has been included in many important group exhibitions, including *documenta X*, Kassel (1997) and the Whitney Biennial, New York (1995).

Mike Kelley **The Thirteen Seasons (Heavy on the Winter)** 1994 acrylic on board thirteen paintings, 62 ½ x 40 in. each Images courtesy Jablonka Galerie, Cologne (checklist)

OPPOSITE **#13 Art** Private collection; Courtesy B.F.A.S., Blondeau Fine Art Services, SA

FOLDOUT (TOP TO BOTTOM, LEFT TO RIGHT)
#1 The Birth of the New Year Fondazione Sandretto Re Rebaudegno per l'Arte, Turin
#2 Fecundity Collection Drs. Michael and Eleonore Stoffel, Cologne
#3 What's Limp in 3D Is Erect in 2D Collection Brandhorst, Cologne
#4 The Dawning of Sexuality Private collection, Cologne
#5 Summer's Rage Collection Magali, T
#6 Fall Peter Stuyvesant Foundation, Amsterdam
#7 The Descent Peter Stuyvesant Foundation, Amsterdam
#8 Cactus Flower (The Purple Twilight of Middle Age) Lang Collection (not in exhibition)
#9 Snow on the Temples Collection Drs. Michael and Eleonore Stoffel, Cologne
#10 The Decay of Year-End Private collection, Essen
#11 The Giving Old Man Collection Hans Böhning, Cologne
#12 Death Collection Drs. Michael and Eleonore Stoffel, Cologne

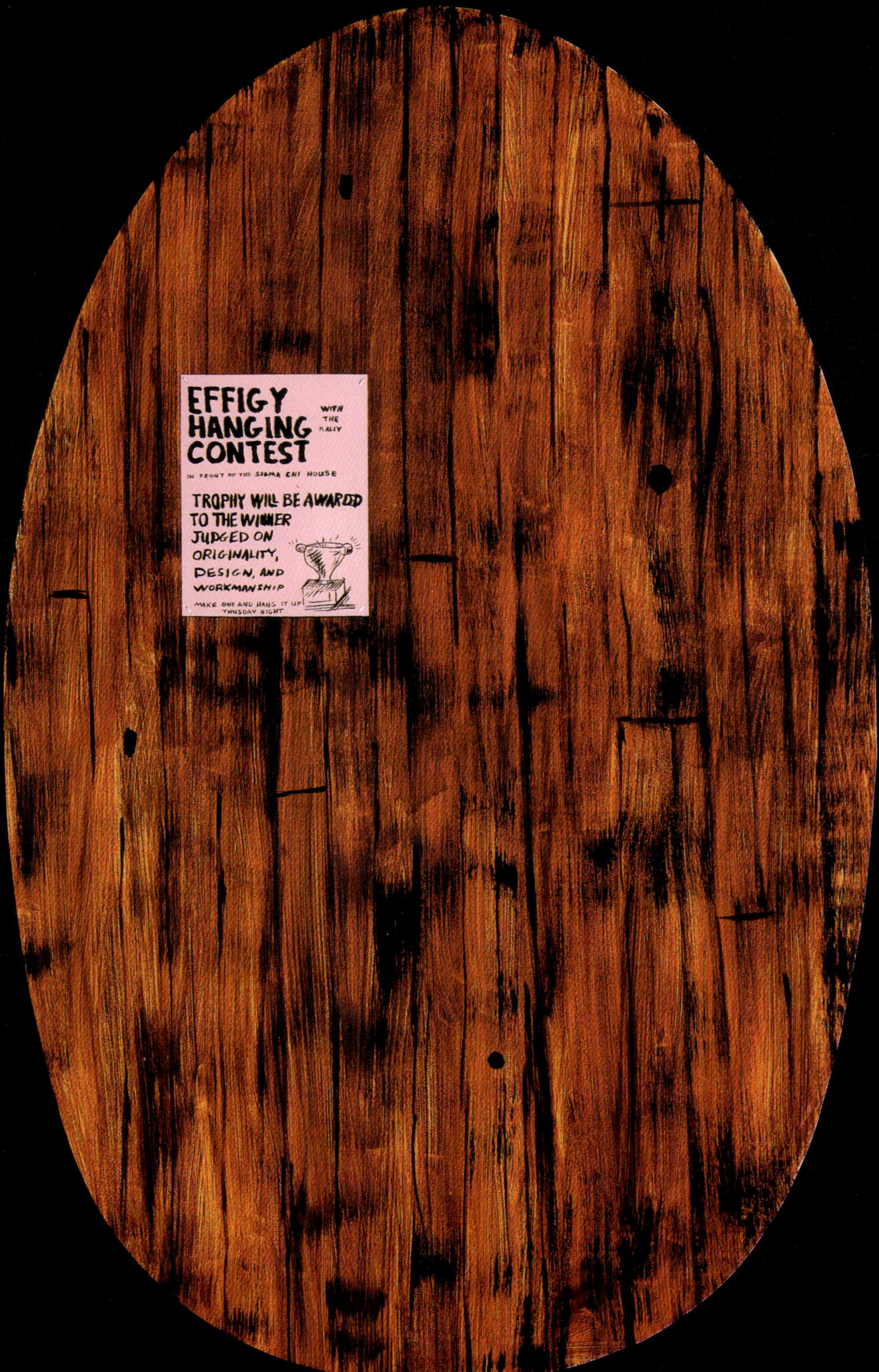
EFFIGY HANGING CONTEST
WITH THE RALLY
IN FRONT OF THE SIGMA CHI HOUSE
TROPHY WILL BE AWARDED TO THE WINNER
JUDGED ON ORIGINALITY, DESIGN, AND WORKMANSHIP
MAKE ONE AND HANG IT UP THUSDAY NIGHT

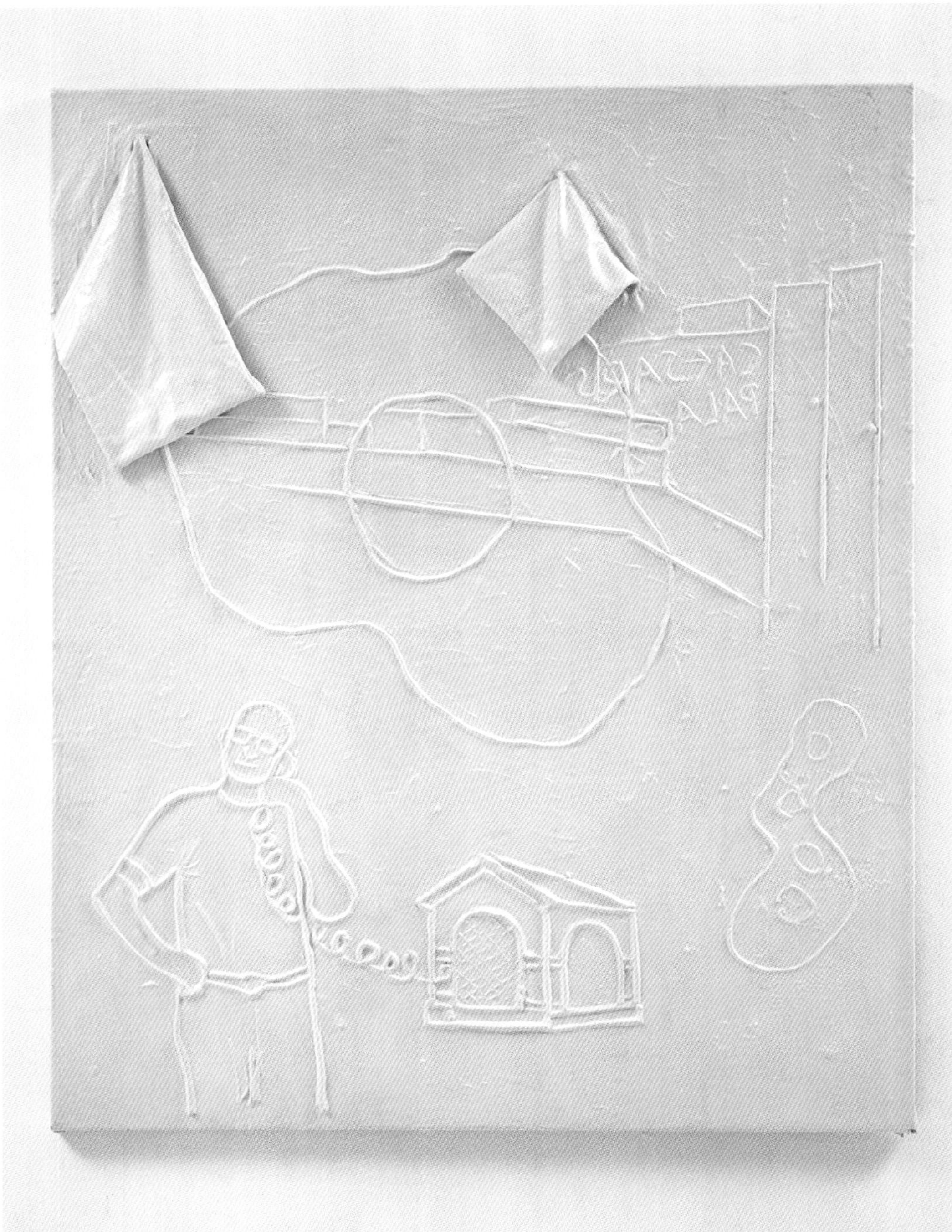

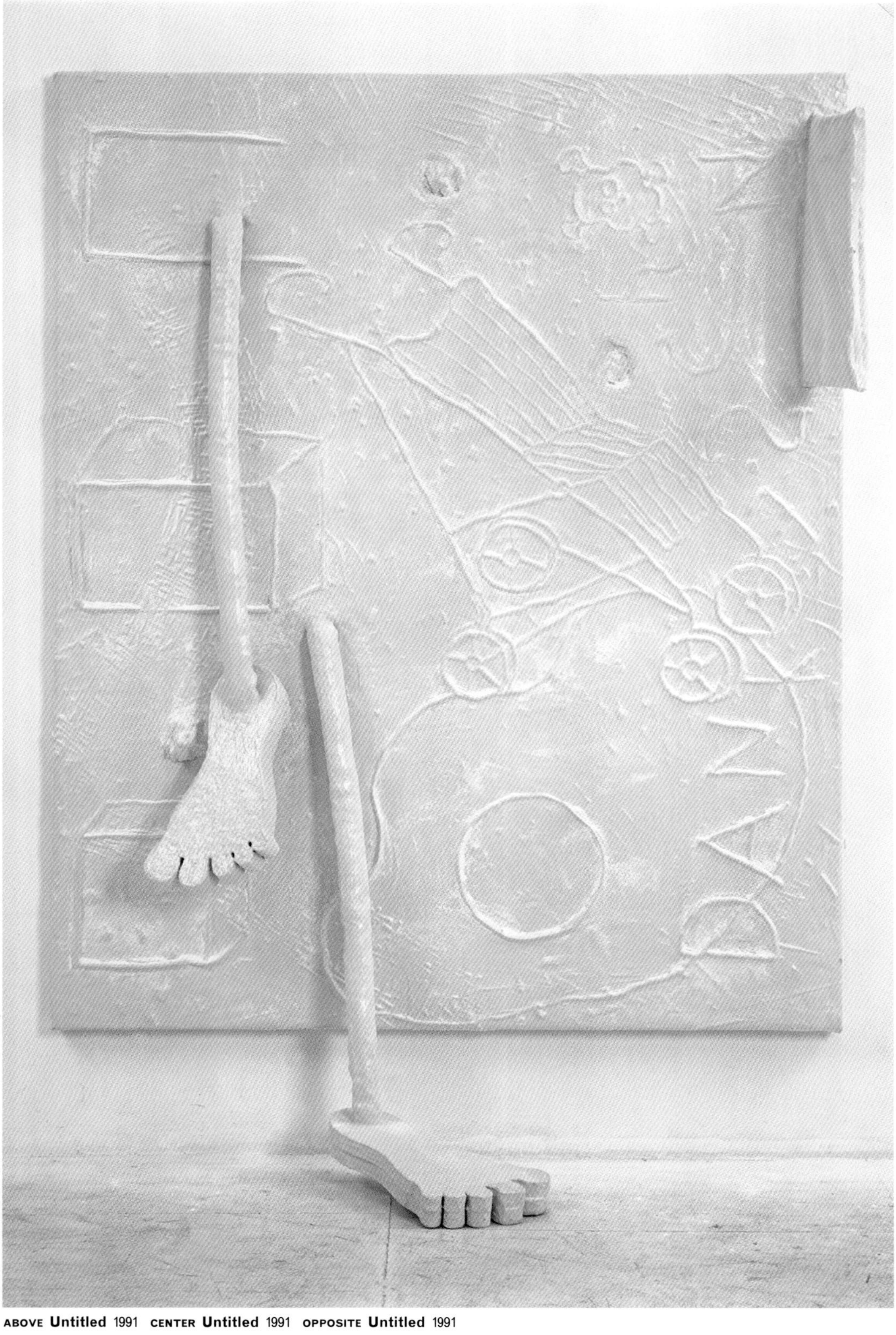

ABOVE **Untitled** 1991 **CENTER** **Untitled** 1991 **OPPOSITE** **Untitled** 1991

Martin Kippenberger

Born 1953 Germany; died 1997
As an artist who emerged in Germany in the early 1980s, Martin Kippenberger worked in every conceivable medium, creating a provocative body of work that challenged dominant art-historical discourses. While ideas about painting were a frequent subject of his artistic project, he exploded the traditional practice of painting, suggesting that "I am a traveling salesman. I deal in ideas. I do much more for people than just paint them pictures." While other artists were earnestly reexamining the painterly gesture, Kippenberger produced intentionally "bad" paintings, hiring professional sign painters to execute them. His installations and hybridized manifestations of painting, such as his cast-rubber works, consistently probed fundamental questions about the nature of art and the boundaries dividing media. A remarkably prolific artist, Kippenberger defies any attempt at categorization, as his practice extended to publishing, curating, and producing music shows and records, among other nontraditional activities. Major solo exhibitions of his work have been presented at the Kunsthalle Basel (1999), the Hirshhorn Museum and Sculpture Garden, Washington, D.C. (1995), and the Centre Georges Pompidou, Paris (1993). His work has also been included in numerous international exhibitions, including the *Carnegie International*, Pittsburgh (1999), *documenta X*, Kassel (1997), and *Skulptur Projekte*, Münster (1997).

OPPOSITE Martin Kippenberger **Untitled** 1991 latex, acrylic, pigments, foam on canvas 70 ¾ x 59 x 15 ¾ in.
Image courtesy Galerie Gisela Capitain, Cologne (checklist)

FOLDOUT (LEFT) Martin Kippenberger **Untitled** 1991 latex, acrylic, pigments, foam on canvas 70 ¾ x 59 x 15 ¾ in.
Image courtesy Galerie Gisela Capitain, Cologne (checklist)
(RIGHT) Martin Kippenberger **Untitled** 1991 rubber, acrylic on canvas 70 ¾ x 59 x 4 ⅝ in.
Private collection Image courtesy Barbara Gladstone Gallery, New York (checklist)

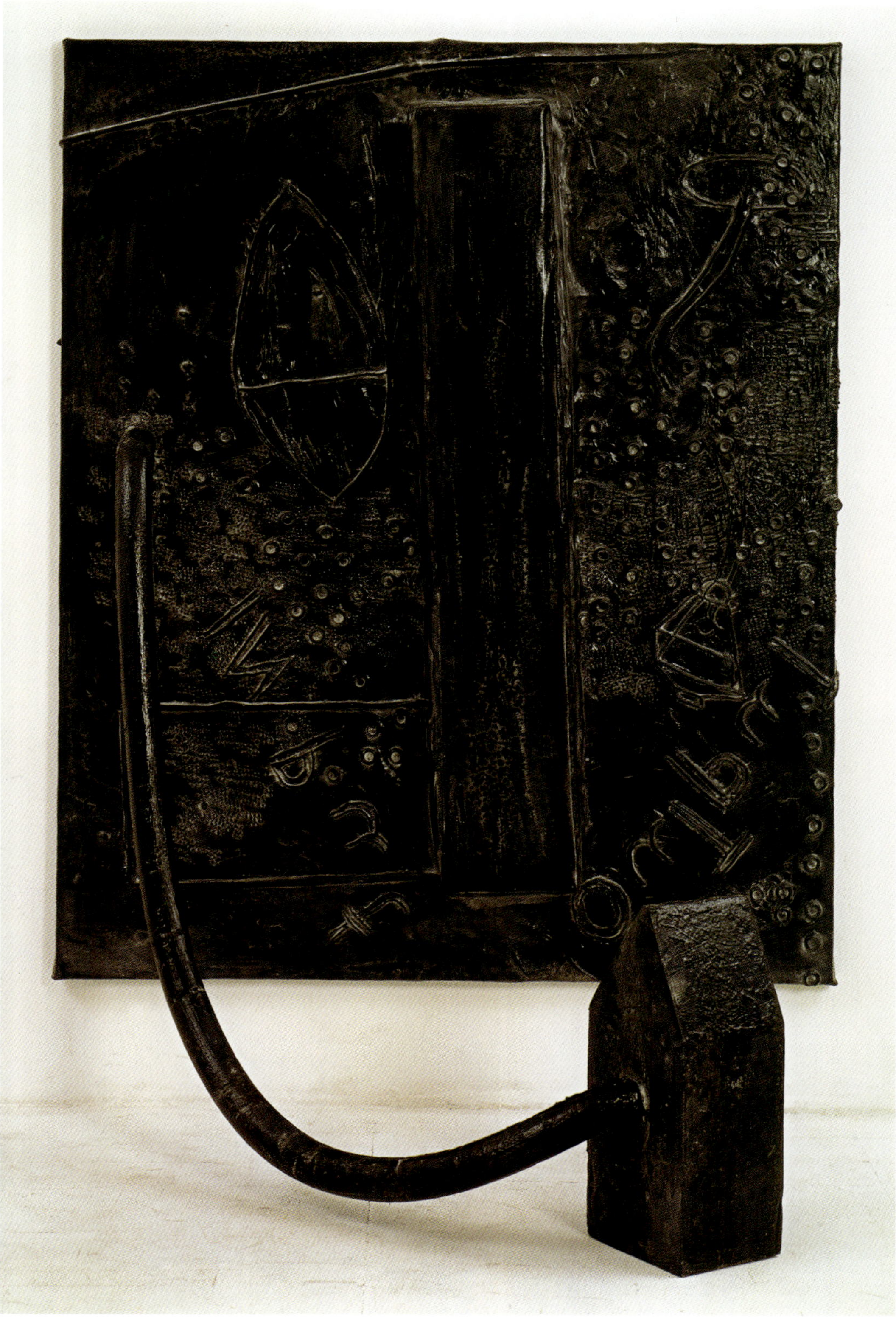

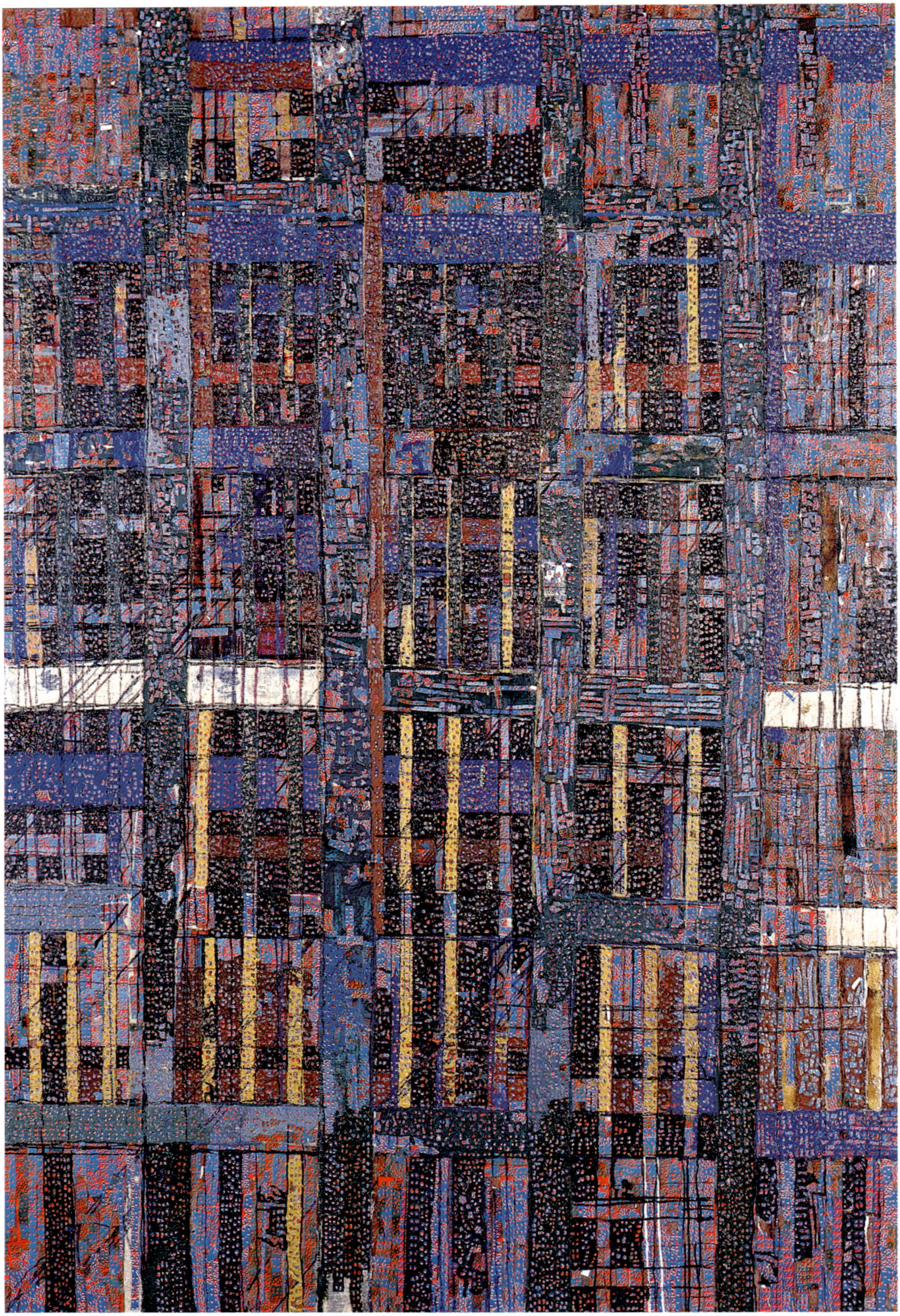

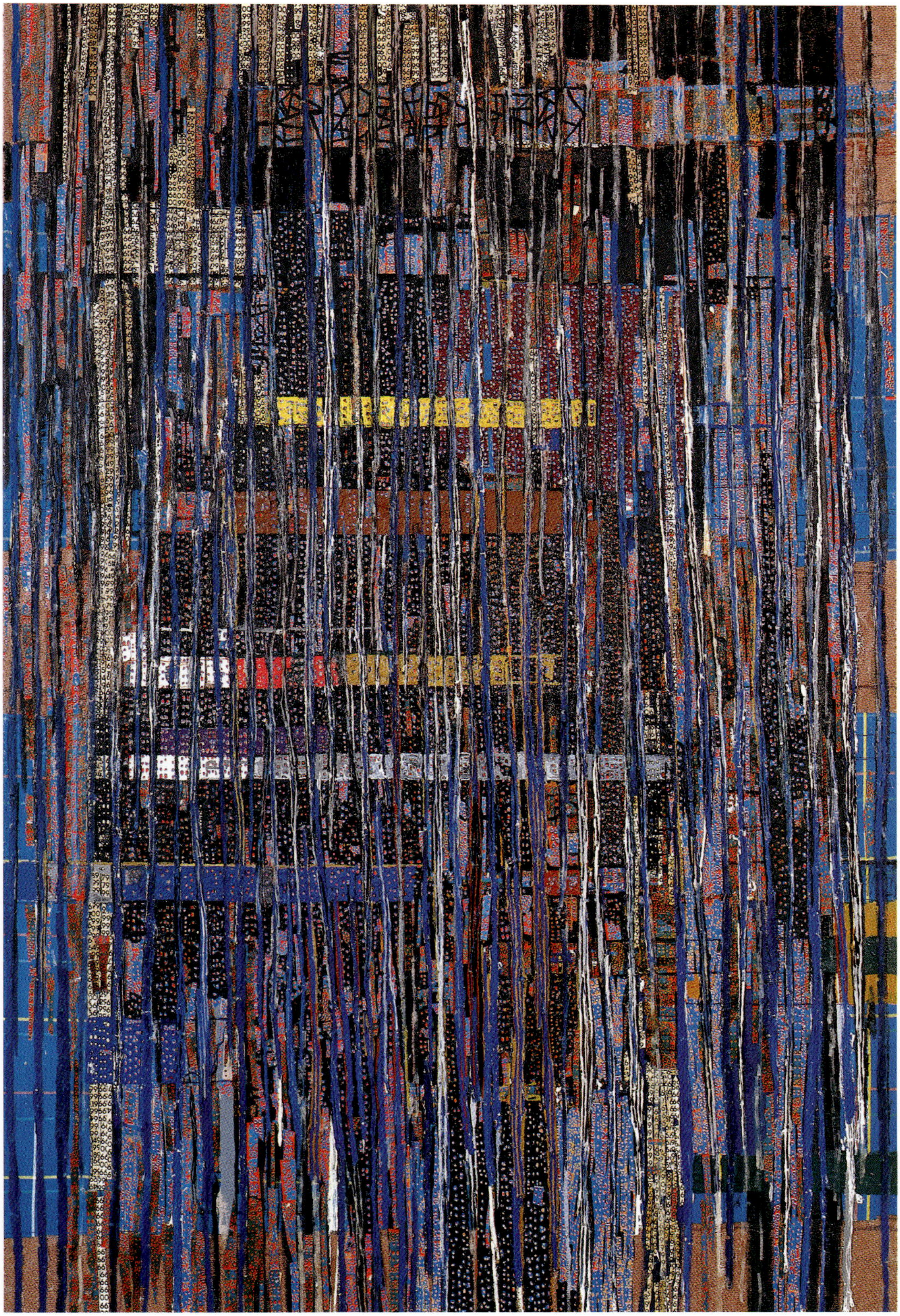

ABOVE **Candy Apple** 2000 CENTER **Road Hole** 2000 OPPOSITE **Avalanche** 2000

Udomsak Krisanamis

Born 1968 Thailand; lives and works in New York City
Udomsak Krisanamis makes use of an eclectic range of materials to create idiosyncratic, personally inflected paintings that investigate the space between abstraction and representation, pattern and gesture, presence and absence. His early works employ a technique adapted from his unique process of learning the English language by reading newspapers and blacking out each word he knew along the way. In these paintings, the obsessively collaged substrate of newspaper is painted over, leaving the unmarked negative spaces inside each letter to emerge as a dense, all-over pattern of circles and ovals. His recent work, in which materials such as price stickers and rice noodles are collaged into physically and symbolically layered surfaces, sustains this investigation of abstraction that opens itself to narrative associations. Krisanamis has participated in numerous international exhibitions, including *Greater New York* at P.S.1 Contemporary Art Center, New York (2000), *Examining Pictures* at the Whitechapel Art Gallery, London, and the Museum of Contemporary Art, Chicago (1999), the Sydney Biennial (1998), and *Truce: Echoes of Art in an Age of Endless Conclusions* at SITE Santa Fe (1997). He has also been the subject of solo exhibitions at the Wexner Center for the Arts, Columbus (2000) and the Henry Art Gallery, Seattle (1997).

OPPOSITE Udomsak Krisanamis **Avalanche** 2000 collage, acrylic, felt-tip pen ink, noodles on cotton fabric 72 x 48 in. Collection Bernardo and Laura Nadal-Ginard, Chestnut Hill, Massachusetts Image courtesy Gavin Brown's enterprise, New York (checklist)

FOLDOUT (LEFT) Udomsak Krisanamis **Candy Apple** 2000 collage, acrylic, felt-tip pen ink, noodles on burlap 72 x 48 in. Collection William Goldiner, Pikesville, Maryland Image courtesy Gavin Brown's enterprise, New York (checklist)
(RIGHT) Udomsak Krisanamis **Road Hole** 2000 collage, acrylic, felt-tip pen ink on blanket 72 x 48 in. Collection Michael Lynne, New York Image courtesy Gavin Brown's enterprise, New York (checklist)

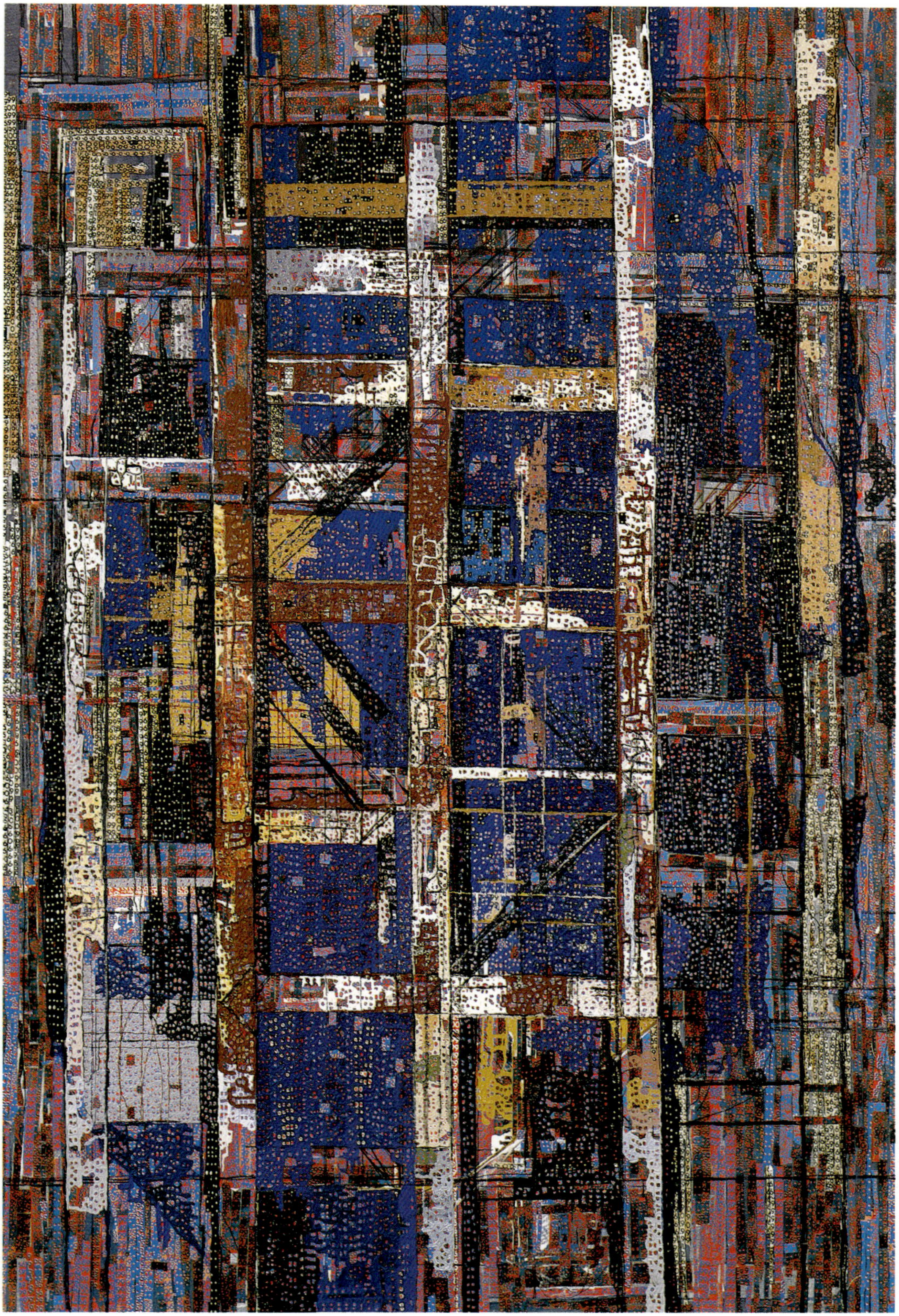

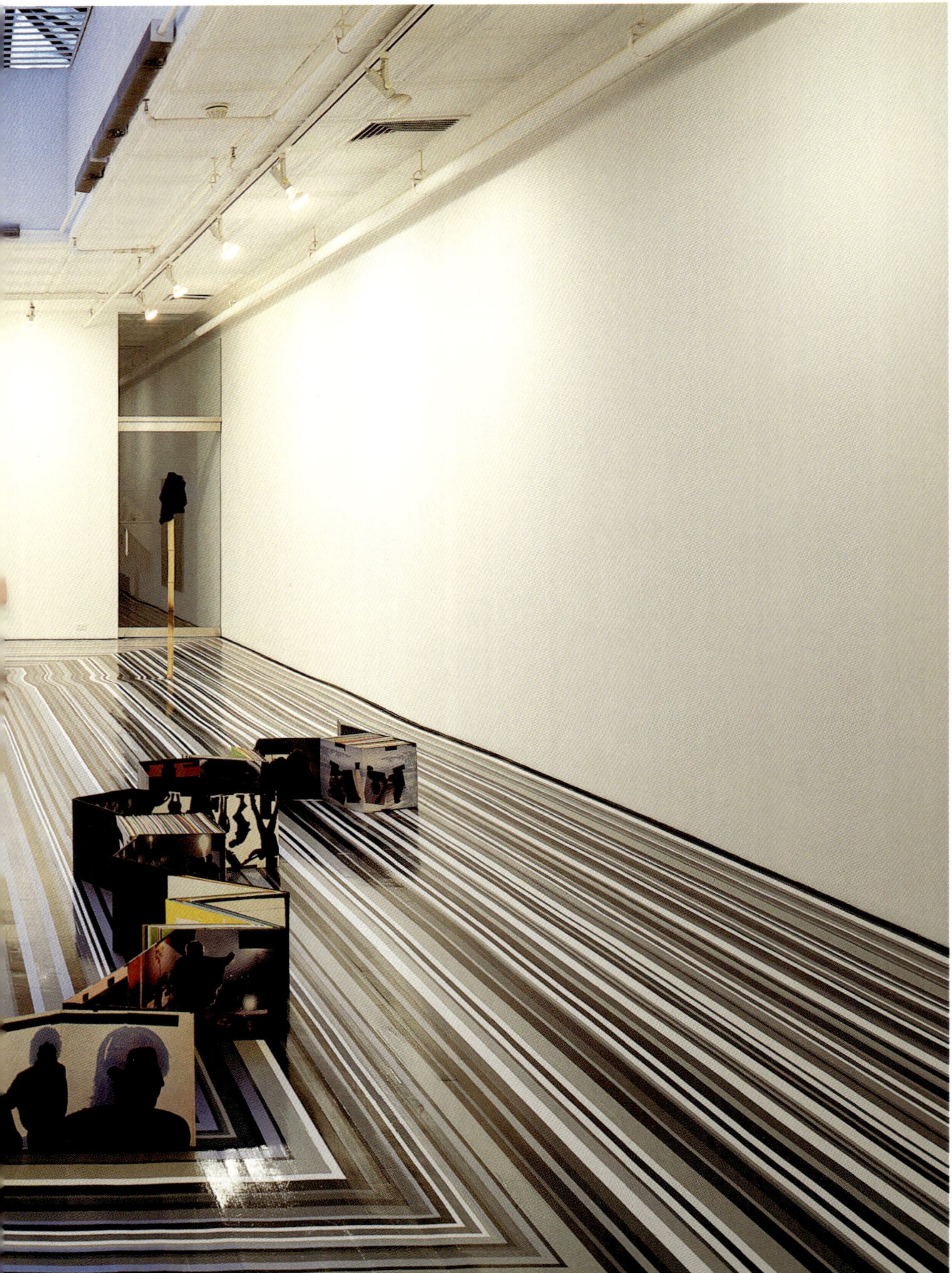

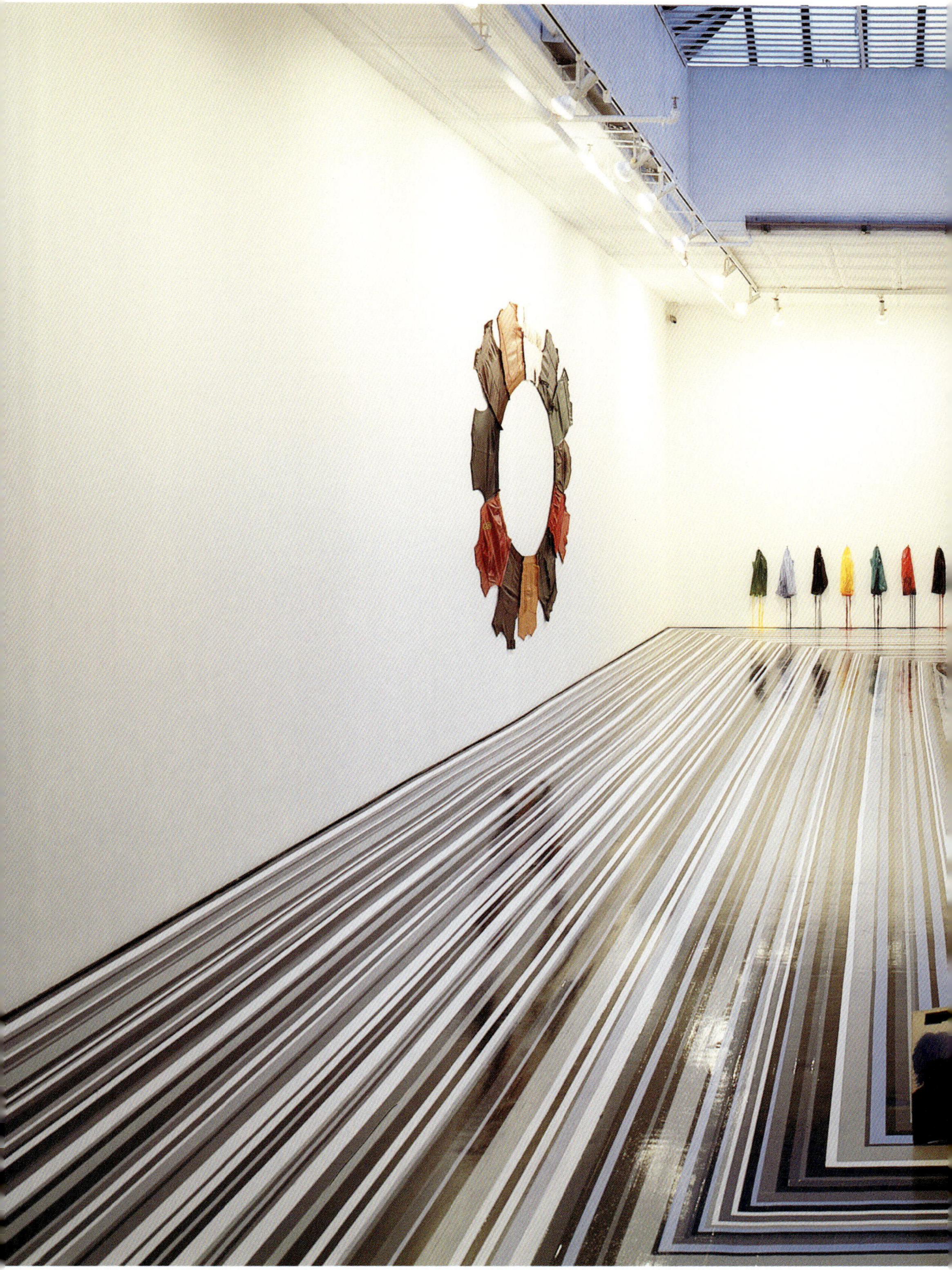

ABOVE installation view of **Blackgloss** at Anton Kern Gallery, New York 2000 **OPPOSITE** **18 Carrots** 1996

Jim Lambie

Born 1964 Scotland; lives and works in Glasgow
Jim Lambie's installations explore the experiential possibilities of spatial perception. In works such as *Blackgloss* and *ZOBOP*, Lambie's interventions "paint" the floor in concentric strips of vinyl tape that respond to the arbitrariness of the given architectural context. Whether vibrantly colored or composed of variations on black and white, the tape follows the contours of the room, in effect highlighting and intensifying the idiosyncrasies of the built environment. His engagement with the floor invites comparison to the radical gesture of Jackson Pollock, while the formal rigor of these installations invokes the legacy of Frank Stella and Sol LeWitt. But Lambie's work is rooted in a particular cultural circumstance—his involvement in the Glasgow club and music scene—and he often incorporates elements such as album covers and band posters into his settings. His artistic practice parallels the potentially transcendent experience of music in the shaping of ambience, which has led one critic to dub his works "Psychedelicsoulspaces." Lambie was selected to participate in *The British Art Show*, Hayward Gallery, London (2000) and he has been included in group exhibitions at the Moderna Museet, Stockholm (2000), Dundee Contemporary Arts, Scotland (2000), Stills Gallery, Edinburgh (1999), and Transmission Gallery, Glasgow (1999, 1997).

OPPOSITE Jim Lambie **18 Carrots** 1996 carrots, gloss paint dimensions variable Image courtesy The Modern Institute, Glasgow

FOLDOUT installation view of **Blackgloss** 2000 vinyl tape dimensions variable at Anton Kern Gallery, New York Image courtesy Anton Kern Gallery, New York

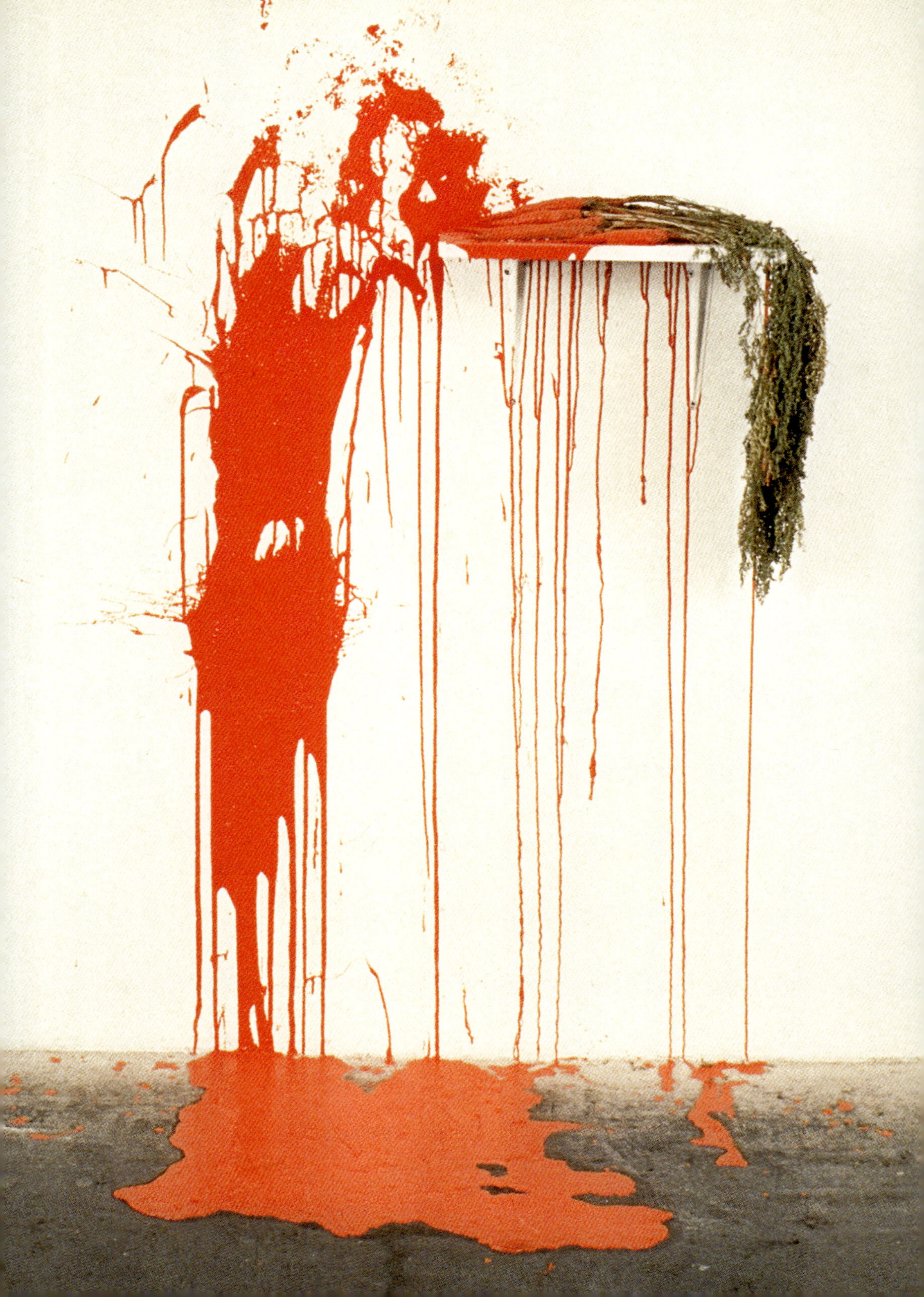

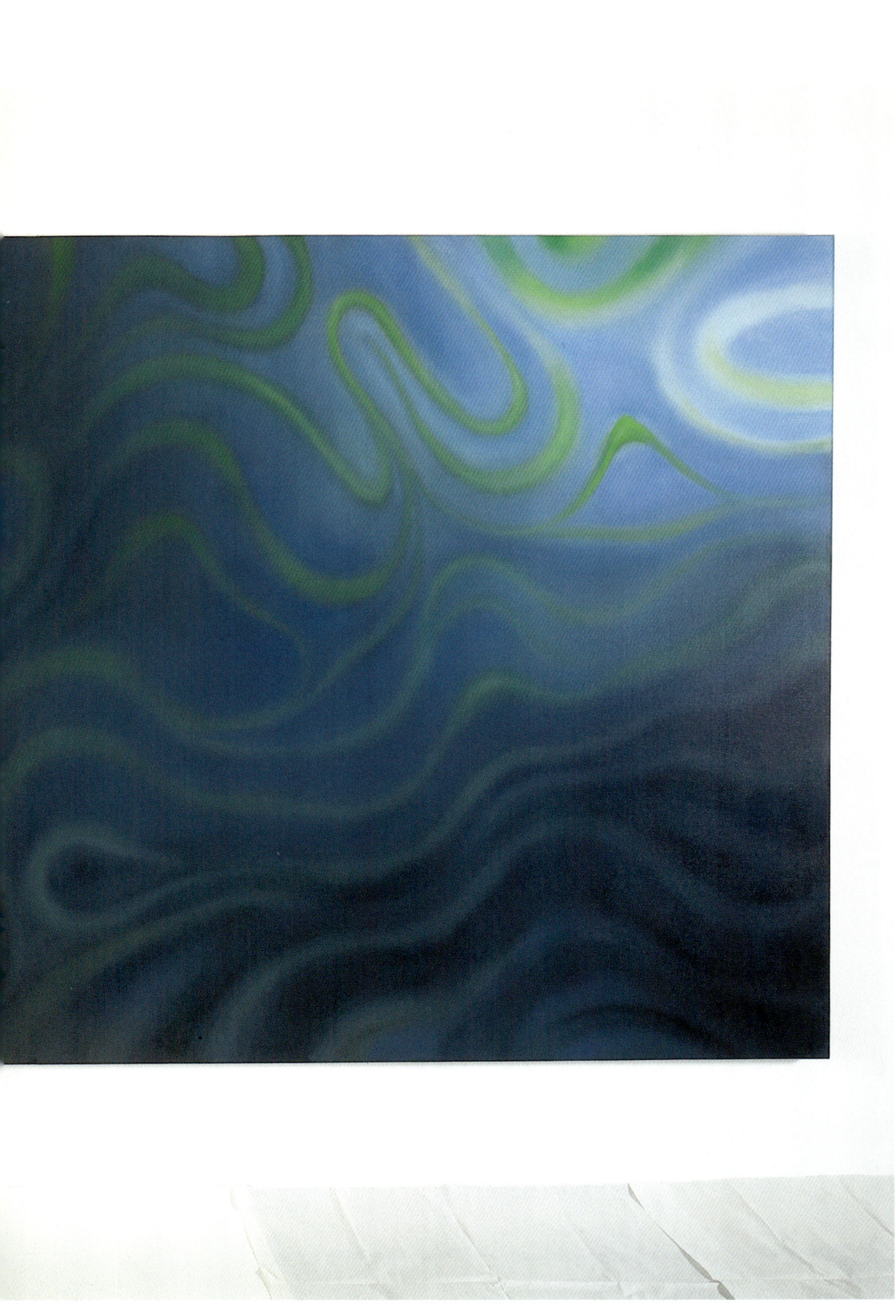

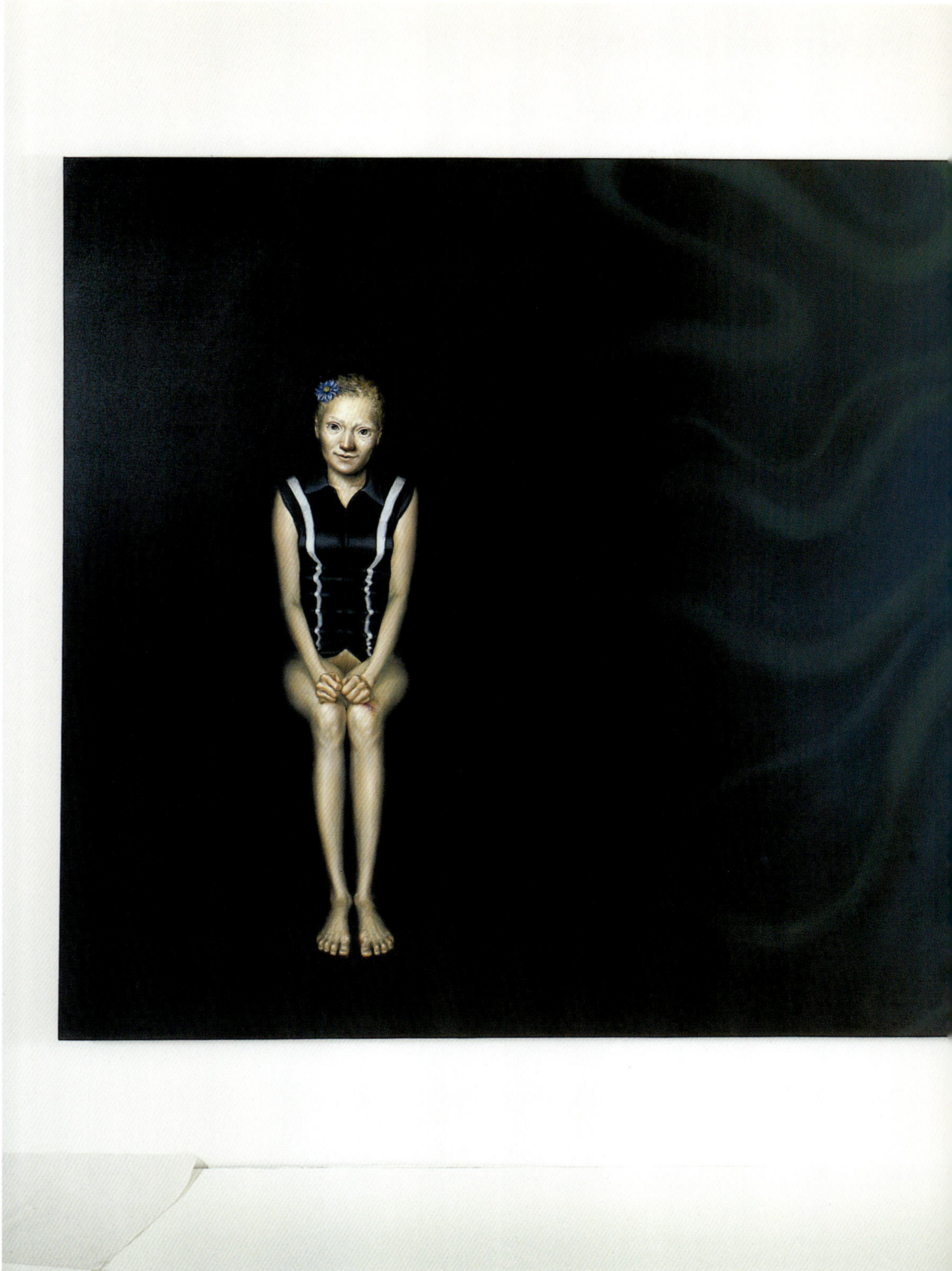

ABOVE **Binaural** 2000 OPPOSITE **Nottem** 2000

Margherita Manzelli

Born 1968 Italy; lives and works in Milan

Although Margherita Manzelli's large-scale paintings are not deliberately intended as self-portraits, they betray a physical and psychic resemblance to the artist. As she states, "I would like them to be different to me. And yet I realize that this very desire is symptomatic of the fact that something of myself remains in them." These invented bodies exhibit distortions of the flesh, in terms of color, proportions, and their slightly unhealthy, emaciated shapes. They inhabit largely empty, abstract, and anonymous spaces and are often frozen in awkward positions. They do not, however, seem caught "off guard." Rather, the inert figures engage directly with the viewer, inviting speculation about their emotional states but ultimately projecting a determined sense of self. Manzelli has been exhibiting internationally since the early 1990s and recently participated in the Istanbul Biennial (1999). Her work was included in *Examining Pictures* at the Whitechapel Art Gallery, London, and the Museum of Contemporary Art, Chicago (1999), as well as in group exhibitions at the Institute of Contemporary Arts, London (1997) and the Palazzo Re Rebaudegno per l'Arte Contemporanea, Guarene, Italy (1996).

OPPOSITE Margherita Manzelli **Nottem** 2000 oil on canvas 98 ½ x 78 ¾ in. Image courtesy Studio Guenzani, Milan (checklist)

FOLDOUT Margherita Manzelli **Binaural** 2000 oil on canvas 71 x 145 ½ in. Private collection Image courtesy Studio Guenzani, Milan (checklist)

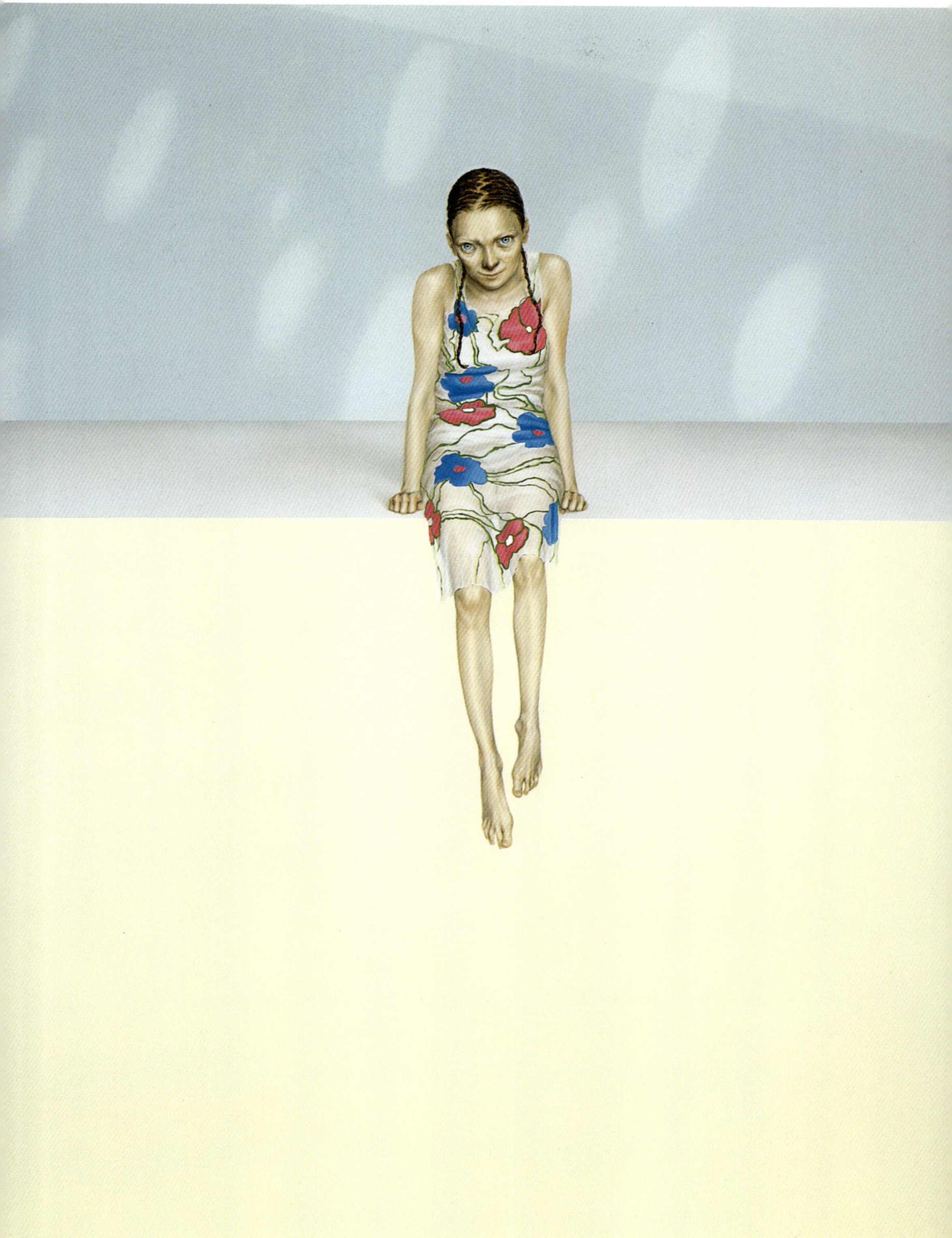

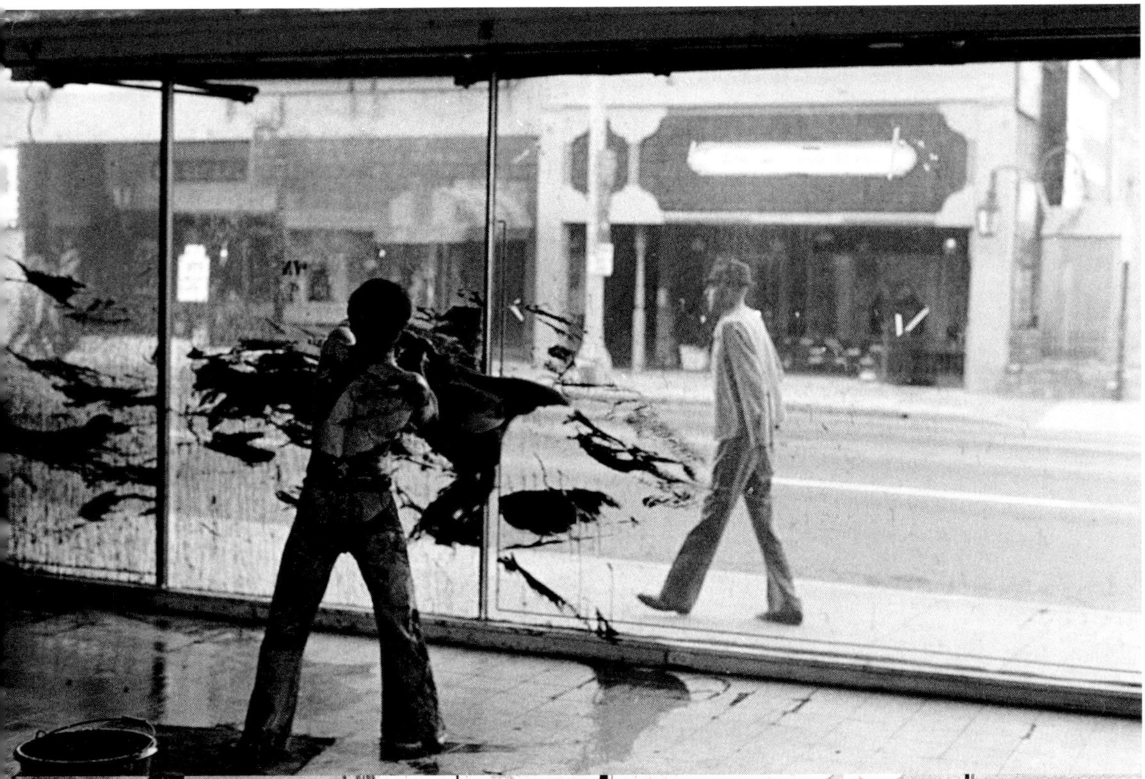

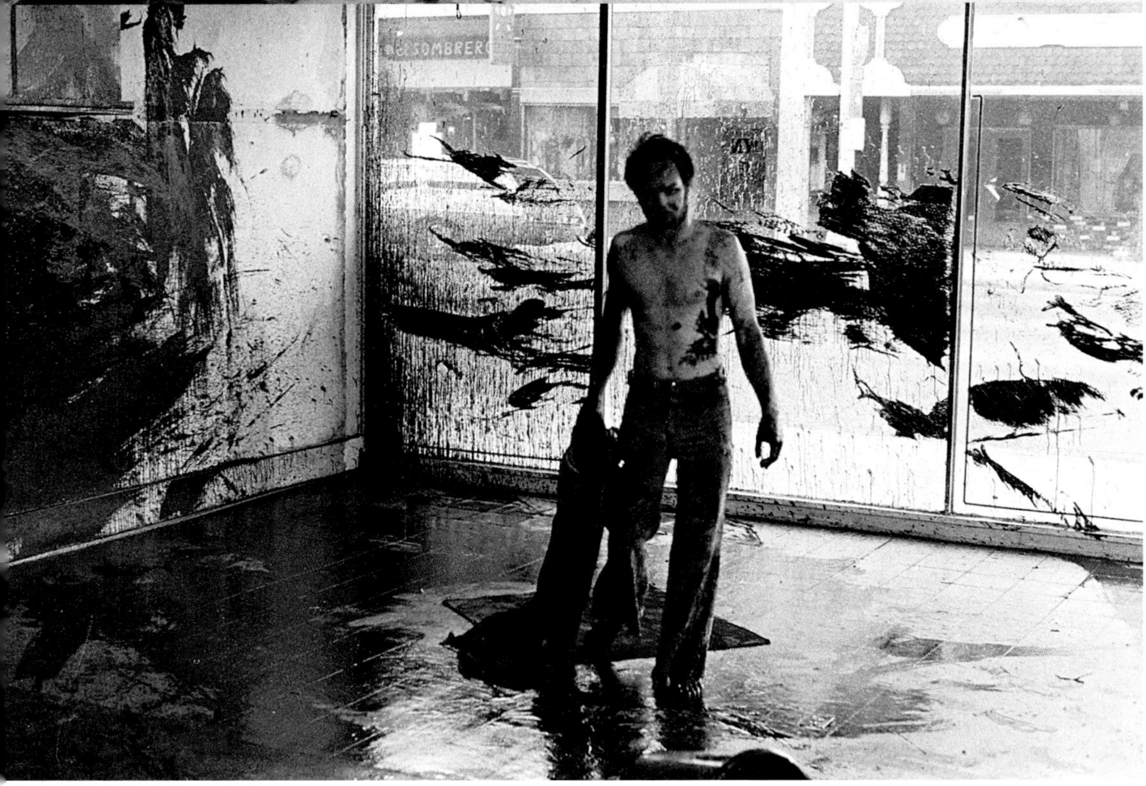

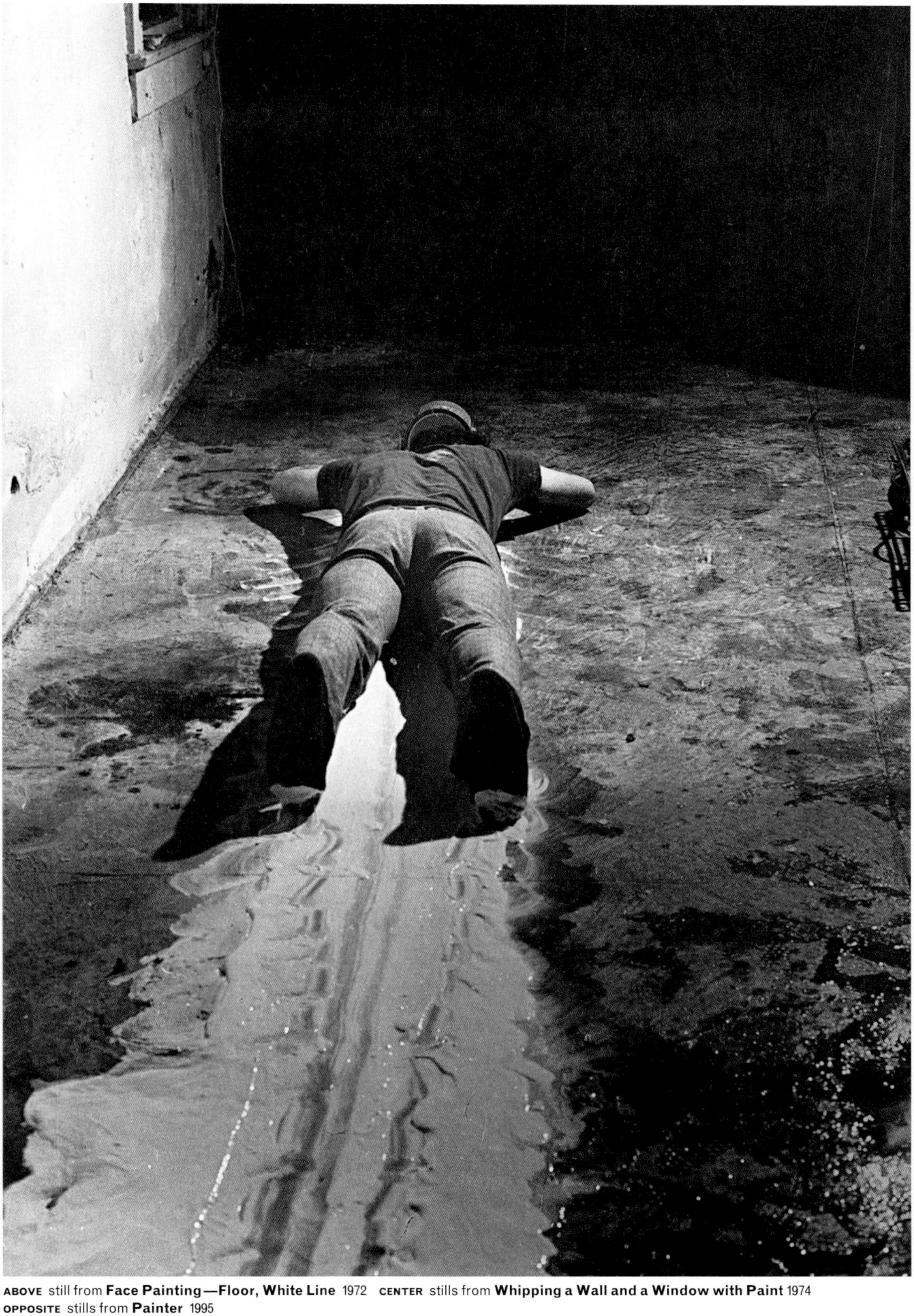

ABOVE still from **Face Painting—Floor, White Line** 1972 **CENTER** stills from **Whipping a Wall and a Window with Paint** 1974
OPPOSITE stills from **Painter** 1995

Paul McCarthy

Born 1945 United States; lives and works in Los Angeles
Since the early 1970s Paul McCarthy has pursued a course of performative art-making that tests the boundaries of conventional art practice and aesthetics, while challenging the physical and psychological limits of the body. Presented as live performances, installations, and video documentation, his work explores notions of artifice and spectacle through the enacting of aberrant behaviors that have little obvious political, cultural, or psychological purpose. McCarthy's orgiastic, performative use of materials such as ketchup, mayonnaise, paint, and surrogate bodily fluids belies his early interest in the action painting of Jackson Pollock and the destructive practices of the Viennese Actionists. Largely improvised, his grueling and psychologically charged works often desecrate traditional notions of family values, colonialism, and even the history of modernist painting in their visual and visceral onslaught. McCarthy's career was surveyed in an important solo exhibition at the Museum of Contemporary Art, Los Angeles, and the New Museum, New York (2000–2001). Other recent exhibitions and venues that have presented his work include the Sydney Biennial (2000), the Museum of Contemporary Art, San Diego (1997), and the Whitney Biennial, New York (1997).

OPPOSITE Paul McCarthy stills from **Painter** 1995 videotape transferred to laserdisc Images courtesy the artist, Altadena, California (checklist)

FOLDOUT (LEFT) Paul McCarthy still from **Face Painting—Floor, White Line** 1972 performance videotape transferred to laserdisc Image courtesy the artist, Altadena, California (checklist)
(RIGHT) Paul McCarthy stills from **Whipping a Wall and a Window with Paint** 1974 performance videotape transferred to laserdisc Images courtesy the artist, Altadena, California (checklist)

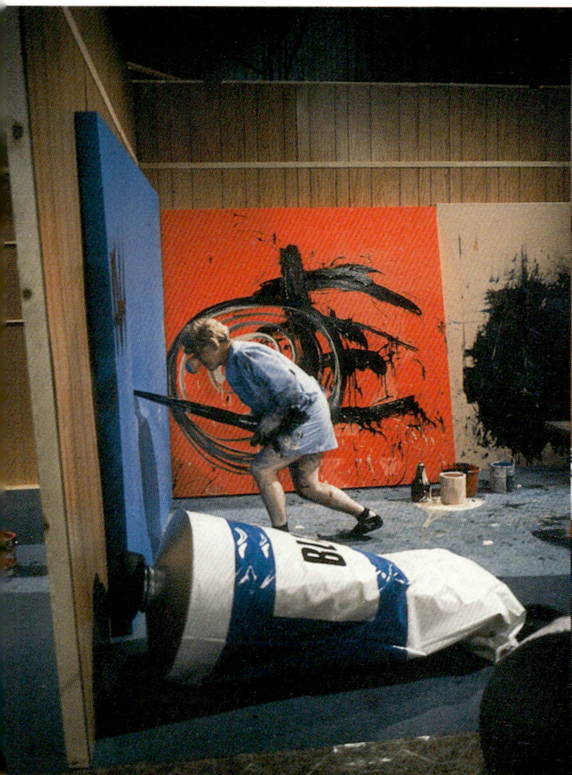
BL

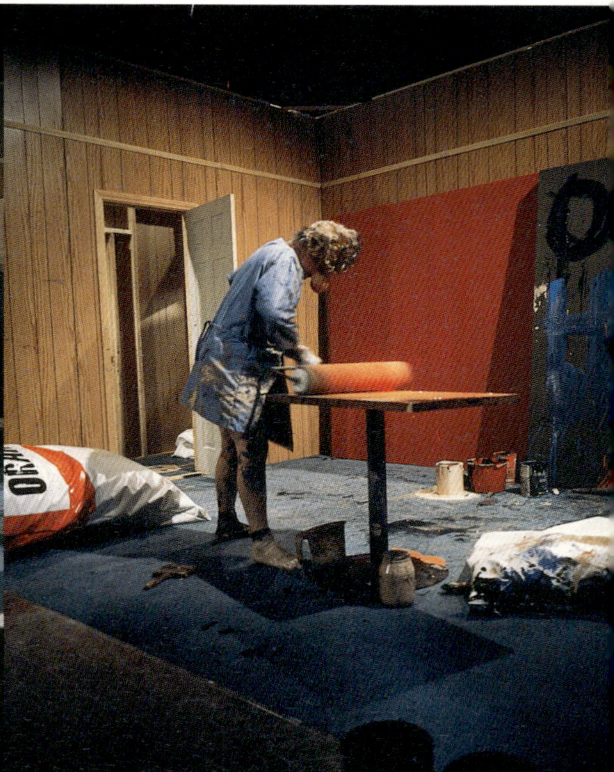

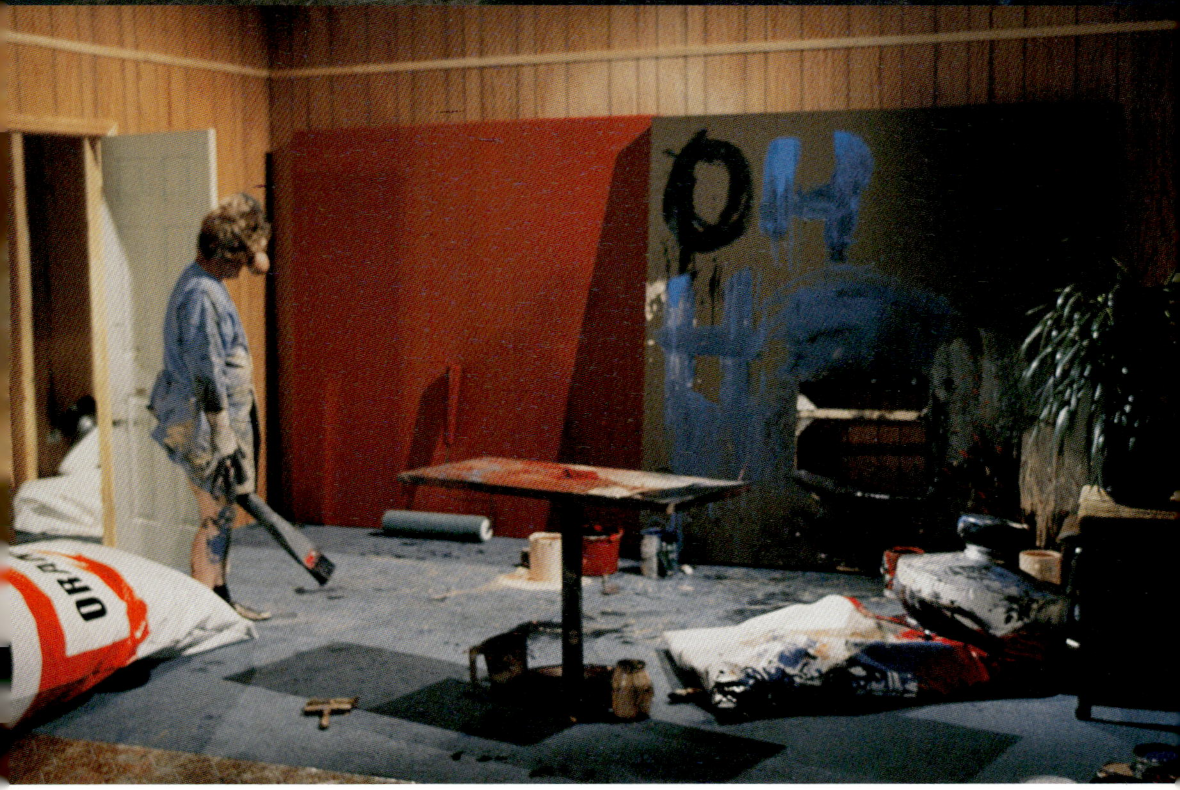
OH

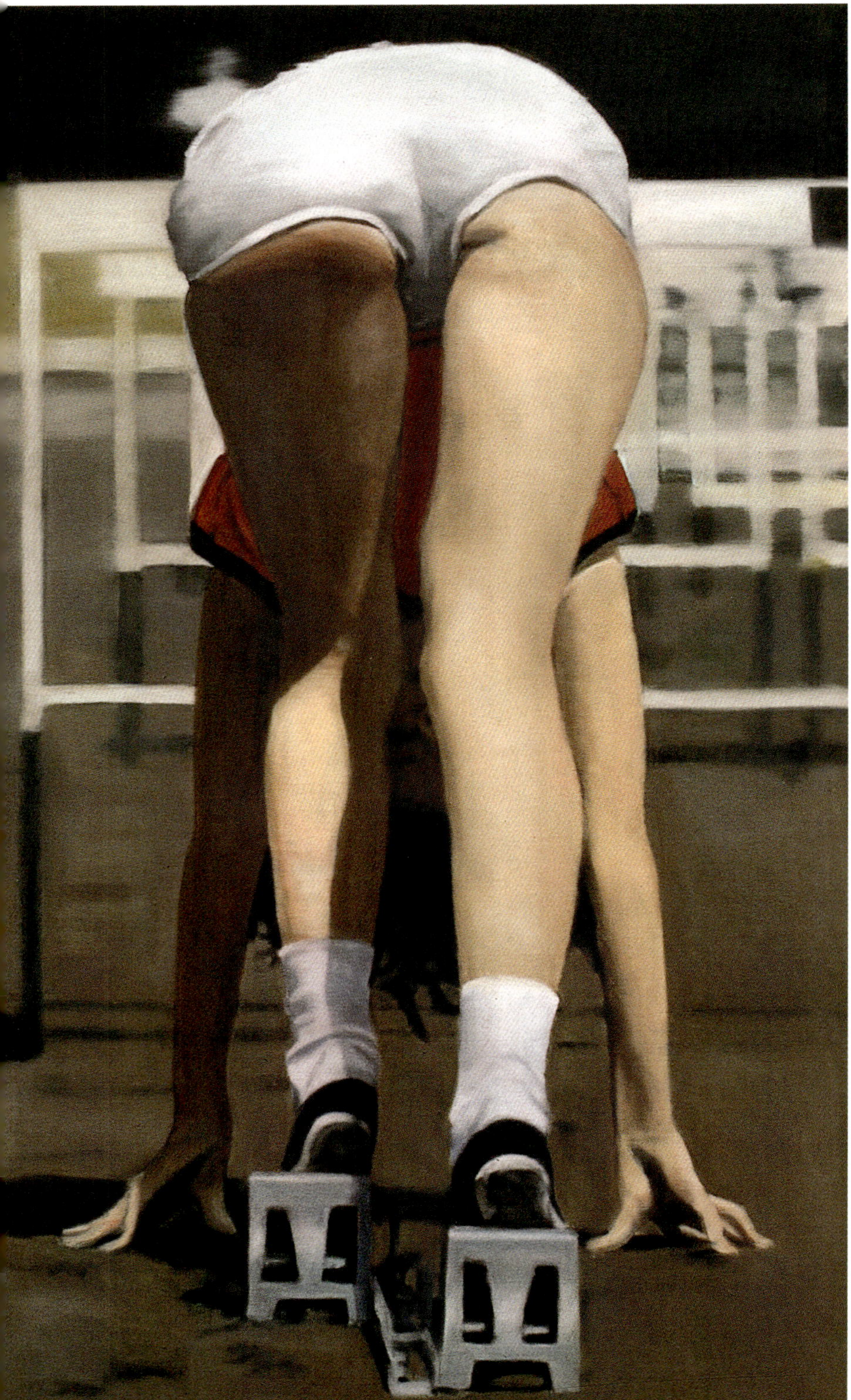

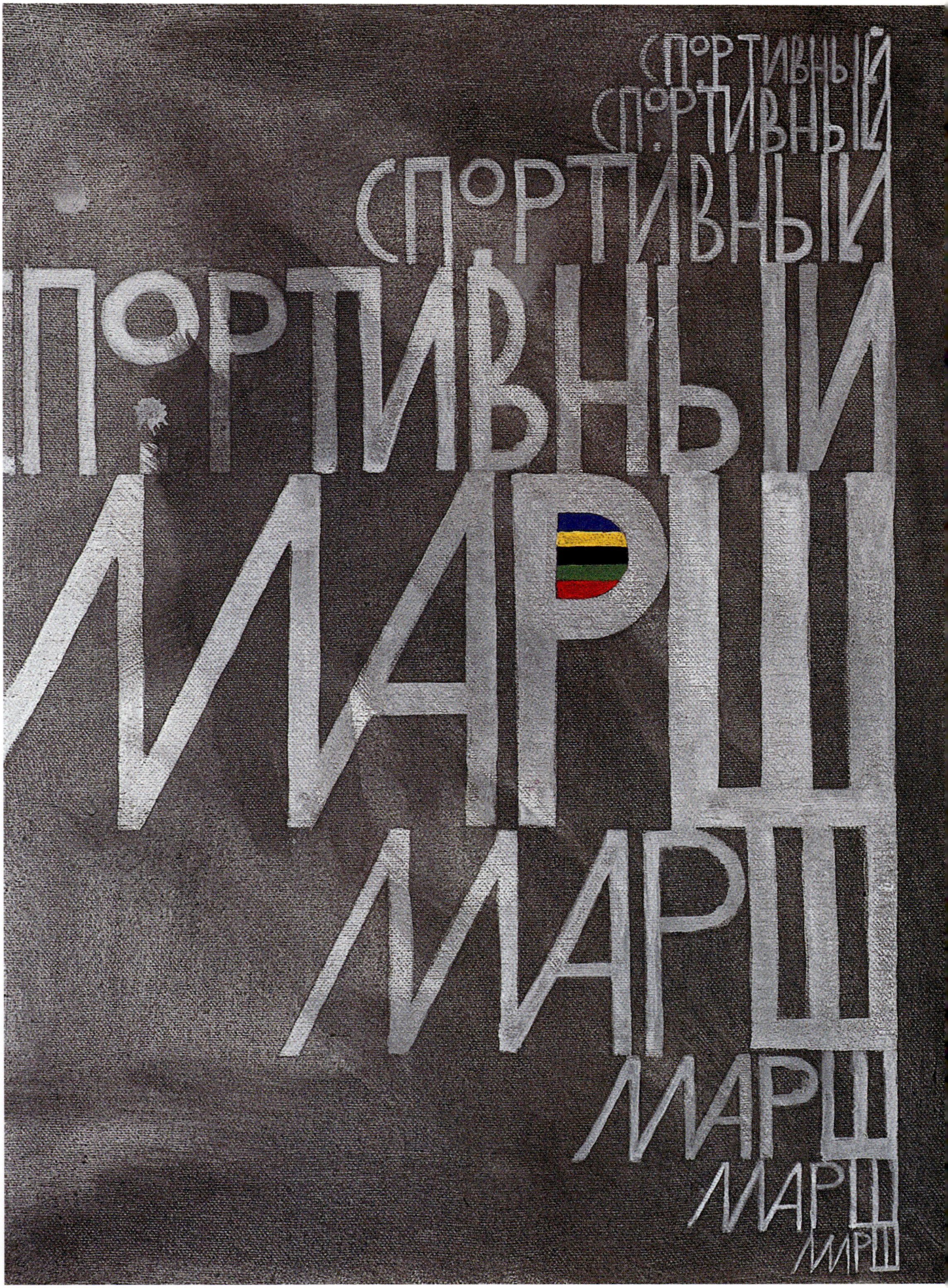

ABOVE **Sport March** 2000 CENTER **Curious** 1998 OPPOSITE **Olympians** 1998

Lucy McKenzie

Born 1977 Scotland; lives and works in Glasgow
Lucy McKenzie's work investigates the social and political undercurrents in celebratory mass spectacles such as concerts and sporting events. As she has said, "I use sport because it is an aesthetic shorthand through which to enjoy twentieth-century malaise, sex, politics, mass culture, girls, totalitarianism, men and women, modernism, and art in general." The idea of discord figures prominently in her project of uncovering the cultural strata of iconic images, and she attempts to rupture the continuity of artifice and content on both visual and metaphorical levels. Recently, she has been preoccupied with images of Olympic athletes from Socialist regimes. Drawn from found photographs of Eastern European competitors, the resulting paintings of young athletes are often rendered as if seen through a refraction lens. In other works, she overpaints found canvases with poster graphics, turning them into "advertisements" for past rock shows by bands such as Depeche Mode. McKenzie was recently selected to participate in the *Beck's Futures* exhibition at the Institute of Contemporary Arts, London (2000) and *The British Art Show*, Hayward Gallery, London (2000). Her work has also been shown at Transmission Gallery, Glasgow (2000) and the Royal Scottish Academy, Edinburgh (1999).

OPPOSITE Lucy McKenzie **Olympians** 1998 oil on canvas 33 x 24 in. Collection Jane Lombard, New York Image courtesy Cabinet, London (checklist)

FOLDOUT (LEFT) Lucy McKenzie **Sport March** 2000 acrylic on canvas 15 x 12 in. Collection Nicholas Lawson, London Image courtesy Cabinet, London (checklist)
(RIGHT) Lucy McKenzie **Curious** 1998 oil on canvas 31 x 19 in. Collection Georg Geyer, Vienna Image courtesy Cabinet, London (checklist)

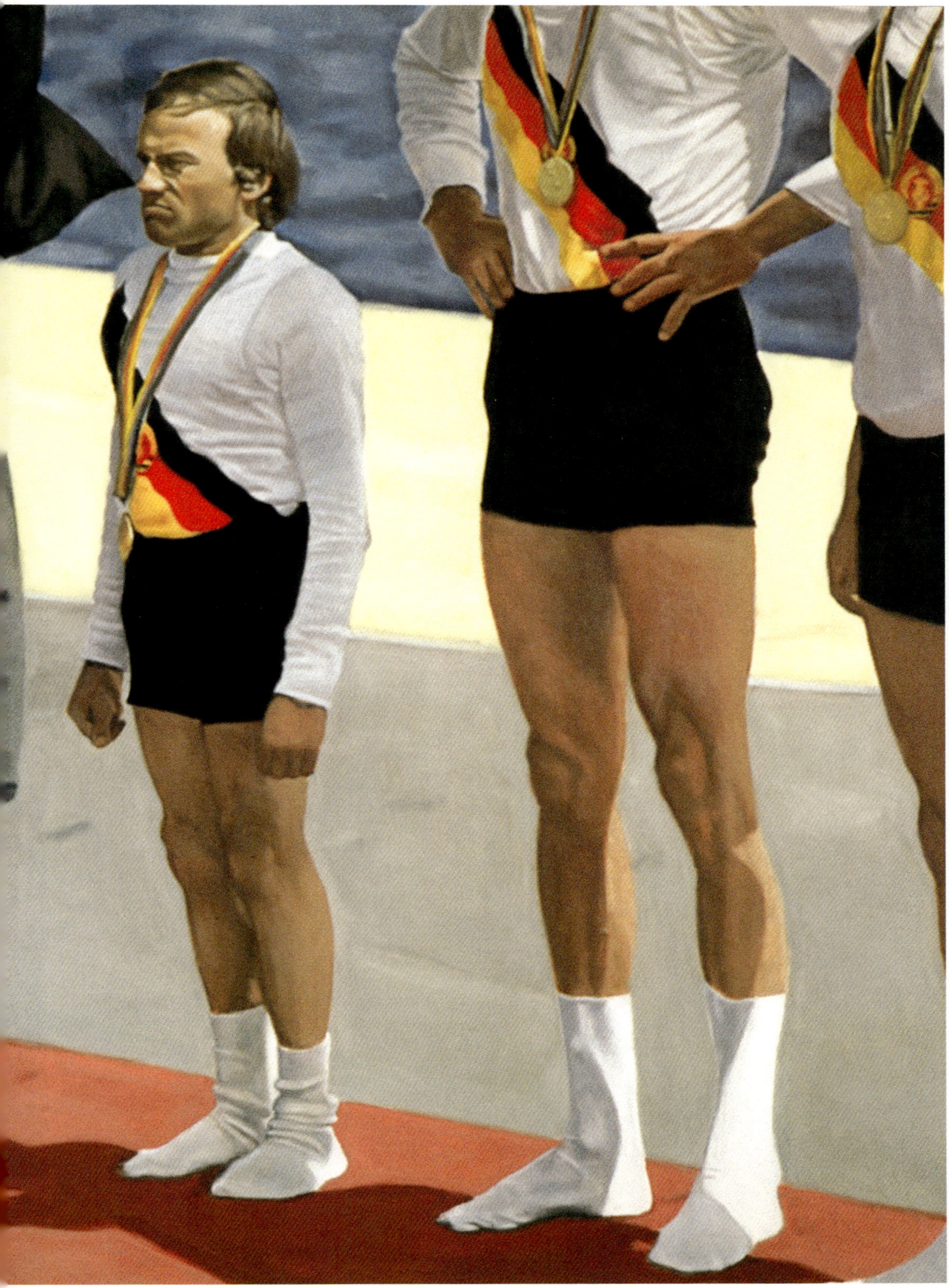

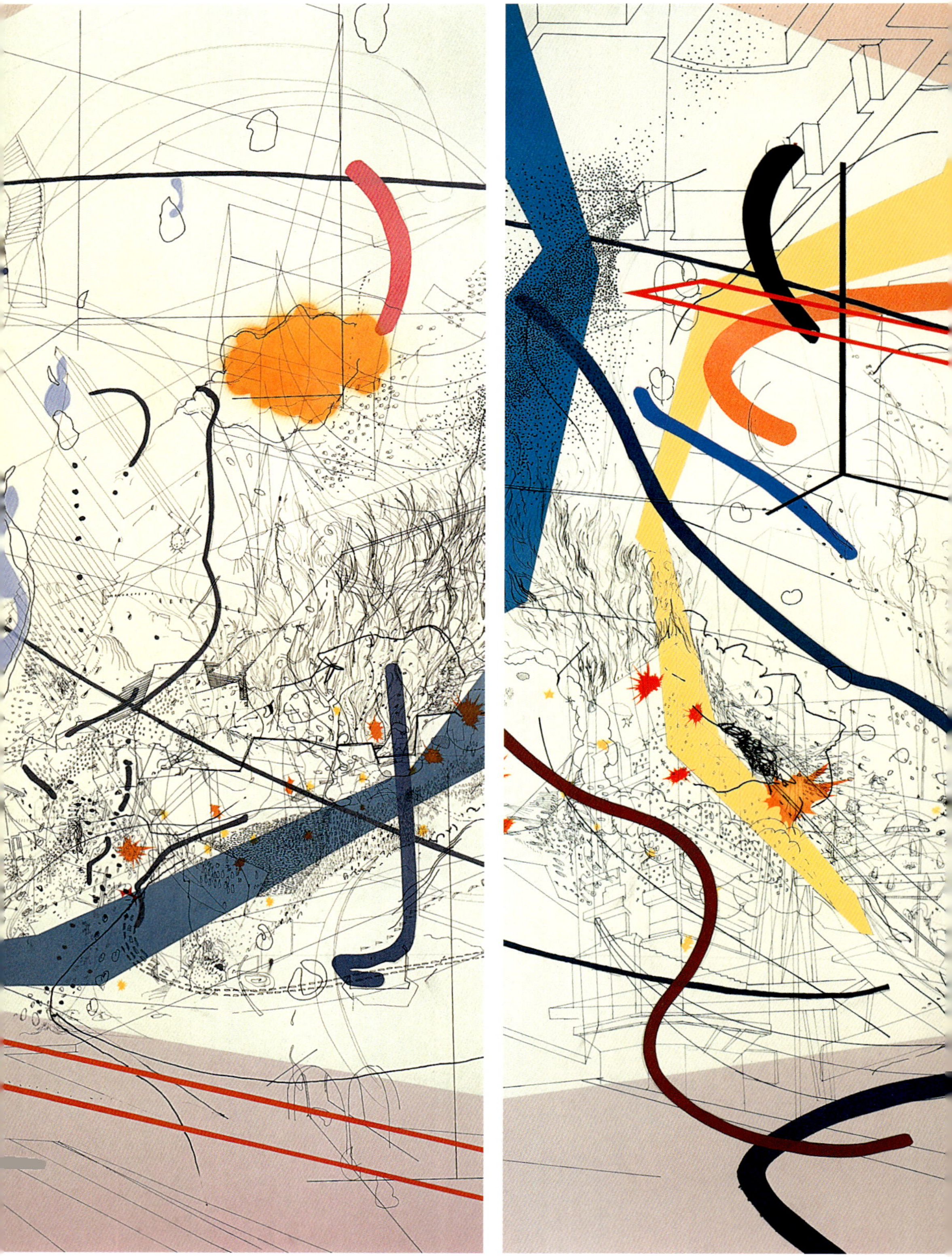

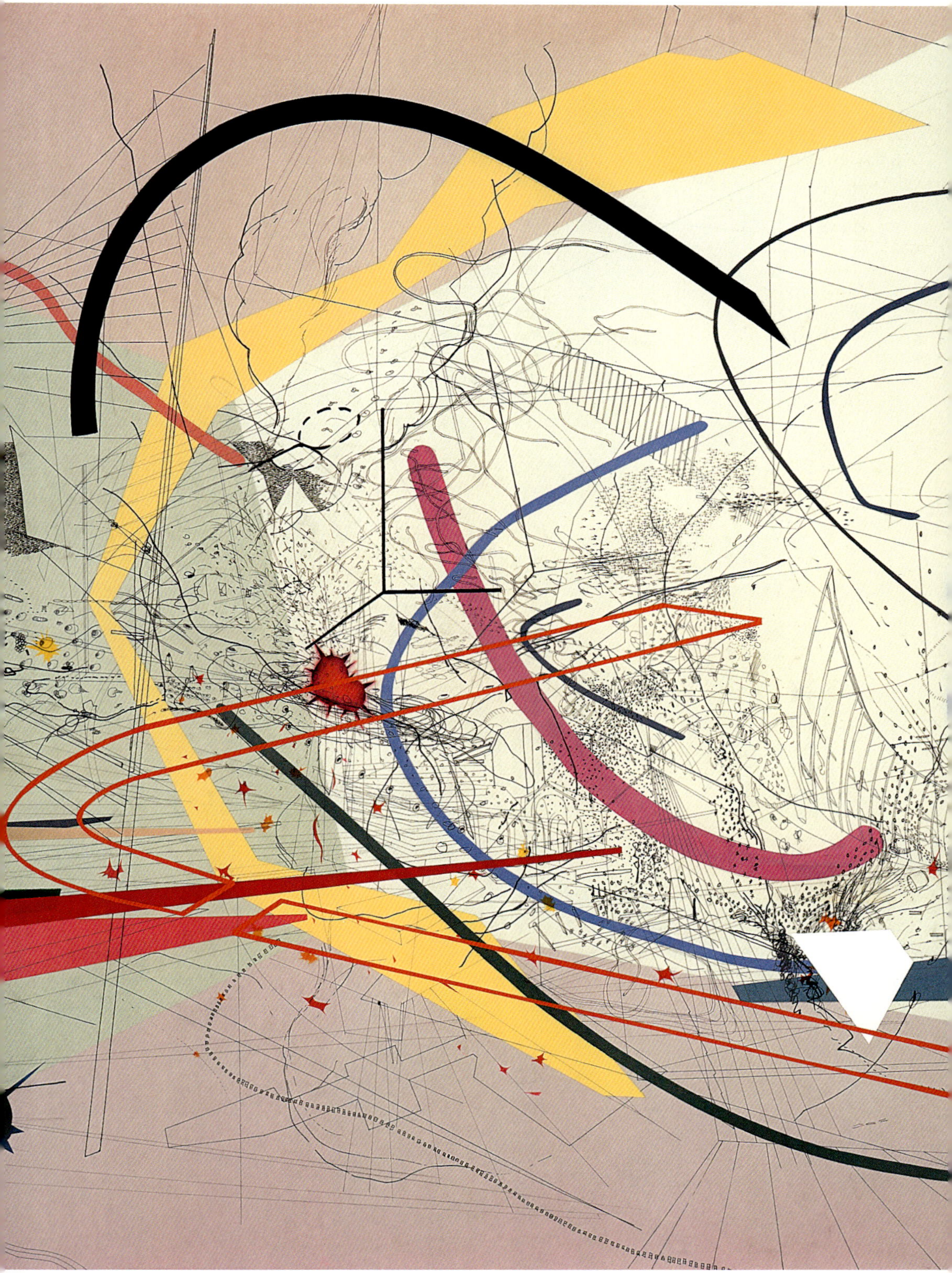

ABOVE AND OPPOSITE **Arcadia and Bushwick Burning** 2000

Julie Mehretu

Born 1970 Ethiopia; lives and works in New York City
Julie Mehretu combines a personal language of signs and symbols with architectural imagery to create elaborate semi-abstractions. Her work simultaneously engages with the formal concerns of color and line and the social concerns of power, history, globalism, and personal narrative. As the artist explains, "I am interested in the multifaceted layers of place, space, and time that impact the formation of personal and communal identity." The underlying structure of her work depicts graphic abstractions of socially charged public spaces—government buildings, museums, stadiums, schools, and international airports—drawn in the form of maps and diagrams. She inscribes her own narrative into these decontextualized, highly controlled spaces through the layering of personal markings. Encased in coats of accumulated resin, these precisely rendered idioms coalesce into an artificial yet highly personal cosmology. Mehretu achieves an effect of compositional maelstrom, as elements advance and recede within the graphically complex, ambiguous architectural spaces. Mehretu's work was included in *Greater New York* at P.S.1 Contemporary Arts Center, New York (2000) and she has participated in group exhibitions at the Center for Curatorial Studies Museum, Bard College, Annandale-on-Hudson, New York (2000), Exit Art, New York (1999), the Contemporary Arts Museum, Houston (1999), and Weatherspoon Art Gallery, Greensboro, North Carolina (1999).

OPPOSITE AND FOLDOUT Julie Mehretu **Arcadia and Bushwick Burning** 2000 ink, acrylic on canvas diptych, 48 x 60 in. each Images courtesy The Project, New York

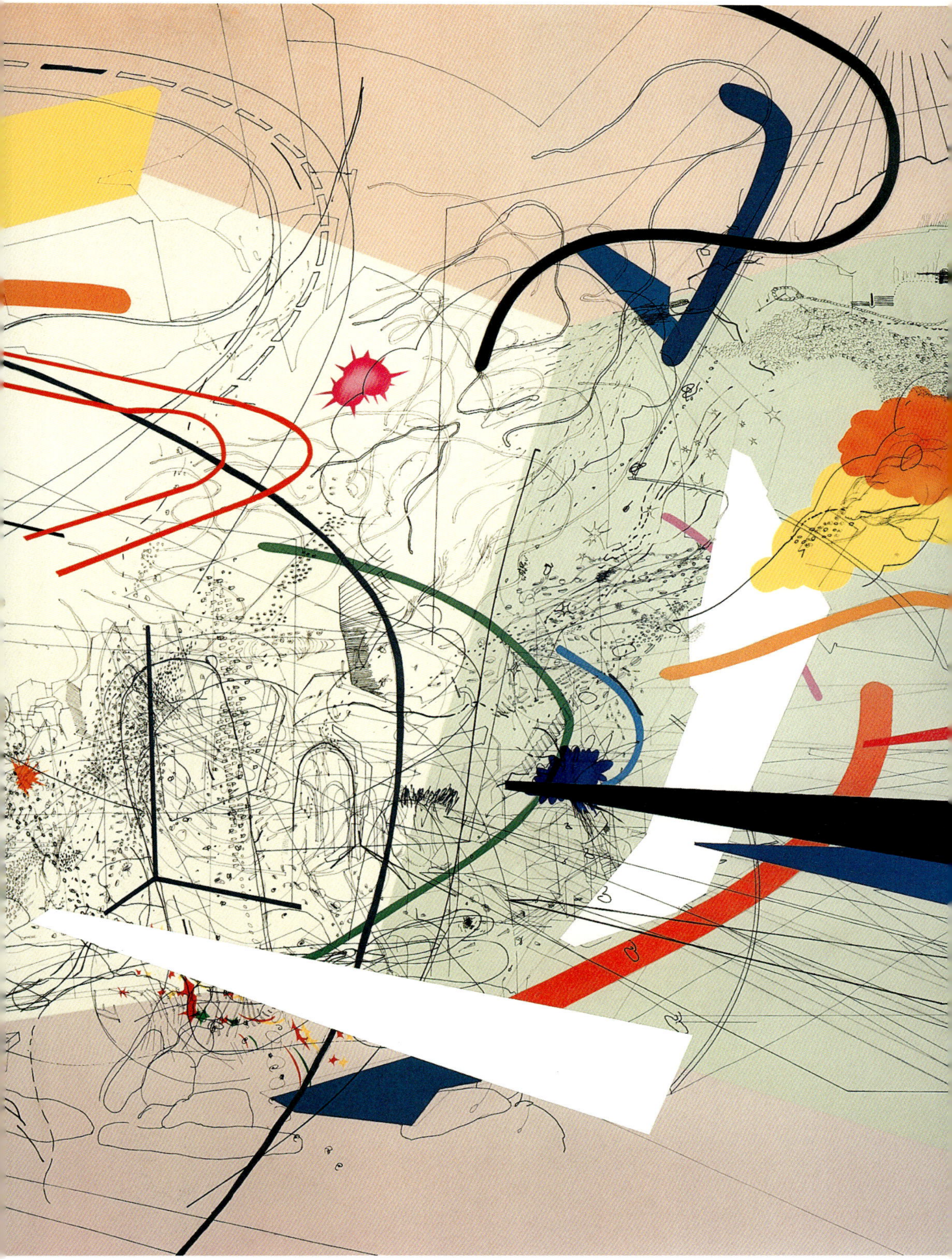

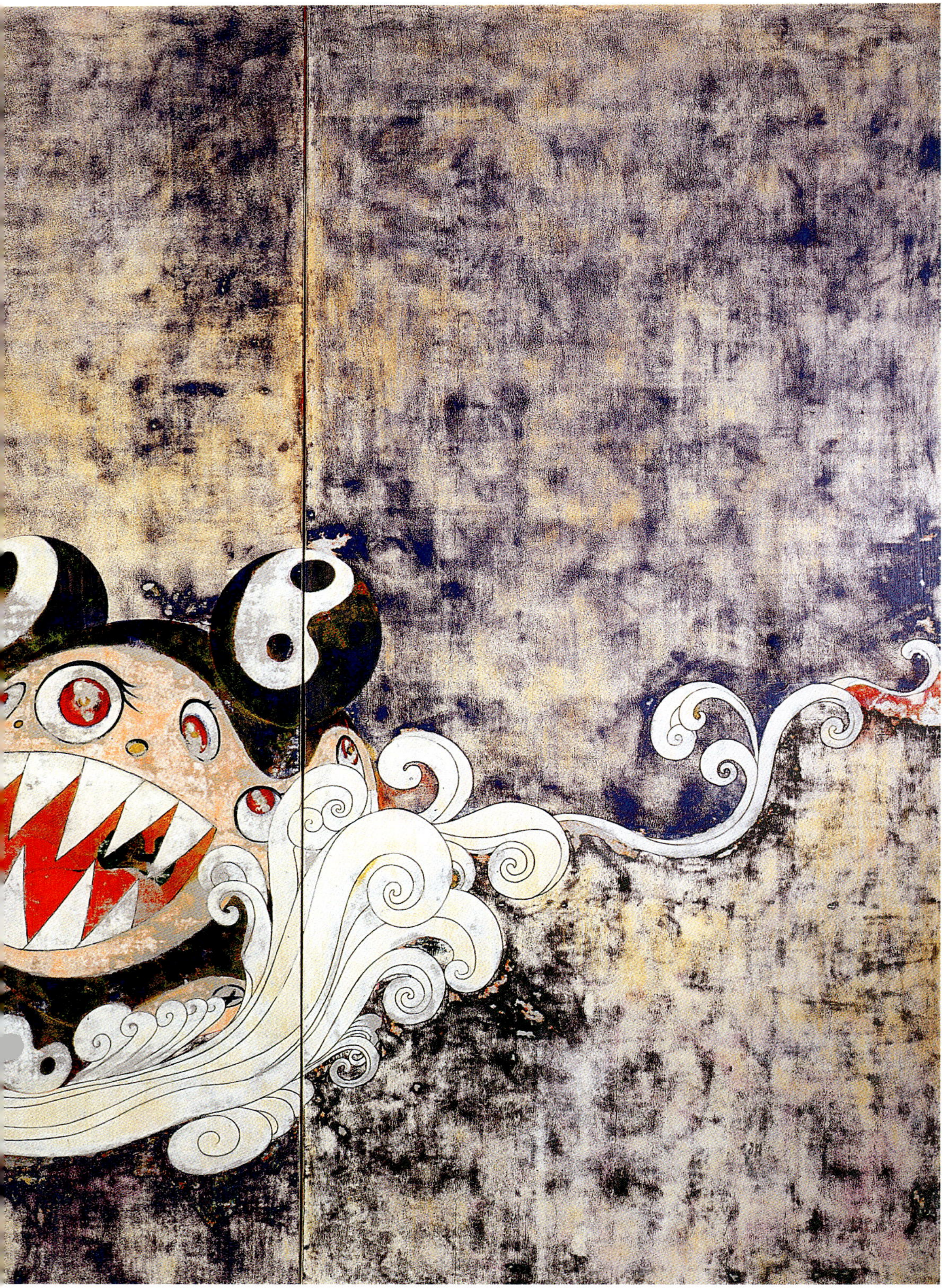

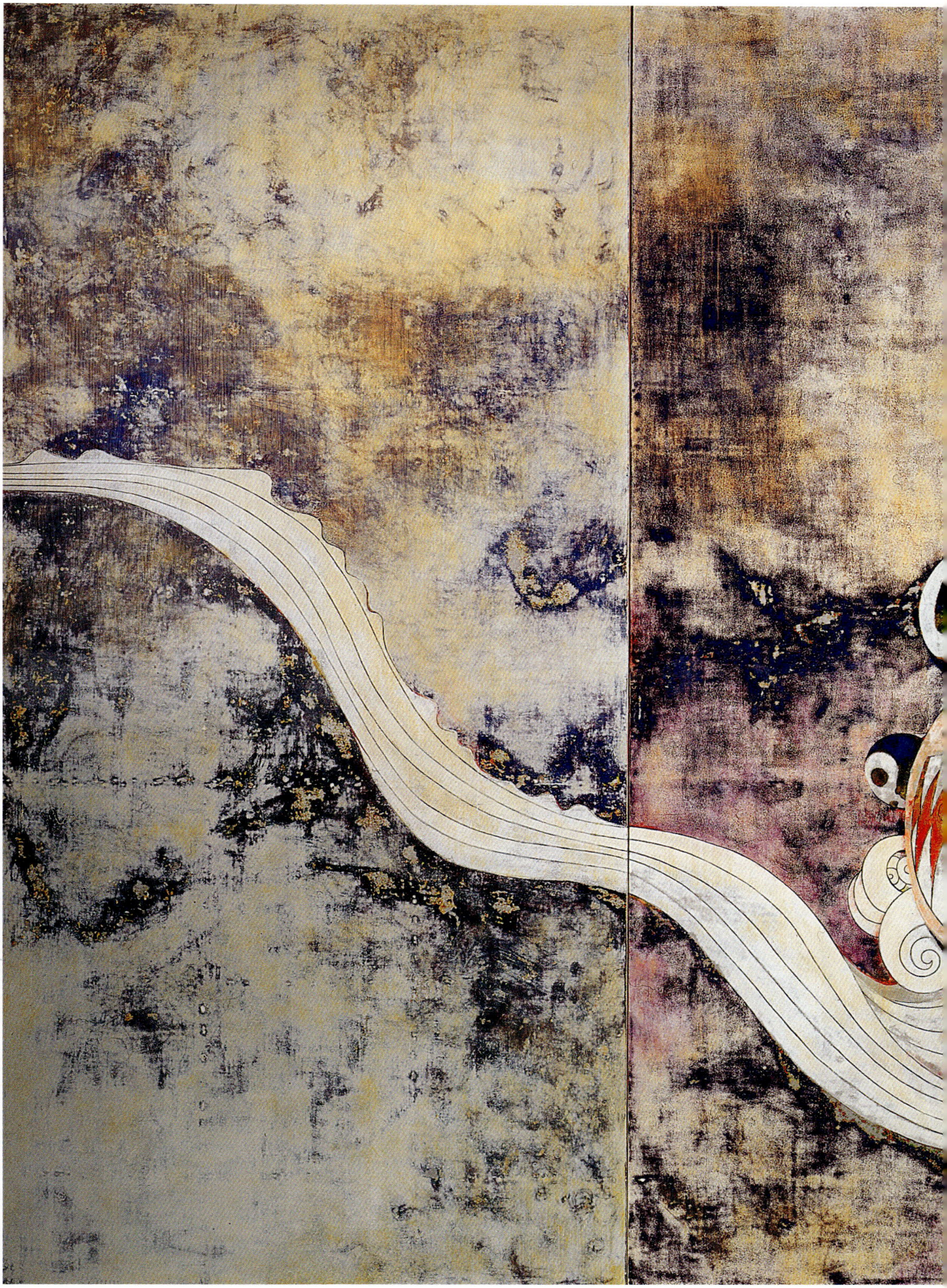

ABOVE 727 1996 **OPPOSITE** The Castle of Tin Tin 1998

Takashi Murakami

Born 1962 Japan; lives and works in Tokyo and New York City
A virtuoso of cross-cultural appropriation, Takashi Murakami explores the collision of divergent influences—craftsmanship and technological innovation, creative practice and scholarship, high art and commercial production, Eastern tradition and Western pop culture—in an astoundingly varied body of work. Originally trained in the Nihonga school of painting, a synthesis of traditional Japanese and modernist Western techniques, Murakami scavenges both from that history and from the ultrasophisticated vocabulary of Japanese *manga* and *anime* to highlight the contradictions and specificity of Japanese culture, particularly in its encounter with the West. He also draws on the legacy of Pop and Conceptual Art strategies, as in the creation of DOB, his own hybridized cartoon character (reminiscent of Disney creations and the Japanese Astro Boy), which he has employed in paintings and sculptures, as well as in a line of commercial products. Murakami has participated in major international exhibitions since 1989, including *Let's Entertain* at the Walker Art Center, Minneapolis (2000), the *Carnegie International*, Pittsburgh (1999), and the traveling exhibition *Cities on the Move* (1997). Solo exhibitions of his work have been organized by P.S.1 Contemporary Art Center, New York (2000) and the Center for Curatorial Studies Museum, Bard College, Annandale-on-Hudson, New York (1999).

OPPOSITE Takashi Murakami **The Castle of Tin Tin** 1998 acrylic on canvas on board 120 x 120 in. Collection Ruth and Jake Bloom, Los Angeles Image courtesy Blum & Poe, Santa Monica, California (checklist)

FOLDOUT Takashi Murakami **727** 1996 acrylic on canvas on board 118 x 177 in. Private collection Image courtesy Blum & Poe, Santa Monica, California; photo: Joshua White (checklist)

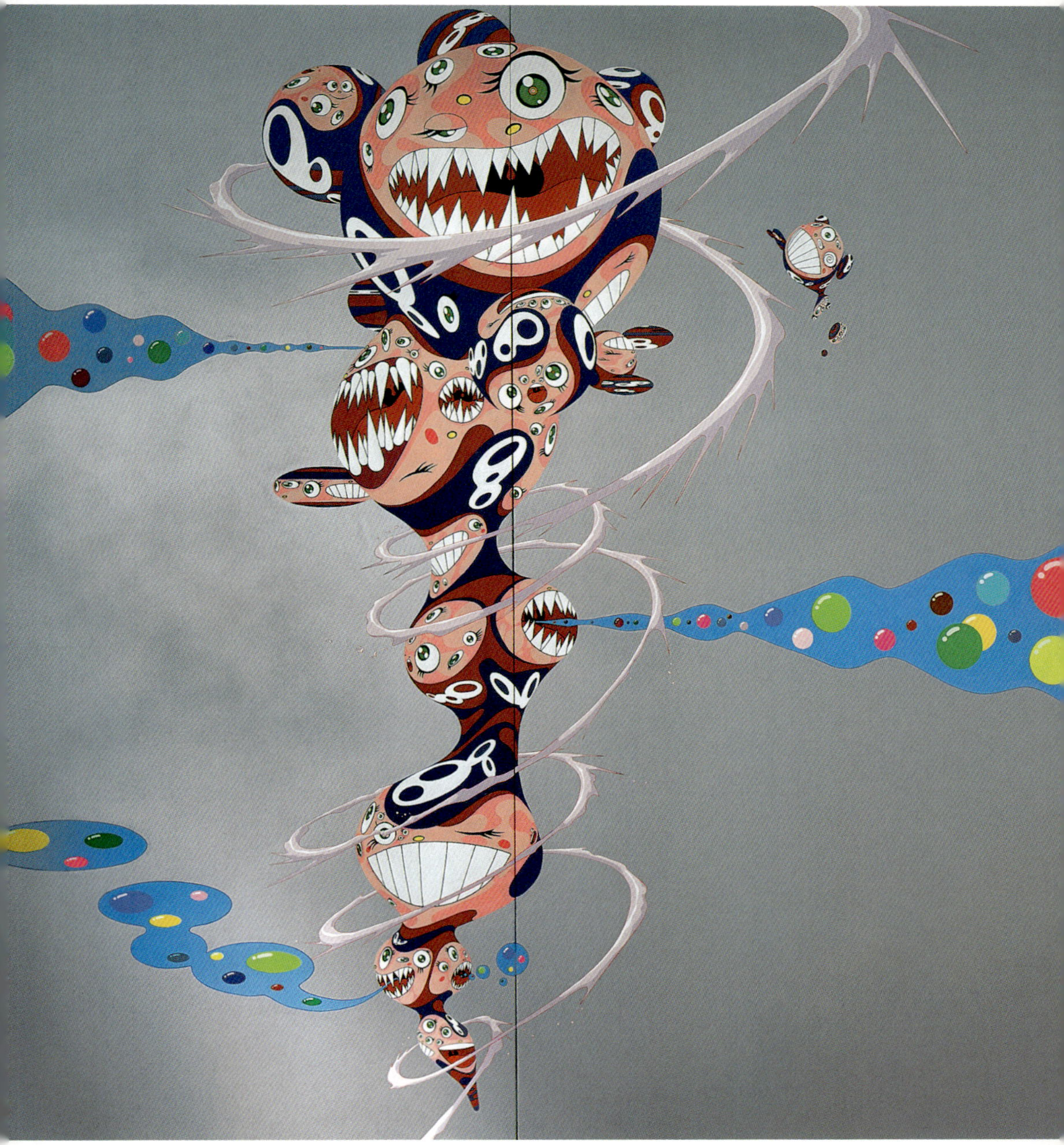

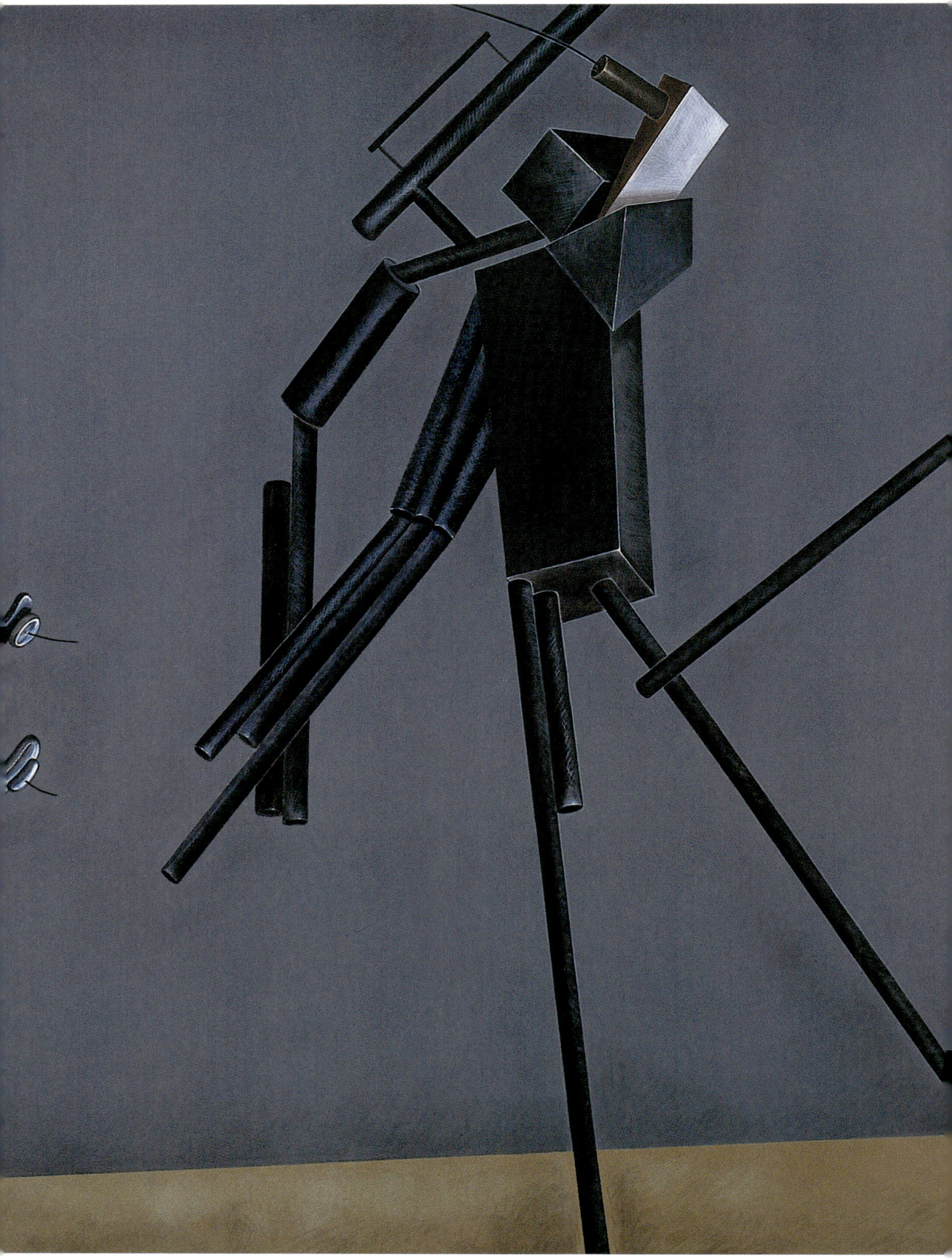

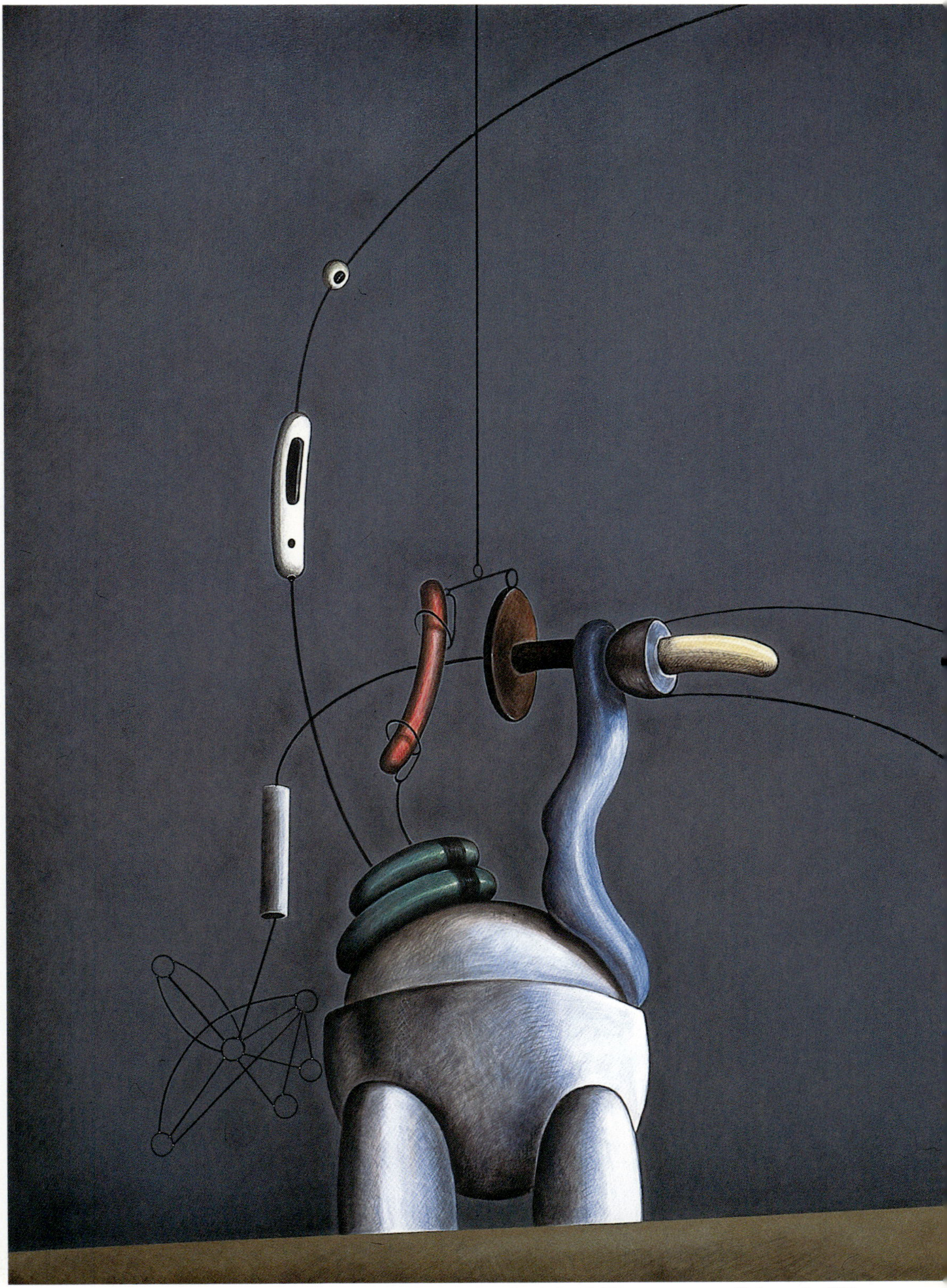

ABOVE **Die Vergewaltigung der Ontologie durch die Logik** (The rape of ontology by logic) 2000 OPPOSITE (TOP) **Nutzung des Bildes zur Entwicklung des Bigreffesder "absoluten Idee"** (Use of the picture for the understanding of "absolute idea") 2000 (BOTTOM) **For Ezra Pound** 20

Nader

Born 1964 Iran; lives and works in Berlin
In canvases populated with enigmatic human-machine hybrids, accompanied by titles laden with philosophical references, Nader ventures to give form to esoteric constructs such as structuralism and existentialism. His mongrel contraptions, seemingly built from the detritus of some postapocalyptic hardware store, inhabit an ambiguous space in which imaginary architectures are rendered in a style of hard-edged abstraction. His paintings lack the slickness of a techno-inflected world informed by the computer age; rather, they bear the imprint of earlier Surrealist evocations of a sci-fi future that never was. As critic Daniel Birnbaum has suggested, Nader's mechanical fantasies are not a wholly serious enterprise: "[A]lthough 'metaphysical' in content, [Nader's paintings] convey a sense of irony and mockery. Philosophy may be dead . . . but his images do not appear to mourn the loss." A former artist-in-residence at P.S.1 Contemporary Art Center, New York (1994), Nader has been included in group exhibitions at the Laboratorio d'Arte Contemporanea, Città Sant'Angelo, Italy and the Init Kunsthalle, Berlin (1999), as well as in *Examining Pictures* at the Whitechapel Art Gallery, London, and the Museum of Contemporary Art, Chicago (1999). He was the subject of a solo exhibition at Kunstalle St. Gallen, Zürich (1997).

OPPOSITE (TOP) Nader **Nutzung des Bildes zur Entwicklung des Bigreffesder "absoluten Idee"** (Use of the picture for the understanding of "absolute idea") 2000 acrylic on canvas 51 x 78 ¾ in. Image courtesy Klosterfelde, Berlin (BOTTOM) Nader **For Ezra Pound** 2000 oil on canvas 51 x 78 ¾ in. Collection Thomas Dane, London Image courtesy Klosterfelde, Berlin (checklist)

FOLDOUT Nader **Die Vergewaltigung der Ontologie durch die Logik** (The rape of ontology by logic) 2000 acrylic on canvas 51 x 78 ¾ in. Image courtesy Klosterfelde, Berlin (checklist)

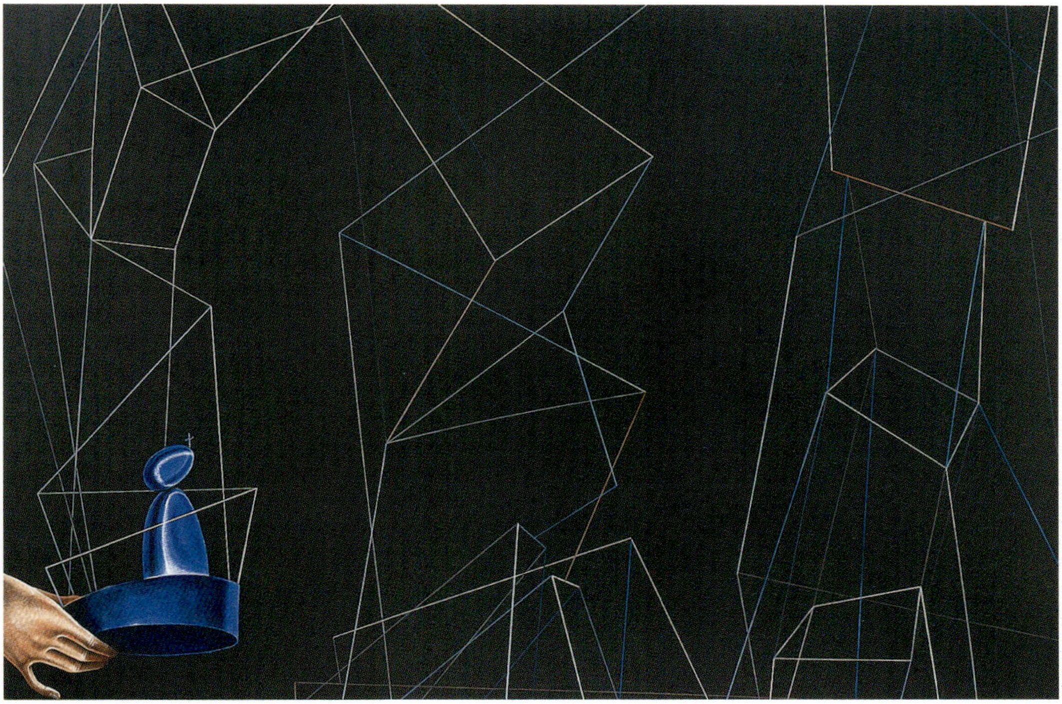

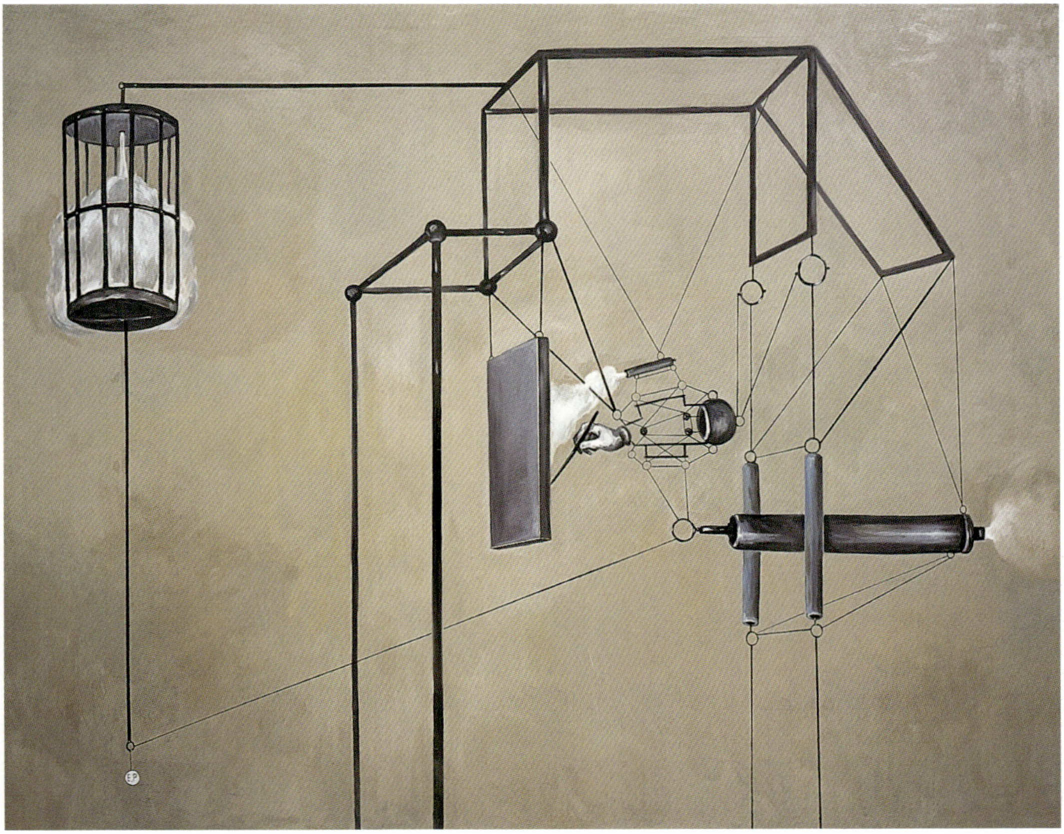

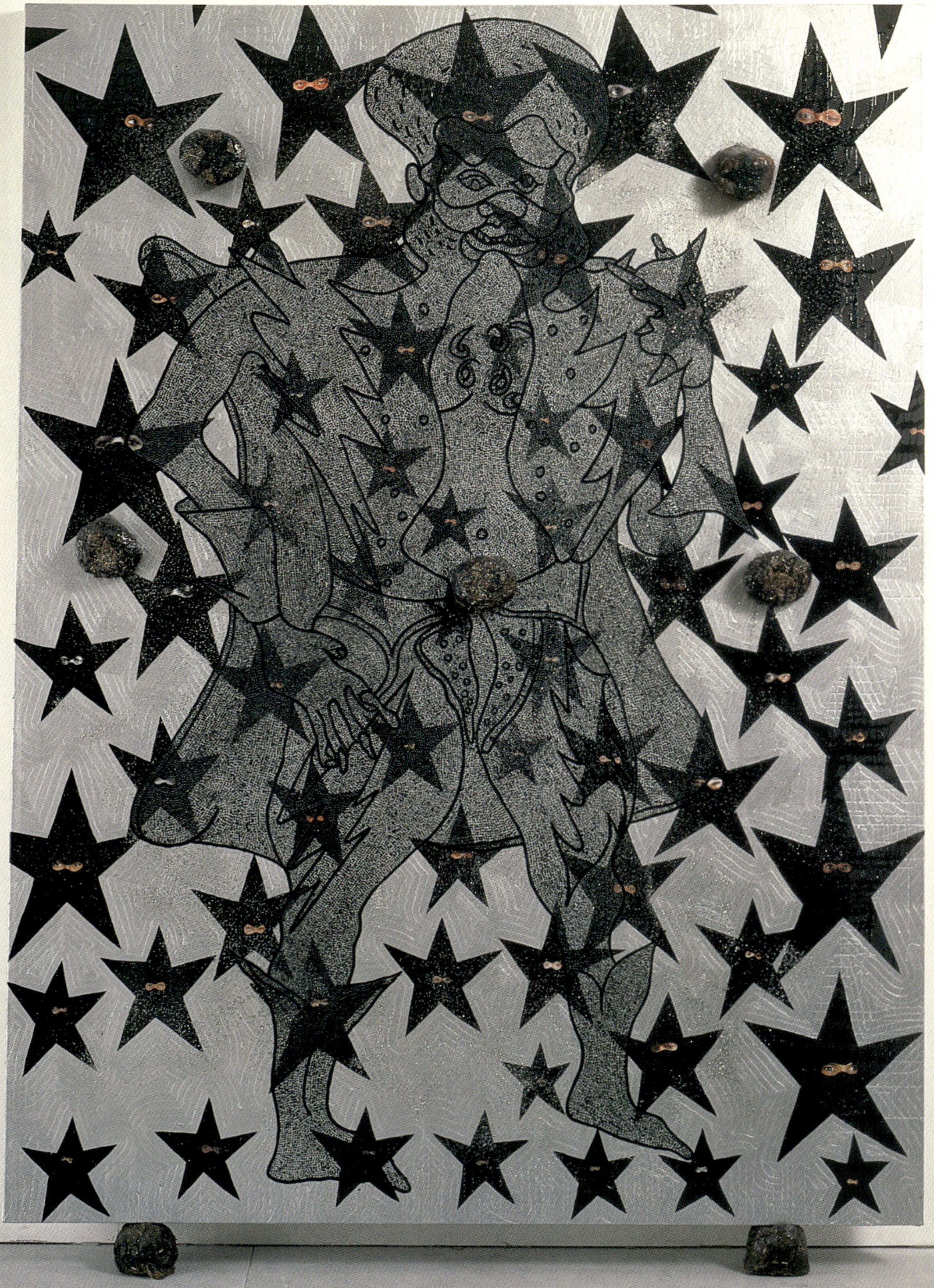

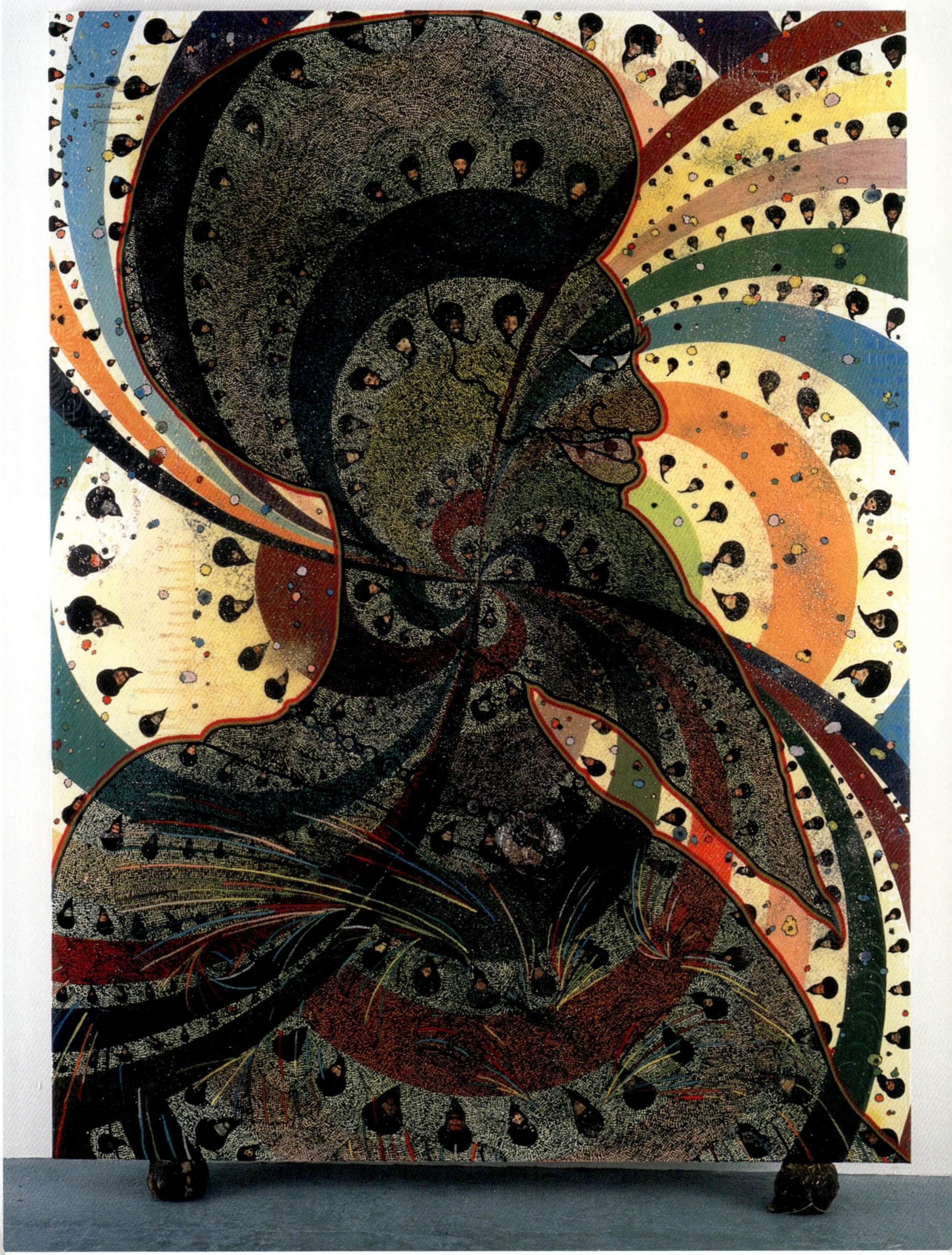

ABOVE **He** 1999 CENTER **The Shadow of Captain Shit and the Legend of the Black Stars** 1998 OPPOSITE **Third Eye Vision** 1999

Chris Ofili

Born 1968 England; lives and works in London
Chris Ofili's paintings are inspired by a wide range of influences from art history and everyday experience, including traditional African art, hip-hop culture, comic books, fashion magazines, and Blaxploitation films. From a distance, his dazzling large-scale works resolve into powerful images that confront stereotypes and address the complex matrix of contemporary black experience. Up close, he meditates on decoration and color using a vocabulary of unexpected materials. Kaleidoscopic, psychedelic patterns emerge from loops and swarms of tiny paint beads that mingle with magazine cutouts of Afro hairdos and figurative details. This culturally charged matter coalesces with kitschy glitter and phosphorescent plastic under layers of colored resin. Since 1992 Ofili has habitually worked with elephant dung (collected from the London Zoo) both as a support for propping the paintings against the wall and as surface decoration. His work was the subject of a solo exhibition at the Southampton City Art Gallery and the Serpentine Gallery, London (1998). Ofili's paintings have also been included in the *Carnegie International*, Pittsburgh (1999) and in group exhibitions at the Royal Academy of Art, London (1999), the Museum of Modern Art, Oxford (1996), and the Walker Art Center, Minneapolis (1995). In 1998 Ofili received the Tate Gallery's prestigious Turner Prize.

OPPOSITE Chris Ofili **Third Eye Vision** 1999 acrylic, collage, glitter, resin, map pins, elephant dung on canvas 96 x 72 3/8 x 6 in. Collection Walker Art Center, Minneapolis; T. B. Walker Acquisition Fund, 2000 (checklist)

FOLDOUT (LEFT) Chris Ofili **He** 1999 acrylic, collage, glitter, resin, map pins, elephant dung on canvas 96 x 72 x 6 in. Collection Warren and Victoria Miro, London Image courtesy Victoria Miro Gallery, London (checklist)
(RIGHT) Chris Ofili **The Shadow of Captain Shit and the Legend of the Black Stars** 1998 acrylic, oil, polyester resin, paper collage, map pins, elephant dung on canvas 96 x 72 x 6 in. The Berardo Collection, Lisbon, Portugal Image courtesy Gavin Brown's enterprise, New York

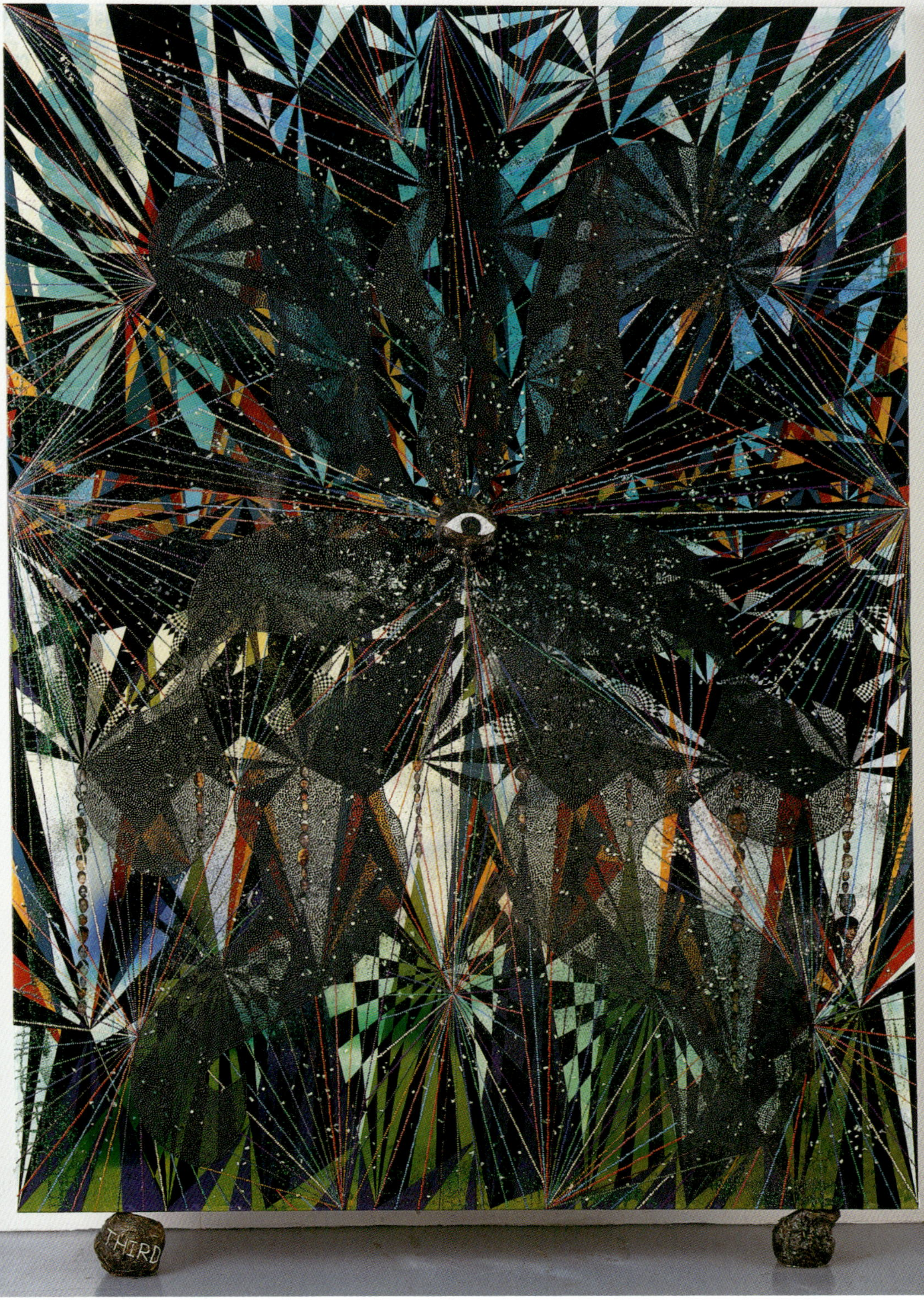
THIRD

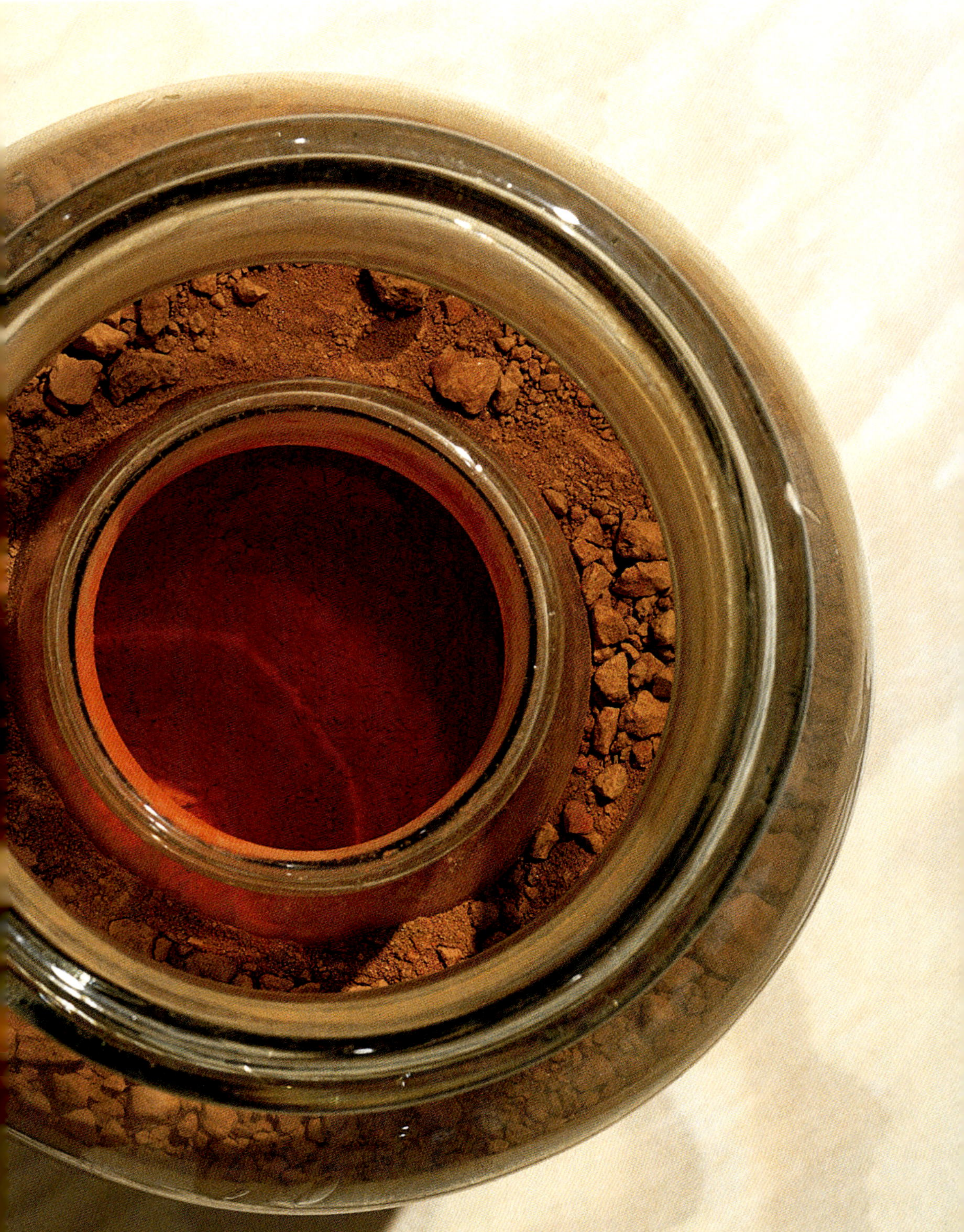

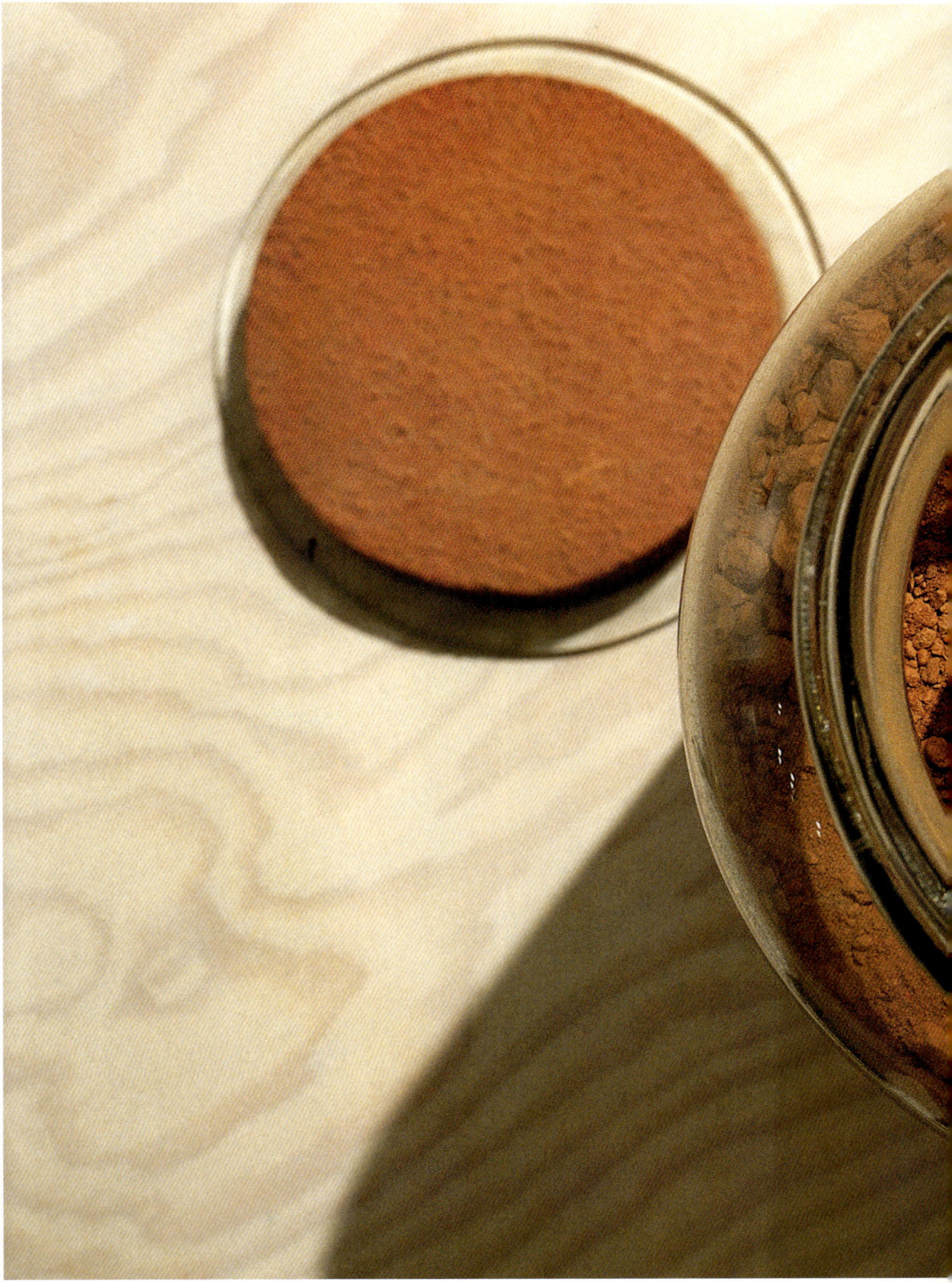

ABOVE **Glass Bolide 1** 1963 OPPOSITE **Nucleus NC 1** 1960

Hélio Oiticica

Born 1937 Brazil; died 1980
A major figure of the Brazilian avant-garde, Hélio Oiticica emerged in the 1960s to radically redefine the relationship of painting to spatial experience. Like other Neo-Concrete artists, Oiticica rejected traditional easel painting: "Already, it was no longer possible to use the plane, that old fashioned element of representation, even when virtualized, because of its 'a priori' connotation of a surface to be painted." He attempted to break free of illusionism by moving the painted surface off the wall and into the room. Oiticica placed great importance on the reinscription of the corporeal and the sensorial into the experience of painting, as well as on the integration of structure and color so that the supporting surface and the surface of the painting became inseparable. In so doing, he challenged the passivity of wall-bound work by creating hybridized three-dimensional constructions, with surfaces arranged architecturally to invite the physical participation of the viewer. In experiments such as the *Bolides*, he attempted to "give color a unique structure" by amassing jars of raw pigments, thereby incorporating painting into the material realm. Oiticica has been the subject of a solo exhibition at the Museu de Arte Contemporânea da Universidade de São Paulo (1987), as well as a traveling retrospective exhibition presented at the Witte de With Center for Contemporary Art, Rotterdam; the Galerie nationale du Jeu de Paume, Paris; and the Walker Art Center, Minneapolis (1992). His work was included in the Bienal de São Paulo (1998), in addition to recent group exhibitions at the Museum of Contemporary Art, Los Angeles (1999) and the Queens Museum of Art (1999).

OPPOSITE Hélio Oiticica installation view of **Nucleus NC 1** 1960 acrylic on wood, mirror dimensions variable from the exhibition **Hélio Oiticica** at the Walker Art Center, Minneapolis, 1993–1994 (checklist)

FOLDOUT Hélio Oiticica installation view of **Glass Bolide 1** 1963 glass jar, glass bottle, earth, pigment from the exhibition **Hélio Oiticica** at the Walker Art Center, Minneapolis, 1993–1994

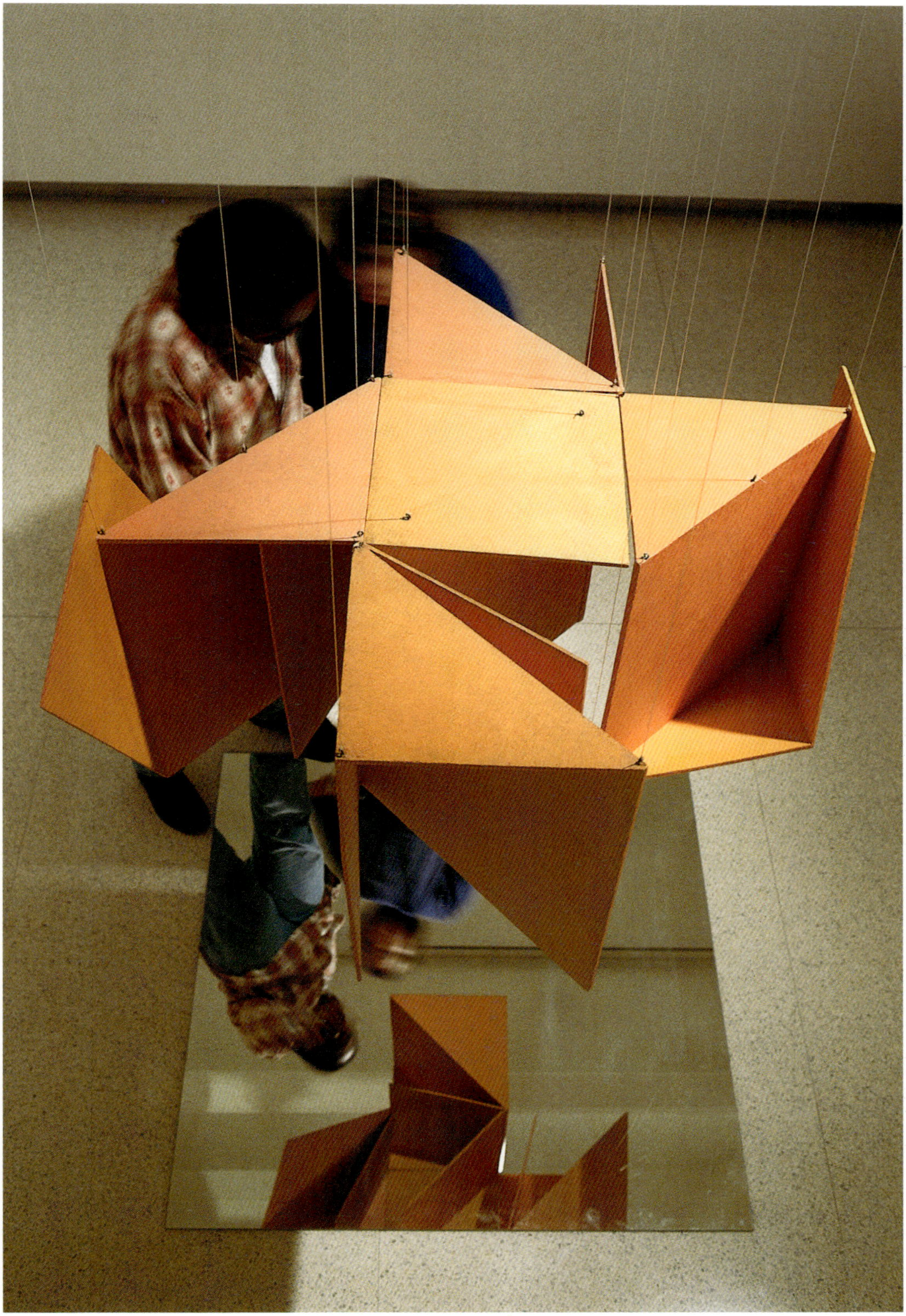

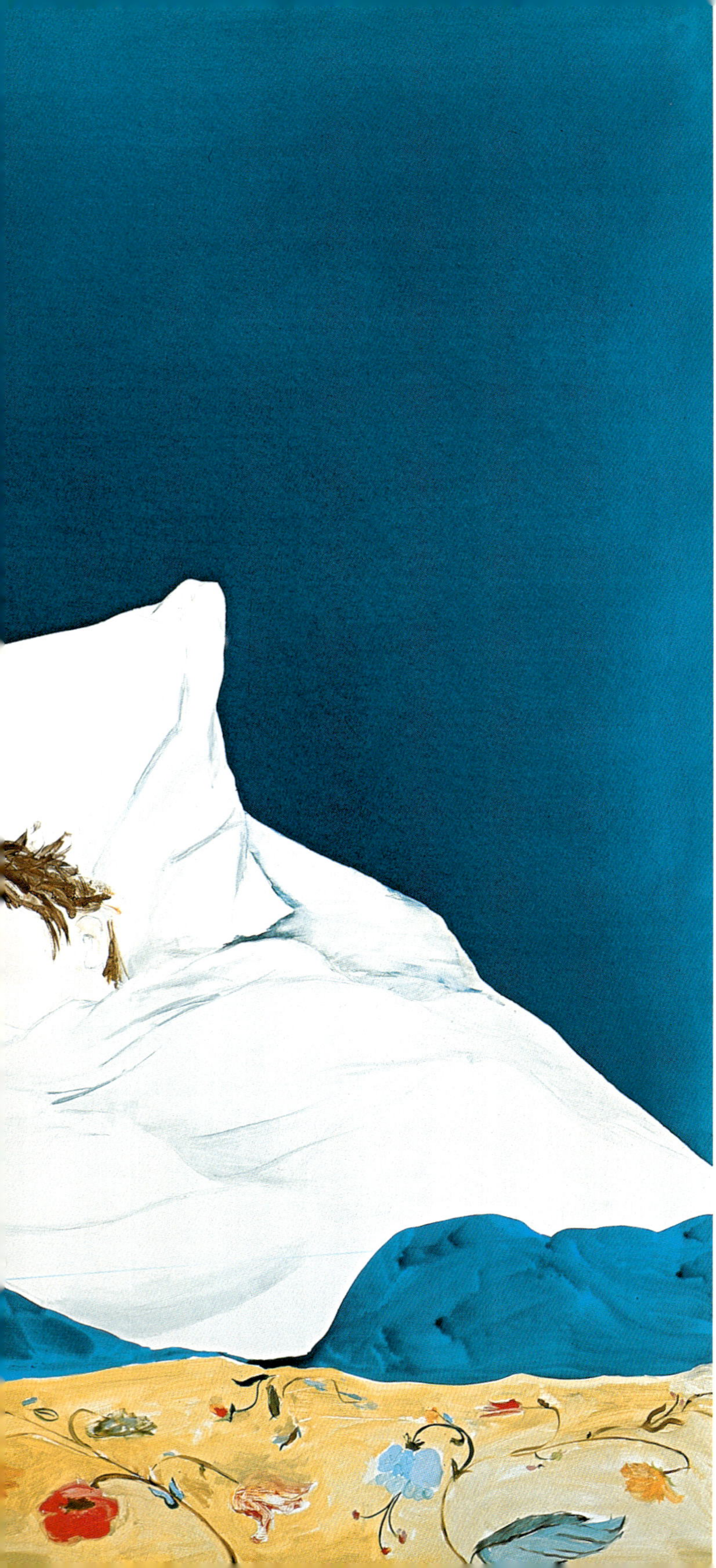

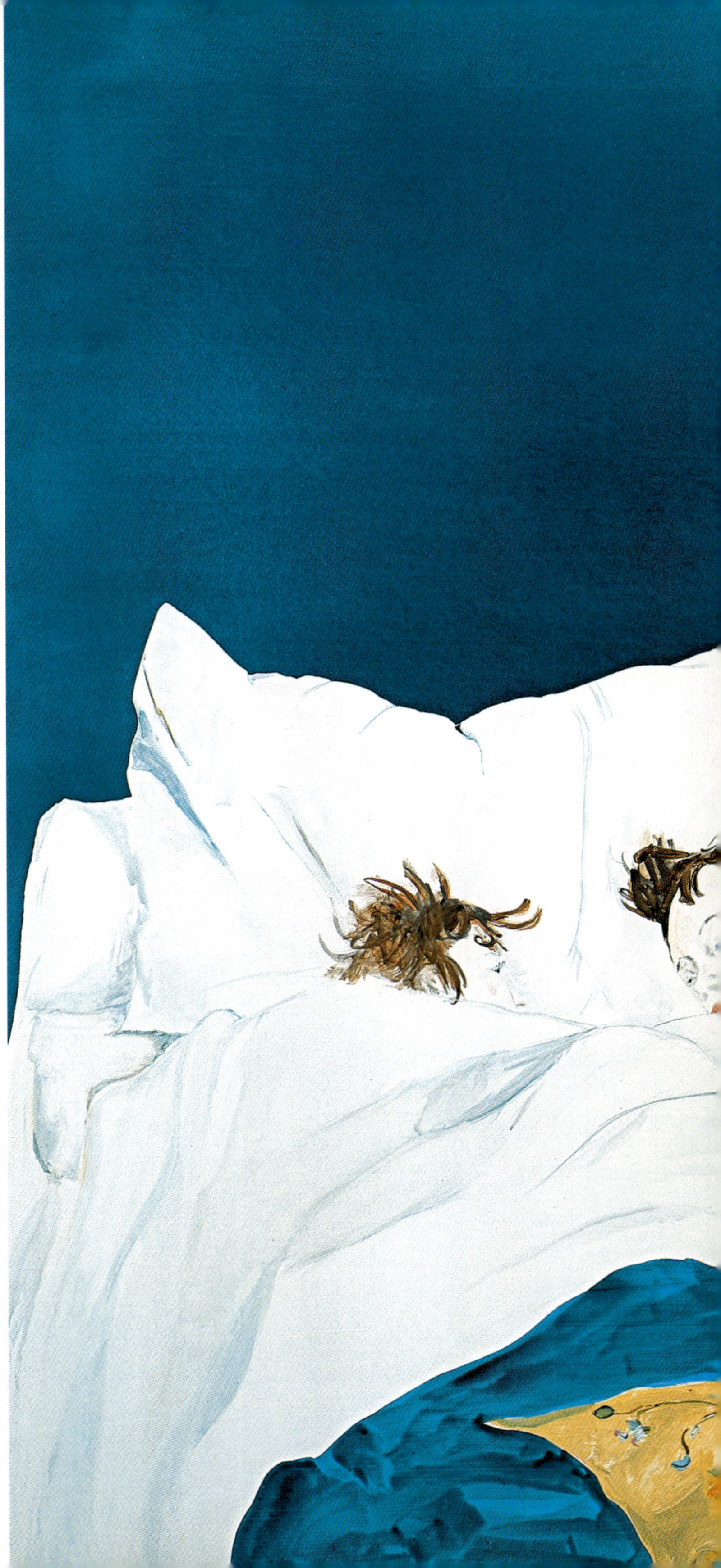

LEFT **Untitled** 2000
RIGHT **Untitled** 2000

Laura Owens

Born 1970 United States; lives and works in Los Angeles
As a painter, Laura Owens assumes multiple identities, assimilating various pictorial styles in a determined investigation of painting's possibilities: "I'm always interested in what a painting can do, and then questioning those things." These explorations take a variety of forms, ranging from decorative canvases that revel in loose, fanciful abstraction to geometrically defined interiors rendered in strict one-point perspective. Within each work she often combines diverse visual languages, using her command of vernacular painting effects to conceptual ends. In the same way that the grandeur of her large-scale canvases is mitigated by a calculated, informal aesthetic, her references to the high-modernist canon are tempered by allusions to the everyday experience of modern forms through design and architecture. Her paintings often project a concern with the phenomenological experience of viewing artworks in space—namely, how the body "walks past and between paintings." Owens was included in the *Carnegie International*, Pittsburgh (1999) and *Examining Pictures* at the Whitechapel Art Gallery, London, and the Museum of Contemporary Art Chicago (1999). She has participated in recent group exhibitions at the Kunsthalle Basel (1999), Artists Space, New York (1997), and the Kunstverein Hamburg (1996).

OPPOSITE Laura Owens **Untitled** 2000 oil, acrylic on canvas 111 x 72 in. Goetz Collection, Munich Image courtesy Studio Guenzani, Milan; photo: Roberto Marossi (checklist)

FOLDOUT Laura Owens **Untitled** 2000 acrylic on canvas 72 ¼ x 66 ¼ in. Image courtesy Studio Guenzani, Milan photo: Roberto Marossi (checklist)

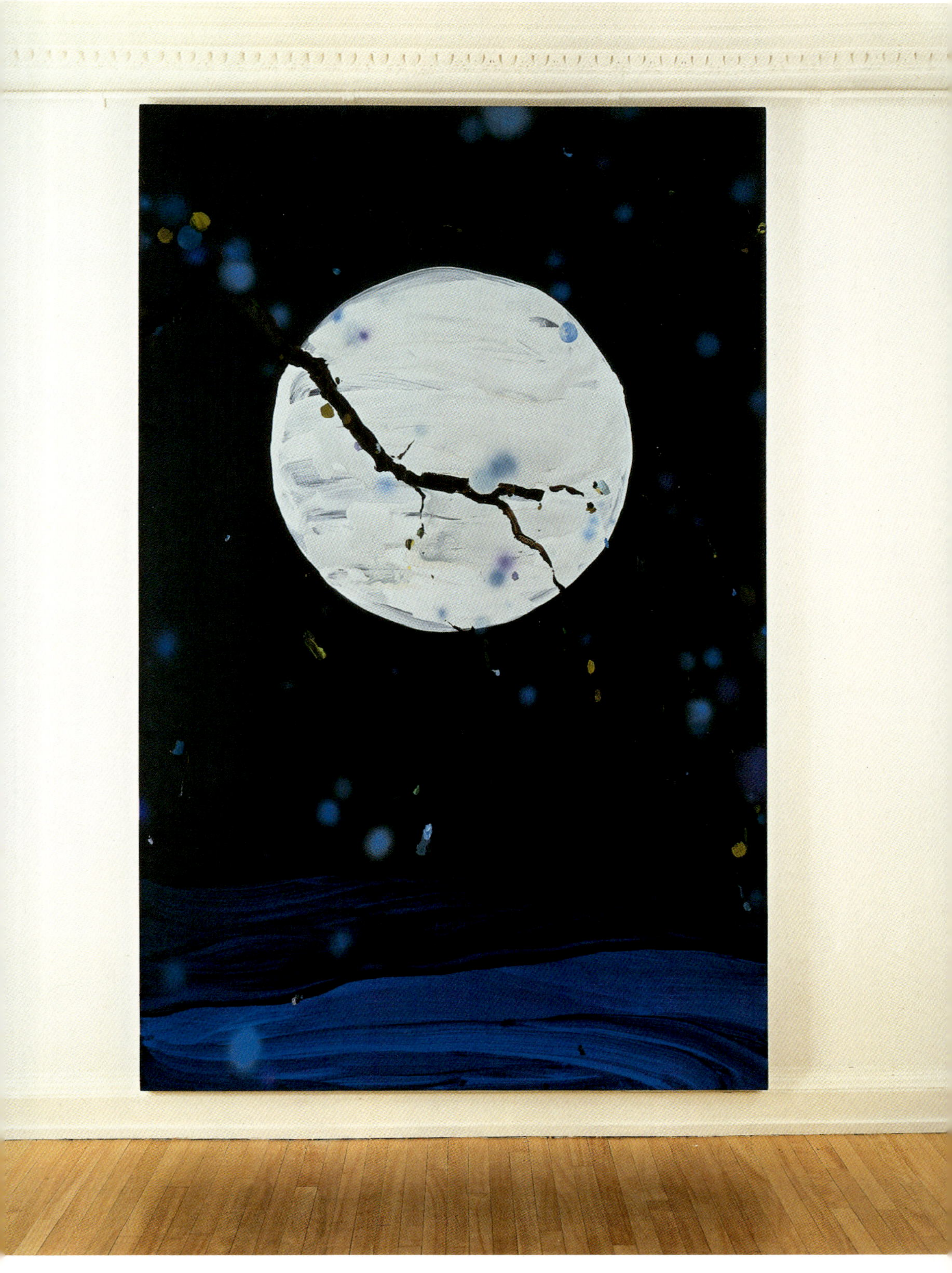

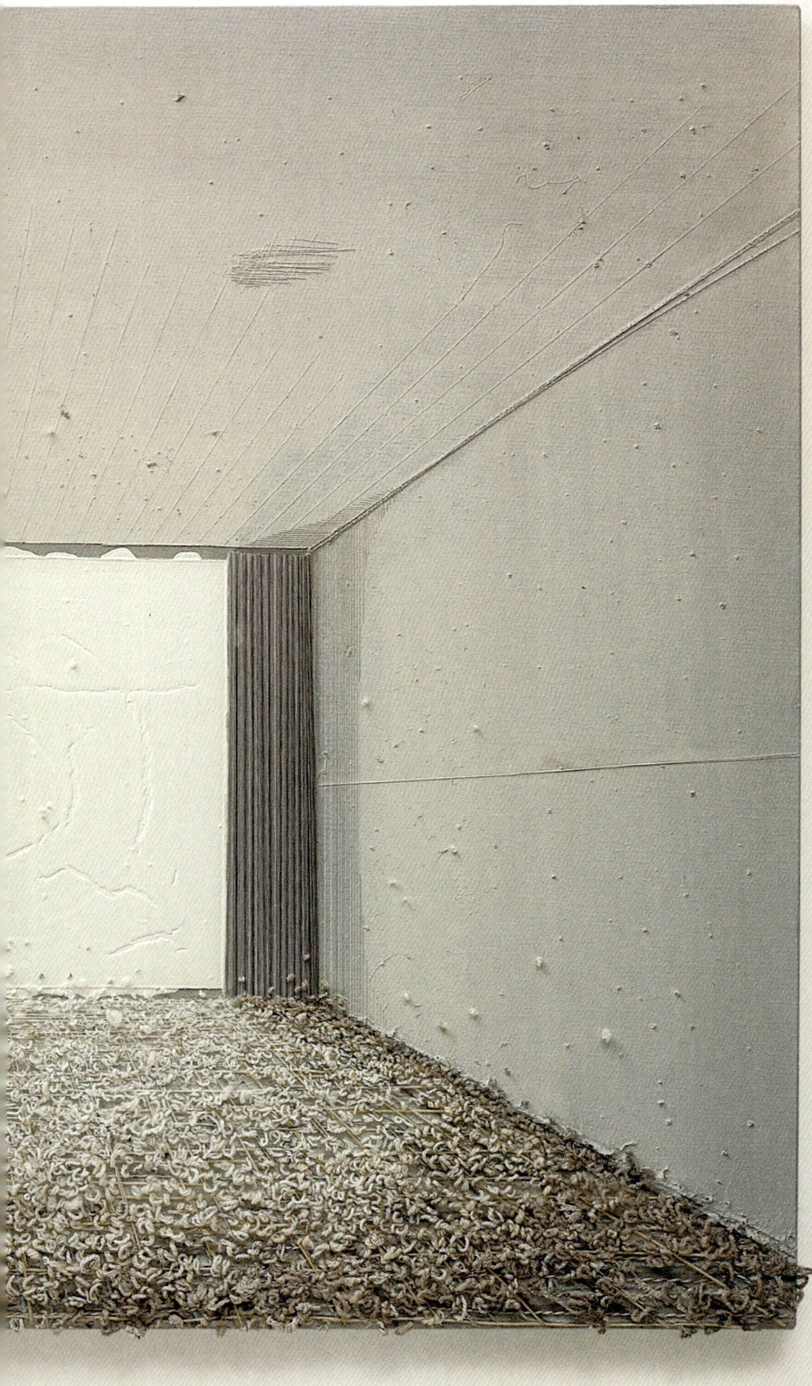

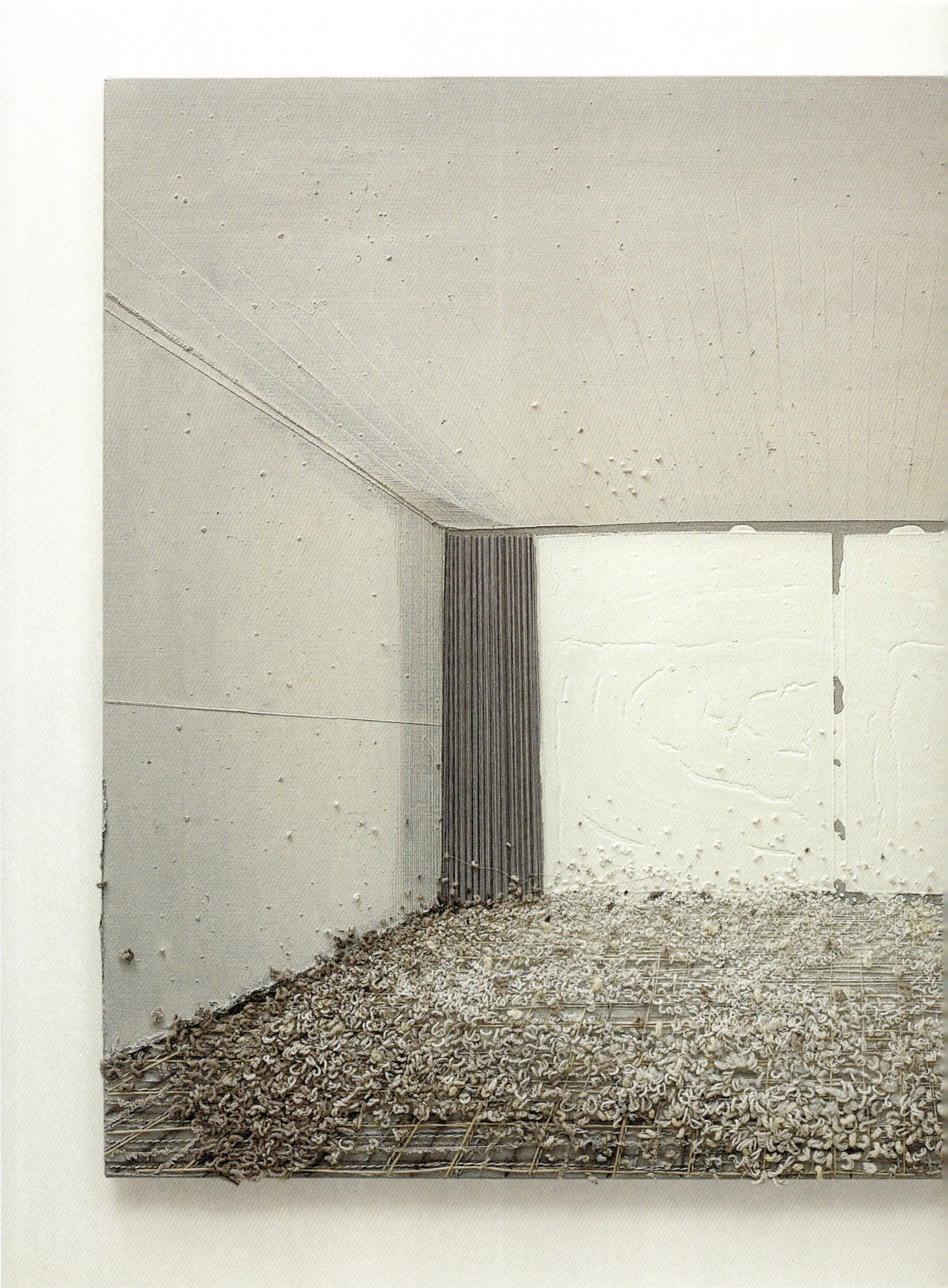

ABOVE **radiate** 2000 OPPOSITE (TOP) **kismet** 1999 (BOTTOM) **phantom** 1999

Michael Raedecker

Born 1963 The Netherlands; lives and works in London
Michael Raedecker's paintings are characterized by an inventive and exquisite use of embroidery and paint. His subjects—ambiguous landscapes, exteriors, and interiors—are rendered in a muted palette with a cinematic sense of framing. Almost sketchlike, the works depict spare spaces with a minimum of gesture; the unconventional compositions are intensified by the selective application of detail. The intermingling of fiber and pigment achieves varied effects of texture and form, and both media are resolutely expressive—the paint thinly washed or impastoed on the surface, the thread looping or knotting or tautly stitched. Raedecker was short-listed for the Tate Gallery's prestigious Turner Prize in 2000, and his work has been included in *The British Art Show*, Hayward Gallery, London (2000) and the Istanbul Biennial (1999). He has participated in group exhibitions at the Van Abbemuseum, Eindhoven (2000), the Whitechapel Art Gallery, London, and the Museum of Contemporary Art, Chicago (1999), the Institute for Contemporary Arts, London (1998), and the Stedelijk Museum, Amsterdam (1997).

OPPOSITE (TOP) Michael Raedecker **kismet** 1999 acrylic, thread on canvas 80 ¾ x 98 7/16 in. Collection Van Abbemuseum, Eindhoven Image courtesy The approach, London; photo: Peter Cox (checklist)
(BOTTOM) Michael Raedecker **phantom** 1999 acrylic, thread on canvas 48 x 58 in. Private collection, Naples Image courtesy The approach, London

FOLDOUT Michael Raedecker **radiate** 2000 acrylic, wool, thread on canvas 50 ¼ x 70 ¼ in. CAP Art Collection, New York Image courtesy The approach, London; photo: FXP Photography

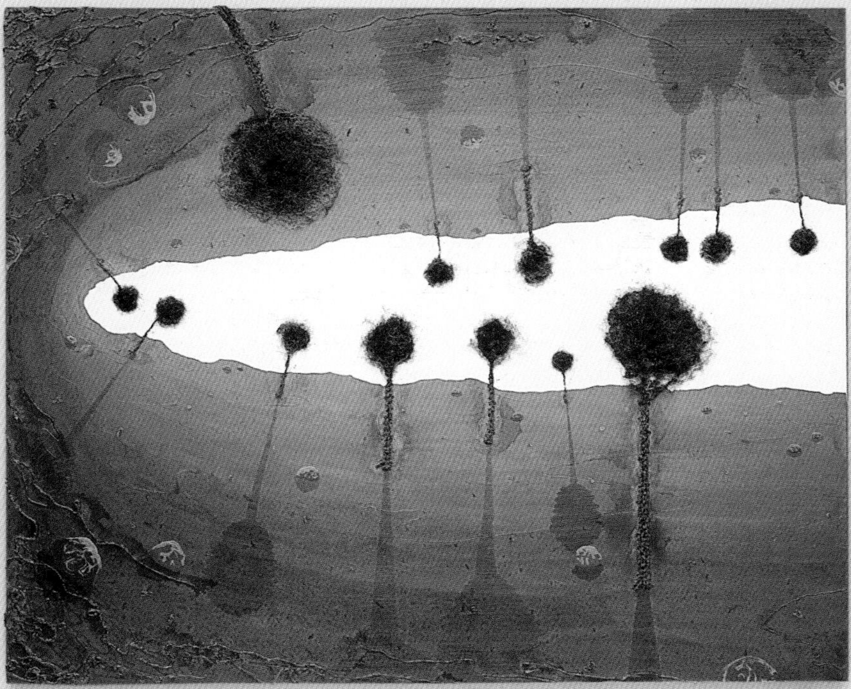

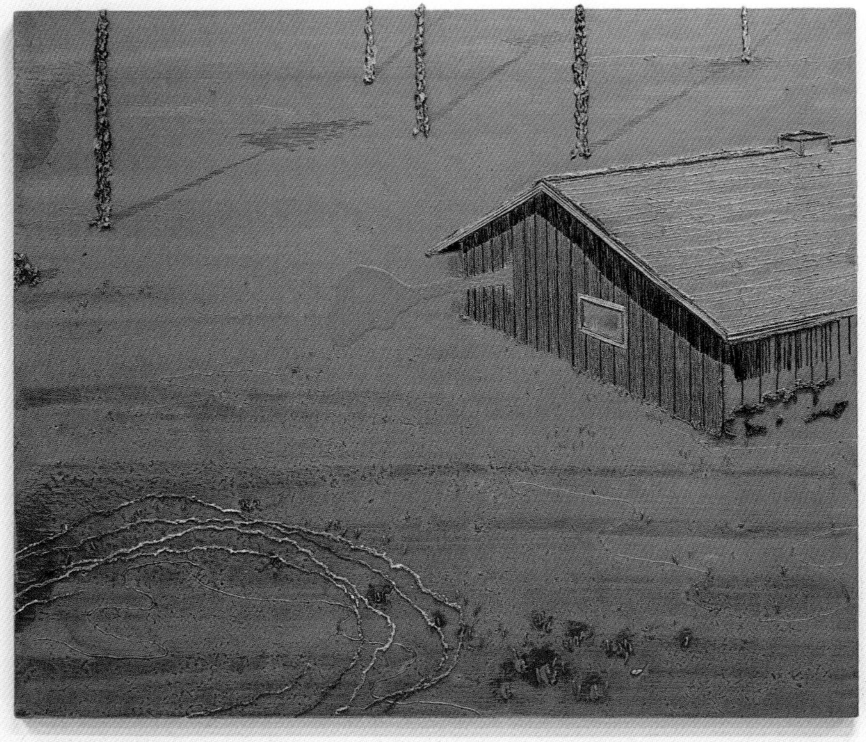

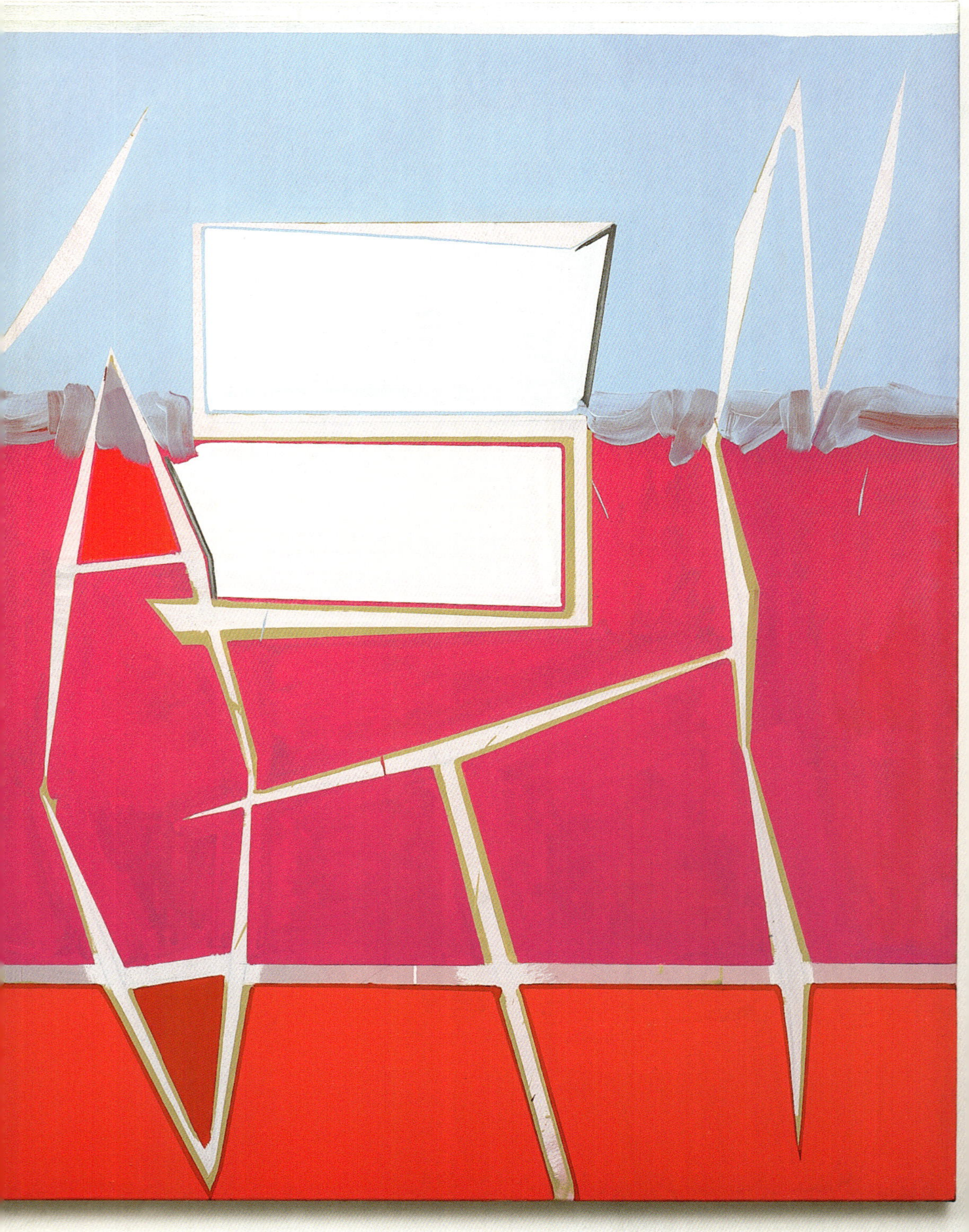

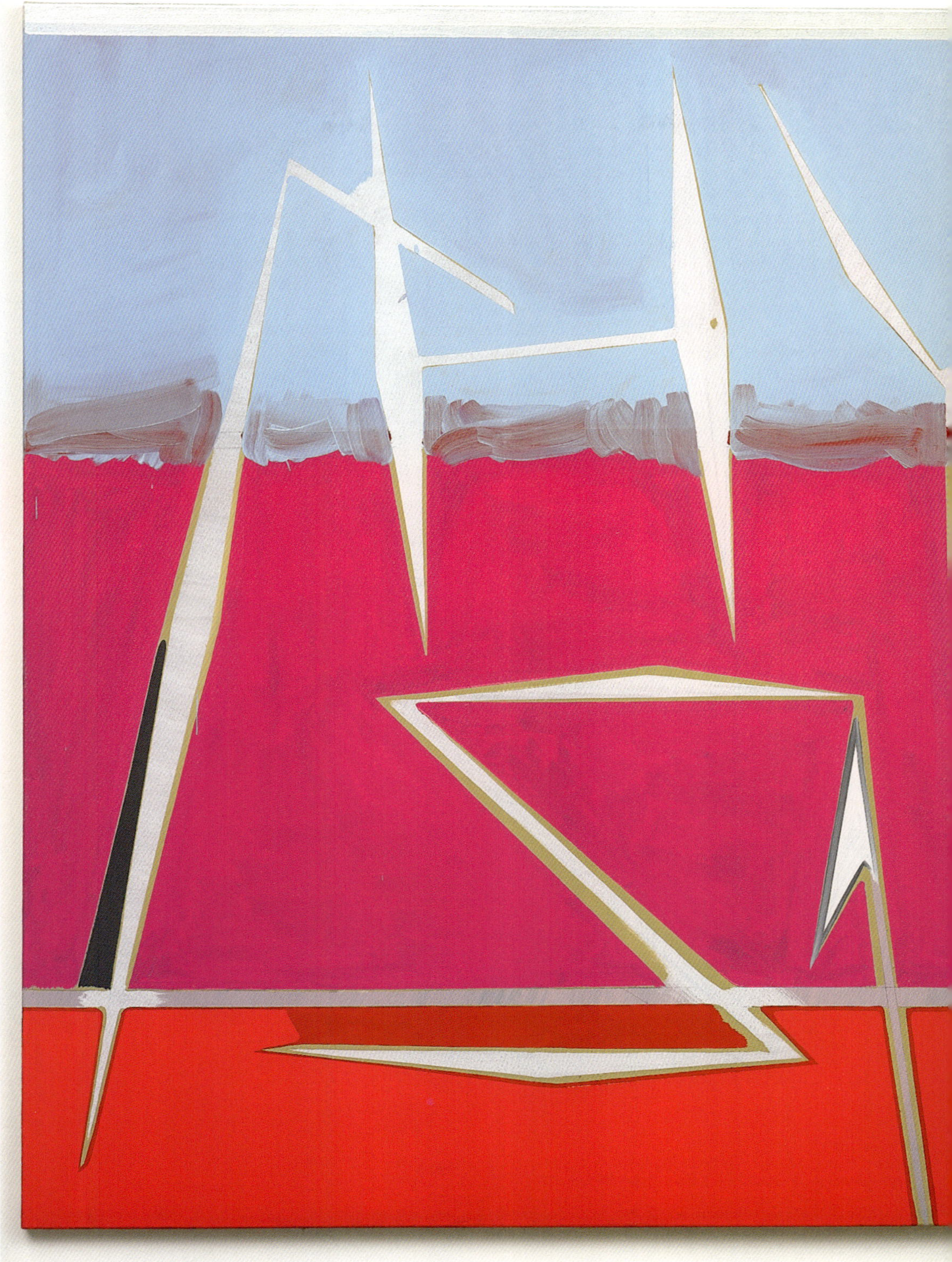

ABOVE **Schriftbild (Writing Picture)** 2000 OPPOSITE **Untitled** 1999

Thomas Scheibitz

Born 1967 Germany; lives and works in Berlin
Thomas Scheibitz makes highly stylized paintings of banal, anonymous subjects that are at once formally simplified and compositionally complex. Whether the subject is landscape or architecture or even abstract painting itself, he mines the fertile ground between pictorial illusion and modernist flatness by constructing aggressively geometric renderings of objective reality that border on complete abstraction. In his hands, the traditional techniques of perspective are propelled to their limit, the illusion of depth teetering on the verge of a breakdown into pure blocks of color and interlocking lines. Scheibitz's paintings owe as much to such art-historical forebears as Matisse, Mondrian, and Picasso as they do to contemporary graphic design, the influence of which is one of style and attitude. Rendered in a discordant palette, the carefully composed paintings betray an immediacy of creation in the errant drips and thick impastoes that cling to the surface. Scheibitz was recently featured in solo exhibitions at the Kunstmuseum Winterthur, Switzerland (2001) and the Institute of Contemporary Arts, London (1999). His work has been included in numerous group exhibitions, including *Examining Pictures* at the Whitechapel Art Gallery, London, and the Museum of Contemporary Art, Chicago (1999) as well as at the Kunsthalle Dresden (1997).

OPPOSITE Thomas Scheibitz **Untitled** 1999 oil on canvas 56 x 42 in. Collection Kenneth L. Freed, Boston Image courtesy Bonakdar Jancou Gallery, New York (checklist)

FOLDOUT Thomas Scheibitz **Schriftbild (Writing Picture)** 2000 oil on canvas 63 x 100 ½ in. Image courtesy Galerie Gebr. Lehmann, Dresden; photo: Jens Ziehe, Berlin (checklist)

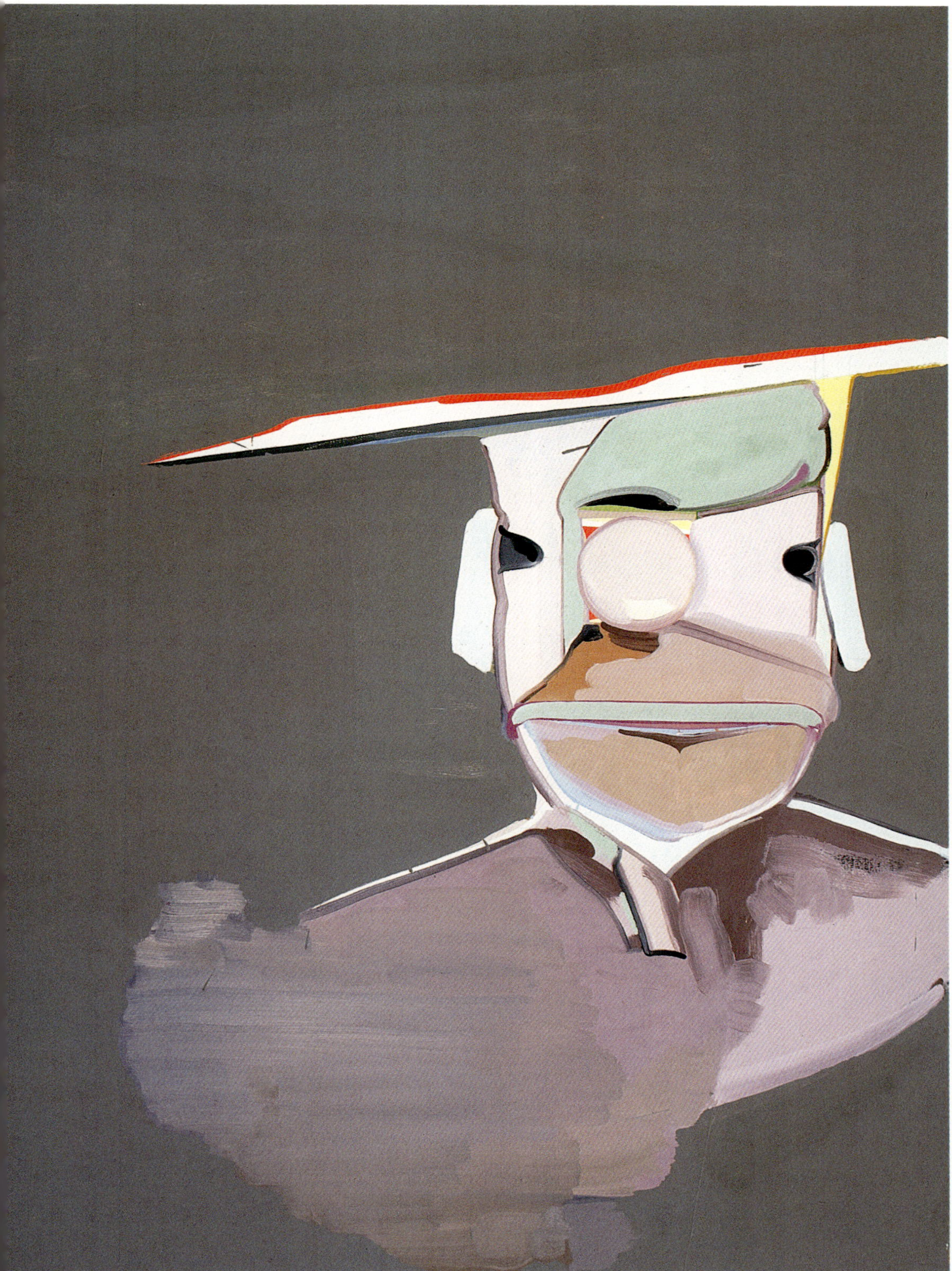

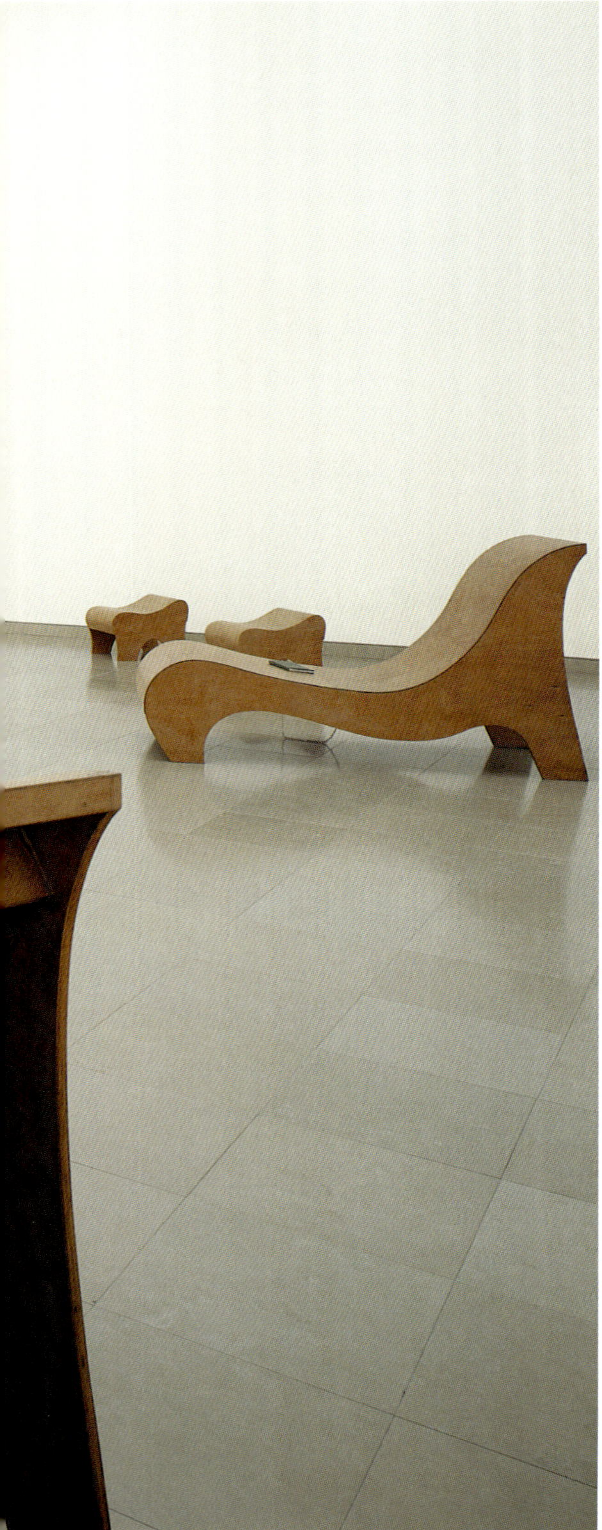
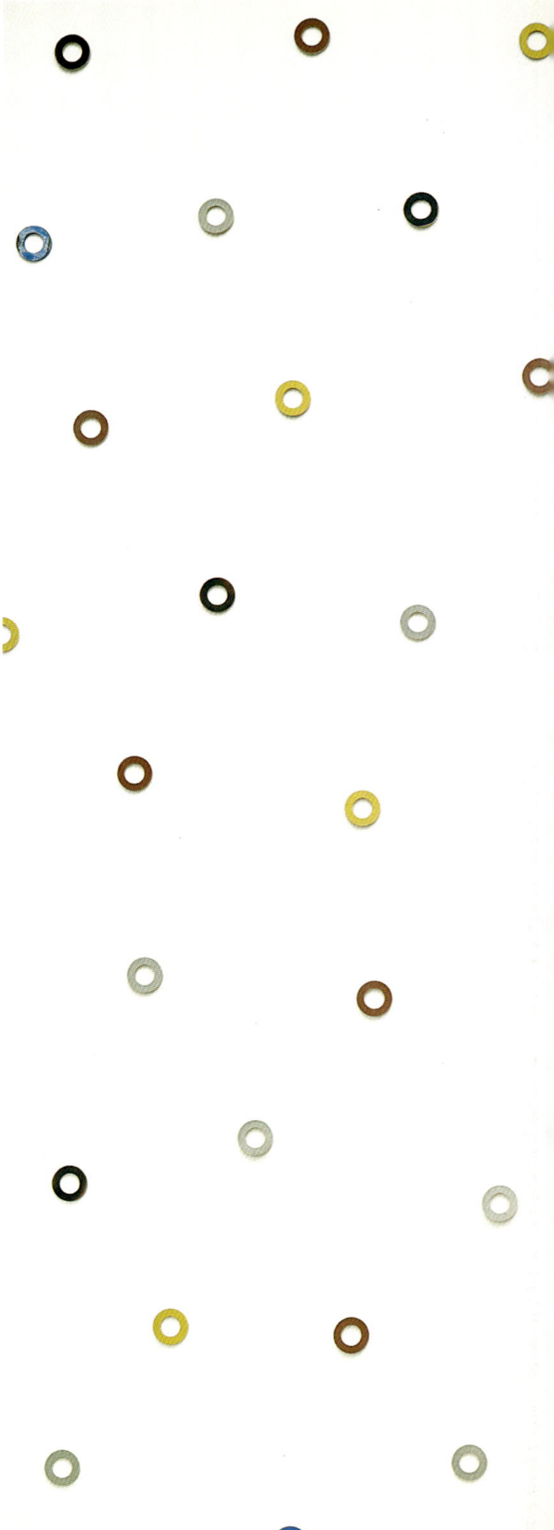

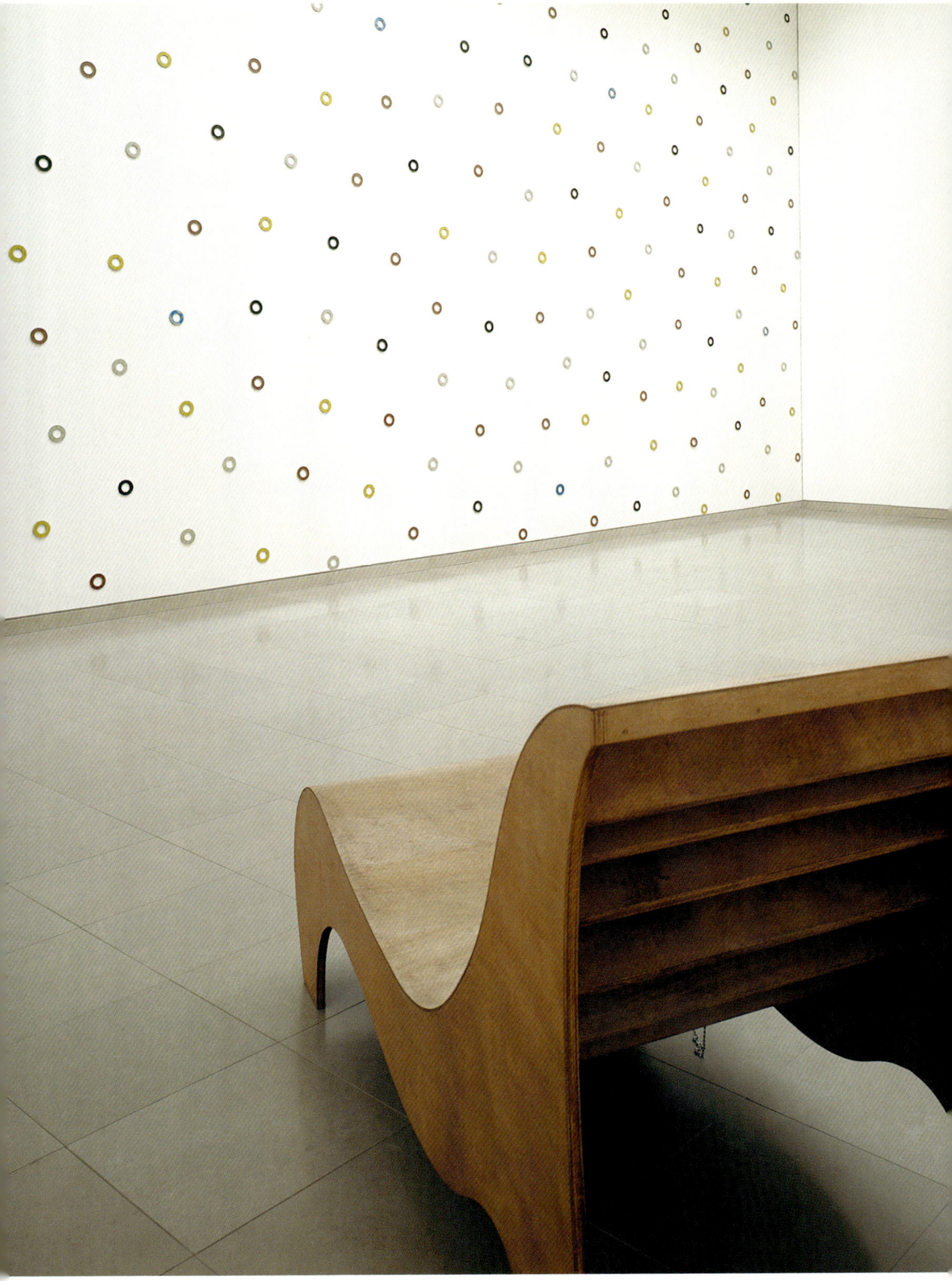

ABOVE AND OPPOSITE installation view of **Ringe (Rings)** 1977/1994 at Carré d'Art, Nîmes

Thomas Schütte

Born 1954 Germany; lives and works in Düsseldorf
Throughout his career Thomas Schütte has eschewed the pursuit of a single artistic purpose, preferring to engage in a type of creative "repertoire" that encompasses a broad array of media, forms, scales, and approaches. Even his painting practice is varied, ranging from small-scale watercolors to large canvases to installations, each transcending the specific conditions of its medium in the construction of meaning. In much of his early work he implicates architectural practice, whether by fabricating precise models or by working in the real space of large-scale installations. In *Ringe (Rings)* (1977/1994), Schütte merged the exhibition space with the work of art by covering the walls in an irregular pattern of colored rings, calling into question assumptions of the systematic conceptualism of Daniel Buren and Niele Toroni while at the same time asserting the value of the decorative as a valid artistic strategy. For Schütte, the physical space shared by the work and the viewer is paramount: "Direct experience is much more touching than media . . . I still believe in enlightenment and inspiration, [in] that moment of sudden awareness of yourself." Major solo exhibitions of Schütte's work have been presented at the Dia Center for the Arts, New York (2000), the Whitechapel Art Gallery, London (1998), and the Kunstverein Wolfsburg (1996). He has also participated in numerous international exhibitions, including *documenta*, Kassel (1997, 1992, 1987) and *Skulptur Projekte*, Münster (1997, 1987).

OPPOSITE AND FOLDOUT Thomas Schütte installation view of **Ringe (Rings)** 1977/1994 oil on wood, nails dimensions variable at Carré d'Art, Nîmes Artesia Contemporary Art Collection, Brussels Images courtesy the artist (checklist)

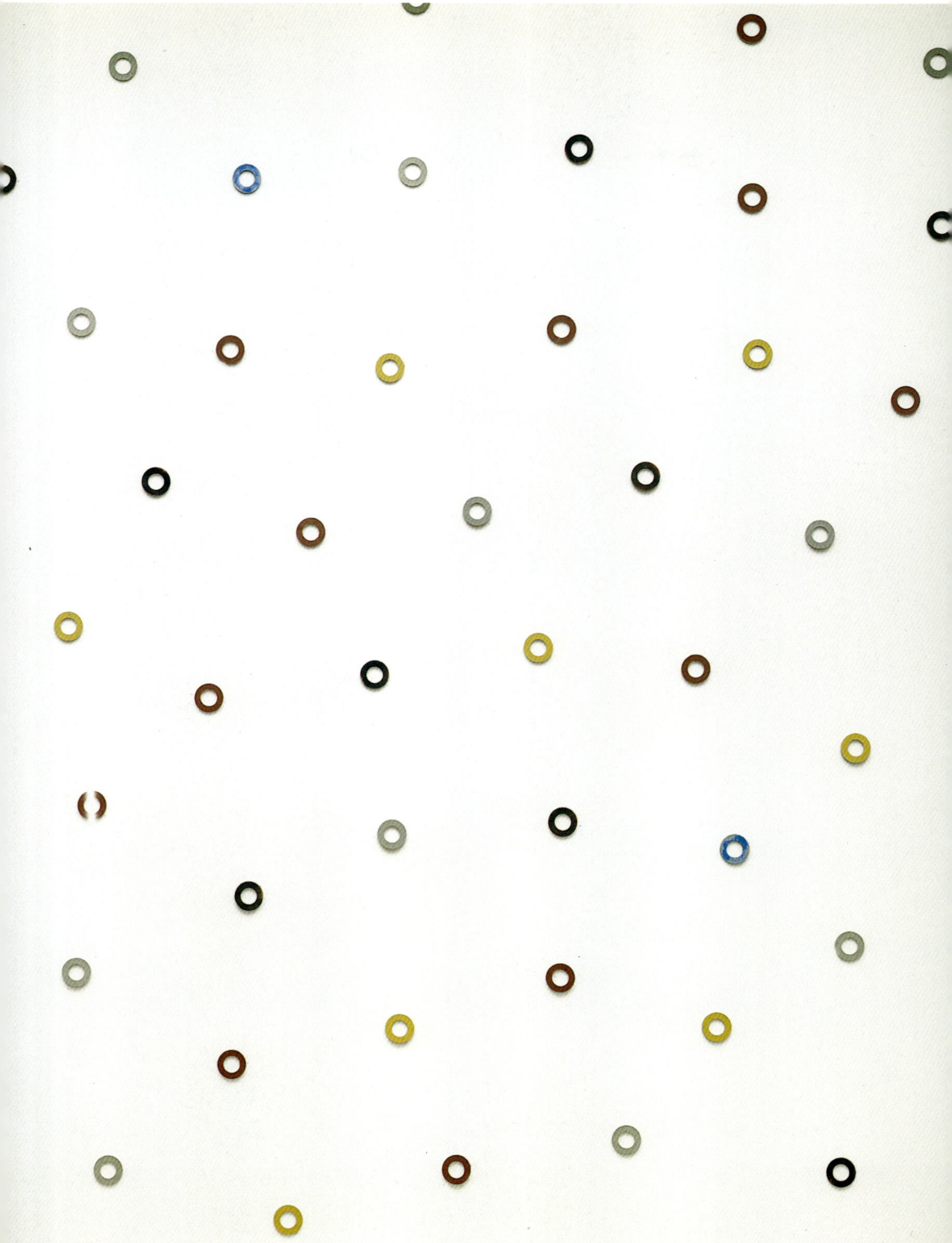

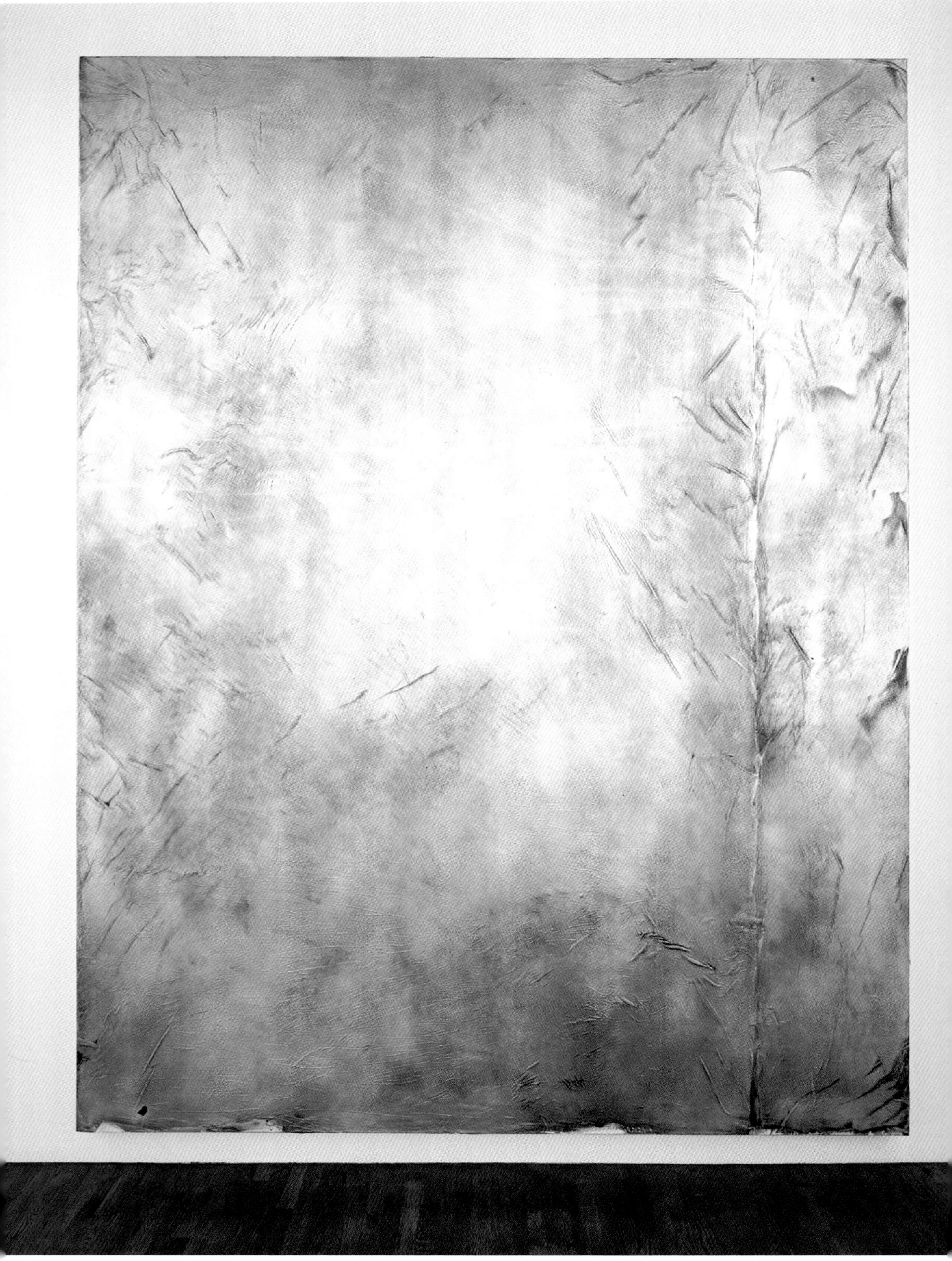

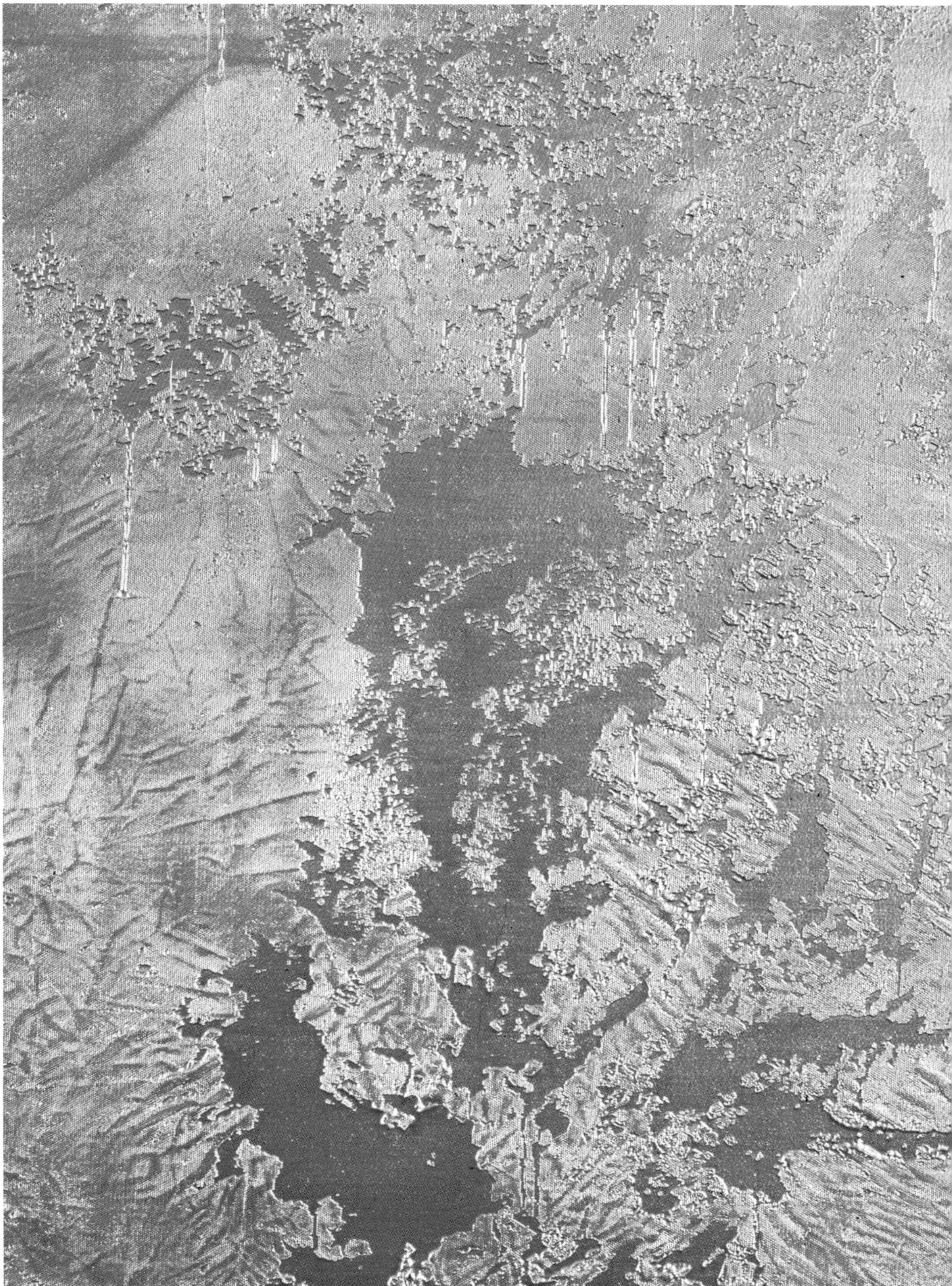

ABOVE detail of **Untitled** 1998 **CENTER** **Untitled** 1994 **OPPOSITE** **Instructions** 1989

Rudolf Stingel

Born 1956 Italy; lives and works in New York City
Upon superficial examination, Rudolf Stingel's paintings could be considered as purely formal investigations rooted in the traditional practice of abstract, monochromatic painting. But his work is based in a highly conceptual effort to deconstruct and demystify the conventions of modernist practice. In his 1989 artist's book *Instructions*, Stingel used the style of an industrial technical manual to outline the process by which he creates a painting. Humorously engaging the legacy of Conceptual Art (such as Sol LeWitt's dictum that "the idea becomes a machine that makes art"), this rule book summarized every step, beginning with the selection of paint and ending with the application of fabric to achieve unique surface effects. However, in contrast to the cool detachment of LeWitt's project, Stingel's work still relies on the expressive qualities of paint. While he exposes the myth of the unique creative act and radically standardizes the technical aspects of painting, the resulting canvases assert their singularity by retaining a subtle sensuality and by exploiting the possibilities of chance within a prescribed system. His work has been included in *Examining Pictures* at the Whitechapel Art Gallery, London, and the Museum of Contemporary Art, Chicago (1999), as well as in group exhibitions at P.S.1 Contemporary Art Center, New York (1997), Second Biennial, SITE Santa Fe (1997), and the Kunsthalle Zürich (1995).

OPPOSITE Rudolf Stingel **Instructions** 1989 screenprints on paper four panels, 42 ½ x 30 ⅝ in. each Edition 1/5 Image courtesy Paula Cooper Gallery, New York; photo: G. Clements (checklist)

FOLDOUT (LEFT) Rudolf Stingel detail of **Untitled** 1998 oil, enamel on canvas 32 x 32 in. Image courtesy Paula Cooper Gallery, New York; photo: Adam Reich (checklist)
(RIGHT) **Untitled** 1994 oil, enamel on canvas 144 x 112 in. Image courtesy Paula Cooper Gallery, New York; photo: James Dee

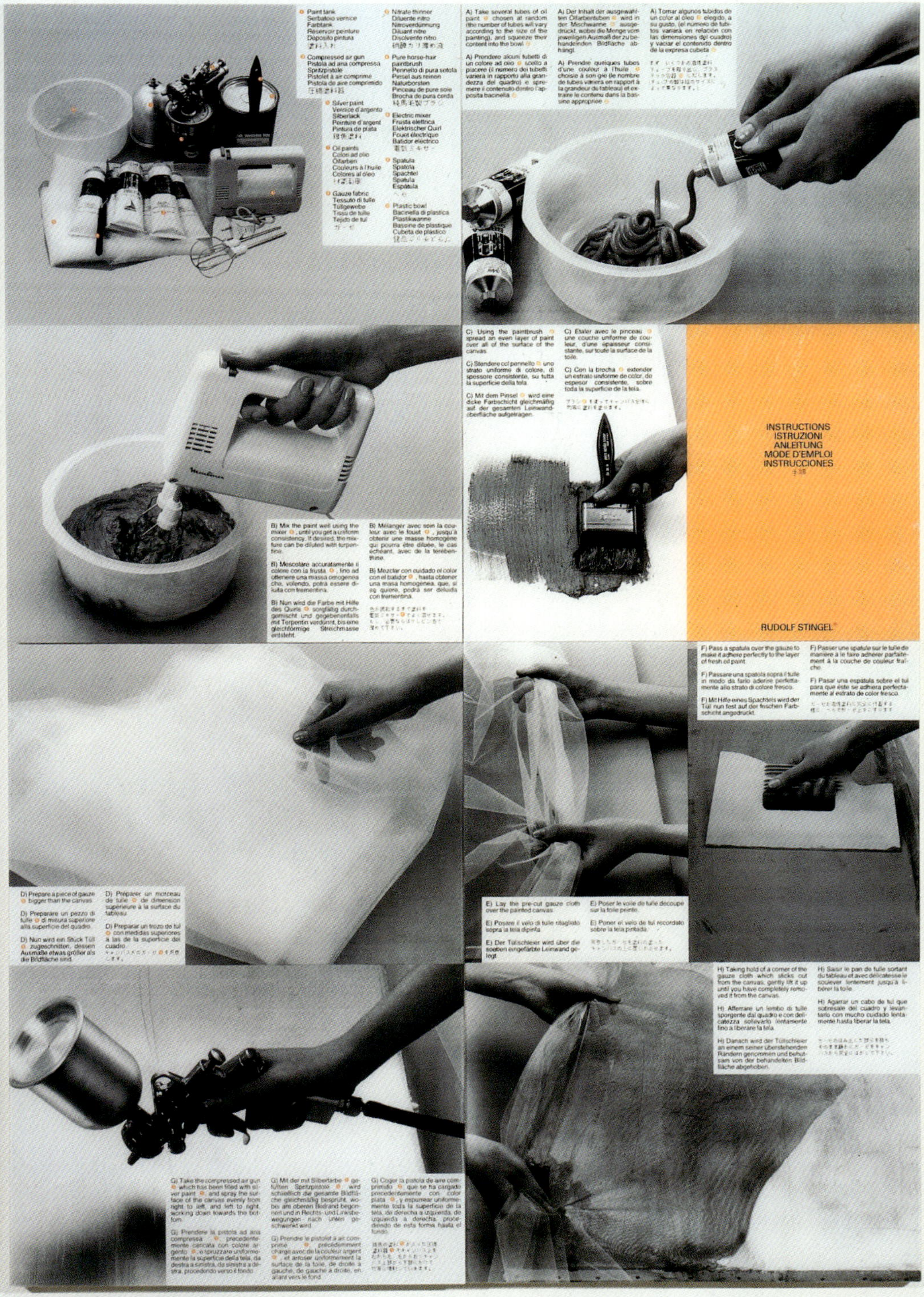
Paint tank
Serbatoio vernice
Farbtank
Reservoir peinture
Depósito pintura
Compressed air gun
Pistola ad aria compressa
Spritzpistole
Pistolet à air comprimé
Pistola de aire comprimido
Silver paint
Vernice d'argento
Silberlack
Peinture d'argent
Pintura de plata
Oil paints
Colori ad olio
Ölfarben
Couleurs à l'huile
Colores al óleo
Gauze fabric
Tessuto di tulle
Tüllgewebe
Tissu de tulle
Tejido de tul
Nitrate thinner
Diluente nitro
Nitroverdünnung
Diluant nitre
Disolvente nitro
Pure horse-hair paintbrush
Pennello di pura setola
Pinsel aus reinen Naturborsten
Pinceau de pure soie
Brocha de pura cerda
Electric mixer
Frusta elettrica
Elektrischer Quirl
Fouet électrique
Batidor eléctrico
Spatula
Spatola
Spachtel
Spatule
Espátula
Plastic bowl
Bacinella di plastica
Plastikwanne
Bassine de plastique
Cubeta de plástico
A) Take several tubes of oil paint chosen at random (the number of tubes will vary according to the size of the painting), and squeeze their content into the bowl
A) Prendere alcuni tubetti di un colore ad olio scelto a piacere (il numero dei tubetti varierà in rapporto alla grandezza del quadro) e spremere il contenuto dentro l'apposita bacinella
A) Der Inhalt der ausgewählten Ölfarbentuben wird in der Mischwanne ausgedrückt, wobei die Menge vom jeweiligen Ausmaß der zu behandelnden Bildfläche abhängt
A) Prendre quelques tubes d'une couleur à l'huile choisie à son gré (le nombre de tubes variera en rapport à la grandeur du tableau) et extraire le contenu dans la bassine appropriée
A) Tomar algunos tubidos de un color al óleo elegido, a su gusto, (el número de tubitos variará en relación con las dimensiones del cuadro) y vaciar el contenido dentro de la expresa cubeta
B) Mix the paint well using the mixer, until you get a uniform consistency. If desired, the mixture can be diluted with turpentine.
B) Mescolare accuratamente il colore con la frusta, fino ad ottenere una massa omogenea che, volendo, potrà essere diluita con trementina.
B) Nun wird die Farbe mit Hilfe des Quirls sorgfältig durchgemischt und gegebenenfalls mit Terpentin verdünnt, bis eine gleichförmige Streichmasse entsteht.
B) Mélanger avec soin la couleur avec le fouet, jusqu'à obtenir une masse homogène qui pourra être diluée, le cas échéant, avec de la térébenthine.
B) Mezclar con cuidado el color con el batidor, hasta obtener una masa homogénea, que, si se quiere, podrá ser deluida con trementina.
C) Using the paintbrush spread an even layer of paint over all of the surface of the canvas.
C) Stendere col pennello uno strato uniforme di colore, di spessore consistente, su tutta la superficie della tela.
C) Mit dem Pinsel wird eine dicke Farbschicht gleichmäßig auf der gesamten Leinwandoberfläche aufgetragen.
C) Etaler avec le pinceau une couche uniforme de couleur, d'une épaisseur consistante, sur toute la surface de la toile.
C) Con la brocha extender un estrato uniforme de color, de espesor consistente, sobre toda la superficie de la tela.
INSTRUCTIONS
ISTRUZIONI
ANLEITUNG
MODE D'EMPLOI
INSTRUCCIONES
RUDOLF STINGEL
D) Prepare a piece of gauze bigger than the canvas.
D) Preparare un pezzo di tulle di misura superiore alla superficie del quadro.
D) Nun wird ein Stück Tüll zugeschnitten, dessen Ausmaße etwas größer als die Bildfläche sind.
D) Préparer un morceau de tulle de dimension supérieure à la surface du tableau.
D) Preparar un trozo de tul con medidas superiores a las de la superficie del cuadro.
E) Lay the pre-cut gauze cloth over the painted canvas.
E) Posare il velo di tulle ritagliato sopra la tela dipinta.
E) Der Tüllschleier wird über die soeben eingefärbte Leinwand gelegt.
E) Poser le voile de tulle découpé sur la toile peinte.
E) Poner el velo de tul recortado sobre la tela pintada.
F) Pass a spatula over the gauze to make it adhere perfectly to the layer of fresh oil paint.
F) Passare una spatola sopra il tulle in modo da farlo aderire perfettamente allo strato di colore fresco.
F) Mit Hilfe eines Spachtels wird der Tüll nun fest auf der frischen Farbschicht angedrückt.
F) Passer une spatule sur le tulle de manière à le faire adhérer parfaitement à la couche de couleur fraîche.
F) Pasar una espátula sobre el tul para que éste se adhiera perfectamente al estrato de color fresco.
G) Take the compressed air gun which has been filled with silver paint and spray the surface of the canvas evenly from right to left, and left to right, working down towards the bottom.
G) Prendere la pistola ad aria compressa precedentemente caricata con colore argento, e spruzzare uniformemente la superficie della tela, da destra a sinistra, da sinistra a destra, procedendo verso il fondo.
G) Mit der mit Silberfarbe gefüllten Spritzpistole wird schließlich die gesamte Bildfläche gleichmäßig besprüht, wobei am oberen Bildrand begonnen und in Rechts- und Linksbewegungen nach unten geschwenkt wird.
G) Prendre le pistolet à air comprimé précédemment chargé avec de la couleur argent, et arroser uniformément la surface de la toile, de droite à gauche, de gauche à droite, en allant vers le fond.
G) Coger la pistola de aire comprimido, que se ha cargado precedentemente con color plata, y espurrear uniformemente toda la superficie de la tela, de derecha a izquierda, de izquierda a derecha, procediendo de esta forma hasta el fondo.
H) Taking hold of a corner of the gauze cloth which sticks out from the canvas, gently lift it up until you have completely removed it from the canvas.
H) Afferrare un lembo di tulle sporgente dal quadro e con delicatezza sollevarlo lentamente fino a liberare la tela.
H) Danach wird der Tüllschleier an einem seiner überstehenden Rändern genommen und behutsam von der behandelten Bildfläche abgehoben.
H) Saisir le pan de tulle sortant du tableau et avec délicatesse le soulever lentement jusqu'à libérer la toile.
H) Agarrar un cabo de tul que sobresale del cuadro y levantarlo con mucho cuidado lentamente hasta liberar la tela.

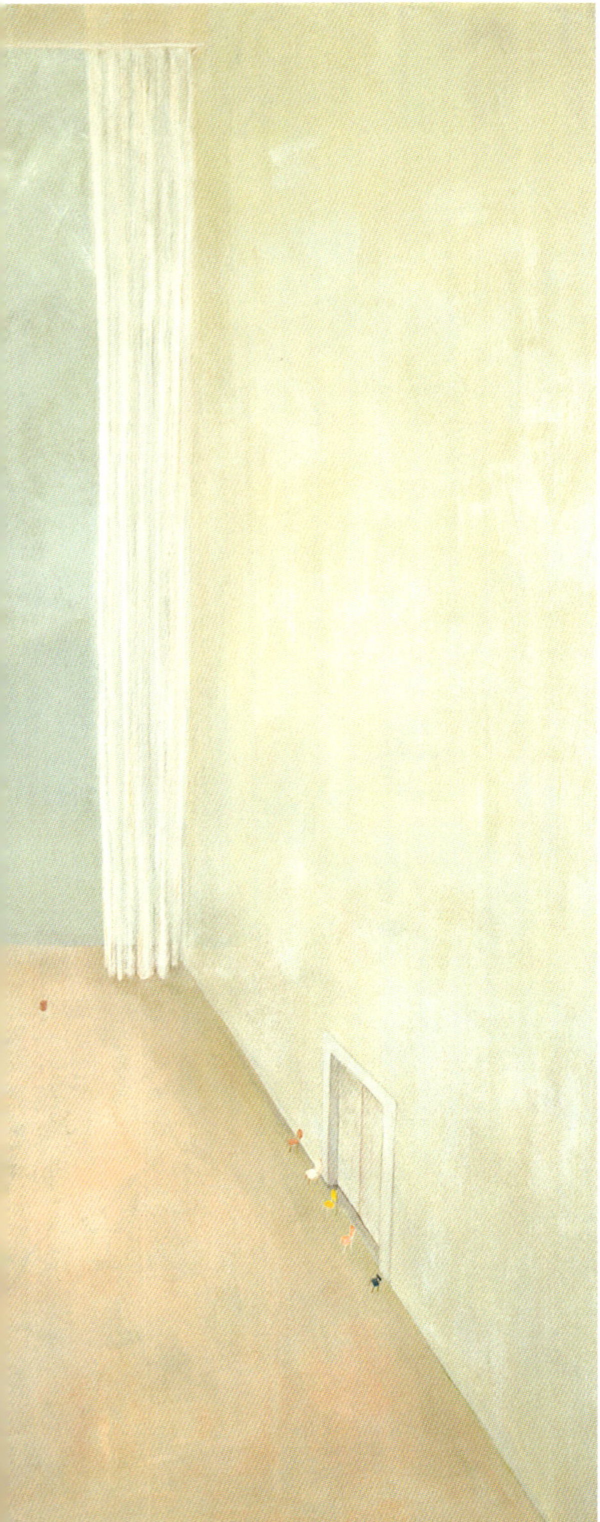

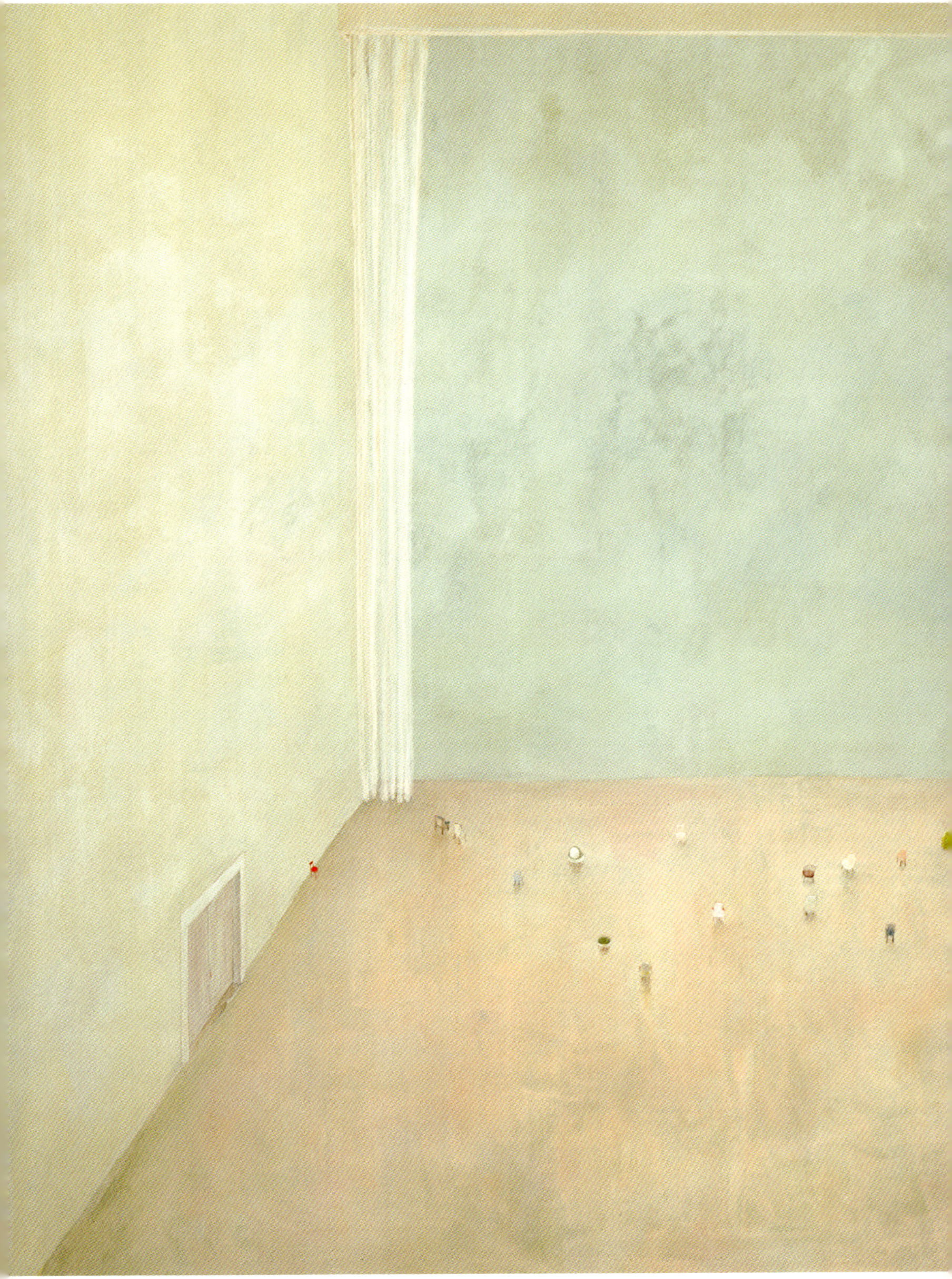

ABOVE **the pink floor** 1998 OPPOSITE **the secret tower** 1998–2000

Hiroshi Sugito

Born 1970 Japan; lives and works in Nagoya
Hiroshi Sugito's paintings negotiate the portrayal of childhood memories and fantasies from a position of grown-up sophistication. With a limited, subdued palette, he paints naively rendered figures that inhabit tentatively delineated settings. The perspective and scale are often off-kilter: enormous seas are populated with miniature battleships; oversized rooms seem empty as the smattering of diminutive chairs cling to the very bottom of the walls. Sugito often incorporates theatrical devices in his work, such as a proscenium stage or curtains drawn back to reveal the subject of the painting. The delicately worked canvases, which evoke the soft-focus world of dreams, often appear sweet but betray an underlying psychological complexity. In his landscapes resembling innocent daydreams that are subverted by the presence of Lilliputian battles and hybrid monsters, he constructs a metaphysical theater of childlike wonder and existential contemplation. Sugito was the subject of a solo exhibition at the Museum of Contemporary Art, Tokyo (1999). His work has been included in group exhibitions at the Gendai Center for Contemporary Art, Ujazdowski Castle, Poland (2000), the Ueno Royal Museum, Tokyo (1998), the Aichi Arts Center, Nagoya (1998), and the Aldrich Museum of Contemporary Art, Ridgefield, Connecticut (1997).

OPPOSITE Hiroshi Sugito **the secret tower** 1998–2000 acrylic, pigment, ink on paper 70 x 90 in. diptych, one of two panels Collection Carlos and Rosa de la Cruz Image courtesy Marc Foxx Gallery, Los Angeles

FOLDOUT Hiroshi Sugito **the pink floor** 1998 acrylic, pigment, graphite, colored pencil on cotton duck 80 x 96 in. Collection Dean Valentine and Amy Adelson, Los Angeles Image courtesy Marc Foxx Gallery, Los Angeles (checklist)

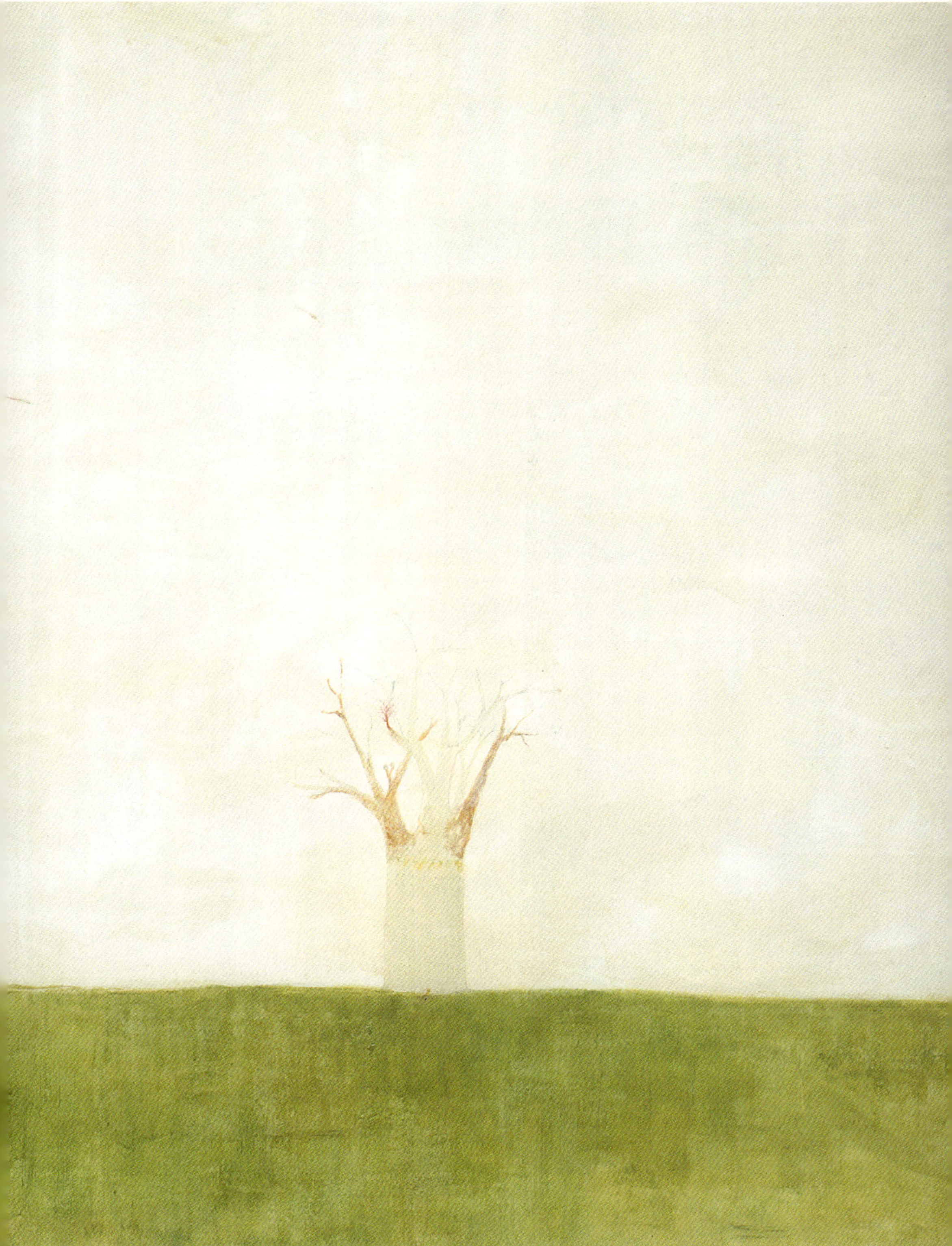

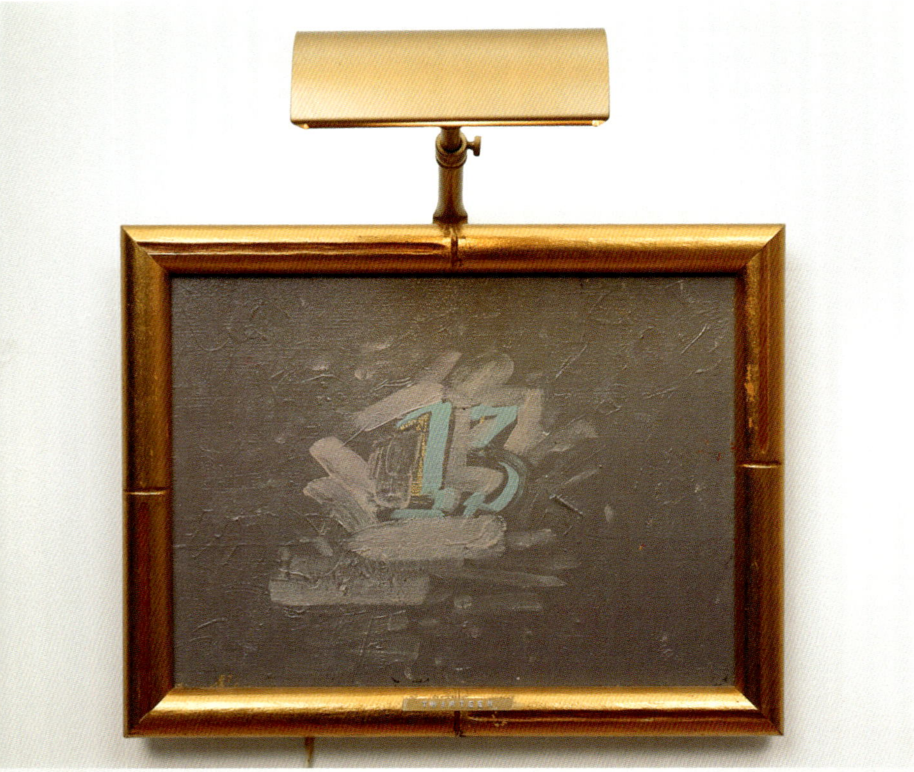
13
THIRTEEN

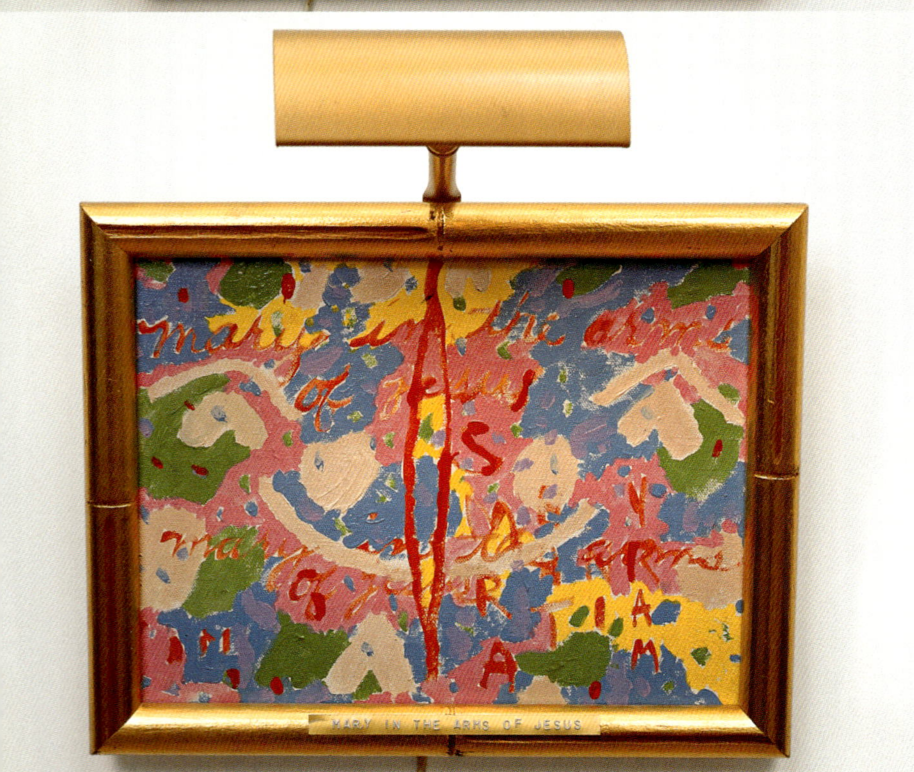
MARY IN THE ARMS OF JESUS

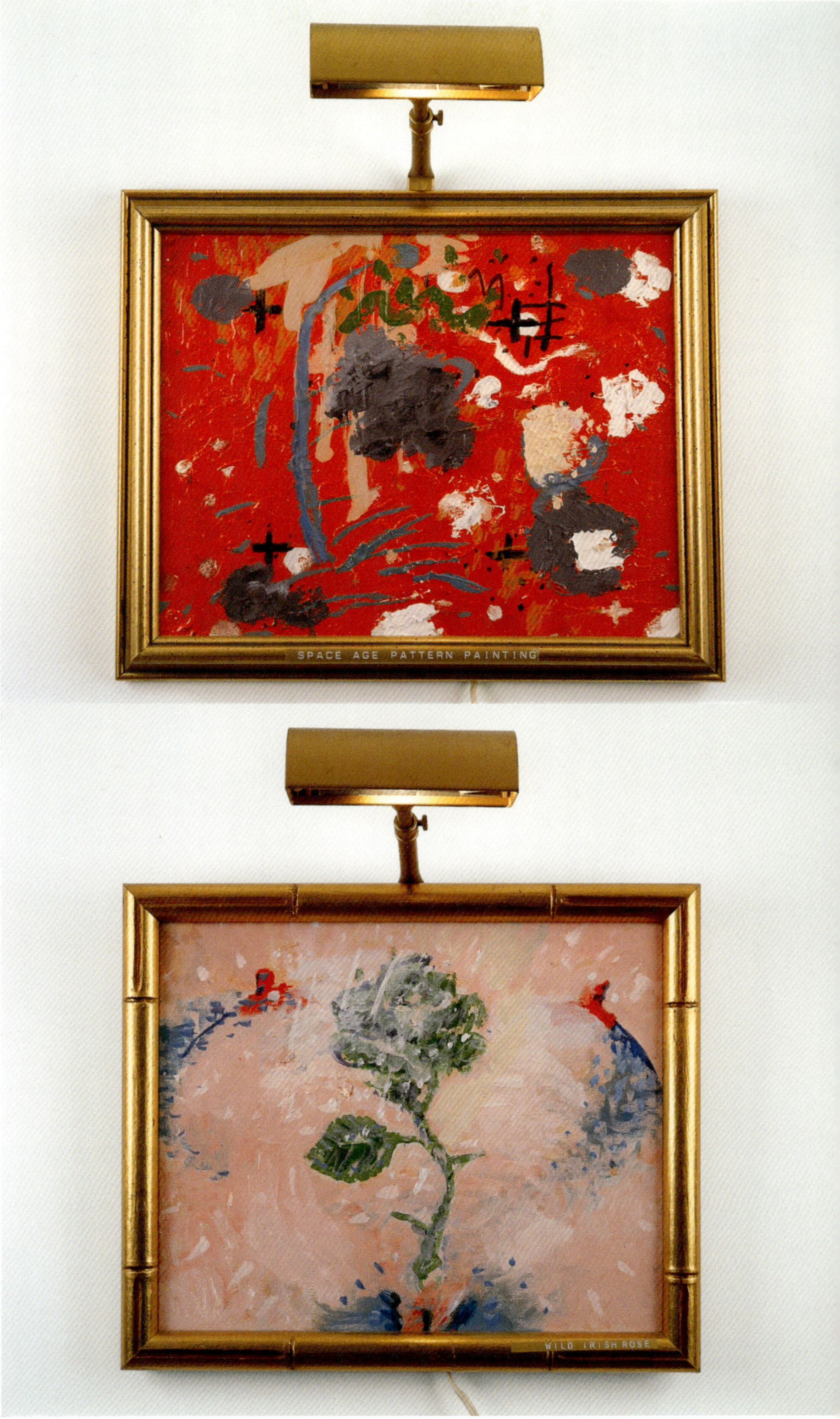

TOP TO BOTTOM, LEFT TO RIGHT **Space Age Pattern Painting** 1980 **Wild Irish Rose** 1979–1980 **Thirteen** 1979–1980 **Mary in the Arms of Jesus** 1979–1980 **Pink Cross and Green Buds** 1975–1980 **Periscope** 1979–1980

Paul Thek

Born 1933 United States; died 1988
Largely under-recognized at the time of his early death, Paul Thek created a remarkably influential body of work that presciently reflected significant shifts in contemporary art practice. During the 1960s and 1970s, Thek's roving interest in diverse media and viscerally charged subjects countered the dominant modes of Minimalism and Conceptual Art. He rejected their cool formalism and veneer of detachment, often incorporating banal, kitschy materials into his sculptures, performances, and installations in the pursuit of an anti-heroic aesthetic. His environments were conceived with the intent of directing the viewer's experience in space, as in his series of "picture light" paintings. These small, faux-naive paintings were set in cheap gilded frames mounted with individual display lamps and installed low to the ground, accompanied by small chairs for careful viewing. Rendered in all manner of painterly styles and genres, they reflect Thek's interest in the mythic and the personal, and their accumulation suggests a sweet reverence for painting itself. A major traveling retrospective of Thek's work was organized by the Witte de With Center for Contemporary Art, Rotterdam (1995). Other solo exhibitions have been presented at the Camden Arts Centre, London (1999) and the Arts Club of Chicago (1999). His work was recently included in group exhibitions at the Museum of Modern Art, New York (1997) and the Whitney Museum of American Art, New York (1993).

OPPOSITE (TOP) Paul Thek **Pink Cross and Green Buds** 1975–1980 acrylic on canvasboard with artist's frame and picture light 12 x 16 in. Collection Carolyn Alexander, New York Image courtesy Alexander and Bonin, New York; photo: Orcutt & Van Der Putten (checklist)
(BOTTOM) Paul Thek **Periscope** 1979–1980 oil on canvas with artist's frame and picture light 9 x 13 ¾ in. Courtesy Galerie Peyroulet, Paris Image courtesy Alexander and Bonin, New York; photo: Orcutt & Van Der Putten (checklist)

FOLDOUT (TOP TO BOTTOM, LEFT TO RIGHT)
Paul Thek **Space Age Pattern Painting** 1980 acrylic on canvas with artist's frame and picture light 13 x 16 in. Courtesy Estate of George Paul Thek and Alexander and Bonin, New York; photo: D. James Dee (checklist)
Paul Thek **Wild Irish Rose** 1979–1980 acrylic on canvas with artist's frame and picture light 11 x 14 in. Private collection; Courtesy Galerie am Lindenplatz AG, Vaduz, Principality of Liechtenstein Image courtesy Alexander and Bonin, New York; photo: D. James Dee (checklist)
Paul Thek **Thirteen** 1979–1980 acrylic on canvas with artist's frame and picture light 10 ½ x 13 ½ in. Collection Kenny Schachter, New York Image courtesy Alexander and Bonin, New York; photo: Orcutt & Van Der Putten (checklist)
Paul Thek **Mary in the Arms of Jesus** 1979–1980 acrylic on canvas with artist's frame and picture light 10 ½ x 13 ½ in. Collection Kenny Schachter, New York Image courtesy Alexander and Bonin, New York; photo: Orcutt & Van Der Putten (checklist)

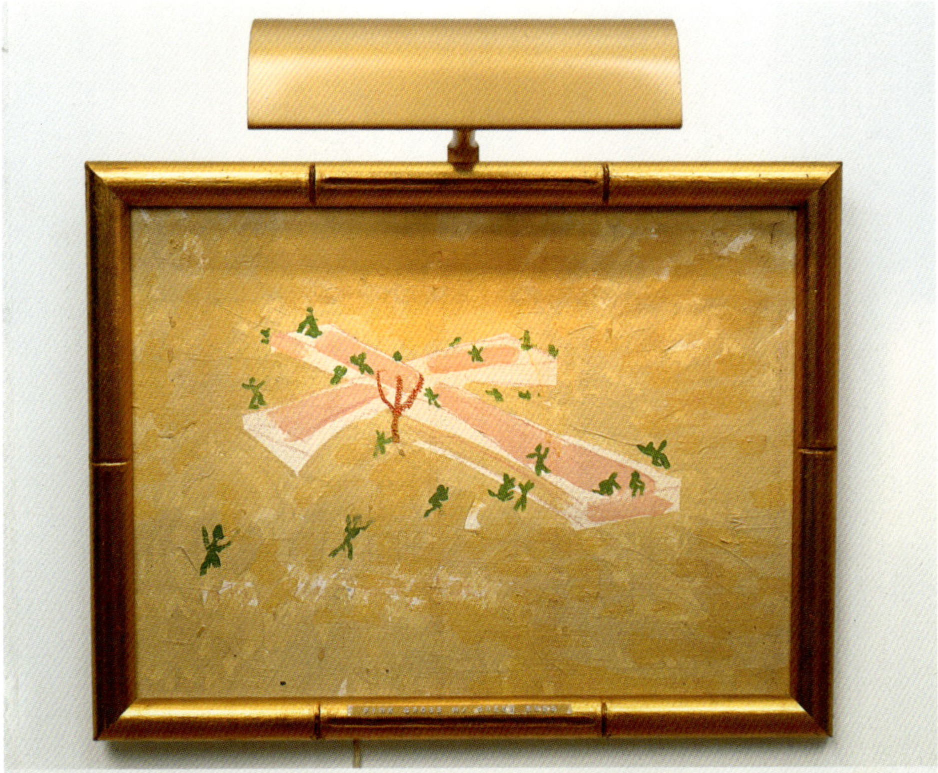
PINK CROSS W/

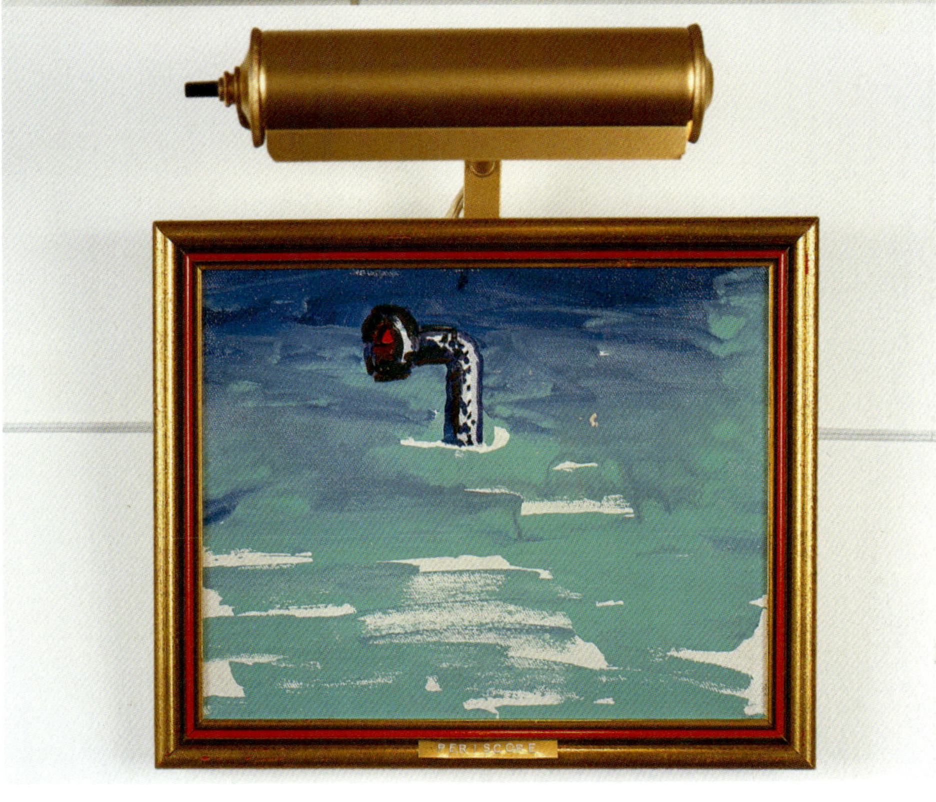
PERISCOPE

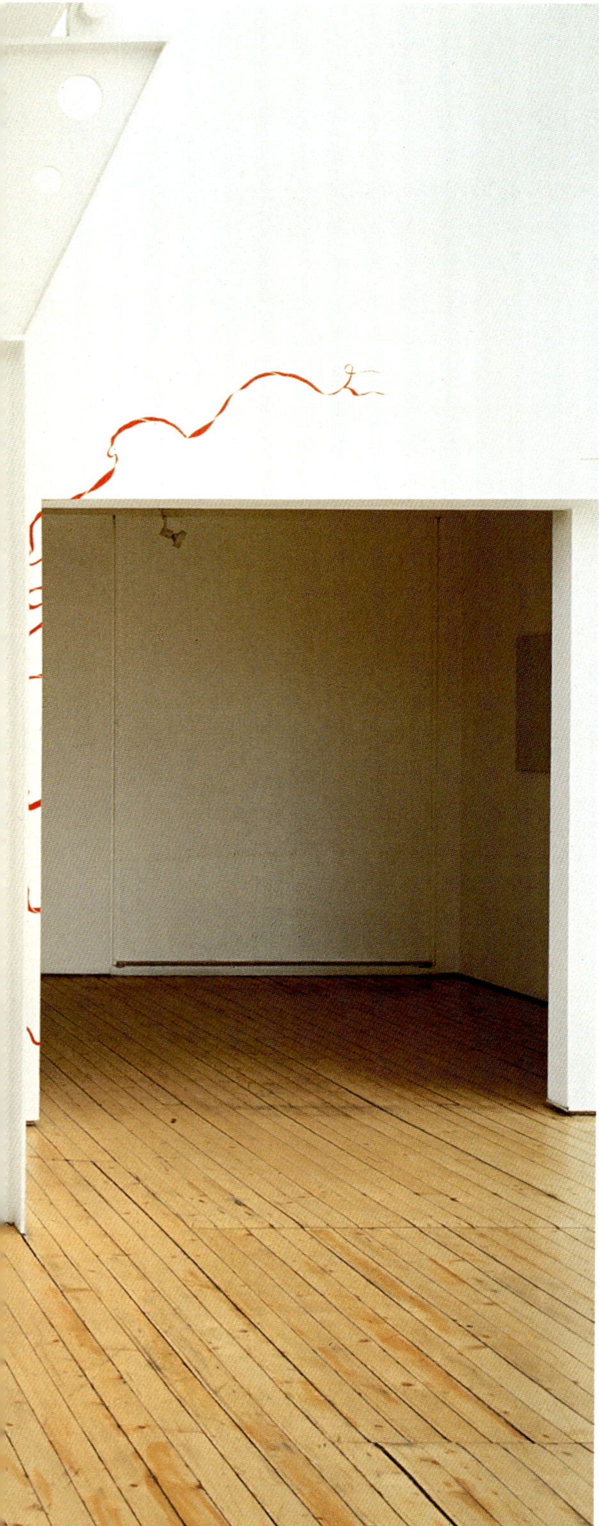

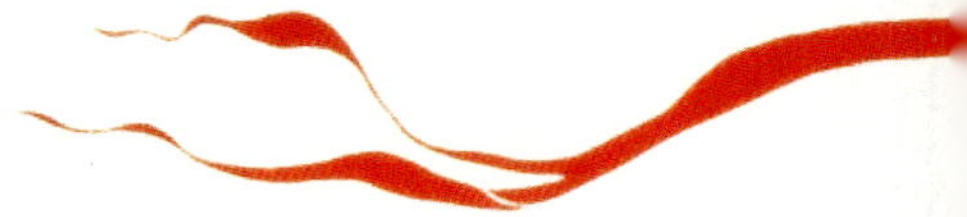

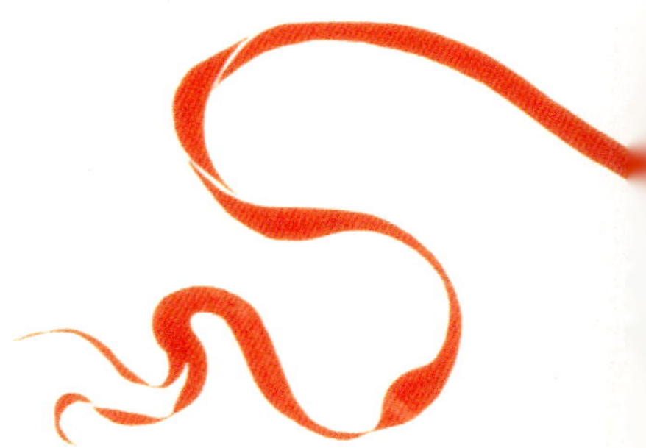

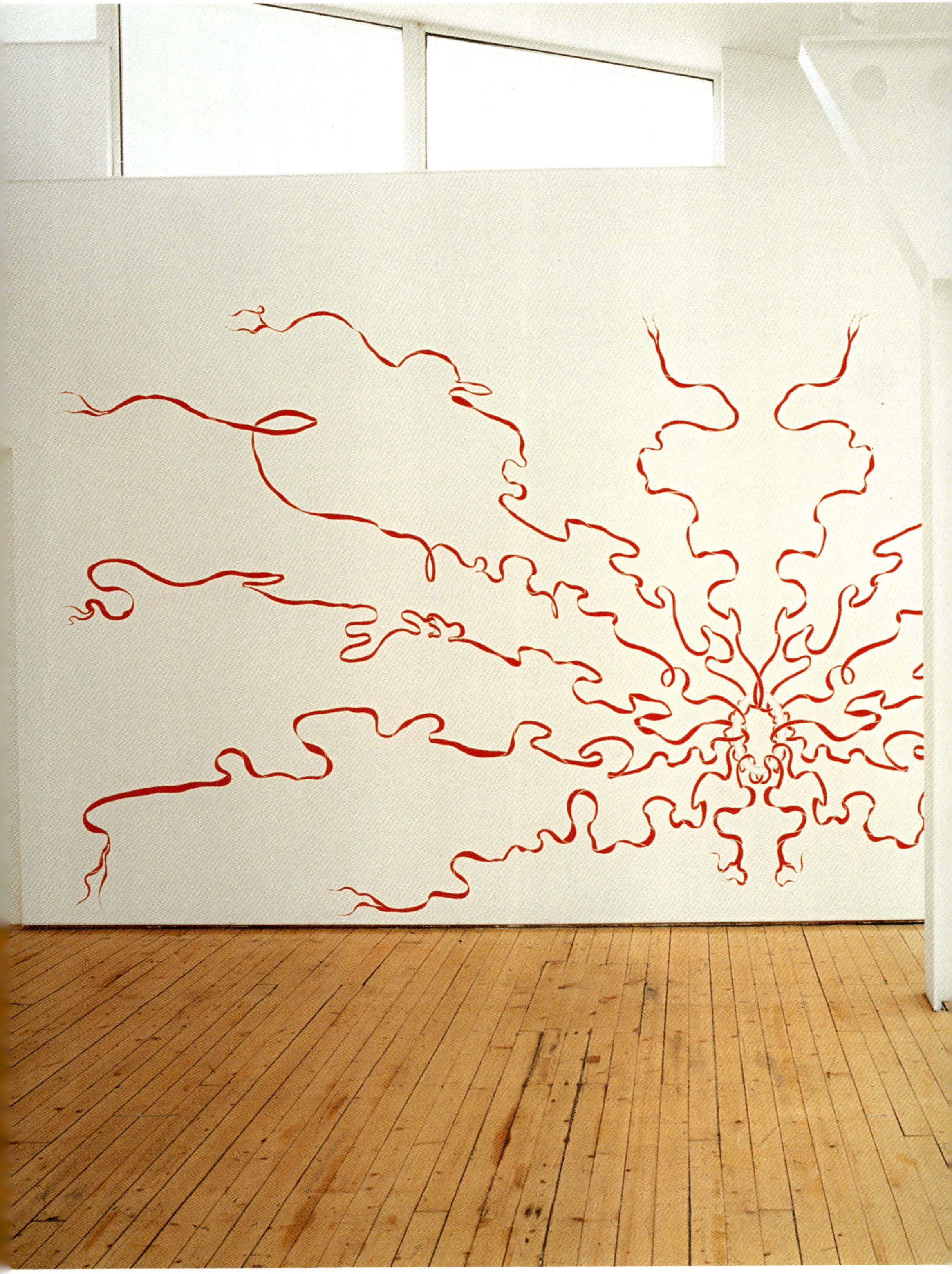

ABOVE AND OPPOSITE installation view at Fruitmarket Gallery, Edinburgh 1997

Richard Wright

Born 1960 England; lives and works in Glasgow
Richard Wright's work engages a paradoxical condition: he doesn't want his work to look like "painting," but that is the very medium he pursues. Wright maintains this tension between painting and nonpainting by eschewing the canvas in favor of the wall. He challenges modernist codes regarding the hand of the artist, the autonomy of the object, and hermetic content by consciously operating in ambiguity—his work is hand-rendered but looks mechanically produced; his work appears carefully composed but is executed spontaneously. By definition site-specific, each of his large-scale works is completed during one intense session, reflecting "the pressure of the live situation." Although he brings resource images with him to a site, the content and process of a composition are largely informed by the external conditions of the given architecture, the presence of other artworks in the space, and the physical limits of his own production. Wright was selected to participate in the Tate Triennial of British Art, London (2000) and *The British Art Show*, Hayward Gallery, London (2000). His work has been included in group exhibitions at the Drawing Center, New York (1999), the Institute of Contemporary Arts, London (1998), Manifesta 2, Luxembourg (1998), and the Musée d'art moderne de la Ville de Paris (1996).

OPPOSITE AND FOLDOUT Richard Wright installation view at Fruitmarket Gallery, Edinburgh 1997 gouache wall painting
Image courtesy BQ, Cologne; photo: Simon Starling

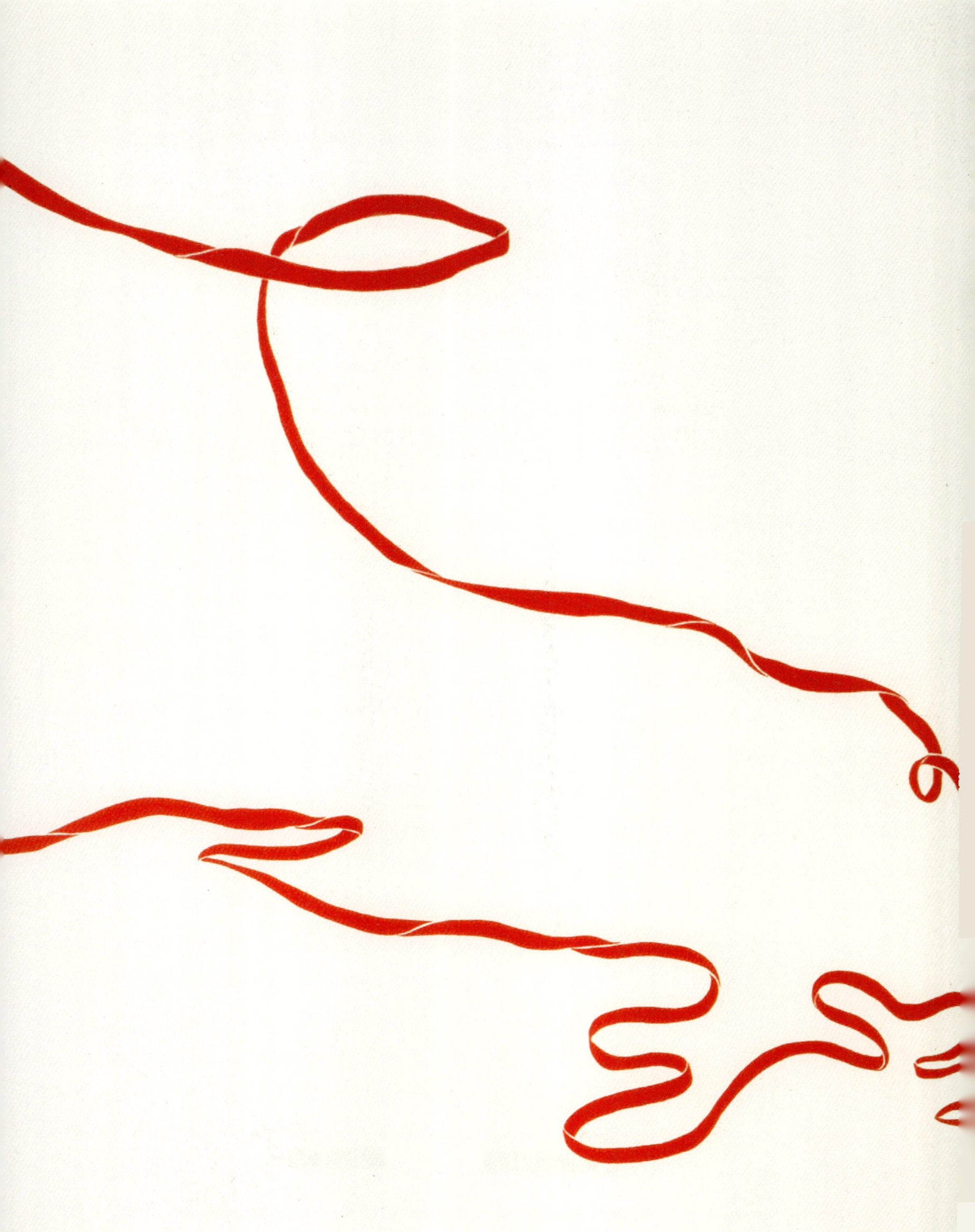

Curator **DOUGLAS FOGLE**
Curatorial Assistant **ELIZABETH THOMAS**
Designers **ANDREW BLAUVELT AND SANTIAGO PIEDRAFITA**
Editor **MICHELLE PIRANIO**
Publication Manager **EUGENIA BELL**

Printed and bound in Germany by Cantz.

Available through D.A.P./Distributed Art Publishers, 155 Sixth Avenue, 2nd floor, New York, NY 10013.

First Edition © 2001 Walker Art Center

Inquiries should be addressed to: Editor, Walker Art Center, 725 Vineland Place, Minneapolis, MN 55403.

Library of Congress Cataloging-in-Publication Data is available from the publisher.